MANAGEMENT AND BUSINESS RESEARCH

5th
EDITION

Mark Easterby-Smith,
Richard Thorpe
Paul R. Jackson

SAGE

Los Angeles | London | New Delhi
Singapore | Washington DC

SAGE Publications Ltd
1 Oliver's Yard
55 City Road
London EC1Y 1SP

SAGE Publications Inc.
2455 Teller Road
Thousand Oaks, California 91320

SAGE Publications India Pvt Ltd
B 1/I 1 Mohan Cooperative Industrial Area
Mathura Road
New Delhi 110 044

SAGE Publications Asia-Pacific Pte Ltd
3 Church Street
#10-04 Samsung Hub
Singapore 049483

Editor: Kirsty Smy
Editorial assistant: Molly Farrell
Production editor: Sarah Cooke
Copyeditor: Solveig Gardner Servian
Proofreader: Lynda Watson
Indexer: Silvia Benvenuto
Marketing manager: Alison Borg
Cover design: Francis Kenney
Typeset by: C&M Digitals (P) Ltd, Chennai, India
Printed and bound in Great Britain by Ashford
Colour Press Ltd

First edition published 1991
Second edition published 2001
Third edition published 2008
Fourth edition published 2012
This fifth edition published 2015

Library of Congress Control Number: 2014952691

British Library Cataloguing in Publication data

A catalogue record for this book is available from the British Library

MIX
Paper from
responsible sources
FSC® C011748

ISBN 978-1-44629-657-8
ISBN 978-1-44629-658-5 (pbk)

At SAGE we take sustainability seriously. Most of our products are printed in the UK using FSC papers and boards. When we print overseas we ensure sustainable papers are used as measured by the Egmont grading system. We undertake an annual audit to monitor our sustainability.

BRIEF CONTENTS

CONTENTS

ABOUT THE
AUTHORS

MARK EASTERBY-SMITH is Distinguished Professor of Management Learning at Lancaster University Management School. He has a first degree in Engineering Science and a PhD in Organizational Behaviour from Durham University. He has been an active researcher for over 30 years with primary interests in methodology and learning processes. He has carried out evaluation studies in many European companies, and has led research projects on management development, organizational learning, dynamic capabilities and knowledge transfer across international organizations in the UK, India and China.

He has published numerous academic papers and over ten books including: *Auditing Management Development* (Gower, 1980), *The Challenge to Western Management Development* (Routledge, 1989), *Evaluation of Management Education, Training and Development* (Gower, 1994), *Organizational Learning and the Learning Organization* (Sage, 1998) and *The Handbook of Organizational Learning and Knowledge Management* (Wiley, 2011).

At Lancaster he has been variously, Director of the School's Doctoral Programme, Director of the Graduate Management School and Head of Department. Externally he spent several years as a visiting faculty member on the International Teachers' Programme, acting as Director when it was held at the London Business School in 1984. During the early 1990s he was national co-ordinator of the Management Teaching Fellowship Scheme funded by the UK's Economic and Social Research Council (ESRC), which was responsible for training 180 new faculty members across UK management schools. He is a former member of the ESRC Post-graduate Training Board and was President of the British Academy of Management in 2006 and Dean of Fellows in 2008.

RICHARD THORPE is Professor of Management Development and Pro Dean for Research at Leeds University Business School. His early industrial experience informed the way his ethos has developed. Common themes are: a strong commitment to process methodologies and a focus on action in all its forms; an interest in and commitment to the development of doctoral students and the development of capacity within the sector; and a commitment to collaborative working on projects of mutual interest. Following a number of years in industry, he joined Strathclyde University as a researcher studying incentive payment schemes. This led to collaboration on *Payment Schemes and Productivity* (Macmillan, 1986).

In 1980 he joined Glasgow University, where he widened his research interests to include small firm growth and development as well as making regular contributions to the Scottish Business School's Doctoral Programme. In 1983 he attended the International Teachers' Programme in Sweden where he met Mark and embarked on a PhD under Mark's supervision. Collaboration continued through the 1990s with the ESRC Teaching Fellowship Scheme. In 1996 he was instrumental in establishing the Graduate Business School at Manchester Metropolitan University and in 2003 joined the ESRC Training and Development Board. There, he was involved in establishing the training guidelines for both doctorate and professional doctorate provision and more recently in initiatives to address capacity building in management and business. In 2003 he contributed to the

ESRC's Evolution of Business Knowledge programme, his research interests including: performance, remuneration and entrepreneurship, management learning and development and leadership. He has published (with others) a number of books including: *Strategic Reward Systems* (Financial Times/Prentice Hall, 2000), *Management and Language: The Manager as Practical Author* (Sage, 2003), *Dictionary of Qualitative Management Research* (Sage, 2008), *Performance Management: Multidisciplinary Perspectives* (Palgrave, 2008) and more recently the *Gower Handbook of Leadership and Management Development* (2010). He was President of the British Academy of Management in 2007, Dean of Fellows in 2012, and is currently Chair of the Society for the Advancement of Management Studies.

PAUL R. JACKSON is Professor of Corporate Communications at Manchester Business School. He has a first degree in Psychology from the University of Sheffield and an MSc in Applied Statistics from Sheffield Polytechnic (now Sheffield Hallam University). His first university post was as a research assistant in studies on impression formation, where he decided that it was worth learning how to write programs in Fortran so that the computer could do the tedious work of adding up and he could do the interesting bits. His research interests have included lab studies of impression formation, large-scale surveys of the impact of unemployment on psychological health, longitudinal field studies of the effects of empowerment and work design on employee health and performance, employee communication and teamworking, mergers and social identity.

He has published widely in journals such as the *Academy of Management Journal, Journal of Applied Psychology, British Medical Journal, Human Relations, Journal of Occupational Health Psychology* and *British Journal of Management*. His books include: *Developments in Work and Organizational Psychology: Implications for International Business* (Elsevier, 2006), *Psychosocial Risk Factors in Call Centres* (HSE Publications, 2003), *Change in Manufacturing: Managing Stress in Manufacturing* (HSE Publications, 2001) and *Organizational Interventions to Reduce the Impact of Poor Work Design* (HSE Publications, 1998).

Over the years he has undertaken various roles including Director of Doctoral Programmes at the University of Sheffield and, at UMIST, Head of the Division of Marketing, International Business and Strategy as well as designing the doctoral training programme at MBS. He has been teaching research methods to undergraduate, masters and doctoral students since 1975 and has contributed to books on research methods teaching as well as workshops for students and teachers on behalf of the British Academy of Management.

PREFACE TO THE FIFTH EDITION

The first edition of this book appeared in 1991, at a time when there were very few management research methods books on the market. It quickly became established as the leading text because it covered all of the essential ground, yet was not too long or intimidating. Students and staff liked it because it tackled difficult issues, but avoided either trivializing them or making them unnecessarily complex. The success of the book was attested by the sales figures, and by the fact that it had become the most highly cited management methodology book in the world according to Google Scholar.

The second edition was published in 2002, and this included a substantial updating of the material since methodology had become a hot topic during the intervening years, and there were many new methods and approaches to management research which needed to be covered. The market had also begun to change significantly, as research methods were starting to be taught at undergraduate level. This resulted in a modest repositioning of our book, but also stimulated the appearance of strong competitors in the market.

The third edition maintained the continuity in the sense that it provided comprehensive treatment of philosophies and methods, plus coverage of both qualitative and quantitative techniques; but it also introduced some radical departures both in terms of content and design. The most significant change was that we strengthened the treatment of quantitative methods, running from the basic techniques for collecting and analysing quantitative data, up to multivariate analysis and structural equation modelling. In keeping with our desire to avoid complications, we covered the principles of analytic methods without introducing complicated algebra. We claimed in the third edition that this part of the book now provided advanced statistics without tears!

The fourth edition was the first edition that deployed full colour. There were additional boxed examples, usually drawn from our own experiences and from those of our students. We also rethought some of the material on philosophy and research design and extended the coverage of qualitative analysis, particularly with the use of computer-assisted methods. The exercises, based on our own extensive methodology teaching, were appropriately updated in response to student feedback. We retained the companion website, developing our guidance to teachers. Perhaps most striking of all to this edition was the addition of a system of icons based around the metaphor of research being like a tree that sucks up nutrients (data, ideas and experiences) from the ground and then converts them into leaves and fruits (reports, publications and theses). Without wanting to labour the metaphor exhaustively, we then went on to develop the icons to illustrate some of the points and as a general orientation tool.

The fifth edition builds on changes made to the book's structure in the fourth edition. We have also changed the order of some of the chapters in order to improve the logic of our arguments and make the text flow better. A new Chapter 1 has been designed to give an overview of the book's content, whilst at the same highlighting what students at all levels need to consider when preparing their research proposals. The chapter on literature searching has been brought forward and updated, and the two qualitative methods chapters have been split into three to mirror the three quantitative methods chapters later in the text. As with other editions, we have offered students an increased number of examples and exercises to help illustrate the points being made or the issues being discussed.

ACKNOWLEDGEMENTS

This book is based on the personal research experience of the authors, but thanks should also go to a number of students and colleagues. Both have contributed to this edition in a number of ways, through their encouragement as well as their ideas. We have tried to reflect their suggestions as far as possible in the text.

Our students have taught us a great deal and we have included a number of their examples, both in this edition and earlier editions. We would like to thank Chavi Chen, Gerard Duff, Ray Forbes, Suzanne Gagnon, Jean Clarke, Anya Johnson, Mohamed Mohamud, Lee Beniston, Kendi Kinuthia, Paul Grimshaw, Anna Zueva, Brian Simpson, Julie Schönfelder, Sanaz Sigaroudi and Geetha Karunanayake.

Colleagues have also assisted us by reading through the transcripts, making comments and suggesting ideas, and to them we are extremely grateful. These include Lisa Anderson, Susan Baker, Joep Cornelissen, Ann Cunliffe, Ardha Danieli, Ashish Dwivedi, Paul Ellwood David Holman, Robin Holt, Ossie Jones, Efthimios Poulis, Christine Reid, Haina Zhang, Liu Wei, Anna Lorbiecki, and Hannah Preston. Jean-Claude Usunier provided a valuable critique of the first edition of the book from a European perspective, and this led to a French translation of the book, which is now in its second edition. Joanne Larty, Mirjam Werner, Daniella Fjellström and Lena Kruckenberg all helped with the preparation and organization of the manuscript from the third edition to the present day, with Lena Kruckenberg being particularly helpful in the restructuring of sections of the book for this fifth edition.

Our editor at SAGE for the first edition was Sue Jones. She provided us with the initial inspiration, and since then Rosemary Nixon, Kiren Shoman, Natalie Aguilera, Delia Alfonso and Alan Maloney offered encouragement, and occasionally hectored us. Our minder for the fourth and fifth edition has been Kirsty Smy.

The authors are grateful to SAGE for permission to include extracts from R. Thorpe and J. Cornelissen (2003) 'Visual media and the construction of meaning' (Ch. 4) in D. Holman and R. Thorpe (eds) (2003), *Management and Language: The Manager as Practical Author*.

We would like to thank our families for their tolerance while this book was being written and rewritten – we hope they will consider the outcome to be worth the effort.

Paul would like to dedicate this book to the memory of Sallie, who died in the final production stages of this edition. She enriched his life beyond measure.

ABOUT THIS BOOK

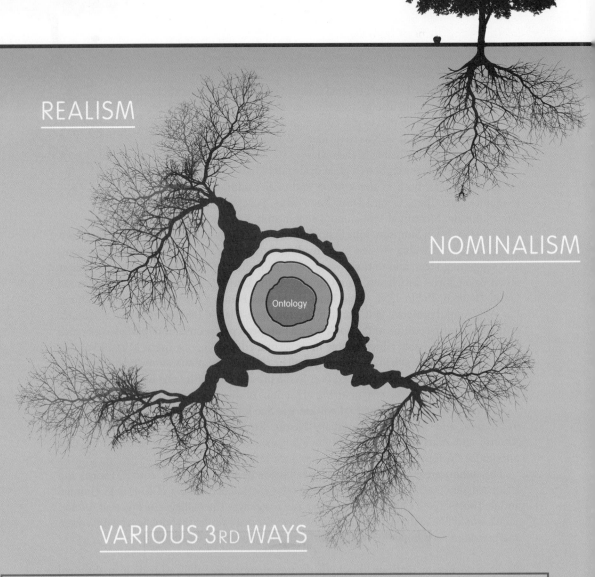

REALISM

NOMINALISM

Ontology

VARIOUS 3RD WAYS

 Ontology

 Epistemology

 Methodology

 Methods and Techniques

We use the metaphor of a tree to represent how the research process unfolds. The key elements of the tree are the roots, the trunk and branches, the leaves, and the fruit – and each of these parallels an aspect of conducting research.

The *roots* symbolize the research traditions within particular disciplines as well as the experiences of past researchers from particular fields. These perspectives, understandings, ideas and beliefs are drawn up (as the tree draws nutrients from the soil) to form the basis of the researcher's ideas in relation to such things as design, methods and forms of analysis.

The *trunk* transports the nutrients from the roots through the branches to the leaves and fruit; it also provides strength and shape to the tree. Here we use a simplified cross-section of the trunk to symbolize four main features of a research design. The inner ring (or heartwood) is the densest part of the trunk, and we use it to represent *ontology*, the basic assumptions made by the researcher about the nature of reality. The next ring represents *epistemology*, the assumptions about the best ways of inquiring into the nature of the world. The third ring from the centre represents *methodology*, or the way research techniques and methods are grouped together to provide a coherent picture. And the fourth ring represents the individual **methods and techniques** that are used for data collection and analysis. The four rings are named and ordered in this way, because the most visible parts of research projects are the methods and techniques used for data collection and analysis and represented by the outer ring. The three inner rings are increasingly hidden from the external observer, yet each makes a critical contribution to the strength, vitality and coherence of the research project.

Moving up and along the *branches*, the leaves and fruit form the tree's canopy. The *leaves* collect energy from sunlight, and represent the collection and analysis of data within a research project. It is the collection of research data that stimulates new ideas and enables the evaluation of existing theories. Here we distinguish between three main kinds of data based on the underlying epistemology (second ring in the trunk), according to whether they are essentially positivist, constructionist or hybrid approaches. To provide differentiation we indicate the positivist approaches in orange, constructionist approaches in green, and hybrid approaches in a combination of these colours.

In the final chapter of the book we focus on the *fruit* of the tree, which represents the way the research is written up and communicated to third parties. Here we show the coherence between the outputs of the research, and the ontology, epistemology, methodology and methods which underpin any research. In this way, the views and

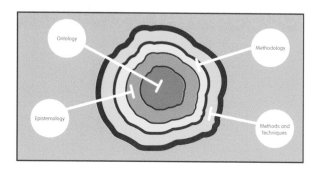

values adopted by the researcher from the early stages of the framing of the research, the design of the research project and the collection of the data are coherently connected and linked.

Within the chapters that follow we have placed a number of these icons in key locations. This is not intended to be exhaustive in the sense that everything is necessarily covered by the icons; nor are we seeking to explain everything through the use of these icons. Our intention is mainly to use them in the light sense as an organizer and as a reminder of the origins of some of the ideas being discussed.

Key of symbols

Ontology

Epistemology

Methodology

Methods and Techniques

Positivist

Constructionist

Hybrid approaches

Output

GUIDED TOUR

LEARNING OBJECTIVES

 To help students think through the issues they will need to consider wh preparing a research proposal.

 To understand the interdepender of philosophy, design and meth in effectively addressing rese questions.

Learning objectives Each chapter starts by setting out clearly what key information you should soon understand, so you can easily track your progress.

research topic i
(Example 1.1)
Having a conceptua
and align their theorizing
through the process outlined
her research and it also helper

Examples Real management and business research examples are highlighted in these boxes, to show you how research happens in reality.

 EXAMPLE
1.1

A PhD student refle

When I initially embarked o
nate, already having an ide
business'. This feeling of
told by my supervisor th
frame my research. D
I eventually came t
consequence l
approach

EXERCISE
2.1

Defining your

a) **Individual exercise**
a short research state
500 to 1,000 words in
ideas and assumptions
work in progress.

b) **Interactive exercise**:
group and ask them to
of your research? Wha

Identifying key

Once the t

Exercises These activities are designed to get you to practise and think about the key research tasks covered in each chapter.

Conclusion Review the contents of each chapter in the Conclusion, an easy-to-read review and discussion of the most important information you've read.

can be
estions of commercial co
the initial client. We discuss iss
mation in more detail in Chapter 5.

CONCLUSION

As we conclude this first chapter, we w
wish to give to their research. This bo
go about conducting such research
need to help in developing practi
and mode 2 research.

need to help in
and mode 2 research.

FURTHER READING

Alvesson, M. and Willmott, H. (eds) (2003) *Stu*
   A collection of chapters for readers who
   management.
Bartunek, J.M., Rynes, S.L. and Daft, R.L. (2
   transfer between practitioners and academ
   This article discusses the role of relationshi
   disseminating knowledge across 'the Gre
Grey, C. (2005) *A Very Short, Fairly Interestin*
   London: Sage.
   As it says on the label, this book prov
   zation, and it is reasonably priced
   for the perspectives of those w
Marshall, S. and Green, N. (200
   Helpful Commentary

Further reading Each chapter ends by highlighting books and articles that provide more in-depth information on the methods presented in each of the chapters and insights into how these methods have been used successfully in existing studies.

CHAPTER 2

Exercise 2.4 Performing literature

b) Individual exercise: *Te*
searches on one specializ
base (such as Web of Scie
(ProQuest), Business Sourc
or JSTOR), on SRRN and
Scholar. Have you found
expected? What were th
How do the results
database compare w
SRRN and Goog

Answers to exercises Turn to the
back of the book to get responses
to those exercises that have
specific answers.

Glossary Key terms appear
in bold in the text, and their
definitions are presented in the
Glossary near the back of the
book.

1-tailed test refers to a directi
tive hypothesis relative to the nu
esis; a prediction of a positive as
between variables, or that one grou
will be bigger than another

2-tailed test refers to a non-dir
alternative hypothesis relative to
hypothesis; association between
may be either positive or negativ
the means of two groups wi
either direction

academic theory expli
through exchang

CHAPTER 1: GETTING S[TARTED:]
THE RESEARCH PROPOS[AL]

Alvesson, M. and Willmott, H. (eds) (2003) *Studyin[g]*
  A collection of chapters for readers who are expl[...]

Bartunek, J.M., Rynes, S.L. and Daft, R.L. (2001)
  between practitioners and academics', *Academy*
  This article discusses the role of relationships b[e...]
  nating knowledge across 'the Great Divide.'

Grey, C. (2005) *A Very Short, Fairly Interesting a[...]*
  Sage.
  As it says on the label, this book provide[...]
  it is reasonably priced. It adopts a cri[...]
  those who are managed, rather t[...]

Further Readings For ease of reference we have gathered the further reading from all chapters into one section.

Bibliography A wealth of reading material is covered here, as all the sources that have collectively informed the writing of this book are gathered in one place.

AACSB (2013) *The Promise of Doctoral Edu[cation:]*
  Quality. Tampa, FL: AACSB International.
Abrahamson, M. (1983) *Social Research Methods.* [...]
Ackermann, F. and Eden, C. (2011) *Making Strategy.* [...]
Ackroyd, S. and Fleetwood, S. (2000) 'Realism in [...]
  S. Ackroyd and S. Fleetwood (eds), *Realist Perspecti[...]*
  pp. 3–25.
Agar, M.H. (1986) *Speaking of Ethnography*. Beverly Hil[...]
Ahmed, S. (1998) *Differences that Matter: Feminist Theor[...]*
  Press.
Ahuja, G. (2000) 'Collaboration networks, structural h[...]*
  Science Quarterly, 45: 425–55.
Aiken, H.D. (1956) *The Age of Ideology*. New York: Me[...]
Alvesson, M. (1990) 'Organization: from substance t[...]
Alvesson, M. (1998) 'Gender relations and identit[y...]
  tions, 51 (8): 969–1005.
Alvesson, M. (2003) 'Beyond neopositivists, r[...]
  sation research', *Academy of Managem[...]*
[Alve]sson, M. and Deetz, S. (2000) *D[...]*
[...] and Kärreman, [...]

$SAGE edge™

edge.sagepub.com/easterbysmith

For the cyber-hungry among you, or for those who are more inclined to read in pixels than in print, this textbook comes with SAGE edge (**edge.sagepub.com/easterbysmith**), a range of free tools and resources that will enhance the teaching and learning experience.

$SAGE edge™ for Students provides a personalised approach to help you accomplish your course-work goals in an easy-to-use learning environment and features:

- **Learning objectives** for each chapter that reinforce the most important material
- Practice **quizzes** that allow you to assess your understanding of course material, with 3 short answer questions per chapter and 10 multiple choice questions per chapter
- Exclusive access to **SAGE journal articles and chapters** which have been carefully selected to support and expand on key concepts and to encourage critical thinking
- Links to **websites and videos** that offer a new perspective and an alternative learning style
- A complete **dataset** so you can practice data analysis with helpful **notes** from the authors
- **Action plan** for a more personalised learning experience
- Mobile friendly **eFlashcards** to strengthen your understanding of key terms and concepts

$SAGE edge™ for Instructors supports teaching by making it easy to integrate quality content and create a rich learning environment for students. **$SAGE edge™** instructor resources for this book include:

- **PowerPoint slides** for each chapter that can be edited for use in teaching
- **Instructor's Manual** containing chapter overviews, hints and tips, guidance on the exercises and examples in the book and additional exercises (some incorporating the use of video).

GETTING STARTED AND WRITING THE RESEARCH PROPOSAL

1

LEARNING OBJECTIVES

 To help students think through the issues they will need to consider when preparing a research proposal.

 To understand the interdependence of philosophy, design and methods in effectively addressing research questions.

 To alert the reader to the impact and engagement agenda.

The landscape of management and business research

Elements of a research proposal

Clear questions and research objectives

Explanation of how the research relates to previous work in the field

Concise description of the research design and methods

The impact and engagement agenda

Conclusion

Further reading

This chapter offers an overview of the book through examining what students need to consider when writing. In doing this, we take the view that the format of proposals is essentially very similar whether for undergraduate projects, postgraduate dissertations or doctorates.

THE LANDSCAPE OF MANAGEMENT AND BUSINESS RESEARCH

Our aim in producing this textbook is to offer an insight into the nature of the landscapes of management and business research and the different skills that will be required to navigate it successfully. The research proposal is, for many students, the first opportunity to test out the logic and content of the research on which they wish to embark.

Within this chapter we set out the thought processes that students might go through, and what they need to consider when writing research proposals. We summarize the nature of the intended project, including what research has taken place before, why it would be useful to conduct a particular study, and why it may be opportune to conduct a study at this time. If the study is at doctoral level, some institutions will require proposals from prospective research candidates before they register; if not, they will certainly do so between three and six months following enrolment. If the purpose of the study is an undergraduate or postgraduate dissertation, then proposals (and their quality) often form part of the assessment process prior to conducting the research. They are often seen as a way of judging to what extent the student has grasped the content of a formal training programme in research methods.

Different types of research also tend to be linked to different levels of degree. *Undergraduate research* tends to be specific and bounded, either as an assignment from tutors or as a question posed by a client. Common projects include small market-research studies, or interview-based studies of employee attitudes. As a consequence, there is more likely to be an emphasis on **applied research**. Again, because of the limitations of time, it is more likely that a single method will be used, and sometimes this might also be specified in advance of the study taking place. The opportunities for choice with these types of project lie mainly around the kind of methods that might be used, and how the results are to be interpreted and communicated. In many cases, undergraduate research projects are also conducted in teams, because – from a teaching point of view – this creates economies of scale, for example when using surveys. It also means that more significant projects can be undertaken in a short period of time, and students can gain the benefits of combining their skills and working together in teams.

Research conducted as part of a *postgraduate taught degree* will normally have greater scope, and more time will be available – often several months over the summer. Again, applied research is likely to predominate. **Evaluation research** is one of the easiest options, and this involves looking at some kind of existing practice and making recommendations for how it might be changed and improved. The advantage of a dissertation that seeks to comment on existing practice is that the company, as well as the student, knows about the organization, and the dissertation will take on some of the features of **action research**. Involvement in change can lead to rich and interesting results, and the student can develop skills that might well be valuable if they are seeking work in consultancy.

Doctoral dissertations are required to produce contributions to knowledge and, as a consequence, an additional element is a certain degree of originality. This suggests that doctoral studies need to contain significant elements of **pure research**. Although doctoral studies may include both applied and action research, the theoretical contribution is a necessary condition for the award of a doctorate. But there are also other contributions that can be made and assessed within a thesis. One of those is the individual's understanding of the research process adopted in the search for new ideas. This might come from the invention of new procedures and methods, the replication of existing studies in new contexts, or the application of new theoretical perspectives to existing research questions. For many students, the thesis is their first exposure to the world of work and organizational life; empirical studies conducted within an organizational context can give students a valuable insight into the world of work. This in turn can lead to insights into how the results of their research study can be of use to management and business practice, and as an applied field of study; this can be a contribution in its own right.

Funded projects are usually conducted by experienced researchers, but require many of the same decisions as projects conducted as part of university degrees. The required outputs will depend on the expectations of the funding body: if funding is provided by a company, there may be an emphasis on applied research; and if it is funded by a research council, then there will be an emphasis on pure research.

Of course, the reader should not assume that research is undertaken only by qualified and trained individuals. In many ways, research is something that managers do as a natural part of their everyday activity, collecting and analysing data and drawing conclusions. Also, consultants conduct research, and many management and business students go on to become consultants in later life.

What often differs, though, is the level of sophistication in the methods used, as well as the speed with which answers are sought.

Thinking about the role of research

Individual or interactive exercise: What is the role of research in relation to the job of academics, compared to the role of research in relation to the job of practitioners who embark on research projects to improve organizational practices, to innovate or to explore new areas of activity?

EXERCISE
1.1

A recent report by the Association to Advance Collegiate Schools of Business (AACSB, 2013) highlighted two dimensions on which scholarship might differ while still remaining of high quality. One dimension focused on whether the research was based on or undertaken by practitioners conducting their own investigations (or perhaps acting as consultants) or by academics whose interest lay in more abstract theories and ideas. The second dimension focused on whether the research being conducted was basic foundational research (aiming to produce 'general theory') or was focused on producing knowledge to be translated into practice (perhaps case-specific research that values the richness of context and explicit solutions to particular problems).

These issues and the main links between types and levels of research are discussed in more detail in later chapters; factors that require a particular emphasis in relation to management and business (e.g. the political and the philosophical factors that can influence the way research is conducted in this field) are highlighted.

ELEMENTS OF A RESEARCH PROPOSAL

Formal research proposals are becoming necessary at most levels. Organizations that fund research, whether academic or applied, have to ensure that their money is being wisely spent, so a paper trail has now become necessary. At the higher level, research councils now require very detailed (but concise) proposals before they will allocate money to applicants; there are similar requirements for those upgrading their registration within doctoral programmes, sometimes referred to as 'the transfer'. Even when there is no formal requirement to produce a research proposal, the exercise of doing so is an extremely good discipline that can help students draw together what they already know, their early ideas and what the literature says on the topic. There is some truth in the saying that 'you don't know what you think until you see what you say'! So, for many, writing a proposal offers the opportunity to begin to see how elements of the research process come together, and to demonstrate for others the coherence of what is being proposed.

To draw an analogy with cooking, a research proposal might be seen as a recipe, for which ingredients are needed. Some of these ingredients are essential for good taste (i.e. quality), while others are less important. Some chefs (researchers) will approach cooking the dish in one way, and others in another. Bringing out certain textures or flavours while suppressing others requires skill, and this both depends on preferences and requires practice, ideas and a vision of what is being aimed for. Thus, the purpose of proposals is to set out the ingredients required, and how the food will be prepared and served. For example, what kind of dish is to be served? Is it fast food of relatively poor quality or high-quality cuisine? What ingredients will be used, and what cooking procedures and kitchen utensils will be required to prepare the particular dish? This translates to the importance of students being both qualified and capable of undertaking their study, and to supervisors being assured that the research is feasible and likely to contribute to generating the knowledge claimed.

Although the requirements for research proposals do differ from institution to institution, there are some common elements that can be discerned.

CLEAR RESEARCH QUESTIONS AND RESEARCH OBJECTIVES

Clarity in relation to the focus of the research is usually achieved by students setting out the main research questions to be investigated and describing the aims that will link to the outcomes of the research. Expressions such as 'to investigate' or 'to study' are not aims in themselves and need to be avoided. In addition, the aims need to be consistent with the method or methodology adopted; in other words, they need to be capable of being achieved through the methods proposed. Overly general or ambitious aims can also be problematic. There have been many occasions when supervisors have been heard to remark that for this research to be completed, six researchers would need to work on it for a lifetime!

There can be several purposes behind a particular research project and these need to be clearly articulated. They include the recognition of patterns in data or information; the development or refinement of a particular methodological approach; the ability to generalize to a wider population; and the ability to describe a problem in a sufficiently detailed way to show the realism of a particular context. We will consider all of these in later chapters of the book.

Having a clear objective is extremely important as it helps students to understand and identify an interesting research project. Students will need to know, for example, what are relevant criteria for deciding that a research idea is worth pursuing and appropriate. Tracy (2013) gives some useful advice on this, suggesting that there are a number of ways for students to generate their research ideas. For example, ideas may stem from:

- the student's personal life – such as family, work, political beliefs and travel
- current societal problems or organizational dilemmas – such as the cost of food waste, or issues relating to ethnicity and employment
- current events – such as societal needs or policy debates
- current research debates – as expressed, for example, in the Point Counterpoint papers in the *Journal of Management Studies* or in review papers on a particular topic, such as in the *International Journal of Management Reviews*.

EXPLANATION OF HOW THE RESEARCH RELATES TO PREVIOUS WORK IN THE FIELD

Understanding the literature in the area in which the student wishes to be taken seriously is an important prelude to a research project. Not only is it the means by which students see what work has been undertaken on the subject before, but also it provides a stimulus to what focus the study might have and how it might be undertaken.

At every level – undergraduate, postgraduate and doctorate – there will generally be an expectation of evidence that the student has an understanding of what literature already exists on a particular subject. Although there is often no specific expectation to be definitive, there should be sufficient evidence produced to indicate that there is a question to be answered. This is because it is through generating knowledge via the research that those in the field will become more knowledgeable. A simple test that might be used here would be to reflect on whether the research proposal would convince someone with a good knowledge of the area that the individual has a sufficiently good grasp of the relevant current literature and the boundaries of that knowledge to claim that the topic warrants further research.

There are a number of different ways of thinking about how knowledge might be created, and students employ different strategies for different reasons. Research is about both a creative and a disciplined sense of curiosity; how researchers employ different strategies (sometimes simultaneously) in order to choose their research questions is dealt with in detail in Chapter 2. One way of crafting a review of previous work in the field that we discuss later is the notion of defining a gap. Gaps can be defined in at least three ways: to take well-understood and mainstream methods from one area of the social sciences and use them (perhaps for the first time) in another; to take a well-understood problem within a particular discipline that has been explored in a particular way, and to investigate the same phenomenon using a different methodological approach; or to identify contradictory results and try, through the research, to reconcile them or produce new findings.

However gaps are defined, the role of the researcher is to show how their research serves to fill the gap and, in so doing, to offer explanations that are new and original, producing knowledge that extends understanding of the problem or the field.

Some academics go even further and suggest that the role of research students, through the way they present their research, is to create gaps. Tom Lupton, an early researcher in the field of management and business, and an anthropologist by training, likened this process to a blind person crawling along a chain-link fence feeling for a gap through which it would be possible to crawl in order to get to the other side. Once the person found even the smallest chink in the fence, the requirement would be to prise out a hole large enough to crawl through.

Another approach, which is quite different, relies on a creative process of 'disciplined imagination', a phrase coined by Karl Weick (1989). This process is undertaken with a high degree of intuition and creative thinking, and contrasts with the 'gap spotting' approach outlined above. The argument being made by Weick is that unlike the natural science model of research, which many social scientists try to emulate, social science is rather different and as a consequence requires a different approach. This approach involves researchers thinking about a subject or problem and 'imagining' the different ways in which they might operationalize their study.

Such an approach would normally surface a range of alternatives and perspectives from which choices can be made (the 'disciplined' part), which in turn are further specified in terms of more detailed hypotheses, research designs and questions which are built into the conduct of the research. Weick also suggests that the thinking process involved in disciplined imagination takes place simultaneously as opposed to sequentially and includes three elements: problem statements, through trials, and finally, the criteria used for selection.

Cornelissen (2006) suggests that it is helpful for researchers to engage in a series of mental experiments which he refers to as 'thought trials', where researchers iterate between the reviewed literature, preliminary analysis, background assumptions and their intuition to consider a variety of metaphors, ideas as representations of the subject or problem in hand (imagination) before selecting and deciding on the way the problem might be conceptualized and, consequently, how the research might be most appropriately conducted (discipline).

Weick suggests that such an approach offers an active role for researchers who can imagine and construe theoretical representations, rather than see theoretical representations as deductively or naturally following on from a literature review. In Weick's words, research and theorizing is more like artificial selection than natural selection, as the research, rather than nature, intentionally guides the evolutionary process of selecting new ideas and theoretical representations (1989: 819).

In practice, this means that all researchers will imagine and construe theoretical representations in their own way, leading to different theoretical representations even though the general topic of the research is the same. Further, the researchers' educational and cultural backgrounds, as well as their previous research experiences, will all serve to affect the way in which they view a research topic conceptually.

An example of someone who has gone through a process of conceptualizing their research topic in this way is offered by Joanne, a doctoral student at Cardiff Business School (Example 1.1)

Having a conceptual model is not meant to restrict the student, merely to help guide and align their theorizing in more productive and focused ways. Joanne indicated that through the process outlined below, she found many new and different avenues to follow in her research and it also helped having a guide to keep the research project focused.

EXAMPLE
1.1

A PhD student reflects on conceptualization

When I initially embarked on the PhD programme I thought that I was quite fortunate, already having an idea of what subject area I wanted to explore: 'the family in business'. This feeling of security quickly changed to a state of anxiety when I was told by my supervisor that I would have to have some kind of 'conceptual model' to frame my research. Despite initially trying to hope this requirement would disappear, I eventually came to accept that I have to have a basis from which to work and as a consequence I would need to have to look for a 'model' which justified my chosen approach. My salvation was my supervisor, who proposed I use his model on networking and 'systems of exchange'. It took some time for me to see how this model would fit with my research area – family business – while making a contribution to organization theory, but, after reading more of the literature, connections began to emerge between these two aspects which I incorporated into the conceptual schema. Social capital literature made a good bridge and other links became apparent and began to fall into place. It was the identification of the linkages that led to the building of the conceptual model below. This was aided by the fact that I was able to use my masters as a pilot study for the PhD, and this really helped me get a sense of how I could apply the features of the model. It also highlighted to me elements that could be included in the model that currently were not, such as trust and the differing orientations to action of the different actors in a relationship. The diagram below represents my thinking of 'if that, plus that, are taken into account, then maybe we may end up with a model looking something like that ...' This has meant that the initial conceptual development is something like a hypothesis or research question and will serve to guide my research and help me stay focused. See Figure 1.1.

FIGURE 1.1

An example of a conceptual framework

The debates and approaches that Joanne refers to are covered and illustrated in Chapter 2 (on reviewing the literature). There, we set out how students might begin to appreciate what a literature review entails at different levels, and why it is necessary to undertake one. It also includes those practical skills that researchers will need in order both to identify and to record relevant literature for inclusion later in either a literature-review chapter or in the analysis and discussion sections of the thesis. Most importantly, the chapter helps researchers to understand what is meant by a critical review, including how researchers might evaluate the literature in order to persuade their audience of the value of their research.

CONCISE DESCRIPTION OF THE RESEARCH DESIGN AND METHODS

The second element of a research proposal is a concise statement of the design to be adopted and the methods which will be used to meet the objectives. We consider that good research design is fundamental to achieving high-quality research, and so we have brought together in Chapter 4 an analysis of design principles and applications in different areas of research.

Before exploring design in detail, we think it is important for students to understand the different philosophical assumptions that underlie management and business research, and in particular to reflect on their own position, and we do this in Chapter 3. Through appreciating the strengths and weaknesses of these different perspectives, students will be able to appreciate how different philosophical assumptions influence the criteria used when judging the quality of research, how the assumptions made about research philosophy directly impact on research design, and how the quality of the design proposed might also be judged.

Having settled on an appropriate research design based on a preferred philosophical position, the next step is to consider the kinds of data to be collected, and research projects may propose to use either **primary data** or **secondary data** sources. Most of the examples we use throughout the book involve the collection of primary data directly by the researchers. Primary data can lead to new insights and greater confidence in the outcomes of the research, which is very useful for students wishing to use their research experience as a basis for subsequent careers in management consultancy. It is normally expected that dissertations at undergraduate, postgraduate and doctoral levels will include some primary data.

However, some subjects – such as economics and finance – rely more on public or corporate financial data and statistics (see Chapter 9). Research using secondary data like this has value through exploring new relationships and patterns within these existing data, and we give some examples later in the book. In Chapter 2, we consider published literature as another form of secondary data, especially in the form of literature surveys. Reinterpreting what has gone before is important so as to avoid repeating something that has already been done, as well as to provide new understandings which can guide empirical research.

The method section of the proposal may well be divided up into discrete stages of the research, and each of these should be clearly linked to the aims of the research. On occasions, some of the stages may have already been completed through a previous research project. If this is the case, it is also worth linking to the nature of this research, how it was conducted, and what conclusions were derived.

The most important feature of a good research proposal is that the study design and the methods of enquiry should be appropriate to answering the research questions. The literature review section should summarize existing knowledge, and identify gaps in that knowledge which are the focus for the research questions. The design and method sections then explain how the researcher intends to answer those questions. Figure 1.2 illustrates the balance that we believe should be struck between the research design and most appropriate methods to meet its requirements; the research questions asked within the field; and the skills of the individuals to carry out the research, undertake the analysis and communicate

FIGURE 1.2

Balancing the components of research

the results. The biggest section of this book is concerned with methods, and we follow conventional practice by looking separately at qualitative methods and quantitative methods.

Chapter 6 offers an overview of the nature of **qualitative data** and why data of this type are collected. It focuses on textual data (both primary and secondary) and how data are created through language. We specifically examine the nature of the qualitative interview and how interviews might be appropriately conducted, as well as textual data (again primary and secondary) through such devices as diaries. Many research participants may never before have considered the answers to the questions posed in a qualitative interview, and so their views may be hidden or only partly understood. A key characteristic of a skilled researcher is the ability to work with study participants to allow their opinions to surface. We conclude Chapter 6 with a reflection on how researchers might gain access to, and collect and store, data – including raising issues of data protection and the avoidance of **bias**.

Chapter 7 focuses on the creation of qualitative data through observation and interactions that take place between researchers and respondents and/or users. The techniques that we explain include **participant observation** and a variety of participatory tools that researchers might use in order to elicit understanding from settings being studied. In studies like this, it is important to be aware of the ethical issues linked to these methods, as well as on the risks and opportunities that occur through involvement and interaction in the field. It is particularly important in qualitative studies for the researcher to reflect on the ways in which they are influencing the individuals from whom information is being collected, the research process and the research outcomes. This kind of **reflexivity** is an important and valuable part of the qualitative research process, and we will examine later how it influences in conducting 'good' research.

Chapter 8 offers an overview of the different types of analysis of qualitative data, explaining how these map on and link to different philosophical traditions. Again, we stress the difference between pre-structured approaches (e.g. **content analysis**) and emergent approaches to analysis (**grounded analysis**), stressing the importance of adopting a systematic approach, while remaining flexible and creative in the analysis. The chapter covers data-analysis techniques, focusing on how patterns within the data can be identified through the way the data are indexed and coded. More recent methods, such as the analysis of visual data, are also included. Chapter 7 also introduces a range of computer-aided analysis tools and techniques, describing how these might be used, offering an overview of the main packages and suggesting how students might find out more about them. Within the qualitative tradition, we highlight the importance of the interplay between theory, data and analysis through the process of research. The concluding part of the chapter discusses the criteria that might be used for assessing the quality of qualitative research.

The next section of the book (Chapters 9, 10 and 11) details opportunities, expectations and methods that would be required if research students decide to undertake their research within a quantitative tradition. Chapter 9 builds on the foundations laid down in Chapters 3 and 4, and focuses on alternative sources of quantitative data and the craft of designing structured questionnaires with well-defined questions and appropriate measurement scales.

The next two chapters cover analysis of quantitative data. Here, we follow the same principle as everywhere else in the book, by focusing on understanding *why* particular methods are used rather than simply knowing *what* to do. Comments in a research proposal such as 'analysis will be undertaken using statistical methods' or 'the analysis will be undertaken using SPSS' will detract from the credibility of the research. SPSS is one of many software packages, and it almost never matters what software is used to achieve a result. What matters much more is the kind of analysis to be undertaken and how that analysis enables the research to answer the research questions specified in the proposal.

Chapter 10 discusses the principles behind summarizing quantitative data, and then considers the way in which significance tests can be used to make inferences from a researcher's sample data. Inference is a vital element in a research proposal, since it provides the link between summaries of sample data and answers to research questions which will be expressed in terms of a more general population. Chapter 11 is more advanced in that it covers **multivariate** analysis, and we include it in the book because the methods we describe reflect more faithfully the reality of management and business research where many factors need to be considered at the same time.

THE IMPACT AND ENGAGEMENT AGENDA

Students carrying out research projects are now facing conflicting demands. They are supposed to deliver parsimonious and abstract theory in order to contribute to academic debate, while at the same time they are expected to provide detailed solutions to practical problems. Closer linking of research to societal needs or challenges is becoming an irresistible pressure within management and business research – and within university research more generally – as there is an increased emphasis given to relevance to the real world in all walks of life.

Because of this pressure, it has been argued that undertaking research differently – by researching in teams, first valuing the perspective of practitioners and focusing on problems that really matter to them – could be a way in which management and business researchers can both write scholarly papers and at the same time create 'useful' knowledge. Gibbons et al. (1994) described two forms of research: **mode 1 research** concentrates on the production of knowledge, with academics working from the perspective of their own discipline and focusing on theoretical questions and problems; and **mode 2 research** generates knowledge through direct engagement with social practice and problems. Some scholars (e.g. Tranfield, 2002) argue that management research should follow the latter approach, with its emphasis on practical application. Others (e.g. Huff, 2000) suggest a compromise position where both theoretical and practical work is required, and this is sometimes characterized as **mode 1½**.

Many institutions now have in place performance-measurement systems that address impact within research. As a consequence, younger researchers need to take the impact and engagement agenda seriously if they are to be successful within their careers.

One of the key features of basic research is that its results are brought into the public domain for debate and disseminated through academic books, articles, conference papers and theses that aim mainly at an academic audience. Dissemination is seen as of primary importance and a major responsibility for the researcher, and career progression for academics depends on getting the fruits of their research published in the most prestigious journals. This is seen as proof of the quality of the work. In contrast, **applied research** is intended to lead to the solution of specific problems, and usually involves working with clients to identify important problems and deciding how best to tackle them. There are several variants of applied research. In evidence-based practice research, practitioner knowledge and the results of previous research into the particular issue being studied – as well as the researcher's own understandings and results of empirical research – are seen as important to comprehending particular phenomena. **Action research** is another approach that involves making changes within an organization or its parts in order to understand the dynamic forces there. Action research recognizes that there can be multiple outcomes: academic outcomes for the researcher; and practical outcomes, often the result of organizational changes made through the research process. **Engaged research** requires close collaboration between academics and practitioners (Van de Ven and Johnson, 2006).

The results of applied research always need to be reported to the client, who is likely to evaluate the quality of the research in terms of its usability. But there is always the potential to publish the results of applied research in practitioner or professional journals, provided the results can be shown to have wider significance, although this possibility often raises questions of commercial confidentiality and the need to maintain good relationships with the initial client. We discuss issues such as ethics, confidentiality and the control of information in more detail in Chapter 5.

CONCLUSION

As we conclude this first chapter, we would like to encourage readers to reflect on the emphasis they wish to give to their research. This book will help them in the choices they make and how they might go about conducting such research. Certainly, the next generation of management researchers will need to help in developing practices that enable new ways of integrating the demands of mode 1 and mode 2 research.

FURTHER READING

Alvesson, M. and Willmott, H. (eds) (2003) *Studying Management Critically*. London: Sage.
    A collection of chapters for readers who are exploring areas for critical research in business and management.
Bartunek, J.M., Rynes, S.L. and Daft, R.L. (2001) 'Across the Great Divide: knowledge creation and transfer between practitioners and academics', *Academy of Management Journal*, 44, 340–355.
    This article discusses the role of relationships between practitioners and academics in generating and disseminating knowledge across 'the Great Divide'.
Grey, C. (2005) *A Very Short, Fairly Interesting and Reasonably Cheap Book About Studying Organizations*. London: Sage.
    As it says on the label, this book provides a succinct overview of theories of management and organization, and it is reasonably priced. It adopts a critical view in the sense that it has a slight preference for the perspectives of those who are managed, rather than the managers themselves.
Marshall, S. and Green, N. (2007) *Your PhD Companion: A Handy Mix of Practical Tips, Sound Advice and Helpful Commentary to See You Through Your PhD*, 2nd edn. Oxford: Cromwell Press.
    A handy guidebook for readers embarking on doctoral study – and a good read.
Thomas, A. (2004) *Research Skills for Management Studies*. New York: Routledge.
    A comprehensive overview of skills required to conduct management research.

Want to know more about this chapter? Visit the ⓈSAGE edge™ website at **https://edge. sagepub.com/easterbysmith** to access practice questions, selected journal articles, useful web links and much more.

REVIEWING THE LITERATURE

2

LEARNING OBJECTIVES

 To appreciate what a literature review in management and business research entails, and why it is necessary.

 To learn the practical skills needed to search, identify and record relevant literature.

 To understand how to evaluate critically different sources of information, and know how to write literature reviews.

What is a literature review and what are its main purposes?

Preparing a literature review: finding and recording relevant literature

Finding relevant literature

Evaluating literature

Writing a literature review

Conclusion

Further reading

This chapter considers how students at different levels can discover what is already known within a particular field, and identify gaps in the literature, for their own study. Whether it is for undergraduate dissertations, masters or doctoral level, a literature review is an essential part of any study. The main differences between levels of study are predominantly the time constraints in place, and the breadth and depth of the literature review required.

The literature review should provide students with a basic understanding of how the topic has developed over time and what remains to be investigated. Anyone starting a research project should be aware of the existing theories and research in their field. A good literature review not only deals with the traditional sources such as books and journal articles, but also may include knowledge gained from experts such as managers, consultants and official bodies. It is important for (management and business) researchers to be in touch with a range of perspectives and sources, whether these are held by the organization or in the public domain. **Search engines** and bibliographic databases make it easy to identify relevant books and articles, but there are now a range of other electronic resources, such as topic-related websites, podcasts and news items. The first part of this chapter defines what a literature review is and details its purposes. It then gives an overview of the literature review process and of different sources of information. The second part outlines how to prepare a literature review, beginning with a section on how to identify relevant keywords, followed by sections on undertaking bibliographical searches, and accessing and recording relevant material. The third part explains how to classify, read and evaluate literature throughout the review process. This leads to the fourth part, which discusses how to align a literature review with the context and approach of a given study, and offers some tips for structuring and writing a literature review. The chapter concludes with some final reflections on the role of the literature review in qualitative and quantitative research. While we hope that the guidance offered in this chapter will assist readers in conducting their own literature reviews, we strongly advise them to complement these insights with those provided by their own local library.

WHAT IS A LITERATURE REVIEW AND WHAT ARE ITS MAIN PURPOSES?

A literature review is an analytical summary of an existing body of research in the light of a particular research issue. In a literature review, researchers describe, evaluate and clarify what is already known about a subject area. There are different types of literature reviews. Stand-alone reviews are published as individual review articles, and provide an overview and synthesis of a particular research topic or field of study. More often, however, literature reviews are a part of a wider research output such as research proposals, reports, papers, dissertations or monographs. Given that the ability to advance current understanding depends on prior knowledge of the subject under study, literature reviews are fundamental to any research endeavour. Literature reviews help researchers to *learn from previous research* but they also serve a number of additional purposes. A well-written literature review *provides a context* for a research project and helps to *refine its topic*. It can help highlight flaws in previous research and outline gaps in the knowledge about a certain topic. In this way, a literature review indicates *what a research project is adding* to the understanding of a field, *justifying* why the research is being undertaken, and ensuring that the research undertaken *fits in* with the existing wider research within the subject area. Chris Hart's expanded definition of a literature review touches upon the multiple purposes of a literature review:

> The selection of available documents (both published and unpublished) on the topic, which contain information, ideas, data and evidence written from a particular standpoint to fulfil certain aims or express certain views on the nature of the topic and how it is to be investigated, and the effective evaluation of these documents in relation to the research being proposed. (2005: 13)

The literature review in the research process

It is important to note that when researchers talk about their literature reviews, they often mean the process of reviewing the literature as much as the selection of literature they work with, and the actual output of this process (i.e. the literature review as a specific type of text). Most literature reviews are continued throughout all stages of the research process. When planning a research project, researchers prepare literature reviews to explore a subject area and to develop ideas about how they can conduct research in this area. By reviewing the literature around their research topic, they improve their understanding of key issues, concepts, theories and methodologies that define their field of study. They identify leading scholars and research organizations, and develop a sense of how past and ongoing debates have shaped the development of their fields. Once a gap has been identified in the area of knowledge that they wish to research, researchers continue to work on their literature reviews as they re-evaluate their position in ongoing debates, revise their research questions, and figure out how to frame their research. As their research progresses, they expand the catalogue of keywords they use for their literature searches, check for new research findings, and venture into related fields. Most reviews require further modifications as the research progresses. This is due in part to empirical findings that might lead the research in a new direction, or the emergence of new findings that have to be taken into account in order to be as up to date as possible. Finally, in the process of writing up a report, thesis or dissertation, most literature reviews have to be revised in the context of the research findings and their contribution to the subject area. The completed review provides the context and justifies the research for which it has been prepared.

Sources of information

What is considered to be an appropriate source for a literature review depends on the aim and topic of the review, and also on the traditions of the discipline. However, in most academic disciplines, _peer-reviewed journal articles_ are considered to be the most important source of information because it is through the peer-review process that the quality and relevance of the research can be judged. _Academic books and reference works_ are another important source of established knowledge; _working papers and theses_ provide access to the latest research, as do some _academic websites, research blogs and podcasts_. Many supervisors advise their students to stick only to peer-reviewed academic literature. But there are topics that require researchers to consider non-academic sources; these sources are known as 'grey' literature. Examples of these are _publications and websites by governmental and non-governmental bodies_, including firms and media outlets. Professional associations and expert groups often run their own _websites, email lists, newsletters and online forums_; and they organize conferences and workshops that facilitate networking and the exchange of information. Last but not least, there is _the Internet_, which allows access to information on all sorts of topics.

A literature review can and should be based on a wide range of information, but it should also aim to give a truthful and balanced account of the research and knowledge that exist on a certain topic. It is evident that some sources of information are more appropriate and more reliable than others: a peer-reviewed article has been reviewed and accepted by several international experts in the field; and a book has been published by a publisher who considers it worthwhile, often after seeking the support of external reviewers. A blog or website, however, might reflect the ideas of just one person – perhaps even an individual with very little understanding of the topic. Data made available through governmental websites, for example, may be much more reliable than data posted by someone from a lobby group. This, of course, does not imply that state-sponsored websites are somehow value-free or neutral; they should still be considered critically.

In our information age, researchers should embrace the opportunities that arise from the World Wide Web of information, while at the same time remaining cautious about the credibility and appropriateness of the information they access. Given the absence of quality controls, many researchers see the Internet as both a blessing and a curse (Fink, 2005; Lee, 2000). It appears to offer them immediate access to 'everything' – but ultimately can be a very time-consuming resource to work with, as it also requires them to assess the quality of each piece of information they wish to include in their review (Fink, 2005). Table 2.1 lists four areas that require thorough consideration before web-based information can be included in a literature review.

TABLE 2.1   Criteria for evaluating sources of information

1. PURPOSE: What is the purpose of this source? What are the motivations or interests that led to its creation?

2. AUTHORSHIP: Who is responsible for the source? Are the authors/producers authoritative in this subject?

3. CREDIBILITY AND ACCURACY: Why should this be credible information? Do the authors give enough information so that their claims and methods can be evaluated? Has this information been taken up or mentioned in peer-reviewed sources? If not, what might be the reason? Is the information it contains objective or biased? How accurate is the information?

4. TIMELINESS: When was the source created? When was it last updated?

SOURCE: BASED ON A SIMILAR SET OF MORE SPECIFIC QUESTIONS DEVELOPED BY FINK (2005)

Types of literature reviews

As can already be seen from these introductory paragraphs, conducting a literature review is a research activity in itself, requiring a wide range of research skills and analytical capabilities. Before moving on to the next sections, which detail what skills are needed to conduct a literature review, it is instructive to draw attention to the fact that there are different types of literature reviews. A *traditional literature review* summarizes a body of literature and draws conclusions about the topic in question (Jesson et al., 2011). This review should aim to be 'systematic, explicit, comprehensive and reproducible' (Fink, 2005: 17). However, some reviewers adhere to stricter criteria than others. Traditional literature reviews are defined by what the reviewer considers to be the most interesting or most relevant sources. While they discuss a bounded area of research, they might leave out debates or issues that the reviewer considers less relevant. For most traditional reviews, the criteria for the selection and evaluation of literature remain implicit; that is, they structure the review but are not openly stated.

In contrast, **systematic literature reviews** strive to 'comprehensively identify, appraise and synthesize *all* relevant studies on a given topic' (Petticrew and Roberts, 2006: 19, emphasis added). They require reviewers to provide explicit and rigorous criteria for identifying, including, evaluating and synthesizing their material. Typically, systematic reviews consider peer-reviewed academic articles only. Through searches of the main bibliographic databases, topic-related peer-reviewed articles are identified that correspond to the search criteria stated in the literature review. Each filtering decision is noted down in order to ensure that articles are not selected on the basis of personal preference. The selected articles are then evaluated against a previously defined set of criteria, using rigorous methods. Systematic reviews have become increasingly common across the academic disciplines, but they have their advantages and disadvantages (see Table 2.2; and see Example 2.3, in the last section of this chapter, for a description of a systematic review). Many academics value systematic reviews as the more objective and 'scientific' type of review, given that they are replicable and more transparent. However, if they cover a wider field, systematic reviews can be rather time-consuming; they tend to favour journal articles over other sources such as book chapters or reports; and many reviewers rely heavily on the assessment of abstracts rather than full-text articles, which can lead to misconceptions and oversights. As noted by Jesson et al. (2011: 15), traditional reviews can provide 'insights that can be neglected or passed over in the steps towards inclusion and quality control that are required in the systematic review model'. The formalized structure of systematic reviews can make it difficult to justify innovative approaches or to start new discourses that break with the predominant understanding of a topic.

TABLE 2.2 Pros and cons of systematic reviews

Pros	Cons
Involving collection from a broad range of sources that might cross over into other disciplinary areas related to management and business	Limiting creativity and intuition
	Overlooking important 'grey' literature, e.g. reports
Aiding interdisciplinarity through highlighting cross-disciplinary themes	Being restricted by the accessibility of sources
	Requiring keyword search strings to be identifiable
Increasing transparency of the review	Failing to reach older 'scanned' texts
Increasing replicability of the review	Relying on databases that support 'keyword' search
Being 'systematic' and so offering a sense of rigour	
Aiding the process of synthesis through the increased scope possible	Relying on the quality of the abstract (often limited to 100 words)

SOURCE: THORPE ET AL., 2005

However, it should be noted that a high-quality systematic review can make an important contribution to the understanding of its field. While literature reviews remain secondary sources (given that they do not report any new research findings), they can synthesize a certain research topic or problem in a novel or particularly illuminating way. Published reviews of literature can be seen in specialist review journals such as *International Journal of Management Reviews*, *Academy of Management Review*, *Annual Review of Organizational Psychology and Organizational Behavior* and *Psychological Review*. These journals act as invaluable resources for those wishing to gain an overview of existing studies in a particular field – and hence are an important source of information when starting a new literature review.

The review process

Conducting literature reviews requires, but also enhances, a broad range of academic skills. First, researchers need to develop appropriate skills in information-seeking, which allow them to identify and access relevant sources of information. Second, researchers enhance their critical-appraisal skills by evaluating existing research in writing. It can be useful to structure the review process, in terms of comprising a number of general stages or steps that require different skills and techniques. Figure 2.1 gives an overview of the review process. It identifies three different stages. First, the topic, scope and aim of the literature review needs to be established, so that keywords and search terms can be identified (top row). Second, literature needs to be found, recorded and evaluated – three tasks that require a transparent and systematic approach, consistent and orderly 'housekeeping', and critical thinking and analytic rigour (middle row). Third, the reviewed literature needs to be summarized and organized around different themes. Once these have been aligned with the wider research project, writing a literature review can be the easiest step of the entire process (bottom row). The arrows

FIGURE 2.1
The review process

between the different tasks indicate that most literature reviews evolve not in a linear process but rather in several loops. For example, it might become necessary to revise the topic or research question throughout the review process and, as a result, to repeat and modify certain literature searches.

PREPARING A LITERATURE REVIEW: FINDING AND RECORDING RELEVANT LITERATURE

Be precise about the *topic, the scope, and the aim of a literature review* from the beginning, as the review might otherwise cover too broad a field or not stay sufficiently focused. The topic of a review arises from the main theme or research question of a given research project. Once the topic is clear, there are numerous ways in which a literature search can be done – but it should always follow the aim of the research. It can be very helpful to start a literature review with a brief written research statement covering the following questions:

- What is the topic of my research?
- Why is this topic relevant, important or interesting?
- How does this project relate to past research in this field?
- What are the main concepts and theories that could be relevant?
- What is the aim of the literature review, and how does it relate to the aim of my research?
- What could be an appropriate working title for this review?

A written research statement marks the official starting point of the review process. While none of the responses has to be perfect, it is helpful to write these down in order to make research questions, expectations and knowledge gaps more explicit.

In series of revisions, the focus and scope of the research topic and the literature review may shift. For example, if the selected topic is one that has already attracted a lot of research, it often makes sense to narrow it down further, in order to avoid becoming overwhelmed by too much information. If the topic is very narrow or innovative, it might be necessary to broaden it out in order to find enough related material.

Defining your topic

a) **Individual exercise**: Decide on a working title for your literature review and write a short research statement that addresses the six questions listed above (about 500 to 1,000 words in total). The statement should help you to articulate your ideas and assumptions. It does not have to be perfect and should be considered work in progress.

b) **Interactive exercise**: Give your research statement to one or two students in your group and ask them to comment on it. Do they understand the topic and intention of your research? What aspects do they find most/least interesting? Why?

Identifying keywords

Once the topic and aim of a literature review are decided, keywords are much easier to identify. This second step can be facilitated by some initial reading of scholarly publications on the topic, noting down important terms and concepts. Sometimes, it can also be helpful to consult a wider range of sources, such as the *Financial Times*, or the *World Investments Report* (WIR), published annually by the United Nations Conference on Trade and Development (UNCTAD). Most articles carry keywords beneath the abstract that identify themes addressed in the study. These can be invaluable filters when looking to focus one's literature review. The most useful source, however, is usually the research statement, which already identifies a number of relevant concepts. By noting down such concepts and their relationships (e.g. when creating a mind-map or a Venn diagram of overlapping circles), researchers can further explore their ideas and identify additional keywords. Figure 2.2 gives an example of a simple Venn diagram for a literature review on the roles played by creativity and innovation in science and engineering.

As the Venn diagram becomes more detailed and includes more keywords, it might begin to look more like a daisy with several overlapping petals (Luker, 2008). In the process of revising the diagram, it is useful to start an accompanying list of keywords, taking into

FIGURE 2.2
Venn diagram of keywords

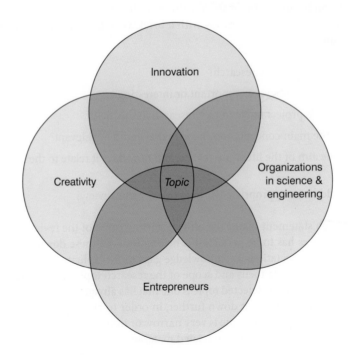

account synonyms and alternative terminologies, and variations in word endings. Library classification systems provide for alternative 'labels' to identify each category. Researchers should try to become aware of the most likely alternatives. An alternative term might be as straightforward as changing the word slightly; for example, when using 'organizational innovation' as keywords, it would also be useful to try 'organizational innovating'. Most databases allow the researcher to truncate when a term can have several endings; for example, 'innovat*' would search for 'innovation' and 'innovative' in some databases. Similarly, 'wildcards' are symbols that can be used to look for variant spellings; for example, in some databases, 'organi?ational' covers 'organizational' and 'organisational'. The symbols used for truncations and wildcards can vary between different databases, catalogues and search engines, so researchers are advised to consult the help pages before they start their searches.

A literature review often starts off from a broad strategy, becoming more focused, with a narrow research scope. Conceptualizing a broad field can be difficult, and bringing together literature from a vast range of traditions and disciplines can be a gargantuan task. Mind-maps can be helpful for identifying linkages between different fields of study, and for establishing the scope and structure of a literature review. Figure 2.3 shows a mind-map that was created for a systematic review on the roles played by creativity and innovation in science and engineering. When compared with the Venn diagram, this mind-map gives a clear indication of the amount of work required to develop such an advanced systematic review. It also shows the way in which literature reviews contribute to the understanding of how a certain research area has developed over time, and how current research trends and debates may shape a given topic.

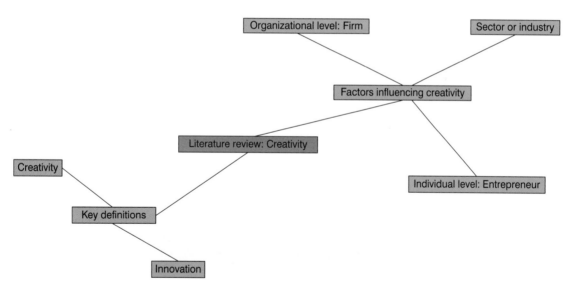

FIGURE 2.3
Mind-map of a literature review

Mapping your topic

a) **Individual exercise**: After re-reading your initial summary once or twice, draw a simple Venn diagram or mind-map for your own research project, adding all the items you think your study should cover. Think about how the different items relate to one another and what keywords could be used to describe

(Continued)

EXERCISE
2.2

(Continued)

them. Prepare a list of keywords, adding alternative expressions and synonyms. Decide what kinds of truncations or wildcards could be useful. For example, the term 'orga*' might turn out too many results but, combined with 'innovat*' and 'manag*', could form part of a useful search.

b) **Group exercise**: Share your Venn diagram with two or three members of your group. Can you use it to explain your research project? What words do you use? Show them your initial list of keywords and ask them to revise this list with you. Do they have any useful suggestions?

FINDING RELEVANT LITERATURE

For hundreds of years, the most obvious place to begin a literature search was the library. Today, this seems to be an outdated approach, given the vast amount of information that can be accessed via the Internet. However, this information age leaves many researchers struggling with 'information overload'; less experienced researchers in particular are likely to feel overwhelmed by the sheer amount and diversity of resources available to them.

A visit to the local university library can help to prevent or overcome such problems. After all, the library remains an important gateway to information – and these days not only to books and journals, but also to online resources. Librarians have an overview of the information that is available, and they know to navigate the various systems by which it can be accessed. As noted by Luker (2008: 85), researchers could hardly afford to ignore their librarian in the past, but today such ignorance can be 'downright suicidal'. Most researchers benefit hugely from getting to know their library early in the research project. Many libraries offer guided tours, handouts and online courses – in addition to the usual support by librarians.

While browsing through stacks of books is still a great way to start a literature search, it is of course not the only way. When searching for literature, different search strategies and search tools (e.g. search engines or databases) will yield complementary results. According to Selvin and Stuart (1966), there are two main ways of tackling a literature search. First, there is 'trawling', which involves a wide sweep to see what information can be brought in to get an overview of a field, and then there is 'fishing', which involves a more targeted search for more specific information. Trawling and fishing should not be seen as opposites, more as different starting points, independent of the extent of the researcher's prior knowledge and focus. Before setting out on a trawl (i.e. sweeping up whatever information exists on a topic), time can be saved by researchers in deciding and being selective in what they are after. When starting a literature search, researchers must be clear about *what* they look for (topic and type of information), *where* they look for it (sources), and *how* they look for it (search queries and search skills).

This means it is necessary for them to consider how the review will develop and benefit their studies and understanding. Systematic reviews can provide a more objective or comprehensive overview, and they can help to identify where gaps in the current research exist. However, they may also unintentionally reduce researchers' ability to use their creativity for opening up new perspectives and fields of research. Whatever the motivations, the decision to conduct a certain type of review has to be taken at the first stage of the review process. This is due to the fact that systematic reviews require explicit review protocols and clear criteria for accessing, retrieving and judging the quality and relevance of studies in the research area.

Searching literature in libraries

Most libraries classify books in subject themes according to one of the major published classification schemes. Browsing among books can be a useful way of providing an overview, but it is always likely to be a partial one. Often subjects are scattered around and range, for example, from economics to industrial sociology to psychology. A library's online catalogue is an index used to search and locate all electronic and print material held in the library. There are two limitations to library catalogues. First, library catalogues tend to list publications such as books or journals, but they do not allow searching of their content (i.e. individual chapters or journal articles). In order to access this information, other databases and search engines have to be used; these will be introduced below. The second limitation arises from the speed in which research accumulates: today, it seems unlikely that any library, however large, will be able to meet all a researcher's needs from its own resources.

Once the stock of books available in the university library has been reviewed, appropriate catalogues should be consulted to see what else has been written. A comprehensive list of links to major libraries is usually available on most university websites. Very large libraries such as the British Library or the Library of Congress (USA) contain almost all publications in the English language, along with many foreign-language publications. In addition, there are national/international online catalogues such as Copac (a merged online catalogue of many major university research libraries in the UK and Ireland), Bibliothèque Nationale (France), Deutsche Nationalbibliothek (Germany) and Biblioteca Nacional (Spain). Specimens of more specific catalogues can be supplied by, for example, the Institute of Chartered Accountants (Current Accounting Literature) and the Baker Library at Harvard Business School. Books, journal articles, maps, recordings and other resources can be ordered from other libraries through the inter-library loan system. This service, offered by most college and university libraries, usually takes a few weeks and is often accompanied by nominal fees.

EXERCISE
2.3

Getting to know your library

a) **Individual exercise**: Look up the webpages of your library and browse through its online support pages. Can you answer the following questions?

- Are there any online courses or workshops that could help you to improve your skills?

- Who is the subject librarian responsible for your topic or discipline?

- On the website, what information can you find on literature searches in your field, such as a list of relevant databases?

- What kind of classification system does your library use?

- What kind of materials can you find using the library's online catalogue (e.g. books, journals, journal articles, videos, book chapters and research reports)? Is there any guidance on how to use the library's online catalogue?

- Is it possible to use truncations or wildcards? What are the relevant symbols?

b) **Individual exercise**: A 'classmark' is a set of letters and numbers assigned to a library item, allowing the item to be shelved with other items on the same topic. Classmarks are used to locate individual items but they can also help to explore

(Continued)

(Continued)

a topical area. With this in mind, conduct a search with your keywords using your library's catalogue. Go to the relevant sections and browse through the sections you have identified as being relevant. Have you found anything useful? If not, ask your local librarian for help. Note down or save the references of all sources that appear particularly useful.

c) **Individual exercise**: Consult encyclopedias, guides, handbooks and dictionaries available in the library under the classmarks for management and business, such as *The International Encyclopedia of Business and Management*. Look up your key concepts and note down definitions, additional keywords and key references that may help you with your literature research.

d) **Individual exercise**: Some libraries offer specialized web portals and guidance for researchers in management and business research. Have a look at the web portals created by the British Library (www.bl.uk/reshelp/findhelpsubject/busmanlaw/mbs/managementpage.html) and the Baker Library of the Harvard Business School (www.library.hbs.edu/guides/). How can the resources offered on these web pages help you to develop your literature review? What resources might be particularly useful for your topic?

e) **Interactive exercise**: Discuss what you have learned from the websites listed above. What resources did you find more/less useful? Why?

Designing literature searches

It is one thing to know where to look for a certain type of literature; it is another to develop the skills to conduct an advanced literature search. The majority of online catalogues and literature databases have a basic search interface in which researchers can enter strings of keywords. Advanced search interfaces allow researchers to define where to search for certain keywords (e.g. in the title, author names, abstract or full-text), and to use result limiters to restrict the output to a specified range of dates (e.g. 2010 to 2014) or publication type (e.g. electronic sources). Some search engines allow for the use of quotes to search for exact phrases such as 'organizational innovation'.

A good search query requires careful consideration. What are the most relevant terms, and how can they be combined so that they retrieve what the researcher looks for and nothing else? In most search operations, Boolean operators should be used to carefully delineate the scope and depth of search results. For example, the operator 'AND' narrows down the scope and leads to more specific results (e.g. articles that contain both 'innovation AND creativity'); 'OR' can be used to cover similar concepts (e.g. 'organization OR firms'); and 'NOT' allows for the exclusion of irrelevant results ('creativity NOT art'), but can also create a filter, inadvertently removing relevant results. Figure 2.4 illustrates the use of Boolean Operators and below is an example of a keyword search

EXAMPLE
2.1

Keyword search

An example of too broad a keyword might be 'management' or 'innovation'; there will be literally hundreds of thousands of articles using this term, in many different disciplines, with different meanings and linked to different concepts. It may refer to different aspects of management or innovation. Too narrow a keyword might be 'crucial'; sometimes this can be achieved by choosing a verb rather than a noun, for example 'innovate' rather than 'innovation'. In the example below, we illustrate how the use of different keywords and combinations of them give different results. The title of this search example is: 'How is management of innovation and new technology dealt with in the corporate social responsibility literature?' The searches are limited to the years 1995 to 2010 in the database ABI (ProQuest). The numbers of hits returned are shown below.

Search string	Number of hits
Manage* AND innovat* AND tech*	71,269
(Corporate responsibility OR environment) AND innovate*	41,904
(Corporate responsibility OR environment) AND innovate* AND tech*	23,051
Corporate responsibility AND tech*	691
Corporate responsibility AND innovate*	374
Corporate responsibility AND environment AND innovate*	140

A well-defined search can save hours of browsing. All searches should always be noted down in a *search record* for future reference (Jesson et al., 2011). This is not only considered to be 'good practice' and a requirement for conducting systematic reviews, it is also very useful as follow-up searches take less time and existing searches can be modified. See Table 2.3 for an example of a simple search record that can be kept in a notebook or digital spreadsheet. Some reference-management software packages offer tailored solutions to save search records and tasks.

The point behind systematic reviews is that each search and filtering decision is noted as completed, making it easy for others to see what has been done, and to judge the relevance

FIGURE 2.4
Boolean operators

How to use Boolean Operators

AND: Articles that cover innovation AND creativity

OR: Articles that cover EITHER *innovation* OR *creativity*

NOT: Articles that cover *innovation* but do NOT include the word *creativity*

TABLE 2.3 Example of a search record

Source	Date	Search/query	Output	Comments
Google Scholar	10/01/2014	Innov* AND creative* AND organi* OR entrepren* NOT art; since 2010	~ 4000 results, examined 100	Revise query, try bibliographic database
PhD Seminar	11/01/2014	Recommendation: review by M. A. Runco	1 reference	Look up/assess review
Literature review: Shalley & Gilson, 2004	11/01/2014	Examined references	4 key references	Look up highlighted references; citation search

SOURCE: BASED ON JESSON, MATHESON AND LACEY, 2011

and substantive nature of a given review. Articles that are returned are not seen to have been selected on the basis of personal preference.

Finding articles and papers using literature databases

Today, most researchers conduct their literature searches using multiple databases. The selection of the 'right' databases depends on the topic and the type of review; for example, systematic reviews require databases of peer-reviewed articles. It is recognized that there are a limited number of searchable databases for book chapters and reports, though currently there are a number of national and university libraries working to increase the number of books available online. Research institutions usually subscribe to some but not all of the databases. With regard to journal articles, there are two types of scholarly databases. Bibliographic databases (e.g. Web of Science and ABI (ProQuest)) simply list search results and often offer a broad range of content. Full-text databases, meanwhile, provide direct access to articles but often are more limited in scope (e.g. Business Source Premier). The Centre for Research Libraries has compiled a detailed overview of the most relevant scholarly databases (see http://adat.crl.edu/databases). In addition to the more general 'abstracts and indices', there are several other databases that focus on specialized fields, such as International Abstracts of Human Resources, International Abstracts in Operations Research, Marketing Information Guide, Packaging Abstracts, Psychological Abstracts and Training Abstracts. Others, such as Public Affairs Information Service Bulletin (PAIBS), are very useful for retrieving information on affairs connected with the international public environment, while the current Technology Index, although being on the margin of management and business studies, can also be very useful.

Journal articles can often be accessed through several search paths, but not all sources provide access to full-text articles. Therefore, one might need to consult different databases or access the journal directly through the university library. Some articles will be available only via an inter-library loan; others can be purchased online, albeit often at a significant cost. Some databases allow researchers to save searches or to receive the results of a saved search on a regular basis (through a 'saved search alert'). Others allow for the setting-up of subject-related or journal-related alerts. For example, Zetoc Alert is a service that automatically emails the tables of contents of journals and articles that match searches for authors' names or keywords from article titles (http://zetoc.mimas.ac.uk/).

Different databases produce complementary but also redundant results. It can be rather time-consuming to integrate several lists with results. This is one of the reasons why Google Scholar has become such a popular search option in the past decade. A quick search in Google Scholar can identify seminal texts across the academic disciplines. The main drawback of this is that it quickly widens the field of research, and this can work against the need for research focus.

Wikis can also be useful sources of information. They are online databases that allow users to add and edit content – the most well-known of these is Wikipedia. As users can change the content of the database, researchers should use their common sense and verify anything they are taking from a Wiki source. Therefore, if approached with caution, a Wiki can be a useful way of gathering preliminary information.

Many researchers publish their most recent work in conference papers and working papers, which can be accessed online via their own university websites or repositories, such as that of the Social Science Research Network (SRRN) – see Table 2.4. Some of these papers are later published in peer-reviewed journals, a process that usually involves several rounds of revisions. Electronic resources have now been extended to include articles approved for publication in future editions, a service that is referred to as 'online early/first' or 'published ahead of print'; this service is usually available via the journal's website. Articles published online in this way are identical to those that will eventually be published in the print journal.

Performing literature searches

EXERCISE
2.4

a) **Individual exercise**: Make it a habit to think about and write down your literature searches before you open a search engine. Have a look at your research statement, list of keywords, and Venn diagram or mind-map, and create a search record. What combinations of keywords could be found in the texts you want to read? What keywords could be too wide or ambivalent in their meaning? Construct a minimum of five searches using Boolean operators (AND, OR, NOT), limiters (such as date of publication), truncations (*) and/or wildcards (?). Next to the searches, note down the reasoning behind the search. What do you hope to find with this combination of keywords?

b) **Individual exercise**: Test your searches on one specialized database (such as Web of Science, ABI (ProQuest), Business Source Premier or JSTOR), on SRRN and on Google Scholar. Have you found what you expected? What were the problems? How do the results of the scholarly database compare with those listed by SRRN and Google Scholar?

c) **Interactive exercise**: In groups, decide one common research question/topic and let each member use different software to collect the literature. Compare and analyse the outcome. If the outcome differs, discuss why it differs and how you used different search terms.

d) **Individual exercise**: Which journal is the most prominent journal in your field? Find the website of the journal and look through the table of contents of the past two volumes/years. Note down the details of three articles you found most interesting. Check whether the journal publishes ahead of print/online first. Set up a 'table of contents' (TOC) alert using the journal's website or **Zetoc**.

e) **Interactive exercise**: Give a short presentation on your chosen journal to a group of peers, covering:

- name, publisher, editor and history of the journal
- subject areas covered by this journal
- two to three topics or debates that were particularly prominent in this journal in the past two years
- why this journal is an important resource for your research.

f) **Interactive exercise**: In pairs, discuss the advantages and disadvantages of using systematic searches compared to a more personally directed approach to the identification of appropriate sources.

Snowballing and tracing citations

When searching for a wider body of literature, most researchers deploy multiple search strategies. They search online databases and library catalogues, but they also consult review articles and trace citations listed in relevant publications. Following citations just as Hansel and Gretel followed breadcrumbs, they can reconstruct the development of an academic discourse or entire field by tracing citations back in time (Luker, 2008). They can identify the key scholars of their fields and, by looking up their CVs and lists of publications, learn more about past and current debates around their topic of interest. The objective is to find a number of key studies; exactly how many will depend on the focus and scope of the review.

Some bibliographic databases also allow accessing the details of all publications that have subsequently referred to a given journal article. This is the only indexing method that enables a researcher to search forwards (rather than backwards) in the literature. Citation searching is available within many databases including Web of Science, ScienceDirect and Google Scholar. Citation searches can be complemented by 'citation alerts' that send out emails whenever a new publication comes out that cites a particular piece.

Citation searches in both directions are a productive technique for identifying the seminal works of a given research area, particularly those that offer an overview of the approaches to an extant literature upon a particular topic. For example, Easterby-Smith (1997) has published a review of organizational learning from the perspective of six different disciplines. A systematic review of knowledge in small and medium enterprises (SMEs) can be seen in Thorpe et al. (2005; see also Example 2.3 in the last section of this chapter). Both reviews could be used as starting points for researchers investigating these particular areas.

Another way of getting started is to begin with studies written on the topic over the years. Some journals give a systematic précis of the articles published in issues of that year. For example, the *Journal of Marketing* includes several pages covering all types of significant articles and publications on all aspects of marketing (e.g. distribution, publicity, sales and strategy) for that volume.

One of the problems with comprehensive reviews is that they often encourage the use of secondary sources at the expense of primary sources. Some academics have made cutting remarks about researchers who are happy to quote material that they have not actually read (instead assimilating concepts and ideas from other articles). One must be clear and point it out if the material is a quotation from a secondary source; it is advisable to rely on primary sources whenever possible.

EXERCISE
2.5

Using citation searches and alerts

a) **Individual exercise**: Pick an article that appears to be particularly useful for your review. Go through the reference section of this article, and look up five references that could be relevant to your literature review. Note them down in a search record. Assess titles, keywords and abstracts (if available). Then, have a look at the reference sections of at least three papers. Can you identify citations that appear in more than one paper? Which citations seem to connect these papers and why are they important?

b) **Individual exercise**: What is the most relevant journal article you have found so far? Set up a citation alert for this article on Google Scholar.

c) **Individual exercise**: Go to the homepage of Zetoc at http://zetoc.mimas. ac.uk. You should be able to log in by selecting your research institution and using your institutional username and password. If you have problems, your librarian should be able to help you. Once logged in, follow the instructions on the site. More detailed information about setting up a Zetoc Alert may be found at http://zetoc.mimas.ac.uk/alertguide.html.

d) **Individual exercise**: Identify a key scholar in your field and Google their profile. Can you access their full list of publications or CV? Evaluate the list and see if they have published more relevant articles or books on your topic.

Alternative sources and networking

When starting a new research project, it is also an excellent strategy to join subject-specific research communities. This can be a very fruitful way of getting to know like-minded colleagues who are working on a similar topic, not just in a researcher's own country but all over the world. The British Academy of Management (BAM) and USA-based Academy of Management (AoM) both have special interest groups or divisions; these cover a range of disciplines and cross-disciplinary topics, hold regular seminars and workshops, and are very welcoming to new researchers. Many useful leads and references can come from participating in email discussion groups. Contacts for such groups are often found at conferences or similar academic associations. For doctoral candidates, this kind of networking is perhaps even more important than for those simply engaged on an individual research topic. Doctoral streams and colloquia are organized at most of the big international conferences; for example, those of BAM, the European Group for Organizational Studies (EGOS), AoM, the European Academy of Management (EURAM), the European Doctoral Education Network (EDEN) and the European Institute for Advanced Studies in Management (EIASM). All these groups enable researchers to submit their current research for discussion and debate.

The Economic and Social Science Research Council's newsletter, *The Edge*, brings the latest and most topical social science research to key opinion formers in business, government and the voluntary sector. Other possible sources of information include the registers of current research published by several leading business schools. In France, there are newsletters such as *Le Courier du CNRS*.

Social-network websites such as LinkedIn, Facebook and Twitter offer a new means to share research ideas and literature-review tips in real time. People who are reading an interesting article or book can update their status to share this article or to have an online discussion about the content or concepts of an article.

Finding your research community

Interactive exercise: Discuss in small groups of three to six students what research groups and professional organizations could be relevant for your research. Conduct a search online and identify at least one academic and one non-academic institution for each member of the group. Sign up to their research newsletters or email lists if possible.

EXERCISE
2.6

Dissertations and theses

For those undertaking research, it is often important to know what theses have already been completed, if only to identify the individuals with whom to make contact. In Britain, many theses are available through EThOS (Electronic Theses Online Service), a service provided by the British Library. At the European level, DART-Europe is a useful portal for finding electronic theses and dissertations. The Networked Digital Library of Theses and Dissertations (NDLTD) attempts to build a wider international database. The commercial service ProQuest Dissertations and Theses claims to be the world's most comprehensive international collection. It can take quite a while to look through these different databases. However, it is an important task since it is helping to ensure that there is no duplication of research. As the cost (in time) of duplication of research is high, searches of this kind can be a very worthwhile exercise – even if no similar theses are found in the end.

Table 2.4 gives an overview of the advantages and disadvantages of using the different sources of information presented above. Figure 2.5 illustrates the different pathways of a systematic search for literature.

Recording and organizing selected literature

It can take some time to develop the skills necessary for searching academic literature in a focused and efficient way, but for many researchers it takes even longer to adopt a consistent system of recording the results of searches. This is unfortunate, given that good housekeeping and consistency in record-keeping in the early stages of the review process can save a lot of time down the line, when patchy notes require endless repeat searches. Once books have been read and returned to the library shelves, or radio programmes have finished and the day they were broadcast has been forgotten, it is extremely difficult and very time-consuming to find references unless the researcher has developed some kind of systematic cataloguing system.

To avoid being flooded with references whose contents and quotations are difficult to control, mechanisms for organizing are essential. We recommend devising a system of storing results – either an electronic database or something much simpler. The simplest option is to use standard hand-written record cards in subject and alphabetical order. For up to a certain number of references, this can be a useful strategy. Reviews based on more than 50 references – or for a project that is likely to lead to follow-up projects – make this strategy less viable in the long term. In this case we would recommend the use of reference-management software or 'reference organizers', which allow fast and easy processing of large amounts of bibliographic data.

Universities and colleges often subscribe to specific packages that help students keep track of their references. Researchers and students can create their own personal databases or libraries into which they can import references from a bibliographic database or Google Scholar. In addition, many packages enable users to insert citations into documents when writing reviews or other academic texts, while at the same time creating a list of references in whatever style required. More elaborate packages (such as Citavi; see Figure 2.7 for an example) facilitate knowledge management more generally; they feature different types of indexing and coding systems that can be linked to individual quotations, comments and ideas. In this way, they turn what used to be seen as 'virtual filing cabinets' into knowledge-management tools, assisting analysis.

Most universities acquire licences to a number of reference-management packages such as EndNote, RefWorks, ProCite and Reference Manager, but there are also a wide range of freely available packages, such as Mendeley or Zotero. Most packages allow the import and export of bibliographic data in different formats. Figures 2.6 and 2.7 illustrate the reference-management systems of two PhD students in management and business. However, researchers are advised to compare packages before they create a digital library for their own research. There are multiple reviews and comparative overviews available on the Internet that can help with the selection process (see references listed in Exercise 2.6).

TABLE 2.4 Overview of sources

Source	Description	Advantages (+) & disadvantages (−)	More information
Library	Libraries collect and organize information, and provide access to printed and digital material; the literature available varies, depending on the kind of library and the main topic areas it covers	+ Gateway to library resources but also to other libraries (inter-library loans) and bibliographic databases + Information available that is difficult to access elsewhere (in particular, printed material) + Access to selected electronic resources and bibliographic databases + Assistance available − Visits can be time-consuming − Hardcopies rarely cover the latest research in the field	Most libraries have online catalogues and webpages with further information on literature searches Look out for dedicated sections for management and business research: http://www.bl.uk/reshelp/findhelpsubject/busmanlaw/mbs/managementpage.html Some libraries have created merged catalogues such as http://www.worldcat.org/ and http://copac.ac.uk/
Google Scholar	Freely accessible search engine that searches full text, and covers most books and online journals of the largest academic publishers, along with working papers and other types of scholarly texts	+ Quick and easily accessible + Easy to get an overview − Tends to broaden the scope of the review − Relative coverage varies by discipline and topic − Does not contain an easy method to sort results	There are special manuals available with tips on how to use Google Scholar, e.g. http://www.otago.ac.nz/library/pdf/Google_Scholar_Tips.pdf
Scholarly databases such as Web of Science, ZETOC, ABI (ProQuest), Business Source Premier and JSTOR	Databases contain journal articles (in the case of Web of Science, Business Source Premier and JSTOR), business news (e.g. Nexis) and reports on market and business research, industries and company profiles	+ Mostly high-quality, peer-reviewed articles + Usually easy to use; lists of results can be saved and exported − Duplicates when using several different services − Fee-based online research service (access via libraries) − Embargo on the current issues of some journals − May not include earlier print issues (with the exception of JSTOR)	There are different databases and subscription services available; some academic publishers have also developed useful search interfaces For further information, contact the librarian and visit http://adat.crl.edu/databases & http://www.brookes.ac.uk/library/business/manage.html

(Continued)

TABLE 2.4 (Continued)

Source	Description	Advantages (+) & disadvantages (−)	More information
SRRN	Website aiming at the rapid dissemination of research across the social sciences, featuring specialized research networks	+ The latest research + Circulates papers at an early stage, permitting authors to incorporate comments + Over 240,000 authors − Mixed quality	See http://www.ssrn.com/en/
Literature reviews	Existing reviews around the subject area give an overview of what is already known	+ Good general overview & starting point + Identify seminal studies − Secondary literature often based on abstracts & summaries − Widen the field of research − Lack depth	For literature reviews in management and business research, search main journals such as *Journal of Management Research* (review issues), *Academy of Management Review*, *International Journal of Management Reviews* and *Journal of Marketing*
Special interest groups & academic networks	Associations and professional organizations aiming at the professional development of their members and the advancement of management and business research	+ Insights into ongoing research + Email lists and conferences + Internal journals and working paper series − Mixed quality of outputs − Usually membership fees	See American, British and European academies of management: • http://aom.org/ • https://www.bam.ac.uk • http://www.euram-online.org/ Or see EGOS: • http://www.egosnet.org/
Theses and dissertations	Can give important insights into recent research and research trends	+ Detailed accounts of recent research + Can help to anticipate new developments (as most PhD students publish after completing their PhD) − Theses and dissertations can be tedious to find and access	http://ethos.bl.uk/Home.do http://search.proquest.com/pqdtft http://www.dart-europe.eu/basic-search.php http://www.ndltd.org/

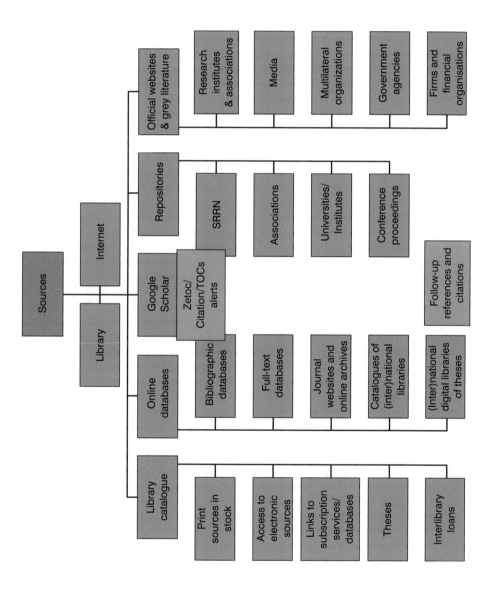

FIGURE 2.5
Systematic searching

FIGURE 2.6
EndNote
reference list

FIGURE 2.7
Main interface
of Citavi

EXERCISE
2.7

Choosing reference-management software

a) **Individual and interactive exercise**: Look up these two lists of reference organizers:

- http://en.wikipedia.org/wiki/Comparison_of_reference_management_software
- www.literaturereviewhq.com/6-tips-on-how-to-choose-reference-management-software/

Then type into YouTube the name of the package you are most interested in. See if you can find a video review and a tutorial. Look at the website for further information. Review the package for the group.

b) **Interactive exercise**: Ask students in your group about their experiences with reference organizers. Establish a list of criteria for choosing a suitable reference organizer.

Whatever system or software is used, there is a need to build bibliographies from the start of a research project. It is important that users make it a habit to store all references to research literature in their 'library' as soon as they come across them. There are different methods of doing this:

- Most references can be transferred directly from bibliographic databases just by clicking on 'download reference' or 'export reference' (see Figure 2.8); this applies to individual references as well as lists of references. References can also be downloaded from Google Scholar (as illustrated in Figure 2.9) and from the websites of most academic journals (as shown in Figure 2.10).

- Some packages are connected to public databases, which can make it easy to download the bibliographic information for books and journal articles just by typing in the respective ISBN or digital object identifier (DOI). A DOI is a character string used as a unique identifier of an electronic document (see e.g. highlighted DOI number in Figure 2.10); hence, it allows for persistent citations in scholarly materials, such as journal articles and book chapters.

Some references have to be registered manually, for example for older material not available online and for 'grey' literature.

FIGURE 2.8
Importing references from ABI (ProQuest)

FIGURE 2.9
Importing
references
from Google
Scholar

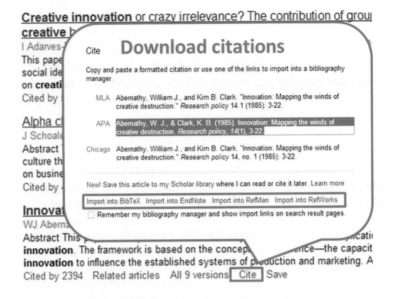

FIGURE 2.10
Importing
references
from a
journal's
website

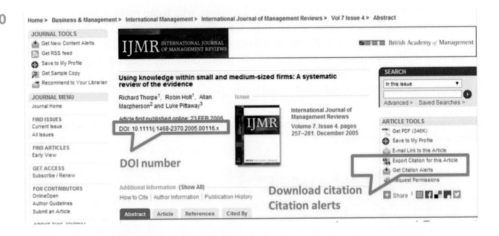

It is essential to double-check downloaded references to make sure that they are complete, and to add appropriate keywords to each reference. Using keywords based on the research statement means that efficient access to the relevant literature is less likely to become a problem once the library has grown beyond a certain size. Keywords should reflect the topic and substantial content of the reference. Additional keywords might relate to individual themes or sections of the literature review.

EVALUATING LITERATURE

After a first overview of the research area has been established, a more thorough examination of the literature is required. A literature review does not merely summarize an existing body of research; it also analyses and synthesizes this body of literature with a view to a specific problem, issue or question. The process of searching and recording literature should therefore always be accompanied by 'a critical evaluation of the literature according to argument, logic and/or epistemological or ontological traditions of the review subject' (Petticrew and Roberts, 2006: 19). The critical reflection of the literature should start as early as possible, as this helps to identify weaknesses in published research and to pinpoint research gaps.

The art of reading and analysing scholarly text is perhaps one of the key skills of a researcher – a skill that is usually acquired over the course of years, if not decades. Not all relevant aspects of this art can be covered in this section. More elaborate and in-depth guidance on how to critically evaluate literature for a literature review can be found in Hart (2005).

Reading techniques

Many students and young researchers feel overwhelmed by the amount of literature they are expected to read – which is often beyond what they can manage. This can lead to two problems. Some students read less and less; others develop a rather passive approach (Jesson et al., 2011), reading and memorizing material for exams but failing to question this. However, *reflection and critical analysis are essential* when it comes to reviewing literature.

The amount of literature to read for a decent review can be difficult to reconcile with time available for its production. For many, the prospect of reading dozens – if not hundreds – of articles and books is not particularly tempting. Against this background, it is essential to develop *different reading techniques* and to learn when to use them. Most important, however, is never to forget that *reviewing is reading with a purpose*, a purpose that arises from the topic and questions of the reviewer – and not the authors of the reviewed literature.

Selection of a piece of literature is usually based on limited bibliographic information about the author, title, keywords and/or context of publication (e.g. edited volume or special issue). Hence, the first evaluative step is to review whether the initial selection is justified. Does a particular book, article, report or newspaper clipping really merit further examination? For this first assessment, it is usually sufficient just to skim through the text, noting its structure and topic.

Systematic reviews require transparent and consistent criteria for judging which studies should be included. With some studies, there may be wholly inadequate abstracts and this may mean that the introduction and/or conclusions of the article need to be examined; this is sometimes referred to as 'examining in detail'. The chosen studies in the literature review need to be discussed and contrasted to justify the use of each, based on explicit criteria.

Once the initial decision to include the material is confirmed, it should be established which parts of the text could be useful for the review. A quick read through the abstract, table of contents, introduction and conclusion usually allows the reader to identify relevant sections that should be perused in more detail. Often, it is not necessary to read the entire book or report, as just a couple of sections address the topic under review.

These sections, however, should be read more carefully. By circling important concepts and marking definitions, claims, arguments and conclusions as such, the reader starts delving into the text. At this stage, it is important to identify the main argument of the text and the authors' position, which becomes visible in their methodologies, theories and questions. If, after this first read, the resource still appears to be useful – that is, topical and non-redundant – a summary record should be created.

Summary records

A summary record allows the reviewer to identify and record the contribution of a piece of literature to the topic under review. Initially, the creation records may appear to be a waste of time. However, summary records make it easier for the reviewer to compare, analyse and synthesize different studies without losing themselves in the details of each one. They also make it easier to track what has been read over months and years, so that acquired knowledge can be sourced and reassessed long after the source has been returned to the library. Table 2.5 presents a simple template for a summary record that can be kept either on paper or as a digital spreadsheet. Some reference organizers also include special tools for creating summary records.

TABLE 2.5   Summary record

Author & year	Research question/ topic/ problem & main findings	Argument	Design: theory, concepts & method	Key references	Why relevant/ problematic	Comments

The following questions can help to create a useful summary record:

- What is the main topic of the study?
- What are the key findings?
- How is the research justified?
- Why is this important for my literature review?
- What is the main unit of analysis (individual, firm etc.)?
- What is the analytical approach of the author(s)?
- How was the topic researched (methodology, data, sampling etc.)?
- What main concepts and theories were used?
- What is the scope of the study?
- What are the strengths and weaknesses of this research?
- Do I find it convincing? Why?
- How did this piece impact on subsequent research (citations, responses etc.)?

Critical assessment

A summary record forces the reader to determine the main message or key contribution of a text. It includes a summary of the main argument, and identifies important features of the theoretical framework and research design (if appropriate). In the first few columns, it invites the reviewer to assess a piece of literature in its own right; this assessment may be supportive or critical. The last columns then draw the attention of the reviewer away from the recorded piece of literature to the literature review. Here, the assessment of the reviewed literature follows the criteria and (emerging) themes of the review. Both steps require critical assessment: an evaluation of strengths and weaknesses, and of appropriateness and interest.

Key sources often merit a deeper analysis of the ways in which they construct an argument. Arguments involve a claim (a statement such as 'heterogeneous teams are more creative'), followed by some evidence to support or refute the claim (e.g. a comparative case study of work teams in the film industry). A critical assessment enquires how the claim and backing are related, and whether this relationship is sufficiently accurate and appropriate.

It is important to note that there are different types of claims. *Claims of fact* – such as 'heterogeneous teams are more creative' – require appropriate backing in order to be accepted; this backing can be based on facts but also on inferences, illustrations, scenarios and analogies (Hart, 2005). Many authors also make *claims of value*, such as 'the more profitable a business is, the better it can serve its customers and community'. While this judgement is widely shared, it remains a judgement in the sense that a business could also be better because it makes an important social contribution to the life of its employees. Claims of value can also relate to *claims of policy* (e.g. 'free childcare has to be expanded in order to achieve gender equality in the workplace'). Some claims arise from the use of certain *concepts and interpretations*; for example, claims regarding tax avoidance and tax fraud could arise from the same case. Finally, there are claims that ultimately rest on *authority* (e.g. 'because a Nobel laureate said it, it is true' or 'because this fact was published in a peer-reviewed article, it is true'). The first challenge for the reviewer lies in identifying what kinds of claims are used, on what assumptions these claims are based, and whether claims and assumptions can be verified. The second challenge arises from the need to then assess the implications of claims, arguments and assumptions for the topic under review.

Evaluating two articles

a) **Individual exercise**: Select two journal articles that are particularly relevant to your research – one that has been published within the last two years, and another published before 1990. Answer the 12 questions in the bullet list above.

b) **Interactive exercise**: In pairs, select, read and discuss a journal article. What are the key findings presented in this article? Underline all conclusions. What argument leads to these findings? By circling all inference indicators such as 'therefore', 'thus' and 'hence', you can identify arguments more easily. Highlight or mark reasons and evidence. Discuss what kinds of claims are used to support the argument. Are there any underlying assumptions that remain unmentioned? What are the strengths and weaknesses of this article?

EXERCISE
2.8

Identifying problems and themes

Throughout the review processes, researchers examine and revise their own research questions as they learn more about the field they wish to study. While, on one hand, it is pivotal for a researcher not to forget about their own questions when reading the work of others, on the other hand their reading can and should influence the way their research evolves. The aim of the literature review can change as a result of critically reviewing more literature, which is a part of flexible research design.

By revising the research statement, and related Venn diagrams and mind-maps, this process becomes more transparent and so easier to control. Initial jottings that stated merely the links between some concepts evolve into more elaborate mind-maps identifying more complex webs or relationships between different concepts, discourses and fields of study. Figure 2.11 shows how the review process that followed Figures 2.2 and 2.3 led to the creation of a much more detailed mind-map that details the scope and structure of the review.

In this example, **common factors** affecting creativity (leadership, hierarchy, creative environments and climates, and individual characteristics) gave a focus and structure to the entire review project. Common themes of this kind can be identified by comparing summary records or by indexing or coding different resources with keywords (a technique that will be introduced in more detail in Chapter 8). The analysis of the reviewed material may aim to establish different categories that facilitate comparison between different studies, such as types of methodology used, titles of journals in which they were published, types of organizations studied, and conclusions reached; each of these can be further classified, and so common themes discovered. The resultant categorization then forms the basis of the structure for writing up the literature review.

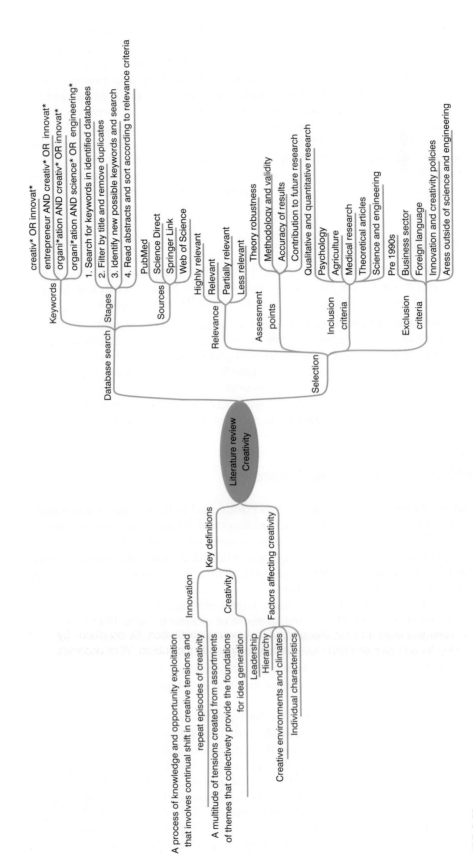

FIGURE 2.11

Elaborate mind-map of a literature review

The creation of overview tables and evaluation sheets can aid the process of comparing the features of different studies and synthesizing their results. Table 2.6 shows an example of an evaluation sheet with four columns that was designed for the review process depicted in Figure 2.11.

TABLE 2.6   Example of an evaluation sheet

Author/year	Definitions of creativity & innovation	Factors affecting creativity identified	Main findings

NOTE: ALIGNMENT WITH STUDY CONTEXT AND APPROACH

A review of the literature may be in a single disciplinary area or in several areas, depending on the nature of the research and its subject area. Regardless of the setting and the issue being investigated, it is paramount that there is some kind of alignment between the research methodology to be adopted, its context and the approach used. Studies concentrating on a narrow subject domain will require a critique of the literature in that specific area. However, multidisciplinary and practice-based studies might require a review that spans different literatures and synthesizes them.

Whether the nature of the study focuses on one discipline or takes a more multidisciplinary approach, the literature review will need to be consistent with the study as a whole. This means that the study's epistemology, strategy, literature review, design, methods and empirical sections should all be linked and should demonstrate an internal coherence (see Chapters 3). At the same time, as we have indicated, a simple description of previous research is not sufficient. Rather, the review needs to incorporate interpretation and analysis, as well as being critical, so as to underpin the research questions identified. Patriotta (2003) offers an example of the way he conducted a literature review (see Example 2.2).

Literature review by Patriotta

In his book entitled *Organizational Knowledge in the Making*, Patriotta (2003) reviews the literature on knowledge within firms and identifies different perspectives, including the cognitive, knowledge-based, 'situated' and techno-science approaches. He offers a critical interpretation of different perspectives, acknowledging their respective strengths while also identifying areas that require clarification. He concludes by arguing for an integrated and multi-faceted approach to the subject. What becomes apparent to him is that the pluralistic approach adopted has led to his ability to propose that there are in fact three methodological lenses, which transcend the narrow epistemological boundaries of current perspectives on organizational knowledge. These three lenses are suggested as being breakdown, time and narrative.

EXAMPLE
2.2

Because research projects can take years, new research is likely to emerge during most research projects. Therefore, a literature review is not something done once but rather a continual process throughout the research project. Sometimes it is necessary to consult and review additional literature after the fieldwork, if a new aspect has emerged from the data. Because new research constantly develops, it is necessary to consult new literature that has emerged, or was not included in the original review. This needs to be done until the very end of the project, to make sure no new important study is omitted.

WRITING A LITERATURE REVIEW

Our argument here is that the writing of a literature review should start early in the life of the project or dissertation. With that in mind we offer here some initial advice on how to craft the review. But as the research develops it may be necessary to update it from time to time. Hence in Chapter 12 we revisit the literature review in the light of needing to incorporate it within the context of the final dissertation or thesis.

We suggest that the literature be written in a discursive style which allows the writer freedom to develop their own arguments and flow, building progressively towards the focal research topic. They should not present just a series of summary records but should start with a rigorous explanation of what is being reviewed, followed by a critical evaluation of the existing knowledge, identifying how the research by the reviewer will relate, complement and/or challenge this knowledge. When engaging with and critiquing previous studies, researchers need to strike a balance that simultaneously displays criticality with regard to the assumptions, theories and methods of previous studies, while at the same time acknowledging the insights and strengths of these studies.

Literature reviews vary significantly in length and depth, and in how they are presented, in articles, reports, books and theses. Some literature reviews are organized around a topic structure of different themes (like the one indicated in the mind-map above) or around a series of research questions or problems; others identify what is known about a phenomenon before exploring what remains unknown. Then, there are reviews that follow a method-oriented order, identifying different types of studies and how they have contributed to a certain field of knowledge.

Ultimately, it is not so relevant which organizational scheme is chosen – as long as it is followed consistently and *corresponds to the aim of the literature review*. For example, a *critical review* assesses the value of existing research in a critical light; a *theoretical review* evaluates and synthesizes a corpus of theory that has accumulated around a concept, theory, or phenomenon; and a *scoping review* maps the territory for future research and develops a new research agenda (see Jesson et al., 2011, for more detail and examples).

Usually, it makes sense to develop a plan for the written review based on the research statement, diagrams and mind-maps, summary records and evaluation sheets. The plan should state the topic and purpose of the review, followed by an abstract summarizing the main points and conclusions of the review. It should then indicate what information should be covered in the introduction, main body and conclusion. Drafting an appropriate structure might take some time, but will enable the reviewer to build up a full draft step by step.

EXERCISE
2.9

Structuring a review

a) **Individual exercise**: Select two review articles related to your research topic and evaluate their structure. What are the aims of the two articles? What organizational themes have been used to structure these articles? How do aims and structure correspond? Think about alternative ways in which the reviews could have been organized.

b) **Individual exercise**: Draft out a plan for your own literature review.

c) **Interactive exercise**: Exchange and discuss your plan or draft with someone else in your group. Have you chosen a different/similar approach? Why?

d) **Individual exercise**: Assess your review using the criteria listed in Table 2.7.

Like most texts, the review then develops in three stages. First, there should be an *introduction* that states the topic, aim and scope of the review; shows why the topic is of interest; and explains the organization of the review. Second, the actual review commences in the *main body* of the text, which is usually divided into a number of sections covering distinct aspects such as methodological and conceptual issues, and different sub-topics or themes. At the end of the main body, the discussion should be drawn together, leading to the identification of key findings. Third, the *conclusion* summarizes the review and relates it back to the introduction, and to the topic, aim and scope of the review. In the conclusion, flaws and gaps in literature are identified that motivate and justify future research.

Once the review is complete, the reviewer should assess the quality of the review, bearing in mind its more specific aim as well as the overall purpose of literature reviews. Table 2.7 lists some general criteria for evaluating literature reviews that can be used as a checklist for most traditional types of reviews. Systematic reviews – with their standardized and protocol-driven methodology – have to meet additional criteria, as they aim at a comprehensive and exhaustive coverage of all relevant literature (see the list of further reading, at the end of the chapter, for recommended literature on systematic reviews). PRISMA (Preferred Reporting Items for Systematic Reviews and Meta-Analyses) is a set of standards that aims to help researchers improve the reporting of systematic reviews and meta-analyses (www.prisma-statement.org/index.htm). PRISMA was developed for systematic reviews of health-care interventions, but its checklist can also be applied to other disciplines and fields of research, such as management and business research.

Literature reviews involve a lot of referencing. While it can be tedious to work through a huge amount of bibliographic data, it is essential that references are included for all materials covered in a review, in order to avoid (unintended) plagiarism. Depending on the context of a

TABLE 2.7   Checklist for literature reviews

Topic, aim and scope are clearly identified
Relevance or significance of the topic are indicated
Context of the topic is established
A clear understanding of the relevant terms and concepts is shown
The review includes appropriate material and states why the material was selected
Key resources and landmark studies are covered
The review includes up-to-date material
Existing research is summarized and critically evaluated
The relationship between theory and empirical research is addressed; main methodologies are identified
Existing research is synthesized in a way that opens up a new perspective
The reviewer shows a reflexive approach when detailing the analysis undertaken for the review
Appropriate quotations and examples are used to justify the main arguments
The review meets expected standards of academic writing (references, spelling etc.)

literature review, the use of different reference styles might be required. Many reference organizers allow the selection of citation templates, so that all references appear in the right style and in the right place. We will be returning to an examination of these issues in Chapter 12 of the book when we consider the writing up of management and business research.

EXAMPLE 2.3

Key stages of the study by Thorpe et al. (2005)

The example presented below gives an overview of the review process of Thorpe et al. (2005), who conducted a systematic review of how SMEs create and use knowledge.

Background preparation

A review panel was first formed, consisting of the study's authors. The panel considered prospective sources of information, and decided to use peer-reviewed journals – both practitioner and academic. Books, reports and book chapters were excluded on the grounds that they did not provide the opportunity for searchable bibliographical databases. The team then used terms relevant to the study as keywords to determine the most appropriate databases, given the peculiarities of the research. Thus, words such as 'know*' and 'learn*' were employed. The asterisk helps retrieve variations on, and words related to, the ones entered in the search. For example, searching for the word 'know*' encapsulates 'knowledge' and its derivatives, including 'knowing'. The returns were analysed and used as guides in narrowing down the type of databases. In this case, the databases with the highest number of returns were chosen: ABI (ProQuest), Business Source Premier and Ingenta (incorporating ScienceDirect). Up to this point, the process involved identifying relevant databases. The next step was to do detailed keyword searches.

Keyword search

Since the topic was knowledge and learning within SMEs, the team's principal keywords and search strings included 'know*', 'learn*', 'SME OR small firms' and 'entrepreneur*'. When keywords were deemed to complement one another, the word 'AND' was used to enable the retrieval of a comprehensive result (e.g. 'know* AND learn*'). When keywords were seen to be substitutes, 'OR' was used instead (an example here is 'SMEs OR small firms'). Of course, 'know*' and 'learn*' may also be viewed as substitutes, and this was reflected in searches, with keyword searches alternating between the formats 'know* AND learn*' and 'learn* OR know*'.

Exporting results

The results were downloaded into a citation software program (ProCite). This gave each paper's keywords and abstracts. In the first instance, the team sifted through the abstracts, determining each article's relevance to the subject of study. Those articles considered irrelevant were excluded, as were those from other fields (such as education and engineering). The key guiding idea at this stage was relevance, rather than the depth of the articles.

Further exclusions

With the articles put together, the next step was to interrogate them based on a number of criteria: theory robustness, implications for practice, coherence between data and arguments put forward, theory, relevance to SME knowledge (on account of findings, methods and theories) and contributions made. The result of this exercise was the identification of papers that dealt with SME knowledge while meeting the set criteria.

Themes and conceptualizations

The study portrayed a landscape of studies into SME knowledge, and produced broad themes as well as sub-themes about the subject. These findings were eventually published as an academic paper. For further information and the published review article, see Thorpe et al., 2005.

CONCLUSION

You should have a clear grasp of what a literature review is – and what it is not; that is, it is not a mere list of sources, a series of summary records or an annotated bibliography. In this chapter, we have aimed to provide insights into where to find relevant literature and other sources for a research project, and what aspects are important when actually writing a literature review. The key points of this chapter, therefore, are:

 A literature review is a continuous process, requiring writing and refocusing throughout the research project. It should be used as a tool to learn about existing research. It should inform the creative development of future research and strengthen the arguments for such research, rather than blindly repeating what has been said before.

 As with research in general, a literature review is about crafting. Conducting a literature review is a research activity all in itself that requires a wide range of research skills and analytical capabilities. It takes time and effort to develop these skills.

 The quality of literature reviews also depends on good 'housekeeping'. It pays to learn the various techniques that enable researchers to search, select, record and evaluate literature in a systematic and efficient way.

We would like to close this chapter with a brief note on the role of literature reviews in different research designs. Literature reviews are defined by their aim, topic and scope. All three aspects are in turn influenced by the research strategy and the underlying philosophical assumptions of the reviewer. Depending on whether the researchers follow a more positivist (theory-testing) research strategy or a more constructionist (theory-generating) research strategy, a literature review plays a different role in their overall research process and is likely to reflect a different style of writing. Theory-testing studies derive their hypothesis from a review of existing research; they value a systematic approach that aims at representativeness. In contrast, theory-generating studies often treat the literature review as a more open exploration of their field of study: an exploration that can help to inform the development of more appropriate questions about the phenomenon under study. Here, the aim of the review is not to come to a generalizable synthesis of existing research but rather to critically assess what has been done, and to identify what has previously been left out of sight. The main differences between these approaches and their underlying philosophical assumptions will be discussed in the next chapter.

FURTHER READING

We recommend in particular the following textbooks on literature reviews:

Easterby-Smith, M. (1997) 'Disciplines of organizational learning: contributions and critiques', *Human Relations*, 51 (9): 1085–116.

Fink, A. (2005) *Conducting Research Literature Reviews: From the Internet to Paper*. Thousand Oaks, CA: Sage.

Hart, C. (1998) *Doing a Literature Review: Releasing the Social Science Research Imagination*. London: Sage. Excellent introduction to how to plan a literature review, which also offers important guidance on how to read and critically evaluate research publications (with a focus on traditional literature reviews).

Jesson, J., Matheson, L. and Lacey, F.M. (2011) *Doing Your Literature Review. Traditional and Systematic Techniques*. London: Sage.

An extremely helpful textbook that covers both traditional and systematic reviews.

The following three publications focus more specifically on systematic reviews:

Petticrew, M. and Roberts, H. (2006) *Systematic Reviews in the Social Sciences: A Practical Guide*. Malden, MA: Blackwell.

Shalley, C.E. and Gilson, L.L. (2004) 'What leaders need to know: a review of social and contextual factors that can foster or hinder creativity', *The Leadership Quarterly*, 15 (1): 33–53.

Thorpe, R., Holt, R., Macpherson, A. and Pittaway, L. (2005) 'Knowledge within small and medium-sized firms: a review of the evidence', *International Journal of Management Reviews*, 7 (4): 257–81.

Tranfield, D., Denyer, D. and Smart, P. (2003) 'Towards a methodology for developing evidence-informed management knowledge by means of systematic review', *British Journal of Management*, 14 (3): 207–22.

Published reviews of literature can be seen in specialist review journals such as *International Journal of Management Reviews*, *Academy of Management Review*, *Annual Review of Organizational Psychology and Organizational Behavior* and *Psychological Review*. The following three articles were chosen to illustrate different kinds of literature reviews:

Want to know more about this chapter? Visit the ⓈSAGE edge™ website at **https://edge. sagepub.com/easterbysmith** to access practice questions, selected journal articles, useful web links and much more.

THE PHILOSOPHY OF MANAGEMENT AND BUSINESS RESEARCH

3

LEARNING OBJECTIVES

 To understand the different philosophical assumptions 'hidden' beneath management research, and to appreciate the strengths and weaknesses of each.

 To appreciate how different philosophical assumptions influence criteria for judging research quality.

 To enable readers to surface and identify their own philosophical assumptions.

The philosophical debates

Ontology: from realism to nominalism

Epistemology: positivism vs social constructionism

Strengths and weaknesses of the main traditions

Paradigms and research approaches

Conclusion

Further reading

'It is a capital mistake to theorise before one has data. Insensibly one begins
to collect facts to suit theories, rather than theories to suit facts.'

Arthur Conan Doyle (creator of Sherlock Homes[1])

The relationship between data and theory has been hotly debated by philosophers for many centuries. Failure to think through such philosophical issues, while not necessarily fatal, as Sherlock Holmes suggests, can adversely affect the quality of management and business research. They are therefore of central concern in its design and evaluation. The aim of this chapter is to consider the main philosophical positions that underlie the designs of research: in other words, how do philosophical factors affect the creation of satisfactory outcomes from the research activity?

There are at least four reasons why an understanding of philosophical issues is very useful. First, the researcher has an obligation to understand the basic issues of epistemology in order to have a clear sense of her/his reflexive role in research methods. The clarity this will bring to issues related to the theory of knowledge, we believe, is essential if researchers are to make a creative contribution to their field.

Second, it can help to clarify research designs (see Chapter 4). This involves considering not only what kind of evidence is required and how it is to be gathered and interpreted, but also how this will provide good answers to the basic questions being investigated in the research. Third, knowledge of philosophy can help researchers to recognize which designs will work and which will not. It should enable them to avoid going up too many blind alleys and should indicate the limitations of particular approaches. Fourth, it can help researchers to identify, and even create, designs that may be outside their past experience. It may also suggest how to adapt research designs according to the constraints of different subject or knowledge structures.

Arguments, criticisms and debates are central to the progress of philosophy. It is unfortunate that, within the social sciences, such debates sometimes take the form of denigrating the other point of view, or of completely ignoring its existence. We believe that it is important to understand both sides of an argument because research problems often require eclectic designs that draw from more than one tradition. Thus, we try to provide a balanced view of the different philosophical positions underlying research methods and designs; with this in mind, we have returned to some of the original sources of these positions. Therefore, the chapter starts by reviewing some key debates among philosophers of the natural sciences and the social sciences. Then we explore these philosophies further, and review a number of alternative positions.

THE PHILOSOPHICAL DEBATES

Most of the central debates among philosophers concern matters of **ontology** and **epistemology**. Ontology is about the nature of reality and existence; epistemology is about the theory of knowledge and helps researchers understand best ways of enquiring into the nature of the world. At this point it is important to note that natural and social scientists generally draw from different ontological and epistemological assumptions when developing their methodologies for conducting research. Sometimes, they do this consciously and deliberately; more often, they simply follow the traditions passed on by those who trained them. For example, most of the time, medical researchers can simply follow the procedures of scientific research when developing new drugs and they rarely need to reflect on the nature of the human soul – unless, for example, they are using human embryos to conduct research into the therapeutic value of stem-cell treatments. In this latter case, the differing views about when human 'life' begins are very important.

---

[1]From Conan Doyle, A. (1982) *The Adventures of Sherlock Holmes.* London: George Newnes.

(See Chapter 5 for further discussion of some of the ethical problems in management and business research.)

Similarly, as we have suggested above, social researchers often follow the traditions of their training without dwelling on more fundamental issues. We think this is a shame. Awareness of philosophical assumptions can both increase the quality of research and contribute to the creativity of the researcher. Furthermore, there is much confusion among researchers about the distinction between terms such as 'epistemology' and 'ontology', and hence in this section we will try to establish some clarity around these terms. The essence of ontology, epistemology, methodology, and methods and techniques is summarized in Table 3.1.

TABLE 3.1 Ontology, epistemology, methodology and methods and techniques

Ontology	Philosophical assumptions about the nature of reality.
Epistemology	A general set of assumptions about ways of inquiring into the nature of the world.
Methodology	A combination of techniques used to inquire into a specific situation.
Methods and Techniques	Individual techniques, for data collection, analysis, etc.

In Figure 3.1, we illustrate the relationship between these four terms using the metaphor of a tree, as explained in the introductory part of the book, under the section 'About this book' (second diagram on page xv).

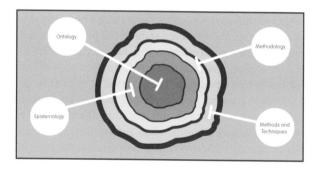

FIGURE 3.1
The four rings model

In this case, it is the trunk of a tree that has four rings. The outer ring – the bark – represents the methods and techniques adopted in a research project, such as interviews and questionnaires. These are the most obvious and visible features of a project, but they depend on decisions and assumptions about methodology, epistemology and ontology that lie behind the scenes, and that are progressively less visible. So, we will start with ontology, represented by the central core (or heartwood) of the tree, and then we will work outwards. Since the second half of the book is concerned with the choice and application of individual methods, we will concentrate in this chapter on the three inner rings: ontology, epistemology and methodology.

ONTOLOGY: FROM REALISM TO NOMINALISM

The first term, ontology, is the starting point for most of the debates among philosophers. Although there are strong parallels between the debates within the natural sciences and the social sciences, there are also differences. Since the scientific community has been debating

methodological issues for much longer than the social scientists, we still start with a summary of the methodological debates among scientists before coming back to social sciences.

Ontologies and natural science

Among philosophers of *natural science*, the main debate has been between **realism** and **relativism**. There are several varieties of realism. A long-standing position emphasizes that the world is concrete and external, and that science can progress only through observations that have a direct correspondence to the phenomena being investigated. This position has been modified by philosophers of science in recent decades, who point out the difference between the laws of physics and those of nature, and the knowledge or theories that scientists have about these laws. This position is labelled by Bhaskar as **transcendental realism**, which assumes that 'the ultimate objects of scientific inquiry exist and act (for the most part) quite independently of scientists and their activity' (1989: 12).

The next position along the continuum is **internal realism**. This assumes that there is a single reality, but asserts that it is never possible for scientists to access that reality directly, and for example, it is only possible to gather indirect evidence of what is going on in fundamental physical processes (Putnam, 1987). A nice illustration is provided by the 'bubble chamber', which was developed in the 1950s to track the paths of sub-atomic particles during experiments. The bubble chamber is a tank filled with an unstable transparent liquid, such as superheated hydrogen; as these high-energy particles pass through the chamber, they make the liquid boil, leaving a track of tiny bubbles that can be photographed immediately. Thus, the bubbles provide a visible record of the activity of sub-atomic particles, which cannot otherwise be 'seen' directly. The problems of observation at this level were summarized more formally by the indeterminacy principle, formulated by Werner Heisenberg in 1927, which states: 'The more precisely the position is determined, the less precisely the momentum is known in this instant, and vice versa.' Thus, it is never possible to obtain full and objective information about the state of a body because the act of experimentation itself will determine the observed state of the phenomenon being studied. Any attempt to measure the location of an electron will, for example, affect its velocity.

Internal realism does accept, however, that scientific laws, once discovered, are absolute and independent of further observations. The position of *relativism* goes a stage further in suggesting that scientific laws are not simply out there to be discovered, but that they are created by people. It has been strongly influenced by the work of Latour and Woolgar (1979), who have studied the way scientific ideas evolve within research laboratories, and noted the amount of debate and discussion that take place about how to explain observed patterns and phenomena. People hold different views, and their ability to gain acceptance from others may depend on their status and past reputation. Thus, the 'truth' of a particular idea or theory is reached through discussion and agreement between the main protagonists. Furthermore, Knorr-Cetina (1983) points out that the acceptance of a particular theory, and hence the 'closure' of a scientific debate, may be highly influenced by the politics of business and commercial resources.

EXAMPLE 3.1

Global warming

The Intergovernmental Panel on Climate Change published a series of reports in 1990 that argued that global warming represented a very serious threat to human civilization. But their own data also showed a period of global warming about 1,000 years ago, when vineyards were widespread in Britain. This opened a question about whether current signs of global warming are caused by CO_2 emissions from fossil fuels burnt by humans, or whether they are just part of natural cycles of global climate change.

The international debate about climate change is a good example of the difficulties in reaching agreement about the significance of 'scientific' evidence (see Example 3.1) and a good illustration of what happens when individuals have no established reflexive sense of self in respect to knowledge and the process of judgement based on evidence. Although the same evidence is potentially available to all protagonists, no single piece of evidence is accepted as definitive by all, and both supporters and sceptics of the climate-change hypothesis tend to select evidence that specifically supports their own views. This links closely to the quotation at the start of this chapter. In addition, there are bodies with very strong, entrenched interests – oil companies, environmentalists and national governments – which see their political and economic concerns as bound up with a particular outcome from the debate. The relativist position assumes that there may never be a definitive answer to the climate-change debate, just different accommodations as the interests of different groups interact with the gradual accumulation and acceptance of scientific evidence. We shall return to some of these political and ethical issues in Chapter 5.

Realist scientists have responded vigorously to the relativist challenge by arguing that even if scientists work through social and political networks, the truth of scientific laws is quite independent of the process of discovery. Richard Dawkins, the biologist, famously comments that even the most dedicated relativist does not believe, when flying at 40,000 feet in a Boeing 747, that the laws of physics that hold the jet in the air are mere constructs of the imagination (Irwin, 1994).

Ontology and the social sciences

Within the *social sciences*, there have been similar debates, although primarily between the positions of internal realism, relativism and **nominalism**. Of course, within the social sciences we are interested in the behaviour of people rather than inanimate objects, and this leads to debate about whether the assumptions and methods of the natural sciences are appropriate to be used in the social sciences (Blaikie, 2007). In our view, the answer depends both on the topic of enquiry and the preferences of the individual researcher. Therefore, concepts such as social class and racial discrimination can be treated as real phenomena, which exist independently of the researcher, and which have real consequences for the life chances and career success of people of different classes or races. In both cases, it can be difficult to agree what these concepts mean or how to measure them, but such disagreements do not alter the reality of their consequences. This indicates the *internal realist* position.

From a *relativist* ontology, it is accepted that social class and racial discrimination are defined and experienced differently by different people, and this will depend greatly on the classes or races to which they belong, and the contexts or countries in which they live. Thus, there is no single reality that can somehow be discovered, but there are many perspectives on the issue. The relativist position assumes that different observers may have different viewpoints and, as Collins (1983: 88) says, 'what counts for the truth can vary from place to place and from time to time'.

The position of nominalism goes further by suggesting that the labels and names we attach to experiences and events are crucial. Postmodern authors, such as Cooper and Burrell (1988), envisage social life as paradoxical and indeterminate, and argue that social reality is no more than the creation of people through language and discourse (Cunliffe, 2001). From this position, there is no truth; and the interesting questions concern how people attempt to establish different versions of truth. Thus, the idea of 'social class' is often used as an explanation of why some people (and families) are systematically more successful than others. For some, it provides a critique of the way privilege is maintained through educational and employment institutions; for others, it may provide a justification of the superiority of some classes (or castes) over others. Similarly, following the racial discrimination line, the label 'institutional racism' provided a sharp critique of the internal practices of the Metropolitan Police following their botched investigation into the murder in London of the black teenager Stephen Lawrence in 1993.

These four ontological positions are summarized in Table 3.2.

TABLE 3.2 Four different ontologies

Ontology	Realism	Internal Realism	Relativism	Nominalism
Truth	Single truth	Truth exists, but is obscure	There are many 'truths'	There is no truth
Facts	Facts exist and can be revealed	Facts are concrete, but cannot be accessed directly	Facts depend on viewpoint of observer	Facts are all human creations

We can illustrate these different positions with two examples, one physical and the other social. First, consider investigating winners in the game of tennis as played on the professional circuits. A *realist* view of tennis would concentrate on aspects of performance that can be measured: the speed of service, the number of 'break points' won or lost within a game, the duration of a match, whether they do better on grass or clay courts, and other past statistics for each player. The *internal realist* would also be concerned with measurement, but with an emphasis on accuracy, and the tension between human judgements made by line-judges and referees, and the technological data provided by technology such as the Hawk-Eye equipment used to determine whether a tennis ball falls within the lines of the court. From this perspective emphasis would be placed on identifying any distinctive physical characteristics of successful players. These features can be monitored and enhanced through fitness training, physiotherapy and practice. Moving to the *relativist* position, the focus would be less on the physical characteristics of the players and more on their mental capabilities. How do they develop their strategies in advance to deal with different types of opponent, and how might these strategies be adapted in 'real time' while playing? Also an important aspect from this perspective is the relation between the players and the crowd: how can they get the crowd to support them rather than the opposition? From a *nominalist* perspective, the focus could be on the way players make sense of particular successes and defeats in post-match interviews, and then what happens in the discussion with the trainer afterwards. Given the impact that partisan crowds can affect the performance of players, the creation of individual images by presenting aspects of themselves to the media could be very important. And then there are other less visible aspects, such as who controls the finances of the professional game, the way careers are forged, and the stories of the vast majority of hopeful young people who never make it onto the professional circuit.

The second example, which is more relevant to conventional business, is the notion of corporate profit. A *realist* view will assume that there is a single figure that represents the difference between income and expenditure, and that the accounts posted by companies at the year-end are an accurate account of how much money came in and went out over the financial year. The *internal realist* will see a more complex position: the boundaries may be permeable, with acquisitions and divestments taking place during the year; highly diverse activities may be woven into single threads; and decisions will be taken about how to divide ongoing activities between one year and the next. Thus, the profit figure posted will be just an approximation of the 'true' profit of the company. From a *relativist* position, it would be recognized that profit is just one indicator of corporate health, and other indicators (such as sales growth, innovation rates and stock-market valuations) may be equally relevant – with no one view taking precedence. The *nominalist* perspective will draw attention to the way profit figures are constructed from many operational decisions about what to show or hide, and at corporate levels may well be manipulated so that tax liabilities are minimized, or so that directors can maximize their annual bonus payments.

EPISTEMOLOGY: POSITIVISM VERSUS SOCIAL CONSTRUCTIONISM

As indicated above, epistemology is the study of the nature of knowledge and ways of enquiring into the physical and social worlds. It is, as we have indicated, the study of theories of knowledge; how we know what we know. It has formed the ground for a sustained debate among social scientists, which has focused on the respective merits of two contrasting views of how social science research should be conducted: **positivism** and **social constructionism**.[2] Each of these positions has to some extent been elevated into a stereotype, often by the opposing side. Although we can draw up comprehensive lists of philosophical assumptions and methodological implications associated with each position, there is no single philosopher who subscribes to all aspects of one particular view. Indeed, an author from one side occasionally produces ideas that belong more neatly to the other side.

Also, when we look at the actual practice of research, even self-confessed extremists do not adhere consistently to one position or the other, as we shall see below. And although there has been a gradual trend from positivism towards constructionism since the early 1980s, there are many research studies – both in management and the wider social sciences – that deliberately combine methods from both traditions. These so-called mixed methods have great potential for finding deeper insights into management and organizational research, but researchers sometimes come unstuck when using them because they are not aware of the pitfalls of combining worldviews that are fundamentally different from each other. It follows that we need to understand these differences at an early stage in the research process, which is why we elaborate on these two traditions below.

The key idea of positivism is that the social world exists externally, and that its properties can be measured through objective methods rather than being inferred subjectively through sensation, reflection or intuition. The nineteenth-century French philosopher Auguste Comte (1853: 3) was the first person to encapsulate this view, saying: 'All good intellects have repeated, since Bacon's time, that there can be no real knowledge but that which is based on observed facts.' This statement contains two assumptions: first, an ontological assumption that reality is external and objective; and second, an epistemological assumption that knowledge is of significance only if it is based on observations of this external reality; it is the result of empirical verification. It isn't simply related to the consideration of a method of inquiry. It also relates to where the judgement resides in respect to evidence. This has a number of implications, although not all of them were proposed by Comte (see Table 3.3).

It is worth repeating that these assumptions are not simply the view of any single philosopher; they are a collection of points that have come to be associated with the positivist viewpoint. Some 'positivists' would disagree with some of these statements. Comte, for example, did not agree with the principle of reductionism. Wittgenstein argued strongly in his early work that all factual propositions can be reduced to elementary propositions that are completely independent of one another. But in his later work, he challenged his earlier view on the grounds that elementary propositions, such as colours, could still be logically related to each other (Pears, 1971). So, philosophers within one school not only disagree with each other; they may also disagree with themselves over time!

The view that positivism provides the best way of investigating human and social behaviour originated as a reaction to metaphysical speculation (Aiken, 1956). As such, this philosophy has developed into a distinctive **paradigm** over the last 150 years. The term 'paradigm' came into vogue among social scientists, particularly through the work of Thomas Kuhn (1962), who used it to describe the progress of scientific discoveries in *practice*, as opposed to how they are subsequently reconstructed within text books and academic journals. Most

---

[2]There are a number of terms which are equivalent to 'social construc*tion*', notably construc*tivism* and interpretivism, which we will encounter again in later chapters.

TABLE 3.3 Philosophical assumptions of positivism

- *Independence*: the observer must be independent from what is being observed.

- *Value-freedom*: the choice of what to study, and how to study it, can be determined by objective criteria rather than by human beliefs and interests.

- *Causality*: the aim of the social sciences should be to identify causal explanations and fundamental laws that explain regularities in human social behaviour.

- *Hypothesis and deduction*: science proceeds through a process of hypothesizing fundamental laws and then deducing what kinds of observations will demonstrate the truth or falsity of these hypotheses.

- *Operationalization*: concepts need to be defined in ways that enable facts to be measured quantitatively.

- *Reductionism*: problems as a whole are better understood if they are reduced into the simplest possible elements.

- *Generalization*: in order to move from the specific to the general it is necessary to select random samples of sufficient size, from which inferences may be drawn about the wider population.

- *Cross-sectional analysis*: such regularities can most easily be identified by making comparisons of variations across samples.

of the time, according to Kuhn, science progresses in tiny steps, which refine and extend what is already 'known'. But occasionally, experiments start to produce results that do not fit into existing theories and patterns. Then, perhaps many years later, a Galileo or an Einstein proposes a new way of looking at things, which can account for both the old and the new observations. It is evident from these examples that major scientific advances are not produced by a logical and incremental application of scientific method. Rather, they also and significantly result from independent and creative thinking that goes beyond the boundaries of existing ideas. The result of this is a 'scientific revolution', which not only provides new theories, but also may alter radically the way people see the world, and the kind of questions that scientists consider as important to investigate. The combination of new theories and questions is referred to as a 'new paradigm'.

A new paradigm has been developed by philosophers during the last half-century, largely in reaction to the limited success that has been achieved from applying the principles of positivism to the social sciences. This stems from the view that 'reality' is not objective and exterior, but is socially constructed and is given meaning by people in their daily interactions with others. The idea of social constructionism, as developed by authors such as Berger and Luckman (1966), Watzlawick (1984) and Shotter (1993), focuses on the ways that people make sense of the world – especially through sharing their experiences with others via the medium of language. Social constructionism is one of a group of approaches that Habermas (1970) has referred to as 'interpretive methods'. We will touch on these, and a number of other approaches, in the course of this and the following chapter.

What, then, is the essence of social constructionism? First, it is the idea, as mentioned above, that many aspects of 'societal reality' are determined by people rather than by objective and external factors. Hence, the task of the social scientist should not only be to gather facts and measure the frequency of patterns of social behaviour, but also to appreciate the different constructions and meanings that people place upon their experience. The focus should be on what people, individually and collectively, are thinking and feeling, and attention should be paid to the ways they communicate with each other, whether verbally or non-verbally. We should therefore try to understand and appreciate the different experiences that people have, rather than search for external causes and fundamental laws to explain behaviour. Human action arises from the sense that people make of different situations, rather than as a direct response to external stimuli.

The methods of social constructionist research can be contrasted directly with the eight features of classical positivist research. They are summarized in Table 3.4. Again, it should be emphasized that these represent a composite picture rather than the viewpoint of any single author.

TABLE 3.4   Contrasting implications of positivism and social constructionism

	Positivism	Social Constructionism
The observer	must be independent	is part of what is being observed
Human interests	should be irrelevant	are the main drivers of science
Explanations	must demonstrate causality	aim to increase general understanding of the situation
Research progresses through	hypotheses and deductions	gathering rich data from which ideas are induced
Concepts	need to be defined so that they can be measured	should incorporate stakeholder perspectives
Units of analysis	should be reduced to simplest terms	may include the complexity of 'whole' situations
Generalization through	statistical probability	theoretical abstraction
Sampling requires	large numbers selected randomly	small numbers of cases chosen for specific reasons

The implications of holding these different views may be seen, for example, in the way researchers can study managerial stress. The positivist would start with the assumption that occupational stress exists, and would then formulate measures of stress experienced by a large number of employees in order to relate them to external causes (such as organizational changes, interpersonal conflicts and critical performance reviews). Measures of stress could be based on standardized verbal reports from the managers or on physiological factors, such as blood pressure. Social constructionists would be interested in the aspects of work that managers consider 'stressful', and perhaps in the strategies that they develop for managing these aspects. They would therefore arrange to talk with a few managers about their jobs, and about the aspects they find more (or less) difficult, and would attempt to gather stories about incidents that the managers had experienced as stressful.

It should be clear by now that there is a link between epistemology and ontology, with positivism fitting with realist ontologies, and constructionism fitting with nominalism. We also introduce here a distinction between fundamental and more practical versions of positivism and constructionism. With regard to positivism, this follows the distinction introduced by the Oxford philosopher A. J. Ayer ([1936] 1971: 50) between statements that are either directly, or only indirectly, verifiable. The idea of 'normal' constructionism refers to those who construct their own knowledge while accepting the existence of independent, objective knowledge, whereas 'strong' constructionism assumes that there is no difference between individual and social knowledge (Ernst, 1996).

The correspondence is therefore summarized in Table 3.5, where positivism and constructionism are linked to internal realist and relativist ontologies, while strong positivism

TABLE 3.5 Methodological implications of different epistemologies

Ontologies	Realism	Internal realism	Relativism	Nominalism
Epistemology	Strong positivism	Positivism	Constructionism	Strong constructionism
Methodology				
Aims	Discovery	Exposure	Convergence	Invention
Starting points	Hypotheses	Propositions	Questions	Critiques
Designs	Experiments	Large surveys; multi-cases	Cases and surveys	Engagement and reflexivity
Data types	Numbers and facts	Mainly numbers with some words	Mainly words with some numbers	Discourse and experiences
Analysis/ interpretation	Verification/ falsification	Correlation and regression	Triangulation and comparison	Sense-making; understanding
Outcomes	Confirmation of theories	Theory-testing and generation	Theory generation	New insights and actions

and strong constructionism are linked to the realist and nominalist ontologies. However, we take the argument further by suggesting that, with the weaker versions of both episte-mologies, there are overlaps in these positions, and the methodologies that follow from them combine different features of each. The table therefore summarizes the main methodologies under the four main positions, and we explain these further below.

In the *strong positivist* position, it is assumed that there is a reality that exists independently of the observer, and hence the job of the researcher is to discover the laws and theories that explain this reality. This is most readily achieved through the design of experiments that eliminate alter-native explanations and allow key factors to be measured precisely in order to verify or falsify predetermined hypotheses. On the other hand, less strong versions of positivism accept that real-ity cannot be accessed directly. The research therefore needs to infer the nature of this reality indirectly through conducting surveys of large samples of individuals, activities or organizations. Data will normally be expressed in quantitative form, but this may be supplemented by qualita-tive data. This should enable patterns and regularities in behaviour to be identified, thus allowing propositions to be tested and new ideas to be developed. Even so, it is only a matter of probability that the views collected will provide an accurate indication of the underlying situation.

From the *constructionist* position, the assumption is that there may be many different realities, and hence the researcher needs to gather multiple perspectives through a mixture of qualitative and quantitative methods, and to collect the views and experiences of diverse individuals and observers. This is sometimes described as **triangulation** (see Example 3.2).

EXAMPLE
3.2

Triangulation

Triangulation is based on the idea that seafarers, wishing to avoid rocks hidden just below the surface in coastal waters, need to identify their position with reasonable accu-racy. In the days before the invention of radar and GPS, this could be done only by taking compass bearings on three different landmarks, and then drawing lines on the chart from these points, thus producing a small triangle that would indicate the position of the vessel. The degree of accuracy is indicated by the size of the triangle (small triangles generally being better than larger ones). The course of the ship can then be plotted on the chart by joining up the series of triangles created by such sightings, and the navigator can then see whether or not they are in danger of hitting the rocks.

The story from the *strong constructionist* perspective is different again because it assumes there is no pre-existing reality, and the aim of the researcher should be to understand how people invent structures to help them make sense of, and influence, what is going on around them. Consequently, much attention is given to the language and discourse that can be used both to create meanings and to influence – or 'enact' – the environment. Researchers following this path are encouraged to be critical of the way meanings can be imposed by the more powerful on the less powerful. Furthermore, the recognition that the observer can never be separated from the sense-making process means that researchers acknowledge that theories that apply to the subjects of their work must also be relevant to *themselves*. Such reflexive approaches to methodology are recognized as being particularly relevant when studies are considering power and cultural differences (Anderson, 1993; Easterby-Smith and Malina, 1999; Cunliffe, 2003, 2011).

Spotting the epistemology

EXERCISE 3.1

Individual or interactive exercise: Researchers normally betray their epistemology in the language they use. Here are seven brief statements of the aims of different papers. Which is which? What clues did you spot?

1. 'We advance research on absorptive capacity by extending and empirically validating the conceptual distinction between potential and realized absorptive capacity' (Jansen et al., 2005: 1000).

2. 'This paper develops a holistic model of the overall process, by integrating knowledge oriented, routine oriented, and social/context of perspectives' (Hong et al., 2006: 1027).

3. 'This article contributes to the study of managerial agency in the absorption of new knowledge and skills … Empirical data are drawn from a longitudinal study of a …' (Jones, 2006: 355).

4. 'We (also) examine the influence of tacit and explicit knowledge on IJV performance. We find that relational embeddedness has a stronger influence on the transfer of tacit knowledge than it has on the transfer of explicit knowledge' (Dhanaraj et al., 2004).

5. 'These findings can be explained by elements of JCT and social exchange theory. As expected, when both LMX quality and empowerment were low the most negative outcomes resulted, and in general, when both variables were high the most positive outcomes resulted' (Harris et al., 2009: 397).

6. 'Organizational routines are ubiquitous, yet their contribution to organizing has been under-appreciated. Our longitudinal, inductive study traces the relationship between organizational routines and organizational schemata in a new research institution' (Rerup and Feldman, 2011: 577).

7. 'This brings me to a discussion of the credibility performance of agency – client relations. In some respects the very structure of a corporation can be seen in how it arranges performances … Like an individual, a corporation may be seen as a performer …' (Moeran, 2005: 917).

STRENGTHS AND WEAKNESSES OF THE MAIN TRADITIONS

Here, we summarize some of the strengths and weaknesses of each position (see Table 3.6). This should help the researcher to choose which methods and aspects are most likely to be of help in a given situation.

We start with quantitative methods, which are based on the stronger version of the positivist paradigm. In this case, the main strengths are that they can provide wide coverage of the range of situations; they can be fast and economical; and, with statistical analysis of data from large samples, their outcomes may be of considerable relevance to policy decisions. On the debit side, these methods tend to be rather inflexible and artificial; they are not very effective in understanding processes, or the significance that people attach to actions; they are not very helpful in generating theories; and, because they focus on what is (or what has been recently), they make it hard for the policy-maker to infer what changes and actions should take place in the future. In addition, much of the data gathered may not be relevant to real decisions, even though they can still be used to support the covert goals of decision-makers.

The strengths and weaknesses of stronger forms of the *social constructionist* paradigm and associated interpretative methods are fairly complementary. Thus, they have strengths in their ability to look at change processes over time, to understand people's meanings, to adjust to new issues and ideas as they emerge, and to contribute to the evolution of new theories. They also provide a way of gathering data, which is seen as natural rather than artificial. There are, of course, weaknesses. Data collection can take up a great deal of time and resources, and the analysis and interpretation of data may be very difficult, and depend on the intimate, tacit knowledge of the researchers. Qualitative studies often feel very untidy because it is harder to control their pace, progress and end points. There is also the problem that many people, especially policy-makers, may give low credibility to studies based on apparently 'subjective' opinions.

TABLE 3.6   Strengths and weaknesses of different epistemologies

	Strong positivism	Positivism	Constructionism	Strong constructionism
Strengths	If it works, it can provide highly compelling conclusions	Can provide wide coverage; potentially fast and economical; easier to provide justification of policies	Accepts value of multiple data sources; enables generalizations beyond present sample; greater efficiency, including outsourcing potential	Good for processes, and meanings; flexible and good for theory generation; data collection less artificial
Weaknesses	Hard to implement social experiments and to control for alternative explanations of results; focus may be very narrow	Inflexible and artificial; not good for process, meanings or theory generation; implications for action not obvious	Access can be difficult; cannot accommodate institutional and cultural differences; problems reconciling discrepant information	Can be very time-consuming; analysis and interpretations are difficult; may not have credibility with policy-makers

The bulk of research in business and management is underpinned by the weaker forms of positivism and constructionism. It is tempting, then, to seek out compromise positions that can combine the strengths, and avoid the limitations, of each of the more extreme positions. To some degree, this is what has happened over the last three decades: a number of new research approaches have developed with the aim of getting the best out of both worlds, and these populate the central space of the epistemological continuum.

In the following section of this chapter, we will introduce another analytic dimension that will help us to map newer methods against some of the established positions. This is intended to help researchers to work out how to fit into the broader philosophical map the methodologies that they devise or borrow.

PARADIGMS AND RESEARCH APPROACHES

In this section, we review the philosophical positions and assumptions that underpin some of the more popular methodologies that have influenced, either directly or indirectly, the approaches that can be used when doing research into business and management.

The map we use is partly inspired by the ground-breaking book published by Gibson Burrell and Gareth Morgan in 1979, entitled *Sociological Paradigms and Organisational Analysis*. In this book they identified four distinct traditions, each with its own assumptions about the nature of reality, the essence of knowledge and the roots of human behaviour. They labelled these as 'functionalism, interpretivism, radical structuralism and radical humanism', and argued that they were distinct paradigms because their underlying assumptions were incompatible with each other. So, for example, the assumption that society needs institutions and organizations in order to *regulate* human behaviour does not compare well with the view that society and organizations are fundamentally designed to maintain, or increase, inequality, and that they can be changed for the better only through *radical* change.

In the context of academic research, some of the current approaches might be considered as *paradigms* because they contain distinct sets of assumptions about ontology and epistemology that are shared by supporters and that largely exclude adherence to other points of view. Others, perhaps less grand than paradigms, might be regarded as schools of thought, or meta-methodologies.

Epistemology and researcher engagement

Up to this point, we have reviewed the fundamental philosophical positions that underlie the practice of management and business research, with an emphasis on the epistemological dimension. In this section, we introduce a second dimension that is particularly relevant to both the status and the future potential of such research. This is the notion of engagement of the researcher with the research context (as mentioned briefly in Chapter 1).

This second dimension contrasts two views on the relationship between researchers and the objects of their research: first, that researchers should strive to be independent of, and 'detached' from, the people and processes that they are studying; and second, that, when studying social systems like complex organizations, there is positive value in getting closer to the things they are studying, and this is increasingly known as an 'engaged' style of research.

Thus, we can take the epistemological dimension of positivist–constructionist, and add this new dimension of detached–engaged. We will treat these as being orthogonal to each other, and this produces a two-by-two matrix, which is illustrated in Figure 3.2.

In order to make sense of this matrix, we have found it useful to take the analogy of the business researcher and the fictional detective. Both are seeking answers to questions, albeit different kinds, and their careers and reputations depend on their ability to solve

FIGURE 3.2
Epistemology
and research
style

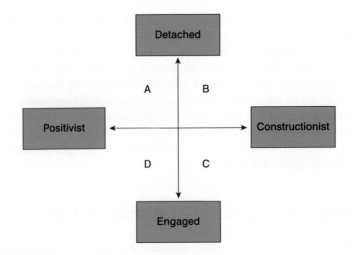

problems. In the case of the detective, to identify the murderer (normally within one or two hours if on TV); and for the researcher, to identify (for example) how the new social media are affecting the value of knowledge held by organizations (within four months if an undergraduate project, or three years if a doctorate).

The point is that there are a number of distinct ways in which fictional detectives operate, and these are similar to the choices that researchers have when they conduct their investigations. On the horizontal dimension of Figure 3.2, which represents two contrasting epistemologies, we can compare the scientific approach of Sherlock Holmes with the more intuitive style of the Agatha Christie character, Miss Marple. Whereas Holmes relies on detailed observation of physical evidence, and the process of logical deduction about the circumstances of the crime, Marple acts as an insider to the scene of the crime and makes use of her intuitive feel about the characters involved. Sherlock Holmes therefore represents the positivist side, and Miss Marple represents the constructionist side.

We can also identify characters who personify the vertical dimension in Figure 3.2. Thus, the other famous Agatha Christie character, Hercule Poirot, is a classic example of the detective who is totally untouched and unruffled by the number of homicides that surround him as he travels around with his high-society friends. His only concern is his apparent inability to solve the crime immediately, although it is his superior intellect – those 'little grey cells' – that always enable him to get there in the end (and well before Superintendent Japp).

Poirot stands in sharp contrast to many of the Hollywood detectives, who operate very close to the world of the criminals they hunt, and who regularly provoke violent exchanges with their quarries. Clint Eastwood's portrayal of Dirty Harry provides an example of a cop who acts first and thinks later – in contrast to the effete, intellectual style of Hercule Poirot, who is all brain and no action.

Of course, the poles in Figure 3.2 represent extreme positions and, in many respects, it is interesting to explore the spaces between the axes, shown in the matrix as the four quadrants A, B, C and D. Continuing with the detective analogy briefly, in quadrant A, we could envisage Dr Temperance Brennan, the straight-laced scientist in the American forensic science drama *Bones*, or Amanda Burton who plays professor Sam Ryan in *Silent Witness*. Both characters have high intellectual ability and demonstrate strong belief in the primacy of scientific technique. In quadrant B, we might find Inspector Morse, also with a combination of his high intellect and his intuitive feel for the community in and around Oxford University. There would be many contenders for quadrant C, but perhaps our favourite would be lead detective Sarah Lund, who wears the same Nordic sweater throughout ten episodes of *The Killing*; highly intuitive, she is always getting herself into dangerous situations. Finally, for quadrant D, our favourite representative would be Lisbeth Salander, heroine of *The Girl with the Dragon Tattoo*, who combines extraordinary technical ability with devastating martial arts performance.

Returning to the matter of research paradigms and schools of thought, we have organized these around the four quadrants, since they rarely fit precisely into any single category, and the quadrants provide greater flexibility. In developing this model, we were influenced by *Sociological Paradigms and Organisational Analysis* (Burrell and Morgan, 1979). Although the paradigms themselves are conceptually distinct, this does not necessarily mean that all research approaches fall neatly into one paradigm or another. Some fit neatly into one quadrant; others may spread over two or more. We list them here in alphabetical order and then in the next section of this chapter we will review them in relation to the four quadrants defined in Figure 3.2.

Critical Realism	Hermeneutics	Scientific Method
Critical Theory	Postmodernism	Structuration Theory
Feminism	Pragmatism	Systems Theory

Alternative paradigms and research approaches

Quadrant A: detached positivism

Scientific method is closely associated with positivism and therefore shares many of the same assumptions, including the need for independence of the observer from the subject of observation; specifying in advance the expected findings; and defining terms in ways that enable them to be measured. There is also a preference for large samples that can enable statistical analysis, in order to establish how far the results can be generalized.

Scientific method is used widely in most disciplines: it underpins most 'hard' sciences (such as physics, chemistry and biology) and medical research, but is also extensively used in business and management research, including in the areas of strategy, human resource management, market research, financial modelling and simulation.

One of the problems in management research is that the top journals are dominated by studies that use this scientific method. Roughly 80 per cent of papers published in the leading US-based journals are positivist, against around 25 per cent in the leading Europe-based journals (Easterby-Smith, Li and Bartunek). The lack of balance here has several consequences. First, it discourages ambitious researchers from getting involved in more qualitative/constructionist approaches. Second, it means that research projects may try to follow positivist methods, when other methods would be both cheaper and more insightful. Third, there is a lack of understanding, and occasional intolerance, from researchers operating out of the scientific model who are evaluating non-positivist work because they unconsciously use the criteria of the scientific quadrant to judge work that is based on another, sometimes incompatible paradigm. We shall come back to this point in several of the later chapters in the book.

Critical realism is sometimes portrayed as a compromise position between the stronger versions of positivism and constructionism, but with more emphasis on the former. Over the last three decades, it has been adopted by a number of management and organizational researchers because it provides a structured way of thinking about social and organizational problems. It starts with a realist ontology, which recognizes social conditions (such as class or wealth) as having real consequences, whether or not they are observed. It then incorporates a relativist thread, which recognizes that social life both is generated by the actions of individuals, and has an external impact on them (Ackroyd and Fleetwood, 2000).

A key feature of critical realism is the idea of a 'structured ontology', which differentiates between three levels: the *empirical* domain, which comprises the experiences and perceptions that people have; the *actual* domain, which comprises events and actions that take place, whether or not they are observed or detected; and the *real* domain, which comprises causal powers and mechanisms that cannot be detected directly, but that have real consequences for people and society (Bhaskar, 1978: 13). These three domains correspond roughly to three of our ontological positions: respectively relativism, internal realism and realism.

Two other features are important in critical realism. First is the idea that causality exists as the potential – rather than the automatic – correlation of events that is normally associated with strong positivism. Second is the idea drawn partly from critical theory that many of these underlying mechanisms do not work in the interests of ordinary people and employees, and that greater awareness of their underlying causes will provide potential for emancipation from their effects.

We have located critical realism as being *just* in the detached positivism quadrant because its proponents are explicit about its realist ontology; also, there is more emphasis on theory-building than on direct engagement with the world through empirical research. Still, there are implications for management and business research, suggesting an agenda that may be critical of the status quo. In addition, since critical realism is located quite close to the middle ground philosophically, it tolerates an eclectic approach to research methods. Nevertheless, there are relatively few research studies that have adopted the methods of critical realism wholeheartedly, but many draw on its ideas to structure processes of data collection and analysis.

Quadrant B: detached constructionism

Although **hermeneutics** were originally developed by Protestant groups in seventeenth-century Germany as a means of interpreting the Bible, the theory still has some relevance to management research. Essentially, it provides insight into ways of interpreting textual material, which can comprise both formal written texts and spoken words that can be recorded. Two of the best-known proponents of hermeneutics are Gadamer (1989) and Ricoeur (1981).

Gadamer is particularly concerned about the context within which texts are written. He points out that contemporary interpretations of earlier texts are influenced by the culture in which the interpreter is located; so, in order to understand a particular text, one must try to understand what was going on in the world of the writer at the time that the text was written. Ricoeur argues that when reading any text, there is bound to be a gap between the author and the reader due to temporal differences – which he refers to as 'distanciation'. Ideally, there needs to be some kind of discourse between the author and the reader at the same point in time, but this is no longer possible in the case of historical texts. Therefore, we have to be aware that there may be no single correct interpretation of a particular text because both the writing and the reading will be context-dependent.

In the context of management research, some of the insights from hermeneutics have obvious relevance if the researcher wishes to analyse corporate documents such as annual reports. In this case, instead of (for example) conducting a content analysis of statements about the environment in annual reports for 1980, 1990 and 2000, one would need to analyse references in each report separately in relation to the social, economic and political context at each point of time. Thus, the analysis would be between context-based observations, rather than simple additions and enumerations of mentions.

Postmodernism first came to wide academic attention with the English publication of Jean-François Lyotard's (1984) book, *The Postmodern Condition*, although the term had been used intermittently in relation to literary criticism since 1926 (Chia, 2008). A loose cluster of other (mainly French) philosophers have been associated with the development of ideas around postmodernity, including Derrida (1978) and Foucault (1979).

There are three key ideas to postmodernism. First, it provides a critique of scientific progress, suggesting that it is not necessarily a good thing. Thus, scientific progress is discontinuous and contested, rather than linear and continuous. Lyotard, for example, examines the impacts of computerization on the control of knowledge, and demonstrates how technology enables many large corporations to become more powerful than states. Second, postmodernism is associated with a somewhat experimental movement in architecture and the arts, which seeks to redress the excesses of modernism, for example the bleak concrete architecture of the 1960s. Thus, postmodern architecture tends to be very eclectic, drawing upon different traditions and ideas, and so avoiding the large-scale regularity of modern architecture. Third, as we have discussed above, postmodernism contains an ontological position, which is opposed to realism, though it is sometimes dismissed as supporting relativism and mere nihilism.

There are several implications for management research. First, the opposition to systematic control and regularity leads to an emphasis on flux and flexibility. Thus, postmodernists do not see organizations as static and monolithic, and this makes their perspective particularly appropriate for studying organizational dynamics and change. Second, the opposition to realism places an emphasis on the invisible elements and processes of organizations, including tacit knowledge and the informal processes of decision making. Finally, postmodernism retains a critical edge and is sceptical about the role and motivation of large industrial organizations, and questions whether they are of lasting value to society.

Quadrant C: engaged constructionism

Pragmatism originated in the writings of early twentieth-century American philosophers, particularly William James ([1907] 1979) and John Dewey (1916). It is often seen as a compromise position between internal realism and relativism: it does not accept that there are predetermined theories or frameworks that shape knowledge and truth; nor does it accept that people can construct their own truths out of nothing. The key point is that any meaning structures must come from the lived experience of individuals. Dewey, in particular, talks about the need to balance concrete and abstract on one hand, and reflection and observation on the other.

Perhaps it is no coincidence, since Dewey was an educationalist, that pragmatism has had a significant impact on theories of learning within organizations. The Kolb Learning Cycle (Kolb, 1984) adopts a pragmatic approach, suggesting that learning takes place as a continual movement from concrete experience, to reflective observation, to abstract conceptualization, to active experimentation and back to concrete experience. It is also consistent with the original thinking of James that organizational theorists have adopted elements of pragmatism because it offers a synthesis between features often regarded as irreconcilable dualisms, such as positivism and anti-positivism (Brandi and Elkjaer, 2008).

Pragmatism is a valuable perspective in management research because it focuses on processes that are particularly relevant to studies of knowledge and learning. Its impact on methods can be seen in the tradition and methods of grounded theory, which we will discuss in some detail in the next chapter.

Critical theory started as an intellectual movement, also known as the Frankfurt School, which sought to critique the effects of society and technology on human development. The key figure in this movement is Habermas (1970), who argues that society leads to inequalities and alienation, yet this is invisible to people who do not realize what is taking place. He therefore argues that there is a degree of irrationality in capitalist society, which creates a false consciousness regarding wants and needs. Thus, people are, for example, seduced into wanting consumer products that they do not really need.

Habermas (1970) also identifies clear differences between the natural and social sciences, the former being based on sense-related experiences, and the latter on communicative experiences. This means that although understanding in the natural sciences is one-way (monologic), with scientists observing inanimate objects, communication in the social sciences should be two-way (dialogic), with both researchers and the researched trying to make sense of the situation. Hence, Habermas suggests that it is only through dialogue that social scientists will be able to work effectively. He also introduced the important idea that knowledge is determined by interests, and that very often it is the more powerful people in society who determine what is regarded as 'true'. Consequently, truth should be reached through discussion and rational consensus, rather than being imposed by one group on another.

Critical theory has several implications for management and organizational research. It casts a sceptical eye on the motives and impact of powerful groups and individuals, which, in an emancipatory way, shows a concern for the interests of the least powerful members. Of course, awareness of the way in which knowledge is determined by political processes is of increasing relevance – especially within knowledge-intensive organizations.

We have found it difficult to pin critical theory to a single location on the map in Figure 3.2. Perhaps this is because scholars working in this area are more concerned with theory than with empirical research. But the distinction made by Habermas (1970) between the natural and the social sciences suggests that research informed by critical theory should be located away from the scientific end of the map, and the importance given to dialogue as a potential basis for change means that it fits best in quadrant C.

Feminism is critical of the status quo, but from a very specific angle: that women's experiences have been undervalued by society and by scientific enquiry. From a philosophical viewpoint, it contains a strong critique of science on the grounds that women's perspectives have been ignored by most scientific enquiry, in at least five respects (Blaikie, 2007): there are very few women employed within science; there is gender bias in the definition of research problems; there is bias in the design and interpretation of research; there are too many rigid dualisms in male-dominated science; and science is not as rational and objective as it claims to be. Furthermore, it is claimed that similar processes operate in the social sciences, especially with **structured interviews**, which create a status difference between the interviewer and respondent, even when the interviewer is a woman (Cotterill, 1992). In particular, it is emphasized that external knowledge is impossible and that we must therefore understand human behaviour from within, through understanding the experiences of women themselves.

There is also an emancipatory agenda to feminism, although in relation to social sciences, there is a split between epistemologies known as 'feminist empiricism' and those known as 'feminist standpoint'. The former assumes that the problem is not with science itself, but with the way it is conducted; therefore, there is a need to rectify the norms and procedures of the natural and the social sciences so that they incorporate a gendered perspective. The feminist standpoint, on the other hand, is more radical. It suggests that social science and its methods are fundamentally flawed, and need to be completely rethought. In particular, social science needs to include issues of power dynamics and gender differences, and should make far greater use of subjective experiences and the procedures of reflexivity.

The relevance of feminism to management research is that it provides not only a spotlight on the historical and continuing inequalities of women working in most organizations, but also sensitivity to other areas of discrimination within organizational life, which may be caused by other factors, such as race and age.

Structuration theory is most associated with the work of Anthony Giddens (1984), who developed the idea of 'duality of structure': that structure and agency should not be regarded as pre-ordained. Instead, he suggested that structures are created and recreated through social action and the agency of individuals, and structure then guides and constrains individual agency. Hence, there is a continual interaction between social structure and social action.

Philosophically, he is at pains to point out that the laws of the natural and the social sciences are fundamentally different, because the former are potentially universal, while the latter depend upon the context (including both structure and action) within which things are taking place. He is also concerned about the use of language, pointing out that words are not precisely 'representational', and that their use depends on agreement about their meaning, which may be the product of debates and reinterpretations. Because language is essentially problematic, he therefore advocates that social scientists should try to avoid specialist language, because it potentially obscures and creates confusion for outsiders. In order to communicate insights from social science, he suggests that social scientists should attempt to use common-sense language in the normal course of their work.

In the context of management research, structuration theory has relevance to understanding the relationships between employees and the organizations within which they work, or between communications and the information systems that are supposed to facilitate them. In other words, it can throw light on aspects of organizations where there is some kind of structural duality.

Quadrant D: engaged positivism

Systems theory was first developed in the 1950s as an interdisciplinary methodology for studying systems, both living and inanimate. The key figure at the start was Ludwig von Bertalanffy, a biologist who developed systems theory from observations of systematic processes within biology. His wider aim was to discover whether the principles of systems theory could be applied usefully in other disciplines. Hence, he drew together a group of leading scientists in other fields (such as sociology and anthropology) and in 1956 established the Society for General Systems Research (now the International Society for the

Systems Sciences), with the aim of developing and testing the application of systems theory to other areas of the natural and the social sciences.

Systems theory has a number of basic assumptions. First of all, there is the assumption that complex systems should be studied as wholes, rather than through breaking them down into their constituent parts. Second is the idea that when studying systems, human or otherwise, it is the relationships between members that provide the most important information. Third is the belief that there are common properties in all systems, which therefore provide the potential for methodological unification across the social sciences.

Two variants of the basic systems theories are soft systems methodology (SSM) and critical systems theory. The former was developed by a group at Lancaster University under the leadership of Peter Checkland, who distinguishes SSM from traditional systems methods thus: 'Whereas systems engineering methodology is a system concerned with achieving objectives, SSM is a learning system. The learning is about a complex problematical human situation, and leads to taking purposeful action in the situation aimed at improvement' (Checkland, 1989: 278). SSM has been very successful as a framework for students doing projects within companies, because it provides some useful analytic tools that give guidance in a highly flexible way. It also has the distinction that it is designed to be used collaboratively when looking for unstructured problems within organizations.

The second variant is critical systems theory, which adds elements of critical theory, such as the need to develop critical social awareness, accept pluralism in organizations, and have a concern for emancipation. This can be most useful when investigating situations that contain conflict or sharp differences in the power of participants.

Within business schools, the proponents of systems theory are most likely to be found in management-science departments, project-management groups or IT units. Since the methodology encourages engagement and active collaboration with companies and other organizations, this approach fits well with the wider agenda (in the UK, at least) of encouraging collaboration between universities and companies. Although we have classified systems theory in general as belonging to the engaged-positivism quadrant, in our view SSM would fit more easily with the engaged-constructionist quadrant because of its concern with human (rather than physical) systems.

Overview

In Figure 3.3, we provide a sketch of how these nine philosophies relate to each other against the two dimensions introduced earlier in this chapter. The positions are intended to be indicative rather than precise mappings.

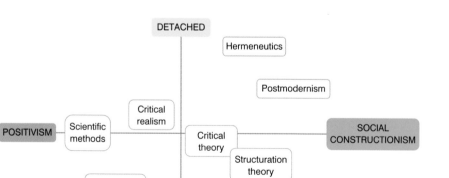

FIGURE 3.3

Mapping research paradigms and schools of thought

CONCLUSION

In this chapter we have concentrated on philosophies that underlie management research. Our main aim has been to help readers to identify philosophical assumptions underlying other people's work, and to understand how these might influence and assist their own research endeavours. At this stage, we can emphasize four key points:

 All researchers hold philosophical assumptions, although these are often tacit rather than explicit positions.

 Researchers need to be aware of their own philosophical assumptions.

 The strongest philosophical contrast is between realist and nominalist ontologies.

 There is often correspondence between ontologies, epistemologies and methodologies.

So far, the discussion has been inevitably theoretical. In Chapter 4 we will start to work on how these philosophical positions influence specific research methods, and will provide a number of illustrations and practical exercises to assist in developing research plans and designs.

EXERCISE 3.2

Identifying your own philosophical position

Interactive exercise: Write down a very brief description of some research that you are planning to do, or might do, including a title, the main question and how you would do it (one sentence for each). Consider: (a) what ontology you are adopting (i.e. realist, internal realist, relativist or nominalist); and (b) what epistemology you are likely to adopt (strong/weak positivist or strong/weak constructionist). Share your answers with two colleagues and try to challenge the analysis that each provides.

EXERCISE 3.3

Debating philosophical positions

Interactive exercise: The idea of a 'balloon debate' is that contestants have to imagine that they are travelling in a hot-air balloon that is running out of fuel and is about to crash into a mountain. In order to save the lives of the majority, it is decided that one person must be tipped out of the basket. Each person in the basket there-fore has to argue why they would represent the greatest loss to society if they were to be sacrificed.

● In the balloon debate, each person normally has to argue the case for a famous person or an ideology. In this exercise, we suggest that groups argue the case for one of the philosophical positions outlined above. So, divide into groups of four or five people. Each group should:

○ pick one general philosophical position described in the penultimate section (i.e. critical theory, feminism, hermeneutics etc.)

○ summarize its main features

○ draw out the methodological implications for researching a question or issue

○ make the case to the rest of the class for why this is a valuable philosophy/ method and why it should not be thrown out of the balloon.

After each group has presented, groups must identify one of two philosophies that should remain in the balloon. (There must be no self-nominations or tactical voting!)

FURTHER READING

Ackroyd, S. and Fleetwood, S. (eds) (2000) *Realist Perspectives on Management and Organizations*. London: Routledge.
A useful collection of readings that cover both the theoretical assumptions of critical realism and their applications to organizational research in different contexts, such as medicine and high-technology companies. Authors emphasize different features of critical realism and do not follow a single party line.

Alvesson, M. and Deetz, S. (2000) *Doing Critical Management Research*. London: Sage.
One of the few books that articulates what 'critical' management research looks like, and how it can be conducted, for example through increasing sensitivity to the aspects of organization life that normally lie hidden. Also provides a much deeper review of critical theory and why it is important.

Blaikie, N. (2007) *Approaches to Social Enquiry*, 2nd edn. Cambridge: Polity Press.
This book provides an excellent overview of different philosophical approaches to social research, with particular attention to the question of whether the research methods in the natural sciences are appropriate for the social sciences. It is quite comprehensive and very useful, provided you are prepared to put in the effort! See also:

Hassard, J. and Parker, M. (eds) (1993) *Postmodernism and Organizations*. London: Sage.
Since postmodernism is such a wide and disparate field, it is probably best to start with edited collections. This book is one of a number of edited works on postmodernism, but has the advantage that it focuses on the relevance and application of postmodernism to organization and management theory. Contributors include many of the leading European management scholars with expertise in postmodernism.

Johnson, P. and Duberley, J. (2000) *Understanding Management Research: An Introduction to Epistemology*. London: Sage.

Want to know more about this chapter? Visit the ⑤SAGE edge˘ website at **https://edge. sagepub.com/easterbysmith** to access practice questions, selected journal articles, useful web links and much more.

DESIGNING MANAGEMENT AND BUSINESS RESEARCH

4

LEARNING OBJECTIVES

 To appreciate how research philosophies impact research designs.

 To understand what is regarded as good theory within each tradition.

 To be able to critique research designs.

 To be able to develop and justify research designs.

THE ESSENCE OF RESEARCH DESIGN

Research designs are about organizing research activity, including the collection of data, in ways that are most likely to achieve the research aims. Let us start with an example.

In 1985, the US businessman Kenneth Lay (see Figure 4.1, for a police mugshot of Lay in 2004) founded Enron after merging Houston Natural Gas and InterNorth. The company expanded very rapidly, first as an energy company and then through diversification, so that by mid-2000 its stock was valued at over $60 billion. But on 2 December 2001, it filed for bankruptcy following the failure of a rescue bid from a rival company. It quickly emerged that the company had systematically developed accounting practices that had inflated revenue while keeping debts and liabilities off the books. Not only had these practices been fostered by Lay and his colleagues at the top, but also the global consultancy firm Arthur Anderson, which had regularly audited Enron, had failed to report any problems.

FIGURE 4.1
Businessman
Kenneth Lay

This raised major implications about the efficacy of accepted practices for auditing corporate accounts. Imagine that you wish to conduct empirical research into the changes in corporate accounting practices following this scandal. In the previous chapter we outlined an ontological dimension containing the positions of realism, internal realism, relativism and nominalism. Following each of these positions in order, your research design might involve: (1) conducting a review of new legislation and accountancy practices published over the period 2002–2005; (2) sending out a postal questionnaire to 200 members of the Chartered Institute of Management Accountants; (3) arranging to interview one accountant from each of 20 different organizations including companies and consultancies; or (4) getting a job for a year in the accounting department of a US energy company.

Each of these brief statements includes at least three decisions about research designs. In (1) there is a decision to focus on two categories of written documents published over a specific period of time; in (2) the decision is to design a questionnaire, which will be mailed to a specific number of people who belong to one professional association; in (3) the aim is to gather views from a medium sample of people likely to have different perspectives and experiences; and in (4) the decision is to invest personal time in observing accountancy practices in a US company within a specific industry. Each of these decisions specifies courses of action in preference to other options. For example, the focus on published sources precludes internal corporate documents; the decision to mail the questionnaire precludes face-to-face interviews; the decision to interview only one person from each company precludes multiple perspectives from any company; and the decision to work in one company precludes obtaining direct data from other companies.

This is the essence of research design: it is about making choices about what will be observed, and how. But each of these designs is incomplete, and there are many other choices to be made, and features to be specified. A research design is a statement written, often before any data is collected, which explains and justifies what data is to be gathered, how and where from. It also needs to explain how the data will be analysed and how this will provide answers to the central questions of the research.

We can also analyse the Enron example against the Detached Engaged dimension identified at the end of Chapter 3. In the first case, since the focus is on documents in the public domain, the researcher remains quite *detached* from the source of the investigation. In each of the subsequent examples, he or she is likely to become increasingly involved with the people who influence the evolution and implementation of accounting practices. This defines a second major dimension of choice for the researcher, which is the degree of *engagement* with the object of the research. It is similar to the pure/applied research distinction, where the former tries to maintain the independence and objectivity of the researcher, and the latter encourages greater engagement and interchange between the researcher and the research setting.

In this chapter we explain: what a research design is; the main choices that need to be made; how research designs vary according to the underlying philosophical position; and how the quality of research designs can be judged. In the later chapters of the book we will be looking in detail at techniques and methods for gathering and analysing qualitative and quantitative data, though questions of research design need to be resolved before gathering (much) data.

We produce the basic dimensions of the matrix in Figure 4.2.

Remember that the poles in the matrix represent extreme positions, and because it is relatively rare for research designs to be purely one or another we will now focus on the space between them, essentially the quadrants, which we have labelled A, B, C and D. We also need to emphasize that the horizontal dimension is a continuum between strong positivism on the left-hand side, and strong constructionism on the right-hand side. In the next two sections we give examples of typical methodologies that fit into each of these quadrants, although we have grouped them as primarily positivist or constructionist methodologies. There are also some methods and designs that bridge across quadrants, or combine elements of constructionism and positivism. We refer to these as mixed methods, and we will cover these in the third section.

FIGURE 4.2
Epistemology and research style

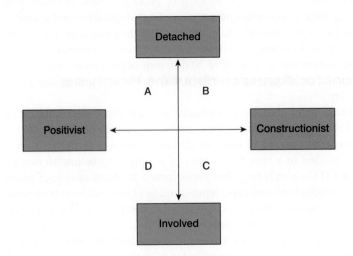

POSITIVIST RESEARCH DESIGNS: QUADRANTS A AND D

As we noted in Chapter 3, positivist methods usually incorporate the assumption that there are true answers, and the job of the researcher is either to start with a hypothesis about the nature of the world, and then seek data to confirm or disconfirm it, or the researcher poses several hypotheses and seeks data that will allow selection of the correct one. The ideal methodologies for doing this are experimental and quasi-experimental methods, and we will describe the key principles of each below. We then look at survey methodologies, which are generally associated with positivism in the sense that they are looking for patterns and causal relations which are not directly accessible.

EXPERIMENTAL METHODS

Classic experimental method involves **random assignment** of study participants to either an experimental or a control group. Conditions for the experimental group are then manipulated by the experimenter/researcher in order to assess their effect in comparison with members of the control group who are receiving no unusual conditions.

Possibly the most famous experimental studies in the field of management were the Hawthorne experiments conducted by Elton Mayo at the General Electric Hawthorne Plant in Illinois between 1927 and 1932. One experiment involved the relocation of six women (the experimenters selected the first two, who were each asked to select two more) into a room separate from the rest of the employees who assembled telephone relays. Their working conditions were modified systematically in order to establish whether there was any link between physical conditions and productivity. An observer was located in this room, making notes of what was happening and also keeping them informed about progress of the experiment and listening to their ideas and complaints. Over a period of many months changes were made, including shortening the working day, introducing increasing amounts of breaks into the day, and eventually providing a hot meal in the middle of the morning shift. With each change, productivity increased, which would suggest a correlation between productivity and the easing of working conditions. However, at the end of the experiment they returned conditions to the situation at the outset, expecting productivity to decrease to the initial level – but it increased once more. This observation led to the development of **human relations theory**, which stressed that positive relationships between employees and their supervisors were more significant than the physical circumstances of their work as predictors of productivity.

Questions for discussion about the Hawthorne experiment

1. What is the primary question/hypothesis of the researchers?
2. What are the key features of the research design?
3. In what ways does the Hawthorne experiment diverge from classical experimental design?

EXERCISE
4.1

There are three important implications from the Hawthorne experiment. First, the study showed that the most significant findings emerged because the experiment went *wrong*, in the sense that the expected results were not obtained. Second, the design was very systematic, including the return to the original condition. These features reflect the ideas of Austin about what leads to scientific breakthroughs as discussed in Chapter 1. The third implication is that it has raised awareness of the **experimenter effect** whereby human behaviour can be affected, and potentially 'distorted', by the presence of an observer. Most people behave differently if they think they are being watched.

The main *advantages* of experimental research designs are that they encourage clarity about what is to be investigated, and should eliminate many alternative explanations because the random assignment ensures that the experimental and control groups are identical in all respects, except for the focal variable. It is also easier for another researcher to replicate the study, and hence any claims arising from the research can be subjected to public scrutiny. The *disadvantages* are practical and ethical. With medical research there is always the danger that volunteers will be harmed by drug tests; hence stringent ethical guidelines have been developed, which are now filtering into social science and management research (see Chapter 5). Also, when dealing with people and business situations it is rarely possible to conduct true experiments with randomization. For example, if a company wants to assess the value of an elite highflier career development scheme, it cannot simply assign managers at random to the scheme because the managers themselves will be aware of what is happening, and there will also be strong ethical, performance-related and employment law objections to this arbitrary assignment. For this reason, quasi-experimental methods have been developed in order to circumvent the problem of random assignment.

Quasi-experimental designs

A key feature of **quasi-experimental design** is the use of multiple measures over time in order to reduce the effects of control and experimental groups not being fully matched (Shadish et al., 2002). Individuals are not allocated randomly to the treatment group and the control group, but rather allocation takes place on some other criterion, usually by using intact groups. As a result, the **validity** of inferences from this type of design depends critically on how equivalent the two groups actually are. Since equivalence cannot be guaranteed in this type of design, some purists insist that they be called **non-experimental designs**; although in practice many forms of quasi-experimental design can allow relatively strong inferences in settings where true experiments would be impossible to achieve.

Quasi-experimental methods share some of the advantages of full experimental methods such as clarity, transparency and repeatability. However, as we have indicated, they have problems accommodating the politics and agency of human beings in work settings. And there are also other subtle problems with pre-test and post-test designs because changes over time may be a consequence of measurement itself (a **testing effect**). The first measurement may get respondents to reflect on their initial answers, and this can lead to them answering differently the next time – not because of the intervention itself, but because they have been measured before. Thus, the process of measurement itself becomes a kind of intervention, but one that cannot easily be directly assessed. Returning to Figure 4.2, the aspiration of quasi-experimental methods is to conduct research without affecting the people under study, which would locate it in quadrant A. But as we have seen, the necessary level of detachment is often difficult to sustain. Figure 4.3 shows four common forms of research design, in increasing order of sophistication.

The cross-sectional comparison

The first form of design (Figure 4.3a) is the commonest in business and management research, but also the weakest. It involves selecting a group of people who have experienced something that you are interested in (attended a training course, graduated from

a) Cross-sectional comparison: the post-test only design

b) Longitudinal design

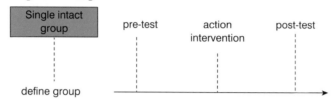

c) Randomized control group design

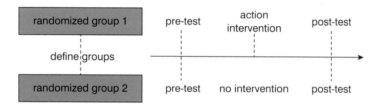

d) Non-equivalent control group design

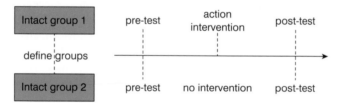

FIGURE 4.3
Common forms of quasi-experimental design

a prestigious university, worked with a charismatic mentor etc.), and then comparing that group with others who have not had the same experience. If we find a difference between the two groups on some variable that is theoretically interesting, it is tempting to jump to conclusions about causality. Although a great deal of the empirical literature relies on cross-sectional comparisons of this kind, it is obvious that no firm conclusion can be reached about cause-and-effect relationships unless groups being compared differ only on those variables (such that no other factor could be responsible for the observed difference in group means). Since this can never be guaranteed outside of the research laboratory, cross-sectional studies have only limited potential for advancing knowledge in a convincing way.

The pre-test/post-test design

It is a commonplace principle that when something changes, you have to measure before and after the change. Figure 4.3b shows a simple form of design with a single group measured twice, with an intervention of some kind taking place between the two measurements. The intervention might be the introduction of group exercises in a classroom, or a new form of recording product defects on an assembly line. In another example, the effects of a leadership course on a group of managers might be evaluated by measuring the managers' attitudes and behaviour before and after the course.

What interpretation could be placed on a change in means from pre- to post-test? The most obvious question to ask is whether the same change would have been observed if the intervention had never taken place. Change could reflect the influence of some other event that took place between pre- and post-test (this is called a *history* effect); or *maturation* in respondents (due to them growing older, wiser, stronger or more disillusioned) in ways that have nothing to do with the intervention. Both history and maturation effects are those that would have happened anyway, with or without the researcher's presence.

More subtly, changes over time may be a consequence of measurement itself (a *testing* effect), arising from effects of the first measurement in leading to respondents reflecting on their answers for the first time. This may then lead to them answering differently the second time, not because of the intervention itself, but because they have been measured before. Thus, the process of measurement itself becomes a kind of intervention, but one which cannot easily be directly assessed. If there is a danger that the properties of a measuring instrument change if it has been answered before, it may make sense to change the instrument from pre- to post-test. However, this brings new problems unless it can be guaranteed that the instrument, though different, measures the same thing in the same way (the *instrumentation* effect).

The randomized control group design

The classical way to deal with history and maturation as threats to the internal validity of a design is by using a control group of individuals who are the same as the treatment group in every way except that they do not receive the intervention (Figure 4.3c). The way in which this is achieved is by randomization in allocation to groups. The consequence of randomization is that the whole of the prior history of individuals is detached from the intervention itself: individuals either receive the intervention or not based on a criterion (tossing a coin, or the equivalent) which is quite separate from any characteristics on which they differ. Any change in the treatment group which is not paralleled by an equivalent change in the control group is thus attributed to the intervention, on the basis that the control group shows what the treatment group would have been like but for the intervention. History effects and maturation effects will show in changes in the control group, and the effect of the intervention can be seen by comparing changes in the two groups.

The non-equivalent control group design

A weaker form of research design, which captures some of the strength of the randomized control group design, is the non-equivalent control group design (Figure 4.3d). Although the formal specification of this design looks similar to design (c), the crucial difference is that individuals are not allocated randomly to the treatment group and the control group, but rather allocation takes place on some other criterion, usually by working with intact groups. As a result, the validity of inferences from this type of design depends critically on how equivalent the two groups actually are. The non-equivalent control group design is the simplest of a family of research designs, which are termed 'quasi-experimental designs'. Since equivalence cannot be guaranteed in this type of design, some statisticians insist that they be called non-experimental designs; though the reality is that many forms of quasi-experimental design can allow relatively strong inference in settings where true experiments would be impossible to achieve. (It is also the case that even where a true experiment is possible, the phenomenon being tested is not of interest because its generalizability to the real world is questionable.)

There are substantial problems when using this form of design in real organizations. For example, the design assumes that 'nothing' happens to the control group during the period that the treatment (for example, course attendance) is being given to the experimental group.

This is a naive assumption, as Easterby-Smith and Ashton (1975) found, when attempting to evaluate a project-based management development programme held at Durham University Business School. While the 'chosen few' were away on the course, several members of the control group seized the opportunity to improve relationships with their bosses and strengthen their political standing in the company, thus harming the career prospects of a number of managers who had attended the course.

Designing a call centre

EXERCISE
4.2

Call centres are important for many companies for lots of reasons. First, they are often the primary point of contact between the company and its customers, and so the call centre staff *are* the company as far as customers are concerned. The company's reputation is in the hands of those people. Second, call centres have to be accessible 24 hours a day for global companies operating in many time zones and in many languages. Finally, the turnover of staff in call centres is very high, and can be over 90 per cent per year.

People who run call centres therefore have to pay attention to recruiting the best people and treating them well so that they stay with the company. There is some truth in the saying that a happy worker is a productive worker (not always, but often); and it is not a coincidence that First Direct (the online banking arm of HSBC) has year after year won awards for the quality of its customer service and also for how it treats its employees.

The task

You have been contacted by a company seeking to set up its own call centre, and your task in this exercise is to design a study to identify which factors are important for the company to consider in the design of its call centre. Consultants have identified the following general factors as being important:

- density of workstations
- layout of the space
- ergonomics of the workstation (the chair, the desk, lighting etc.)
- colour of the walls
- the view – is there a view out of the windows?

Discussion questions

What primary questions/hypotheses would you investigate?

Based on the list of factors identified by the consultants, how would you go about designing a study for the most effective call centre?

Validity of positivist experimental designs

Experimental methods are particularly concerned to ensure that results provide accurate reflections of reality. They distinguish between internal and external validity, with the former relating to *systematic* factors of bias and the latter being concerned with how far the conclusion can be generalized across other types of person, settings and times.

The aim of experimental designs is to maximize **internal validity**, and this requires the elimination of plausible alternative explanations for any differences observed between groups. That is why full experiments require random assignment to control and experimental groups, and efforts are then made to ensure that the subsequent experiences of the two groups are identical in all respects, except for the focal variable. But there are many threats to internal validity, including history (experiences of the two groups diverge in some unexpected way), maturation (group members get older or other life changes take place) or mortality. The latter can be a problem in medical research where people literally die before the experiment is completed, and in organizational studies people may vanish from the research because they move jobs, leave the company or lose interest. Threats to internal validity are systematic rather than random, and they tend to focus on factors that cloud the interpretation of differences between groups in change over time.

External validity is about generalizability of results beyond the focal study. In the physical sciences we assume that Newton's laws of motion will have equal validity whether applied in New York, Bogota, Xi'an or on Mars. If they do not apply in the same way everywhere, then there should be a clear way of understanding how they vary in different circumstances. Thus Albert Einstein predicted through his theory of relativity that bodies do not follow Newton's laws when they are moving at relative velocities near to the speed of light, and that light does not travel in straight lines when subject to strong gravitational forces. The latter prediction was confirmed by observations of the total eclipse of the Sun in 1919 (see Example 4.1).

EXAMPLE 4.1

Relativity and the 1919 total eclipse of the Sun

Probably the most important eclipse in the history of science occurred on 29 May 1919. Just six months after the end of the First World War, British astronomers used it to test a new idea that came from Germany in 1915. Expeditions of astronomers photographed the eclipse in difficult tropical conditions in Brazil and on the African island of Principe. At the time, the Sun was in front of a useful cluster of stars, the Hyades. The astronomers compared the relative positions in the sky near the Sun with the positions of the same stars as previously photographed in the night sky.

The proposition was that gravity affected light, space and time itself, and as a result the Sun would deflect starlight passing by it. Changes in the apparent location of stars in the sky, seen close to the Sun during a total eclipse, could confirm the idea. It was predicted that for stars almost in line with the Sun, the shift in apparent position would be slightly less than two seconds of arc, or a few ten-thousandths of a degree. The 1919 measurements confirmed that the Sun bent the light rays by roughly the right extent – less than predicted in Principe, more than predicted in Brazil.

Source: www.esa.int/esaSC/SEM7I9R1VED_index_0.html.

However, in order to demonstrate external validity, management research designs need to demonstrate a number of features. First, they need to demonstrate that the results observed are not just a product of the selection of individuals or organizations. Sometimes the people who volunteer to take part in research are open minded and keen to help; sometimes they will put themselves forward because they have strong opinions or 'axes to grind'. Managers will often 'volunteer' employees to take part in research because they believe they will show the organization in a positive light, and will not offer individuals who are likely to be critical; or they will allow access to the organization because they hope research will add legitimacy to a new innovation or policy that they wish to promote. These issues of access and sampling are discussed further in later chapters (Chapters 5 and 8), but the key point to remember is that selection should avoid sources of bias as far as possible.

Other threats to external validity come from the setting and history. In the first case, the results of a piece of research in the health service may be difficult to generalize to an automobile manufacturer. Similarly, research conducted in large organizations may not apply to small organizations; and there is also increasing awareness that research conducted in one national setting may not apply to other national settings. With regard to history, it is important to note that patterns and relationships observed in one era may not apply in another era. For example, at the present time, with the emergence of new economies such as China and India as global economic forces, the theories about the behaviour of financial markets that were developed during the era of US dominance are now having to be rewritten. Similarly, a study on reward systems conducted in one country where the supply of skilled labour is plentiful might not be relevant in another country where there is a marked shortage of skilled labour.

SURVEY RESEARCH

The dominant epistemology underlying survey research methods is positivism. As explained in the previous chapter, this assumes that there are regular, verifiable patterns in human and organizational behaviour, although they are often difficult to detect and extremely difficult to explain due to the number of factors and variables that might produce the observed result. Consequently, survey research tends to use cross-sectional designs with large samples, which enable multiple factors to be measured simultaneously and hence potential underlying relationships to be examined.

There are three main types of survey that seek to take a detached viewpoint: factual, inferential and exploratory studies. **Factual surveys** can also be used in an engaged way, where they are established as survey feedback processes. The three main types generally fit with quadrant A of Figure 4.2, whereas engaged factual surveys fit into quadrant D. We will briefly describe and illustrate each type here. More detailed information on the technical design of surveys can be found in Chapter 8.

Factual surveys are most often associated with opinion polls and market research, and involve collecting and collating relatively 'factual' data from different groups of people. Thus, in order to assess market share or loyalty we might be seeking to identify what percentage of the population of Manchester entered either an Aldi or a Tesco supermarket at least once in the previous week. This is reasonably factual data, which could be gathered by a postal questionnaire or structured interviews; however, it could be affected by people's ability to recall what they did in the previous week, and possibly by social desirability factors where they claim loyalty to one supermarket over another in order to project a particular image of themselves to the researcher.

A common use of factual surveys within companies is survey feedback. This involves distributing a questionnaire to all employees asking for their views on the management of the organization, the quality of communications, their job satisfaction, feelings of security and so on. Data is then aggregated by department, level or job category and results are discussed in public. This puts pressure on management to change systems, procedures and their own behaviour in order to get 'better' results next year.

Inferential surveys predominate in academic management research, particularly in the fields of strategy, marketing and organizational psychology. They are aimed at establishing relationships between variables and concepts, whether there are prior assumptions and hypotheses regarding the nature of these relationships. Inferential surveys generally assume an internal realist ontology, although epistemologically they involve a weaker form of positivism than experiments. The usual starting point for inferential surveys is to isolate the factors that appear to be involved, and to decide what appears to be causing what. This means that researchers have to identify the main dependent variables and predictor variables:[1] it is the latter that are assumed to be causing the former.

---

[1] The term independent variable is often used instead of 'predictor variable'. We prefer the latter term because in practice, even independent variables tend to be related to each other, and therefore use of the former term is misleading.

In Figure 4.4, we are suggesting (hypothesizing) that the predictor variables of salary, leadership and responsibility have an impact on the dependent variable, motivation at work. In order to test this hypothesis it would be necessary to define ways of measuring each of these variables, generally through a small number of items in a questionnaire, and this would need to be completed by a sample of employees in one or more places of work. Naturally, this requires that the measures of the four variables are accurate, and that the sample is appropriate in terms of size and constitution in order to test the hypothesis; we discuss how to do this in more detail in Chapter 8. Moreover, the four factors identified in Figure 4.4 could be examined in more detail. For example, one might be interested in the interactions between some of the variables, such as whether some forms of leadership result in greater responsibility being distributed around the workforce; or one might be interested in whether some of the arrows might work in other directions, so that a highly motivated workforce would lead to particular styles and strategies of leadership. These are some of the relationships that can be analysed, particularly with more complex models, through the use of structural equation modelling (see Chapter 10). Studies of this kind are often known as **cross-sectional surveys** because they involve selecting different organizations, or units, in different contexts, and investigating how other factors, measured at the same time, vary across these units.

Similarly, Lyles and Salk (1996) were interested in the conditions that led to greater transfer of knowledge from foreign parent companies into international joint ventures. So they selected a sample of 201 joint ventures that were regarded as small or medium-sized across four manufacturing industries in Hungary. Through comparing indicators of performance across the whole sample, they were able to conclude first that there was a strong link between knowledge transfer and performance, and second that this transfer was most likely to take place when the foreign and domestic parents had equal (50/50) equity stakes in the new venture. The sample size of 201 was sufficient for them to demonstrate that the results were statistically significant, but one of the key problems for researchers using cross-sectional designs is to know how large the sample needs to be.

Geert Hofstede's (1980/1984) study of national cultural differences provides an example of an exploratory survey. He attempted to develop a universal set of principles against which any culture can be measured, in the hope that this would provide a basis for predicting the behaviour of individuals and organizations in almost any country. However, he did not start with an explicit set of hypotheses; rather, he had a large number (about 216,000) of questionnaires completed by employees of IBM with regard to their views and values, and he was looking for patterns in the data. His four dimensions – power distance, individualism/collectivism, uncertainty avoidance and masculinity – emerged from his data, and by demonstrating that they fitted reasonably well with prior research into this topic, he was able to substantiate his claim to the importance of these four dimensions.

FIGURE 4.4
Possible predictors of motivation at work

Which variable is which?

EXAMPLE
4.2

Chen's (2008) doctoral thesis examined how workers in virtual teams doing different tasks used instant messaging to support their work. Her respondents were all Chinese-language speakers in China or Taiwan. Some of them worked with people in the same location (building or city), while others worked with colleagues in other countries (such as Canada, USA, Germany).

- Instant messaging is not a variable because everyone in the study used it; but other communication technologies (such as email, videoconferencing and face-to-face meetings) are variables because some people use them while others do not. Similarly, dual-language use (Chinese and English) is not a variable because the whole sample spoke both languages.

- The focus of the study was on what led people to switch communication media or languages, and this therefore was the *dependent* variable. The *predictor* variables were task characteristics, indices of relationship quality (how well people knew each other), and whether they worked in the same or different locations.

Principles in judging the quality of a sample design

When decisions are made that can have significant consequences for people it is important that those decisions are based on evidence. The trustworthiness of the evidence base for decisions depends on many factors. We begin with the difference between a **population** and a **sample** drawn from that population. The term 'population' refers to the whole set of entities that decisions relate to, while the term 'sample' refers to a subset of those entities from which evidence is gathered. The **inference** task then is to use evidence from a sample to draw conclusions about the population. Samples are very commonly used, both for research and for policy-making.

Companies estimate morale among employees from quantitative surveys of samples of employees (either by deliberately picking names from the payroll, or by letting employees choose whether or not to respond). Here, the population is the whole set of employees within the organization, and management want to gain a picture of their staff by summarizing the results from a sample of those who respond to the survey. For example, companies such as Gallup and Towers Watson are leaders in carrying out such opinion surveys, and one of the benefits that they claim is that they can compare the profile of a company (and sub-units within it) with that of other companies where the same survey questions have been used. This gives a method of benchmarking, which senior management often find very informative and powerful in shaping their strategy.

Many companies also use small-scale surveys repeated frequently (perhaps once a month) as a kind of barometer of how employees or customers are feeling. Companies may set up a panel to represent the entire body of employees, and their responses are used to monitor the state of the organization at that time. This can be very valuable during the course of a period of major change. During the UK general election in 2010, opinion polls appeared every day monitoring the state of the electorate and their response to the offerings of the political parties.

The UK government uses sample surveys of companies on their annual pay negotiations in order to get an estimate of wage inflation in the economy. In most countries, estimates of activity in the labour market (whether people are unemployed, self-employed, economically inactive etc.) are derived from samples and not from complete counts.

Researchers who are interested in the rhythms of working life often use diary methods to study what employees are doing during their working day and how they feel about those activities. This is often done by using a bleeper (or a mobile phone) set to go off at specific times, and individuals are asked to answer a set of specific questions. Here again, sampling is involved since it is impossible to collect information continuously (unlike, for example, a heart rate monitor which someone might wear). The researcher will generally want to consider a 'typical' working day, or perhaps compare responses obtained while carrying out different kinds of work activities. In this example, the working day could be considered as the population, and the bleeps could be considered as samples of activities during the day.

Sometimes, a research project involves collecting evidence from every member of an organization (or every member of a project group), but more often this is not the case and the researcher needs to decide on a sampling strategy. A sample might be a proportion of employees in an organization, a selection of companies operating in a specific market, a number of specific periods of time for assessing the quality of customer responses in a call centre, or a selection of transactions for audit purposes. For each of these examples, the researcher has to make a decision about what the sampling unit is (the person, the company, the transaction etc.), how many sampling units to take, and on what basis sampling is to be undertaken.

Generally speaking, the purpose of collecting data from a sample is to enable the researcher to make statements about a larger group that the sample is drawn from. Many people say that they only want to talk about their sample data, but we almost never believe them. Even if there is no formal generalization beyond the sample, both the writer and the reader are interested in what this study's findings tell us that would be useful when thinking about other settings. This places a responsibility on researchers, whether we like it or not, to say where our findings might be relevant.

The claims that can legitimately be made from sample data depend absolutely on the relationship between the sample and the population (the larger group that the researcher wants to make claims about). Get the sampling wrong, and accuracy in calculating the results is of no consequence. The opposite is also true: get the sampling right, and even rough-and-ready calculations or 'eyeballing' of the data can be immensely valuable. There are two basic principles that underlie decisions about sampling design: **representativeness** and **precision**.

Representativeness in sampling

The accuracy of conclusions drawn from a sample depends on whether it has the same characteristics as the population from which it is drawn. If the sample is systematically different in some way, then the sample is biased. A simple definition of bias in sampling is that it occurs when some members of the population have a higher chance of being included in the sample than others. There are two steps involved in defining a sampling design: first, to draw up a **sampling frame**, a list of all who are eligible to be included in the study; second, to achieve a valid response from all those included in the sampling frame. **Bias** can be introduced into a sampling strategy in many ways, through choices made in the design of the study itself and also through features of the process of collecting research data:

1. *Exclude groups of people*: leave out home-workers, casual staff, new recruits, part-timers. If your study involves selecting people to interview, it is tempting to prefer people who are articulate and have 'interesting' stories to tell, or people who have been cooperative in previous studies within the organization.

2. *Distribution method*: send out a questionnaire survey using an out-of-date list of mailing addresses to exclude those who have recently moved; distribute an invitation to interviews or a focus group by email to exclude those without a PC on their desks.

3. *Language used*: use English to exclude those who don't speak English, and introduce biasing factors for those who do because of differences in how well people can use the language.

One of the key ways of judging the representativeness of a sample is to compare the characteristics of the sample to those of the population; this kind of information is commonly reported in published papers that are based on quantitative surveys but less so in interview studies. Even if the sampling frame accurately represents the population, non-response is a major source of problems in getting outsiders to believe the results. In itself though, non-response is not a problem, as long as those who do take part in the study have similar characteristics to those who do not. Of course, there is usually a big problem in assessing whether this is true, because (obviously) you do not have data from those who did not take part. It is sometimes possible to get some idea about potential bias due to systematic non-response by comparing those who respond quickly to a questionnaire survey or an invitation to attend an interview with slow responders on demographic variables and also on the central variables in the research. The idea is that the slow responders will be more similar to non-responders than are those who reply quickly. If the slow responders have similar characteristics to rapid responders, then the researcher can have greater confidence that non-responders would also have been similar, and this helps to build credibility in a study.

Precision in sampling: sampling proportion and sample size

Precision is about how credible a sample is. For example, opinion polls conducted before the 2014 general election in India used samples that are very much smaller than the population of registered voters. How confident is it possible to be about predicting election outcomes from opinion poll samples? Does the precision of the estimate depend on how big the sample is? It seems plausible that it should. Does it also depend on what proportion of the population the pollsters talk to? If the number of electors is 10,000 then a sample of 1,000 (i.e. 10 per cent) might be OK. However, many people would be less happy with a sample of 1,000 if the number of electors was one million instead (0.1 per cent). Intuitively, this proportion seems too small. However, the first intuition is correct, but the second is not.

Nguyen (2005) provides a clear and graphic example of cooking chicken soup to show why the size of a sample matters but how big a proportion the sample is of the population (the **sampling proportion**) does not. Consider three scenarios: cooking at home for four people using a small pot; cooking for a dinner party with 12 guests using a medium-size pot; and cooking a banquet for 200 wedding guests using a huge pot. Regardless of the number of guests, the only way to tell if there is enough salt in the soup is to taste it. The way to find this out is: first, stir the soup so it is well mixed and is the same all the way through, and second, use a tablespoon to draw off some soup. A tablespoon will do because there is no point taking more than that: taste it all and there is no soup left for the guests; taste more spoonfuls and each will taste just the same, so nothing is learned. It is not necessary to use a large ladle to sample from the large pot simply because the pot is bigger, or a tiny spoon to sample from the small pot because the pot is smaller: the same sized tablespoon is enough to judge the adequacy of the seasoning regardless of how big the batch of soup is, as long as the pot is stirred first.

The soup in the pot is the *population*; the spoonful to taste is the *sample*. The size of the spoon is the **sample size**, and that is what matters. The cook needs to taste enough soup to be able to make a judgement about the pot as a whole. Now apply these principles to the task of making judgements about attitudes in a society towards an issue of concern. Consider the question of whether organizations should aim to maximize their profit or should consider their social responsibilities. The precision of the answer to this question has nothing to do with the size of the population but rather depends on the size of the sample. Small samples will always be less precise than large samples.

Combining precision and representativeness to achieve a credible sample

We have looked at the two design principles of bias and precision, and clearly both are important in achieving a credible sampling design for a quantitative research project. Low bias means that conclusions from a specific sample can reasonably be applied to a larger population, and high precision means that the margin of error in the claims that are made will be low – the researcher can expect to be precisely right (see Table 4.1). However, high precision is no way of saving a study where the sample is biased (the claims the researcher makes are precisely wrong). Giving very precise answers to the wrong question will not endear a researcher to his or her supervisor, just as it does not help in getting high marks in an examination! Most projects carried out by students (at whatever level) are a compromise in some way, simply because resources are limited. As a result, there will always be trade-offs when it comes to decisions about design. Is it better to have a large sample (giving higher precision) if the cost of achieving it is to introduce bias into the sample achieved? Put more simply, which is better: to be imprecisely right or to be precisely wrong? In our opinion, the answer is straightforward. Imprecisely right is better: it is preferable to have a sample that properly represents the population even if the precision is lower because of a small sample.

TABLE 4.1   Principles in designing a sample

		Bias	
		High	Low
Precision	High	Precisely wrong	Precisely right
	Low	Imprecisely wrong	Imprecisely right

Probability sampling designs

This section describes forms of sampling design where the probability of each entity being part of the sample is known. Some sampling methods have the same probability for every entity in the sample, while others have the same probability within segments of the design but differing probabilities across segments.

Simple random sampling

With **simple random sampling**, every sample entity (company, employee, customer etc.) has an equal chance of being part of the sample. In the past, this was done using printed random number tables. Now computers are used for this, and it is easy to draw up a list of random numbers as a basis for selecting a sample.

Stratified random sampling

One drawback of simple random sampling is that it can mean that small but important parts of a population are missed altogether or sampled so little that the researcher cannot make confident statements about them. For instance, customer surveys of a healthcare facility would be badly served by a simple random sample. Most users of a healthcare facility have relatively minor ailments and perhaps visit only once or twice in a year. There will, however, be a small number of patients with major health problems whose treatment is perhaps extensive. It is quite reasonable to expect that a sample should be informative about the chronically ill minority as well as the occasionally ill majority. The way to achieve this is to divide the population up into homogeneous groups called *strata*, and then take a simple random sample within each stratum. **Proportional stratified random sampling** has the same sampling proportion within all strata; but this has the disadvantage that rare groups within the population would be badly represented. The way to deal with this problem is to take a larger proportion of sample units in small strata, and a smaller proportion in the larger strata. This is called **non-proportional stratified random sampling**.

Systematic random sampling

Systematic random sampling relies on there being a list in some form or other of the units in the population that the researcher is interested in. This might be a customer database, or a list of employees of a company or students registered in a university. Suppose that a researcher wants to achieve a sample of 500 students in order to assess their satisfaction with the virtual learning environment (VLE) system that a university has just introduced. If there are 20,000 students, then 500 represents a sample of 2.5 per cent, corresponding to selecting 1 in 40 students from the population. This proportion could be achieved by choosing a number at random between 1 and 40. If that number were 27, then the researcher would go down the list taking every 27th student in order to derive a sample list of 500 names. What this process relies on is that the population list is essentially organized randomly, so that picking in this systematic way does not introduce bias. There could be a problem if the list is ordered alphabetically by individuals' last name, since all those students with the same name will be listed together and individuals with the same name will have less chance of being selected than if the list were randomly ordered.

Cluster sampling

Any method that involves random sampling will lead to practical problems where the population units are spread very widely, such that the cost of approaching them is very high. Cluster sampling deals with this by first dividing up the population into what are called 'clusters', and then by sampling all the units within the selected clusters. A study of company success in emerging economies might first identify all the countries where the company operates, select randomly a number of those countries to study in detail, and then approach all the relevant contacts in those countries. This would allow the study to use local research staff who are familiar with the language and culture of each country.

Multi-stage sampling

Multi-stage sampling combines together the methods described above in order to achieve higher operational and technical efficiency. For example, stratified random sampling divides the population into strata and then samples from within all of them. Instead, a study might use a sampling approach at each level, and this is very common in large-scale social research. Suppose there was a national change in the organization of schools to give greater management autonomy to head teachers, and researchers wanted to know whether this change had any effect on the performance of students in schools. It would be very inefficient to select students at random, even if the research team actually had a national database of all school students. It makes more sense to divide the country up into regions, select some regions for detailed attention, identify all the schools in the targeted regions, and then select a sample of schools. Having defined a sample of schools within selected regions, the same process could be used to sample classes within the selected schools, or perhaps take a sample of students from all of the classes in a selected school. In this example, the criterion of randomness applies at each of several stages in the design of the study; hence the name 'multi-stage sampling'. The aim is to balance the need for representativeness of the sample with the highest possible cost effectiveness.

Why are probability sampling designs valuable?

It is only with probability sampling that it is possible to be precise about the relationship between a sample and the population from which the sample is drawn. Knowing what this relationship is allows the researcher to make a firm judgement about the relationship between characteristics of a sample and characteristics of the population from which the sample was drawn. All forms of probability sampling design have this feature in common: it is always possible to state the probability of each individual respondent being selected for inclusion in the research study. The statistical theory behind the inference process (often called 'significance testing' – we discuss this in Chapter 10) relies fundamentally on sampling based on probabilities. There is always uncertainty about any claim made from data, but using probability sampling designs can allow the researcher to quantify that uncertainty. Thus, sample data can tell us whether the risk associated with using a mobile phone while driving is higher, but only a properly constructed sample design can allow us to decide how worried we should be about that extra risk.

Non-probability sampling designs

Non-probability sampling designs all share the same characteristic: that it is not possible to state the probability of any member of the population being sampled. As a result, it is harder for the researcher to be confident that claims made about the sample can apply to the larger group that the sample is taken from.

Convenience sampling

Convenience sampling involves selecting sample units on the basis of how easily accessible they are, hence the term 'convenience sampling'. A student who uses a list of friends on Facebook for their dissertation is taking a convenience sample. Such a sample may well reflect the individual's own social network, but is clearly not representative of students as a whole or of the population of the UK. This may not matter: it depends what claims the researcher wants to make. Facebook may be the medium of choice for Generation Yers and their social networks, but is much less common for Baby Boomers. Convenience samples are very common in research because they are – well – convenient! It is impossible to guarantee that any sample achieved in this way represents a specific population that may be of interest. However, they can still have a value. It rather depends on what the purpose is for collecting data. For a very long time, people thought that all swans were white because no one had ever seen one of any other colour. It only takes an Australian researcher with a convenience sample of one black swan to prove the old generalization to be wrong.

Quota sampling

Quota sampling divides the relevant population up into categories (perhaps male/female, or country of origin for students) and then selection continues until a sample of a specific size is achieved within each category. The aim is to make sure that each of the categories is represented according to the quota proportions. For example, in doctoral research on whether the Internet empowers consumers, quota sampling enabled the researcher to ensure that she had users of a variety of ages, while a convenience sample would be more likely to result in a preponderance of people similar to the researcher and her friends.

Purposive sampling

In **purposive sampling**, the researcher has a clear idea of what sample units are needed according to the purposes of the study, and then approaches potential sample members to check whether they meet eligibility criteria. Those that do are used, while those that do not are rejected. The guiding principle for sampling might be theory (theoretical sampling), and the basis of sampling could therefore change as a study is carried out if analysis of initial data is used to guide theory development.

Snowball sampling

Snowball sampling starts with someone who meets the criteria for inclusion in a study who is then asked to name others who would also be eligible. This method works well for samples where individuals are very rare and it is hard to identify who belongs to the population. Dissertation students often do this by starting out with people they or their supervisor know personally, and then ask those people to pass them on to others who would also be suitable. It works well too for individuals, groups or companies that are part of networks whose membership is confidential (LinkedIn is a useful resource here, and its owners actively promote the professional network as a useful way of finding interesting people to get in touch with).

Why are non-probability sampling designs valuable?

The sampling approaches described in this section are answers to a variety of practical problems that researchers have encountered in carrying out their work. But how do these sampling methods stack up against the key quality criteria of bias and precision that we started this section with? *Precision* is most straightforward, since its main focus is the size of the sample achieved. A convenience sample can meet the first requirement of a big-enough sample most easily; quota sampling and purposive sampling both aim to ensure that every sector in a sampling design is filled, while snowball sampling addresses the problem of ensuring an adequate sample of hard-to-find people.

However, the principle of *bias* is where non-probability sampling methods can most easily fall down, especially for convenience sampling. Many management researchers have been seduced by the lure of large samples for quantitative studies (perhaps feeling themselves under pressure from journal editors to report large samples) and achieved them simply through collecting respondents by any means (MBA classes, lists of Facebook friends etc.). There is no guarantee that the findings reported are credible, since the credibility of findings relies in large measure on the character of the sample. It is not surprising then, that reviews of research often highlight contradictions in findings between different studies, given that researchers often take little care in defining their sampling design. Qualitative researchers are not immune to issues of bias, and can be seduced by the richness of data from small samples. Rich data can be powerful persuaders, but every research study involves a sample, and it is vitally important to the credibility of results that the researcher considers how the sample used sits within the larger group from which the sample is drawn.

Validity in survey research

Since *survey designs* are informed by internal realist ontology, the issues of validity are reasonably similar to those of strong positivist studies. Thus, there is a major concern about whether the instruments and questionnaire items used to measure variables are sufficiently accurate and stable. Most of this is done through pre-testing instruments before the actual research is carried out, and hence measures of reliability are important because they assesses whether an instrument will produce the same score for each occasion that it is used. There is also the question of external validity: whether the patterns observed from the sample data will also hold true in other contexts and settings. And again, the technicalities of assessing reliability and validity with survey data will be discussed further in Chapter 9.

Which supermarket gives the best deal?

EXERCISE 4.3

This exercise examines the methods used by different UK supermarkets to answer the question 'Who gives you the best deal?'.

Which?

Which? uses a basket of 100 popular branded food and grocery products sold by four online supermarkets, and it calculates the average price of each individual product for each month. It then compares the prices for each supermarket to answer the question 'Who gives you the best deal?'.

MySupermarket.co.uk

MySupermarket is an online comparison site which shows the cost of items at Tesco, Asda, Sainsbury's, Waitrose and Ocado. It has recently included Aldi in its list of supermarkets, as a result of the increase in popularity of the low-cost supermarket

(Continued)

(Continued)

in the UK. Since Aldi's range consists mostly of own-label products, MySupermarket compares them to the equivalent own-label products at other retailers.

Waitrose price match promise

Waitrose selects 1,000 everyday branded products from their food and drink grocery ranges, and checks the prices against the online price at www.tesco.com for a post-code served by large Tesco stores (excluding Tesco Metro or Tesco Express). The standard individual unit selling prices are matched for identically branded products; but this does not include multi-buy promotions.

Tesco price promise

Tesco check the price of a shopper's basket of items against the prices at its three main supermarket competitors. If the comparable grocery shopping would have been cheaper there, then they give a voucher for the difference. There must be at least ten items in the basket in order to qualify for the comparison.

Sainsbury's brand match

Sainsbury's check the price of an identical basket of branded products (same size, flavour, colour etc.) at Asda. If the identical basket bought on the same day would have been cheaper at either of those supermarkets, then they give the shopper a coupon at the till for the difference.

There are several different sampling issues involved when trying to decide who gives the best deal, for example:

- *Sampling of supermarkets* – where do you buy your products? Each supermarket compares itself against selected others in order to persuade the consumer that they offer the best deal. What are the implications of the different alternatives?

- *Sampling of items* – what products do you buy? Each of the comparisons takes a different approach to deciding what to compare. Which option (if any) do you find most convincing as giving an answer to the question 'Who gives you the best deal?'.

CONSTRUCTIONIST RESEARCH DESIGNS (QUADRANTS B AND C)

Constructionist research designs are linked to the relativist and nominalist ontologies. They start from the assumptions that verifiable observations are potentially subject to very different interpretations, and that the job of the researcher should be to illuminate different truths and to establish how various claims for truth and reality become constructed in everyday life. Hence it is not surprising that there is a wide range of methodologies which fit within the constructionist paradigm. Here we cover some of the main methodologies – action research and cooperative inquiry, archival research, ethnography and narrative methods – which are primarily based on constructionist designs. In the subsequent section we will look at methods that often bridge the epistemological divide, notably case method, grounded theory and so-called mixed methods.

Action research and co-operative inquiry

One of the key assumptions of positivism, and of natural scientific methods, is that the researcher should be objective, maintaining complete independence from the object of study. In the social sciences, where claims of the researcher's independence are harder to sustain, many people have tried to turn this apparent problem into a virtue. This is the tradition of **action research**, which assumes that social phenomena are continually changing rather than static. With action research, the researchers are often part of this change process itself. The following two beliefs are normally associated with action research designs:

1. The best way of learning about an organization or social system is through attempting to change it, and this therefore should be an objective of the action researcher.

2. The people most likely to be affected by, or involved in implementing, these changes should as far as possible become involved in the research process itself.

Some forms of action research appear to follow the principles of positivism, for example by attempting to change the organization from the outside and then measuring the results. Kurt Lewin (1948), who originated the action research tradition, used experimental designs when investigating the efficacy of different ways of getting housewives to change their nutritional habits during the Second World War (see Example 4.3).

An early example of action research

EXAMPLE
4.3

During the Second World War, Kurt Lewin and his associates experimented with groups of American housewives to see if they could be persuaded to serve unpopular types of meat, such as beef hearts, sweetbreads and kidneys, to their families. They used two methods to try to persuade them to change their habits. In the first case, a lecturer gave an attractive talk to members of the group on the dietary and economic value of using these meats, and offered some good recipes. In the second case, the same information was provided to the housewives, but they were invited to discuss the information and at the end to indicate by a show of hands whether they intended to serve the new meats. In a follow-up study it was found that only 3 per cent of the members of the lecture groups served one of the meats, compared with 32 per cent for the discussion/decision groups.

Similar results were obtained when persuading mothers to give orange juice and cod liver oil to their infants, although in these cases the discussion/decision method was only found to be twice as effective as the lecture method.

Source: Krech et al., 1962: 229–30

Kurt Lewin's studies were, however, different from traditional experimental research because there was an emphasis on changes in behaviour, and his housewives were active participants in deciding whether or not to change. The weakness with his initial experimental design was that it did not allow him to discover *why* the changes took place. This required subsequent experiments and qualitative studies in order to build up deeper understanding of why behaviour changed under these different circumstances. Given the strong emphasis on intervention as part of the research process, and the focus on debate and discussion, these later studies fit within quadrant C in Figure 4.1.

Involvement in the research process is taken a stage further in what has come to be known as **co-operative inquiry** (Reason, 1988; Heron, 1996). This has been developed for researching human action mainly at individual and community, rather than at organizational levels.

It starts with the idea that all people have, at least latently, the ability to be self-directing, to choose how they will act and to give meaning to their own experiences. It fits with stronger versions of constructionism, and rejects traditional positivist methods where people are studied as if they were objects under the influence of external forces. Cooperative inquiry not only focuses on the experiences and explanations of the individuals concerned, it also involves them in deciding in the first place what questions and issues are worth researching. Thus the 'subjects' become partners in the research process.

A study of the development of Afro-Caribbean entrepreneurs in the West Midlands adds a further dimension. Ram and Trehan (2010) have worked for five years with a group of eight entrepreneurs. The group meets on a monthly basis and determines its own agenda, and more importantly controls its own membership. The primary goal for the entrepreneurs is to gather ideas and develop strategies from their interaction with other owners, which will enable them to grow their businesses (none of the businesses are in competition with each other). The academics are present at these meetings in the roles of process consultant, facilitator and researcher; they are also given access to company documents and conduct interviews with group members. This approach, known as **critical action learning**, is driven largely by group members and takes place within a social and political context. The academics thus become partners in the problem solving of the group, and contribute particularly through surfacing the feelings and emotions of members.

Archival research

It is not always necessary to gather new data when conducting research. An enormous amount of data already exists in the public domain as corporate and government reports, and the statistical and financial databases that can be accessed online. Our focus here is mainly on textual information and its analysis, which we call **archival research**. Given the focus on words and on existing texts, this type of research fits with quadrant B in Figure 4.1.

Favoured sources of archival data in management and business research are the annual reports from companies where statements from chief executives review achievements from the past year and outline plans and priorities for the next year. Analysis of the language used over time can demonstrate, for example, the emerging concern among large companies about sustainability issues, or increasing emphasis being placed on employee engagement. By analysing policy statements produced by central and local government in the UK between 1997 and 2008, O'Reilly and Reed (2010) were able to follow the changing rhetoric about the desirable behaviour of public sector managers over this period (see Example 4.4).

EXAMPLE
4.4

An archival study

O'Reilly and Reed (2010) analysed 29 'high-level' government documents published between 1997 and 2008, which focused on the management of the public sector. They searched these documents for strings of text containing <profession>, <manag> and <leader>. By looking at the frequency of usage they were able to show how the discourse of leadership, which emphasizes change and reform, has started to take over from the older 'New Public Management' discourse of managerialism, which emphasized efficiency and performance.

Ethnography

The key principle of **ethnography** is that the researcher should 'immerse' him or herself in a setting, and become part of the group under study in order to understand the meanings and significances that people give to their behaviour and that of others. It is thus a strong form of constructionism. Most outsiders who are new to an organization or group will encounter things that they do not understand. These are what Agar (1986) calls 'breakdowns': events or situations where the researcher's past experience gives no help in understanding what is going on. This breakdown therefore represents something unique about that organization, and which was previously unknown to the researcher. For example, most groups have 'in-jokes', based on experiences shared only by members of the group. In order for an outsider to make sense of the breakdown provided by an in-joke it will be necessary to track back to the original experiences (Roy, 1952; Collinson, 2002). The breakdown provides a kind of window into exploring aspects of the experiences and meaning systems of groups and organizations. It will only be possible to resolve the breakdown when the researcher has understood these meaning systems.

Another important distinction is between what are known as **emic** and **etic** perspectives. These two terms were first coined by the American linguist Kenneth Pike (1954): *emic* refers to the sounds within a language which can only be distinguished by speakers of that language; and *etic* refers to features of a language that are easily identified by outsiders, but are largely inaudible to people who speak that language. For example, the four Chinese tones are *emic* because they cannot easily be distinguished by a non-Chinese speaker, yet are absolutely critical to understanding the language. On the other hand, most native English speakers are unaware that their speech is seen (from an *etic* perspective) as tight-lipped and monotonic by French and Italian speakers.

The distinction has also led to the view that better insights can be gained into management and organizations through combining insider and outsider perspectives. Thus, Bartunek and Louis (1996) advocate methods which involve research teams that combine people working inside the organization with people working from the outside. Using methods like this the ethnographer has the opportunity to challenge and extend conventional wisdom, and to generate new insights into human behaviour. However, in many organizations it can be difficult to conduct full ethnographic research because of access restrictions, although it is often possible to combine observation of meetings with interviews of participants. We provide an example of a contemporary study in the aerospace industry in Example 4.5, which shows both the limitations on access and potential that researchers have to influence their informants. In Chapter 6 we develop the idea of participant observation further. The emphasis of involvement of the researcher in the research setting, combined with the strong constructionist element, locates ethnography within quadrant C in Figure 4.2.

A study of organizational decision making

EXAMPLE 4.5

Winston Kwon and colleagues (2009) were interested in the way managers used discourse and rhetoric in meetings to influence strategic decisions. They conducted interviews and observations over a two-year period with senior managers in a large aerospace company. Regular team meetings and conferences were observed over a six-month period and all key participants were interviewed before and after the observation period. Due to other commitments of the researchers and constraints imposed by the company they were not able to be present all the time, and hence access was intermittent. They were also asked to provide non-evaluative feedback about their observations to the company, and on several occasions this feedback led managers either to change, or clarify, decisions that they thought they had already made.

Narrative methods

Another group of constructionist research designs have been given the general label of **narrative methods** (Boje, 1995, 2001; Czarniawska, 1998; Daiute and Lightfoot, 2004).

These contain both ontological and epistemological elements. The ontological view suggests that stories and myths form a central element of organizational reality, and therefore organizational research, which ignores stories, is necessarily incomplete. The epistemological position is that by collecting organizational stories, the researcher will gain insights into organizational life which could not be reached by more conventional means. This may involve participant observation, where the researcher can become part of the process of constructing and transmitting stories, or they may be collected through interviews by asking people for the stories that they have heard about particular events (see Example 4.6). In essence, the method relies on literary theory (Hatch, 1996), and hence both the position of the narrator and the role of the analyst are very important.

EXAMPLE
4.6

A narrative-based study

Humphreys and Brown (2008) investigated the way corporate social responsibility (CSR) was introduced as an important function within a financial services company. The authors, consistent with our definition above, saw stories and narratives as central to the way managers and employees make sense of what was going on in the company. But their research design also involved the collection of stories from key actors involved in the establishment of corporate social responsibility within the company. From the analysis of semi-structured interviews with 64 employees, they identified three major themes/narratives associated with CSR – idealism and altruism, economics and expedience, and ignorance and cynicism – which summarized the conflicting perspectives on CSR in that company.

One of the criticizms of narrative methods is that they do not offer much that is distinctive or additional to 'normal' qualitative research. Nevertheless, they do have a number of strengths: they provide a holistic perspective on organizational behaviour; they are particularly useful in developing social histories of identity and development; they are useful in helping to examine relationships between individuals and the wider organization; and they introduce values into the research process. Returning to the map in Figure 4.1, narrative research may be seen as more detached (quadrant B) if the collection of existing stories is emphasized, or more involved (quadrant C) if the researcher plays a role in encouraging people to invent new stories that illustrate their feelings.

Validity of constructionist designs

There is much concern about how to assure and demonstrate the quality of constructionist designs, although authors rarely use the term 'validity'. In a classic paper, Golden-Biddle and Locke (1993) identify three key criteria:

- authenticity
- plausibility
- criticality.

Authenticity involves convincing the reader that the researcher has a deep understanding of what was taking place in the organization; *plausibility* requires the research to link into some ongoing concern/interest among other researchers; and *criticality* encourages readers to question their taken-for-granted assumptions, and thus offer something genuinely novel. More recently Amis and Silk (2008), in discussing 'non-foundationalist' qualitative research, suggest that good research within the constructionist tradition should be partisan, taking the side of the less powerful members of society and organizations, and supporting a 'moral-sacred' philosophy. Thus quality would be indicated by the presence of the audience in the text, the sharing of emotional experience, stressing political action, taking sides, moving people to reflect and act, and providing collaborative, reciprocal, trusting and friendly relations with those studied.

Another perspective is provided by Silverman (2000), who argues for a more objective stance (and hence a weaker form of social constructionism) because there are few safeguards to prevent researchers from picking evidence out of the mass of data to support their particular prejudices. In order to defend themselves against charges of 'anecdotalism' he suggests several principles, including refutability, constant comparison, comprehensive data treatment and tabulations. *Refutability* involves looking for examples that might disconfirm current beliefs; *constant comparison* follows the principles of grounded theory (see next section) in looking for new cases and settings, which will stretch the current theory; *comprehensive data treatment* involves carrying out an initial analysis of all of the data available before coming up with conclusions; and *tabulations* imply greater rigour in organizing data, and accepting that it can also be useful to add up the occurrence of phenomena sometimes.

Our own view is that the results of constructionist research should be believable, and they should be reached through methods that are transparent. Thus it is very important for the researcher to explain how he or she gained access to the particular organization, what processes led to the selection of informants, how data was created and recorded, what processes were used to summarize or collate it, how the data became transformed into tentative ideas and explanations, and how he or she felt about the research.

CASE METHOD AND GROUNDED THEORY

There are several methods that, despite having a single label, can be used in quite different ways by different proponents. This is particularly true with **case method** and **grounded theory**. Although the dominant texts about case method come from the positivist end, the method can also be designed in ways consistent with relativist and constructionist perspectives. On the other hand, grounded theory was designed as a constructionist alternative to positivist methods, yet some respected versions now contain positivist elements.[2]

Case method

Essentially the case study looks in depth at one, or a small number of, organizations, events or individuals, generally over time. There is a very extensive literature on the design, use and purposes of case studies. In the management field authors tend to coalesce around those who advocate single cases and those who advocate multiple cases. Advocates of single cases generally come from a constructionist epistemology; those who advocate multiple cases usually fit with a more positivist epistemology.

Robert Yin is the best-known exponent of case method in the social sciences (Yin, 2013). His concern is that case studies are vulnerable to a number of criticisms from more *positivist* researchers. In particular, it is suggested that they do not have the rigour of natural scientific designs; they rarely allow generalizations to be made from specific cases to the general population; and they produce huge piles of data, which allow researchers to make any interpretations they want. In response to these criticisms, he suggests that all case studies should have clear

---

[2]Our focus here is on single methods, which may be interpreted and practised in significantly different ways. This is distinct from 'mixed methods', which involve using combinations of different data collection methods and types for the same study (see Creswell, 2014).

designs produced before any data is collected, and these designs should cover: the main questions or propositions, the **unit of analysis**, links between data and propositions, and procedures for interpretation of data. He is anxious to demonstrate that case studies may contain the same degree of validity as more positivist studies, and therefore his exposition of the method contains both rigour and the application of careful logic about comparisons.

The contrasting position, which is informed by a *constructionist* epistemology, is much less concerned with issues of validity, and more concerned with providing a rich picture of life and behaviour in organizations or groups. Robert Stake (2006) writes about qualitative case studies, and distinguishes between *instrumental* and *expressive* studies. The former involves looking at specific cases in order to develop general principles; the latter involves investigating cases because of their unique features, which may or may not be generalizable to other contexts. An example would be Andrew Pettigrew's research into organization development within the chemical company ICI during the 1970s and early 1980s. In those days ICI was the most powerful manufacturing company in Britain, so there was naturally a lot of interest in understanding how they were managing and developing themselves. In that respect the study was expressive, but there was also an instrumental element since Pettigrew was interested in understanding the phenomenon of organization development, and ICI was regarded as one of its leading proponents. His research involved numerous interviews with key actors in the company over several years, and this provided a longitudinal element to his research, which enabled him better to understand both the contextual and historical settings of the company (Pettigrew, 1985).

From a similar perspective, Nikkolaj Siggelkow (2007) provides a spirited defence of cases arguing that they are particularly valuable for demonstrating the importance of particular research questions, for inspiring new ideas and for illustrating abstract concepts. He also points out that even single cases can provide very convincing tests of theory by quoting the famous 'talking pig' example. Thus we only need to produce a single talking pig to demonstrate the error of the popular idea that pigs are incapable of intelligent speech. The logic being that we only need one example of an anomaly to destroy a dominant theory – as in the case of Einstein's refutation of Newton's theory. And although we are unlikely to identify a 'talking pig' organization, there are many examples where single cases can be uniquely interesting; for example, the company that does significantly better (or worse) than all others in the same industry, or the entrepreneur who builds a fortune from small beginnings.

EXERCISE
4.4

A longitudinal case study

A study conducted by Prieto and Easterby-Smith (2006) explored the links between dynamic capabilities and knowledge management through a case study of the evolution of a single company over several years. Because the researchers were interested in dynamic capabilities – which are by definition about continuous change – it made sense to observe processes over time so they could examine how, for example, the introduction of knowledge-sharing routines led to greater strategic flexibility. Accordingly, the researchers spent time observing management meetings, talking with participants at meetings, and interviewing other managers. They also followed information exchanges with partner organizations by conducting visits to their sites, repeating interviews with key informants, and feeding back emerging insights to senior managers to 'validate' their interpretations and to stimulate further insights.

Questions

1. How would you justify that this research was 'valid'?

2. What possibilities are there for generalizing the findings from this research?

3. Do questions about validity and generalizability make any sense in this instance?

A few points are important about constructionist studies. First, they are based on direct observation and personal contacts, generally through interviews. Second, they take place within single organizations, but then involve sampling from numbers of individuals. Third, the collection of data takes place over a period of time and may include both live observations and retrospective accounts of what has happened. Thus the unit of analysis is either the individual, or specific events such as the exchange of a piece of knowledge, or strategies employed to transfer or retain control of knowledge.

There is also an intermediate position, which has been developed particularly through the work of Kathy Eisenhardt (Eisenhardt, 1989; Eisenhardt and Graebner, 2007). This view draws inspiration from both the positivist and constructionist positions, and has been adopted widely by researchers using case methods, particularly in North America. She is eclectic in her advice about methodology: using designs that are established at the outset, but then being flexible about their adaptation; recommending data collection through using multiple methods; and conducting both within case and across case analysis.

Above all, Eisenhardt is concerned about building theory from case-based research, and this takes the form of developing hypotheses. She recommends that hypotheses can be formed, or shaped, through three main stages. The first stage involves sharpening-up the basic constructs, and this is essentially an iterative process of moving back and forth between the constructs and the data. The second stage involves verifying that emergent relationships between constructs fit with the evidence from each case. In this respect she comments that 'Each case is analogous to an experiment, and multiple cases are analogous to multiple experiments' (Eisenhardt, 1989: 542). The third stage involves comparing the emergent theory/concepts/hypotheses with the existing literature. In particular, she suggests paying attention to literature that is contradicted by the evidence, both because any evidence of having ignored contradictory findings is likely to reduce confidence in the final conclusions, and because the highlighting of contradictory conclusions is likely to make the original contribution from the research most explicit.

Comparative case study design

EXAMPLE
4.7

In a comparative study of investment decisions in Chinese and UK companies (Lu and Heard, 1995), case studies of 16 decisions in 8 companies were compared and contrasted in order to establish the cultural and institutional variations in business decision making between China and the UK. The study involved collecting both qualitative and quantitative data, including extensive site visits to companies in both China and the UK. Each UK company was matched, in terms of size and industry, with the equivalent Chinese company. This allowed for a number of comparisons, between different industries, and between China and the UK, which led to new insights. For example, in the latter case the researchers noticed that the mean time between the inception and implementation of a major investment decision (approximately £100 million) was virtually identical in both China and the UK (approximately 3.4 years). This significantly contradicted existing theory about the speed of decision-making, which suggested that decision making in China was far slower than in the UK. Of course, with the benefit of hindsight it is now possible to see how fast Chinese companies have been developing over the last two decades, but this study was one of the first to demonstrate the speed of economic development in China.

Although the variations in case study design and application are complex and sometimes blend into each other, we summarize in Table 4.2 some of the main distinctions in the use and application of case method at three points along the epistemological continuum.

TABLE 4.2 Key features of case method informed by different epistemologies

	Positivist (Yin)	Positivist and Constructionist (Eisenhardt)	Constructionist (Stake)
Design	Prior	Flexible	Emergent
Sample	Up to 30	4–10	1 or more
Analysis	Cross-case	Both	Within case
Theory	Testing	Generation	Action

Grounded theory

Grounded theory was first formulated by Glaser and Strauss (1967). They saw the key task of the researcher as being to develop theory through 'comparative method', which means looking at the same event or process in different settings or situations. For example, the researcher might be interested in the workings of performance appraisal interviews and would therefore study a number of interviews handled by different managers, in different departments or in different organizations. As a result of the studies it might be noticed that most appraisal interviews either focus on reviewing performance in relation to last year's objectives, or they focus on future goals and how the subordinate may be helped to achieve these. They might then be labelled as 'judgemental' or 'developmental' interviews, and the distinction would represent a *substantive theory* about appraisal interviews.

However, the theorizing could be taken further. For example, it might be observed that neither form of interview has much effect on individual performance, nor on the relationships between the managers and their subordinates. Then we could conclude that both forms of interview are simply organizational rituals, which have the function of demonstrating and reinforcing hierarchical power relations. This would be the beginning of a more generalized *formal theory* about power and organizational rituals. Glaser and Strauss consider both substantive and formal theory to be valuable, and they propose two main criteria for evaluating the quality of a theory. First, it should be sufficiently *analytic* to enable some generalization to take place; at the same time it should be possible for people to relate the theory to their own experiences, thus *sensitizing* their own perceptions.

It is important to note that 'I'm doing grounded theory!' should not be used as a justification for doing some vaguely qualitative research without any clear view of where it is supposed to lead. Grounded theory contains precisely articulated methods and presuppositions. The problem is, as Locke (1997) explains, that methods have evolved and developed since their initial exposition, and at the heart of this was a rather acrimonious debate between Barney Glaser and Anselm Strauss.[3] In essence, Glaser now believes that researchers should start with no pre-suppositions, and should allow ideas to 'emerge' from the data (Glaser, 1978, 1992), whereas Strauss recommends familiarizing oneself with prior research and using structured, and somewhat mechanistic, processes to make sense of the data (Strauss, 1987; Corbin and Strauss, 2015). The implication is that the researcher should be aware that there are different versions of grounded theory, and hence needs to articulate his or her own position when writing up the research. Agreed features are shown in Table 4.3, and differences between Glaser and Strauss are summarized in Table 4.4.

---

[3]We understand that Glaser and Strauss did meet up and resolve their differences shortly before the untimely death of Anselm Strauss (personal communication).

TABLE 4.3 Agreed features of grounded theory

Grounded Theory	
Must:	fit the substantive area; be understandable and useable by actors; be sufficiently complex to account for variation.
Key analytical operations are:	cycle of theoretical sampling; constant comparisons; evolving theory, *leading to*... theoretical saturation.

TABLE 4.4 Points of disagreement between Glaser and Strauss

	Glaser	Strauss (and Corbin)
Researcher Roles	Maintain distance and independence.	Active interrogation of data.
Theory	Emerges from data itself.	Arises from theorist/data interaction.
Ontology	World is 'out there'.	Reality and experience are constructed.
Pre-understanding	Avoid literature from immediate area.	Flexible approach. Insights from many sources.

The debate is extended further by Kathy Charmaz (2000), who characterizes the methods of both Glaser and Strauss as 'objectivist'. Her complaint is that both authors separate the researcher from the experiences of the subjects of the study. She also feels that the recommendations from Strauss and Corbin (1998) about detailed analysis of transcripts, including line-by-line analysis and 'fracturing of data', reduces the ability to represent the whole experience of individuals involved. In her view, a constructionist should recognize 'that the viewer creates the data and ensuing analysis through interaction with the viewed' (Charmaz, 2000: 523). As such she is located a little further in the constructionist direction than Strauss because she emphasizes the interaction between the researcher and the researched, rather than between the researcher and the data.

In order to make sense of these differences, we need to look both at the ontology and epistemology of the authors. Ontologically, Glaser comes across as a realist, or possibly an internal realist, whereas both Strauss and Charmaz have a more nominalist ontology because they assume that the social world is created through the interaction of actors. Epistemologically, Strauss, who was significantly influenced by Corbin (personal communication), adopts a weak positivist position, which emphasizes systematic and reductionist approaches to the analysis of data. Glaser, on the other hand, promotes a more relaxed epistemology, insisting that the data should be analysed in its entirety, and should not be reduced to discrete elements. In some respects this is similar to the constructionist perspective of Charmaz, though she goes further in emphasizing the primacy of the stories and experiences of her research subjects.

Before completing this section, it is important to note that the methods of grounded theory have been developed mainly within educational and health settings where the researcher can have relatively easy and flexible access to data and cases. But access is far more difficult within commercial organizations, and researchers are rarely given the freedom to select their samples on theoretical grounds – hence some of the assumptions of grounded theory have to be amended further to deal with this kind of situation (Locke, 2001). Organizational researchers have to accept the interviewees assigned to them by powerful organizational members who act as gatekeepers (see the discussion on strategies for gaining research access in Chapter 5); there are also limits imposed in terms of timing, topics and the use of data. This often requires a number of compromises to be made in terms of research design, as can be seen from the reflections of Suzanne Gagnon in Exercise 4.5 about her study of identity formation among highflying managers in two different international organizations.

Grounded theory, in its different guises, is one of the most popular qualitative methods in business and management research. Suddaby (2006) gives much helpful advice for researchers seeking to use grounded theory methods and publish their work. He lists common misconceptions:

1. Grounded theory is not an excuse to ignore the literature.

2. Grounded theory is not presentation of raw data.

3. Grounded theory is not theory testing, content analysis or word counts.

4. Grounded theory is not simply routine application of formulaic technique to data.

5. Grounded theory is not perfect.

6. Grounded theory is not easy.

7. Grounded theory is not an excuse for the absence of methodology.

EXERCISE
4.5

How grounded is this? A letter from a doctoral student

Hi Mark

I started with a general area for study – the interplay of personal and organizational identities in multi-nationality, multicultural organizations (how important is organizational culture in such settings, and why? What identities do people see themselves as having in these settings, and why?).

Once having been in the sites for some time and gathered some data through interviews, I found that *identity regulation* was a term (perhaps even a central category in Strauss' and Corbin's words) that had explanatory power; I got this term from the literature, having continued to iteratively study the literature and the data, while continuing to gather data.

My 'sample' was more or less set from the beginning (all participants on two management development programmes), so in this sense I did not use theoretical sampling. However, I did add questions and change emphases in the interviews as I proceeded.

Whether I reached theoretical saturation, I am not fully sure. In a sense it was more a question of talking to everyone, and then sampling the data (with some follow-up and changes to subsequent questioning and focus, as above).

I see this as a kind of 'theory elaboration' rather than deduction per se. But there is definitely a deductive side to it. It may also be the case that I come up with my own theory (hope so), especially, perhaps, in comparing results across the two cases.

That's as far as I can go at the moment. What do you think? How grounded is this?

Suzanne

Questions

1. How grounded is this?

2. Should she be sticking more closely to grounded theory principles, and if not, why not?

MIXED METHODS

In recent years there has been growing interest in the use of research methods that draw from both positivist and constructionist epistemologies, and which combine both qualitative and quantitative methods in the same study. This has been stimulated by several influential books (Creswell, 2003; Tashakkori and Teddlie, 2010; Teddlie and Tashakkori, 2009) and by the founding of the specialist *Journal of Mixed Methods Research* in 2007.

There has also been a debate between proponents of mixed methods and those who are sceptical about their value. Those in favour argue that by using a range of different methods within the same study the researcher will increase the validity and generalizability of results and the potential theoretical contribution; the sceptics point to practical limitations such as the competence of researchers in conducting different methods, and to possible contradictions between the paradigms underlying different methods.

There are many variants of mixed methods in social research, but the key idea is that they involve combinations of qualitative and quantitative methods for data collection and analysis. We will therefore start by discussing the choices with regard to data collection, then we consider different strategies for analysis, and finally we consider some of the arguments for and against the use of mixed methods.

Designs for data collection

There are two main considerations in the design of studies that use both qualitative and quantitative methods to conduct research: **sequencing** and **dominance**. Sequencing refers to whether one method goes before the other, and if so which goes first. Dominance is a matter of whether one method uses significantly more time and resource than the other, or whether they are roughly balanced in importance. These considerations are summarized in Table 4.5.

By combining these choices we can identify three distinct designs, which incorporate both quantitative and qualitative methods. We call these master-servant, partnership and compensatory designs.

With *master-servant* designs the key point is that one method serves the needs of the other. There is usually a definite sequence in the use of methods, and naturally one method dominates the other. The most common format is the qualitative pilot study based on interviews or direct observation, which is used to develop, and maybe test, the items for the main study, which involves a questionnaire survey. Here the questionnaire survey

TABLE 4.5   Choices in designing mixed methods research

Design Features	Alternatives to Consider
Sequencing of methods	Qualitative first, or quantitative first, or both at the same time
Dominance of methods	Predominantly qualitative, or quantitative, or balanced

is dominant, and the pilot study serves no function in the final result of the work, other than helping the researchers to design a questionnaire that is likely to yield accurate and reliable data.

There are also contemporary examples of the reverse process, where a survey is used to identify a small number of 'interesting' cases for in-depth investigation, and then the survey results are largely ignored in the final results. For example, Macpherson et al. (2010) conducted a survey based on single interviews with 92 entrepreneurs. From this sample they identified three critical cases where they conducted repeated interviews over a year in order to establish how various artefacts (such as knowledge management software, benchmarking and problem-solving forums) contributed to the learning processes of the SME. In this case it is the qualitative study that dominates the published paper, with the survey merely in the background. Similarly, Detert and Edmondson (2011) investigated why employees usually fail to speak their minds to those in authority through a four-stage design. In the first stage they conducted interviews in one company to identify the implicit theories from employees about why it was unwise to speak up; the second stage used an open survey questionnaire circulated to 185 managers in different organizations to test the generalizability of these theories. Stages three and four then developed and validated quantitative survey instruments, which could be used to examine the phenomenon on a much larger scale.

Partnership designs typically involve combining more than one method, such as a questionnaire survey and interviews, where both assume similar importance in the study. For example, entrepreneurial behaviour can be investigated by interviewing a small sample of entrepreneurs about their origins, motives, strategies, successes and failures, supplemented by a questionnaire containing similar questions sent out to a larger sample. When combined, the interview data will contain greater detail, clarifications and added explanations; the questionnaire data will contain shorter answers, possibly more focused, but will be able to cover responses from a wider range of entrepreneurs who could be divided into subgroups to explore possible differences according to family history, levels of funding, types of technology and so on.

Compensatory designs combine qualitative and quantitative studies where each is used to make up for the weaknesses of the other. Typically qualitative studies are seen as weak on generalization, and quantitative studies are weak at explaining why the observed results have been obtained. Thus there is a growing trend in leading US publications such as the *Academy of Management Journal* for quantitative studies that establish statistical relationships between variables to be supplemented by quotations from substantial numbers of interviews focusing on the mechanisms and processes, which may provide explanations of the observed results.

Analysis

Another form of mixed methodology can be introduced at the analysis stage. Although qualitative and quantitative data are normally analysed within their respective traditions, there is also the possibility of cross-over designs. Thus quantitative data can be analysed in qualitative ways and qualitative data can be analysed in quantitative ways. The most common form of the latter is when frequency counts are made of the use of particular words, phrases or themes from a sample of interview transcripts. The study by O'Reilly and Reed (2010) (see Example 4.4) provides an example of qualitative archival data in the form of government policy documents being analysed quantitatively for the occurrence of particular words and expressions. Slightly less common is when quantitative data is analysed by techniques such as factor analysis, and **principal components analysis,** which look for patterns that are largely hidden. Techniques such as the **repertory grid** technique (see Chapter 7) involve starting with qualitative data, which then becomes quantified and analysed statistically, and the result is then interpreted qualitatively.

Arguments for and against mixed methods

As we have outlined above, there are many reasons why mixed methods are regarded as a good thing: they have the potential to throw new perspectives on research questions, to increase the credibility of results, to demonstrate generalizability, and to provide deeper insights that explain why things take place. But there are also plenty of reasons for being cautious about their wholesale adoption. We summarize some of these pros and cons in Table 4.6 based on the arguments of Jick (1979), Tashakkori and Teddlie (2010) and Bryman and Bell (2007).

There is, however, a more fundamental critique of the use of mixed methods, which hangs on the notion of paradigm incommensurability (Burrell and Morgan, 1979; Morgan and Smircich, 1980). The argument is that it is unwise to combine different paradigms within the same study because the different underlying assumptions mean that it will not be possible to join the two parts of the study together. At the extreme this can produce a **semi-detached design**, because like two semi-detached houses, they are physically linked together, yet there is no adjoining doorway between the two parts of the house.

The weakness of the incommensurability argument is that it assumes that paradigms are always distinct and that there can be no overlaps. Recent thinking about paradigms suggests that boundaries are more fluid than originally portrayed (Cunliffe, 2011), and hence it may be acceptable to combine paradigms up to a point. In our view the limits can be defined by the continuum presented in Figure 4.1, where it is possible to combine adjacent ontologies and epistemologies within a mixed methods study, but increasingly problematic when combining more distant positions. For example, a positivist study might demonstrate that 80 per cent of corporate performance could be predicted by three variables: size, market share and growth rate. But when combined with an ethnographic study exploring the micro-politics of constructions of corporate performance, this would not contribute in any way to identifying the remaining 20 per cent in the predictive formula. It would be more likely to undermine the credibility of the main study by arguing that the concept of 'performance' is a sham.

The use of mixed methods can often lead to contradictory results. If the ontologies are very different there will be no way of resolving the confusion. However, if they are close enough then resolution may be possible, as illustrated in Example 4.8.

TABLE 4.6 Pros and cons of mixed methods

Arguments for Mixed Methods	Arguments against Mixed Methods
• They increase confidence and credibility of results • They increase validity • They stimulate creative and inventive methods • They can uncover deviant dimensions • They can help synthesis and integration of theories • They may serve as a critical test of competing theories • They can combine confirmatory and exploratory research at the same time • They present greater diversity of views • They provide better (stronger) inferences	• Replication is difficult • The research design must be relevant to the research question • They provide no help if you are asking the wrong questions • They take up more resources than single method studies • Their use requires a competent overall design • The researcher needs to be skilled in the use of both methods • It is not helpful if one method simply provides window dressing for the other (an extreme version of the handmaid design discussed above)

EXAMPLE
4.8

Problems with mixed methods

Morgan Tanton and Mark Easterby-Smith carried out a comparative evaluation study of two executive management programmes (Courses A and B), held in two different business schools (respectively, Institutions A and B). Observations during the course, and qualitative data obtained from follow-up interviews, showed quite clearly that Course A was superior to Course B, but the quantitative data in the form of student ratings about the two courses showed clearly that Course B was preferred to Course A. Was this discrepancy caused by the methods used, or could it highlight some unusual features of the two courses being examined?

To resolve this dilemma we showed the survey results to participants and asked for their explanations. First, participants commented that they were cautious when filling in multiple choice rating forms, because they could never be sure what the data would be used for; therefore, they usually avoided unduly negative responses. Second, the course designs and institutional settings affected the criteria that participants used for evaluating the two courses. In Institution A the emphasis was on the longer-term application of what had been learnt; in Institution B the emphasis was on the immediate quality of sessions conducted within the classroom. Thus it was not surprising that the rating forms which were completed at the end of the course showed one pattern, whereas follow-up interviews conducted some months later showed another pattern. In this case it was possible to combine the two sets of data because the survey and interviews were respectively backed by internal realist and relativist perspectives, and both parts shared a common research question.

Finally, we can note that much of the interest in mixed methods comes from those on the positivist side of the spectrum, who hold at least an internal realist view of the world, on the grounds that added data and more perspectives will enable them to get closer to the intangible objects of their enquiries and cynics might say that positivists need to incorporate more constructionist methods to make up for the shallowness of their traditional methods!

Summary

We accept that in some circumstances mixed methods can be advantageous, but think it is important that a clear rationale for their use is worked out in advance, and care needs to be taken to ensure that the methods are reasonably compatible. There is always a danger in using mixed methods just because they might add to the overall credibility of the research, because the ad hoc combination of different kinds of study means that neither may be done properly. As Bryman and Bell (2003: 493) comment: 'multi-strategy research should not be considered as an approach that is universally applicable or as a panacea'.

COMMON DESIGN DILEMMAS

In this section we identify five areas that require decisions when formulating research designs, irrespective of the ontology or epistemology that informs the study. These are:

- identifying the unit of analysis
- universal theory or local knowledge
- theory or data first

- cross-sectional or longitudinal
- verification or falsification.

Identifying the unit of analysis

The unit of analysis is the entity that forms the basis of any sample. Thus, samples may be formed from one or more of the following: countries, cultures, races, industrial sectors, organizations, departments, families, groups, individuals, incidents, stories, accidents, innovations and so on. In positivist forms of research, including multiple case studies informed by an internal realist perspective, it is important to be clear about the unit of analysis in advance, because this is the basis for collating data that will subsequently be analysed. It is not essential in constructionist forms of research, but with highly unstructured data it can help to provide an initial guidance for analysis. In the above example from our research, which compared decision-making between China and the UK (Example 4.7), the unit of analysis was the company, but there was a subsidiary unit of analysis (what is sometimes referred to as an **embedded case**), which was the investment decision. Hence it is possible to have more than one unit of analysis provided the theoretical aims of the research justify this, but it is not advisable to have too many.

Universal theory or local knowledge?

One of the key principles of scientific methods and positivist knowledge is that theories and observations made in one context should be applicable to other defined contexts. As we have discussed above, being able to provide assurances of **generalizability**, or external validity, are critical features both of experimental designs and the statistical procedures that are employed to interpret realist research data. In these cases, as with the guidance of Kathy Eisenhardt on case method, the objective is to produce **universal theories**.

On the other hand, a number of scholars argue that **local knowledge** is more significant. For example, according to post-colonial theory many theories of race, economic development and culture are constructs of scholars in Western countries, which typically cast non-Western culture and institutions as being somehow inferior to their own (Said, 1978). Similarly, from feminist theory there is a strong view that many of the dominant theories of social behaviour are blind to the effects of gender and patriarchy (Ahmed, 1998). In both cases the argument is that any generalized statement about the social world is likely to contain within it assumptions that mask relations of power between those who formulate theories and those to whom they are applied. Moreover, there is a strong view that significant social theory should be understood in relation to the context whence it is derived.

Local knowledge is also important for management and organizational research. First, it is suggested that the practical knowledge used by managers is essentially contextually bound, and is learnt through engaging in practice (Cook and Brown, 1999; Rouleau, 2005). If this is the case then it follows that for research to have theoretical value it should focus on these local practices – which may well be unique to that situation. Second, some people argue that managerial behaviour is culturally relative, including both national and organizational cultures (Boyacigiller and Adler, 1991). Hence researchers should formulate their ideas separately within each cultural context, and should not try to generalize across cultures.

For example, it has been accepted for some time that models derived from Western management research are unlikely to be relevant in Asian contexts, as Nor (2000) found in his study of Malaysia, because of Malaysia's unique cultural, political and institutional circumstances. Over the last decade there has been much interest in the development of entrepreneurial capabilities in Asian countries such as China, Vietnam, Malaysia and India. It is increasingly accepted that the cultural and institutional differences between these countries are such that local theories to explain entrepreneurial behaviour are necessary in each country (Taylor, 1999; Hobday and Rush, 2007).

Theory or data first?

The third choice is about which should come first: the theory or the data? Again this represents the split between the positivist and constructionist paradigms in relation to how the researcher should go about his or her work. The Straussian view of grounded theory assumes that pre-conceptions are inevitable. After all, it is common sense to assume that someone will not be interested in a research topic or setting without knowing something in advance about it. Hence he argues that the researcher should make him or herself aware of previous work conducted in the general field of research before starting to generate his or her own theory.

Recent developments in organizational research have led to a wide range of designs, some of which extend the range of fieldwork methods, and others that provide intermediate positions between the two extremes. In a recent research project looking at absorptive capacity within European companies, Easterby-Smith et al. (2008) became increasingly aware that the relationship between theory and data needs to be an interactive process. When researchers observe something that seems surprising or novel in a company, it is important to go back to the literature in order to see whether anybody else has remarked on it. This ongoing dialogue between existing knowledge and what the data have to say that is novel is one reason why initial literature reviews are almost always modified before the final write-up of a research project. Similarly, when a new paper gets published it may have a direct impact on the ongoing collection and interpretation of data.

Cross-sectional or longitudinal?

Cross-sectional designs, particularly those that include questionnaires and survey techniques, generally belong to positivist traditions. As we have noted earlier, they have undoubted strengths in their ability economically to describe features of large numbers of people or organizations. But a major limitation is that they find it hard to describe processes over time and to explain *why* the observed patterns are there. Thus, although Lyles and Salk (1996) were confident that balanced equity stakes led to the highest chance of knowledge transfer, their study itself could not explain what mechanisms or processes led to knowledge being transferred.

In order to understand processes of change over time it is necessary to adopt longitudinal designs. From the positivist side these include quasi-experimental methods and diary methods because repeated measurements are taken over time, but it is more often associated with constructionist research, where repeated visits are made to the same individual or companies over months or years, or when the researcher conducts an ethnographic study working continuously in the same location.

Verification or falsification

This final decision is slightly different from the four preceding ones since it is not linked to resolving the broader debate between positivist and constructionist views. However, it is very important both for researchers and for managers, as we will explain below. The distinction between **verification** and **falsification** was made by Karl Popper (1959) as a way of dealing with what has become known as Hume's 'problem of induction'. This is the philosophical problem that, however much data one obtains in support of a scientific theory, it is not possible to reach a conclusive proof of the truth of that law. Popper's way out of this problem is to suggest that instead of looking for confirmatory evidence one should always look for evidence that will *disconfirm* one's hypothesis or existing view (as in the 'talking pig' example on page 90). This means that theories should be formulated in a way that will make them most easily exposed to possible refutation. The advantage then is that one only needs one instance of refutation to falsify a theory, whereas irrespective of the number of confirmations of the theory, it will never be conclusively proven.

The example often given to illustrate this approach takes as a start the assertion that 'all swans are white'. If one takes the verification route, the (non-Australian) researcher would start travelling around the country accumulating sightings of swans, and provided that he or she did not go near a zoo, a very high number of white sightings would eventually be obtained, and presumably no black sightings. This gives a lot of confidence to the assertion that all swans are white, but still does not conclusively prove the statement. If, on the other hand, one takes a falsification view, one would start to search for swans that are *not* white, deliberately looking for contexts and locations where one might encounter non-white swans. Thus, our intrepid researcher might head straight for a zoo, or perhaps book a flight to Western Australia where most swans happen to be black. On making this discovery, the initial hypothesis would be falsified, and it might then have to be modified to include the idea that 'all swans have either white or black feathers'. This statement has still what Popper calls high 'informative' content because it is expressed in a way that can easily be disproved, whereas a statement like 'all swans are large birds' would not be sufficiently precise to allow easy refutation.

Much of the debate about verification and falsification fits within the positivist view because ideas of 'truth' and 'proof' are associated mainly with that paradigm. But there are also important lessons that the constructionist might take from this discussion. For example, Alvesson and Deetz (2000) advise 'critical sensitivity', and Reason (1988) advocates 'critical subjectivity', which involves recognizing one's own views and experiences, but not allowing oneself to be overwhelmed and swept along by them. If the idea of falsification is to be applied more fully to constructionist research, then one should look for evidence that might confirm or contradict what one currently believes to be true. Indeed, a falsification strategy is an important element of abductive research (Dubois and Gadde, 2002) which emphasizes ways in which data can generate new theory rather than either confirm or disconfirm existing theory.

This advice not only applies to researchers but also to managers who are concerned to investigate and understand what is taking place within their own organizations. Most managers are strongly tempted to look for evidence that supports the currently held views of the world. This is not surprising if they are responsible for formulating strategies and policies within a context that is very uncertain, and hence they will be looking for evidence that demonstrates that their strategies were correct. The logical position that follows from the above argument is that, even if *disconfirmatory* evidence is unpopular, it is certainly both more efficient and more informative than confirmatory evidence. Moreover, if managers adopt the falsification strategy and fail to come up with evidence that disconfirms their current views, then they will be able to have far more confidence in their present positions.

CONTRIBUTING TO THEORY

Good research designs need to have some link to theory. In the case of student projects and dissertations it is generally necessary to *use* theory, whereas for doctoral theses and papers in academic journals it is necessary to demonstrate a *contribution* to theory. This is not as daunting as it might seem, and in this section we elaborate on the types and purposes of theory, and explain how they can be incorporated into research designs.

The term 'theory' often has negative connotations. Someone might report back on a lecture saying, 'It was all a lot of theory!', meaning that it was either difficult to understand or just plain boring. Or someone might react to a new idea saying, 'Well that's all right in *theory*, but …', meaning that although the idea sounds plausible, it would not work in practice. So, in this case theory is seen as the opposite of practice. On the other hand there is the well-known saying, 'There is nothing so practical as a good theory' (Lewin, 1948). In order to unscramble this confusion we offer distinctions between everyday and academic theory, the latter subdividing further into middle-range and grand theories.

Everyday theory refers to the ideas and assumptions we carry round in our heads in order to make sense of everyday observations. For example, if you observe an old man walking down the street arm in arm with a young woman, you might conclude that they were grandfather and granddaughter. In order to reach this conclusion you might hold two assumptions about family relations: that grandparents often live close to their family members, and that grandparents often have very close relations with their grandchildren. If the man is leaning slightly on the woman, then it would strengthen the grandfather–daughter hypothesis; but if the man's walk was very unsteady this might suggest a new theory, that they are patient and nurse. On the other hand, if the man is well dressed and the woman is conspicuously glamorous, an alternative hypothesis might suggest itself: that the man is a wealthy philanderer and the woman is a mistress or 'trophy' wife.

Although everyday theories enable people to make sense out of specific events or situations, **academic theories** tend to look for higher levels of generalization. Following the above example for just a moment, in order to explain what was going on, a sociologist might draw on theories about the power of male patriarchy, palliative care for the elderly, or the evolution of the institution of marriage. The distinction between **middle-range theories** and **grand theories** is a matter of scale and formality. An example of the former would be the key idea of absorptive capacity: that the ability of an organization to absorb new external knowledge depends on whether it already possesses related knowledge (Cohen and Levinthal, 1990). It is middle-range because it is a generalizable proposition that can potentially be tested empirically.

On the other hand, grand theories tend to be more abstract and contain whole edifices of assumptions that are often not testable. The theory of psychoanalysis is one example because it provides a self-contained set of ideas to explain human behaviour. Similarly, personal construct theory (PCT) contains a set of propositions starting with the fundamental postulate that 'A person's processes are psychologically channelled by the way they anticipate events', which is linked to a series of corollaries about human sense-making and communications (Kelly, 1955; Bannister and Fransella, 1971). In the management field, elements of PCT have been used to make sense of group decision making and strategy formulation (see Chapter 7). A number of the integrated philosophies summarized at the end of Chapter 3, such as critical theory or structuration theory, are grand theories in the way we have described them here.

Where researchers are seeking to build theory, this is normally at the level of middle-range theory, and is an incremental process. Thus recent work by Todorova and Durisin (2007) has argued that Cohen and Levinthal's (1990) model of absorptive capacity is too rational and unduly focused around R&D, and consequently more attention needs to be paid to political and systemic processes. This leads to a question about how we can evaluate the quality of theories, or theoretical contributions, and how can we distinguish a good contribution from one that is less good? The answer is that some criteria are fairly obvious: good theories need to be simple, have good explanatory power, and be relevant to issues that need explaining. But beyond this the evaluation of contribution is largely a matter of judgement among people who already know the field quite well, which is why peer review is normally used to evaluate the theoretical contributions of research proposals and academic papers. We will be returning to these issues at various points later in the book, especially in Chapter 12.

CONTRASTING VIEWS ON VALIDITY AND RELIABILITY

There is an underlying anxiety among researchers of all persuasions that their work will not stand up to outside scrutiny. This is very understandable since research papers and theses are most likely to be attacked on methodological grounds, and one of the key justifications for doing 'research' is that it yields results that are more accurate and believable than common everyday observations.

The technical language for examining this problem includes terms such as 'validity', 'reliability' and 'generalizability'. But as we have indicated above, these mean different things within different research traditions. In Table 4.7 we therefore summarize how these terms are discussed from the philosophical viewpoints of positivism, relativism and constructionism.

The implication of Table 4.7 is fairly obvious: that depending upon where people stand on the epistemological continuum, they are likely to use different criteria for judging the quality of research. This will affect how they design and conduct their own studies and how they assess the quality of others' work, particularly when they are acting as examiners, reviewers or just colleagues.

TABLE 4.7 Four perspectives on validity, reliability and generalizability

Viewpoint	Strong Positivist	Positivist	Constructionist	Strong Constructionist
Validity	Has the design excluded all rival hypotheses?	Does the design make it possible to eliminate plausible alternative explanations?	Have a sufficient number of perspectives been included?	Does the study clearly gain access to the experiences of those in the research setting?
Reliability	Do the measures correspond closely to reality?	Do the measures used provide a good approximation to the underlying concepts of interest?	Will similar observations be reached by other observers?	Is there transparency about data collection and interpretation?
Generalizability	Does the study confirm or contradict existing findings in the same field?	Are the patterns observed in the sample data consistent with findings from other studies?	Is the sample sufficiently diverse to allow inferences to other contexts?	Do the concepts and constructs derived from this study have any relevance to other settings?

RESEARCH DESIGN TEMPLATE

We have argued throughout this chapter that research designs should take account of epistemology, and hence formal research designs need to focus on different issues. In Table 4.8 we list some of the main headings that need to be covered within each epistemology. The key point about this table is that a research proposal will need to consider different issues and to use different language according to where the researchers, and more importantly any external assessors, stand. The way to use this template is to decide which epistemology is most appropriate to your research study and then follow the questions down the relevant column.

TABLE 4.8 Research design template

Epistemology	Strong Positivist	Positivist	Constructionist	Strong Constructionist
Background	What is the theoretical problem and what studies have been conducted to date?	What is the theoretical problem and what studies have been conducted to date?	What are the ongoing discussions among researchers and practitioners?	What are the ongoing discussions among researchers and practitioners?
Rationale	What is the main gap in existing knowledge?	What are the main variables, and how are they related to one another?	What perspectives have been covered and what are missing?	What are the limitations in the discussions so far?
Research Aims	Specify testable hypotheses.	List main propositions or questions.	Identify the focal issue or question.	Explain how the research will add to the existing discussion.
Data	Define variables and determine measures.	Define dependent and independent variables and determine measures.	Explain and justify a range of data collection methods.	Identify main sources of data. How will interviews be recorded/transcribed, etc.?
Sampling (see Chapter 8)	Explain how group selection and comparison will eliminate alternative explanations.	Justify sample size and explain how it reflects the wider population.	How will the sample enable different perspectives to be included?	Explain sampling strategy. Will it be opportunistic, emergent, comparative, etc.?
Access (see Chapter 4)	How are experimental subjects to be recruited?	How can responses to questionnaires etc. be assured?	What is the strategy for gaining access to individuals, organizations?	How will insights from co-researchers be combined?
Ethics (see Chapter 4)	Is participation voluntary?	Could results be used to harm any participants?	Will the interests of individuals and organizations be protected?	How 'open' is the research? Will there be any deception?
Unit of Analysis	Differentiate between control, experimental groups, etc.	Specify whether individuals, groups, events or organizations.	How will units/cases be compared with each other?	What are the entities that are to be compared with each other?
Analysis (see Chapters 7, 9 and 10)	Statistical procedures for examining differences between groups.	Statistical procedures for examining relationships between variables.	Arrangements for coding, interpreting and making sense of data.	How will co-researchers be involved in sense-making?

Epistemology	Strong Positivist	Positivist	Constructionist	Strong Constructionist
Process	Explain stages in the research process.	Explain stages in the research process.	Explain what can be pre-planned and what can be open-ended.	Provide realistic timing including adequate provision for contingencies.
Practicalities (see Chapters 6 and 8)	How will groups be recruited? Where will experiments take place?	Who will gather data? How will it be recorded/ stored? Who will analyse it?	How will researchers share observations? Who will do transcriptions, etc.?	How will co-researchers be engaged?
Theory	How will hypotheses be tested?	In what ways will the results add to existing theories?	Will the research build on existing theory or develop new concepts?	Will the research build on existing theory or develop new concepts?
Outputs (see Chapter 11)	Where will the research results be published?	What is the dissemination strategy?	What is the dissemination strategy?	How will insights be shared with colleagues and collaborators?

CONCLUSION

In this chapter we have discussed some of the key philosophical debates underlying research methods in the social sciences, and we have looked at the implications these have for the design of management research. Some key points are:

 There is a clear dichotomy between the positivist and social constructionist worldviews, but the practice of research involves a lot of compromises.

 Each position has its own language and criteria for evaluating research designs.

 There is considerable diversity of methods and designs, especially within the constructionist research tradition.

 Differences in opinion about research methods are often underpinned by ontological differences.

The worldview held by an individual researcher or institute is an important factor, which affects the choice of research methods. But there are other factors, too. Senior academics can exert pressure on junior colleagues and students to adopt methods that they favour. Governments, companies and funding organizations can exert pressure on institutions to ensure that the aims and forms of research meet with their interests. The politics of research are complex, and researchers neglect them at their peril. That is why we have chosen to devote the next chapter to a discussion of these issues.

Discussion questions (for small groups in class)

Classify the following according to whether you consider them to be ontologies, epistemologies, methodologies or methods: grounded theory; unobtrusive measures; narrative; case method; ethnography; critical realism; participant observation; experimental design; falsification; theoretical saturation. If it is a weak association put * into the corresponding box, ** for a moderate association, and *** for a strong association. Explain your reasoning. (Note: many of them could be more than one thing.)

	Ontology	Epistemology	Methodology	Method
Grounded theory				
Unobtrusive measures				
Narrative				
Case method				
Ethnography				
Critical realism				
Participant observation				
Experimental design				
Falsification				
Theoretical saturation				

FURTHER READING

Charmaz, K. (2014) *Constructing Grounded Theory: A Practical Guide Through Qualitative Analysis*, 2nd edn. London: Sage.
A good textbook that introduces how to design and conduct a grounded theory study. Charmaz is a prominent advocate for constructionist approaches to grounded theory, distancing herself from the more positivist leanings of the founders of grounded theory.

Creswell, J.W. (2003) *Research Design: Qualitative, Quantitative and Mixed Methods Approaches*, 2nd edn. Thousand Oaks, CA: Sage.
A great beginner's overview of the three different paradigms.

Locke, K. (2001) *Grounded Theory in Management Research*. London: Sage.
This is an excellent overview of the origins of grounded theory including the differences of opinion between Glaser and Strauss, the key methods and approaches as currently practised, and the specific adaptations that may be required when conducting organizational or management research.

Miller, D.C. and Salkind, N.J. (2002) *Handbook of Research Design & Social Measurement*, 6th edn. Thousand Oaks, CA: Sage.
A useful, albeit slightly dated, handbook for further reference with excellent chapters on how to develop a research design, formulate a research problem and compose a research proposal. It also includes a section on applied and evaluation research.

Shadish, W.R., Cook, T.D. and Campbell, D.T. (2002) *Experimental and Quasi-Experimental Designs for Generalized Causal Inference*. Boston, MA: Houghton Mifflin.
An updated version of the classic book on experimental forms of social research.

Teddlie, C. and Tashakkori, A. (2009) *Foundations of Mixed Methods Research: Integrating Quantitative and Qualitative Approaches in the Social and Behavioral Sciences*. London: Sage.
Chapter 7 of this authoritative text on mixed methods research considers research designs for studies which combine quantitative and qualitative methods.

Want to know more about this chapter? Visit the ⓈSAGE edge™ website at **https://edge. sagepub.com/easterbysmith** to access practice questions, selected journal articles, useful web links and much more.

POLITICS, ACCESS AND ETHICS

5

POLITICS AND POWER IN RESEARCH

A common view about research is that it is essentially an 'ivory tower' activity, which is carried out by independent scholars, dedicated selflessly to the pursuit of knowledge. For them questions and issues are defined as interesting according to the current state of knowledge and the curiosity of the researcher's intellectual curiosity.

Although this characterization may be an admirable aspiration, especially for scientists, it is rarely possible for researchers to divorce themselves from the realities of everyday life. For a start, scholars have regularly got themselves into trouble for following beliefs that were politically unpopular. The Greek philosopher Socrates was condemned to drink a cup of hemlock because he did not seem sufficiently respectful of current Athenian divinities; and Galileo was forced to recant his belief, which was based on careful observation of sunspots and planetary orbits, that the Earth moved around the Sun. In China the first Qin emperor is reputed to have buried alive some 400 scholars because he did not like their opinions.

Although many academics have tried in the past to maintain their independence, it has never been altogether possible to separate scholarship from politics. But what do we mean by 'politics'? Our basic premise is that it concerns the power relationships between the individuals and institutions involved in the research enterprise, plus the strategies adopted by different actors and the consequences of their actions on others. Crucial relationships may be between: students and supervisors/tutors, funders and grant holders, authors and journal editors, companies and research institutes, managers and their bosses and so on. Influence within these relationships may be exerted over: what is to be researched, when, by whom; how information is to be gathered and used; and how the products of research are to be evaluated.

For those doing empirical management and business research there is an important difference compared to other forms of social and psychological research. This is that it usually needs to be carried out in the context of organizations. Access to organizations usually has to be negotiated through managers, who are responsible for controlling, influencing and structuring the awareness and actions of others. It is the central process whereby organizations achieve the semblance of coherence and direction. This process is political, and various authors have commented on the same point (Hardy, 1996; Buchanan and Badham, 2008). It is very hard to think of an organization which is not political in some way!

This highlights a comparison with the wider social sciences, where the work is carried out on members of society who are often less powerful than the researchers. That is why so often studies are conducted on members of an organization's workforce, and less often on the senior management team. As Slater (1989) remarks, it is 'the mad, the bad, and the ill' who have received most attention from social researchers in the past.

In contrast, when conducting research into management and business, the subjects of research are very likely to be more powerful than the researchers themselves. Furthermore, most organizations are both tightly structured and controlled, so that gaining access to the corporate boardroom, for example, is exceedingly difficult. Managers are usually in a position where they can easily decline to provide information for researchers; they are also adept at handling face-to-face interviews and at managing interactions with strangers. So, in the case of research into management and business, the boot is firmly on the other foot.

Our aims in this chapter are: first, to understand how political factors are often near the surface when research is being conducted in organizations; second, to appreciate the importance of power when negotiating access to organizations; third, to review ethical codes and practices that have been developed to redress power imbalances; and fourth, we look at the way ethics and politics can help or hinder the utilization of research. These aims correspond to the four main sections of this chapter.

Although some of the material in this chapter may seem to have little relevance to undergraduate researchers, the section on ethical issues is critical since most universities now require clearance for *all* external research and data collection in advance of the work being done. The other three sections are also important in making sense of the ethical 'minefield', but can be treated as stand-alone sections.

POLITICAL INFLUENCES ON RESEARCH

Most positivist researchers are not keen on self-disclosure because the admission of personal motives and aspirations might be seen to damage the image of independence and objectivity that they are at pains to cultivate. Hence they rarely explain precisely where their ideas and questions have come from.

Fortunately things are beginning to change, for two reasons. First, because social studies of the development of scientific knowledge (Latour and Woolgar, 1979) have started to show that the formal view of scientific progress differs from what most scientists do in practice. Second, because there is a growing acceptance among social scientists of the need to be reflexive about their own work, and this has led to more autobiographical accounts of research in practice (e.g. Czarniawska, 1998). Consequently there is less reliance on traditional 'linear' models of scientific progress.

Although it is recognized that a thorough knowledge of prior research is very important, it is rare for good research ideas to be derived directly from the literature. Indeed, qualitative researchers often develop post hoc theoretical rationales for their work and findings, which are explained when the thesis, or academic paper, is submitted (Golden-Biddle and Locke, 2007). Our argument in this chapter is that there are many other factors that can influence the kind of questions which are seen as worthy of research, and that these include both the personal experiences of the researcher, the attitudes and influence of external stakeholders, and the broader context within which he or she works and studies. These factors are summarized in Figure 5.1. We do not regard this as a mechanistic model; we see research ideas evolving in an incremental way through a continual process of negotiation with these factors.

Before tackling each of these factors in turn we would like to offer a simple model, which we have found useful in making sense of the politics of research. This is based on the classic study by Boissevain (1974) of social networks, especially in the Sicilian Mafia.

Study of Sicilian Mafia

EXAMPLE
5.1

In the early 1970s, the anthropologist Jeremy Boissevain conducted a study in Sicily of the roles and relationships between members of the Mafia. He identified two distinct roles played by participants: brokers and patrons. *Brokers* are social 'fixers' who use their secondary resources, such as information and a wide range of contacts, in order to achieve their ambitions. *Patrons* have direct control over primary resources, such as people and money. But when they need information or the resolution of a problem the patrons turn to brokers who have the contacts and a past record of solving problems. A skilful broker will also specify a tariff that is only part of the real cost – so that when the transaction is made he will have built up further goodwill with the patron. This will in turn increase the broker's overall credit for future problem solving.

While we would not wish to suggest a direct correspondence between the worlds of Mafiosi and business researchers, there are a number of parallels. In the research world, senior academics and tutors can act as brokers because they know the way round the system, and are known by others. They may be able to arrange for access to a particular organization; clarify and negotiate assessment criteria, to advise on how to obtain funds from research councils; identify appropriate external examiners, or to make links with journal editors who are most likely to be interested in a particular paper. Within companies, training and human resource managers can often act as brokers because, although they have little formal power, they usually have a wide range of contacts at all levels of the organization. Successful researchers can also develop brokerage skills. Thus

FIGURE 5.1
Sources of political influence

HR managers are more likely to help provide access to their company if they think the researcher may be able to provide them with something in return – whether it be expertise, credibility or other contacts.

The experience of the researcher

Motivation

Individual interests and experience provide a good starting point for research, especially if you have observed aspects of working life that strike you as 'odd'. Student projects and dissertations provide an excellent opportunity to deepen, or widen, some areas of understanding or practice.

Personal background affects what the researcher is able to see, because experience acts both as a sensitizer and as a filter. Other factors such as social class, race and gender will affect the ease with which the researcher can gain access to different settings, and this may also pre-determine responses from different client groups.

A large portion of management and business research is carried out by students and academics working on their own. But increasingly teams are being used, both as student project groups and as teams of funded researchers. A team that balances perspectives, backgrounds and skills may be much more effective than individuals at conducting research. Teams can also be established to take advantage of the insider/outsider perspective (Bartunek and Lewis, 1996). This follows the ethnographic principle that insiders will be able to see and understand things that will make no sense to outsiders, while outsiders will notice things that may have become quite invisible to insiders.

Team dynamics

Although teams can have the advantages of efficiency, and positive educational outcomes, there are always tensions that arise at some stage. These usually come down to disagreements over the right direction to take, whether everybody is pulling their weight to the same extent (sometimes called the 'free-rider' problem). Various solutions can be applied to problems in group dynamics including: doing team-building exercises at the beginning of the project; agreeing roles that fit with people's skills/interests; formally allocating regular time to review how the team is working; and, if all else fails, go and see the tutor!

Externally-funded research projects which employ research staff on fixed-term contracts also have plenty of problems (see Example 5.2).

EXAMPLE
5.2

The power of knowledge

Patrick Barwise, a professor at London Business School, working with two other professors, succeeded in obtaining a grant for a multidisciplinary investigation of strategic investment decisions. Although the project was conceived and 'sold' to the funders by these professors, it was carried out by a junior half-time researcher who was recruited specifically for the project. The senior academics initially gave clear instructions over what to do and how to do it, treating the researcher as their 'eyes and ears'. But about half way through the project they were forced to acknowledge that the researcher was the only one who fully understood the data and its interpretation, and that she was indispensable to the team if any further projects were going to be negotiated.

Source: Barwise et al., 1989

There is much potential for conflict in this example. The power of the senior professors lay in their control of funds and their potential influence on the future career of the researcher. The researcher's power, on the other hand, was based on intimate knowledge of the research process and the potential to withhold cooperation. Thus both parties are in a position to exert influence throughout the project, although the relative balance changed in favour of the researcher as the project evolved.

Academic expectations

The relationship between students and supervisors is an obvious power dynamic, but there are many other dynamics within the academic world. Research councils exert influence on the direction of research through control of funds; disciplinary associations determine quality criteria in their own fields; journal editors, referees and conference organizers act as final arbiters of academic quality; and senior academics control career rewards. In almost all circumstances, members of the academic community operate with a high degree of probity and professionalism; nevertheless, given the amount of competition for relatively few prizes, there are bound to be criteria and processes which are not totally transparent. Our aim in this section of the chapter is to make these relationships and criteria more visible.

Funding bodies

Academic funding bodies, such as research councils, have to respond to political pressures from the governments that fund them. A common response is to target resources towards specific initiatives such as entrepreneurship or competitiveness. At the present time, political pressures in the UK are demanding that government-funded research should demonstrate usefulness, which means that user engagement is very much on the agenda.

But there is also a danger if funding becomes *too* responsive to political priorities and pressures, because research results may be used by one group directly to harm another group, and it is very easy for researchers to become compromised in the process. An extreme example of this is the work carried out by scientists in Nazi Germany on concentration camp inmates. The majority of those involved appeared to be highly principled, as scientists, and strongly denied any anti-Semitism. Yet in a review of a careful study of surviving evidence, Billig (1988: 476) comments:

In Murderous Science, we see academics continually writing grant applications, guessing what projects the controllers of the funding agencies will be considering socially useful: is it the Gypsies, or the degenerates, or the ability to withstand cold, which will bring the grants this year?

He who pays the piper not only calls the tune, but can also define what a good tune is. One hopes that exercises such as these would never take place in or around modern organizations. But the personal and social consequences of losing a power struggle, or a job, can be very profound indeed. Researchers should therefore be very wary of the ends that they may be serving, and this is why increasing attention must be given to ethical issues, as we will see later in this chapter.

Funding bodies always receive more proposals than they can accommodate. Proposals in the UK are given an *alpha* rating if the independent referees consider them to be technically worthy of funding, but the ESRC only has funds for around 20 per cent of the alpha-rated proposals, and so it has to take into account other criteria such as the track record of applicants. This is an advantage for established professors, but a major obstacle for the newcomer. Hence we offer some advice to newcomers wishing to get their feet on the ladder:

- Start with modest-sized proposals.[1]
- Make the best use of your own experience through highlighting any related work or publications you may have.
- Get known by key people in the field by going to conferences and submitting papers for publication.
- Take the opportunity to attend workshops that provide guidance on crafting proposals.[2]
- Make use of networks, possibly by submitting proposals jointly with people who are already established, and by sending drafts to potential referees. In both of these cases, senior colleagues may be able to act as brokers by establishing initial contacts, or they may be willing to collaborate directly.

Supervisors and institutions

For those working on projects or research degrees, the main pressures come from supervisors, colleagues and gatekeepers. At the undergraduate level, supervisors will sometimes use their personal contacts in local firms to identify viable projects. More commonly, the sourcing of projects is left to a specialist department which has to make sure that the project meets the requirements of the company. Research degree supervisors worry about whether parts of the thesis will be publishable, possibly as joint papers between the student and the supervisor(s); they also worry increasingly about completion rates because both they and their institutions get judged on these factors.

The rise of professional doctorates in subjects such as education, psychology, social administration and business has added another dimension to the work of business schools. In our view they offer a distinct opportunity for working on the relationship of theory to practice. Students are encouraged to produce their results for both academic and practitioner audiences through conference presentations and journal articles. These professional specialisms have the distinct advantage that students find it much easier to obtain research access, because they already have both experience and contacts.

---

[1]Most research councils have schemes that fund relatively small grants (say, up to £100,000) which are available exclusively to younger researchers who have never received grants before. Individual universities often have much smaller 'starter grants' of £3,000 to £10,000.
[2]The British Academy of Management runs excellent workshops on grant applications every year.

House style

Academic departments usually have their own house styles, which support and encourage particular kinds of work, whether quantitative or qualitative, and there is also much pressure on departments to prioritize their research interests. This can make it hard to find the right supervisors and examiners. The ideal external examiner not only needs to share the same research philosophy as the candidate, but also needs to know a lot about the subject of investigation. It is advisable in most cases to start looking for potential external examiners at a fairly early stage in a research degree. This helps to focus the research project, because it requires the candidate to be clear about the boundaries of the field in which he or she is operating, and also to know who are the key movers and shakers in the field. Although the supervisor will need to approach the external examiner, it is important that the candidate is able to provide a list of potential examiners. If the candidate does not have such a list, it is a worrying sign because it suggests he or she may not be sufficiently on top of the field.

Conferences

As we have mentioned above, conferences provide a valuable form of contact within the academic community, and it is essential for anyone doing a doctorate to get onto the right conference circuits. Some conferences are not too competitive, and will accept papers on the basis of 1,000-word abstracts; those that are more competitive, such as the US or British Academies of Management, often run a separate conference for doctoral researchers who may not have succeeded in getting papers accepted for the main conference. The British Academy of Management also offers some very attractive funding schemes for a limited number of doctoral students.

The benefits of conference participation should be obvious, but here is a list of points:

- they provide visibility for you and your ideas
- they enable you to get feedback on papers that you will subsequently submit to journals
- they enable you to identify others working in your own field
- they give access to early copies of publications that may not appear in journals within two or three years
- they help you to spot potential external examiners.

In addition, conferences act as recruitment fairs, explicitly in the USA and implicitly in the UK. Gibson Burrell (1993: 75) provides an entertaining account of how the system works at the Academy of Management Conference:

> Doctoral candidates, looking for university positions, are glaringly obvious in the hotel lobbies. The males dress in blazers and grey trousers, the women in blue suits. Prestigious professors dress in Bermuda shorts and sandals. One's position in the hierarchy therefore is marked by dress, so the 'smarter' the attire, the lower is one's standing.

We offer this quote partly for those who agonize over what to wear at conferences – the message being to dress down rather than up – but also to highlight aspects of power within the academic game, which is often expressed through (not so subtle) symbols. And if you are tempted to wear Bermuda shorts and Hawaiian T-shirts, remember that they should be well ironed.

Corporate stakeholders

We use the term 'corporate' loosely here, to include companies, public organizations and others generally within the user community. These are becoming very significant because they are both sponsors and users of management research. Many companies invest heavily in executive education, sponsoring managers to attend MBAs and other programmes, and most of these involve projects conducted within the sponsoring organization. There is also growing interaction between companies and universities through enterprise development networks, knowledge transfer partnerships, and the sponsorship of consulting/research projects for both undergraduates and postgraduates.

Undergraduate projects

At Lancaster University, undergraduates on the Bachelor of Business Administration carry out consulting projects with local companies, which involve tackling live problems concerning human resources, marketing or internationalization. These run for about ten weeks and require both practical presentations for the companies and academic reports for the university. In the course of these projects, students have to appreciate and deal with many issues. They have to learn to manage their own time and make effective use of their own resources; they have to take responsibility for managing the relationship with the company, gaining the support both of the initial sponsor and key actors; they have to help the company work out what it actually wants from them, and then deliver it; and they have to strike a balance between producing useful consulting reports and providing good academic support for their recommendations.

In the case of postgraduate projects, there are several potential sets of expectations. A production manager attending a part-time MBA might, for example, want to set up a three-month project in the marketing department. This means that the main stakeholders will include: the project sponsor in the marketing department; the academic supervisor; the training department that has organized sponsorship in the first place; and the manager. Again, there is often tension between the sponsor who wants a solution to a problem, and the academic supervisor who will be looking for a well-argued case that uses recent literature and is supported by tangible evidence. Sometimes it is necessary to write two separate reports. Occasionally the two sets of expectations can be met with one seamless report that blends academic theory with practical action. Alternatively, there is the 'sandwich' model where the client report is prefaced by an academic introduction and literature review, and then followed by a methodological and substantive critique.

One residual consideration is whether research that is conducted for corporate clients will become 'contaminated' because of the funding relationship. There are two ways in which this might happen. As we have already noted, funders are likely to exert some influence on the direction of research and the kinds of questions that are considered to be significant. But this is likely to be the case with all forms of funded research, whether following a positivist or constructionist approach, and we think that the differences due to the presence or absence of corporate funding are merely a matter of degree. The other form of contamination may come from people within the organization deliberately feeding information into the project, which is likely to support their political agendas.

Given that contamination inevitably arises from political factors, the question is how best to deal with it? Our view is that these political factors and their consequences should not be kept hidden, rather they should be incorporated explicitly into the reports of the research process. The researcher's own interests, the process of gaining access or funds from organizations, or discussions about dissemination of results may all be relevant. Thus we would advise researchers to keep regular records not only of formal research data, but also to chronicle their own views and moods, and the processes of organizing and conducting the research. Further, we think it important that researchers are prepared to reflect critically on all of these influences on their research, and to make these thoughts available to others. As we mentioned in Chapter 7, this requires an element of reflexivity – which should increase, rather than decrease, the credibility of the results.

The subject of study

The subject or topic of study may also exert considerable influence on the nature and direction of the research enterprise. By the 'subject' we mean the problems or issues to be considered – rather than the people and data that will be looked at within the study. Each academic discipline, whether it be mathematics, engineering, sociology or organizational theory, tends to have a number of key debates and issues at any one time. There is also a tendency among researchers to follow fads and fashions with regard to both method and focus (Calhoun et al., 2011).

For example, in the early 1990s when the first edition of this book was published, some of the fashionable debates stimulated by academic management researchers in Europe were postmodernism, ethics and critiques of the enterprise culture. A decade later some of the hottest areas were the knowledge economy, globalization and e-commerce. Now there is particular interest in the rising economies of India and China, dynamic capabilities and innovation. There are clear advantages to situating one's work close to the mainstream: others will be interested in the subject, debates will be lively, and there will be conferences and special issues of journals being commissioned on the topic. On the other hand, there will be a lot of competition for space and to establish ownership of new ideas. And the fashion may also turn, so that unless the research topic is defined in a flexible way there is a danger of being stranded with good ideas and materials that excite no further interest.

A 'strategic' approach may be to try to spot issues that are currently regarded as mundane, in the hope that they will suddenly pick up interest. This is another reason for working the conference circuit to find out what the 'industry leaders' think will be important issues for the future. At a wider level, though, the focus on fashion may result in other important or 'ordinary' issues being overlooked. Very often it is the ordinary and commonplace that can be most revealing. Ryave and Schenkein (1974), for example, describe a study of the relatively trivial topic of how people walk. Their results show how a number of social rules can be identified with regard to space, control and propriety – which are by no means mundane, and which have direct relevance to architecture and the design of public spaces.

If the research is to be carried out in a corporate setting, it is always worth talking to managers and other employees to find out what they consider to be the emergent issues for them. Often practitioners are ahead of mainstream academics in identifying key problems and relevant solutions. Sometimes this can lead to tension between corporate sponsors and academic supervisors around the questions they consider to be important. But there are plenty of examples of the appropriate combination being achieved. One of our research students was asked by her sponsoring company to investigate how appraisal systems were working in practice in different parts of the company. The researcher was able to answer this practical question to the satisfaction of the company. At the same time she was able to use data from her interviews to show how organizational systems, such as appraisals, are a product of wider cultural value systems in those parts of the organization; and conversely how such systems are a channel for the transmission and articulation of value systems, particularly as defined by senior members of the organization.

EXAMPLE
5.4

Collaborative research project with engineering companies

The Knowledge and Information Management (KIM) project was funded by the Engineering and Physical Science Research Council (EPSRC) between 2006 and 2009. It involved teams from 11 universities looking at the social and technical problems of information management within engineering companies that were seeking to add a significant service element to the products that they sell. The project had a steering committee comprising representatives of 16 companies, which provided general guidance on the direction and potential outputs of the project.

There were many forms of collaboration here: between universities; between engineers and social scientists; between companies and universities; and between companies (some of which are normally in direct competition with each other). Sponsoring companies were able to exert influence by allowing research access only to those projects that had potential to contribute to the business, but they also contributed significantly to the quality of the academic debates by making presentations at the universities, and organizing workshops and seminars on their own sites.

Thus there is no particular reason why academic and practical goals should not be achieved simultaneously; indeed, as in Example 4.4, we have found that many practitioners will become enthusiastically involved in theoretical debates created from the academic perspective. Such managers are not only likely to be familiar with academic debates about culture and values; they also wish to contribute substantially to these debates. This increasingly leads to the possibility of managers, sponsors and gatekeepers being seen as collaborators in the research process itself.

POLITICS OF ACCESS

In this section we consider the politics that are involved in gaining access to research sites. We distinguish between *formal* access, which involves gaining permission from senior management to gather data from within the organization, and the *informal* process of gaining access to people and documents. Similar to Buchanan et al. (1988), we would argue for an opportunistic approach.

Most researchers seriously underestimate the amount of time and patience that can be required to gain this initial access. In the following paragraphs we provide some 'war stories' of how hard it can be, and offer some advice on how access may be eased. The good news is that there seems to be a growing acceptance of the value of in-company projects – possibly because a growing number of middle managers have now been through business schools themselves. Consequently they are not so likely to be threatened, and they may be genuinely interested in what is being investigated.

It is extremely difficult to gain access to companies out of the blue (sometimes called 'cold calling'). In our experience it is essential to start with some kind of personal contact, however tenuous. If one's supervisor or institution does not have the right links, then it is often worth trying the relevant trade or professional associations, or using contacts in related organizations. We have found associations to be very helpful here, and they rarely object to being mentioned as the source of the contact – because, of course, brokerage is the lifeblood of most trade and professional associations (see Example 5.5).

Once the initial contact has been made by phone, letter or email, the gatekeeper is likely to consider two questions: (1) is this individual, and his or her project, worth supporting; and (2) will it be possible to 'sell' to others whose cooperation is being requested? The latter question hangs on a consideration of whether the potential benefits will outweigh the likely costs, or potential risks, of the project. Given that information about costs and benefits will be very imprecise, it usually helps at this stage if:

- the project has potential relevance and benefit to the organization
- the time and resources requested are minimal
- the project appears not to be politically sensitive
- the individuals concerned and their institution have a good reputation.

Trade associations and access

EXAMPLE 5.5

Selen Kars wanted to explore dynamic capabilities in medium-sized Turkish companies. She decided to focus on three different sectors – olive oil, motor components and tourism – which represented increasing degrees of dynamism. Within each sector she needed matched pairs where two companies should be as similar to each other in all respects, except that one would have a reputation with the industry for being particularly innovative, and the other would be well known for sticking with 'traditional' methods. Accordingly, she visited the national industry association for each sector, and they helped her both to identify companies that fitted her criteria and then provided introductions to the chief executives.

However, projects can still go wrong. In a recent ESRC-funded project on the evolution of business knowledge, the research design required us to gain access to four distinct companies. Within the first six months of the project we obtained access, and had commenced fieldwork, to the first three companies – and these all yielded valuable data and stories. We also gained an official letter of invitation from the fourth company, but before we were able to arrange the first meeting our sponsor, who had written the letter, abruptly left the company. Three months later at a dinner, Mark mentioned the problem to a senior manager from the company, and she agreed to provide another introduction. We attended a meeting and presented our proposals to a new group of managers, but were informed a few weeks later that the company had taken a policy decision to engage in research links with a very small list of universities, and ours was not on that list.

A few months later Mark discovered that a Lancaster alumnus was working as PA to the UK managing director of the company. She offered to organize a meeting with the top man, which meant that we might be able to outflank the earlier policy decision. Unfortunately, a week before the meeting the company announced an international structural reorganization, which threatened the role of the UK managing director, and hence the meeting was cancelled. By this time we were three months from the end of the project and it was too late to replace that company with another company. The moral of this story is that it is always important to plan for contingencies: don't count your chickens, and keep something in reserve!

The principle of reciprocity is important: the more the company gives, in time or money, the more it expects in exchange. Another feature that is common to the above examples is that the initiative usually comes from the researcher, and organizational brokers may then be used to reach the patrons. However, there are occasions when patrons themselves may wish to initiate some research. At least six reasons for sponsoring research are common, and these are summarized in Table 5.1.

As we have suggested above, official access is only the start of the story: the next problem is to obtain cooperation and trust inside. In our experience these relationships are complex because of political issues within the organization, and we divide these into two types:

TABLE 5.1   Six Reasons Why Companies May Fund or Sponsor Research

To gain support for a new idea

To demonstrate the success of a recent project

To help the individual or unit defend against attack

To act as a sounding board

To support research for its own sake

As a means of enhancing legitimacy and reputation

micro-issues, which are about relationships between individual employees; and macro-issues, which are to do with the wider organizational politics.

At a *micro-political* level it is important to be able to develop a cooperative relationship with each informant. In our own research about knowledge management and retention in aerospace companies, informants were quite mixed and included managers, technical specialists, designers and others (Lervik et al., 2010; Fahy et al., 2014).

With most informants the relationship begins when you try to negotiate an appointment. As employees work under increasing pressure, they are becoming very protective over their time, and will make assessments of the likely costs and benefits of cooperating. Some informants will get interested in the topic during the interview and will want to keep talking, others will give very short replies, and you will wonder how you are going to get through the allotted hour. We will discuss the dynamics of field entry and interview situations in more detail in Chapters 6 and 7, but for the time being we note some of the typical problems for researchers.

EXAMPLE
5.6

Internal blockages to access

Barbara Czarniawska (1998) provides a fascinating account of her experiences in Warsaw, where she had obtained agreement to conduct a ten-day observational study of the director of finance of the city council. Most of this period seemed to be taken up with the director finding excuses not to talk to her, or to exclude her from meetings. Even when the director, in a moment of helpfulness, tried to arrange for Barbara to meet the deputy mayor, she only managed a passing contact and never managed to schedule an actual interview.

Barbara Czarniawska (see Example 5.6) is a senior professor with an international reputation, so perhaps it was hard for the director to resist her openly. With younger researchers more direct 'put downs' may be used. One technique is for the interviewee to cross-examine the interviewer at the outset in order to establish that she has very little relevant experience of the organization or context that she is apparently studying, and is very naive about the realities of anything outside the academic environment. Having established who is really in control of the interaction, the senior manager may then be prepared to sit back for 40 or 50 minutes and respond honestly to questions.

Even experienced researchers occasionally get caught out by this tactic. Beynon (1988) provides a nice example of a senior National Coal Board manager attacking the credibility of an expert academic witness involved in a colliery enquiry by asking such direct questions as: 'Are you qualified to manage a coalfield?', 'What practical management experience have you had in operating?', 'Have you any personal knowledge of selling to commercial buyers?'. This form of discrediting the external expert provides a very effective form of corporate defence, and perhaps the minor 'put downs' given to researchers by senior employees may be an anticipatory form of defence just in case the 'wrong' results are produced by the study.

Sometimes it is a *macro-political* problem, for example, when the researcher becomes trapped between two major groups or factions. When Mark Easterby-Smith was researching for his PhD he had been asked by the Works Manager of a large chemical company to conduct a study into the consequences of a large plant closure. This exercise had apparently been handled very successfully and had led to the voluntary redundancy of over 1000 workers, without any overt industrial relations strife occurring. This was exceptional at a time when industrial relations were riven with conflict.

About a week after starting the study he noticed that people were beginning to become less available for interview, especially those with access to personnel records. He was, however, very much reassured to be invited to lunch one day by a Director of the wider company. Discussion ranged over the research project which had recently started, and the manager showed much interest in some initial observations. It was later the same day that Mark met one of the personnel managers from the site who informed him regretfully that a meeting had been held that same morning to discuss the research project, and that one person who had been very insistent about stopping it was the Director with whom Mark had just dined.

This was unexpected, since nothing had been mentioned at lunchtime. It was even more surprising that the personnel manager thought there was nothing unusual about the Director's behaviour. It later emerged that the decision to ban the project was the focal point in a major battle between the Works Manager and the Director with regard to the appropriate management style on the site. The former was backing a rather paternalistic line of management, and the results of the study would no doubt have helped him in his argument. The Director was arguing for a much harder form of managerialism, and unfortunately for the research project it was an argument that the latter won. Mark was simply 'collateral damage' in this wider dispute.

The lesson from these political examples is that the researcher needs to be aware of conflicts that may be far deeper and more complex than will be evident to a relative newcomer in the organization. We can offer three pieces of advice on how to deal with such politics. First, try to identify one or two 'key informants' who may be prepared to help in a disinterested way. They need to be generally well informed but not directly concerned with the issues under investigation. Key informants may be able to advise on whom to talk to, and they should be able to explain why things are, or are not, happening. Second, deliberately look for people who have different perspectives on key issues. Talk further to them and others in order to understand *why* they hold different views. Third, always assume that there is more than meets the eye. People may withhold information because they think it is not important, or irrelevant, or they may genuinely have forgotten things. In organizations that have a policy of moving people around every two years, the collective memory may be very short. The departmental secretary may be the only person who knows that your topic has already been researched and written up twice in the last five years!

Role-play about access

Your group has the possibility of being given access to a local internet company, which sells broadband and associated services to small- and medium-sized businesses across the country. The task is to conduct fieldwork into 'leadership', and you

EXERCISE 5.1

(Continued)

(Continued)

need to complete a number of interviews in a real organization in order to complete your assignment. The initial contact with the company is through the training manager, and she has arranged for a meeting with the chief executive to discuss the possible research. The meeting will take place on site, and the chief executive has a busy schedule. He has also indicated that he would like to see just two members of the team on this first instance.

Roles

- *Student 1, student 2*: Their aim is to gain access on behalf of their colleagues for a project that both fits their academic needs and is also ethically acceptable.
- *Chief executive*: He is prepared to provide access providing the project uses minimal resources/time, offers some potential benefit to the company, and carries absolutely no risks for the company or individuals within it.
- *Training manager*: She is a former employee of the university at which the students are studying, but her own position in the company is slightly insecure.
- *Other group members*: Should act as observers during the role-play and as facilitators of the debrief afterwards.

Role-playing process

The chief executive is in control of the meeting throughout. He has given himself 15 minutes in which to make a decision about whether or not to let the students in.

Timescale

- 15 minutes: preparation. Student representatives; CEO and training manager; observers to discuss in separate groups their agendas and how they will handle/monitor the role-play.
- 15 minutes: role-play.
- 20 minutes: debrief. To be chaired/facilitated by the observers. Try to cover: pre-meeting strategies of different parties; degree of satisfaction with the outcome; what was unexpected; general lessons learnt about the process of access.

ETHICS

There are ethical issues bubbling under the surface of many of the examples we have given above. In this section we focus on the ethical issues which can arise when doing research into management and business. We start with a brief overview of the historical evolution of ethics; then we look at the kind of ethical problems that are most commonly encountered in organizational research; and we finish with a critical review of the measures that universities are introducing to ensure that staff and student behaviour is ethical when conducting research.

History and evolution of ethical concepts and practices

The Greeks were the first people to write about ethics. Philosophers like Socrates, Plato and Aristotle spent much of their time discussing whether there could be principles to guide the moral behaviour of people, and if so, what form these principles might take. Socrates was one of the first philosophers to tackle problems of day-to-day life, and was particularly keen to focus on topics which could engage the imagination of normal people, such as the mutual responsibilities of people within the same city or country. Plato followed on and in his numerous books both represented Socrates' views and also developed his own ideas. Arguably, the most important of his books was *The Republic*, which outlines an ideal city with a class structure, and defines the moral obligations between members of different classes towards each other.

Aristotle went one better, because not only did he publish a book specifically about ethics (*Nichomachean Ethics*), but he was also given the role of tutoring the young prince who subsequently became Alexander the Great.[3] He also developed the view we would recognize today as self-actualization. The essence of this is that each individual would both be personally content and be doing good, if they strived to make the best of their given talents and should try to achieve their full potential. Alexander had conquered half of the known world by the age of 33, so he must have paid great attention to the lessons with his tutor!

The other enormous influence on present thinking about ethics in research is Hippocrates, a doctor also from the 5th Century BC. The Hippocratic Oath is still extremely important for modern doctors, although it contains within it clear opposition to invasive surgery, including aiding in 'assisted' suicides, or abortions (issues that remain highly divisive among doctors and the general public). So it is not surprising that when it comes to modern research ethics, the medical people are well in the lead as a discipline. This means that the medical model of ethics tends to dominate those developed more recently by scientists and social scientists.

Current issues

These are of particular concern in the medical sciences because of the danger that experiments might be conducted that would bring genuine harm to participants, and also because of the enormous financial muscle of commercial funding bodies such as drug companies, which might well seek to influence results in directions that would give an advantage to their products.

The serious outbreak of the Ebola virus in West Africa during the summer of 2014 (see Figure 5.2) has led to ethical dilemmas (which are ongoing at the time of writing). So far there is only one drug that has been developed to deal with Ebola and it has not yet been tested on humans. Initial stocks of the drug have been given, with some success, to four western aid workers, and shortly there will be the possibility of extending the treatment to larger populations of Africans, with or without their consent.

This leads to a number of ethical questions. First, is it ethically fair that the drug should be made available to Western visitors but is not yet available to locals? Second, would it be right to distribute a drug which has not been clinically tested to large numbers of people already infected? Third, although new drugs may only be tested on humans in developed countries if the patients have given their 'informed consent' in advance, should this also apply in a non-developed country where the survival rate for victims is less than 50 per cent, and most of them are highly superstitious about the disease?

Ethical codes and principles in business and management research

Although management and business researchers generally do not undertake studies which could put at risk the lives of those who take part, many of the principles discussed above still

[3]For an account of this, see: http://books.google.co.uk/books?id=37kerL_zdJUC&lpg=PR11&ots=GpoViNVh-z&dq=aristotle%20tutor%20prince%20Alexander%20the%20Great%20%20&lr&pg=PP1#v=onepage&q=aristotle%20tutor%20prince%20Alexander%20the%20Great&f=false

FIGURE 5.2
Nurses in Liberia briefing the public about the risks

apply. Certainly, research could lead to economic harm through plant closures or changes in work patterns or payment systems. Informed consent and the right of confidentiality are also just as important for management and business research as they are in medical research. Up until about ten years ago, management researchers, and their professional associations such as the British Academy of Management and the (American) Academy of Management, were relatively relaxed about the provision of ethical codes. But there is growing pressure from other academic disciplines, such as medicine and psychology, for all universities to adopt definite ethical codes and practices, and there is growing coherence, especially in the social sciences, around a common set of principles. Bell and Bryman (2007) conducted a content analysis of the ethical principles of nine professional associations in the social sciences. They identified ten principles of ethical practice, which were defined by at least half of the associations. These principles are summarized in Table 5.2.

Essentially, the first six of these principles are about protecting the interests of the research subjects or informants; the last four are intended to protect the integrity of the research community, through ensuring accuracy and lack of bias in research results.

TABLE 5.2 Key principles in research ethics

1	Ensuring that **no harm** comes to participants.	*Protection of research participants*
2	Respecting the **dignity** of research participants.	
3	Ensuring a fully **informed** consent of research participants.	
4	Protecting the **privacy** of research participants.	
5	Ensuring the **confidentiality** of research data.	
6	Protecting the **anonymity** of individuals or organizations.	
7	**Avoiding** deception about the nature or aims of the research.	*Protection of integrity of research community*
8	Declaration of affiliations, funding sources and **conflicts** of interest.	
9	Honesty and **transparency** in communicating about the research.	
10	Avoidance of any **misleading** or false reporting of research findings.	

(ADAPTED FROM BELL AND BRYMAN, 2007)

The circumstances of management and business research are largely similar to the social sciences in general, but are distinct in one important respect, which we have already mentioned. Although the interests of informants still need to be protected, it can no longer be assumed that the researcher is in the all-powerful position held by clinical and social researchers. Indeed, when research is conducted into companies, it is the researcher who is often the least powerful party to the transaction.

While researchers should normally protect interests of the organizations they are investigating, there may be times when they come across illegal or unethical behaviour within the organizations themselves – and some people would argue that this should be published in a way that will expose the organization. An extreme example of this would be the case of Julian Assange who, between 2006 and 2010, took on the might of the US military and State Department by publishing over a million secret documents on his website, WikiLeaks. Consequently he is still in hiding in the Ecuadorean embassy in London.

The debate about whether or not Assange was morally justified in what he did has been highly divisive. So, even though most organizational research is on a far more modest scale, it becomes difficult to establish hard-and-fast ethical principles, and good practice requires considerable judgement from the researcher.

There are three main areas where management researchers are likely to get into trouble. The first refers to the use of participant observation research methods, which, as Ditton (1977) says, are essentially deceitful. That is, if you are participating in a situation, and at the same time observing and recording (perhaps later) what has taken place, you cannot avoid some deception about your real purposes. Although, as will be seen in Chapter 7, observations do not have to involve deception. Our preference is to be as open as possible when people ask challenging questions about the purpose of the research, for two main reasons: first, because they may well be interested in the nature of the research and might have valuable insights into what you are investigating; and second, because if they suspect that you are withholding information they are most unlikely to be cooperative if you ask for their help. Trust is important.

The second is about trade-offs when conducting fieldwork. Within organizations there is always the possibility of betraying the confidences given by employees if one comes under pressure from senior managers. Informants who are politically adept can often read a great deal into the questions that the interviewer is asking. For example, on one occasion, one of the authors happened to be interviewing the head of a national investigatory organization about the longer-term effects of a particular management development programme. He asked a carefully focused question about how the reward system was working, to which the director immediately came back with: 'I take it you have been talking to John Dawson about that … Well in that case …' Even though most managers are not professionally trained as investigators, they will often be able to work out the nature and sources of information already collected by researchers who are sufficiently unfamiliar with the detailed political context of the organization to be aware of the significance of the questions that they are asking.

The third ethical issue is around the control and use of data obtained by the researcher. In most cases he or she has control and ownership of the data, and therefore must exercise due ethical responsibility by not publicizing or circulating any information that is likely to harm the interests of individual informants, particularly the less powerful ones. There is an interesting story, however, where this particular assumption was neatly turned upon its head. A senior British professor happened to be interviewing a royal duke, and at the end of the interview he offered to have the tape transcribed and to send a transcript to the interviewee who could then strike out any passages to which he objected, whereupon the Duke stretched out a hand saying 'No. I shall retain the tape and will let you have the portions that I am prepared to have published.'

Finally, there is an ongoing debate about the value, or otherwise, of ethical codes in relation to research. It is argued that at least some codes need to be made explicit in order to ensure that people are alerted to some of the likely ethical dilemmas that they may face. Such codes should also provide some kind of sanction in cases of blatant abuse and exploitation. But there is a problem here. As Snell (1993) points out, ethical issues are extremely complex. They involve not only the dynamics of power but also the competing claims of different ideologies. The danger is that ethical guidelines will not only be too rigid and simplistic to deal with real cases, they will also contain the biases that are inherent in one or another ideological position.

Mason (1996) and Bell and Bryman (2007) make similar points about ethical codes being generally written in abstract terms, aimed at preventing serious and unambiguous cases of abuse. The problem is that most of the ethical issues faced by the researcher are small-scale, incremental and ambiguous. Mason argues that researchers should operate as thinking, reflective practitioners who are prepared to ask difficult questions about the ethics and politics of their own research practice on a regular basis. Although ethical review procedures have been criticized for being overly bureaucratic, they can help students and researchers to reflect on critical issues.

Ethics in business and management research

Most universities in the UK have listened to the criticisms about bureaucracy and inflexibility with ethical reviews, and have responded by allowing departments and faculties to develop their own procedures with regard to ethical clearance. They have also encouraged self-assessment wherever possible.

At the universities where we work, for example, all students (and staff) who are involved in research that collects data from human 'subjects' are required to follow a two-stage process during the early stages of their work. The first stage consists of a multiple-choice questionnaire and acts as a diagnostic filter: in the vast majority of projects in management and business there will be minimal risk and the form gets signed off by the supervisor. If any of the answers at stage one suggest the possibility of risk, then there is a more detailed second-stage form to be completed, and if there are serious doubts then the project will have to be reviewed by the central ethics committee.

The chief value of these procedures is that they provide formal encouragement for researchers to start thinking of possible ethical issues before they arise. The big problem with this approach is that it is built around the model of scientific research where the full research design must be specified *before* the research is conducted. It is less helpful for management and business researchers who use methods that have emergent designs which evolve, sometimes in an opportunistic way, as the project progresses.

Summary, and a way forward

We have argued in this chapter that most organizational research will have some political dimension to it. We have summarized the various ways that different 'stakeholders' may want to influence the direction and outcomes from research. We then looked at the key problem of access and provided some advice on how to increase the chances of getting past the gatekeepers. Now we have just been looking at some ethical dilemmas and at the principals and codes that may be introduced to deal with them.

By way of a summary we have put together Table 5.3 which summarizes the main stages in a student project and the possible ethical dilemmas that may arise in each of these stages.

TABLE 5.3 Main Project Stages and Ethical Issues that might arise

	Potential Problems	Ethical Responses	Grey areas/Issues that might raise concern
Stage 1 *Determining the direction*	Undue pressure from tutor or sponsor to fit with their ideas.	You write the proposal and present for ethical clearance.	Clarify stakeholders' interests. Negotiate between what you and they want.
Stage 2 *Gaining access*	Try to avoid deception when proposing your research. It can be difficult to define privacy and confidentiality for individuals and host organization.	Frame the relationship with the company in non-judgemental terms. Introduce principle of informed consent for all individuals. Preparation of access proposal (see Chapter 7).	Quid pro quo: what does the organization want in exchange for access?
Stage 3: *Gathering and interpreting data*	Organizational politics and conflicts can inhibit access and lead to biased accounts. Interviewees may withhold information or they may try to mislead you. Certain questions can reveal the identity of informants.	Be sensitive to the context of your research including organizational politics and potential conflicts of interests. Look out for areas of agreement and disagreement. If everyone tells the same story, be suspicious.	Try to cultivate someone (maybe your gate keeper) who can interpret information you are receiving if it doesn't 'add up'…
Stage 4 *Writing-up and dissemination*	You might publish information that could harm both the company and/or individuals within it.	Stick to all confidentiality/anonymization requirements, especially for individuals. Consider carefully the key principles listed in Table 4.2 before disseminating any results.	Check through data to ensure that it doesn't reveal the identity of respondents. Send drafts of reports and publications to the company and ask them to let you know if there are any problems (within 2–4 weeks if possible).

CONCLUSION

At this point we can identify some general implications for the researcher:

 It is important to recognize that power and political issues will be significant even when they are not obviously present.

 There are no easy answers, nor solutions, to the political web. It exists in the form of ideologies, of personal interests, of power differences and of ethical dilemmas.

 The researcher needs both clarity of purpose and much flexibility in tackling problems.

 Clarity of purpose can come from self-awareness of one's own interests and assumptions about the world, and these can be incorporated into reflexive accounts.

We have discussed the issues of ontology, epistemology, research design, politics and ethics in the last three chapters. In the next part of the book we consider the range of methods and techniques that are at the disposal of the researcher. We stress consistently that these should not be seen as entirely free-standing: they should be subordinated to the considerations of purpose and philosophy, which have been outlined above.

EXERCISE
5.2

Political dilemmas in conducting student project (group discussion)

You have to do an in-company project as part of the assessment for your degree. Your tutor has arranged access to a local supermarket to investigate the quality of customer relations, and the contact, who is deputy manager, has suggested that you talk to members of two departments: one appears to be very successful, and the other is regarded as problematic. Here are some possible scenarios. What would you do?

1. When you arrive for the initial meeting with the deputy manager you are informed that she has been called on urgent business to the regional head office and cannot see you.

2. When you meet the deputy manager she asks you to sign a non-disclosure agreement.

3. During a one-to-one interview with a checkout assistant she comments that there have been incidents of sexual harassment in her department. What do you do with this information, if anything?

4. After conducting a number of interviews in both departments the deputy manager asks you for your opinion of the qualities of both supervisors.

5. During the project, one team member persistently fails to pull his weight. How do you deal with this?

FURTHER READING

Bell, E. and Bryman, A. (2007) 'The ethics of management research: an exploratory content analysis', *British Journal of Management*, 18 (1), 63–77.

    The authors suggest that management researchers face ethical issues that are distinct from those encountered by other social science researchers. They provide a review of ethics codes formulated by nine social scientific associations, and argue that reciprocity is a central principle for management research.

Buchanan, D. and Badham, R. (2008) *Power, Politics and Organizational Change: Winning the Turf Game*, 2nd edn. London: Sage.

    This edition, which focuses on how managers can act as internal change agents, emphasizes the contexts in which they initiate and achieve change. It provides an accessible overview of organizational politics, which is useful for the researcher both in conducting and implementing research.

Saunders, M., Lewis, P. and Thornhill, A. (2012) *Research Methods for Business Students*, 6th edn. Harlow: Pearson.

    This is a competitor textbook which provides an extensive discussion of ethics and access in Chapter 6 (pp. 208–57). Somewhat less coverage of politics, though.

Want to know more about this chapter? Visit the $SAGE edge˚ website at **https://edge.sagepub.com/easterbysmith** to access practice questions, selected journal articles, useful web links and much more.

CRAFTING QUALITATIVE DATA THROUGH LANGUAGE AND TEXT

6

LEARNING OBJECTIVES

 To gain an overview and general understanding of different approaches and methods for collecting qualitative data through language and text, and to appreciate their advantages and disadvantages.

 To get practical insights into how to prepare for the collection of qualitative data using language and text.

 To learn about how to plan qualitative interviews and focus groups, and to become aware of the skills needed to conduct such interviews.

Many of the approaches that are included in this chapter are quite loosely specified. This offers researchers considerable opportunity to use their creative abilities. We have attempted to move away from presenting a simple list of methods and have instead grouped them into headings that depict the basic approaches that are available. We examine a number of approaches and techniques for creating qualitative data. Today, management researchers have an astonishing array of inquiry approaches at their disposal.

In the first of the two chapters, we give a general introduction to qualitative data collection, followed by a more in-depth discussion of approaches that create information (data) through language and text. **Natural language data** can be collected from individuals and groups of individuals whether they are managers or employees. In management research, language data are used to gain insights into social and organizational realities. This takes place through discovering the views, perceptions and opinions of both individuals and groups through the language they use in conversation as well as in writing. The main methods to achieve this are the **in-depth qualitative interview** and participatory methods based on interviews, such as mapping and repertory-grid techniques. Valuable information can also be gained from diaries and the examination of a range of textual data, such as company reports and written correspondence.

In Chapter 7, we explore a different range of approaches for creating qualitative data through observation and interaction, such as observational, ethnographic and participatory techniques. Here, the ways in which data are collected are rather different; they include the examination and understanding of symbols, settings and observations in a context. There are various methods that fall into this category, including visual methods, participant observation and the researcher interacting closely and directly, and cooperating with, individuals or groups.

Both chapters contain sections that look at some general issues that surround qualitative methods of data collection. In Chapter 6, we discuss practical issues surrounding the preparation of interviews; in Chapter 7, we include a brief discussion of the use of case studies, field access, confidentiality, and the necessity of reflexivity of the researcher's own involvement. Then in Chapter 8, we discuss strategies for data management and present different approaches for framing and analysing qualitative data.

CRAFTING QUALITATIVE DATA

Qualitative data are pieces of information gathered in a non-numeric form. The most common types of qualitative data are accounts of what research participants have said or done; for example, interview recordings and transcripts, written notes of observations, and images, videos and documents (e.g. company reports and meeting minutes). Qualitative data can be defined by their form (non-numeric) and by the interactive and interpretative process in which they are created. Contrary to what the term 'data collection' suggests, data rarely are discovered and collected like mushrooms. More often than not, qualitative data have to be developed by the researcher: interviews must be prepared for, conducted and transcribed; pictures must be taken; and field notes must be written. It is the process of creating qualitative data that will be explored here and in the following chapter. The creation of quantitative data will be covered in Chapters 9, 10 and 11.

While there is some overlap between some of the techniques used by qualitative and quantitative researchers, it must be noted that the strategy of data creation, and its degree of standardization and structuration, vary in significant ways. Qualitative research tends to be of a more explorative nature and involves open-ended rather than pre-coded questions and responses. This makes it important to record the entire interaction between researcher and research participant. The lack of standardization of many techniques for creating qualitative data restricts the numbers of individuals or organizations an individual researcher can work with; it also limits the aggregation of data and the use of statistical comparisons.

There are different ways of categorizing the impressive array of methods and approaches for the creation of qualitative data. In this book, we discuss different approaches along two dimensions: first, we distinguish methods that aim primarily at the collection and creation of textual/language data from those that aim at observational/interactive data; and second, we consider the extent to which the process of data creation requires the active involvement of the researcher. For example, when collecting existing reports or videos, researchers have little influence on their content. However, if the reports are written by the researchers themselves and the videos are co-produced in a joint endeavour with research participants, researchers gain a more direct influence over the form and content of the data they later analyse. This does not imply that qualitative data created by the researchers themselves are more or less valuable or useful. Nonetheless, the mode of data creation has important implications for how data should be analysed and presented. In the remaining sections of this chapter, we discuss a number of approaches to collecting and creating qualitative data through *language and text*, starting with more passive forms of collecting existing **secondary data**, such as company reports and letters. We then move towards more interactive forms of creating **primary data**, such as field diaries. The main emphasis of the chapter then shifts to **qualitative interviews** and interview-based participatory techniques.

TEXTUAL DATA

Secondary textual data are written sources of information produced for a purpose other than research but with some relevance to a given research project. Secondary data sources include company and government reports, archival data, advertisements, newspaper articles, books and blogs. They can provide information related to a specific company, market, customer, product or supplier. Search engines on the Internet can facilitate the quest for secondary sources. Secondary data are often used to complement primary data (such as interviews), and sometimes data consist only of secondary sources.

The advantages of secondary data are, first, savings in time and effort for the researcher. Second, the data sources often appear to be of high quality, especially when published by firms and governments. However, notwithstanding an excellent first impression, one should always critically evaluate the sources of secondary data and assess their credibility. Third, secondary data can open up a historical perspective to a given project, which might not be feasible through the collection of primary data. The main difference between secondary data and primary data is that primary data are collected by the researcher and thus may better aid data collection in respect to the research questions. The main disadvantage of secondary sources is that the data do not necessarily fit into the research we want to investigate. Therefore, it is essential to let the research questions guide and frame the data – and not the other way round (Ghauri and Grønhaug, 2010). The collection of some secondary textual data, such as internal reports or written correspondence, can require the development of a strong and trusted relationship between the researcher and the research participant who has access to these texts. Such a relationship might be developed during interviews, participant observation and action research. Whatever method is chosen, the processes of data creation through language and text require a fair amount of strategic thinking and planning that goes beyond the development of an appropriate research design (see Chapter 2).

EXERCISE
6.1

Gathering secondary data

a) **Interactive exercise**: When thinking of secondary data, most of us think about company reports, but individuals and organizations produce all kinds of written documents that are rarely analysed. For example, complaint letters can tell us a lot about stakeholder relations, and seasonal greetings can reflect a firm's values, as can its guidelines and manuals for employees. In pairs, prepare a list of unusual secondary sources that could be analysed for a management research project. Who came up with the most innovative ideas? Whose suggestions are the most practical?

b) **Individual and interactive exercise**: Conduct a search for corporate sustainability reports online, and select and download three of them. (Many firms post such reports or reviews on their websites.) Examine their content, make a list of the issues covered, and identify who has authored them. In class, discuss what we could learn from an analysis of these reports. How important is it to consider authorship when analysing secondary data?

Diary methods

In contrast to research aiming at the collection and analysis of secondary data, primary research aims at the creation of original (primary) data. A useful – but rather unusual – technique for creating *primary textual data* is the use of diaries. There is quite a long history of diary methods in the UK, one of the most interesting examples being the Mass Observation studies during the Second World War. Here, a substantial number of ordinary people (including Nella Last, subject of the TV dramatization *Housewife 49*) were recruited to keep diaries of everything they did for one day each month, and to report on specific days, such as bank holidays. Analysis of these diaries was intended to show how the British population in general was reacting to different aspects of the war (Calder and Sheridan, 1984). Diaries can be either quantitative or qualitative, depending on the kind of information that is recorded. They can be useful in management and organizational research on a number of levels. At one level, diary-keeping by organizational members can provide a simple journal or record of events. A quantitative analysis might take the form of activity sampling, from which patterns may be identified statistically. This approach is sometimes used by management-services practitioners who wish to measure the frequency of certain activities so that they can reorganize or 'improve' the work. At other times, it is used by managers to reflect on aspects of their own work, as in time-management analysis (see, for example, Stewart, 1967, 1982). At another level, diaries might take the form of a personal journal of the research process, and include emergent ideas and results, reflections on personal learning, and an examination of personal attitudes and values, which may be important at the data-analysis and writing-up stages. At yet another level, diaries can provide a rich qualitative picture of motives and perspectives, allowing the researcher to gain considerable insight into situations being examined. It is this latter use of a diary that we wish to explore in a little more detail here.

There are a number of advantages to using diaries. First, they provide a useful method for collecting data from the perspective of the employee. In participant observation, researchers cannot help to some extent imposing their own reference frame as the data are collected, but in a diary study, the data are collected and presented largely within the reference frame of the diary-writer. Second, a diary approach allows the perspectives of several different writers to be compared and contrasted simultaneously, and it allows the researcher greater freedom to move from one situation or organization to another. Third, diaries allow the researcher to collect other relevant data while the study is in progress and to carry out much more analysis than would be possible for the participant observer in the course of fieldwork. There is the opportunity to collect information not only from the perspectives of different individuals, but also through using different data sources. Finally, although diary studies do not allow for the same interaction and questioning, they can sometimes be an alternative to participant observation when, for example, it is impractical for a researcher to invest the time in an extended longitudinal study as observer.

A number of important lessons were learnt from a multiple diary study conducted by Bowey and Thorpe (1986) in an English coal mine during a national study into incentive schemes. These lessons are described in Example 6.1.

EXAMPLE 6.1

Diary study of incentive schemes

First, it was found to be important to select participants who were able to express themselves well in writing. In cases where a group of associates had been asked to keep a diary and where there was doubt about one member's writing ability, a judgement had to be made as to the likely consequences of the individual taking offence if excluded. Second, some structure was found necessary to give the diarist focus. To assist this, a list of general headings developed from an earlier pilot study was provided:

Please write about the following:

1. Your relationships with other people, including your supervisor, your workmates, anyone you supervise, and other people you come into contact with.

2. Any particular difficulties you encountered during the day with machinery, raw materials or people.

3. Whether the incentive bonus scheme affected you at work, and if so in what way.

4. Anything that you were especially pleased about or that made you feel angry.

5. Anything else you feel is important, especially if it has something to do with the incentive bonus scheme.

A third lesson highlighted was the need for continued encouragement and reassurance during the study. An earlier pilot study had left diarists very much to their own devices, and they had continued to write for only four to six weeks. In the main study, where regular contact was maintained and feedback given in the form of additional questions or clarifications, almost two-thirds of the sample kept writing into the third month, and more than one-quarter completed the full three-month period. An improvement we might have made would have been to supplement the diaries with interviews. This would have enhanced the effect of maintaining interest, as well as providing the opportunity to probe areas of interest further.

Fourth, the importance of the need for confidentiality was confirmed. In a pilot study, jotters had been issued to record instances that occurred during the day, and this had led to problems. One particularly uncomplimentary entry in a respondent's jotter had been left in an accessible place and was read by the person described. This caused the relationships between the two people to be soured, even though thoughts entered 'in the heat of the moment' did not generally reflect the opinions of the individual. It was therefore decided that, even at the cost of a loss of spontaneity, it was preferable for diaries to be written up away from the workplace.

Finally, the study confirmed individuals' willingness to cooperate at every level, and their enthusiasm for doing so. There was no evidence to justify the view that individuals might be nervous of participating in this kind of research. The experience showed that there was more nervousness among the researchers themselves who felt that they 'dare not ask' or that asking people to maintain a diary for up to three months would be unacceptable to those under study.

Source: Bowey and Thorpe, 1986

All diarists in the study described above (including those who stopped writing before the end of the three-month period) maintained that they had welcomed the opportunity to express their feelings, observations and opinions about their life and work to somebody who was interested. All maintained that they enjoyed writing them, and some confided that they were flattered that outsiders were taking an interest in them as individuals. No payment or other inducements were made, although pens and folders were regularly provided. This was sufficient reward for many, and it shows how important it is to find out what individuals wish to gain from participating in the research. The practicalities of undertaking diary research are fully discussed in Bowey and Thorpe (1986).

Keeping a research diary

EXERCISE
6.2

a) **Individual exercise**: It is a good idea to keep a research diary in which you record the current stage of your research, your ideas about what is emerging that might represent findings, and your contribution – as well as how you are currently feeling about the research. If there are difficult issues in relation to the research process, these should also be recorded.

b) **Interactive exercise**: In pairs, discuss whether you think keeping a research diary could help you, particularly in relation to your research approach.

Written correspondence

Postcards, *e-postcards* and *emails* can also be used to create and gather primary textual data; they can also provide a means of overcoming some of the recognized difficulties of organizational research, such as problems of access (Thorpe and Holt, 2008). Postcards combine elements of asynchronous mediated interviews with a research strategy that can also be used for short quantitative surveys. A postcard is designed as the traditional postcard from the nineteenth century, with a picture, addressee and sender details, and a few questions with space to answer these. The picture is often a metaphor of the research, or of something that can be associated and related to the research topic. The postcard design attracts immediate attention and has an easy structure. It is simple and quick for the respondent to answer a few questions and send the card back to the researcher. The response time is shorter with e-postcards than with mailed postcards. The use of e-postcards can also save money if they are sent to a large sample. One further advantage of this method is that the data arrive 'transcribed'; that is, in written form, ready for the researcher to start the analysis. Figure 6.1 illustrates how a postcard can take form.

Diaries, letters and postcards used to be 'hard copy' ways of creation of a wide range of primary textual data. More recently, e-postcards, blogs, emails, Twitter, Instagram and WhatsApp offer new opportunities for data collection. They give evidence to the rapidly changing ways in which we communicate, and illustrate how new information technologies enable innovative research strategies and methods for data collection (Fielding et al., 2008). Whereas, in the past, data collection based on asynchronous written communication (such as letters) appeared to be quite a traditional undertaking, the development of social networking and video conferencing has reduced the gap between the creation of textual data and interviewing techniques.

QUALITATIVE INTERVIEWS

Qualitative interviews are directed conversations evolving around questions and answers about a certain topic (Lofland and Lofland, 1984). Interviews differ from everyday conversations in that they are based on series of questions that follow a particular purpose,

Images of Britain: Stonehenge – Just a bunch of old stones or a pinnacle of human achievement in astronomy, engineering and spiritual insight?

Please answer the four questions below by clicking on and typing in the spaces and return as an email attachment to Professor Richard Thorpe at rt@lubs.leeds.ac.uk. **Many thanks**

What do you regard as your ultimate goal in business?	To be well known as excellent in ability to challenge thinking and develop the true potential of others, in a variety of ways, while enhancing my own life situation.
Why is this your goal?	Because I have realized that this is what I have always wanted to do from being a small child, and because it gives me great 'job' satisfaction.
Who/what helps or hinders you in reaching your goal?	Who/what helps? Having time allocated separately from family life helps me to focus on what needs doing My new found ability to strike up relationships and make opportunities by just ringing people up Persistence and determination Listening to what others say and then if necessary ignoring it Belief that I am doing the right thing for me at this time Finding a network of like-minded people Who/what hinders? Organizing house and family Working alone
If you could picture your goal – what image or object would best symbolize it?	It would be a purple shiny runner bean seed – which embodies the development and growth which I support in every area of my life, from my garden to my business to my family and in my art-work.

(GOLD, 2008: 159)

FIGURE 6.1
Postcards

usually the in-depth exploration of a particular topic or experience (Charmaz, 2014). An interview is always contextual and negotiated, and – in contrast to an interrogation – its purpose has to be negotiated between the interviewee and the interviewer. As noted by Tracy (2013: 132), 'interviews provide opportunities for mutual discovery, understanding, reflection, and explanation […] and elucidate subjectively lived experiences and viewpoints.' Interviews therefore enable researchers to access information in context, and to learn about phenomena otherwise difficult or impossible to observe.

The label 'qualitative interview' has been used to describe a broad range of different interviewing techniques, from those that are supposedly totally non-directive, or open, to those where the interviewers have prepared a list of questions, which they are determined to ask, come what may. While, as Jones (1985) outlines, there is a range of practices – and therefore theory – between these two extremes of interviewing technique, the main aim of qualitative interviewing is generally seen as attempting to gain an understanding from the respondent's perspective, which includes not only what their viewpoint is but also why they hold this particular viewpoint (King, 2004). As Kvale and Brinkmann (2009) note, the aim of qualitative interviews should be to collect information that captures the meaning and interpretation of phenomena in relation to the interviewees' worldviews (see Chapter 8, on phenomenographic analysis). Researchers must therefore be able to conduct interviews so that the opportunity is present for these insights to be gained. Failure to achieve this might well result in a superficial exchange of information, which might have been better achieved via a semi-structured questionnaire.

In order to be able to achieve these insights, the researcher will need to be sensitive enough and skilled enough to understand the other person's views, but also, at times, to assist individuals to explore their own beliefs. Charmaz (2014) offers a useful approach as to how researchers' might do this to advantage, and a number of techniques are discussed later in the chapter. Interviews, both semi-structured and unstructured, are therefore appropriate methods when the following apply:

1. The aim of the interview is to develop an understanding of the respondent's 'world' so that the researcher might influence it, either independently or collaboratively – as in the case with action research.

2. It is necessary to understand the constructs that the respondents use as a basis for their opinions and beliefs about a particular matter or situation.

3. The step-by-step logic of a situation is not clear; the subject matter is highly confidential or commercially sensitive; or there are issues about which the interviewee may be reluctant to be truthful, other than confidentially in a one-to-one situation.

Remote interviewing

Managers sometimes choose mediated interviews that are conducted via telephone, email or chat, in preference to the more traditional face-to-face interviewing. Remote interviewing offers more flexibility, and managers feel less committed, because they do not have an obligation to host the researcher or to meet them at a certain time. However, exactly because of these reasons, remote interviewing does not always benefit the researcher. Mediated interviews lack the immediate contextualization, depth and non-verbal communication of a face-to-face interview. Therefore, it is important to consider carefully whether mediated interviews are an appropriate choice for a given research project.

Synchronous mediated interviews – such as telephone conversations and internet-based chats – resemble face-to-face interviews in the sense that interviewer and respondent converse at the same time (O'Connor et al., 2008). They may, for example, prove very effective in the context of real-time and process-based research. In such research projects, researchers are interested in understanding the detail of a situation and an exact 'real-time' chronology of events. In order to establish chronologies, it is perfectly reasonable for the researcher to have frequent telephone conversations centered around current activities and decisions rather than retrospective developments.

Other remote interviews, such as interviews conducted via emails or in internet forums, are asynchronous in that they allow individuals to participate at different times, giving them greater flexibility. Asynchronous interviews give interviewees more time to think about their responses and so increase their ability to control their representations. Depending on the topic of the research, this can be a problem or an advantage. Asynchronous interviews can also be more affected by distraction and sudden drop-out (Tracy, 2013).

Interviews conducted in writing save the researcher the time and costs of transcription, but by having the participants 'transcribe' their own responses, the likelihood of short responses and drop-out increases. Some topics lend themselves more to remote interviewing than do others. A biographic interview about a manager's professional career requires a stronger relationship between the interviewer and the respondent than does an expert interview with a government official that aims to collect data on a particular policy framework. Once a good relationship of trust has been established between the researcher and the research participant, remote interviewing can also be a useful approach for conducting follow-up interviews.

EXERCISE
6.3

Exploring the potential of qualitative interviews

a) **Individual exercise**: There are various types of qualitative interviews, not all of which are discussed in this chapter. Conduct a literature search for more information on different types of qualitative interviews, using the resources and search strategies introduced in Chapter 2 on literature reviews. Identify at least five types of qualitative interviews. Prepare a short briefing (1,000 words) on the more specific features, advantages and disadvantages of expert interviews, narrative interviews and ethnographic interviews.

b) **Interactive exercise**: In pairs, discuss the advantages of qualitative interviews for different research projects. What kind of interviews could be useful for your own research project or assignment? Would you prefer face-to-face interviews or remote interviewing? Why?

Focus groups

Interviews need not take place on a one-to-one basis, and for some types of investigation, group interviews or focus groups can be very useful. Focus groups take the form of loosely structured, guided conversations among a group of individuals. Focus groups are a useful approach for learning how certain groups of individuals react to an issue or shared experience; they are therefore used extensively in market research and politics. The quality of focus groups depends on their composition; if the participants of a group do not share an experience or point of reference, it can be difficult to moderate their discussion (Tracy, 2013).

In any interview, the skill of the interviewer both as initiator and facilitator is of vital importance. In focus-group interviews, this role is called 'moderator', and the added complexity of the situation means that the skills of initiating and facilitating are of particular relevance. As Walker (1985) outlines, a group interviewer should attempt not to conduct numerous interviews simultaneously, but rather to create a situation where all participants feel comfortable expressing their views and responding to the ideas of those around them. Although the focus interview is loosely structured, it should never be entirely without structure (Stokes and Bergin, 2006). The format of the interview should be organized by using what is called a **topic guide**. This is a résumé of the main areas of interest that are to be explored. It is designed so that, while still covering the general areas of interest, it allows unforeseen areas to emerge. However, the problems of group interviews can sometimes outweigh the advantages. Social pressures can condition the responses gained, and it may well be that people are not willing to air their views publicly or are too shy to do so. This effect might be less pronounced in some mediated forms of focus groups, such as internet forums.

Our own view is that such criticisms illustrate the mistake of applying the wrong criteria for assessing the technique. Focus-group interviews can be extremely useful in applied market-research studies, and are used to great effect as an exploratory tool in other types of qualitative research. Curran and Downing (1989), for example, used the technique to good effect as a means of validating the questionnaire responses made by owner-managers in a largely quantitative study that sought to understand the utility of the UK government's consultation strategies with small- and medium-sized firms. Further reading is given at the end of the chapter for those who wish to study this method in more detail.

Conducting individual and group interviews

Interactive exercise: In groups of two to four, discuss the advantages and disadvantages of individual interviews and focus groups. For what kind of research would you choose to conduct individual interviews? What kinds of projects would benefit from the use of focus groups? Prepare a list of three projects (title and short abstract) that could be undertaken using just one of these two approaches (individual interviews or group interviews) without stating the approaches you have chosen on your list. Exchange the list with another group. Can you guess whether the list suggests projects for individual interviews or focus groups? Which group did a better job in identifying suitable projects? Why?

EXERCISE
6.4

Critical incident technique

One method of teasing out information, which is often used alongside interviews, is the **critical incident technique** (CIT). Proposed by Flanagan (1954), the technique offers an opportunity to go straight to the heart of an issue and to collect information about what is really being investigated, rather than gathering large quantities of data that may or may not be directly relevant to this. CIT is often used to identify behaviours that contribute to the success or failure of an individual or organization in a particular situation, based on the analysis of retrospective data on events or 'past incidents' gathered through an interview or questionnaire.

The technique has been used by qualitative researchers to great effect, particularly in conjunction with **in-depth interviews**, as we have indicated above. Respondents might, for example, be asked to track back to particular instances in their work lives, and to explain their actions and motives with specific regard to those instances. In his PhD research, Thorpe used the technique to ask owner-managers of small companies what had been their particular barriers to growth. At a given point in the interview, he would ask if there had been any particular problems in the development of the company. He would then encourage the manager to explain that problem in some detail and to illustrate how the problem was eventually surmounted. From this example, Thorpe would begin to develop ideas about how individuals managed particular problems and about the information they used in doing this. It is important to use material that can be substantiated, since there are criticisms of the technique relating to recall, and the natural tendency of individuals to use hindsight in rationalizing the past.

PREPARING FOR DATA COLLECTION

The first step in the preparation for data collection is the development of a sampling strategy that informs the selection of potential research participants and methods for data collection. For quantitative studies aiming at representativeness, sampling strategies aim to generate samples that are *representative of a larger population*; they adhere to a number of rigorous rules (see Chapter 4). Different qualitative research traditions also have established distinct strategies of how to select and compare pertinent data to develop an emerging theory (see, for example, Charmaz, 2014, on theoretical sampling in constructivist grounded theory). On the most general level, qualitative sampling strategies aim to identify reasonable *instances of the (larger) phenomenon under research* (Luker, 2008). Such a non-probabilistic strategy is guided by considerations of a more or less theoretical nature; it seeks to select a purposeful sample, while at the same time reducing the likelihood that the way a sample is chosen influences the outcome of the research. Whether or not this is the case depends to a large extent on the research design of a study, how it frames the population and phenomenon to be researched, and what kind of comparisons it uses to develop or enhance theory.

Table 6.1 gives an overview of some of the most prominent non-probabilistic sampling strategies. Most researchers aiming to collect qualitative data through language and text design a sampling plan based on one or more sampling strategies when they start data collection; such a plan helps them to identify and contact research participants. The size of the sample and the amount of data to be collected depend on the study and its objectives. Ideally, the selection of cases, the collection/creation of data, and the analysis of these data should evolve in a circular process until the further collection and analysis of data on additional instances appear less and less likely to reveal new or relevant information.

 ## Interview preparations

Before adopting any method of data collection, it always helps to be clear about the overall objectives of the research. This applies to the choice of the in-depth interview or focus group as a method, as well as to the wide range of ways in which interviews may be conducted. Jones (1985) highlights a number of issues that researchers need to consider in order for interviews to be successful. The first is the problem that all researchers must resolve: how much structure to put into the interview.

TABLE 6.1 Sampling strategies

Sampling strategy	Procedure and purpose
Random sampling	Probabilistic selection of cases or interviewees such that the sample is likely to reflect the target population (see Chapter 9 on creating quantitative data)
Ad-hoc sampling	Cases are selected based on availability and ease of access; this strategy is most appropriate in situations where the priority is speed of data collection and low cost
Snowball sampling	Selected participants recruit or recommend other participants from among their acquaintances; useful strategies in settings with limited/difficult access
Maximum-variation sampling	Selection aims to include a wide range of incidents of a given phenomenon, including extreme cases
Typical-case sampling	Selection that aims at identifying the most typical instances
Theory-guided sampling	Selection of cases depending on whether they meet certain theoretical characteristics/embody specific theoretical constructs
Negative-/deviant-case sampling	Selection of cases or interviewees that are likely to contradict a theory or explanation

(BASED ON TRACY, 2013, AND MILES ET AL., 2014)

Jones argues that no research exists without presupposition, by which she means that all researchers have some level of understanding prior to the interview of the research surrounding the interview topic. She further outlines that researchers often enter the interview situation with some key questions; however, these are likely to change as new and interesting areas are uncovered, and researchers may want to tailor their questions depending on the participants' positions or responses.

Interviews can be highly formalized and structured; for example, in market research, where interviews follow a detailed interview schedule listing all questions that are asked in a predefined order, sometimes with a selection of predefined responses (*highly structured interview*). Other interviews are based on a list of questions that can be addressed in a more flexible manner (*semi-structured interview*). Finally, there are interviews where questions are used to stimulate a conversation rather than to guide responses. In the context of ethnographic research, such 'conversations' are often of a rather spontaneous nature and, as such, difficult or impossible to prepare for (*unstructured interview*). Table 6.2 gives an overview of different types of interviews, according to their degree of structuration.

Although interviewing is often claimed to be the best method of gathering information, its complexity can sometimes be underestimated. It is time-consuming to undertake interviews properly, and they are sometimes used when other methods might be more appropriate. If researchers wish to obtain answers to a number of fairly simple questions, then a questionnaire might well be more appropriate. Highly structured interviews are based on carefully prepared sets of questions piloted and refined until the researcher is convinced of their 'validity'. The assumption is made that the interviewer will ask each interviewee the same question in the same way. The simplest form of such interviews is where there are short answers to questions, the interviewer simply ticks boxes, and no deep thought is required by either party. Large numbers (hundreds or thousands) will be required in order to have confidence that the responses obtained can be generalized to the population at large; this is very much the territory of the professional political pollster, for example.

Particularly in the case of using less-structured interviews, we would encourage researchers, as they collect their data, to make choices as to which lines of questioning to explore further, and which to discard. Certainly, researchers need frameworks from which to plot out the developing themes, but – as Jones (1985) reminds us – although they are to some extent tied to their frameworks, researchers should not be 'tied up' by them. One way in which this can be achieved is to prepare a **topic guide**, which can be used as a loose structure for the questions. What a topic guide might look like is explained later in the chapter. Although there may be some deviation from the sequence in order to follow interesting lines of inquiry and to facilitate an unbroken discussion, the interviewer should attempt to cover all the issues mentioned.

Finally, on the subject of structure, the researcher should be warned against assuming that a 'non-directive' interview, where the interviewee talks freely without interruption or intervention, is the best way to achieve a clear picture of the interviewee's perspective. This is far

TABLE 6.2   Types of interview

Level of structure	Type of interview	Guidance and preparation
Highly structured	Market-research interview	Detailed interview schedule: questions in a predefined order, some of them with a narrow selection of predefined answers
Semi-structured	Guided open interview	Topic guide: selection of topics or issues to be covered
Unstructured	Ethnographic interview	Individual questions stimulate an informal conversation; no interview schedule or guide

from true. It is more likely to produce no clear picture in the mind of the interviewee of what questions or issues the interviewer is interested in, and no clear picture in the mind of the interviewer of what questions the interviewee is answering! Too many assumptions of this kind lead to poor data, which are difficult to interpret. Researchers are therefore likely to be more successful if they are clear at the outset about the exact areas of their interest. In the section on avoiding bias, this issue is dealt with in more detail.

It is important to be aware of the advantages and disadvantages of the different ways of conducting interviews. Whereas structured interviews allow for a high degree of standardization of questions and answers, more open (or semi-structured and unstructured) interview questions often give a higher degree of confidentiality, as the replies of the interviewees tend to be more personal in nature. In addition, the interviewer has the opportunity to identify non-verbal clues (e.g. in the inflection of the voice, facial expressions or clothes that the interviewee is wearing), which can be used to develop secondary questions. Sometimes, these verbal clues may offer important reasons for misinformation (Sims, 1993).

This chapter deals primarily with in-depth qualitative interviews, where the main purpose is to understand the meanings that interviewees attach to issues and situations in contexts that are not structured in advance by the researcher. For more detail on the use and application of highly structured questionnaires, readers should refer to Chapters 9 and 10.

Creating a topic guide

As noted above, interview schedules involve standardized scripts of questions that follow a predefined order. In contrast, topic guides refer to more informal lists of topics and questions that can be addressed in no particular order. Hence the difference lies in the degree of structure and the way in which respondents are addressed. When preparing a topic guide or interview schedule, researchers first revisit their research questions, research design and sampling strategy. This helps them to clarify the purpose of the interviews that they would like to conduct. There is often a tendency to approach interviews as an exercise of 'data extraction' as opposed to 'meaningful conversation'. This can create problems not only for the respondent but also for the interviewer. Respondents who face difficult, unsuitable or inappropriate questions tend to disengage, and the outcome of such interviews is likely to be unsatisfactory for both parties. Therefore, when designing a topic guide or preparing individual questions, it is important to reflect on how potential respondents might understand and feel about certain questions, in order to ensure that questions relate to the world and identity of the respondent as well as to the research interests of the interviewer.

In contrast to research questions, interview questions should avoid abstract theoretical concepts, jargon and scholarly talk. Instead, they should be clear and easy to understand. Good questions promote open-ended answers and allow respondents to report or reflect on an experience and certain pieces of information; they are followed up by appropriate 'probes' or other questions (e.g. 'Please tell me more about this'). Research questions should not be too leading. A question such as 'Don't you admire your managers for their excellent track records?' is likely to produce a predictable response. It is important to bear in mind that natural conversations tend to be organized around stories, and so organizing research interviews in a similar way can be useful. There are interview situations in which challenging questions are required and appropriate, but great care should be taken that such questions are worded in the right way. If abstract concepts such as 'innovation' or 'collaboration' cannot be avoided altogether, respondents should be asked to clarify their understanding of these concepts, and they should be provided with some examples that can help to develop a shared definition.

Topic guides may be more flexible than interview schedules, but they should nonetheless be organized into at least three sections: opening questions, questions around a number of key topics, and closing questions. Topic guides should remind the interviewer to ask for the consent of the respondent to be interviewed, and they should include 'icebreaker' questions that build rapport, as well as closing questions or comments that make the respondents feel appreciated. Towards the end of the interview it can be useful to ask respondents whether they have anything to add. Depending on the sampling strategy, closing questions should also include a question about follow-up contacts and recommendations.

Informed consent

The planning of interviews also involves a couple of formal steps to address issues arising from data protection, confidentiality and informed consent. Most universities require students and staff to have all research activities with human participants approved in an ethical-review process, a procedure that we will discuss in more detail in the following chapter. At this stage, it is sufficient to know that permission to conduct research has to be given by the university and that the review process involves the preparation of a consent form to be signed by each research participant. Consent forms should be understandable by the target population. They should confirm that research participants were informed about the research and its expected benefits ahead of the data collection, and that they have a right to withdraw voluntarily from the research at any time. Consent forms also detail how the confidentiality of the respondents is protected. If appropriate, they include a statement about risks that could arise from participation.

CONDUCTING INTERVIEWS

Various skills are required for interviewing; these can take quite a while to learn. Understanding issues from an interviewee's point of view can be extremely difficult, especially when the respondent may not have a clearly articulated view of the answers to the questions posed, or may not wish to divulge sensitive information. It is here that the skills of the interviewer come to the fore.

McClelland (1965) conducted careful studies about common-sense notions of 'motivation'. He concluded that people cannot be trusted to say exactly what their own motives are, as they often get ideas about these from commonly accepted half-truths. For example, a person may claim to be interested in achievement because of having made money. But a careful check using different probing methods may reveal quite a different picture. Often, people simply are not aware of their own motives. Mangham (1986), in his studies of managerial competence, met this problem. From survey work conducted quantitatively, he found that many managers sought subordinates who could better motivate staff and act in leadership roles within their organizations. In follow-up interviews, he was able to ask managers exactly what they meant by 'leadership'. Some gave ambiguous answers and became confused, offering examples of leadership that ranged from highly autocratic styles to highly democratic forms.

From a positivistic standpoint, the fact that there is ambiguity about the meaning of 'leadership' invalidates the research, but for the in-depth interviewer who probes, questions and checks, these are important data. The fact that people are confused and cannot agree on what they mean by leadership, or the way they construct particular situations, is the essence of the research.

The skills of an interviewer, then, centre on the ability to recognize what is relevant and remember it, or tape it, so that afterwards detailed notes can be made. This requires one to be perceptive and sensitive to events, so that lines of inquiry can be changed and adapted as one progresses. Above all, interviewers need to be able to listen, and to refrain from projecting their own opinions or feelings into the situation.

This is more difficult than it sounds, since one of the ways of obtaining trust is to empathize with the respondent. The interviewer needs to *listen to what the person wants and does not want to say*, without helping (Charmaz, 2014). In recognizing these situations, non-verbal data might be crucial in providing clues, for example the loss of eye contact or a changed facial expression. From time to time during the interview, as patterns or uncertainties arise, it is useful to check that one understands by summarizing what has been said. This should be presented as a way of seeking clarification. The process of 'testing out' is a way of safeguarding against assuming too quickly that understanding has been achieved.

Laddering

As questions are asked, the researcher might like to think about how to get more from a question. Employing the technique of **laddering up** will help the respondent move from statements of fact or descriptive accounts about the questions posed upwards so as to begin to reveal the individual's value base (Bourne and Jenkins, 2005; Wansink, 2003). The best way to achieve this is to ask 'why' questions. An example of this process can be seen in Example 6.2, and the hierarchical value map to which it relates is shown in Figure 6.5. The technique is very valuable for qualitative researchers; however, sensitivity and common sense do need to be applied, as persistent use of 'why' type questions can spoil an interview since the respondent will eventually run out of things to say. Vary the way in which the question 'why' is asked is one strategy, as Susan Baker does in Example 6.2, to make the exchange more varied and interesting as she explored the reasons why individuals purchased a particular make and style of running shoe.

Laddering down is where the researcher seeks to obtain illustrations and examples or occurrences of events. For example, the researcher might say 'Could you give me an example of that?' or 'When was the last time that happened to you?' Through such a process it is possible to explore a person's understanding of a particular construct. A laddering up-and-down using five or six questions (the number of themes contained in a topic guide) will quite easily fill out the whole of an interview, while gaining significant insights into the topic under investigation.

EXAMPLE 6.2

Laddering

Question: Anything else about the design?

Answer: I think the weight of the shoe is important. The shoes shouldn't be too heavy.

Question: Why is this?

Answer: Because a lighter shoe is more comfortable.

Question: Why is this important to you?

Answer: It means I can move around quickly at tennis …

Question: Tennis is important to you?

Answer: Yes … I like it … It means I can get some fresh air … It's good for the heart, the nerves and your cholesterol … It makes me feel better. I feel good when I play tennis.

Source: Baker and Knox, 1995: 85

Laddering up and down

EXERCISE
6.5

Interactive exercise: In pairs, ask each other a simple question that relates to a personal view or preference the person might have. Then try to ladder up from this question to see if you can learn something about the person's values (normally this can be done by asking 'why' questions). Then ladder down to see if you can learn something about the detail that surrounds these preferences. (This is normally done by asking about specific instances.)

Avoiding becoming biased

Readers will see in Chapter 9, on quantitative research methods, that **interview bias** – where the process of conducting an interview might influence the responses given – is regarded as crucial. With in-depth interviewing, the issue is a slightly different one. Since the aim of in-depth interviews is to uncover the meanings and interpretations that people attach to events, it follows that there is no one 'objective' view to be discovered that the process of interviewing may bias. However, there is a very real concern about interviewers imposing their own reference frames on the interviewees, both when the questions are asked and when the answers are interpreted. The researcher is in something of a dilemma, because – as has been suggested in an earlier section – open questions may avoid bias, but they are not always the best way of obtaining the information one may wish to have; nor are they always the best way of putting an interviewee at ease. But the issue of bias gives a pull in the other direction. In order to avoid bias, there is often the tendency for researchers to leave questions open. There will be some occasions when researchers will want to focus on discovering responses to specific alternatives, and in this case **probes** can be useful as an intervention technique to improve, or sharpen up, the interviewee's response. A number of probes are listed in Example 6.3.

Probes in data collection

EXAMPLE
6.3

- The basic probe involves simply repeating the initial question, and is useful when the interviewee seems to be wandering off the point.

- Explanatory probes involve building onto incomplete or vague statements made by the respondent. Ask questions such as 'What did you mean by that?' and 'What makes you say that?'

- Focused probes are used to obtain specific information. Typically, one would ask the respondent 'What sort of …?'

- The silent probe is one of the most effective techniques to use when respondents are either reluctant or very slow to answer the question posed. Simply pause and let them break the silence.

- The technique of drawing out can be used when interviewees have halted or dried up. Repeat the last few words they said, and then look at them expectantly or say, 'Tell me more about that' or 'What happened then?'

- Giving ideas or suggestions involves offering the interviewee an idea to think about, for example, 'Have you thought about ...?', 'Have you tried ...?', 'Did you know that ...?' and 'Perhaps you should ask Y ...'.

(Continued)

(Continued)

● Mirroring or reflecting involves expressing in your own words what the respondent has just said. This is very effective because it may force the respondent to rethink the answer and reconstruct another reply, which will amplify the previous answer 'What you seem to be saying/feeling is ...'. To avoid bias, probes should never lead. An example of a leading probe might be: 'So you would say that you were really satisfied?' Instead of this, the interviewer should say, 'Can you explain a little more?' or 'How do you mean?'

General interview concerns

Using interviews as the main method of obtaining qualitative data in a successful way, however, does not depend only on researchers' personal interview skills, capacity to organize and structure interviews, and ability to avoid bias. Researchers should be aware of six important practical issues involved in conducting interviews; these may affect the outcome of an interview. These are: obtaining trust; being aware of social interaction; using the appropriate attitude and language; getting access; choosing the location for the interviews; and recording interviews.

Obtaining trust is an important element in ensuring that interviews will provide the researcher with the information sought. Obtaining trust can be difficult, especially in one-off interviews where the people involved have not met before. Failure to develop trust may well result in interviewees simply resorting to telling the researcher what they think is expected. But an open and trusting relationship may not be possible or sufficient when dealing with particular elites or individuals in positions of power, as we have discussed in Chapter 5. One way to obtain trust is to make sure that one is well informed about the company. A scan through the company's website will give a quick impression of the issues that are currently considered significant. Another way to obtain the trust of the company one wishes to research is to present the research in a professional and enthusiastic way so that the company sees a benefit, as managers will be weighing up the likely costs and benefits of the potential intrusion.

Social interaction between the interviewer and the interviewee is another important factor that may influence the interview process. Jones (1985) suggests that people will attribute meaning and significance to the particular research situations in which they find themselves. The questions that an interviewer may ask and the answers that an interviewee gives will often depend on how their situations are defined. Similarly, Jones (1985) points out that interviewees will 'suss out' what researchers are like, and make judgements – from their first impressions – about whether they can trust the researchers with their data, or whether they might be damaged in some way by sharing information. Such suspicions do not necessarily mean that interviewees will refuse to be interviewed, but it might mean, as Jones indicates, that they just 'seek to get the interview over as quickly as possible, with enough detail and enough feigned interest to satisfy the researcher that he or she is getting something of value but without saying anything that touches the core of what is actually believed and cared about in the research' (1985: 50). It is, furthermore, important to be able to recognize when an interviewer is being misinformed (Sims, 1993). Individuals will often select answers that they think will be easily understood by interviewers, rather than providing the 'whole truth', simply because it would take too long to give all the nuances.

Appropriate attitude and language should also be kept in mind when preparing for and conducting one's research. Interviewers should appear knowledgeable, competent, humble and sensitive. They should be attentive and avoid judgements. It is not a good strategy to baffle a potential gatekeeper by mentioning too many theoretical concepts, but clarity also needs to be ascertained with respect to the interviewee's use of language, as what is said may not always be what is meant; the sky might indeed be blue like an orange! Clarifying probes can help to reveal the latent interpretations and understandings of the interviewee. In Table 6.3, we provide a few examples of the way words may be interpreted. Towards the end of the interview, interviewers should leave time for respondents to reflect on the interview and to volunteer additional information they consider relevant. Whether or not an interview has turned out to be helpful, interviewers should never forget to thank respondents for their time in a specific and appreciative way.

Getting access In terms of getting access preliminary phone calls or e-mails are best followed by something more formal prior to the interview date. This fulfils a number of purposes. One is that it gives some additional credibility, particularly if the communication is from the University or the letterhead signifies the independent nature of the research. Secondly, this kind of attention to detail might assist with cooperation in the future, and thirdly, it provides the opportunity to send the respondent further information about the research and set out in detail what is required. But all the above assumes that interviews need to take place informal setting, which leads to the next point.

The location of the interview and the setting in which the interview takes place is a fifth element that can be important. Good locations are those which are easy for both parties to access, are comfortable (e.g. the furniture and temperature), and characterized by low levels of noise and distractions (without lots of people coming and going, and with no loud music or TV in the background). One should also be careful to understand the impact of spaces on people's understanding of the interview situation. A manager's office, for example, might not be perceived as a neutral space by other employees, as experienced first-hand in a study by Thorpe (Bowey and Thorpe, 1986). One strategy used by a PhD student, Neil, was to conduct interviews well away from the workplace. When researching aspects of management development, he undertook this fieldwork by sitting in the first-class compartments of trains. He would sit next to executive-looking individuals, armed only with a folder marked 'Management Development' in the hope that managers would talk to him. This they usually did, and – without prompts – he was able to elicit their views on a range of management-development issues. What struck Neil was the extent to which the views and opinions expressed by managers, off-guard and to a person they were unlikely ever to meet again, contradicted the 'reality' contained in much contemporary management literature. Had the interviews taken place in the managers' offices, the results might well have been quite different. This example not only illustrates how a researcher managed to obtain data that the manager may have found hard to articulate in the office, it also shows how a method can be undertaken in a 'natural setting', where each person views the other as having equal status. This kind of research would

TABLE 6.3   Use of words and the different impressions they can give

Words	Impression given
Student	Implies an unskilled 'amateurish' inquiry, which may be a waste of time, although unthreatening
Researcher	Implies a more professional relationship, although questions of access might need to be managed more carefully
Interview	Implies a formal structured interrogation, which is under the control of the researcher
Discussion	May make managers feel more relaxed and less threatened, with the potential for genuine exchange

normally be extremely costly, yet it does illustrate the lengths that might have to be gone to in order to obtain data.

Recording interviews is a sixth aspect that may affect the outcome of an interview. The decision of whether or not to use a voice recorder lies with the interviewee. Some interviewees harbour concerns about confidentiality and the use to which any information divulged can be put (see Chapter 5). Therefore, the question of whether or not a meeting can be recorded should be approached with tact. Concerns can be addressed, for example, by handing over the responsibility for switching the voice recorder on and off to the interviewee, so that the latter has control over which parts are recorded. The main reasons in favour of using a voice recorder are that it aids the listening process and gives the opportunity of an unbiased record of the conversation. Good audio recordings are essential for accurate transcripts and also enable the researcher to listen again to the interview, possibly hearing things that were missed at the time. It is important to test the chosen recording technology ahead of the interview, if possible in the proposed location. If interviewees oppose the recording of interviews, researchers should depend on their own ability to take accurate notes and write down everything they are able to remember as soon as possible after the interview has ended. Even if allowed to record conversations, interviewers are advised to take notes during the interviews. This makes the interviewees feel more appreciated, can aid the researchers in developing probes and follow-up questions, and reduces the time of direct eye contact (which many interviewees find uncomfortable). What is particularly important is for researchers to create a verbatim account as soon as possible after the interview is completed.

EXERCISE
6.6

Interviewing

a) **Individual exercise**: The qualitative researcher needs to have good personal engagement to gain trust so that 'good' data can be obtained. Think about a time when you have been interviewed, either as a research respondent or at a recruitment interview. Did the interviewer do anything to gain or lose your trust?

b) **Interactive exercise**: Think about which of your own characteristics and traits could affect your relationship with research participants. In pairs, discuss these traits and write them down. What characteristics or traits are likely to have a positive or negative impact on your data collection?

c) **Individual exercise**: Pick a general topic that relates to an experience that most students in your group are likely to have had (such as recount how you felt when you arrived at your first school, completed your first application for a job, or had your first job interview) or to attitudes and expectations (such as career expectations, environmental protection, or growth of local business). Prepare an interview guide of at least ten questions, including an opening question and a closing question. Write down what you expect to find in your interview (500 words). Conduct the interviews in pairs, so that everybody plays the part of the interviewer and that of the respondent at least once each. Each interview should last a minimum of 20 to 40 minutes. Discuss how you have experienced the interview as interviewer and as respondent. What would you do differently next time you conduct an interview?

d) **Individual and interactive exercise**: Search online for information about your university's ethical-review process. What is the procedure at your university? Who assesses the applications? What issues are covered? Look online for some templates of consent forms (e.g. www.lancaster.ac.uk/researchethics/1-4-samples.html). What issues are covered in these templates? Discuss the merits and challenges created by the use of consent forms.

INTERVIEW-BASED MAPPING TECHNIQUES

After having discussed qualitative interviews as an interactive way of creating qualitative data on a more general level, we now introduce two interactive mapping methods that combine interviewing techniques with participatory methods: repertory-grid technique and cognitive mapping. Both techniques help researchers to identify an individual's or a group's view of the world, and enable the simple and relatively immediate presentation of complex information. To this end, both techniques integrate processes of data collection with those of data analysis.

Repertory-grid technique

Based on personal-construct theory (Kelly, 1955), a repertory grid is a special interviewing technique that is used to identify the ways in which respondents interpret their experience, draw conclusions about patterns of cause and effect, and behave according to those conclusions. A better understanding of these processes can be useful to explore the meaning that respondents assign to a certain problem, and what kinds of solutions they could envisage. The technique is useful for investigating areas that the respondent might not have thought much about, or that they find hard to articulate. It has been used extensively in areas such as career guidance, and for the development of job descriptions. In the case of Example 6.4, a housing manager within a large metropolitan council used the approach to assist in identifying what householders valued in terms of bathroom and kitchen design.

Repertory grid

EXAMPLE
6.4

Mackinlay (1986) used the repertory-grid technique to elicit the values and perceptions that householders in a particular housing district held of different types of bathroom and kitchen colour schemes and layouts, as elements to be compared and contrasted. He showed photographs to householders, and asked them to compare and contrast the different photographs; in so doing, he elicited the 'constructs' they used to differentiate between the photographs, and to reveal their likes and dislikes. The method proved extremely useful, with the photographs helping to resolve differences and deal with the complex issues involved in the notion of what people valued and preferred. This demonstrates that grids can elucidate what might not be immediately observable, so that new insights or perspectives can be gained.

Repertory grids help individuals to look not only at the words people use, but also at the wider constructs employed when making decisions and taking action. Often, these may not be known even to the individuals themselves, so representation in the visual form of a grid can be the beginning of a process whereby individuals learn more about the ideas they have, how they might have been formed and how they might be changed.

Grids can also be used in group situations as a basis for discussion about how different people view the world; they enable complex relationships to be represented with the objective of building up shared understandings (Easterby-Smith et al., 2010). The technique is used to understand individuals' perceptions and the constructs they use to understand and manage their worlds. A repertory grid shows how constructs and elements are related to each other; the space can be shown geometrically through principle components analysis. The principal components analysis gives a mathematical relationship between the underlying dimensions and the constructs and elements. Repertory grids can also be used with people who have low verbal ability and can be used with either dyads or triads. An example of how a repertory grid might be constructed is presented below.

The standard procedure for generating a repertory grid is as follows:

1. Decide on the *focus* of the grid. This should be quite specific, and the interviewee should be reminded of it at regular intervals. The focus might be on the qualities required of a manager in a particular function, the work content of a given job, or the features of products currently competing with one's own.

2. Select with the interviewee a group of *elements* (between five and ten) that are relevant to the chosen focus, and that are also likely to provide a good range. If, for example, the focus of the grid was on the skills required of a manager, it would be appropriate to choose individuals who were familiar to the interviewee, some of whom the latter regarded as particularly able, some of average ability, and some of below-average ability.

3. *Constructs* are elicited, usually by asking the respondent to compare and contrast elements in groups of three, known as 'triads'. Each element is written onto a card and then three cards are selected at random. The interviewee is asked to decide which pair of cards is similar in a way that also makes them distinct from the third. They are asked to provide a word or phrase that describes the pair, and a contrasting word or phrase to describe the remaining card. For example, in the case of a grid with the focus on the competencies required of a manager, someone might choose two cards of named people as similar because they see them both as *dynamic*, and the third as *staid*. In this case, the construct elicited is a continuum on which *dynamic* is at one end and *staid* is at the other. This process is repeated with different triads of elements until a reasonable number of constructs (perhaps six to ten) has been produced.

4. Each of the elements needs to be *linked* to, or rated against, each of the constructs. This can be done in several different ways: by deciding which of the two 'poles' of the construct provides the best description of the element; by determining the position of the element on a rating scale (often with seven points), constructed between the poles of each construct; or by rank-ordering each of the elements along the dimension indicated by each of the constructs. The results of these ratings or rankings are recorded as ticks and crosses, or as numbers in a matrix.

Small grids can be analysed manually (i.e. by eye), by looking for patterns of relationships and differences between constructs and elements. This can form the basis of an interesting collaborative discussion between interviewer and interviewee. With larger grids (say, five-by-five or more), it is more common to use computer analysis packages. Figure 6.2 shows a marketing example analysed using GridSuite, in which a PhD student studying in the mid-1990s was interested in aspects of brand preference in relation to mobile phones. The study recognized the very different approaches being adopted (even by the same company), and aimed to identify how consumers were influenced by brands.

The completed grid shows how the respondent questioned has made comparisons between various mobile phones. In the example, phones by Siemens have been compared with phones from Nokia, Motorola, Sony, Ericsson, Philips, Panasonic and Alcatel. The comparisons range from answers that mention the 'personality' of the phones to practical dimensions, such as ease of use. The example shows that respondents have been asked to rate the constructs elicited on a scale (one to seven) and the computer has colour-coded the results (the darker the shading, the higher the score given by the respondent for a given construct). The colour coding offers a visual impression of which phones score more or less highly on the constructs elicited.

1	Nokia	Motorola	Sony	Siemens	Ericsson	Phillips	Panasonic	Alcatel	7
Innovative product									Unchanging product
Sophisticated features									Basic features
Easy to understand									Complicated to use
Modern design									Conservative design
Attracts young users									Older users
Phones with personality									No differentiation
Strong image for mobile phones									No clue about brand
Brand with good ideas / innovative									Followers
Close to the consumer									Factory-oriented
Brand image of phone is v. clear									V. Unclear Image
Brand image of company clear									V. Unclear image
Overall Preference									

FIGURE 6.2
Repertory grids in the mobile market

In terms of analysis, there are two very different kinds of output in terms of visual representation: a map and a dendrogram. The map type plots the elements within dimensions and axes, defined by the constructs. The map in Figure 6.3 shows that two main components explains nearly 70 per cent of the variance: component 1 (54.8 per cent) and component 2 (16.1 per cent). Names have been assigned to these components in order to catch the essence of the components, in this case component 1, it is suggested, indicates phones that inspire users whilst the other end of the dimension characterizes phones that are less inspiring. Component 2 (which explains a smaller variance) might be named 'uninspiring'. From this grid, principal component analysis enables the mobile phones under investigation to be represented within the two axes, which indicates the extent to which they possess the constructs elicited from the grid.

Another way of representing the analysis of a grid takes the form of a dendrogram (Figure 6.4). Dendrograms show how close the constructs are to one another in terms of how they have been scored. Where the 'tree' branches are close, the indication is that the two constructs have something in common and therefore might be connected. Figure 6.4 shows a dendrogram using the same data as used in Figure 6.3.

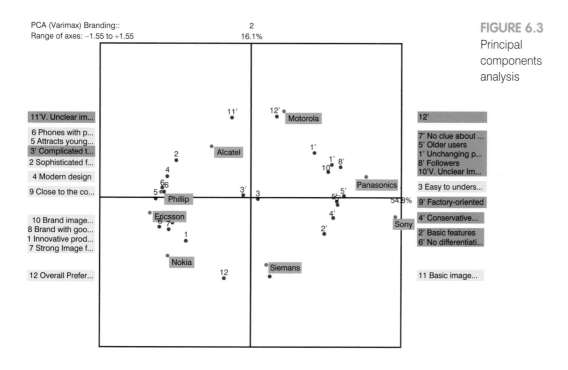

FIGURE 6.3
Principal components analysis

In Figure 6.4, instead of a researcher dealing with 12 constructs, the dendrogram in this example also suggests that it may be possible to collapse the constructs into only four main categories. This process is analogous to the process that researchers undertake when conducting grounded approaches to data analysis. In this case, researchers would look for similarities in the suggested links and assign a name to the higher-level construct.

Grids have both advantages and disadvantages, as shown in Table 6.4, which indicates the main advantages and disadvantages of using repertory grids, identified by Stewart et al. (1981). Our view is that grids not only offer assistance in seeing patterns and associations – and, as a consequence, new insights – but they also provide a medium of communication that

FIGURE 6.4
Branding of mobile phones

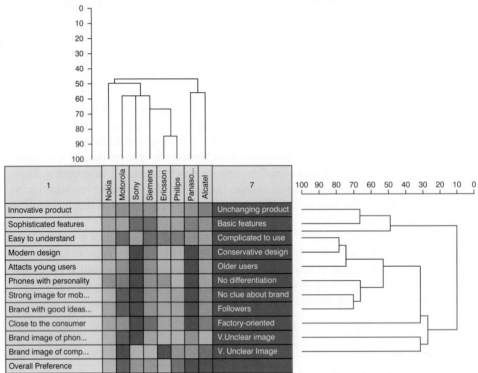

Dendrogram Grid: Branding - Client

TABLE 6.4 Pros and cons of using repertory grids

Advantages	Disadvantages
They involve verbalizing constructs that otherwise would remain hidden	Grids are hard work to complete and can take considerable periods of time: a 20 x 10 matrix can take up to 1.5 hours
They are based on the individual's own framework, not that of the expert	They require a high degree of skill from the interviewer if the interviewee's construct framework is to be fully explored
They provide insights for both the researcher and the researched	They can be difficult to analyse and interpret, and there is some danger that individuals will rely on the structure of the technique to produce packaged (rather than meaningful) results
	The technique has become 'popular' and, as a consequence, is sometimes used mechanistically, forgetting the underlying theory of personal constructs

can spur new understandings and new acts of sense-making (Easterby-Smith et al., 2010). So, they are not simply a graphical representation of an individual manager's concerns and beliefs, but operate in a reflexive manner (see Harper, 1989), helping managers respond to the map or picture that is produced.

For those interested in learning more about the repertory-grid technique, further reading is provided at the end of this chapter, and Easterby-Smith et al. (2010) illustrate a number of applications in the field of management.

Cognitive mapping

This method of data collection is based on the same personal-construct theory as repertory-grid technique. **Cognitive mapping** is a modelling technique that aims to portray managers' ideas, beliefs, values and attitudes – and to show how they interrelate. A cognitive map represents the relationships between the constructs of a number of individual managers regarding a managerial issue or problem (Eden et al., 1983; Huff and Jenkins, 2002). A cognitive map is not supposed to be a scientific model of an objective reality in the way that some influence diagrams are, but instead should be a presentation of part of the world as a particular person sees it – it can never be shown to be right or wrong, in an 'objective' sense (Eden et al., 1983: 44). Cognitive maps therefore capture managers' professed theories-in-use, and their conceptual and symbolic uses of language.

Cognitive maps can work at either an individual or group level, and can be used *statically* as a method of simple data collection (instead of field notes) or *dynamically* with groups of managers. As with repertory grids, various *tools* have been produced that help mediate the intervention; many are computer-based and offer added promise to enhance strategic thinking. We begin with suggesting individual approaches and then give some examples of the collective uses of cognitive mapping.

Individual cognitive maps

Figure 6.5 shows a typical individual map produced by a PhD student (Baker, 1996) undertaking a comparative study of consumer perceptions. In this example, we provide a map about running shoes.

The map is produced through questioning and laddering. The lines running between the numbers (content codes) represent the linkages. Readers will notice that there are fewer *values* (those constructs at the top of the map) than *attributes* (those constructs at the bottom), with consequences tending to come towards the middle. This map might be interpreted in the following way. The main value (primary value 26 at the top of the map) is *well-being*. Below this, there are three further elements, each of which has a large number of elements leading into it. These are: *design* (value 2), *weight/shape* (value 3) and *enhanced performance* (value 14). Baker and Knox's (1995) interpretation is that it is the design of the shoes that enhances what they call 'the performance and well-being chain', and that this is illustrated by the high number of relations among its respective elements, which implies that the product was purchased for the perceived benefits it might deliver in terms of performance.

In order to gain understanding and to interpret the map, the interviewer again needs to go through a process of laddering, in order to explore the person's understanding in more depth. As the constructs deployed in this map are presumed to have a hierarchical relationship, the process of laddering employed in the interviews helps to gain a better understanding of a person's construct system. *Laddering down* (also called 'pyramiding') is where the interviewer explores a person's understanding of a particular construct; *laddering up* is where the interviewer explores why a particular construct is important to the person and helps to explore the latter's value system.

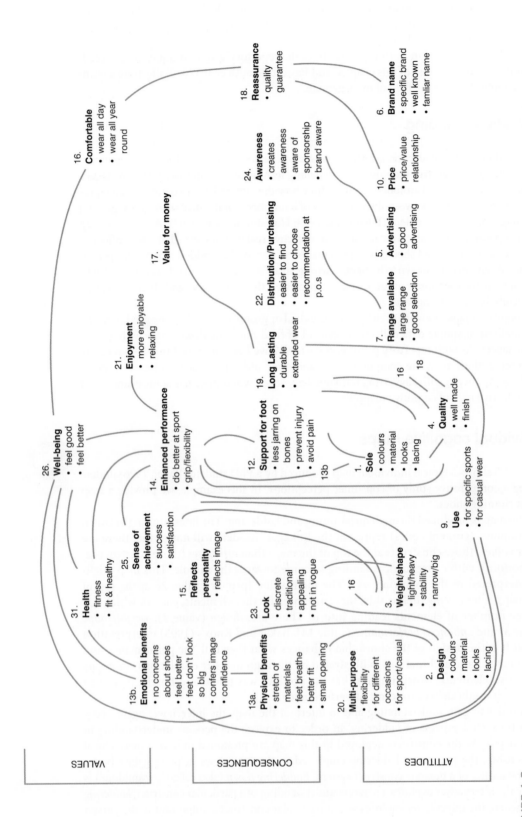

FIGURE 6.5

Hierarchical value map: combined trainers

Dominoes

A less systematic way of developing constructs – and one that might be preferred, particularly where there are issues of power and control (e.g. when working with senior managers) – is to use a process called 'dominoes'. This method allows the manager more control over the process and can save considerable time. The process involves the researcher simply identifying elements (whether these are people or objects) and placing them in front of the manager all at the same time. The managers are then asked to place the elements into groups. Elements that come together are then given a name or phrase (labelled) based on what it is that all the elements have in common. Managers are then encouraged to explain the relation between these groups and this is done by encouraging them to explain aloud how the different groups of elements relate together to form a pattern. Their comments are then recorded by the researcher and questions can be asked to obtain clarification as necessary. Using this approach, the managers often find the exercise 'fun' to complete, and differences between elements that produce the constructs can be drawn out.

Using the dominoes technique

Ask a colleague to:

- identify seven people – a mixture of people the person likes and dislikes

- write the people's names down on cards and place them on the desk in front of you

- find a feature that differentiates some of these individuals from the others

- place the names of those with similar features adjacent to each other

- supply a word or phrase that best describes the common attributes held – this is one construct.

Now repeat the process and see how many different constructs can be found.

EXERCISE
6.7

Group maps

Cognitive maps are now being used by researchers in a whole variety of contexts, from helping managers clarify and design strategy to providing tools of mediation. Used interactively, they can help groups think around issues as well as formulate plans. Such approaches have spawned an industry known as 'strategic support', and the improvement in computers and software has enabled a large number of software products to be designed; these can sit within a group of managers or employees to help them map out their perspectives on problems or issues within an organization and, from this collective set of views, clarify next steps. Used in this way, the research clearly takes on an action-research flavour, where change is decidedly part of the process of data collection, making the approach an attractive proposition for those undertaking consultancy.

As a consequence, cognitive-mapping methodologies have been increasingly used in action research, where groups of individuals, managers or employees collaborate to model the complexity of their organizational problems as *they* see them so that they can subsequently be analysed and solved. Here the focus is not just on collecting and presenting large amounts of data, but on stimulating new learning that will lead to change – hence its use in strategy development. Originally a manual system, the computer packages now available (e.g. Decision Explorer) provide powerful support both to assist the analysis process and to explore an organization's strategic options (Eden, 1990).

Eden is critical of the traditional view that the formulation of strategy can be conducted quite independently from its implementation. One of the advantages of cognitive mapping is that the process enables those taking part to challenge the views and perspectives of others, and it is often the realization of differences between individual managers – together with the following discussion – that proves most useful, by giving prominence to distinctions and making connections that might otherwise be overlooked (Ackermann and Eden, 2011). A final beneficial outcome of the cognitive-mapping process is that it helps managers reach a collective judgement about issues that are ambiguous, complex and often contested. In the words of Thomas and Thomas (1928: 47), 'If men define situations as real, they are real in their consequences.'

In practice, members of an organization are brought together in a room facing a blank wall or large projector screen. The focus of the session or problem on which they are to work is presented to them by a researcher or facilitator. In comfortable surroundings and with a continuous supply of coffee, the individuals then begin to consider aspects of the situation. Each contribution made is either written down on sticky notes (called 'ovals') or stored by computer, and the unfolding cognitive map, which represents the individuals' view of the issue, is projected onto the screen or posted on the wall for participants to alter and refine.

The approach not only allows individual managers to offer their perceptions of a problem, but also gives those responsible for strategy formulation the opportunity to understand the perspectives of others. In this context, interaction among participants – and collaboration between researcher and researched – is a decidedly good thing. An example of using a cognitive-mapping approach is described below and represented in Figure 6.6.

This example involved the use of a cognitive-mapping approach in the strategy-development process when working to surface issues and produce an agenda for change in a hospital merger. Both hospitals were 'hot' sites and, as such, had the prestige of dealing with accident-and-emergency patients. As a consequence, both hospitals had maternity wings (for which accident-and-emergency on site was a necessity), each location was represented by a different Member of Parliament who represented their local catchment, and each hospital had historically been part of a different regional health authority (and as a consequence developed a very different culture, organizational structure and set of uniforms). Following pressure to merge from both the government (for reasons of efficiency) and the Royal Colleges (for reasons of improved clinical practice), researchers undertook an action-learning approach to change. At one stage in the change process, they introduced the concept of cognitive mapping as a tool to surface the views of the senior management team, and to engender debate. Working with the management team (all managers and all clinical directors) from both hospitals, the researchers created maps to depict both collective and individual perspectives of the issues faced by the hospital in the context of the impending merger. By first interviewing managers and clinicians individually, they created a number of maps, which were then discussed and debated within a larger group. The trigger questions for discussion were:

1. What is your vision for what needs to be done for the merger to be a success?

2. What actions need to be taken for this to be realized?

The maps were then modified, with the views expressed captured, grouped and structured into a causal map offering a synthesis of each participant's view on the two questions. Simultaneously, managers were asked to discuss the suggested clustering of concepts, and the content and priorities of the strategic issues. One of the early observations was the speed at which it helped the group to surface the strategic issues facing the hospital.

An initial review of the map, part of which is shown in Figure 6.7, indicated the complexity of the problem. There was a multiplicity and a diversity of social, economic

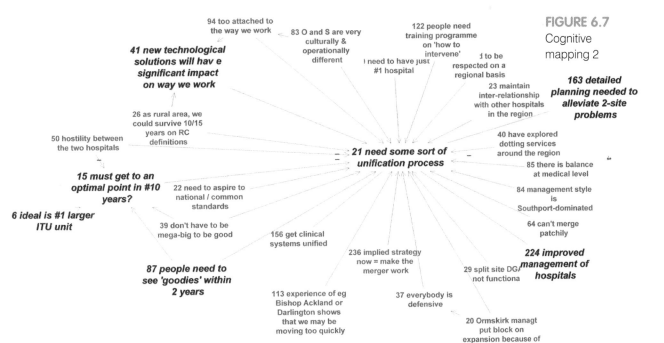

FIGURE 6.6
Cognitive
mapping 1

FIGURE 6.7
Cognitive
mapping 2

224 improved
management of
hospitals

286 seek a balalnce
between centralised
control and
decentralised
operations

285 budgets based on
zero-based review
every year

250 issues around
pay need to be
resolved

258 new NHS pay
system needs to be
incorporated

275 nursing cultures
and rates of
development at #2
sites are very
different

222 John, Eric &
Peter took over much
of CD's role

251 expectation that
pay will be
difficult

276 waiting list
initiatives have
distorted pay (via
implied sovertime working)
iow = make the
merger work

252 competences /
quality / conditions
on the #2 sites are
different

155 student nurses
being trained on #2
different systems /
policies [UCPreston,
Edge Hill]

121 not enough skill
(or competence) in
the system

56 merger is good
thing to achieve
critical mass eg
anaesthetology

216 strategy now is
murky and
ill-defined

257 seen as a
takeover by
Southport

19 need critical
mass in eg intensive
care, path labs,
midwifery

231 relationship wrt
purchasers will be
difficult

269 changes in
junior doctors'
hours & training

235 potential for
good relationships

217 group stopped
couple of years ago

220 CD structure
changed into 3
business groups

114 have had
clinical
directorates

27 population size
served =main reason
for merger

oblems will
arise from now
having #2 HA's, #2
Regions, and #2
Deaneries

234 prefer to deal
with GP's as F256 not been able to
deliver on promises

214 strategy group
was successful

doctors haven't
performed well as
clnical directors

229 accepted wisdom
= Ormskirk got more
money from HA than
Southport !

232 policy of equal
service for all not
realistic or tenable

218 changes in GPF

219 lots of
restrictions

129 lots of dotted
lines

94 too attached to
the way we work

83 O and S are very
culturally &
operationally
different

122 people need
training programme
on 'how to
intervene'

41 new technological
solutions will hav e
significant impact
on way we work

d to be
respected on a
regional basis

163 detailed
planning needed to
alleviate 2-site
problems

need to have just
#1 hospital

23 maintain
inter-relationship
with other hospitals
in the region

26 as rural area, we
could survive 10/15
years on RC
definitions

40 have explored
dotting services
around the region

50 hostility between
the two hospitals

21 need some sort of
unification process

85 there is balance
at medical level

15 must get to an
optimal point in #10
years?

84 management style
is
Southport-dominated

6 ideal is #1 larger
ITU unit

22 need to aspire to
national / common
standards

64 can't merge
patchily

39 don't have to be
mega-big to be good

156 get clinical
systems unified

224 improved
management of
hospitals

236 implied strategy
now = make the
merger work

29 split site DGA
not functiona

87 people need to
see 'goodies' within
2 years

113 experience of eg
Bishop Ackland or
Darlington shows
that we may be
moving too quickly

37 everybody is
defensive

20 Ormskirk managt
put block on
expansion because of
merger possibilities

and governmental issues facing the hospital, as well as conflicting views about the current state of the organization and the likely challenges it faced. Despite these differences, we observed that during the cognitive-mapping process, we faced few difficulties achieving interaction between team members as they negotiated their way through the dynamics of reaching consensus on the key strategic issues presented. As Churchill (1990) has observed, this kind of process can be seen to indicate a collective form of organizational learning. The main issues, broken down by cluster, related to politics, performance, staff development, communications and reputation. We found that using this technique enabled all those involved to experience the difficulties of other departments and, with this insight, to begin to understand how the hospital as a whole functioned. The resultant map reduced the messiness and ambiguity that characterized the situation, and enabled the different groups to:

- manage the resultant complexity by identifying emergent themes
- prioritize these themes so that they could subsequently be developed.

As a consequence, group discussion of the cognitive map not only enabled the transmission of information and of the implications of the issues raised for the management of the local authority, but it also helped to overcome disagreement about goals, the interpretation of issues, and subsequent courses of action.

CONCLUSION

In this chapter we have provided an overview of some of the main methods for creating qualitative data through the modalities of language and text. The key points of this chapter that we would like to emphasize are:

 Qualitative research is a creative process, which aims to understand the sense that respondents make of their world. If done well, processes of data collection can be beneficial for everybody involved, both researchers and participants.

 There are many techniques for creating qualitative data in a spoken or written form. Although we can give guidelines, each piece of research is unique, and the decision must be taken on which of these alternative and often-competing approaches is most appropriate.

 The flexibility of qualitative research does not mean that anything goes. Processes of data creation require a fair amount of planning and strategic thinking, and the time and skills needed to create useful data should never be underestimated.

In Chapter 7, we explore a different set of approaches for creating qualitative data, namely those based on *observation and interaction*, such as observational, ethnographic and participatory methods. This next chapter also addresses some overarching issues, such as field access, confidentiality, the role of the researcher, and the necessity of reflexivity of the researcher's involvement. In Chapter 8, we then present strategies for data management, along with different approaches for framing and analysing qualitative data.

FURTHER READING

Alvesson, M. (2003) 'Beyond neopositivists, romantics, and localists: a reflexive approach to interviews in organisation research', *Academy of Management Review*, 28 (1): 13–33.

Bourne, H. and Jenkins, M. (2005) 'Eliciting managers' personal values: an adaptation of the laddering interview method', *Organizational Research Method,* 8 (4): 410–28.

Butterfield, L.D., Borgen, W.A., Amundson, N.E. and Maglio, A.T. (2005) 'Fifty years of the critical incident technique: 1954–2004 and beyond', *Qualitative Research* 5 (4): 475–97.

Cassell, C. and Symon, G. (2004) *Essential Guide to Qualitative Methods in Organizational Research.* London: Sage.

Useful guide with chapters on how to use different methods and techniques in organizational research (including interviews, critical incident technique, repertory grids, cognitive mapping and other methods).

Eden, C. (1992) 'On the nature of cognitive maps', *Journal of Management Studies*, 29 (3): 261–65.

Fielding, N., Lee, R.M. and Blank, G. (2008) *The SAGE Handbook of Online Research Methods*. London: Sage.

Useful collection of chapters on how to conduct research using the Internet, including a chapter on internet-based interviewing. Also:

Gubrium, J.F., Holstein, J., Marvasti, A.B. and McKinney, K.D. (2012) *The SAGE Handbook of Interview Research: The Complexity of the Craft*, 2nd edn. Thousand Oaks, CA: Sage.

Excellent resource with chapters on all aspects of interviewing.

Krueger, R.A. and Casey, M.A. (2009) *Focus Groups: A Practical Guide for Applied Research*, 4th edn. Los Angeles, CA: Sage.

Explains in detail how to plan and moderate focus groups. Similarly useful:

Kvale, S. and Brinkmann, S. (2009) *InterViews: Learning the Craft of Qualitative Research Interviewing*, 2nd edn. Thousand Oaks, CA: Sage.

Useful overview of different interview methods.

Nadin, S. and Cassell, C. (2006) 'The use of a research diary as a tool for reflexive practice: some reflections from management research', *Qualitative Research in Accounting & Management*, 3 (3): 208–17.

The following references provide a useful starting point for those interested in critical incident technique, repertory grids and cognitive maps:

Rogers, B. and Ryals, L. (2007) 'Using the repertory grid to access the underlying realities in key account relationships', *International Journal of Market Research*, 49 (5): 595–612.

Tracy, S.J. (2013) *Qualitative Research Methods: Collecting Evidence, Crafting Analysis, Communicating Impact*. Chichester: Wiley-Blackwell.

Excellent textbook for students planning to conduct a qualitative study; Chapters 7 and 8 cover many practical aspects of interview planning and interview practice.

Want to know more about this chapter? Visit the $SAGE edge™ website at **https://edge. sagepub.com/easterbysmith** to access practice questions, selected journal articles, useful web links and much more.

CRAFTING QUALITATIVE DATA THROUGH OBSERVATION AND INTERACTION

7

LEARNING OBJECTIVES

 To find out about a range of different methods for creating qualitative data through observation and interaction with research participants.

 To understand the potential and limitations of these methods.

 To gain some practical insights into how to prepare for data collection in the field and how to secure access.

 To reflect on the role of researchers in the field, and to understand the ethical premises for conducting observational and interactive research.

Visual data

Observational research

Interactive and participatory methods

General concerns related to the creation of qualitative data

Conclusion

Further reading

Having introduced a range of text-based and interview-based methods in the previous chapter, we discuss in this chapter a number of approaches for creating qualitative data through observation and interaction, including visual methods, participant observation and participatory methods. We address these methods along a continuum from the relatively passive collection of existing secondary data to intrinsically interactive methods aiming at the co-creation of qualitative data with research participants. We then discuss a number of general issues that surround qualitative data collection, such as how to gain access to research participants and research sites, ethical issues, and the necessity of reflexivity of the researcher's own involvement. Together with Chapter 6, this chapter gives a cursory overview of the manifold approaches and techniques that facilitate and structure the crafting of qualitative data. It is intended to inspire a creative and reflexive attitude towards data collection, acknowledging that it often requires some effort to identify the most appropriate methods for a given research project, since this decision depends on the research question as much as on the field under study.

VISUAL DATA

Despite the pervasive nature of the visual in our everyday lives, management research has continued to privilege verbal over visual forms of communication. Historically, visual methods of data collection have been viewed as being highly subjective, difficult to interpret and prone to researcher bias. Consequently, most qualitative management research has been limited to textual data-gathering techniques. Yet, as Secrist et al. (2002) note, despite writers' eloquent verbal descriptions of their research experiences, it is often suggested that words alone cannot communicate the complex and intricate situations they encounter. Consequently, there has been an increasing interest in what visual methods can offer management researchers.

Following Knoblauch and colleagues (2008: 3), we define visual data as 'any kind of visual material, either produced by actors (such as lay photographs) or social scientists (such as video records of social interactions) that depend in their meaning and significance on […] visualized records, be it diagrams, photographical reproductions or video-taped records.' In line with the notion of social poetics, visual data offers the opportunity for a situation to be held captive or frozen in time (Wittgenstein, 1953). Whether we look at organizational charts or pictures accompanying news reports, or watch videos on YouTube, visual data provide us with a sense of the situation and reveal meaningful insights into all kinds of human experience. Researchers can investigate the meaning of visual data as well as the ways in which they are created and interpreted.

Secondary visual data

A growing number of qualitative studies involve the analysis of secondary visual data, such as videos from the Internet or photographs taken for purposes other than research. The range of potentially relevant visual data is as broad as the capacity of humans to express themselves in a visual way. Buildings, cartoons and complex academic figures: in one way or another, these all reflect human experience. The proliferation of information technologies has led to an unprecedented increase in the use of visual forms of communication. Through the growth of digital media, researchers can get access to contemporary records made by research participants (e.g. pictures taken with mobile-phone cameras), in this way blurring the distinction between the researcher and the researched (Back, 2006).

Photographs taken from archives can open up a historical dimension to research projects. For example, Figure 7.1 shows photographs of market traders' gestures in 1869, 1987 and 1925. Such pictures could be used to explore how communication between traders has changed over time. Images, however, would not need to be the main focus of attention; they

FIGURE 7.1
Historical photographs of market traders

could be complemented with written accounts, video material, interviews, and the observation of traders engaging in increasingly decentralized practices of trading. Indeed, as Pink (2001) highlights, the relation of images to other sensory, material and linguistic details of the study will result in the images being of interest to most researchers. It is important to bear in mind, however, that secondary data are produced for purposes other than research – and, for that reason, they might not fit into a given research project. If we cannot understand or if we misinterpret the background or purpose of a data fragment, this can compromise the quality of our research. Students are also reminded to consider any copyright implications when collecting visual material. If this is not taken into consideration at the outset they may find their research difficult to publish later down the line.

EXERCISE
7.1

Collecting secondary visual data

Interactive exercise: Pick a picture, video, organizational chart or other visual data fragment that could be analysed for a study in your field. Present your data fragment to the group and explain why you have chosen it, where you have found it and the context of the fragment (who produced it, when and where, and for what purpose). Who has identified the most fascinating data fragment? Who has come up with the most innovative idea for a research project? Who has outlined the most practical research project?

Primary visual data

In contrast to secondary visual data, primary visual data such as photographs or videos are specifically created for a research project or study. A body of research known collectively as 'workplace studies' has made extensive use of video recordings to examine the effects of the material environment and technologies on action and interaction in a variety of organizational settings (Luff et al., 2000; Heath and Hindmarsh,

2002). Example 7.1 gives an example of the utility of methods for the creation of visual data, based on a recent study by Clarke (2011), who employed a visual ethnographic approach to explore entrepreneurs' use of visual symbols in the creation of legitimacy for their ventures. Although visual ethnographic approaches, which involve video-taping individuals in contexts of natural interactions, have a long-standing tradition in the fields of visual sociology and anthropology, this is the first attempt to employ such an approach in the management domain.

Using visual tools in a research study

EXAMPLE
7.1

Clarke (2011) incorporated visual tools into her research in order to explore how entrepreneurs use visual symbols to create legitimacy for their ventures. This study is based on material collected during visual ethnographies of three entrepreneurs, during which she captured videos of entrepreneurs in a range of different interactions with investors, employees and customers over a three-month period. She was aware of the influence that the video-camera could have on the unfolding interactions, and attempted as much as possible to reduce the 'reactivity' of participants. Over time, participants became accustomed to the camera and reacted less to its presence. Also, the camera used was small, compact and portable, making it as unobtrusive as possible. Approximately 60 hours of raw video-taped interactions were digitized and captured for audio and video analysis. She found that entrepreneurs use a range of visual symbols during performances to stakeholders, namely settings, props, dress and expressiveness. Entrepreneurs used these visual symbols in order to present an appropriate scene to stakeholders, to create professional identity and emphasize control, and to regulate emotions. When used systematically, visual symbols help entrepreneurs access much-needed resources through addressing the low levels of legitimacy that typically exist when novel ventures are launched. More experienced or serial entrepreneurs are likely to be more effective at employing a wider range of visual symbols systematically during interactions with stakeholders. By studying in detail how entrepreneurs use their visual surroundings during performances with stakeholders, this study shows that language is only one of the symbolic tools used by entrepreneurs. This study illustrates not only the rich information garnered about entrepreneurial processes using a visual approach, but also the potential future utility of visual ethnographies and other visual methodologies in the field of management.

OBSERVATIONAL RESEARCH

Video recordings such as those undertaken by Clarke stand in the tradition of observational research; that is, research based on researchers observing research participants in particular settings. Table 7.1 gives an overview of the different stances that researchers may take when conducting observational research. First, there are *complete observers*, who maintain a detached distance when observing research participants in the field. Second, there are *observers-as-participants*, who participate in activities in the field but seek to reduce the impact of their presence as much as possible. The third stance, *participant-as-observer*, implies more direct interaction with the field. Participant observers of this kind are more active in their engagement with the field they study. Finally, there are *complete participants*, whose primary role is that of participant (e.g. employee or consultant). Some complete participants conceal their intention to conduct research; this can facilitate access but also gives rise to critical ethical issues, which we will discuss below.

TABLE 7.1 Four types of observational research

I. *Complete observer:* Researcher maintains distance to the object and context, and avoids all direct engagement.

II. *Observer-as-participant:* Researcher engages with the field in a relatively passive way, e.g. by asking questions, while trying not to influence the field under study.

III. *Participant-as-observer:* Researcher does not conceal the intention of observation and participates in the context as researcher and participant. This is the most common type of participant observation in management and business studies.

IV. *Complete participant:* Researcher conceals the intention to study and adopts more fully the role of a participant when observing the field.

(ANDERSON, 2008a)

As this overview shows, different types of observational research differ in their understanding of the *role of the researcher*. Depending on their role, researchers employ different methods of data creation. Researchers conducting complete observation usually create observational records (such as written records, audio recordings and videos) and collect secondary data. Adopting the role of a participant as well as an observer opens up additional avenues for the creation of qualitative data (such as conversations and field interviews) and the (co)creation of visual data (e.g. by drawing an organizational chart with a group of employees). Such methods allow researchers not only to observe certain activities or interactions but also to explore *why* they are pursued. In the following sections, we explore the four types of observational research in more detail.

All observational methods usually require researchers to record their observations. In some cases, this can be done using video or audio recordings, but the most common technique is to make some preliminary scribblings in a notebook, and to return to the notebook later in the day in order to transform the notes into comprehensive written accounts. Writing detailed field notes requires method, skill and practice – and involves an active process of interpretation. In Table 7.2 we include a list of some tips for writing field notes. Readers who wish to conduct an observational study are advised to obtain more in-depth guidance on how to write field notes (see, for example, Emerson et al., 2011).

TABLE 7.2 Tips for writing field notes

1 *Discreetness:* Be careful not to irritate or annoy research participants when taking notes.

2 *Write-up:* Write up your full accounts/field notes as soon as you can, and before speaking to anyone about what you have observed

3 *Headings:* Never forget time, date, place and a list of the participants involved.

4 *Detail:* Be as detailed as possible. Things that appear unimportant at first can turn out to be very important later down the line. Don't forget to describe characters and settings.

5 *Openness:* Just write and do not worry about style or grammar. Your field notes are *your* material.

6 *Perspective:* Ask yourself why you chose a certain perspective on an event or episode – and whether some participants could have experienced this episode in a different way.

7 *No analysis:* Avoid evaluative or judgemental language. Field notes should record facts – analysis comes later.

8 *Quotations:* Indicate direct quotations as such.

9 *Emotions:* If you are tired or emotional, it can be useful to write in the research diary (mentioned in the previous chapter) first.

10 *To-do list:* Note down follow-up questions at the end of the interview.

Exploring the role of the researcher in observational research

a) **Interactive exercise**: Burawoy (2009: 204) notes that as participant observers, 'we don't have access to some Archimedean standpoint' (a hypothetical vantage point from which an observer can objectively perceive the subject of inquiry): instead we are always located somewhere 'in the site, which has grave consequences to what we say'. In groups or pairs, discuss how this statement relates to the four types of observational research presented above. What are the implications of the different standpoints for researchers and research participants? What kind of observational research is the most useful/the most problematic?

b) **Individual exercise**: Reflect on what kind of observational research could be useful for your own project, and what standpoint could be most appropriate when taking into account the objectives of your research and the nature of the field you wish to study.

Complete observation

By *complete observation*, we refer to observations conducted by researchers who avoid any interaction with the field. This type of observation is most commonly used in the field of management services where, for job design and specification purposes, requests are made for 'objective' accounts of the content of work. As a research method, complete observation is of limited use to those interested in a social constructionist view. Even when used in the discipline of management services, practitioners conducting complete observation usually do not ask people for accounts of their own actions because of the requirement for detachment. This limits the depth of the data obtained in significant ways.

Complete observers are often disliked by those whom they observe, since detached observation can appear like snooping, and prevents the development of trust and rapport between researchers and research participants (which, as we have noted before, is fundamental for the creation of qualitative data). However, for trained practitioners, complete observations can give accurate pictures of specific activities in the workplace, and inform assessments of how long they take, even if they fall short of giving a full account of why things are happening in a certain way. While, in the past, detached accounts of non-participant observers were valued as more 'neutral' and so more scientific than participant observations, the artificial character of such observations has given rise to many anecdotes.

In *Kitchen Stories*, a film by the Norwegian director Bent Hamer (2003), scientific observers placed on tall chairs attempt to survey the kitchen habits of old single men in an attempt to optimize their kitchens. The observers are instructed not to communicate with the 'objects' of their research, as a result of which the observed men avoid their kitchens and engage in a similarly detached observation of the unusual behaviour of the scientific 'intruders' until both sides cannot avoid direct engagement. This and similar films and anecdotes show how the artificiality of complete observation can have as strong an impact on the field as open interaction and engagement. This raises questions about the kind of settings that allow for *complete* (i.e. *non*-participant) observations.

Practicing complete observation

EXERCISE 7.3

Individual exercise: Conduct about 20 minutes of complete observation in a public space. For example, observe people doing their shopping in a market place, commuters on a bus, people having a lunch break in a coffee shop, students in a seminar, or tourists visiting a tourist site. Be careful to pick a site where your behaviour won't cause any inconvenience to those being observed or arouse undue suspicion. When observing, try to be as focused as possible. Immediately after the observation, and *before talking to anyone about it*, write down your observations. Do not worry about the format or language you use, just be as specific and detailed as possible. What kind of details can you remember, and what details slipped your mind? Can you explain why? Give your observation record to a friend or colleague. Do they have any comments on your observations or the style in which you noted down your observations?

Participant observation and ethnography

Participant observation is the principal method to document 'moments when belief and action come together' (Luker, 2008: 158). Participant observers accept their role as researchers while they also engage with their field in an active way. Roy (1970: 217) describes the advantages of this approach: he suggests that the participant as observer not only makes no secret of their investigation but is also at pains to make it known that it is the research that is their overriding interest. They are 'there to observe'. As a consequence the participant observer becomes not so tied down and is free to 'run around as research interest beckons'.

Methods of participant observation are defined by a continuum, running from very limited observations to answer specific questions (such as where to place the sink in kitchens for single retired men) to rather open and general observations of an entire social system or culture (such as the life of elderly single men in rural Norway). Looking at participant observation from this perspective helps us to determine the difference between *participant observation* as a method and *ethnography* as a research strategy, two concepts many consider as synonymous. Participant observation can be used as a method for just a couple of hours to answer very specific research questions. The observer can be present sporadically over a period of time: moving, for example, in and out of an organization to deal with other work or to conduct interviews with, or observations of, different people across a number of different organizations.

In contrast to such interrupted involvement, *ethnography* usually refers to the long-term and in-depth use of participant observation, often in conjunction with other methods (such as interviews or the collection of demographic data), to understand an entire social system or culture (Macdonald, 2010). Ethnography requires a systematic and sustained engagement with a field, where the researcher becomes immersed in a new context that poses unexpected challenges and puzzles to solve. Ethnographic research can be an overwhelming experience. Many researchers find it challenging to remain aware of themselves as observers. Hence, ethnographers do not only observe research participants, they also observe themselves and how they engage with their environment.

Example 7.2 illustrates a participant observation study conducted in a tea plantation by a PhD student in Sri Lanka. It shows the 'insider–outsider' conflict that studies like this produce, and it also illustrates the importance trust plays in getting data and making the most of opportunities that present themselves.

EXAMPLE
7.2

A social constructionist perspective on conducting a rural ethnography

In conducting this research, a PhD student aimed to understand how different communities construct, maintain and change their self-identities. The research took place within the particular context of workers on a tea plantation in Sri Lanka (see Figure 7.2). During the fieldwork phase, the student became far more aware of her own identity as a researcher than had hitherto been the case, and she was able to see and understand her identity both as an academic and as a Sri Lankan national. The latter enabled her to understand the social and cultural values, and her Buddhist background enabled her to live with the community and adapt to the prevailing social norms. At times she saw herself as an outsider, while at others she became an insider within the research site. Living both outside and inside different tea plantations, developing close relationships with local people, she was able to make sense of the practices and rituals she was able to observe. At times, some of the elders became protective and supportive of her as a young female researcher. When inside the plantation, she seized the opportunity to spend as much time as possible with those on the plantation, talking and observing. Due to the size of the plantation, when 'on site' she was often accompanied by a representative from management; although this was meant to be helpful, it made it difficult for her to get close to people and to establish the kind of trusting relationship she would have liked. She later learnt that part of the difficulty experienced was due to the fact that workers had been warned by the police not to talk to strangers inside the plantation. This made them hesitant to approach her, although, as she got to know them, she developed sufficient trust to win their confidence. The PhD student summarizes her experiences of an ethnographic approach as being a complex process. The process is not a logical step-by-step approach, and skills of sensitivity are required, as well as a flexibility and willingness to change the plan and to be open to where the research might lead.

FIGURE 7.2
Tea-leaf
picking

There is extensive literature on participant observation and ethnography, particularly in sociology and anthropology (Bernard, 2011). Since organizations can easily be viewed as 'tribes', with their own strange customs and practices, it is by no means surprising that participant observation has also been used in organizational and management research – where it usually implies some kind of close involvement in an organization, with the purpose of uncovering accounts that may not have been accessed by other methods, such as interviews (Anderson, 2008a; Watson, 1994). The object is to gain an insider perspective that enhances a researcher's understanding of other people's realities. In Table 7.3, we list some examples of research involving participant observation in business and management studies.

TABLE 7.3   Examples of observational research in business and management studies

Articles

Knox, H., O'Doherty, D., Vurdubakis, T. and Westrup, C. (2008) 'Enacting Airports: Space, Movement and Modes of Ordering', *Organization*, 15 (6), pp. 869–88. DOI: 10.1177/1350508408095818.

Lok, J. and Rond, M. de (2013) 'On the Plasticity of Institutions: Containing and Restoring Practice Breakdowns at the Cambridge University Boat Club', *Academy of Management Journal*, 56 (1), pp. 185–207. DOI: 10.5465/amj.2010.0688.

McCann, Leo, Granter, Edward, Hyde, Paula, Hassard, John (2013) 'Still Blue-Collar after all these Years? An Ethnography of the Professionalization of Emergency Ambulance Work', *Journal of Management Studies*, 50 (5), pp. 750–76. DOI: 10.1111/joms.12009.

Roy, Donald (1952) 'Quota Restriction and Goldbricking in a Machine Shop', *American Journal of Sociology*, 57 (5), pp. 427–42. DOI: 10.2307/2772323.

Roy, Donald (1954) 'Efficiency and "The Fix": Informal Intergroup Relations in a Piecework Machine Shop', *American Journal of Sociology*, 60 (3), pp. 255–66. DOI: 10.2307/2772683.

Books and Chapters

Van Maanen, John (1991) 'The Smile Factory: Work at Disneyland', *Reframing Organizational Culture*, edited by P.J. Frost, L.F. Moore, M.R. Louis, C.C. Lundberg and J. Martin. Newsbury Park, CA: Sage.

Dalton, Melville (1959) *Men who manage. Fusions of feeling and theory in administration*. New York: Wiley.

Kunda, Gideon (1993) *Engineering culture. Control and commitment in a high-tech corporation*: Temple University Press.

EXERCISE
7.4

Exploring ethnographic studies in management

Interactive exercise: Conduct a brief literature research to identify a recent article or book on an ethnographic study in management research, or pick one of the publications listed in Table 7.3. Read and evaluate the publication to answer the following questions in writing:

- How do the authors describe their methodology? How do they describe their role in the field? Do they detail the length/depth of their engagement with the field? What was their role in the field? Are there any important details missing?

- How does the methodology of the study relate to its outcome?

- Do you think it would have been possible to conduct the study with other methods? If yes, what would have been the advantages and disadvantages of using different methods?

Complete participation and covert research

In contrast to complete observation and participant observation, *complete participation* implies that the role of the researchers in the field is defined by their roles as participants (e.g. as colleagues, employees or consultant). Donald Roy (1952) used the method to great effect when working as an employee in the machine shop of a large company. He was able both to show how workers manipulated the piecework incentive scheme and to understand the motives behind this. For anyone wishing to learn about the craft of participant observation and how the methodology might be written up, they would do well to read one or two of the original articles that Roy produced from his research (see Table 7.3).

Complete observation usually implies that researcher participants either are unaware of the fact that a particular co-worker, manager or employee conducts research (i.e. in covert observation) or do not consider this fact relevant. Researchers who are creating data as complete participants and members of organizations may find themselves negotiating a minefield of ethical issues. *Covert research* is generally difficult to reconcile with the key principles of research ethics (stated in Chapter 5). When reflecting upon this dilemma, it can be helpful to consider whether the potential benefits of the research can really outweigh the ethical issues created through covert observation. The final section of this chapter will briefly return to this thorny issue and to related questions of research ethics in data collection, giving some insights into the ethical-review procedures that are now in place in many universities to ensure the ethical conduct of social research.

Semi-concealed research

Semi-concealed research is not the same as covert research, in that researchers are more open about their rationale for studying the company. The aspect of concealment relates to the way the focus of the research is defined, and the view the researcher takes on the practices under observation. An example of this would be the research of Collinson (1992), who conducted his study into the recruitment and selection practices in large companies without emphasizing that his particular focus was on how the mainly white, male, middle-aged managers controlled entry into the companies in ways that had the effect of excluding women. In this way, he could negotiate access into organizations that otherwise could have inhibited his access for fear of being presented in an unflattering or critical light.

In another study conducted by Thorpe (1980), the researcher was able to gain an understanding of how management's failure to address the motivational needs of the workforce led to disillusionment and apathy (see Example 7.3). Not all individuals involved were aware of the research taking place. However, the company chairperson and the works convener had agreed to the research being conducted, as they considered it useful.

Researcher as employee

Poor planning of work meant that workers were often bored: by experiencing this boredom himself, Thorpe was better able to understand its causes and the ways in which the employees attempted to alleviate it. His team developed a pattern of activity where they worked for the first hour or so, and then took a break, and had a wash and a walk outside. On certain days, they changed their overalls in the laundry, which involved a walk of about 600 yards and a break of about half an hour. After mid-morning, the pace became much slower; and after lunchtime, very little work was done at all.

EXAMPLE
7.3

(Continued)

(Continued)

On one occasion (a Wednesday afternoon), the researcher saw that the conveyor belt was beginning to back up for no apparent reason. On questioning his colleagues about it, he learnt that they saw this as a good strategy to put pressure on management and guarantee themselves overtime at the weekend (at time-and-a-half pay). Since overtime working had to be notified to the employees three days in advance, it was important to slow things down on Wednesday. By Friday, the backlog had all but been cleared but the promise of the overtime remained, making for a fairly easy Saturday morning's work!

Naturally, Thorpe's questioning did not stop at this observation, for it then became of interest to know why the extra pay was required, and why this strategy was used in preference to others.

Auto-ethnography

Participant observation requires researchers to reflect on their own role. If researchers give up the awareness of their own position as participant *and* researcher, they risk becoming assimilated into the field in a way that limits their analytic ability. Practices with which researchers are well acquainted go unnoticed or remain unchallenged more easily than those that appear unfamiliar. Most classical anthropological ethnographies were undertaken in fields that were alien to the researcher, as the incremental reduction in the distance between the researcher as an 'outsider' and a field of 'insiders' was seen as aiding the observational process. While there is certainly some truth in this argument, it can also be difficult for an 'outsider' to understand the motivations and interpretations of 'insiders': something that complete participants have less trouble with.

Being an 'insider' can (literally) 'open doors' that an external observer would not even be aware of; it reduces resource requirements, and facilitates the establishment of trust and rapport (Karra and Phillips, 2007). At the same time, it also can imply role conflict and a lack of critical distance, and begs the question of to what extent the focus of the observation is on *other insiders* or on the experiences, practices and identity of the *researcher as an insider*. Ethnographic studies that shift the focus from the field to the observer are usually referred to as **auto-ethnographies** (or self-ethnographies). An interesting example of an auto-ethnography with a strong autobiographical dimension is a study by Goodall (2007) entitled *A Need to Know*, in which he explores how his father's work for the CIA during the Cold War shaped the history of his family, and his own biography. It could be argued that much management research conducted for postgraduate qualifications is at least partially auto-ethnographic, as students set out to study their own work context and observe their colleagues, as well as their own activities.

INTERACTIVE AND PARTICIPATORY METHODS

Having discussed the collection of visual data and a number of observational methods, we illustrate in this section the use of interactive and participatory methods for the creation of qualitative data. Many of these methods combine techniques of methods we have introduced earlier, such as qualitative interviews, participant observation and the creation of primary visual data. What makes interactive and participatory methods stand out is that they aim at the *interactive (co)creation of qualitative data* in a process that encourages researchers and respondents to develop a joint understanding of what is taking place. Used in this way, interactive and participatory methods become 'tools for thinking' that stimulate discussion and debate, leading to a reduction in uncertainties and ambiguities that so often surround management situations. To develop this notion, we point to Daft and Lengel's (1986) study, which suggested that most organizational situations are characterized by uncertainty and that this uncertainty is very often caused by an absence of information or by ambiguity, caused by equivocality. What researchers need to do, therefore, is to find ways of reducing the uncertainty and the equivocality, both in obtaining data to analyse and in the way that the information is exchanged. Participatory methods involving diagramming and visual techniques can stimulate the exchange and debate needed to achieve this aim, as these methods embrace complexity and open up ways to recognize multiple realities. An additional feature of participatory and interactive methods is that they can be beneficial for the research participants as well as the researcher, as in many cases both parties learn from their application.

A number of methods that aim at stimulating reflection and discussion among research participants involve the (co)creation of data. In Chapter 6, we discussed some interview-based and text-based techniques that are used in this way (repertory grid and mapping techniques). Here, we introduce a number of additional approaches that employ a visual-media component, such as participatory methods that involve videos, photographs and pictures.

Video recordings, photographs and pictures

One attempt at applying a visually based methodology is Cunliffe's (2001) postmodern perspective on management practice, where she video-taped interviews she conducted with a number of managers. She subsequently played these video-taped interviews back to the managers to explore with them how they had co-created meaning through the course of the interview. In this way, the meaning of the interviews was discussed and deciphered in collaboration with the participant, as a form of co-inquiry.

Photographs can be a useful way of gathering information when there is only a small amount of data on an issue to begin with, when getting information is proving difficult, or when the matter under discussion is seen as contentious or problematic. The general public and employees of an organization can contribute to research through the use of photographs. Just as newspapers often request updated pictures from the public, researchers can do the same. Researchers can also ask employees and participants to take pictures of specific events that the researcher is interested in. This can serve to complement other sources – say, interviews, diaries and postcards. Assessing the role that photography has played in organizational research, Buchanan (1999) found that while it has enjoyed a rich tradition in disciplines such as sociology and anthropology (Collier and Collier, 1986; Harper, 1994; Banks, 1995), it has been used far less within the field of management. As a consequence, he deliberately planned his research so as to use photographs to stimulate discussion and debate between members of staff at a hospital as part of a programme to re-engineer the patient's experience. He argued that if something of relevance can be seen, it can be discussed and possibly altered. Buchanan's purpose was to collect photographs in order to record complex scenes and processes that could provide 'non-reactive' records and observations. He found that the photographs helped the study. The use of photographs triggered informants to talk much more about the ideas they had around the images, and this helped to develop a more complex understanding of the chains of activity that occurred. Photographs of the process also contributed to a more accurate sequencing of this, as well as to a more detailed written analysis of the process. Once accomplished, the sequence was shown to a number of groups within the hospital, and again additional complex details were added in the discussions and debates that they engendered.

Pictures and drawings are another form of visual data that can be used to elicit the views of individuals or groups. Individuals, for example, might be asked to represent the issues that concern them in the form of pictures or drawings. Birgit Schyns et al. (2011) have used this approach to great effect in their studies of how leaders are perceived by followers in different cultures. In her and her colleagues' research, people from different nationality groups were asked to draw pictures of leaders; from these, understandings were gained into the dimensions and perspectives of very different national groups in relation to leadership. Figure 7.3 shows one of the outputs from this study, illustrating the wider societal purpose of leadership in relationship to followers seen by students from East Asia. In this example, it can be seen how effective leaders are expected to take responsibility for employees' and their families' well-being.

FIGURE 7.3
Drawing depicting an effective East Asian leader

SOURCE: SCHYNS ET AL., 2011: 403

Visual metaphors

The use of **visual metaphors** can be a powerful way of developing a common understanding of an issue – and for groups to move forward with a vision for the future. An example of a group of managers being asked to draw a picture of the organization as if it were a person is shown in Example 7.4.

EXAMPLE
7.4

A visual metaphor

In research conducted in a large multinational organization, this approach was used to explore how the senior staff viewed their organization (Simpson, 1995). The research was conducted using a series of focus-group interviews. At each session, the groups were asked the following questions:

1. If the organization were a parent, how do you think it would relate to its children?

2. If you were asked to write an honest character reference for the organization, what would it say? Some guidance here included how well it performed in its most recent job, what its most recent job was, its achievements, and anything else that individuals thought was important.

3. Try to imagine the company as an old friend whom you have not seen for the last ten years. How would you judge whether the friend's personality had changed?

4. Finally, individuals were asked to draw a picture of the company as the 'person' is today.

The questions produced very rich data indeed, which was taped and analysed, but perhaps the most interesting aspect of this metaphor approach was the drawings that the individuals produced and their interpretation. An example is shown in Figure 7.4.

FIGURE 7.4

The way the group discussed the drawings was as follows:

Jean: He's a man again, is he?

Mirjam: Yes.

David: Yes, I think he is a man.

Mohamed: It's impossible to get away from that, I think.

Jean: Tell us about your picture; what does your picture show for us?

Mohamed: Shall I defend this? Since I drew it, I got the short straw! Well, I was thinking of the bumbling-uncle-type person: perhaps not the sharpest person in the world, but at least you might get your pocket money off him. Next time you meet him, he's got 30 years younger; he's got a flat top, a nice suit and a BMW. What was I trying to show [indicating hand on the drawing]? I'm not much of an artist as you can see – was basically just 'No!'. It looks like 'On yer bike!', which is just as appropriate.

Lisa: What's this in his other hand?

Mohamed: It's a mobile phone; it's trying to show he's a yuppie, flat-top hair, double-breasted suit, trendy glasses, small chin.

Lisa: It's interesting about the other hand because we thought there would be a lot of gesticulation rather than the sort of verbal interaction; it's sort of hi over there …

Liam: We were going to put him with a bag of money in one hand …

Lisa: But the portable phone gets that across.

Jean: So he's gone from being a friendly uncle to a yuppie?

(Continued)

(Continued)

Mohamed:	Yes.
Clare:	And younger instead of older?
Mohamed:	Yes, yes.
Jean:	Perhaps we should all find out what he is on then!
Lisa:	Didn't that also happen to the bloke who sold his soul to the devil?
Jean:	I don't know.
Mohamed:	What's the film called? It's a baseball film, basically about an old guy who sold his soul to the devil – it's the Faust legend – and became a young baseball player. I don't know what happened to Faust, whether he got younger.

The above interpretations of the changes that had occurred revolved around the symbolism of a more business-like future – the more conservative style of dress (double-breasted suit) and a more frantic (even harassed) appearance – and symbolized the increasing pace of organizational change and activity. An overall theme of the pictures from all the groups was the recognition of the change there had been from a friendly, caring, calm demeanor to an aggressive impersonal characterization of the organization. This example illustrates how, by making comparisons – in this case with something invented – a metaphor picture can help people to articulate their hopes and fears in a relatively non-threatening, non-confrontational and even humorous manner. Drawing pictures and drawing metaphors in groups may also enable employees to work to create a shared landscape, to which they all have contributed and in which they can all see their contribution and role.

EXERCISE
7.5

Exploring the creative use of visual data

Interactive exercise: Discuss the potential use of visual data for different kinds of management research. Think about some research projects that you know about or are planning to do. What participatory methods could be useful for these projects? Try to be creative when considering how different participatory methods could help to engage with research participants. What are the opportunities and challenges that are presented by different kinds of tools? For example, some research participants might not be inclined to draw pictures, instead preferring the use of digital tools, such as the creation of an interactive photo story or a digital memory game on a tablet. Others might lack the experience of working with such technologies.

Action research

As we have discussed in Chapter 3, action research is a particular method that is about change and intervention, and within which researchers work with practitioners on matters of concern (Eden and Huxham, 1995; Saunders et al., 2009). Eden and Huxham (1996) suggest that as the interventions will naturally be 'one-offs', they can be criticized for their lack of replicability and lay themselves open to a claim of lack of rigour. Those contemplating their use do need to be clear on their endeavour, which bring theory and practice together for a process of change and improvement. Action research transcends descriptive and explanatory accounts of organizations. According to Gummesson ([1988] 1991), a researcher comes with a theoretical trajectory or a 'pre-understanding' of a research topic and setting. While it is common for other research approaches to be explicit about the assumptions a researcher might be making at the outset of a research project, it is important for action research to resist making too many assumptions before the project, because alternative interpretations are likely to emerge if pre-understanding is suppressed (Eden and Huxham, 1995). Although Eden and Huxham recognize that this might be difficult to achieve in practice, at least it should be pushed into the background as far as possible. As a result, the analysis of the research may be enriched, which in turn may facilitate finding new insights and concepts.

Researchers who want to use the action-research method should be aware that the skills required are not entirely the same as those needed for other research methods. Eden and Huxham (2007: 539) identify 15 characteristics of action research which they think need to be considered even though they recognize that some might be hard to achieve (see Table 7.4).

TABLE 7.4   Characteristics of action research

15 characteristics of action research

1   Action research demands an integral involvement by the researcher with an intent to change the organization. This intent may not succeed – no change may take place as a result of the intervention – and the change may not be as intended.

2   Action research must have some implications beyond those required for action or generation of knowledge in the domain of the project. It must be possible to envisage talking about theories developed in relation to other situations. Thus, it must be clear that the results could inform other contexts, at least in the sense of suggesting areas for consideration.

3   As well as being usable in everyday life, action research demands valuing theory, with theory elaboration and development as an explicit concern of the research process.

4   If the generality drawn out of the action research is to be expressed through the design tools, techniques, models and methods, then this alone is not enough. The basis for their design must be explicit and shown to be related to the theories that inform the design and that, in turn, are supported or developed through action research.

5   Action research will be concerned with a system of emergent theory, in which the theory develops from a synthesis of that which emerges from the data and that which emerges from the use in practice of the body of theory that informed the intervention and research intent.

6   Theory-building, as a result of action research, will be incremental, moving through a cycle of developing theory, to action, to reflection and to developing theory, from the particular to the general in small steps.

7   What is important for action research is not a (false) dichotomy between prescription and description, but a recognition that description will be prescription, even if implicitly so. Thus, presenters of action research should be clear about what they expect the consumer to take from it, and present it with a form and style appropriate to this aim.

8   For high-quality action research, a high degree of systematic method and orderliness is required in reflecting about, and holding on to, the research data and the emergent theoretical outcomes of each episode or cycle of involvement in the organization.

9   For action research, the process of exploration – rather than collection – of the data in detecting emergent theories and developing existing theories must be either replicable or at least capable of being explained to others.

(Continued)

TABLE 7.4 (Continued)

10 The full process of action research involves a series of interconnected cycles, where writing about research outcomes at the latter stages of an action-research project is an important aspect of theory exploration and development, combining the process of explicating pre-understanding and methodical reflection to explore and develop theory formally.

11 Adhering to characteristics 1 to 10 is a necessary but insufficient condition for the validity of action research.

12 It is difficult to justify the use of action research when the same aims can be satisfied using approaches that can demonstrate the link between data and outcomes more transparently (such as controlled experimentation or surveys). Thus, in action research, the reflection and data-collection process – and hence the emergent theories – are most valuably focused on the aspects that cannot be captured by other approaches.

13 In action research, the opportunities for triangulation that do not offer themselves with other methods should be exploited fully and reported. They should be used as a dialectical device, which powerfully facilitates the incremental development of theory.

14 The history and context for the intervention must be taken as critical to the interpretation of the likely range of validity and applicability of the results of action research.

15 Action research requires that the theory development, which is of general value, is disseminated in such a way as to be of interest to an audience wider than those integrally involved with the action and/or with the research.

Of course, the researcher needs to be skilled in techniques for probing and eliciting information from respondents. But the researcher is also required to have good facilitation skills, and the ability and flexibility to alternate between the roles of co-interventionist with practitioners and academic researcher who steps back and derives abstractions about the immediate experience. Example 7.5 offers an understanding of what action research may entail. For a more detailed list of literature on the use of action research, further reading is suggested at the end of the chapter.

EXAMPLE 7.5

Action research

Huxham (2003) relates a retrospective account of how a particular research team set about analysing data on leadership in a health-promotion partnership with which the research team worked. In the first instance, each of the researchers individually studied the data and identified what occurred over the course of the interventions, either through verbatim quotations or through general and interpretive descriptions. Then, the team convened meetings and started negotiating on meanings of those interpretations, and why these were considered of relevance to leadership within the particular setting. The researchers proceeded to form categories of related issues and interpretations. Huxham explains:

> Gradually clusters of data and interpretations began to emerge. We also added in concepts deriving from the literature. On this occasion we used the mapping software, Decision Explorer. [...] Decision Explorer is a convenient tool because it allows large volumes of data to be handled flexibly. (2003: 244)

In the example given, **Decision Explorer** was not the only means of data analysis; sticky notes were also employed at times. A third stage involved sifting through and dissecting the contents of each cluster with a view to identifying linkages from which a conceptual framework was created. Here, again, the researchers first attempted to identify the linkages individually, and then came together to discuss and agree how the various clusters might be linked. The outcome was a combination of the acceptance of some of the clusters and an abandonment of others for lack of adequate data. At the end of this third step, a core number of clusters were formulated, all linked with leadership.

The subsequent step incorporated reflection on what had been achieved up to that point, but it also encompassed testing the emerging framework in contexts other than the setting in which it was generated.

The fifth and final stage focused on refining the different clusters into a framework, enriching this with theoretical justifications, and disseminating it in academic circles through conferences, while at the same time ensuring a practice link by engaging with other practitioners.

GENERAL CONCERNS RELATED TO THE CREATION OF QUALITATIVE DATA

Researchers who engage in the creation of qualitative data face some common problems independent of the methods they use. In this section, we want to address some of these more general concerns, namely the issue of how to secure access to a field one wishes to study; ethical issues surrounding qualitative research, and how these are addressed in ethical-review processes; common challenges that researchers face when conducting field research; and the necessity of reflexivity when creating and analysing qualitative data.

Access

Having decided on the research objectives and research questions of a qualitative study, researchers need to identify a suitable setting or sample of research participants. Once a first point of contact has been identified, the question arises of how to gain entry. As noted by Tracy (2013: 66), 'qualitative researchers study *with* participants, rather than conduct research *on* them' – and potential participants may or may not be open to such engagement. Negotiating access to the field can be one of the biggest challenges of the research process, and can develop into a struggle between a potentially intrusive researcher and a stubbornly resistant insider (Burawoy, 2009). More often than not, researchers rely on participants to volunteer a significant amount of time; time they could spend on other things they consider more entertaining or more useful. How many researchers are keen to participate in other people's research projects? The answer to this question alone gives an indication of the importance of an appropriate and well-prepared strategy for achieving access to the field. The phenomenal growth in business and management courses over the last two decades has had both negative and positive effects on the likelihood of gaining access. On the one hand, there are now a lot of other students and institutions competing for access to a limited number of organizations; on the other hand, there are now large numbers of managers who have taken management degrees themselves (and some may still be studying on part-time schemes), and they are likely both to understand and to be sympathetic to the researchers' objectives.

Preparing for a first contact with the field requires a significant amount of background research in order to get a clearer picture of whom to contact and how. At this stage, researchers are advised to consider whether access to their chosen field is actually a realistic option – and whether they have a direct or indirect personal link to the field (e.g. a friend, neighbour, family member or colleague) who could help with getting a first contact.

Once this first contact or potential *gatekeeper* is identified, the best way of contacting this individual or institution needs to be established; this may be by letter, email, appearing in person, or a phone call. While preparing for the first attempt to secure access, it is important to think about the research project from the perspective of the potential participant. Why should this person be interested in this project? How can such interest be sparked in the best way? Lengthy academic proposals, unrealistic promises and sloppy template letters are unlikely to be successful. A contact request or access proposal should be polite, personal and appropriate in style and language. It should include:

- a *short introduction to the study and its purpose*, written in clear language
- an *overview of what kind of data collection* the study will involve
- a (flattering) *statement about why the contact person is particularly qualified* to contribute to the study
- a *summary of the experience or background of the researcher* (if it is thought it will help)
- a *section addressing issues surrounding confidentiality and data collection.*

Credibility can be enhanced by using the headed notepaper of an independent body, such as a university, institute or college. The language used in the access proposal merits particular attention. Certain presentations or framings of a research project can make it appear overwhelming, inappropriate, threatening or simply too inconvenient. Such considerations point towards the importance of a patient and incremental approach. While negotiations should not be rushed, continuous follow-up and initiative are likely to be required in order to get the first appointment, telephone call or email, which will decide whether or not access can be established. Whatever choices researchers make about how to approach the field, they should be guided not only by their own research interests but also by considerations about how their behaviour or appearance might be received in the field. One way to obtain trust is to make sure that one is well clued-up about the company. A scan through the company's website will give a quick impression of the issues that are currently considered significant. Another way to obtain the trust of the company one wishes to research is to present the research in a professional and enthusiastic way so that the company sees a benefit. We believe there to be two kinds of benefit which might be offered:

1. Outcomes from the research itself.
2. Contributions to issues within the company which the researcher can offer as a side-benefit of the research. This might be through adding extra topics or themes into interviews or surveys, or carrying out extra work on analysing company data which do not directly benefit the research but add value to the company.

These can both serve to build a stronger relationship with key people in the company, and can also build up 'credit' where the research itself is of more value to you than it is to the company.

EXERCISE 7.6

Preparing an access proposal

Individual exercise: Prepare a sample access proposal for a planned or hypothetical research project. Reflect on how the access proposal might have to be amended when used for different audiences. Ask friends or colleagues to comment on your proposal. Would they be willing to get involved? What elements of the proposal would convince them to do so, and what elements could have the opposite effect?

Another issue that researchers have to consider before entering the field is the role they will assume when conducting their data collection. Some factors that may be kept in consideration when making this choice are:

- *The purpose of the research* may provide a researcher with an indication of which role is most appropriate. Does the research require continued longitudinal involvement, or will in-depth interviews conducted over time give the kind of insights required?

- *The cost of the research* is another factor that needs to be kept in mind. To what extent can the researcher afford to be committed for extended periods of time, and are there any additional costs involved, such as training or housing costs?

- *The extent to which access can be gained* may seem a simple issue, but is also important to be aware of when choosing a researcher's role. Gaining access where the role of the researcher is either explicit or covert can be difficult and may take time.

- *The extent to which the researcher is comfortable in the role* is of course vital to the choice. If the researcher is uncomfortable about taking on a false identity, will it be possible to develop the kind of trusting relationships that are important? Even when permitted, covert research is particularly stressful for the researcher, and not necessarily suitable for inexperienced researchers (Goodall, 1989).

- *The amount of time available* can also be influential. Some methods involve a considerable commitment of time.

Whichever role is chosen, each provides the means to obtain a detailed understanding of values, motives and practices. As Fairhurst (1983: 321) comments, 'The crucial personal skill is to be seen as someone who can be trusted no matter what role is adopted – this will enable much to become possible.'

In a recent example, a PhD student was able to gain access to conduct a three-company case comparison of the effect of performance-related pay on the behaviour of school teachers by taking a job as a lunchtime assistant in one school, a playground supervisor in another, and a classroom assistant in another. Although the lunchtime-assistant role was not ideal as the student would have preferred to be more closely involved in the practice of teaching, it served its purpose in enabling the researcher to get close to teachers, and in helping the early formulation of ideas. As we have indicated above, research of this kind invariably raises ethical dilemmas, and gaining access can be extremely difficult. However, students who require part-time work to undertake their studies can be sitting on very rich research material without realizing it.

Formal access usually has to be granted by decision-makers or authorities that bear some responsibility for the setting that the researcher wants to study. However, this does not generally imply that all potential participants are equally happy to engage with the researcher. Eileen Fairhurst (1983) chose for her research a geriatric ward, and this is where she met her first problem. It took a considerable amount of time to obtain agreement to conduct her research in a particular unit, for two reasons, which illustrate a number of problems involved in this type of research. The first was that consultants in the hospital viewed 'research' in two distinct ways: some saw it as something in which they must become personally involved and that they must 'vet'; others saw it as a self-indulgent activity in which they wanted no part. Even after she had gained agreement for the location of the research, there were additional problems associated with the sensitive focus of the study. Old people are especially vulnerable, and there was real concern that researching them might be viewed as a form of exploitation. To experience delay in the setting up of this kind of study is not in any way unusual. In the case of Thorpe's researcher-as-employee study (see Example 7.3), establishing access took a number of months.

Researchers, as we have discussed in relation to interviewing, must find strategies that will allay people's fears, and offer the organization (or the managers and employees who control access) either reassurance or something in return. This might involve many meetings, and even presentations to the employees, about the aims and potential value of the research. Once accepted, Fairhurst explained how a principal task was to move from a position of stranger to that of friend – someone who could be trusted. When she had achieved this, she found individuals were very willing to tell her about the organization – whether they were nurses, cleaners or ward clerks. While on the wards, she felt it appropriate to help make beds and assist generally; for example, with distributing food and drink at meal times, and collecting bed linen and clothes for patients. At such times, she was not only participating but also strengthening relationships. She recalls that there were times when she simply had to observe, for example when patients were spending time with occupational therapists or physiotherapists (and on other occasions when she did not possess the technical qualifications to take on any role in the work). People understood this and accepted it.

The key skill is to be sensitive enough to know just what role is required in each situation. This is influenced almost entirely by the circumstances at that particular time. For example, Fairhurst explains that it would have been conspicuous if she had stood or sat apart (rather than offering help) when the wards were short-staffed. On the other hand, night staff were always short of work and, as a consequence, she spent much of the time during this period observing, listening to and talking with nurses. Far too often, researchers are perceived to be 'all cost and no benefit' (Luker, 2008: 147), when there are in fact opportunities for them to give something back in a way that enhances their relationships with research participants. At the very least, researchers should never forget to thank research participants in an individual way that reflects their appreciation of the contribution they have made – whether or not this contribution is likely to be helpful.

Ethical issues

Considering the key principles in research ethics listed in Chapter 5, one will notice that the creation of qualitative data can give rise to a number of ethical issues. For example, take key principle 1, which requires researchers to ensure that no harm comes to any participant. While we would like to assume that this principle is fully accepted by all researchers, this does not mean that it is always easy to uphold. A careless sentence that reveals the identify of a particular critical informant to the manager, an ethnographic study discovering shocking shortfalls in a healthcare institution, a notebook full of the names of interviewees lost somewhere on site: there are many ways in which researchers can cause harm to research participants without having intended this at all. The same applies to the other principles. It might not be possible to fully anonymize the identity of an organization that operates in a very small market (protecting anonymity: key principle 6). In a semi-concealed study, we may not want to inform all research participants about the ultimate aim of our research (avoiding deception: key principle 7). What these examples show is that when collecting qualitative data, ethical dilemmas are always likely to arise. Given that we cannot fully avoid them, we should address them in the best possible way.

One way of doing this is to carefully consider the implications of our activities *before* we embark on any fieldwork or data collection. The list of key principles (see Table 5.2) can be used to stimulate reflection on how different activities and data can create ethical issues. Many universities have introduced mandatory review processes called *ethical* or *institutional review* in which a panel of experienced researchers evaluate the ethical implications of a given research project. Researchers are required to submit a review proposal for consideration, and they are prevented from conducting any data collection before they have gained the panel's approval.

The difficulty of getting ethical approval for some projects is something that shouldn't be underestimated. This is particularly the case when projects are more action-oriented with emergent designs. Ethics committees are far more used to positivistic projects where the aims, methods and instruments to be employed can be specified in advance. It is much harder to persuade ethics committees to approve if projects where the type and level of intervention might well change or where the interactions with members of the organization might change over the period of the research.

It is in the process of writing this proposal (at the very latest) when researchers should start thinking about how they can conduct their research in the most ethical way. The exact rules for the structure of such proposals vary, but they generally include:

- a brief *description of the project*, its guiding research questions, objectives, duration and scope
- an *overview of the methods used for data collection*, and how data will be stored and safeguarded
- an outline of *how participants will be recruited* (with a sample contact letter, information sheet and consent form, if required)
- a *reflection on potential issues and how they can be addressed*.

Some review processes also evaluate potential risks to the researchers, and therefore require a statement of how the lead researcher can protect the health and safety of all individuals involved in the research (including participants and assistants). Sometimes, review bodies require researchers to make changes to their plans, and there may be the odd occasion when they refuse to give approval. Many researchers experience the preparation of a review proposal as an unnecessary chore. While this might be true in some cases, it is important not to forget how awful it could be to discover that one's research has harmed research participants in one way or another. It also needs to be noted that attempts have been made to prevent researchers who have foregone such review from publishing their results (Tracy, 2013).

EXERCISE
7.7

Considering ethical-review procedures

a) **Individual exercise**: Find out about whether your institution has established a review process or review mechanism. What are the requirements for postgraduate students? What are the requirements for research staff? Think about how you would approach the preparation of a review proposal. In your view, what issues should be addressed? Do you think you should cover up or remain silent about issues that could be tricky?

b) **Interactive exercise**: In the past, researchers could conduct research without the need for approval by some review panel. For example, most of the studies listed in Table 7.3 were undertaken without such approval. Discuss whether or not you find the introduction of ethical-review procedures useful. What are the strengths and weaknesses of such procedures? Why is it so important to ensure the ethical conduct of research?

Entering the field

In this and the preceding chapters, we have already provided some general guidance on how to conduct research with research participants, and we have highlighted the importance of obtaining trust, being aware of social interaction, and using the appropriate language. Table 7.5 lists some more rules and tips for conducting research with research participants. Many of these may resemble the simple rules of behaviour that our parents taught us (Luker, 2008); their simplicity makes them no less important.

TABLE 7.5 Rules for (co)creating data with research participants

1   Accept the rules that are important to your field, and try to adapt to the customs of your research participants.
2   Be well-prepared, polite and friendly.
3   Listen.
4   Avoid speaking negatively about any of your research participants.
5   Make yourself familiar with the context and background of your research participants.
6   Look out for relevant secondary data.
7   Do not steer all of your conversation towards your research. Allow research participants to meet you as a person.
8   Assess people's practices and responses without judging them prematurely. Allow for conflicting accounts and try to explore the reasons for different interpretations.
9   Do not seek recognition or affirmation.
10 Allow yourself (and others) to laugh about your mistakes and to learn from them.
11 Be open to new experiences.

This list is of course an open-ended one – and we are sure that others might give different advice. Legend has it that Evans-Pritchard, a very eminent anthropologist, would advise all his research assistants before they set off to distant lands to go and get themselves a decent hamper from Fortnum & Mason, and to keep away from the native women (Barley, 1986: 17)! Evans-Pritchard also advised students to 'get a large notebook and start in the middle, because you never know which way things will develop.'

This latter point raises another issue related to observational research. Participant observation is not just a matter of balancing two different roles in the field and keeping a research diary. It involves observing, participating, talking, checking, and understanding and making interpretations. For those who find starting a new job and meeting new colleagues stressful, interactive research methods have a lot to offer. Self-conscious engagement with strangers challenges our self-perceptions. Like people we meet in other realms of life, research participants are usually agreeable and supportive individuals, but there are also those who are cautious, arrogant or difficult. Experiences of disappointment are likely to occur and to have to be dealt with. Combined with the requirements that come with adopting a new role, such experiences can give rise to a crisis of identity.

Getting to know people quite well (even being invited into their homes) and then analysing their behaviour for a research report is a difficult task for most researchers, regardless of ethics. One of the authors vividly remembers his own experience of conducting the semi-covert participant observation study in an engineering works (Example 7.3). He was some 300 miles from his academic base, unable to obtain help or support from colleagues, and found it difficult not to experience a confusion of roles.

Finally, the process of data creation can be both a physical as well as an intellectual challenge. In the case of Thorpe's research, for example, it required the researcher to complete a day of manual work, and then in the evening to continue the process of interpretation so that new lines of enquiry could be picked up the following day. Creating qualitative data can be physically and emotionally draining as much as it can be a thrilling adventure. Keeping a research diary helps to deal with these experiences, as does comprehensive preparation and planning in sufficient time for taking breaks and for recovery.

EXERCISE
7.8

Thinking about fieldwork

Individual exercise: Imagine yourself conducting interactive research. What kinds of situations might you find particularly challenging? A sneering interviewee? Being left aside? Think about how you would react to such situations. Now try to put yourself into the position of your research participants. What kind of behaviour could be challenging for them? Do you have any habits or personal traits that could make it more difficult for them to engage in your research? Make a personal list of rules that could help you with your own fieldwork. Don't forget to consider ethical aspects as well as practical ones.

Reflexivity

Last but not least, some attention needs to be given to the issue of reflexivity. When collecting data, researchers need to think about their roles and the way they affect the research process. A research diary or reflective journal is a way of being reflective and using a critical mindset about the research in progress. As discussed earlier on in this chapter, qualitative research attempts to capture subjective understandings of the external world from the perspective of participants, and abandons the task of representing an 'objective' unchanging external reality. Rather, qualitative research aims to develop knowledge on how participants' understandings are created through patterns of social interaction. In this way, communication is seen as a 'formative' process in which individuals' worldviews are created through interaction with the social world around them. In relation to this, qualitative researchers suggest that meanings are continuously negotiated and renegotiated. However, failing to take account of the place of the researcher in the construction of these understandings enables researchers to remove themselves from the processes that are occurring and allows them to make pronouncements on the role of others. This unfortunately brings a static understanding to meanings that are inherently fluid in nature (Alvesson and Sköldberg, 2000).

For this reason, the notion of reflexivity has become central to any discussion of the collection and representation of qualitative data. While reflexivity may be seen to involve the questioning of 'the threads of philosophical and methodological certainty implicit in the goal of mainstream social science to provide an absolute view of the world' (Cunliffe, 2003: 984), it is difficult to find a commonly agreed definition of reflexivity. In effect, a range of diverse definitions from all corners of the social sciences have been put forward. However, what they all share is a deep underlying scepticism for the truth claims put forward in any form of social-science research. One definition commonly used, which may be helpful to students in attempting to understand what is meant by reflexivity, is that outlined by Alvesson and Sköldberg (2000: 5), who define reflexivity as continuous awareness and attention to 'the way different kinds of linguistic, social, political and theoretical elements are woven together in the process of knowledge development, during which empirical material is constructed, interpreted and written'.

Anderson (2008b) defines reflexivity as that quality that enables the researcher to be aware of their effect on the process and outcomes of research based on the premise that 'knowledge cannot be separated from the knower' (Steedman, 1991). Denzin (1994) comments that in the social sciences, there is only interpretation as nothing speaks for itself and as a consequence in carrying out qualitative research it is impossible to remain 'outside' the subject matter as the presence of the researcher will have an effect of some kind. Reflexive approaches then, as Anderson argues, take into account researcher involvement.

Aiming to incorporate reflexivity into their research practice, many qualitative researchers aim to be aware throughout the research process of how the various elements of their identities become significant, and write this into the research presentations (e.g. Brewer, 2000; Pink, 2001). This often involves paying tribute to social categories such as race, gender and class, and writing these attributes into the research process. This strategy, it is proposed, allows the researcher to understand how their personal characteristics may have in some way influenced the research process and affected their understanding of the results. However, there has been increasing criticism of such approaches to reflexivity. As Cunliffe outlines (2003: 990), 'critics of reflexivity argue it has little to offer […] questioning what is real, what is knowledge, and who (or what) is self, leads only to intellectual chaos, self-indulgent navel-gazing aporia […] and politically motivated subjectivism.' Therefore, some qualitative researchers argue that reflexivity involves too much introspection on the part of the researcher, which may both problematize the research process and paralyse the researcher. While reflexivity has been discussed in this chapter, these issues are no less relevant in the representation of this data; therefore, readers should keep these ideas in mind when reading the chapter on qualitative data analysis.

CONCLUSION

In this chapter we have aimed to provide an overview of some of the main methods for collecting qualitative data through observation and interaction. The key points of this chapter that we would like to emphasize are:

 Qualitative research requires researchers to engage with the field they wish to study.

 Observational, participatory and interactive methods are particularly useful for conducting research on social practices as they allow researchers to explore how intention and action come together.

 Observational and interactive methods of data creation can give rise to serious ethical issues. This is no reason not to use these methods, but rather an opportunity to be more reflexive about our research and its benefits.

 Whatever the method, qualitative data collection should not be unnecessarily burdensome to research participants, but should instead seek to stimulate their interest and involvement.

Together with Chapter 6, this chapter has provided a broad overview of different methods for creating qualitative data, and has discussed a number of key issues concerning the practical use of these. Now it is time to shift our attention from data creation to how the created data may be stored, managed and, most importantly, analysed. Chapter 8 will elaborate further on this.

FURTHER READING

Banks, M. (2008) *Using Visual Data in Qualitative Research*. London: Sage.
    A helpful overview of visual methods. See also:
Coghlan, D. and Brannick, T. (2014) *Doing Action Research in Your Own Organization*, 4th edn. London: Sage.
    Practical manual on how to prepare for action research in your own organization. See also:
Cunliffe, A.L. (2003) 'Reflexive inquiry in organizational research: questions and possibilities', *Human Relations*, 56 (8): 983–1003.
Cunliffe, A.L. (2010) 'Retelling tales of the field: in search of organizational ethnography 20 years on', *Organizational Research Methods*, 13 (2): 224–39.
Eden, C. and Huxham, C. (1996) 'Action research for management research', *British Journal of Management*, 7 (1): 75–86.

Emerson, R.M., Fretz, R. and Shaw, L.L. (2011) *Writing Ethnographic Fieldnotes*, 2nd edn. Chicago, IL: University of Chicago Press.
  Very helpful guidance on how to write – and work with – fieldnotes.
Galman, S.C. (2007) *Shane, the Lone Ethnographer. A Beginner's Guide to Ethnography*. Lanham, MD: AltaMira.
  Entertaining (cartoon) introduction to ethnography for novice researchers.
Karra, N. and Phillips, N. (2007) 'Researching "back home": international management research as autoethnography', *Organizational Research Methods*, 11 (3): 541–61.
Margolis, E. and Pauwels, L. (2011) *The SAGE Handbook of Visual Research Methods*. Los Angeles, CA: Sage.
  Excellent collection of chapters on a broad variety of methods and techniques for creating (and analysing) visual data, including participatory approaches.
Reason, P. and Bradbury, H. (2006) *Handbook of Action Research: The Concise Paperback Edition*. Thousand Oaks, CA: Sage.
  Concise student version (400 pages) of the most comprehensive compendium on action research.
van Maanen, J. (2011) 'Ethnography as work: some rules of engagement', *Journal of Management Studies*, 48 (1): 218–34.
Ybema, S., Yanow, D., Kamsteeg, F.H. and Wels, H. (eds) (2009) *Organizational Ethnography: Studying the Complexity of Everyday Life*. London: Sage.
  Collection of chapters in which authors explore the particular challenges faced by scholars and students conducting ethnographic research in and with organizations. To be complemented by:

Want to know more about this chapter? Visit the **SSAGE** edge™ website at **https://edge. sagepub.com/easterbysmith** to access practice questions, selected journal articles, useful web links and much more.

FRAMING AND INTERPRETING QUALITATIVE DATA

8

LEARNING OBJECTIVES

 To get an overview of different approaches to qualitative data analysis, and to understand how they frame qualitative data in different ways.

 To learn about different methods and techniques for analysing qualitative data.

 To understand how different software packages can assist with the preparation, management and analysis of qualitative data.

 To gain insights into how the quality of qualitative research is assessed.

Preparing and managing qualitative data

Framing and interpreting qualitative data: seven approaches

Computer-aided analysis

Quality in qualitative research

Conclusion

Further reading

One of the most common issues that qualitative researchers face is how to condense highly complex and context-bound information into a format that tells a story in a way that is fully convincing to others. In the case of management research, this goes beyond the requirements of 'good journalism' (where sources are well referenced and interpretations are 'balanced'); it requires both a clear explanation of how the analysis was undertaken and how the conclusions were reached, as well as a demonstration of how the raw data were transformed into meaningful conclusions. Chapter 4 has outlined how to design management research; Chapters 6 and 7 have given the reader some ideas of how qualitative data might be collected; and Chapter 12 discusses how findings could be written up in the project or thesis. This chapter, then, indicates a number of ways in which we might make sense of qualitative data, and how systems can be developed that will make explicit the links between the data collected, the analysis undertaken and the inferences drawn.

In this chapter, we use the term **framing** to refer to a range of ways in which information or data can be made sense of. The analogy is akin to a window that limits and frames what is observed. There are many ways in which data can be 'framed' and looked at, and these ways shape our analysis and our understanding of these data. When analysed through the micro-frame of conversation analysis, interview transcripts can reveal the complexity of decision making in management in great detail. Meanwhile, an analysis of the same interviews using a wider frame can open up a panoramic view on how corporate strategy shapes (or does not shape) everyday decisions in middle management. Some frames focus our view of how managers make sense of their work, whereas others allow us to evaluate the impacts of their decisions. Hence, the way in which we approach data analysis does not depend merely on our research design and the type of data we have collected, but also on our research questions and how we frame our data.

Different approaches to qualitative analysis combine distinct frames, such as a focus on discourse or sense-making, with a set of methods and techniques for interpreting and comparing data, and for building and testing theories. As we have seen in the previous chapters, qualitative research requires rigour, reflexivity and flexibility in equal measure. As this chapter will show, this applies to data analysis as well as to data creation.

Before data can be analysed, they have to be *organized*. While this appears to be common sense, many researchers still waste significant amounts of time and energy on poor data management. With this in mind, we have decided to start this chapter with a short introduction into how to prepare and organize data for qualitative data analysis. We then proceed with an overview of seven different approaches for analysing qualitative data. We begin with approaches that frame qualitative data as proxies for human experience, and then move towards approaches that treat the data themselves as the main object of analysis (Ryan and Bernard, 2003). For each analytical approach, we give a brief introduction into how the approach frames qualitative data, and then present some of the methods and techniques that are associated with this approach. After outlining these seven approaches for framing and analysing qualitative data, we show how specialist software packages can facilitate data analysis, and we advise readers on how to identify tools that are appropriate for their own research. We conclude this series of three chapters on qualitative methodologies and methods with a discussion on how the quality of qualitative research can be assessed.

PREPARING AND MANAGING QUALITATIVE DATA

Before embarking on the analysis of qualitative data, researchers should prepare and organize their data in a way that facilitates the analytic process. As noted by Tracy (2013: 185), such preparation of qualitative data can be seen as akin to the preparation of ingredients for a celebrity chef on TV who wants to create a perfect dish rather than search the kitchen for salt or sugar. Before starting the analysis, *all* relevant data that have been collected should be filed *systematically and in an appropriate format*; digital data should be *formatted* and *labelled in a consistent way* so that individual data fragments can easily be identified and retrieved. Lists of contacts and pseudonyms, and an *overview of all data*, should also be prepared and regularly updated.

It is important to ensure that all data are stored in a way that *prevents unauthorized access*, for example in a locked filing cabinet or as password-protected files on a computer. In the Digital Age, data protection has become more of an issue; this is because digital databases have important implications for the ownership of data and raise complex issues around confidentiality, anonymity and consent (Parry and Mauthner, 2004). These issues should be covered in the research proposal submitted for ethical or institutional review (see Chapter 7 for details). The principles stated in the reviewed proposal should be adhered to at all times. All data should be *backed up and archived* in a place that meets the same standards of data protection. Depending on the study, data might be archived for the duration of the study or for long periods of time. Again, this is an issue to be covered in the review proposal and consent form.

It can be argued that the process of preparing data for analysis is a first analytical step in itself (Bailey, 2008). Researchers sift through their data and get an overview of what they have got; they identify fragments of particular interest, and look at some of their material for the very first time. Data preparation also involves writing up and organizing field notes. Qualitative data collected as audio or video recordings are usually transcribed into written text, a process often experienced as a tedious chore, albeit one that can be facilitated by the use of specialist software. Depending on the guidelines used, different transcripts can be created from the same audio file. When transcribing their data, many researchers already frame these in a certain way. Some just type what they hear word by word; others also note other verbal utterances, silences and hesitations; and then there are some who also cover certain non-verbal dimensions of interaction, such as gestures. The level of detail required for a transcript depends on the aims and methodological approach of a study; that is, whether it is important to note a prickly undertone in the discussion between two managers (e.g. when analysing their decision making) or not (e.g. when it is merely the decision or outcome of the meeting that is relevant).

Depending on the research design and analytic approach, contact-summary records may be used instead of full written transcripts. See Figure 8.1 for an example of such a contact form; this was used to document observations in a study of a new school curriculum (Miles and Huberman, 1994: 53). A contact-summary form of this kind implies a significant reduction of the richness of the data at a relatively early stage, as information that does not relate to the questions listed in the form will not be further considered. Detailed field notes would also reduce the richness of the initial observations, but in a less rigorous and less structured way.

EXERCISE
8.1

Preparing your data

a) **Interactive exercise**: In pairs, prepare a list of issues you need to consider when preparing qualitative data for analysis. Discuss how you would organize your data (chronologically, thematically, by type of data etc.) and how you would label them.

b) **Individual and interactive exercise**: Do an online search to find out more about tools and guidelines for preparing interview transcripts. Have a look for tutorials online, including video tutorials on YouTube. Pick a free method or tool of your choice and learn how it works. Transcribe an audio file of five minutes' length, such as a conversation with a friend, a podcast or a scene in a film, using your method. Present the outcome in class. Who has identified the most practical tool? Who has prepared the most accurate transcript?

Contact Summary Form: Illustration (Excerpts)

FIGURE 8.1
Contact-
summary form

Contact type:		Site:	Tindale.
Visit	X	Contact date:	11/28-29/79
Phone		Today's date:	12/28/79
	(with whom)	Written by:	BLT

1. <u>What were the main issues or themes that struck you in this contact?</u>

   Interplay between highly prescriptive, "teacher-proof" curriculum that is top-down imposed and the actual writing of the curriculum by the teachers themselves.

   Split between the "watchdogs" (administrators) and the "house masters" (dept. chairs & teachers) vis a vis job foci.

   District curriculum coordinator as decision maker are school's acceptance of research relationship.

2. <u>Summarize the information you got (for failed to get) on each of the target questions you had for this contact.</u>

Question	Information
History of dev. of innov'n	Conceptualized by Curric. Coord'r, English Chairman & Assoc. Chairman; written by teachers in summer; revised by teachers following summer with field testing data
School's org'l structure	Principal & admin'rs responsible for discipline; dept chairs are educ'l leaders
Demographics	Racial conflicts in late 60 × 2 's; 60 × 2 % black stud. pop.; heavy emphasis on discipline & on keeping out non-district students slipping in from Chicago
Teacher response to innov'n	Rigid, structured, etc. at first; now, they say they like it/NEEDS EXPLORATION
Research access	Very good; only restriction: teachers not required to cooperate

3. <u>Anything else that struck you as salient, interesting, illuminating or important in this contact?</u>

   Thoroughness of the innv'n's development and training.

   Its embeddedness in the district's curriculum as planned and executed by the district curriculum coordinator.

   The initial resistance to its high prescriptiveness (as reported by users) as contrasted with their current acceptance and approval of it (again, as reported by users).

4. <u>What new (or remaining) target questions do you have in considering the next contact with this site?</u>

   How do users really perceive the innov'n? If they do indeed embrace it, what accounts for the change from early resistance?

   Nature and amount of networking among users of innov'n.

   Information on "/" stubborn "/" math teachers whose ideas weren't heard initially–who are they? Situation particulars? Resolution?

   Follow-up on English teacher Reilly's "fall from the chairmanship."

   Follow a team through a day of rotation, planning, etc.

   CONCERN: The consequences of eating school cafeteria food two days per week for the next four or five months . . .

   (MILES AND HUBERMAN, 1994: 53)

FRAMING AND INTERPRETING QUALITATIVE DATA: SEVEN APPROACHES

In many ways, approaches to qualitative data are closely linked to the different research philosophies discussed in Chapter 3. For example, when conducting a social construction-ist study, researchers assume a relativist ontology (multiple realities) and a subjectivist epis-temology (knowledge is co-created). These assumptions suggest a research process that evolves in a cyclical rather than linear manner: as realities become negotiated, knowledge is created by researchers interacting with research participants. In such a research process, it makes little sense to draw a distinction between data creation and data analysis. In contrast, researchers conducting a study with a more positivist research design usually assume a realist ontology and an objective epistemology. As a result, they will see a sharper distinction between data and the process of analysis, to the extent that the data collection and analysis may well be performed by different people. They will also be more concerned with examining frequencies within qualitative data, which will enable them to turn their data into numbers. Such an approach can be persuasive since, for many managers or for funders, the political need for numbers wins against attempts to provide rich descriptions.

Most approaches to qualitative data analysis frame data in a way that allows for a systematic reduction of their complexity and facilitates the incremental development of theories about the phenomenon under research. However, the ways in which *complexity is reduced* (i.e. which window or frame is chosen) and how *theories are developed* (i.e. how data are organized and interpreted to achieve meaningful conclusions) vary between different approaches. In this section, we will examine seven different approaches to qualitative data analysis: content analysis, grounded analysis, visual analysis, discourse analysis, conversation analysis, argument analysis and narrative analysis. Each of these approaches frames data in a certain way, and involves a number of methods and techniques for exploring, interpreting and comparing data. As will be seen, some of these methods and techniques are closely related to a particular approach, while others are employed across a wide range of different approaches. In this section, we present approaches that frame qualitative data as windows into human experience as well as approaches that focus more explicitly on the structure of language and text, treating the data themselves as the main object of analysis.

Content analysis

Content analysis is an approach that aims at *drawing systematic inferences from qualitative data that have been structured by a set of ideas or concepts*. Researchers interrogate their data for the presence, meanings and relationships of these ideas or concepts, which are derived from a pre-existing theory or hypothesis, from the research questions or from the data themselves (Hsieh and Shannon, 2005; Flick, 2009). In this way, content analysis can be used for hypothesis testing as well as for theory building. The major differences between types of content analysis arise from:

- how organizing ideas or concepts are determined
- the ideas and concepts themselves and how they frame the data
- the methods and techniques used for organizing and evaluating data.

Although content analysis is an interpretative, qualitative method, its underlying positivist framework makes it possible to introduce some element of quantification into the process. For example, some researchers count the occurrence of certain words, phrases or ideas as part of their analysis. Content analysis can be used with all kinds of data, although researchers tend to stick to textual data, including (but not limited to) company reports, observational records, interview transcripts and diaries. Content analysis is also used for conducting systematic literature reviews. For example, Duriau and colleagues (2007) have used content analysis itself to examine how content analysis has been used in organization studies. After drawing a sample of 98 journal articles, they used an indexing (or 'coding') technique to examine what research themes, theories, frames and methods were used in the management literature, based on content analysis. The indexing scheme they used was organized around nine themes; for example, the topical focus of an article was determined according to the various divisions and interest groups of the Academy of Management. More formal methods of content analysis have also been used successfully in the examination of historical artefacts; for example, to determine the authorship of anonymous plays (by analysing the use and recurrent patterns of words and phrases) and, more recently, to determine whether criminals' statements have been added to, or amended, by others at a later date!

The procedure for conducting content analysis is quite straightforward. The first step is usually to *determine a number of criteria for the selection of relevant material* based on the main research question(s) of the study. The selected material is then analysed with a view to what emerging factors or concepts appear relevant for answering the research question(s). As we have seen above, these factors can be determined by a pre-existing theory or by the research question, or they can be identified and refined in the process of analysing the selected material. Once the factors are established, a table, matrix or network diagram can be used to identify variations within and between these factors. One of the most influential source books on content analysis is by Miles and Huberman (1994). They describe a range of ways whereby information might be analysed in order to capture the complexity of all sorts of qualitative data in a variety of circumstances. At the heart of their procedure is a matrix format, which creates an 'intersection' between two different lists that are set up as rows and columns (Miles et al., 2014). In these matrices, ideas or concepts are on one side, and the respondents or instances on the other. Like checklists, matrices of this kind can be used to facilitate the display and analysis of factors and their relationships.

Table 8.1 shows an example of a matrix that Miles and Huberman (1994) used to assess the presence (or absence) of supporting conditions for the uptake of a new reading programme in a school. It shows widespread support for the programme among teachers and key administrators, but also reveals a lack of understanding about the implementation of the programme.

Matrices like that used by Miles and Huberman are particularly useful when a new area is explored. The matrix can develop during the analysis, so one starts with a few easily identifiable components. The checklist can also facilitate data collection, make it more systematic and encourage comparison. However, it is important to justify the selection of quotes and how rankings are made. Table 8.1 illustrates only one type of matrix design, constructed for

TABLE 8.1   Checklist matrix: conditions for supporting preparedness at Smithson School

Condition	For Users (Teachers & Aides)	For Administrators
Commitment	*Strong* ('wanted to make it work')	*Weak* at building level. Prime movers in central office committed; others not
Understanding	*Basic* for teacher ('felt I could do it, but I just wasn't sure how') *Absent* for aide ('didn't understand how we were going to get all this')	*Absent* at building level and among staff *Basic* for two prime movers ('got all the help we needed from developer') *Absent* for other central-office staff
Materials	*Inadequate*: ordered late, puzzling ('different from anything I ever used'); discharged	Not applicable
Front-end training	*Sketchy* for teacher ('it all happened so quickly'); no demo class *None* for aide: ('totally unprepared. I had to learn along with the children')	Prime movers in central office had training at developer site; none for others
Skills	*Weak-adequate* for teacher; *none* for aide	One prime mover (Robeson) skilled in substance; others unskilled

one particular purpose. What we want to draw attention to is the degree of flexibility that is possible. As such, matrix designs can range from simply counting the occurrence of various phenomena to complex matrices that order variables against the dimension of time (for an example of this, see Miles and Huberman, 1994: 201). Matrices can also be complemented by network diagrams or 'mind maps' that help researchers to reflect on and illustrate the relationships among a larger number of factors.

Content analysis with a research team

EXAMPLE 8.1

In the study of payment systems (see Bowey and Thorpe, 1986: Ch. 6), content analysis was used to analyse the data collected for the large number of companies which took part in the research into the introduction of payment systems. This approach was taken so that a number of researchers would be able read the transcripts and apply a comment framework, dramatically speeding up the process of analysis. A number of problems became apparent at the outset of the data analysis process: given the large number of people involved, control over the data collection process had been poor. Not all the core questions had been asked of each respondent and, due to a shortage of tape recorders, field notes had been taken but transcripts were not available for all the interviews, which made comparability difficult. This was far from satisfactory. However, to solve this difficulty, all the material was read by each member of the research team. Subsequently, three substantial interviews were chosen and read in detail and coded by three researchers. Issues that appeared to require elaboration in further interviews were identified. Then, the coding frame that had been developed was discussed with all the researchers and modified in the light of inconsistencies. At the same time, definitions were agreed in relation to the three pilot interviews and detailed notes were made of how answers might be interpreted. Finally, all the interviews were distributed to all the researchers and the same analysis framework used to interpret them. Regular checks were made to reduce the number of inconsistencies between coders. Once all interviews had been coded, they were transferred into SPSS to sit alongside data derived from a large-scale survey of over 1,000 employees. In this example, all the information had derived from interviews, although many of the themes had been identified as relevant in advance. However, new unexpected themes could be accommodated and added into the framework. At a later date, using this method, it was possible to compare answers derived from interviews with those derived from questionnaires – and, moreover, to separate these into definite and probable responses.

We have seen in the above example that more than one hypothesis was tested, and multiple interviewers and coders were used. Moreover, the separation between the collection and the analysis stages is clear. There are also issues raised about how common understandings were arrived at between those involved. The study offers an example of how qualitative data were coded, and then imported into a quantitative dataset and analysed together. This was an example of qualitative data being used to offer behavioural explanations to data collected through a survey instrument.

EXERCISE 8.2

Exploring content analysis

a) **Individual exercise**: Think back to Chapter 4 on how to write a literature review. What concepts or ideas could you use to structure your literature review? Would you derive this scheme from an existing theory, from your research question, or from what you have already read? Make a mind map of the concepts/ideas that you have thought of, and consider how they relate to one another. How could what you have now learned about content analysis improve your literature review?

b) **Interactive exercise**: In pairs, discuss what ideas or concepts could be used in a study about the advantages and disadvantages of doing an MBA earlier or later in life. Create a checklist matrix that could be used to analyse interviews with current MBA students and alumni.

c) **Interactive exercise**: It has been argued that content analysis can be a qualitative, theory-building – as well as quantitative, theory-testing – approach. Why is this so? Discuss the criteria that determine whether content analysis is used in a qualitative or quantitative way.

Grounded analysis

The second approach we are discussing here, **grounded analysis**, is a more intuitive and 'open' approach to qualitative data analysis than is content analysis. While content analysis and grounded analysis share some techniques, they use them in rather different ways, as will be seen below. Researchers who conduct grounded analysis do not start by imposing external structure on their data in the form of concepts or predefined ideas. Instead of testing and elaborating existing theories, grounded analysts aim at building theory from categories that are 'grounded' in the data, meaning that they are identified by a systematic analysis of the data themselves (Charmaz, 2014). Hence, grounded analysis tends to be more holistic than content analysis as it aims to *derive structure (i.e. theory) from data in a process of comparing different data fragments with one another*, rather than framing data according to a pre-existing structure. This is what makes grounded analysis 'open' to new discoveries. Grounded analysts also try to *understand the meaning of data fragments in the specific context in which they were created*. This implies a stronger commitment to the voices and views of research participants, and requires researchers to engage with the cultural and historical dimension of their data. Although we characterize content analysis and grounded analysis as competing alternatives, between them there is a raft of practice, and in many ways the choices that researchers face lie on a continuum (see Table 8.2).

Grounded analysis as an analytic approach is closely linked to grounded theory, which is a more comprehensive research strategy comprising methods for sampling, data collection and data analysis. Researchers conducting studies using grounded theory usually engage in a research cycle, alternating between phases of data collection and data analysis. Originally conceived by Glaser and Strauss (1967), grounded theory has a long tradition and prominent standing across the social sciences. However, what is considered to be grounded

TABLE 8.2   Qualitative data analysis: content versus grounded methods

Content analysis	Grounded analysis
Searching for content	Understanding of context & time
Causally linked concepts & ideas structure analysis	Holistic associations guide analysis
Objective/subjective	Faithful to views of respondents
More deductive	More inductive
Aims for clarity & unity	Preserves ambiguity & illustrates contradiction

theory has also changed significantly over the course of two (and soon three) generations of researchers working with it. This history has been marked by grounded theorists who encouraged researchers to be more creative when developing theory while, at the same time, forwarding rather rigorous, 'recipe-like' sets of methods for conducting such research.

In this section, we outline grounded analysis as a practical approach to sifting through volumes of qualitative data with the aim of teasing out themes, patterns and categories that can be developed into theory. Readers who plan to conduct a study using grounded analysis are encouraged to engage with a well-developed body of literature on grounded theory, which will offer them deeper insights into the manifold methods and techniques that constitute grounded theory today (Charmaz, 2014). Here, we aim to make the general procedure of grounded analysis more understandable by explaining it in the way both we and colleagues have used it. We consider that there are seven steps to grounded analysis:

1. *Familiarization* – First, it is important to sift through all available data, drawing on unrecorded as well as recorded information. This is where any additional field notes and a personal research diary can be important to the process of analysis. Glaser (1978) suggests that, at this initial stage, researchers should remind themselves just what the focus of the study is, what the data suggest and whose point of view is being expressed. The relationship between the researcher and the people interviewed should also be accounted for.

2. *Reflection* – At this stage, desperation may begin to set in. There is usually so much rich data that trying to make sense of them seems an impossible task. Evaluation and critique become more evident as data are evaluated in the light of previous research, academic texts and common-sense explanations. This does not mean that a rigorous conceptual framework should be imposed. Rather, it is suggested to bring into dialogue the data with existing knowledge on the problem or phenomenon under research. The kind of questions researchers might ask themselves are:

   - What are these data about?
   - Do they support existing knowledge?
   - Do they challenge it?
   - Do they answer previously unanswered questions?
   - Are they different?
   - What is different?

3. *Open coding* – A code is a word or a short phrase that summarizes the meaning of a chunk of data, such as a statement, a sentence, or an element in a picture (Charmaz, 2014; Saldaña, 2009). Codes create a link between messy and overwhelming data and more systematic categories, which are developed from sets of codes that appear similar or related. Open coding is guided by open questions such as:

   - What are these data about?
   - Whose point of view is reflected in the data?
   - How is this view expressed?
   - See Table 8.3 for additional information on **open or first-cycle coding**.

4. *Conceptualization* – At this stage, the researcher seeks to discover patterns among the codes that are characterized by *similarity, difference, frequency, sequence, correspondence* or *causation* (Saldaña, 2009). By comparing codes and organizing them into different categories, the researcher identifies concepts and themes that seem to be important for understanding what is going on. For example, in an examination of performance, these might include: management style, technology, absence rates, demographic qualities of the labour force, and locus of power.

Charmaz (2014) suggests that codes should be simple and that the researcher should try to stay close to the data when identifying relevant codes and categories. Writing a short description for each code and an analytic note (or 'memo') on each emerging category helps the processes of identifying and cataloguing concepts.

5. *Focused re-coding* – Once the most significant codes and categories have been established, the researcher codes and re-codes large amounts of data with a limited number of more focused codes. This process of **focused or secondary cycle coding** is usually highly iterative; it can require the researcher to go back to check against the original data, comparing incidents in order to identify particular properties. It may well be that individuals in the same organization were interpreting what appears to be similar concepts in very different ways. While the first coding cycle aims at the development of a framework, the second coding cycle frames data in a way that allows for a more in-depth analysis of what is deemed important.

6. *Linking* – At this stage, the analytical framework and explanations should be becoming clearer, with patterns emerging between concepts. This is achieved by conceptualizing how key categories and concepts relate to one another, and how emerging hypotheses can be integrated into a theory (Charmaz, 2014). Based on analytic memos, diagrams of concepts and lists of quotations, a first draft can be produced, which can then be tried out on others (both colleagues and respondents), so that the argument and supporting data can be exposed to wider scrutiny and some degree of verification. It is important that all data that form the basis of the research conclusions remain available for scrutiny.

7. *Re-evaluation* – In the light of the comments of others, the researcher may feel that more work is needed in some areas. For example, the analysis may have omitted some factors or have over-emphasized others. This stage takes some time; as with the other stages, it may have to be undertaken more than once.

Figure 8.2 illustrates the 'codes-to-theory model' for grounded analysis that is implied in the seven stages listed above (Saldaña, 2009: 12).

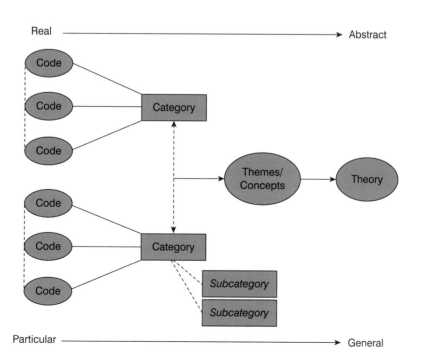

FIGURE 8.2 'Codes-to-theory model' for grounded analysis

(SALDAÑA, 2009: 12)

The researcher may well feel that, for much of the time, the analysis of qualitative data is chaotic and extremely messy. Since grounded analysis reduces the complexity inherent in qualitative data in a slow, incremental process, it often feels overwhelming at the initial stages. This can be seen as an advantage and disadvantage of grounded analysis. On the one hand, grounded analysis opens up a way of developing new insights, because it keeps the researcher open and close to the data until relatively late into the research process. This can make research explorative and exciting. On the other hand, maintaining such openness can be difficult and time-consuming, and researchers can easily get lost in the confusing complexity of their data. By using systematic coding and memo-writing techniques, they can avoid some of these problems. Table 8.3 gives a general introduction into techniques for coding qualitative data. For a more comprehensive overview, see Saldaña (2009).

TABLE 8.3   Coding qualitative data

Coding qualitative data

A **code** is a word or a short phrase that summarizes the meaning of a chunk of data, such as a statement, a sentence, or an element in a picture (Charmaz, 2014; Saldaña, 2009). However, as Miles and colleagues (2014: 93) note, 'a code is more than a filing system'. Coding is an interpretative exercise; it involves not merely labelling data but also linking them, thereby leading researchers from their 'data to the idea, and from the idea to all the data pertaining to that idea' (Richards and Morse, 2007: 137). Many – if not most – approaches to analysing qualitative data involve some kind of coding method. In content analysis, codes are often used to frame data according to a predefined coding scheme (deductive coding); in grounded analysis, they are usually the first step for the development of categories and concepts (inductive coding). As the research progresses, researchers compile an annotated list of codes, and later a more systematic **codebook** that includes definitions and examples for all codes.

Coding can be undertaken on paper – e.g. by highlighting lines of texts and writing on the margins. For such manual coding, three copies of all data (transcripts, observational records, documents etc.) are required. The first one is the reference copy, the second one is used for the first coding cycle, and a copy of this one is then used in the second cycle (Luker, 2008). Some researchers cut out particularly important quotations and paste them on index cards, which can then be arranged in network diagrams to reflect on how they relate to one another. **Computer-assisted qualitative data analysis software** (CAQDAS) has become increasingly popular in the past decades, as CAQDAS software packages facilitate the management of larger data sets, and support an impressive range of analytic methods and techniques – including coding, memo-writing and diagramming. Most of these packages not only assist in the coding of data and development of codebooks; they also feature search tools that operate with Boolean operators to retrieve data that have been assigned with several codes. For more information, see the section on computer-aided analysis below. In grounded analysis, there are two different types of coding procedures: open or first-cycle coding, and focused or second-cycle coding.

Open or first-cycle coding techniques are used by researchers as a first analytical step. Such codes often are *descriptive* or aid the *organization of the data* (e.g. coding of actors and attributes). For example, a line of an interview stating 'now that they have sent us these new machines, we spend less money on electricity and produce twice as much' could be labelled with 'new technology', 'cheaper' or 'production increase'. Open codes are used to break up long texts and complex pictures into manageable chunks, for example by assigning a code to every single line of a text (line-by-line coding). If appropriate, several codes can be assigned to the same section or visual element. First-cycle codes reflect the 'what, who, where and when' of a social phenomenon, the 'how' and 'why' usually being addressed at the second stage (Tracy, 2013). Codes slowly become more systematic as the coding progresses, and similarities and differences are noted when comparing data with other data (Charmaz, 2014). While each analysis is unique in its material and topic, and hence will generate different codes, the coding strategy as such varies with the analytical approach chosen. For example, a researcher conducting a grounded analysis will ask different questions and create different codes from a researcher embarking on a narrative analysis. Saldaña (2009) presents an impressive range of coding first-cycle techniques – such as process coding (using gerunds to code action in the data), values coding (a framework for examining attitudes, values and beliefs expressed by participants) and evaluation coding (assigning judgements about the value or impact of a programme or activity).

Focused or second-cycle coding techniques build on the previous coding cycle and aim at developing a sense of the categorical and conceptual order arising from the open codes. Based on a thorough examination of all codes created in the first cycle, researchers organize and synthesize them into more analytic secondary codes (Saldaña, 2009). For example, the codes above could become part of a group of codes on 'energy efficiency'. Focused codes are usually more abstract, because they are based on a preliminary analysis of more descriptive first-cycle codes. They should be accompanied by an analytical note explaining how the code was generated, how it is defined, and how it relates to other codes and emerging categories. Second-cycle coding techniques aim at comparing codes to other codes and categories in order to advance theory-building. They help the researcher to develop a more elaborated 'cognitive map' of their research (Miles, Huberman and Saldaña, 2014).

Memo-writing is a method of crucial importance for grounded analysis (Charmaz, 2014). Memos are written notes that allow researchers to document and reflect on codes, categories and concepts, as well as research questions and emerging ideas (Saldaña, 2009). When coding and re-coding, researchers make many important decisions about where they take their analysis, and how they frame their data. Analytic memos serve to document and justify these decisions. Successive memo-writing also aids theorizing by enabling researchers to slowly increase the degree of abstraction in their thinking. Memos are usually written in an informal way as they are notes to the researchers themselves and not intended to be shared with a wider audience. However, as the quality of memos improves over the course of a study, they can develop into important building blocks for a research report or thesis.

A study of a Northern park

EXAMPLE
8.2

Thorpe and Danielli's study was into the use of a local park, and information was collected from ten different groups of park users. These included a parent-and-toddler group; representatives from two schools who used the park as a consequence of changes in the requirements of the national curriculum; an Asian women's group (the area was predominantly built up, with a high ethnic population); a disabled group (who used the uncongested pathways to exercise in their wheelchairs); and a young Asian youth team (who used the bowling green to play football!). Interviews were transcribed and analysed using the grounded theory approach described. It was striking that, from the data collected from each group, fear emerged as a central category. Further analysis showed that the manifestation of fear was quite different in each group. For the parent-and-toddler group, it was fear of large groups of Asian boys playing football on the bowling green. For the Asian boys, it was fear of being intimidated by white youths if they went to the sports hall in the town centre. For the Asian women's group, it was a fear of spirits, which they believed to inhabit parts of the park, particularly those that were poorly lit where the trees hung over the walkways. Through focused coding, it was possible to connect the category of 'fear' to other categories, such as 'absence'. Over the years, for a variety of reasons, there had been a gradual withdrawal of park staff, which created a situation in which antisocial behaviour had become more widespread.

(Continued)

(Continued)

Understanding the interrelationships between categories in this way is central for all qualitative research. It is also important, however, to relate such findings to the wider context of the phenomenon under study. So, for example, when explaining and presenting the results of the above park study, Thorpe and Danielli placed the concept of a Northern town park in the context of its role in civic society in late nineteenth- and early twentieth-century Britain, when transport was limited and expensive, and parks were seen as places where local people could meet and promenade in 'Sunday best' clothes. The increase in affluence, changes in the population of the neighbourhood, changing hours of work, and advent of Sunday shopping all have contributed to the decline of town parks. Problems that emerged around 'fear' and 'absence' have to be understood in this context.

One final lesson from this particular study is perhaps apocryphal and relates to what happened when the findings were presented to the council. The leader of the council sub-committee thanked Richard Thorpe for his presentation but questioned him as to the validity of the study as there were no large samples or statistics. Later, during the coffee break, park-warden staff approached him to say that the report revealed something very close to their experiences on a day-to-day basis.

EXERCISE
8.3

Coding and memo-writing

a) **Individual exercise**: Take two pages of an observational record or interview transcript produced in one of the previous exercises. (If no such material is at hand, copy a random email, news report or entry from an online forum into a text document with a wider margin.) Read these two pages carefully and then try to assign codes that summarize the meaning of each line – just the line, not the entire sentence or paragraph. After you are done with the whole text, go slowly through the codes and think about whether they tell you something new about the text. What have you coded: people, actions, locations? Have you considered any implicit views, assumptions or actions when you have coded? Are there any codes that relate to one another? How? Write a memo about the relationship between the two codes that appear most interesting to you.

b) **Interactive exercise**: Discuss what kind of information should be included in a code book and how it should be organized.

We have now discussed two of the most prominent approaches for analysing qualitative data as a proxy for human experiences. Along the way, we have introduced a number of methods and techniques for qualitative data analysis, such as coding, memo-writing and the creation of analytic matrices. While these are important methods that can be used for a wide range of data, there are many more that can be helpful. For example, there is **template analysis**, a method located at the interface between content analysis (predetermined codes) and grounded theory (where codes emerge during the analysis) as it involves the development of a template of codes to reveal patterns in the data (for more information, see King, 2014). Then there are *ethnographic decision models*, which combine many of the techniques employed in content analysis and grounded analysis for the creation of decision trees or yes/no flow charts from ethnographic data (Ryan and Bernard, 2003). Such decision trees are used to document and predict decisions under specific circumstances, for example how fishermen decide where to fish (Gatewood, 1983), or how people decide whether to recycle cans (Ryan and Bernard, 2006).

As is the case with qualitative data collection, the art of conducting qualitative research lies in identifying and refining the approaches, methods and techniques that are most appropriate for a given study. This depends on the research design as much as on the research questions, the field under research, the kind of data collected, and the researcher's experience, skills and creativity. We encourage all our readers to learn more about *how* qualitative data analysis is undertaken by different researchers in their particular fields of interest.

Visual analysis

As we have noted in the previous chapter, methods for the creation of visual data have opened up new perspectives for management research. Visual data can be analysed using existing approaches such as content analysis, grounded analysis or **discourse analysis**. The problem is that most of the methods and techniques developed for these approaches were developed for textual data. True, visual data can be regarded as text: 'Photos tell a story' (Flick, 2009: 246). In many cases, however, **visual analysis** is conducted via transcripts, descriptions and summaries of visual material, which are then studied using methods for the analysis of text, with the visual data merely illustrating what is ultimately a textual analysis. Methods and techniques that are tailored for the analysis of visual data still appear underdeveloped (Flick, 2009). While newer generations of CAQDAS software packages assist in the coding of audio and video material, it is not just the practice of assigning codes that needs modification but also the questions we ask when we code visual material. Like art historians interrogating the composition of a picture to learn more about its production, we need to think about how visual data relate to their site of production and to their audience. With this in mind, we discuss some of the issues that should be considered when analysing visual data. We have positioned this section between approaches for analysing data as proxies for human experience and approaches that look more into the structure and internal organization of the data themselves. This is because the analysis of visual data can entail both.

In her textbook on visual methodologies, Gillian Rose (2001: 30) has included a figure that illustrates the different dimensions of visual analysis (see Figure 8.3). It shows how the analysis of visual data can focus on the context of their *production*, on the *imagery and its effect*, or on their *reception by an audience*. The three sites are represented in the form of three different segments of a circle. Analytical approaches, such as content analysis or different variants of discourse analysis frame data in a way that anchors the analysis in one of these sites. What the figure also illustrates is that there are different modalities to analysing visual data: the technical modality of how visual data are created or transmitted (inner circle); the composition modality of how the data are embedded in a genre or relate to other visual data (second circle); and the all-encompassing social modality that refers to the wider social context (outer circle).

What this figure suggests is that visual imagery is constructed through various practices and interpretations. Consequently, when researchers analyse visual data, they need to be clear what sites and modalities they are looking at – and what aspects they are ignoring.

The process of conducting a visual analysis can be described in six steps (Flick, 2009; Rose, 2001):

1. *Familiarization* – Getting a sense of an image or film as a whole, while noting down first impressions and questions.

2. *Exploration* – Reflection on how the meaning of the image or film is created on the three sites (site of production, the image itself and the audience: see Figure 8.4 for guiding questions).

3. *Framing* – First attempt to interpret the meaning of the data with a view to the research question, noting down key observations, elements or scenes.

Adapted from (ROSE, 2001: 30)

FIGURE 8.3
Sites, modalities and approaches to analysing visual data

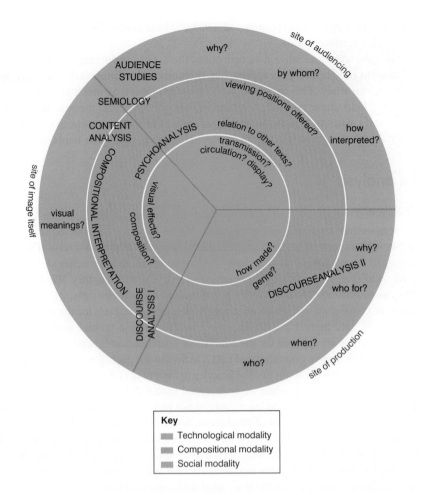

Key
- Technological modality
- Compositional modality
- Social modality

4. *Micro-analysis* – Examination of details or sequences (film) that appear particularly relevant. How do these details contribute to the overall meaning? What patterns emerge?

5. *Re-contextualization* – Critical examination of the 'agency' of the image or film (what does it do with the producer and different audiences?). This should be informed by complementary information on the background of the data and their reception by different audiences.

6. *Interpretation* – All notes prepared in steps 2 to 5 should be reviewed, with a view to the research question.

Coding and memo-writing can assist in the analysis of visual data, as they do when working with textual data. Depending on the chosen approach, codes may be derived from an external theory or framework, or they can be developed throughout the analytic process. However, it is important to decide *which of the three sites is most relevant for a study before choosing an approach for analysing data*. For example, content analysis of visual data is usually limited to the site of an image itself and does not cover its production or reception. Grounded theory can integrate an interpretation of a picture itself with an analysis of other types of data that reveal more information about its context. Some variants of discourse analysis treat visual data themselves as the main object of analysis (see *Discourse Analysis I* in Figure 8.3), whereas others frame visual data as reflecting the practices and institutions that enabled their production (see *Discourse Analysis II* in Figure 8.3).

(BASED ON ROSE, 2001: 188–90)

FIGURE 8.4
Analytic questions for the interpretation of visual data

Discourse analysis

According to Cunliffe (2008), *discourse analysis* is a term that covers a range of approaches that focus on language itself or the much wider relationship of how language is used in a particular context. Research with this focus can develop our understanding of aspects of social action and social theory more generally.

Discourse analysis has become a more prominent approach since the 'linguistic turn' of the social sciences, by which we mean the wider recognition that language not only reflects our social world but also creates it. Since then, more research has been undertaken into *how* language is used for achieving inter-subjective understanding. In this context, a number of analytic approaches have been developed that combine methods used in the social sciences with those coming from linguistics and psychology, including discourse analysis and conversation analysis.

As we have seen in Figure 8.3, different types of discourse analysis exist. These types have developed from different backgrounds, in particular linguistics, psychology and sociology. In this section, we present discourse analysis as an approach for analysing the *content of 'talk' in its wider social context* (Cunliffe, 2008). Discourse analysis of this type (type II in Figure 8.3) goes beyond the detailed micro-analysis of conversations (an approach we will discuss in the next subsection) and aims at wider discourses that can be traced in conversations, writing, visual data, observation of social practices, symbolic artefacts and media items. In management research, discourse analysis has been used in a number of studies (Phillips et al., 2008). Examples include Munir and Phillips' (2005) study of 'The birth of the "Kodak moment"', in which they showed how the meanings and uses of new technologies are discursively constructed.

There are three main ways of viewing discourse: as structure, as rhetoric or as process (Gergen, 1999). Gergen suggests that to view *discourse as a structure* is to see it as a set of recurring conventions (such as metaphors or narratives) that are woven throughout both our speech and ways of living. The second perspective of *discourse as rhetoric* suggests that there is a hierarchical aspect to how social realities are created in discourse. Here, the concept is seen not simply as about the art of persuasion but also as about power. Recognition will therefore need to be made of, for example, why some groups within organizations are favoured over others and how this is manifested in rhetoric. The third perspective is to analyse how lives are influenced and 'constituted' through *discourse as an ongoing process* of conversation and sense-making.

As noted by Alvesson and Kärreman (2011), organizations are settings defined by talk and text. An analysis of such language-in-use provides a specific framework for exploring how organizations work. Discourse analysis then becomes the study of individual fragments of discourse (text), which form a discourse that is embedded in a wider social context (Phillips et al., 2008). Figure 8.5 illustrates this way of framing qualitative data.

Cunliffe (2008) notes that within organizational and business studies, the analysis of discourse has essentially been divided into two main streams: discourse analysis and **critical discourse analysis**. Discourse analysis, she argues, takes a social constructionist perspective, while critical discourse analysis takes more of a postmodern and poststructuralist point of view, and examines discourse from the perspective of *rhetoric*. Where other approaches focus on the effects of dominant logics on organizations, critical discourse analysis provides us with a frame for exploring *how dominant logics are created* (Phillips et al., 2008). In a conversation with Gavin Kendall, Ruth Wodak describes the more particular focus of critical discourse analysis: '"Critical" means not taking things for granted, opening up complexity, challenging reductionism, dogmatism and dichotomies, being self-reflective in my research, and through these processes, making opaque structures of power relations and ideologies manifest' (Kendall, 2007).

Critical discourse analysis has been a useful approach for both social scientists in general and for management-studies scholars in particular, as it facilitates an examination of aspects of power and persuasion within organizations. Critical discourse analysis places an emphasis on aspects of where power lies within relationships (Chouliaraki and Fairclough, 2010) as well as 'ideologies that are created by and represented in language' (Fairclough and Hardy, 1997; Cunliffe, 2008). An example of this is Prasad and Elmes' (2005) study of the language of practicality in environmental management. For Cunliffe, it is the *emphasis that is placed on context* that distinguishes critical discourse analysis from traditional linguistics. The context, she argues, is influenced by factors such as space, time, practice, change and frame (Chouliaraki and Fairclough, 2010; Leitch and Palmer, 2010).

FIGURE 8.5
Critical discourse analysis: analytical framework

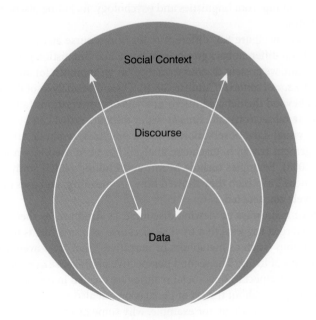

Social Context

Discourse

Data

(BASED ON PHILLIPS ET AL., 2008: 774)

According to Fairclough (1992), discourse analysis should integrate an analysis of the levels of discourse:

1. *Textual level* – by involving techniques used in critical linguistics.
2. *Discourse level* – by investigating how the text is produced and interpreted, and what kinds of 'preferred' reading it suggests.
3. *Social practice level* – by scrutinizing the institutional practices a text may imply, and then exploring whether it reproduces or upholds dominant discourses or social practices characterized by asymmetric power relations.

Due to the wide range of approaches for conducting discourse analysis, it is difficult to give an overview of the various methods and techniques that are used. Some argue that discourse analysis works better as a frame or 'scholarly orientation' (Locke, 2004: 2) than as a methodological approach. Researchers who plan to conduct a study of discourse are advised to think carefully about their research questions, their framing and the scope of their study before engaging with the exuberant literature on discourse analysis for identifying the methods and techniques best suited to assist them in their study.

Using discourse analysis

EXERCISE
8.4

Interactive exercise: Discuss the use of discourse analysis for research in management and business. What kind of research questions could be answered using critical discourse analysis? Remember that the emphasis of critical discourse analysis is on *discourse as rhetoric* that is shaped by – and shaping – context. Come up with two or three topics and discuss what framing and what methods could be appropriate to research them.

Conversation analysis

An *approach* closely related to discourse analysis is **conversation analysis**. This stems from an ethno-methodological tradition and was developed to facilitate the formal analysis of the *structure* of everyday 'interaction as a continuous process of producing and securing meaningful social order' (Bergmann, 2004: 296). The term 'conversation analysis' is actually somewhat misleading, as the data of interest are not limited to everyday casual conversation, but encompass any naturally occurring interaction between two or more people (e.g. telephone calls, talk at the dinner table, job interviews). For this reason, conversation analysts often describe their interest as being in 'talk-in-interaction' rather than 'conversation'. However, even this can be confusing as, in addition to 'talk', the non-verbal aspects of interaction, such as eye gaze and gesture, are also significant (Psathas, 1995: 2).

There are three fundamental assumptions to conversation analysis:

1. That all interaction exhibits stable, organized patterns irrespective of who is talking, and that people orient to and produce that order themselves when they interact with each other.
2. That interaction is organized sequentially, and that it is possible to make sense of a statement only in relation to an ongoing sequence of utterances.
3. That analysis should be grounded in a detailed empirical examination of the data.

The job of the analyst is to discover and describe this order, and the underlying rules and practices from which it is built. In order to do this, the analyst will examine audio or video recordings of interactions and, using detailed transcripts based on the recordings, look for the practices that people use in interaction, and the interactional significance of these and of where they occur. A key question that conversation analysts keep in mind when looking at something of interest in a piece of interactional data is: 'Why that now?' (Schegloff and Sacks, 1973: 299).

There are four main areas of technical findings in conversation analytic research: sequence organization (the order in which utterances are produced in talk); turn-taking (how speakers manage the taking of turns); repair (how speakers deal with problems in hearing or understanding); and word selection (the words chosen by speakers). The level of detail looked at when doing conversation analysis ranges from how whole utterances are constructed, through what individual word choices speakers make, to where silences occur and how long they last (with even a pause of a tenth of a second potentially being inter-actionally significant). This emphasis on detailed empirical analysis has resulted in very precise conventions for transcribing recordings of interactions. We give some examples in Table 8.4. (For the full list of transcription conventions and an accompanying discussion of their benefit, see Jefferson, 2004.)

When approaching a piece of data from a conversational analysis perspective there are several things to take into consideration:

- How is the taking of turns managed by the speakers? Does one speaker select another, or do speakers select themselves? Is there a pre-determined order to the turn-taking, such as in particular institutional settings (e.g. in a news interview the interviewer asks a question, followed by the interviewee providing the answer, similarly in a courtroom interaction)?

- What actions are done by speakers' turns, for example are they requesting, complaining, inviting, assessing etc.?

- How are the speakers' turns constructed? The basic unit of talk is the turn constructional unit (TCU), which can range in length from a sentence to a phrase or just one word, and that is hearably complete grammatically, intonally and in terms of the action it is doing. Are the turns made of one or more TCUs?

TABLE 8.4 Simplified transcription symbols

Symbol	Example	Explanation
[	A: for quite a [while B: [yes, but	Left bracket indicates the point at which the current speaker's talk begins to be overlapped by another's talk
=	A: that I'm aware of = B: = Yes. Would you confirm that?	Equal signs, one at the end of a line and one at the beginning, indicate no gap between the two lines
.hhhh	I feel that .hh	A row of h's prefixed by a dot indicates an in-breath; without a dot, an out-breath; the number indicates the length of breath
( )	future risks and ( ) and life ( )	Empty parentheses indicate an undecipherable word
___	What's up? _____	Underscoring indicates some stress through pitch of amplitude

(SILVERMAN, 1993: 118)

- How do these actions fit together to form a sequence? Actions generally come in pairs known as 'adjacency pairs' made up of a first pair part (FPP) and a second pair part (SPP); for example, a question is followed by an answer, an invitation by an acceptance or a declining, a greeting by a return greeting. Are there any turns that do actions prior to the main 'base' first pair part, for example a pre-request ('Are you busy this afternoon?') before the request is produced? Are there any that come between the 'base' first pair part and the 'base' second pair part, for example a request for clarification?

- When you notice something of interest in the data, such as choice of words or instances of silence, think about where they occur in the interaction: what action is being done by the utterance, where is it in the sequence, was there any problem with its production or understanding? When you find a phenomenon of interest, think about why it occurs in the sequence where it does.

Conversation analysis has been used extensively to examine workplace interactions, including in classrooms (e.g. Macbeth, 2004), in doctor–patient consultations (e.g. Heritage and Maynard, 2006), on calls to emergency services (e.g. Zimmerman, 1992) and helplines (e.g. Baker et al., 2005), in job interviews (e.g. Glenn and LeBaron, 2011) and even in airport operation rooms (e.g. Goodwin and Goodwin, 1996). The findings from these institutional settings can be used to change practice in the workplace.

What a difference a word makes

EXAMPLE 8.3

An example of the significance of one word can be seen in research carried out with family doctors and their patients in the USA. Patients frequently have more concerns than those that they give as their primary reason for making their appointment with a doctor. Family-practice doctors are encouraged to ask patients whether they have concerns – typically with a question such as 'Is there anything else that we need to take care of today?' – but patients still frequently come away from their appointment with unmet concerns. Heritage et al. (2007) wanted to see whether altering the recommended question might have an effect on patients raising more concerns in their appointments. They instructed 20 doctors to pose one of two questions during appointments with patients, just after the patient had stated their main reason for seeing the doctor: 'Is there anything else you want to address in the visit today?' or 'Is there something else you want to address in the visit today?'. The researchers found that patients were more likely to have their extra concerns met when 'some' was used in the question, and suggest that the problem of patients not raising concerns can be reduced just by substituting one word when asking whether they have other concerns.

Looking at conversation analysis

EXERCISE 8.5

Individual exercise: Conduct a literature search on studies that have used conversation analysis. Pick one article you find interesting and examine how the authors of this article have used conversation analysis. What kind of data did they use? How did they frame their data? What methods and techniques did they use in their analysis? If you cannot find any relevant articles, pick one of those listed in the further reading at the end of this chapter.

Argument analysis

Another approach for analysing discourse is framing it as series of *arguments* that reflect people's negotiations of the social world and their role in it. Gold et al. (2002, 2007) employed **argument analysis** as part of a management-development intervention, using arguments to interpret research participants' understanding of their role in the management process as well as in a developmental way (see Example 8.4). Managers were asked to write stories of events at work and then to reflect critically on what they had produced. The exercise aimed at making them more aware of their views and arguments; of how these views and arguments were formed and justified; and of how they could be changed.

This subsection explains how argument analysis can be used in an interactive research design in which both data creation and data analysis require the active involvement of research participants. Two approaches are illustrated; the first one employs the ideas of Toulmin (2001); the second is based on the work of the philosopher Gadamer (1989). Both examples should encourage our readers to reflect on how applied management research can help to develop critical thinking in research participants, and how this may enhance the impact of management research.

EXAMPLE
8.4

Helping managers become more reflective

In their study of Barclays Bank managers, Gold, Holman and Thorpe (2002) asked eight managers to write accounts in which they reflected on their work. The research process was part of a programme for career development. The participating managers were asked to address the following issues:

1. **Story** – They were encouraged to write about significant incidents or 'stories' at work that involved themselves and others.

2. **Statement** – They were asked to explain why they cared about the particular issues described and what they believed was the explanation for events as they emerged in the story. *This part of the task was completed in small groups*.

3. **Claims** – They were then asked to identify the claims that they had made in the stories, and provide an explanation for these claims.

4. **Evidence** – Having returned to their organizations, managers were requested to identify and substantiate evidence for their claims (e.g. the data on which these claims were based).

What became apparent was that some managers lacked sufficient evidence to support the claims they made, while others found that the evidence that they had offered was at best spurious, and at worst wrong. For example, one manager had misread someone else's opinion as a fact. For many participants, the impact of the programme was profound, as they had gained an insight into how to understand and analyse arguments, a skill they considered even more useful after the study had revealed how much they had just taken for granted without ever checking properly.

The study reported above was based on the work of Toulmin (2001), one of the most prominent exponents of argument analysis. His approach frames arguments as having three components:

1. *Claims* – Arguable statements.

2. *Evidence* – Data that are drawn on to support the claims.

3. *Warrant* – Explanation why claims and data are connected.

When this framework was used in the management-development context outlined in Example 8.4, the text of the story was seen as the 'data' from which underlying claims and the warrants could be derived.

Toulmin's (2001) framework can also be applied when evaluating literature for a literature review (see Chapter 2). Identifying the main claim (or hypothesis) of an article, evaluating the evidence that is provided to support this claim (e.g. data and analysis), and interrogating the warrant that connects the evidence to the claim, comprise one of the principal methods to evaluate academic publications (Hart, 2005).

As we can see from the discussion, argument analysis (like discourse analysis) connects a wide range of methods, and can be applied to very different kinds of data. It can inform an analysis of operational manuals for an investigation into how different rules and routines are backed up and explained; or of observational data, for example when analysing how different parties negotiate in a shareholder meeting. It can also be used as a framework for analysing the recording of an employment tribunal in all its linguistic detail, looking into how arguments are formed. Having discussed a more linguistic approach in the previous subsection, in this subsection we want to remain focused on argument analysis as an approach that treats data as windows to human reasoning.

Our second example is based on Gadamer (1989) and his work on the importance of the 'practice of understanding'. This approach frames *thinking and doing as being part of the same process*, and not separate to managers immersed in the flux of everyday life. Gold et al. (2007) used this approach in a critical study of difficult situations experienced by managers, in which they hoped to enhance the managers' critical faculties by developing new perspectives on their problems.

Argument analysis to enhance reflexivity

EXAMPLE
8.5

In Gold, Thorpe and Holt's study (2007), managers were asked to reflect on their experiences at work by drawing a diagram in the shape of a circle with three segments (see Figure 8.6). In the first segment, managers were asked to write about a difficult situation they had encountered; in the second segment, they were asked to read and interpret what they had written in a reflexive way; and in the third segment, they were encouraged to 'reason authoritatively': taking into account the interpretations they had drawn, they were asked to consider possibilities that might lead to some solutions, and articulate the solution they saw as having the most potential. Each manager agreed to keep a record of the use of the diagrams over a period of ten weeks in the form of a small log or memo. A review took place after four weeks and again after ten weeks, when the findings were discussed. All the managers who conducted the exercise demonstrated a considerable willingness to embrace the approach. As they worked through the process, it was clear that they acquired new understandings and gained in experience by engaging critically with their own ideas and assumptions. The researchers gained valuable insights into the perspectives of the management team.

The two examples presented in this subsection are examples of an analytic approach to analysing discourse that does not focus on the structure of discourse (as in conversation analysis) or on the context in which it is produced (as in critical discourse analysis), but rather aims to improve our *understanding of how discourse is used in management as a process* (applied management research). However, argument analysis can be a useful approach for a wide range of research projects. As the example of the literature review has shown, it can be used for a formal analysis of a written text, as well as for an informal discussion of management decisions. The methods and techniques used for argument analysis ultimately depend on the research question, on the data and on *how they are framed* by the research question.

FIGURE 8.6

From the three
'Rs': writing,
reading and
reason

(GOLD ET AL., 2007)

An alternative but related way of framing arguments can be found in Charles Tilly's (2006) book *Why?*, in which he describes four varieties of *reasons*: conventions, stories, codes and technical accounts. The first type, the *convention*, is a widely accepted reason for why something works out a lot better or worse than anticipated (e.g. 'She managed to catch the train because it was late' or 'because she is a lucky girl'). The second type of reason, the *story*, is defined as a narrative that explains an unfamiliar phenomenon or exceptional event in terms of cause and effect. Stories are used when a simple statement is not enough and when some kind of justification is required (e.g. 'She had to take the train because the day before, her car had been stolen). The third type of reason, the *code*, does not have to bear the same explanatory power as the story because it refers to widely accepted rules, whether these are religious or legal (e.g. 'Without a ticket, she was not allowed on the train'). The fourth reason is a *technical account* (e.g. of how a faulty power line delayed the arrival of a train, or how car theft has become a bigger problem in an area of rising unemployment). As can be seen from Table 8.5, reasons can be based on common popular knowledge (in the case of conventions and stories) as well as on more specialized knowledge (in the case of codes and technical accounts); they can be based not only on accepted rules and formulas (conventions and codes), but also on cause-effect accounts (stories and technical accounts).

Tilly argues that each way of offering reasons contains distinctive properties, and that these properties can be used in strategic ways. Bankers who have to account for a major loss need to consider whether their technical accounts are likely to be understood by the general public, or whether they would be better off with a story or an explanation based on conventions. What kind of reasoning is appropriate depends on the situation and on who is

TABLE 8.5 Tilly's four varieties of reason

	Popular	Specialized
Formulas	Conventions	Codes
Cause-effect accounts	Stories	Technical accounts

involved. If we frame argument analysis in this way, we can see how this opens up another approach to analysing discourse, an approach that may help us to better understand *exactly how* the formal configuration of an argument relates to both its content and its context.

EXERCISE
8.6

Applying argument analysis

Individual exercise: Pick one journal article that is relevant to your studies or research and conduct a thorough argument analysis based on Toulmin's (2001) framework introduced above. What claims are made? What kind of evidence is provided? Is the warrant connecting claims and evidence convincing? After conducting the argument analysis, what do you think about the article? What are the strengths and weaknesses of the arguments it presents?

Narrative analysis

Unlike conversation analysis (which focuses on the formal structure of interactions) and argument analysis (which examines the patterns of reasoning), **narrative analysis** is concerned with the ways in which people create and use stories to make sense of the world. Narrative analysis is based on collecting people's stories and then analysing them through a narrative methodology. These stories are usually not treated as sets of facts but as 'devices through which people represent themselves [and their worlds] to themselves and to others' (Lawler, 2002: 242). We all have numerous experiences every day, but we pay particular attention to those we perceive to be part of our 'story' (see Table 8.6 for examples). As we have seen in the section on Tilly's types of reasons, stories help us to explain the unfamiliar, unexpected or exceptional; they infuse with meaning what could otherwise be a confusing sequence of random events.

Narrative analysis can reveal valuable insights into how organizations shape social life. Storytelling is a common way of communicating within and about organizations, and it can occur among individuals or collectively. Organizations can be seen as 'collective storytelling system[s] in which the performance of stories is a key part of members' sense-making' (Boje, 2003: 43). Managers, entrepreneurs and employees tell stories as a way to describe and accomplish their everyday work. Stories can be used to evaluate the past, but they also lend themselves to expressing visions and goals, exchanging information (and knowledge), communicating emotions and instructing others how to act. Managers are taught and socialized to evaluate stories in complex and ambiguous circumstances.

Narrative analysis can be applied to all kinds of data that communicate stories, whether these are in-depth interviews, corporate texts, videos, blogs or autobiographical accounts. Researchers have studied organizational narratives such as founding myths about how a company came to embody certain values; see, for example, Boje's (1995) study on Disney. Others have researched individual narratives of organizational life and identity, such as

TABLE 8.6 Elements of stories

Stories:

- are concerned with the temporal ordering of ideas
- usually tend to focus on the sequential patterning of events and the role of various actors within them
- enable a researcher to build a complex picture of social situations in order to examine the actions of the various actors in a story, and explore their values, ideas and beliefs.

Sims' (2003) research into the 'vulnerability of middle managers' storying'. Narratives of change and resistance have also been examined (e.g. Humphreys and Brown, 2002). In doing so, researchers have identified plots, characters, tropes and different types of narratives that offer insights into issues such as organizational culture, strategy, change, identity and the nature of management. Narrative analysis invites researchers to recognize the producers of a story, the context of its production, and how it is performed, shared and controlled.

Boje (2003) suggests there are four main streams of storytelling in organization and business studies: bureaucratic, quest, chaos and postmodern. In *bureaucratic storytelling*, stories are linear and rationalized, and attempt to make controlling the employees and the organization more predictable. The *quest* is the second form of storytelling, in which the mission is to have the most compelling story. This often begins with a call, journey and return; often, it is the voice of the CEO of the company that gets the most attention here. The third type of storytelling is *chaos*, where the stories are lived and not told. Therefore, it is anti-narrative, without coherence, and inherently non-linear – here, no one is in control. The fourth type of storytelling has been referred to as *postmodern*, which (like chaos) lacks coherence; but (unlike in chaos) the postmodern storyteller works in a conscious, self-reflexive manner (Boje, 2003: 43).

Within these streams, there are a number of trends that can be discerned. The first is where stories are investigated out of context, for example interview text. A second is where stories are produced within a particular context, for example from a functionalist standpoint (in organizational cultural work). Yet another trend is where a managerialist perspective is taken. Here, storytelling is used as a tool; these stories are often positive, with a happy ending. One might suggest, for example, how a complex organizational change might turn out to be ignoring all the possible problems that might result. The fourth and final trend is a story that takes a functionalist/managerialist perspective, and includes research within critical theory, postmodernism and poststructuralism. The main focus of this approach is for the researcher to highlight the multiple approaches to interpretation of the story, and to attempt to uncover hidden stories and perspectives (in contrast to reporting only the storyline of one spokesperson). Here, pluralism is celebrated so that there might be perspectives that pick up themes in relation to gender or race. Boje (2008) argues that the critical issue is how knowledge becomes transferred from individuals to the organization. Managerialist and functionalist researchers set about transferring 'knowledge' and ideas, whereas critical theorists see their role as liberating individuals through the plurality of the perspectives set out, while those undertaking storytelling from a postmodern perspective examine a variety of storytelling forms. Again, the main message here is that the researcher's approach to the story will differ, depending on its purpose and focus (Boje, 2008: 214).

We have now identified different ideal types of stories commonly encountered in organizations, and we have discussed some of the more recent trends in how stories are used and researched. We have shown how narrative analysis is yet another approach to frame qualitative data in a way that sheds light on the structure and process of discourse – and, in some cases, on its rhetoric. But what methods and techniques are used to conduct narrative analysis? In general, narrative analysis follows a few simple steps that are similar to the ones we have identified for discourse analysis, visual analysis and argument analysis:

1. *Selection* – Stories or storytellers are selected based on the research question. There are various kinds of data that lend themselves to narrative analysis, including in-depth interviews, field diaries and correspondence. It is important to accompany the collection of stories with information on the background and context of these stories.

2. *Analysis of the narrative* – This usually involves a detailed examination of the plot of the story; the main actors, activities and places that appear in the story; and any problems that the story addresses. As stories are not always presented in a chronological order, it can be useful to reorganize or rewrite the story in order

to evaluate causal links. The rewritten story can be compared with the original to trace patterns of storytelling. It can be useful to identify formal elements such as beginning, middle and end, and then to divide the story into episodes and sequences. These sequences can then be analysed one by one, with a special emphasis on how they relate to each other and how transitions are made. Key elements such as conflict, surprise and predicament can be identified. Postmodern narrative approaches deconstruct stories further, looking for dichotomies, contradictions, subtle hints and disruptions.

3. *Re-contextualization* – At this stage, stories are re-examined with a special view to the context in which they were told, for example the social, cultural and political background of the story; the position of the storyteller; the relationship between the storyteller and the audience (in some cases, the researcher); and the historical context (including, for example, the history and current situation of an organization of which the storyteller is a member). The timeline of a story can be contrasted with a more general timeline of its context, in writing or using a diagram. Finally, the researcher should also enquire into underlying assumptions that might have gone unnoticed without a detailed understanding of the context. Sometimes, it can be useful to involve participants in this step.

4. *Interpretation and Evaluation* – Against this background, the meaning and the function of a story can be assessed. What were the reasons for a story to be told? What made it interesting to the storyteller or the audience? Why was it told in a certain way (of all the possible ways in which it could have been told)? How does the story relate to other stories in its content, structure and context? Coding, diagramming and the preparation of matrices can help to identify different types of narratives. Finally, the researcher should reflect on the contribution of the story to the research endeavour as a whole: what makes the story relevant to this research?

While this process appears relatively straightforward, albeit time-consuming, it is important to note that different models of narrative analysis exist that emphasize different steps of this process (Riessman, 2003). For example, the emphasis can lie on the second step – the examination of the content of stories with the aim of developing common themes, like those created in grounded analysis. Such *thematic analysis* focuses on *what is being said* as opposed to how it is said, and the context in which it is said. This decontextualization can be problematic because it ignores the fact that different people can attach very different meanings to their stories, or have different reasons to tell them (Riessman, 2003). Whether this translates into a weakness of a study depends on its research questions and objectives.

Other studies on narratives emphasize structure. *Structural analysis* still requires an examination of the content of a story, but its main focus is on *how the story is told*. Here, language is not ignored but becomes an 'object for close investigation – over and beyond its referential content' (Riessman, 2003: 706). *Interaction analysis* shifts the attention of the researcher to the *context* and to the *effect* of a story, and hence to the third and fourth steps outlined above. It acknowledges the fact that stories evolve in a dialogue between the storyteller and an audience situated in a certain context (Riessman, 2003). For the study of direct interaction, such analysis tends to involve techniques akin to those used in conversation analysis. Studies of mediated and indirect interactions may employ methods we have presented in the section on discourse analysis. Interaction analysis becomes *performance analysis* when the analysis focuses on non-verbal interaction as well as verbal interaction. This type of narrative analysis can be useful for studies of communication and identity construction. An example could be a study of how Steve Jobs performed the introduction of new products in a way that affirmed his position and the 'story' of Apple as a company.

We want to conclude this section on framing and interpreting qualitative data with an exercise that asks readers to develop their own example of a narrative analysis, giving them the opportunity to apply some of the methods and techniques presented in this section.

Narrative analysis

a)   **Individual exercise**: Download the transcript of a biographic interview with a Bay Area venture capitalist from the website of the Venture Capitalists Oral History Project at the Bancroft Library: http://bancroft.berkeley.edu/ROHO/projects/vc/transcripts.html.

Browse through the document and identify the section in the beginning in which the interviewee's *background, upbringing, schooling* and *early work experience* are described. Read this section carefully and think about a research question that could require the analysis of this section. Write down the research question and analyse the section as if it were the first document to be examined for this study. Think carefully about how you want to frame your data, what model of analysis would be appropriate, and the elements you will need to emphasize. You may wish to collect additional information on the context of the biography on the Internet. Apply at least two of the following methods in your analysis: coding; creation of a timeline or diagram; re-organization/rewriting of the story in chronological order.

b)   **Interactive exercise**: Give a short presentation about your experience in class. Explain the choice of your research question, how you have framed the data, and the methods you have used. What has been the main result?

c)   **Interactive exercise**: Based on a number of presentations, discuss differences and similarities between the different approaches that were chosen. Would it be possible to link some of the presentations into a group project because they focused on similar themes, used similar frames or employed similar methods?

COMPUTER-AIDED ANALYSIS

CAQDAS is the general term describing the software packages that can be used to aid the analysis of qualitative data, such as text, audio, video and graphics. In the past two decades, such packages have become an essential tool for many researchers working with qualitative data who value the wide array of tools offered by CAQDAS packages for the management and analysis of large volumes of data. However, concerns have been raised that the use of such packages can divert the attention of less experienced researchers away from the actual analysis to the software (Gibbs, 2014). This is indeed a problem, as CAQDAS packages do not analyse data; they merely *facilitate the application* of methods and techniques by the researcher, who (in most cases) could just as well work with paper and pencil. There is certainly an argument to be made that basic techniques such as coding should be practised on hard copies of data before moving to software packages – an approach we have taken with the exercises in this book. However, once the researcher attempts a bigger research project, which requires the analysis of larger amounts of data, CAQDAS packages can become an indispensable tool (Saldaña, 2009). Moreover, as research becomes more collaborative, some CAQDAS packages become even more attractive because they enable researchers to share and analyse their data in research teams.

There are many CAQDAS packages available, with the most prominent being **ATLAS.ti**, **NVivo** and MAXQDA. These and other CAQDAS packages provide some common functions for project management, data management, searching and mapping data, data analysis (in particular coding and the development of categories and themes) and visualization (see Table 8.7).

TABLE 8.7   Core features of CAQDAS packages

Task	Features
Project management	Assistance in organizing and managing a larger research project using memos, a project diary and other features
Data management	Organization and management of large volumes and different kinds of data; creation of an 'audit trail' that assists in documenting the analysis and developing ideas. Hyperlinking allows data to be linked to other data files
Searching and mapping data	All CAQDAS packages have an array of search capabilities – from simple word searches through to complicated multiple-attribute searches – that can interrogate data sets and retrieve coded data. Additionally, most packages include tools to map data and codes in diagrams
Analysis	Coding functions facilitate the analysis of data. Further, the capability to re-code data, to organize and change codes, and to link themes to developing ideas in memos aids continuity and can increase the overall transparency of the analysis process
Visualization and outputs	Most CAQDAS packages have the ability to generate outputs such as reports, models and charts, which can help to visualize data that are being conceptualized and relationships that are being made. Further, this enables data and analysis to be easily shared among the research team

Choosing the right package

Setting aside the tools that most of the packages have in common (such as basic search capabilities), different software packages come with various additional features. Whether or not these are relevant to a certain study depends on the design of the study and the kind of analysis the researcher wants to conduct. There are a number of general factors to consider when choosing a CAQDAS package, which can be summarized in the following key points:

- **Availability:** Most universities and research institutes acquire licences for only one or two of the major packages. As a result, research students or researchers employed in bigger projects usually work with the package they were trained on and have access to. There are also a number of free/open-source packages available. Some of these feature a graphical user interface, but others do not. The price for commercial packages varies; for students, licences can usually be obtained at a reduced price. Before purchasing such a licence, it is important to check that the program can be installed (i.e. that the operating system and capacity of the computer are suitable).

- **Requirements**: Researchers should be clear about what *kind of data* they will be analysing (text files, PDF documents, audio or video files, images etc.), what *kind of analysis* they wish to undertake, and the *methods and techniques* they will be using before they set out to choose a particular software. For example, a content analysis of interview transcripts that is part of a mixed-methods study will require different features (such as word-crunching tools) from a grounded analysis of company reports (which might require more advanced diagramming tools, and the facility to process formatted PDF files). See Example 8.6 for how such an assessment can be made.

- **Skills and training:** Many CAQDAS packages have advanced significantly over the past decade and already offer features of which many of their users are not fully aware. In some cases, the selection of the program should also be guided by consideration about how much time the researcher wants to spend on learning how to use the software. At least for the bigger packages, plenty of manuals and tutorials can be found online (e.g. on YouTube and university websites). More advanced packages or specialized techniques might require more extensive training, using courses that may not be available free of charge.

- **Teamwork:** Not all packages support teamwork. If a project requires several researchers to work on the same dataset, this will limit the choice of suitable packages to some degree.

Once these points have been considered, websites like that of the CAQDAS Networking Project of the University of Surrey can be consulted for guidance on choosing the right package (see the list of further reading at the end of this chapter). Such sites provide up-to-date information on the features and limitations of all major packages, along with detailed reviews and further guidance on where to look for training and support. On the companion website accompanying this book, readers will find an introduction to the main features of Atlas.ti, NVivo and WordSmith (a linguistic analysis software). Given the rapid development of these platforms, such information quickly goes out of date. For this reason, we have decided not to include this material in the print version of this book and instead to advise readers to consult the webpage of the CAQDAS Networking Project and the homepages of CAQDAS packages. Useful tutorials can also be found on YouTube.

EXAMPLE
8.6

Choosing a CAQDAS package

Imagine for a moment that you have just conducted a case study, and you have generated data using semi-structured interviews and observation. You decided early on that you are particularly interested in gaining a deeper understanding of the substantive area, and therefore you have opted for a grounded theory method of analysis. Now you are faced with the first consideration: what are you looking for from your data? There is little empirical evidence in your substantive area from which to structure search queries or inform rigorous, in-depth searching of the data; therefore, you are more interested in what will emerge from the data. Thus, in this scenario, you are more concerned with conceptualization and thematic analysis of the data. The answer to the first consideration then brings you to the second consideration: will you be primarily searching or coding the data? Coding relates to the practice of assigning 'codes', which are essentially descriptions, to selections of data; this is usually conducted in an iterative fashion and results in the conceptualization of data. Consequently, for this consideration, you necessarily decide you are looking for emergent concepts from the data. Last, you arrive at the data-preparation stage. You need to decide whether you code your interviews as audio files, assigning codes to certain sequences (such as 'INNOVATION STRATEGY' for minute 02.30 to minute 5:30) or whether you transcribe your data. Not all packages support the coding of audio material, and if you aim at a very detailed and in-depth analysis of the material, coding audio files might not be practical. If you decide to transcribe your data, you still need to consider the level of detail. Do you want to create summary records for your interviews because you are interested in very specific aspects, or do you choose to fully transcribe them? If you decide to transcribe them, what level of detail will be required? As we have seen above, conversation analysis requires *naturalized* transcripts that record every slightest detail, such as involuntary vocalizations. In contrast, for a grounded analysis aiming at the identification of common themes, less detail is required (*denaturalized* transcripts). Similarly, decisions will have to be made about the field notes. If, for example, you decide just to scan your handwritten notes, you will be able to code them like pictures – a certain section of the scan can be selected and then a code can be assigned. The limitation of this technique is that several packages do not support such coding, and none of them will read in your handwritten notes. As a result, when you retrieve material by code, you will be able to retrieve only pictures (instead of quotations). Therefore, most researchers still type up their field notes so that they can take advantage of the advanced search and query tools included in most packages. Having addressed these considerations, you may be somewhat clearer on the choice of software package. On the most general level, your aims, data and analytical approach suggest the use of a 'code-based' package such as NVivo or ATLAS.ti. You will then have to check which code-based package offers the best support for coding the kind of data you have created and wish to analyse.

To demonstrate the other extreme, briefly consider this alternative scenario. You have conducted the same study, using the same methods. However, this time there is a substantial empirical foundation to the substantive area, and your study is particularly concerned with analysing discourse. Prior to undertaking the study, you have conducted a literature review and have generated a list of keywords that you would like to search for during the discourse analysis; in other words, you are looking for patterns and word frequencies (quantitative insight). Consequently, you decide that you will primarily conduct word searches during your analysis. Last, your overall analytical approach necessitates naturalistic description, because every small detail may be of importance. With this different set of answers, you conclude that you will need to use a software package that is purpose-built for the deeper level of textual analysis that you require; such packages are known as 'text-based' packages. Table 8.8 provides an overview of the considerations discussed. You will notice that there is a column labelled 'Both', which suggests there are CAQDAS packages that cater for all needs. While this is the case, it is only so to a certain extent: code-based packages such as NVivo and ATLAS.ti also have some of the functionality found in text-based packages, such as keyword search and the capacity to search for strings of words. However, an important point that should be borne in mind here is that while such packages can be considered as 'hybrids', they are not purpose-built for handling both text- and code-based work. For example, the use of a package such as WordSmith could facilitate more in-depth, broad work on a textual level.

TABLE 8.8   Type of CAQDAS package

Type of CAQDAS package				
Considerations	**Project factors**	**Text-based**	**Code-based**	**Both**
What are you looking for?	Patterns and quantitative insight	X		X
	Concepts and themes		X	X
What do you need to do with the data?	Search	X		X
	Code		X	X
What is the state of the data?	Naturalized	X		X
	Denaturalized		X	X

Finally, we would like to consider three important points regarding the use of computers for analysing qualitative data. First, the success and the strength of the analysis always depend on the judgement of the researcher; computers cannot substitute for this. If we come back to Tracy's (2013) analogy, the best pan can be used to produce the most unenjoyable food if the chef does not know how to cook.

This brings us to the second point, which is about the importance of developing the right skills. Before undertaking work with any CAQDAS package, it is essential to undertake sufficient training and allow for a period of familiarization. Learning about a software package is not the same as using it. In combination with the software developers' guides and any training courses they may offer, another excellent source of reference is *Using Software in Qualitative Research* (Silver and Lewins, 2014), which offers a step-by-step guide, including detailed sections on NVivo and ATLAS.ti. For Atlas.ti, we would also recommend Friese's (2012) excellent introduction.

Third, we would like to add a word of caution. Even if a suitable package has been found and sufficient training has been undertaken, researchers should be aware of the fact that CAQDAS packages affect how researchers relate to their data, and how they process and frame them. For example, Luker (2008) observes that she tends to generate many more sub-codes when coding on the computer, and that this changes the way she creates and reflects upon her categories. Code-based programs facilitate the retrieval of coded segments or quotations, making it easier to compare fragments of text sourced from different data. However, in contrast to piles of coded hard copies, it also makes it a lot easier to decontextualize what has been coded. This can be very problematic when individual sentences taken from different sources (e.g. an internal report, an interview, a legal statement and a field note) are treated as if they were derived from the same document or context. When coding diverse material, it is therefore essential always to remind oneself that words are used in different ways by different people situated in different contexts. Even if an analysis aims 'merely' to identify themes, it should aim also to be accurate – which brings us to the more general issue of how we can assess the quality of qualitative research.

QUALITY IN QUALITATIVE RESEARCH

If we want our research to be useful, we need to consider how to make it relevant, credible and attractive to others. But how can we assess whether the findings that emerge from our analysis are any good? In this section, we explore some answers to this question. We start by arguing that the quality of qualitative research ultimately depends on how researchers approach their research – from the development of the proposal to the publication of their work. Researchers who aim at conducting their research in a reflexive and transparent way rarely produce bad research. To illustrate this point, we discuss some of the main problems around the quality of the data, the analytical process, the documentation of this process, and the evaluation of outcomes. We will then conclude this discussion with an overview of relevant criteria for the assessment of qualitative research.

Earlier in the chapter, we argued that just as good and well-prepared ingredients are vital for a chef, so good and well-prepared data are vital for a researcher. A chef who, without much thought, just uses whatever can be found in the kitchen is unlikely to produce a great meal. One cannot overemphasize the importance of closely examining the quality of data before embarking on their analysis. This starts with a reflection on what kind of data were collected – and what kind of data were *not* collected, i.e. are missing. For example, a study finding that the damage caused by a fire is greater when more firefighters were involved in extinguishing it would suggest that an important mediating factor has been overlooked. While this might be a rather simplistic example, it should be considered that the complexity of phenomena examined in management research can easily give rise to problems, which may be much less obvious.

Sampling strategies, and the potential bias they can introduce, should be examined carefully to assess what kind of inference can be drawn. Qualitative research aims at transcending anecdotal evidence. If relevant material is ignored or omitted from the analysis, this kind of 'cherry-picking' can limit severely the inferences and generalizations that can be made (Barbour, 2014). Researcher effects should also be considered. Interviews are based on a short period of interaction between an interviewer and an interviewee, and they usually do not give the interviewer much opportunity to fully assess the background of the interviewee, or the motivations of the interviewee to respond in a certain way. Interviewees might wish to impress interviewers or try to enlist them in their own cause (Maxwell and Chmiel, 2014). The triangulation of different data sources, different methods of data collection, and different kinds of data can reduce such problems (Miles, Huberman and Saldaña, 2014) – but triangulation can make the analysis more complicated too. Whenever possible, evidence should be carefully weighed and checked against 'hard facts'.

A good qualitative study is systematic and thorough. Superficial thematic analysis based on anecdotal evidence rarely advances our thinking. Themes should be developed, and the relationships between them explored, with the aim of contrasting, evaluating and integrating findings. Many studies are simply not useful because researchers stopped their analysis somewhere in the middle (Barbour, 2014). Negative evidence that can inform alternative interpretations is essential for good theory-building, as it can inform rival explanations that are needed to assess the robustness and scope of a theory. Such alternative interpretations are part and parcel of the process of constant comparison on which qualitative research builds; as such, they should not be fought against, but should be welcomed as an opportunity to improve the analysis. Alternative interpretations can be developed by researchers who critically examine their analysis in a reflexive way, but they can also be put forward by research participants, colleagues and supervisors. Seminars that allow researchers to present work-in-progress, including ambiguous fragments of data, in order to obtain alternative interpretations, provide an invaluable opportunity to enhance the quality of a study. Table 8.9 presents

TABLE 8.9   Questions enhancing self-reflexivity and transparency

Data:

- What information is included in my data? What information is missing?
- What sampling strategy was used to collect these data?
- What status do I attach to my data (e.g. facts, opinions, views and stories)?
- To what extent do my data include 'outliers', or negative or deviant cases?
- Do I like some data fragments more than others? Why?
- How do my data help me to address my research topic?
- What other data might be needed to answer my research question?
- To what extent is the quality or scope of my data limited by practical issues (e.g. time, funding and access)?

Analysis:

- How do I frame my data?
- Are my framework and perspective appropriate to my data and to my research question?
- On what grounds have I chosen my methods and techniques?
- Am I clear what I am doing?
- Have I included all my data in my analysis? If not, why not?
- What are/were the most important decisions I have/had to make in this analysis?
- Does my analysis go beyond a simple list of descriptions and themes?
- What is my theoretical contribution (however small)?
- Am I making too large claims about my research?

questions that can help in the preparation of such seminars, and in the development and documentation of a *good* study.

Good feedback and honest evaluations can only be given to those who disclose what they are doing. Detailed documentation and 'reflexive accounting' (Barbour, 2014: 505) of the research process (e.g. by answering questions like those listed in Table 8.9) enhance the quality of the study. Transparency is also essential when it comes to convincing others of the quality of the research undertaken. Audiences have to gain some insights into how a study was done in order to consider it credible. Moreover, few audiences are interested in research that does not relate to their own interests or that simply replicates what has already been done. Only through continuous engagement with debates among practitioners and academics can practitioners ensure that their research can be understood in the context of what has already been done. A good literature review is the foundation of a good study.

It is important to be honest about what a project can – and cannot – achieve. Qualitative researchers tend to acknowledge subjectivity where quantitative researchers claim objectivity; qualitative research usually aims at *internal generalizability* (capacity to explain what has been researched within a given setting) and not *statistical generalizability* (inferences beyond those that have been studied), which is the gold standard of quantitative research. More often than not, qualitative studies cannot be replicated as they have been conducted by individuals engaging with a particular setting at a particular point of time. The contribution of qualitative research often lies in its *uniqueness* – and not in whether it can be replicated (Janesick, 2003). As a result, qualitative research may fail some of the standards used for quantitative research (e.g. objectivity, statistical generalizability and replicability). This does not mean, however, that it is not *good* research.

As we noted earlier in the book, qualitative research aims at theory-building. While qualitative researchers often cannot know whether their theories can be transferred to

TABLE 8.10 Checklist of eight criteria for assessing the quality of qualitative research

Criterion	Questions to consider
Worthy topic	Is the research topic relevant, original, timely, significant and/or interesting?
Rigour	Does the study use appropriate data, concepts and methods?
Sincerity	Is the study characterized by (self-)reflexivity and transparency? Does it provide me with the information I need to evaluate the study?
Credibility	Is the study marked by detailed descriptions, the explication of tacit knowledge, and triangulation?
Resonance	Does the research affect readers/audiences through evocative representations, appropriate generalizations, and transferable findings?
Contribution	Does the research make a significant contribution in one or more of the following areas: theory/concepts, methodology/methods and practical impact?
Ethics	Does the research consider ethical issues?
Meaningful coherence	Does the study fulfil its aims? Do the methods and techniques used fit with the stated aims? Does the research meaningfully connect literature, research questions and findings?

(BASED ON TRACY, 2010: 840)

settings beyond the one they have studied, they can identify factors that are likely to determine the *transferability* of certain theories, thereby giving readers room for informed speculation about the settings in which their theories can be applied. As noted by Barbour (2014: 507), 'unlike claims to "statistical generalizability", which purport to provide a universal answer, the invoking of "theoretical generalizability" can simply involve posing a general (but clearly articulated) *question* or tentative hypothesis.' A clearly articulated question can go a long way towards addressing some of the complex phenomena with which management research is concerned.

Finally, this leaves us with the question of whether there are any formal criteria for the quality of qualitative research, given that some of those developed for quantitative research seem not to be suitable. In Chapter 3, we showed how different epistemological stances translate into different views on validity, reliability and generalizability – so these 'traditional' criteria can be used if they are re-interpreted in order to better accommodate research conducted within the qualitative paradigm (Miles, Huberman and Saldaña, 2014: 311). However, several attempts have been made to develop lists of criteria that qualitative researchers would acknowledge to be genuine. Given the impressive range of methods that are considered to be 'qualitative', mainly because they are 'not quantitative', this has not been an easy exercise (Flick, 2007). In Table 8.10, we present an abridged version of a checklist that was developed by Tracy (2010) to facilitate the assessment of the quality of qualitative research. While we belief that such a checklist can only complement a previous and in-depth consideration of the issues raised above, we consider it a useful tool for assessing the quality of one's own research and the research of others.

CONCLUSION

In this chapter we have attempted to provide an overview of some of the main approaches for framing and interpreting qualitative data. We have shown how different approaches frame data in different ways, and how they create links between the data collected, the analysis undertaken, and the inferences drawn. We have then advised readers on how they can identify CAQDAS packages that can assist them in their research. Finally, we have discussed how the quality of qualitative research can be assessed.

The main points raised are:

 The methodology of each qualitative study is unique as it has to be appropriate to the research question, and to the setting or phenomenon under research.

 Different analytical approaches frame qualitative data in different ways and prescribe different methods for their analysis and interpretation. Researchers may wish to adapt and combine different approaches as long as they can be integrated in a coherent research design.

 Good qualitative research builds on the creativity, focus and reflexivity of the researchers, and on their willingness to account for the research process in a transparent way.

While there remains a continual tension between those who aim at building theory and those who aim at assessing its generalizability and exploratory value, a growing number of mixed-methods studies suggest that the long-assumed abyss separating the qualitative and quantitative paradigms is shrinking, and indeed easy enough to bridge. In the next two chapters, we cross this bridge, discussing the merits and methods of quantitative research.

FURTHER READING

Banks, M. (2008) *Using Visual Data in Qualitative Research*. London: Sage.
  Discusses a wide range of visual data produced by researchers and research participants, whereas the following chapter focuses more on the analysis of video data:
Bazeley, P. (2007) *Qualitative Data Analysis with NVivo*. London: Sage.
Bergmann, J.R. (2004) 'Conversation analysis', in U. Flick, E. Kardorff and I. Steinke (eds), *A Companion to Qualitative Research*. London: Sage, pp. 296–302.
Boje, D.M. (1995) 'Stories of the story-telling organization: a postmodern analysis of Disney as "Tamaraland"', *Academy of Management Journal*, 38 (4): 997–1035.
Boje, D.M. (2003) 'Using narratives and telling stories', in D. Holman and R. Thorpe (eds), *Management and Language*. London: Sage.
  Offers a guide for researchers to examine alternative discourse-analysis strategies. The book sets out eight options for use in organization and communication research. See also:
Charmaz, K. (2014) *Constructing Grounded Theory: A Practical Guide Through Qualitative Analysis*, 2nd edn. London: Sage.
  Seminal textbook on how to conduct data creation and data analysis using Grounded Theory.
Cunliffe, A.L. (2008) 'Discourse analysis', in R. Thorpe and R. Holt (eds), *The SAGE Dictionary of Qualitative Management Research*. London: Sage.
Dawson, A. and Hjorth, D. (2012) 'Advancing family business research through narrative analysis', *Family Business Review*, 25 (3): 339–55.
DeCuir-Gunby, J.T., Marshall, P.L. and McCulloch, A.W. (2011) 'Developing and using a codebook for the analysis of interview data: an example from a professional development research project', *Field Methods*, 23 (2): 136–55.
  Details steps on how to create a codebook for coding interview data.
Duriau, V.J., Reger, R.K. and Pfarrer, M.D. (2007) 'A content analysis of the content analysis literature in organization studies: research themes, data sources, and methodological refinements', *Organizational Research Methods*, 10 (1): 5–34.
  A great example for applied content analysis and a useful overview of how it has been used in organization studies.
  The following website is a great starting point for readers wanting to find out more about template analysis:
Flick, U. (2007) *Managing Quality in Qualitative Resear0ch*. London: Sage.
  In this slim volume, Flick goes a long way in explaining how to distinguish good from bad qualitative research. See also Barbour and Maxwell and Chmielin in Flick's *SAGE Handbook of Qualitative Data Analysis*.
Flick, U. (2014) *SAGE Handbook of Qualitative Data Analysis*. London: Sage.
  Comprehensive collection of chapters on a wide range of approaches, methods and techniques for analysing qualitative data.
Friese, S. (2012) *Qualitative Data Analysis with ATLAS.ti*. London: Sage.
Galman, S.C. (2013) *The Good, the Bad, and the Data: Shane the Lone Ethnographer's Basic Guide to Qualitative Data Analysis*. Walnut Creek, CA: Left Coast Press.
  Comic-style textbook for novices to qualitative analysis.
King, N. (2014) *Template Analysis Website*, University of Huddersfield. Available at www.hud.ac.uk/hhs/research/template-analysis/ (last accessed 14 August 2014).
Knoblauch, H., Tuma, R. and Schnettler, B. (2014) 'Visual analysis and videography', in U. Flick (ed.), *SAGE Handbook of Qualitative Data Analysis*. London: Sage, pp. 435–49.
  The following four publications give useful introductions into discourse analysis and conversation analysis:
Lawler, S. (2002) 'Narrative in social research', T. May (ed.), *Qualitative Research in Action*. London: Sage, pp. 242–58.
  Some examples of applied narrative analysis:
Leitch, S. and Palmer, I. (2010) 'Analysing texts in context: current practices and new protocols for critical discourse analysis in organisational studies', *Journal of Management Studies*, 47(6): 1194–212.
Locke, K. (2001) *Grounded Theory in Management Research*. London: Sage.
  Offers a comprehensive overview of the debates and possibilities available to researchers when considering grounded approaches to data collection and analysis.
Miles, M.B., Huberman, A.M. and Saldaña, J. (2014) *Qualitative Data Analysis*, 3rd edn. Thousand Oaks, CA: Sage.
  One of the leading textbook on qualitative data analysis in the social sciences. Miles, Huberman, and Saldaña cover a wide range of methods for exploring, describing, analysing and explaining qualitative data as well as drawing and verifying conclusions.
Saldaña, J. (2009) *The Coding Manual for Qualitative Researchers*. Los Angeles, CA: Sage.

A practical introduction into coding which also provides an excellent overview of different frameworks for coding qualitative data.

Sidnell, J. (2011) *Conversation Analysis: An Introduction*. Malden, MA: Wiley-Blackwell.

Silver, C. and Lewins, A. (2014) *Using Software in Qualitative Research: A Step-by-step Guide*, 2nd edn. Los Angeles, CA: Sage.

A comprehensive introduction into how to use CAQDAS packages with text, video and mixed data. For readers working with Atlas.ti and NVivo we also recommend their online tutorial along with:

Suddaby, R. (2006) 'From the Editors: what grounded theory is not', *Academy of Management Journal*, 49 (4): 633–42.

Article that discusses common misconceptions of what constitutes 'grounded theory'.

Tracy, S.J. (2010) 'Qualitative quality: eight "big-tent" criteria for excellent qualitative research', *Qualitative Inquiry*, 16 (10): 837–51.

A more recent compilation of quality criteria for qualitative research.

Want to know more about this chapter? Visit the ⓢSAGE edge™ website at **https://edge.sagepub.com/easterbysmith** to access practice questions, selected journal articles, useful web links and much more.

CRAFTING QUANTITATIVE DATA

9

This chapter is divided into three main parts. The first part covers three sources of quantitative data: collecting data through surveys, collecting data through observation and using secondary data sources. Each has benefits and drawbacks, and we consider how to make choices between them. The second section looks at the process of measurement in two parts: how to design structured questions for surveys and interviews, and alternative forms of measurement scale for recording responses. The third section examines the conceptual basis of measurement models.

SOURCES OF QUANTITATIVE DATA

In thinking about where to get data that could be analysed using quantitative methods, there are broadly two ways of going about it: researchers can collect their own primary data, or they can use secondary data already collected and stored within archival databases. Each approach has advantages and disadvantages. Broadly, collecting one's own research data gives control over both the structure of the sample and the data obtained from each respondent. This gives greater confidence that the data will match the study objectives. However, that benefit comes at a price since it can be much more expensive (in time and effort) to collect one's own data, compared with using secondary data from an existing archive. The downside of using secondary data sources is that the quality of the data may be more uncertain, and the researcher does not have control over either the sample or the specific data collected.

Collecting data through surveys

Surveys can be good ways of collecting data about the opinions and behaviour of large numbers of people, as long as they are done well. The choice between them will depend on many factors, so that there is no single best way. Survey data can be collected either through self-completion questionnaires where respondents record their own answers, or can be administered by interviewers face-to-face or over the telephone. While these two methods still have an important place, advances in communications technology have brought a variety of new options within the scope of the researcher in business and management. The new methods offer many advantages, and bring challenges, which are also opportunities of course.

Types of survey

Self-completion questionnaires
Postal questionnaire surveys have the advantage that the cost per respondent is low for large samples compared with any method that requires face-to-face contact with individuals, especially when the sample members are widely dispersed. However, response rates can be very low (for many researchers, a 20 per cent response rate would be regarded as good) because there is no personal contact with the respondent that can encourage cooperation. Financial or other inducements are sometimes effective, but the normal guarantee of anonymity makes it difficult to reward people for responding because the researcher has no way of knowing who has replied and who has not. The researcher has little control over whether the person targeted is the one who answers the questions (CEOs are reputed to hand survey questionnaires over to their PAs to fill in on their behalf), and also over how they answer them. As a result checking the quality of data from postal surveys, both completeness and accuracy, is particularly important.

Another application of modern communications technology is the **web-based survey**. As the Internet becomes a taken-for-granted part of business and domestic life, carrying out web-based surveys (Gunn, 2002) is rapidly becoming commonplace. Instead of mailing a questionnaire to each potential respondent and asking them to mail it back, the questionnaire is located on a website, and each respondent is sent the web address in order to access it. The survey is then completed online, and responses are stored directly in an online database for statistical processing later. Tools such as Qualtrics, SurveyMonkey and Verint have dramatically reduced the cost of web surveys by making each step in the process easy for those without technical training. The Internet offers a number of attractions for web surveys. Internet-based surveys can be customized for individual respondents much more easily than can postal surveys. Moreover, the interactivity of web technologies gives a number of advantages: pop-up instructions and drop-down boxes can explain parts of the web survey that are more difficult to understand; questions at different points in a survey can be personalized using responses to earlier questions; and through skip-logic and conditional branching it is easy to skip over topics that are not relevant based on answers to earlier questions. It is also possible to build in dynamic error-checking of answers to ensure that people respond consistently throughout. Finally, data can be downloaded directly into analysis programs such as Excel or SPSS, avoiding the cost of data entry and transcription errors. Berghman et al. (2006) provide a good example of a web survey.

Web surveys are attractive to researchers but they are not always feasible. For example, a student was not able to distribute her questionnaires to staff in telecoms companies in Nigeria by email because many large companies restrict the access that their employees have to the Internet in order to avoid abuse. Email was only allowed from registered email addresses, and so the student had to make paper copies of her survey and distribute them individually to her respondents.

Interviewer-administered questionnaires

Structured interview surveys are much more expensive per head because an interviewer has to be present while each respondent's answers are recorded. The cost of interviews includes the time of the interviewer, which has to cover initial training, time spent in setting up each interview, travel to where respondents are located, and an allowance for broken appointments. They are most often used when accurate data are the main priority, and where there are complicated instructions for how to answer survey questions or where different questions need to be asked depending on individual circumstances. It is almost always better to have a smaller dataset of accurate answers than a larger dataset riddled with errors. Many people are understandably reluctant to divulge confidential or personal sensitive information in a postal questionnaire, and a skilled interviewer can build a relationship of trust with respondents that can reassure them about why the data are needed and how they will be kept secure. An interview method may be the most effective way to collect survey data for groups such as customers in a shop or a service facility, where postal addresses or other contact details are not available.

Telephone interview surveys are now commonplace in many research projects, since they combine the low cost of the postal survey with the interactivity of the face-to-face interview. So much of day-to-day business is conducted now by phone that most people are very familiar with the technology. Collecting data by telephone is of most value where the design of the research project requires contact with respondents who are widely dispersed (so that travelling to them would be time-consuming and expensive) or where the researcher is located in a different part of the world (e.g. many Asian students studying in the UK want to conduct their research in their own country, but cannot afford to travel there to collect data). This task has been made much cheaper in the last few years by the rapid development of voice-over-IP (VOIP) technologies such as Skype (www.skype.com), which use the Internet to transmit voice, so that the cost of a call does not depend on distance.

Advantages and disadvantages of alternative survey strategies

EXERCISE 9.1

Below are three different research projects where survey methodology might be appropriate. Taking into account the topic, the resources available to you and the target group, make a list of the advantages and disadvantages of the four methods of administering your survey. Which method will you use and why?

	Postal survey	Web survey	Face-to-face interview survey	Telephone interview survey
1. A project in a small business to assess views on introducing charging employees for car parking				
Advantages				
Disadvantages				
2. A worldwide survey in a multinational company of staff attitudes to HRM practices				
Advantages				
Disadvantages				
3. An investigation to understand the nature of bullying within the Social Services Department of a local authority				
Advantages				
Disadvantages				

Improving response rates in surveys

A high response rate in a survey is clearly important: it gives a larger body of data, which the researcher can use to address research questions, and it makes it much more likely that the sample is representative of the population of interest. This section draws on advice by Dillman (Dillman, 2007; Dillman et al., 2007), and gives a number of steps that the researcher can take to increase response rates as well as the quality of the information that respondents give. Underlying these steps is a simple principle derived from social exchange theory. Providing data is a cost to each respondent, so you should increase the perceived benefit as much as possible (see Table 9.1) and reduce the effort involved as much as possible (see Table 9.2).

Ways of establishing trust

A survey is a request for people to do something (in this case, answer questions and return the survey) based on the expectation that something will follow. As with many things in life, willingness to act depends on trust that the other person will fulfil what they promise. So, when you contact people to ask them to take part in your survey, it makes sense to increase as much as possible their trust in the promises you make. This can be difficult, since you will almost certainly not know your respondents personally, and so they do not know if they can trust you.

The first way to increase trust is to obtain sponsorship by a legitimate authority. Compliance is higher if the request comes from a source that is regarded as legitimate. If you are a student, it may be better to describe your survey as part of the research being carried out by

TABLE 9.1 Ways of increasing the rewards for participation

- ***Show respect for participants*** – for example, explain why the survey is being done, offer a point of contact for questions, address people by name where possible
- ***Say thank you for taking part*** – through a follow-up letter or email
- ***Frame the survey as a request for their help or advice*** – an example request to patients in a GP practice could be: "I am writing to you because the only way that we know whether we are doing a good job is by asking people who use our service"
- ***Appeal to the values of a group*** – explain the survey in terms of what matters to the group of people involved
- ***Give token rewards*** – offering a small reward can increase the sense of obligation to give a completed survey in return
- ***Make the questions interesting*** – better responses are obtained for topics that matter to the people taking part
- ***Social validation*** – you can increase participation by showing that people similar to them have completed it already
- ***Opportunities to respond are limited*** – telling people that they only have a limited time to respond can increase participation rates

TABLE 9.2 Ways of decreasing the costs of participation

- ***Make it as convenient as possible to respond*** – for a web survey, include a link in an email; for a postal survey, include a reply-paid envelope
- ***Don't talk down to people*** – consider the difference between the following requests to take part in a survey of student satisfaction:

  o 'as a student, you are required to respond to this survey of school administration'
  o 'as a student, you are the best person to help us to improve the service that the school gives you'

  The first is likely to lead to resistance, since most of us don't like being told what to do, while the second puts the respondent in charge.

- ***Make the survey short and easy to complete*** –surveys with fewer questions achieve higher response rates. Don't try to cram as many questions as possible onto a page just to make it look shorter. Sometimes going to the other extreme is actually beneficial. If your target sample consists of older people, then using a bigger font and spreading the text out to make it easier to read is almost certainly more important than skimping on the number of pages used.
- ***Minimize requests for personal or sensitive information*** – many people are reluctant to divulge information about their income, and health, so only ask questions about such topics if they are essential. If you absolutely need to know these things, then explain why this is important and show how you will respect the person's confidentiality. In workplace surveys, we have also found that personal information is better placed at the end of a survey after questions on neutral and less sensitive topics rather than at the beginning.

your supervisor (who of course is wise and experienced). Throughout many years of carrying out employee opinion surveys, we have also found that it makes a big difference that we are academics working in a university rather than paid consultants (we are not being paid to carry out the survey). We work *with* the company (which gives us the legitimate right to be there), but we are not working *for* the company (which would mean that the company controls what we are allowed to ask, and how the answers will be used). We often insist that replies come directly to us rather than to a company HR department, in order to avoid the possibility that employees' answers might be seen by management.

The second way to increase trust is to make the current task appear important. You can increase trust in a survey by showing how the findings from previous surveys have been used to make significant changes. Of course, such claims need to be credible, and you should think about how your own study will be used to make a difference. Doing nothing with your results makes the study less important in the eyes of your participants, and it can be very harmful. There is nothing more likely to damage credibility than asking people's opinions and then doing nothing with their answers.

The third way to increase trust is by ensuring confidentiality and security of information. Most of us are sensitive these days about information about ourselves, who has access to it and how it might be used. Many people seem to be relaxed about sharing some things about themselves on social media such as Facebook, but the same people might be much more cautious about answering questions in a survey. What is now called 'big data' offers the potential to collate fragmented health information in order to identify (for example) rare combinations of treatments which would be effective for devastating diseases. But there continues to be debate in the UK about how to use data for these purposes in a way that protects privacy. You should make sure that data are kept confidential and anonymous (unless there is a really good reason otherwise), and telling your participants that this is so will make it easier for them to trust you and to give their informed consent to take part in your study.

Collecting data through observational methods

Observational methods are used in order to code and analyse behaviour, which may include visual data as well as behavioural data (Banks, 2008). Observational data are uncommon in business and management research, but could be very useful in areas such as the study of team-working, managerial decision making and negotiation. Observing what people do during a task gives a directness and richness which cannot be achieved by asking people to describe what they did. Behaviour may either be coded live or be recorded (e.g.using audio or video or by capturing key presses and screen displays on a PC) for later coding. The most common way in which observational methods are used is with the observer as a non-participant, although participant observation can also be used, as we discussed in Chapter 7.

Types of observational data

There is no single way of classifying observational data, because behaviour is very complicated and the purposes of studies vary enormously. The most obvious distinction is between verbal and non-verbal aspects of behaviour. The researcher may be interested in *verbal* behaviour – the words that people use to express meanings through the content of messages, complexity of syntax, formal versus informal language – in order to explore different ways of explaining how to perform a task. *Non-verbal* behaviour is divided into vocal aspects to do with tone of voice (angry, apologetic, loving, calm etc.), pitch (high or low) and the pacing of speech (talking quickly or slowly), and also visual aspects to do with facial expressions, gestures, body posture and so on. A detailed analysis of the success or failure of a negotiation exercise would need to include an analysis of these aspects of non-verbal behaviour since they carry a substantial proportion of information. For example, Mehrabian's (1981) experimental studies of communications of feelings and attitudes led him to the following formula:

Total Liking = 7% Verbal Liking + 38% Vocal Liking + 55% Facial Liking.

In other words, most of the information about whether one person likes who they are talking to comes not from what is said (only 7 per cent) but on how it is said and on their facial expressions (93 per cent). We can conclude that relying for data only on a written transcript of what was said during a conversation or a meeting will miss much of the most important information about what is going on, particularly regarding relationships between people.

Factors affecting observational data

There are a number of things that need to be kept in mind when designing studies that will use observational data. First, observer effects are common, which refers to the fact that most of us behave differently when we know (or think) that we are being observed. Often, initiatives within local communities rely on exactly these effects to influence the behaviour of members of the public: those boxes on poles at the side of the road often do not contain speed cameras (but they might, so we slow down). From the perspective of positivistic research, observer effects are bad news since they alter the very thing that the researcher is interested in learning about. Consider how difficult it is for many people to pose naturally for a photograph: it is easy to tell the difference between a natural smile and a posed smile since the muscle groups used are different. In practice though, people whose behaviour is being recorded quickly get used to being observed and forget about the cameras. One way to avoid observer effects is to act covertly so that no one knows that they are being watched, but this violates one of the basic principles of ethical research, that research participants give their informed consent to take part in a study (see Chapter 5). Indeed, recording of telephone calls without consent is illegal in the UK, and that is why calls to companies often start with a message saying that calls may be recorded or monitored for security and quality control purposes.

The second factor to bear in mind in using observational data relates to how decisions are made about *what behaviour is sampled*. Some kind of selectivity is inevitable, simply because human behaviour is so rich and complex. One approach is to try to obtain a complete record, and then sample from within it later. A popular TV programme in many countries is *Big Brother* (first developed in the Netherlands), where individuals live in the 'Big Brother House' and a large number of cameras record what they do. Each person also wears a microphone at all times so that what they say is recorded. Even if the output from every camera and every microphone is available for analysis, some kind of selectivity is essential. The programme editors broadcast a tiny proportion of all that material, and their editing judgements can be a source of complaint and comment. For example, inmates of the house often complain that the programme did not show the 'real me' when features of their behaviour that show them in a particular way are selected and others neglected. A second approach is to record only a sample of behaviour: either by *time* sampling (e.g. take a photo every two seconds, or record for five minutes every hour through the day) or by *activity* sampling (e.g. record every phone call that is a customer complaint, or select company orders for a specific range of products).

Coding observational data

One of the most widely used systems for coding behaviour in small groups is *interaction process analysis* (IPA), originally developed by Bales (1950, 1970) and later modified. The original system grouped behaviour into 12 categories according to a focus either on social-emotional aspects of the relationship (e.g. liking vs disliking) or on aspects of the task (e.g. giving answers vs asking questions). The categories form six pairs; for example, seems friendly vs unfriendly; gives vs asks for information. Using the IPA requires substantial training for observers to break behaviour down into discrete units and then classify each unit into one of the categories. A more detailed elaboration of the IPA is the *system of multiple level observation of groups* (SYMLOG) (Bales et al., 1979; Bales, 1988). The two forms of the system code either values or behaviour into 26 categories, which can then be combined to give a position in a three-dimensional interpersonal space: dominance, friendliness and task-orientation.

Using observational data

EXAMPLE
9.1

A Masters student sat in as an observer on selection interviews for engineering apprentices and coded some aspects of the verbal and non-verbal behaviour of each candidate during the interview. Interviews were classified according to the outcome (accept or reject) and were then examined for differences in the behaviour of the candidates. All the candidates treated the interview as a formal situation and were nervous: they sat upright in the chair with their legs together in front of them and their hands together on their knees. The candidates who were *accepted* showed that they were interested in the interviewer by lots of eye contact, and smiling. They reinforced their replies to the interviewer's questions by moving their head – nodding or shaking. By contrast, the *rejected* candidates avoided eye contact with the interviewer, and showed their apparent lack of interest by wandering eyes when the interviewer was talking, and they were much less expressive in their non-verbal behaviour.

Types of questions that observational data can answer

EXERCISE
9.2

Group exercise: In groups, consider the research questions in the box below. Each group selects one of the research questions. The task is in two parts:

1. Draw up a coding scheme for the types of behaviour that the group is interested in.
2. Design a sampling strategy for collecting the data.

Then bring the groups together to present their coding schemes, and compare them. What factors influence the content of the coding scheme and the choice of sampling strategy?

Research question	What data to collect	How to sample
Do people buy more cold drinks in hot weather, and more soup in cold weather?		
Does the presence and type of background music in a store alter customers' buying behaviour?		
How do people use online help sources?		
When do people who work in different places (virtual teams) switch between media (instant messaging, email, video-conferencing, and phone) in order to manage a project?		
How does the conversational style adopted by a call handler influence the effectiveness of telephone helplines?		
In negotiations, how do same-sex and mixed-sex groups differ?		

Using secondary data: databases

The final method of getting quantitative data that we consider in this chapter is using archival sources of secondary data. Most research areas in business and management have data collected by other people. Organizations and individuals keep many different kinds of data for a variety of reasons: regulatory reasons (e.g. personal tax records), for monitoring past and present performance, and as a protection in the event of requests for information about the basis for past decisions. Although much of this data is confidential, a research study may gain access to data provided they meet confidentiality conditions. It is also the case that data of many kinds have to be deposited in archives, which can then be accessed for research purposes. Some of that data is in the public domain, though access to other material may depend on licence agreements of some kind, which the researcher's host institution may have negotiated.

The UK Data Service (www.data-archive.ac.uk/) is a comprehensive resource for some kinds of research and it contains data sets which are accessible to registered users free of charge. These data collections are immensely valuable for social scientists, though of much more limited use to the researcher in business and management. You can search through the UK Data Service archive using the Discover interface; other tools include ReShare (http://reshare.ukdataservice.ac.uk/), Relu (http://relu.data-archive.ac.uk/) and the European CESSDA catalogue (www.cessda.org).

Much more useful for business and management researchers are databases that include different kinds of company data. Examples of **financial databases** include:

- Compustat (www.compustat.com) provides annual and quarterly income statements, balance sheets, cash flow and supplemental data items for North American companies.
- Datastream (www.datastream.com) is one the largest financial statistical databases, and holds current/historical financial data for international companies/indices and bond data.
- SDC Platinum (http://thomsonreuters.com/sdc-platinum/) is an international mergers and acquisitions database.
- The Wharton Research Data Service (WRDS; www.whartonwrds.com) provides access to databases in the fields of finance, accounting, banking, economics, management, marketing and public policy.
- The Center for Research in Security Prices (CRSP; www.crsp.com) holds a variety of databases including: monthly/annual security prices, returns, and volume data for the NYSE, AMEX and NASDAQ stock markets.

The study by Berrone et al. (2013) is a good example of a study using archival data which could not realistically have been carried out in any other way. They collated data from a variety of databases in order to explore whether regulatory and institutional pressures leads to greater environmental innovation among US firms in polluting industries. Table 9.3 summarizes the concepts in their research framework, the indicator variables that they used to measure each concept and the source of the data.

It can be very valuable to work with data collected for another purpose, but it is most unwise to plunge straight into a data archive without thinking carefully. The most important factor affecting the quality of what can be done with secondary data is the design of the database. Generally speaking, archival data will have been collected according to a specific design, which means that the researcher's first task in assessing the value of secondary sources is how close the study objectives are to those that influenced the original collection of the data. For example, someone who is interested in how small- and medium-sized enterprises (SMEs) are using the Internet to internationalize their businesses is unlikely to

TABLE 9.3 Derivation of variables used in the study by Berrone et al., 2013

Concept	Indicator	Source of data
Environmental innovation	Number of citations of environmental patents registered between 1983 & 2001	CHI Patent Citation Indicators database
Regulatory pressures	Number of environmental agency inspections in a US state weighted by the number of focal firm subsidiaries in that state	ECOS report listing state enforcement & compliance activities 1995-1999; Orbis database of location of firm subsidiaries
Normative pressures	Number of environmental NGOs in a state divided by number of regulated entities in a state	National Center for Charitable Statistics
Deficiency gap	Total emissions of facilities belonging to a firm weighted by toxicity (relative to the sector average)	US Environmental Protection Agency Toxic Release Inventory data
Slack resources	1. Ratio of working capital to sales 2. Ratio between net income and revenues	COMPUSTAT
Asset specificity	Ratio of book value of a firm's machinery & equipment to total number of employees	COMPUSTAT
R&D intensity	Ratio of total R&D expenditure to total number of employees	COMPUSTAT
Number of patents	Total number of patents granted	US Patent & Trademark Office
Firm size	Number of employees	COMPUSTAT
Sector	Business sector	COMPUSTAT
Year	Year	

find an archive of publicly quoted companies of much use, since SMEs are much smaller than a typical publicly quoted company.

Using databases

EXAMPLE
9.2

A doctoral student in her PhD work looked at cross-border mergers involving a British company taken over by a non-UK company. She started her search using the Thomson Financial M&A database to identify mergers that met her criteria. Here is her story:

> In my thesis, I needed to draw up a list of acquisitions with particular characteristics, which I would later contact. I needed only majority acquisitions, and it allowed me to search for above 50 per cent acquisitions. I also needed only

(Continued)

(Continued)

UK companies that were bought by foreign companies – the database allowed me to 'include' or 'exclude' acquirers and targets from particular countries from my search. For example, by 'excluding' UK acquirers I was able to search only for foreign acquisitions. It also allowed me to search for deals of a certain age, completed as opposed to only announced deals, deals of a certain value, deals in a specific industry and so on. The database also contained very small as well as very large M&As. Overall, I found it an incredibly versatile tool. I was able to get the list of M&As with the precise specifications that I wanted in a matter of minutes. Thomson Financial, however, did not provide me with addresses or websites of the companies, so I had to search for these myself.

Many archives contain company records for each year (things like profit figures etc.). Databases differ in their coverage of companies: some are more comprehensive for US companies, others for European companies, while yet other databases only contain data for companies above a minimum size. A researcher interested in other regions, for example the growth of Latin American companies, may find it difficult to locate sources of data. Another problem is that of linking data over time for organizations in a world where companies are formed, they grow, they merge with others and they die. Thus profits data for a company will only be available for those periods where it is independent, so that a takeover will mean that it becomes part of a larger organization, while re-structuring may leave the name intact but changes the sub-units that make it up. It may thus prove impossible to compare like for like over a lengthy period of time. The practical consequences of dealing with such changes are outlined in Example 9.3.

EXAMPLE 9.3

Designing a study to assess the impact of the Sarbanes-Oxley Act 2002

Consider the research question of assessing the impact on companies of the Sarbanes-Oxley Act of 2002, which changed the governance regulation and reporting obligations of US public companies after the Enron scandal. The obvious way to assess its impact is to use data for companies before and after the Act came into force. The first task is to decide on a sampling frame (whether to select companies within specific sectors, or companies of a specific size) and the second is to decide what time points to look at (e.g. three years before and after the Act came into force). The research could end up with four kinds of sample, and there are issues with all of the sampling strategies.

● The first approach is to select only companies with complete data throughout the study period. This makes the most sense on the face of it, since it gives a complete picture for the whole of the study period. It gives good answers to the question of how key variables change for companies whose ownership structure stays the same throughout. However, it misses out: companies that went out of business at any time on the study period; start-ups during the study period; and companies that were involved in merger and acquisition (M&A) activity.

● The second approach is to select all relevant companies at the start of the sampling period regardless of whether they still exist. This strategy would ensure that the researcher has a sound sample at the start of the study period, but then the study design suffers from the same problem of incomplete data for companies that went out of existence or changed their structure through M&A activity. This would make it impossible to compare data before and after, but it could still be possible to assess a slightly different question: the likelihood of a company surviving intact until the end of the study period (this is called 'survival analysis' in statistics).

- The third approach is to select all relevant companies at the end of the sampling period regardless of when they came into existence. This ensures a sound sample at the end of the study period, but suffers from incomplete data at the start for companies that are newly formed or re-formed from M&A activity.

- The fourth approach is to select a representative sample of companies at each sampling point, with varying amounts of data for each. This would give a representative picture of companies at each point, but the analysis of change over time would be greatly complicated by different patterns of incomplete data.

Given that there is no ideal solution, a researcher will need to weigh up the relative merits of each alternative and the risks involved. Much will depend on how much change there has been in organizational structures during the study period, and the precise nature of the research questions under consideration.

Where companies are required by regulation to report particular kinds of information, then that is what they will do. When regulations change, there will be an associated change in what is recorded. As a result, great care needs to be taken by the researcher to make sure that the data have a consistent meaning throughout the study period. For example, Wall et al. (1992) were interested in whether empowering shop-floor workers by allowing them to manage machine breakdowns had an effect on productivity. Each machine had a tachograph (similar to those used in vehicles to record driving performance), which automatically logged when the machine was working and when it was not. Production managers also kept their own records of production within each of the departments for which they were responsible. However, the research team had to design their own productivity measures, once they found that company managers had made several changes during the study period to how they recorded productivity. Line managers had designed productivity indices that helped them to achieve the objectives set for them by the company's senior management, but there were frequent changes to corporate priorities during the study period and managers responded to shifting priorities by adjusting what they measured and how they measured it.

The task of the researcher is to interpret the data recorded in a secondary data archive in terms of particular study objectives. This might mean forming *derived* measures by aggregating variables together to form an index, or by creating rates rather than absolute amounts. For example, comparing absolute change rarely makes sense, while percentage change relative to a starting point is generally more informative. Other examples are: measures of earnings per share, which take into account differences in company capitalization; productivity indicators (such as those used in the study in the previous paragraph), which relate outputs to the resources needed to deliver them; and sickness rates for companies, which adjust number of days of recorded sickness absence according to the number of employees.

QUESTION DESIGN

In this section of the chapter, we look at how to structure the wording of questions in interviews and surveys and how to record the responses that people give to them. Research on how politicians respond to questions asked by probing journalists showed that there are apparently 46 ways of avoiding answering a straight question. If that really is true, then how much more difficult is it to interpret answers when the questions themselves are not well-structured?

Principles in designing structured questions

There are five principles of good design when thinking about how to word questions. The first principle is that *each item should express only one idea*. If a question asks more than one thing at the same time, then it is not possible to know which one people are thinking of when they give an answer; for example, 'Do you subscribe to or read magazines or periodicals related to your profession?'

The second principle is to *avoid jargon and colloquialisms*. Jargon is insider knowledge in the form of expressions that some people (but not others) know. So using it only makes sense where it is possible to be confident that respondents are all 'in the know'. Colloquialisms are informal expressions in a language that may not be familiar to people who are not native to that country, or do not belong to a specific group. Mobile phone text-speak is becoming that, where 'cu l8r' is simple for some ('see you later') but impenetrable to others. The message is clear: play safe and use plain language.

The third principle is to *use simple expressions*. Using the active rather than the passive tense is generally better ('I did it' is better than 'It was done by me'). Dividing up complicated statements into a series of simple steps is better than expressing it all in one long sentence. In asking questions such as 'my superior gives me feedback on my performance', what we typically do is adjust the wording according to the custom and practice of the organization. In the UK, the word 'superior' is unlikely to be recognized as referring to the person that you report to, and this person might be called the immediate manager, supervisor, team leader or section head. We would prefer to use a term that is familiar in that organization, rather than stick rigidly to the same word as used in a standard question. Our view is that changing the wording makes it more likely that respondents will understand who it is that they should think of when answering the question. Keeping the wording the same actually reduces consistency in responding – the opposite of what is intended. Consider the question 'How many times did you eat together as a family last week?' At first glance, this seems to be unproblematic, but the following questions arise: 'Where did you eat – at home, in the car, in a restaurant?', 'What does "eat" mean – main meal, snack, take-out pizza?', 'What does "as a family" mean?'

The fourth principle is to *avoid the use of negatives*. In English, this is often done by adding 'no' or 'not' to a verb in order to give the opposite meaning, but two problems can arise. The first is that a quick read of a sentence may miss the negative, so that the respondent answers a question the wrong way around. There is research by Schmitt and Stults (1985) which suggests that around 10 per cent of respondents in large-scale studies may make this kind of mistake; and it obviously disturbs the clarity of data analysis. The second problem is that response scales such as the **Likert scale** are bipolar – they go from negative (*disagree*) through neutral (*not sure*) to positive (*agree*). People who feel good about something would have to show it by disagreeing with a statement worded negatively. This means it can get tricky to work out how to report what they feel.

The fifth principle is to *provide appropriate time referents* – memories fade and so asking people to think back over a long period may not give accurate responses. In general, we prefer to ask people to think about the last week or month rather than the last year when they are asked about regular day-to-day activities. However, some events have a specific pattern which should be reflected in question wording. For example, asking about the setting of exam papers would appropriately be phrased in terms of the 'last academic year' since such activities only occur at specific times.

The final principle is to *avoid leading questions*. The concept of a **leading question** comes from legal settings, where the way that a question is phrased gives a strong lead on what answer is expected. All research has an element of 'leadingness' about it – the researcher chooses what to ask about, and this focuses attention on some areas and not on others. However, leading questions do more than this: they make it easier for the respondent to give the answer that the researcher wants, instead of the answer that the respondent thinks is right.

EXERCISE
9.3

Examples of poor question wording

For each question below:

1. What is the problem?
2. Which of the principles is violated?
3. Re-write the question, and explain why your version works better than the original. (Clue: this might involve replacing it with more than one question.)

How strongly do you agree that smoking is harmful to health?

  □ Not at all   □ Slightly   □ Quite strongly   □ Very strongly

How good is your voting record in local elections?

  □ Not at all   □ Quite good   □ Very good   □ Excellent

If you wanted to express your opinion about genetically modified foods would you consider taking part in a boycott of your local supermarket?

  □ Not at all   □ Probably not   □ Not sure   □ Probably   □ Definitely

How much do you agree or disagree with the following: Politicians never keep the promises they make before an election, once they are in office.

  □ Strongly disagree   □ Disagree   □ Not sure   □ Agree   □ Strongly agree

How much do you agree with the following: My supervisor is dynamic and well organized.

  □ Strongly disagree   □ Disagree   □ Not sure   □ Agree   □ Strongly agree

How much do you agree with the following: I am not satisfied with the progress of my research.

  □ Strongly disagree   □ Disagree   □ Not sure   □ Agree   □ Strongly agree

How much do you agree with the following: The presence of humorous literary allusions is conducive to an accessible presentation mode in academic pedagogy.

  □ Strongly disagree   □ Disagree   □ Not sure   □ Agree   □ Strongly agree

Exercise 9.3 gives some examples of poorly worded questions that might be asked in a questionnaire survey or an interview. Some have been taken from real research, while others have been invented to make a point. The exercise invites the reader to think through the design principles, work out what is wrong with each example question and then devise a better form of words. Like many things in life, asking clear questions seems remarkably easy until we set out to do it ourselves.

Positively and negatively worded items

Some authors recommend that sets of items which are designed to measure a concept should include both positively and negatively worded items. The idea is to avoid the tendency that some people have of just answering all of the questions in the same way, without paying too much attention to the specific wording of each one. While the worry can be a real one, negatively worded items are often harder to understand (disagreeing with a negative means that you agree with the concept – difficult, isn't it?). Making the items harder to follow is not a very smart way to increase respondent engagement with the purposes of the survey. It is generally agreed now that making items simpler to read is more important than balancing positive and negative wording.

Guidelines for ordering questions within a survey

First, group together related questions that cover similar topics. This will allow respondents to think through different aspects of a topic and give more thoughtful answers. In employee opinion surveys, we often introduce each group of questions like this: 'The next group of questions are about how you feel about working conditions where you work.'

Second, ask about facts before opinions. In employee opinion surveys, it is better to ask factual questions first so that respondents are guided to think through what they do in their job, features of the work environment, technology and so on. This primes people by 'walking through' their work before asking them questions about their emotional responses to work features. Starting with questions on job satisfaction runs the risk of giving ill-considered responses which may then colour everything that comes later in the survey.

Third, place sensitive or objectionable questions near the end. Once people have answered several questions and thought through interesting issues, they are less likely to stop if they encounter something more objectionable. Well-designed surveys lead respondents to think about issues on which they may not have already worked out opinions, and so giving them time to reflect on less contentious issues may reduce their objections to 'difficult' topics.

Fourth, it is usually better to ask questions about events in the order that they occurred. In asking about different periods of employment, start from now and work backwards or start from the past and work forwards.

Measurement scales for recording responses

There are two kinds of measurement scales that researchers commonly use, and they differ according to the number of distinctions between alternative points on the measurement scale. **Category scales** consist of few distinctions, while **continuous scales** consist of many distinctions.

Category scales

Category scales may be either unordered (these are called nominal scales) or ordered (these are called ordinal scales). The difference between nominal and ordinal category scales lies in whether shuffling the assignment of numbers to categories makes any difference to the meaning of the variable. **Nominal scales** have no natural ordering. A study by Goldacre et al. (2004) considered the ethnic origin of UK medical consultants, recorded as White, Black, Asian, Chinese and Other. It makes no sense to treat a concept such as ethnic origin as anything other than a nominal scale since the five ethnic groups could equally well be written in any order. Similarly, studies of branded consumer products coding countries of origin could list them in any order. By contrast, **ordinal scales** have a natural ordering. An example of an ordinal scale is socio-economic status, such as the classification scheme used by the UK government (the Registrar General's classification: I professional, II Intermediate, IIIa Skilled non-manual, IIIb Skilled manual, IV Semi-skilled, V Unskilled), which is based on such criteria as educational qualifications and occupation. Similarly, honours degrees awarded to UK undergraduates are graded as first class, upper second class (2:1), lower second class (2:2) and third class. The higher the aggregate mark in assessed work, the higher the degree classification.

Sometimes, however, the status of a variable in a research study is less clear. For the purpose of recording trade flows, country of origin would be recorded on a nominal scale. However, a project on boycotts within Arab countries of consumer products might well rank countries according to how closely they are associated with the USA, thus giving an ordinal scale. This illustrates an important point: that concepts or variables do not carry around with them a measurement scale that is intrinsic to them. Rather, the properties of scales are just that: properties which apply when we measure something.

The measurement of attitudes and opinions

Psychologists are not alone in being interested in what people think about things: the effect of the Lisbon Treaty on political relationships within Europe, the reputation of the company that supplies their electricity and so on. Everyone has opinions, and there is a lot of money to be made out of knowing what those opinions are. It is no surprise then that a lot of attention has gone into understanding effective ways of measuring attitudes and opinions.

Consider the statement 'My organization is a friendly place to work' (see Example 9.4). The simple-minded approach would be to ask people whether or not they agreed with the statement. However, this approach misses out on a lot of useful information because strength of opinion varies. There is a world of difference between someone who likes to listen to rock music from time to time and the fanatic who has every Guns N' Roses CD plus bootleg copies of their live concerts. To capture some of this subtlety, Rensis Likert developed a five-point response scale that still bears his name, the **Likert scale**. The scale has a neutral mid-point to allow for the possibility that an individual may have no opinion on an issue. Then, on each side of the mid-point there are two alternative response options to record moderate and extreme views for or against. Both types of attitude response scale are ordinal scales in that *agreeing* reflects a more positive attitude towards the issue raised than does *disagreeing*.

Alternative attitude response scales

EXAMPLE 9.4

My organization is a friendly place to work. How much do you agree or disagree with this statement?

☐ Agree   ☐ Disagree   (agree/disagree scale)

☐ Strongly disagree   ☐ Disagree   ☐ Not sure   ☐ Agree   ☐ Strongly agree (Likert scale)

Continuous scales

Continuous scales are types of ordered scale so that it is possible to speak about more or less of whatever is being measured according to the value on the scale. The difference between the two types of continuous scale, interval and ratio, lies in whether there is a true zero point. If there is a true zero point on a scale, then that gives a **ratio scale**; it is possible to speak meaningfully of a data point of 20 being twice as high as another data point with a value of 10 (for example). Height is measured on a true ratio scale, and we can meaningfully speak of an adult being twice as tall as a child. Time is also measured on a ratio scale, for example how long it takes for MBA graduates to get a job after their programme finishes. A graduate's income compared to what it was before joining the MBA programme is also measured on a ratio scale.

If there is no true zero point (as, for example, temperature where we have Celsius and Fahrenheit scales), then we have an **interval scale** at best. On an interval scale, differences between alternative values can be described meaningfully, but ratios cannot. Suppose we have four data points with values of 1, 2, 9 and 10 measured on an interval scale. We may say that the difference between the first two data points is the same as the difference between the last two, but not that the last data point is ten times bigger than the first. Travelling from England with a temperature of 15° to Hong Kong with a temperature of 30° is a doubling of temperature when we measure in degrees Celsius but not in degrees Fahrenheit (15° Celsius is 59° Fahrenheit, while 30° Celsius is 86° Fahrenheit). Many continuous measurement scales in social science are truly interval scales rather than ratio scales. The difference is captured succinctly by asking the question: is the data still meaningful if a fixed value (say 50) were subtracted from each score? For much data on attitudes or preferences, scales are arbitrary and such an adjustment would not matter.

MEASUREMENT MODELS

Rationale for measurement models

It is often not possible to measure directly the characteristic that a researcher is interested in, and it may be necessary to rely on indirect indicators of it. This is very common in studies using secondary data sources (see using secondary data above) where variables that are present in a dataset are often used as *proxies* for constructs that are the main focus of interest but are not themselves available directly. For example, Berrone et al. (2013) used the ratio of working capital to sales as a proxy for the concept of 'organizational slack' (see Table 9.3).

Where a construct cannot be observed directly, it is common practice to select a set of items that are assumed to reflect the construct. A measurement model is the relationship between a set of observed variables and the construct that they are intended to measure. Then answers are combined together to form a composite variable to represent the construct (Spector, 1992; DeVellis, 2012).

The rationale behind this approach is that many of the characteristics that management researchers are interested in are complex (particularly in marketing and work psychology), being made up of different elements. A simple-minded approach to measurement would take the following view: if we want to measure how people see the reputation of an organization, then just ask them 'Does company X have a good reputation?' While this approach has some appeal on grounds of simplicity, it scarcely does justice to the complexity of the concept of corporate reputation (Davies et al., 2002). Individuals' attitudes, motivation and commitment are all impossible to observe directly, but understanding them is key to explaining why consumers buy what they do, and why workers stay in a job or leave it. In such circumstances, the researcher is faced with the choice of whether to select a single variable for analysis or to combine several variables together into a single index.

The latter approach has many advantages: it allows greater richness in measurement, capturing nuances of a construct, and it also allows the researcher to assess how reliably the construct has been measured.

Identifying measurement models

EXAMPLE
9.5

A hot topic among HR and communications professionals is that of employee engagement and its possible link to business success. Investigating this relationship would require great care, and involves a number of steps:

1. The first step identifies the variables involved. The sentence above proposes a causal relationship between two variables (let us call them EE for employee engagement, and BS for business success). EE is a predictor and BS is the dependent variable in this relationship: EE ➜ BS.

2. In the second step we consider both variables in turn, and it quickly becomes pretty clear that we cannot measure either of them in a direct way. The success of a business could be assessed in a variety of ways, and the same applies to employee engagement. So both EE and BS are really latent variables, and for each one we need to specify a number of observed variables, which can be used to indicate the value of the latent variable. For example, the kinds of behaviours we might associate with an engaged employee are: putting effort into work over and above what is required; staying in the organization despite offers of better pay elsewhere; taking the initiative to solve work-related problems; praising the organization as a good place to work.

The structure of measurement models

The basic logic here is that items that reflect features of an underlying construct will show common patterns of answering. For example, a manager who feels good about his or her job will tend to respond in a consistently favourable way to questions about different aspects of that job. Consistency in responses from study participants will produce correlations among items, and these correlations are the starting point for identifying patterns that reflect underlying constructs. In a measurement model (see Figure 9.1), the **observed variables** are those that are measured directly by the researcher, and the **latent variables** are the constructs that the researcher assumes are causal factors influencing how sample members respond to the observed variables.

Figure 9.1 shows a measurement model for six measured variables and two unmeasured latent variables. The model distinguishes between two influences on how respondents answer for each observed variable:

1. Those that reflect common features of the constructs being assessed, indicated by the two common factors. The first common factor is what respondents are assumed to have in mind when they respond to variables 1–3, while the second common factor is assumed to influence answers for variables 4–6. The stronger the influence of the common factors (this is the value attached to each of the paths in Figure 9.1, and is called a **factor loading**), the higher will be the correlations among the observed variables.

2. Those that are idiosyncratic to the wording of each variable, indicated by the specific factors, one for each observed variable. These are unique to that question and will not influence answers to other questions.

FIGURE 9.1
Measurement
model for
six observed
variables and
two latent
variables

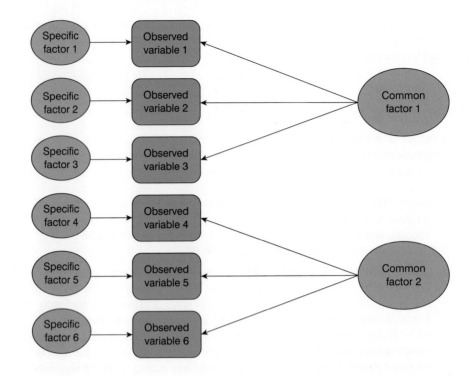

The **reliability** of a composite scale depends on the average correlation among the observed variables and is measured by the **Cronbach's alpha coefficient** (a value greater than 0.70 indicates an acceptable level of reliability).

Table 9.4 shows what the pattern of correlations would look like if the factor loadings for all observed variables were set at 0.60. Taking the correlation between observed variable 1 and observed variable 2 as an example, the value of 0.36 for the correlation between them is calculated by tracing the paths linking the two variables in the figure and multiplying the loadings for each path. Thus, 0.6 * 0.6 = 0.36. The first three observed variables are all correlated with each other, shown by the shading, reflecting the fact that they share loadings on the first common factor; and the second three observed variables, again shown by shading, are also correlated reflecting the influence of the second common factor. Furthermore, the bottom left unshaded area of the correlation matrix contains only zero correlations because the two blocks of variables (1–3 and 4–6) do not share loadings on a common factor with each other.

TABLE 9.4   Hypothetical correlation matrix showing the pattern of correlations for six observed variables and two latent variables

	1	2	3	4	5	6
1	–					
2	.36	–				
3	.36	.36	–			
4	0	0	0	–		
5	0	0	0	.36	–	
6	0	0	0	.36	.36	–

Analysis methods for measurement models: CFA and EFA

Sometimes, the researcher has a set of questionnaire items with no clear idea of what constructs might underlie them, and here the method of choice for analysing the measurement model is **exploratory factor analysis** (EFA). More commonly, though, researchers know what constructs they are trying to measure and design their questionnaires to do just that. In that case, the aim is not to explore what constructs there might be but rather to confirm (or otherwise) a structure that has been designed into a study. This leads to **confirmatory factor analysis** (CFA) as the method of choice. Both types of model share a distinction between common factors and specific factors. Where the methods differ is in the prior specification of a measurement model. EFA analyses can be carried out by many general purpose statistical packages, such as SPSS (Bryman and Cramer, 2004; Blunch, 2008; Field, 2009); while CFA requires one of the specialist structural equation model programs, which we consider in Chapter 11.

In the EFA method, there may be as many common factors as there are observed variables, and all the observed variables have loadings on all the common factors. Two methods in use are common factor analysis and principal components analysis, and both methods derive estimates for the factor loadings of each of the common factors and the specific factors, and give summary indices (called **eigenvalues**) of the importance of each of the common factors, shown by how much of the covariation among the observed variables each one accounts for. The researcher uses these estimates to select a subset of common factors, usually retaining only the largest. The size of the loadings for the common factors determines the correlations among the observed variables. The size of the loadings for the specific factors determines the reliability of the common factors.

In the CFA method, the researcher defines in advance how many common factors are expected and the pattern of predicted loadings for observed variables. The common factors represent the latent variables that the researcher is interested in measuring: one factor for each latent variable. Observed variables are selected specifically to measure each of the latent variables, and so these observed variables are usually assumed to load on only one factor. The method derives estimates for each of the factor loadings for common factors and for specific factors, and gives an overall test statistic for how well the measurement model fits the data. Ullman (2006b) gives a readable introduction to CFA with particular reference to personality assessment, and shows how measurement models can be fitted and tested using SEM software.

Measurement models for measures of work design characteristics: EFA and CFA results

EXAMPLE
9.6

This example takes six variables from the dataset used by Sprigg and Jackson (2006) in their study of the impact of work design on the health of call handlers in UK call centres. The variables fall into two groups: three items measuring timing control, the extent to which call handlers had control over work timing (TC); and skill utilization (SU), how much their work enabled them to use the skills they had. The sample was large, over 1,000 people drawn from a large number of call centres throughout the UK.

The matrix of correlations is shown in Table 9.5(a), and the high correlations are emboldened. It is clear that they form two groups reflecting the constructs that the items were designed to measure. The factor loadings from exploratory factor analysis are shown in Table 9.5(b). The first thing to note is that there are two factors, as would be expected, and that all six variables have loadings on both factors. The second

(Continued)

(Continued)

thing to note is that the loadings of the three timing control items are very high on the first factor, but very low on the second factor, while the reverse is true for the skill utilization items (again the high values are emboldened). It would be reasonable to label the two factors according to the content of the times that load on them, and that is what we have done in the Table. However, this is an inference on our part; the statistical analysis is agnostic about what these latent variables are called.

Table 9.5(c) gives the factor loadings for confirmatory factor analysis, and the major difference is that each item is constrained to load onto one factor. The values of zero are called *fixed values* because they were constrained as part of the input specification for CFA. The reason is that we hypothesized that the first three items would measure a timing control construct and the second three items would measure a skill utilization construct. The factor loadings from CFA are not identical to those given by the EFA analysis because the models that were fitted to the data are different, but the conclusion is broadly the same. Finally, the measurement model from CFA is shown diagrammatically in Figure 9.2.

TABLE 9.5 Measurement model for measures of work design characteristics: EFA and CFA results

(a) Matrix of correlations among variables

	TC1	TC2	TC3	SU1	SU2	SU3
TC1	–					
TC2	.40	–				
TC3	.48	.45	–			
SU1	.16	.16	.14	–		
SU2	.16	.18	.15	.52	–	
SU3	.16	.15	.13	.55	.56	–

(b) Factor loadings from exploratory factor analysis

	Timing control	Skill utilization
TC1	.78	.10
TC2	.76	.11
TC3	.82	.06
SU1	.09	.82
SU2	.12	.82
SU3	.09	.84

(c) Factor loadings from confirmatory factor analysis

	Timing control	Skill utilization
TC1	.61	0
TC2	.67	0
TC3	.63	0
SU1	0	.78
SU2	0	.73
SU3	0	.71

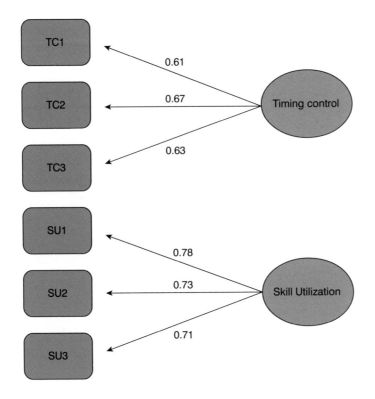

FIGURE 9.2
Measurement model for measures of work design characteristics: CFA results

CONCLUSION

The assumption that underlies the methods described in this chapter is that the researcher uses quantitative data derived from a sample in order to draw conclusions about a defined population. The material we have covered in this chapter is:

(Continued)

(Continued)

 Types of sampling design and the criteria that the research can use to select a form of design that is appropriate for a specific purpose.

 Sources of both primary and secondary data, emphasizing the issues involved in using each source which can affect the quality of data that are available for analysis.

 The process of measurement.

At each stage of the data collection process, decisions made by the researcher can influence the quality of data that can be obtained and the inferences that can be made from that data about the character of the population of interest. The next two chapters describe methods for analysing quantitative data. In Chapter 10, we first consider ways of summarizing key features of data and then examine the principles and practice of hypothesis testing that allow the researcher to make inferences about populations based on evidence from samples. Chapter 10 considers univariate tests, taking one variable at a time, and Chapter 11 extends this treatment to cover the multivariate case where many variables are dealt with simultaneously.

FURTHER READING

Bales, R.F., Cohen, S.P. and Williamson, S.A. (1979) *SYMLOG: A System for the Multiple Level Observation of Groups*. New York: The Free Press.

Bales, R.F. (1988) 'A new overview of the SYMLOG system: measuring and changing behavior in groups', in R.B. Polley, A.P. Hare and P.J. Stone (eds), *The SYMLOG Practitioner*. New York: Praeger, pp. 319–44.

Couper, M.P. (2008) *Designing Effective Web Surveys*. Cambridge: Cambridge University Press.
This is a useful source for web-based surveys.

DeVellis, R.F. (2012) *Scale Development: Theory and Applications*, 3rd edn. Thousand Oaks, CA: Sage.
Covers the foundations of scale construction and measurement in an accessible manner.

Dillman, D.A., Smyth, J.D. and Christian, L.M. (2009) *Internet, Mail, and Mixed-Mode Surveys: The Tailored Design Method*, 3rd edn. Hoboken, NJ: Wiley.

George, G., Haas, M.R. and Pentland, A. (2014) 'Big data and management', *Academy of Management Journal*, 57, 321–6.
Discussion of emerging trends around 'big data' in business and management research.
The following two texts describe the System of Multiple Level Observation of Groups (SYMLOG), which is a more detailed elaboration of the IPA:

Miller, D.C. and Salkind, N.J. (2002) *Handbook of Research Design & Social Measurement*, 6th edn. Thousand Oaks, CA: Sage.
A comprehensive handbook with a useful introduction to assessing social variables, scales and indexes.

Sapsford, R. (2006) *Survey Research*, 2nd edn. London: Sage.

Waters, C.D.J. (2011) *Quantitative Methods for Business*, 5th edn. Harlow: Financial Times/Prentice Hall.
A practical introduction into quantitative methods for beginners with a helpful part on data collection.
The following two books offer a comprehensive introduction to different kinds of sampling design for social science research and the principles that inform how a researcher might choose between them.

Want to know more about this chapter? Visit the ⑤SAGE edge™ website at **https://edge. sagepub.com/easterbysmith** to access practice questions, selected journal articles, useful web links and much more.

SUMMARIZING AND MAKING INFERENCES FROM QUANTITATIVE DATA

10

Management and business is maturing as a discipline, and this maturity is shown in many ways. Its conceptual thinking is becoming more sophisticated, and there is increasing evidence that scholars are not just developing clever ways of thinking about the business of business but are also putting their ideas to the test. The process of gathering quantitative data has been dealt with in the previous chapter. Here, we will look at the tools that management scholars use when their empirical evidence is in the form of numbers: quantitative data.

The most obvious feature of quantitative data – evidence expressed in the form of numbers – is their sheer quantity. It is generally expensive in time and money to accumulate good quality data, and so researchers make the most of each study participant by collecting as much data as possible from each person, and quantitative research designs also often involve large samples. The big challenge then is seeing the wood for the trees – identifying patterns in numerical data and making sense of those patterns. In this chapter, we address this in two parts. First, we consider the key features of numerical data and the common indices that are used to assess those features. The second part of the chapter introduces the logic of statistical inference as a tool for 'going beyond the data' and introduces a variety of statistical tests for looking at data one variable at a time.

Quantitative methods are an important part of the research process in management and business, something which, as we discussed in Chapter 5, is especially true of American journals. Table 10.1 gives some examples from two of the leading journals in strategy and marketing of research questions that have been addressed using quantitative data. Behind the most sophisticated research question and the most complex datasets, however, is a simple basic principle. All quantitative researchers do the same two things: they identify what features tell the best story about the data (we call this **summarizing** the data); and then they look for patterns in the data that can be used to draw conclusions about the study's research questions (we call this making **inferences** about populations based on sample data).

The idea behind summarizing and making inferences is a simple one, which can be illustrated quite easily. The year 2010 was a bad one for BP, following the explosion on the Deepwater Horizon drilling rig, which killed 11 people and led to a massive leak of oil into the Gulf of Mexico. The company's share price showed a high of 655 and a low of 302 for the year, reflecting the impact of the explosion on the investment community's view of BP's reputation and its future viability. Behind the bald figures of share price movements is also an inference process – one might say a kind of guesswork or betting – that predicts what the future profits of BP will be, based on its past performance. The judgements of investment analysts are based on an inference process (not formal statistical inference, but rather informed guesswork) about future data on the performance of BP. Management researchers follow the same kinds of inference processes when they make judgements about the world based on their data.

Example datasets for the chapter

This chapter uses datasets from a variety of sources. Table 10.2 shows the midday temperature for selected world locations on Thursday 2 December 2010. The lowest temperature recorded in the table is a distinctly cold −15°C in Moscow; while the highest temperature is a very pleasant (but perhaps rather humid) 33°C in Bangkok. The table itself is presented in alphabetical order according to the name of the location, and so it is not easy to gain much of an impression of what this body of data looks like. Figure 10.1 uses a stem and leaf plot to organize the data in a rather more helpful way.

Stem and leaf plot
This form of display groups the data into a number of categories (called 'stems'), and then shows the number of data points within each category (each data point is called a 'leaf'). The stems are labelled according to the second digit of each data value. At the bottom of

TABLE 10.1   Examples of studies using quantitative methods from *Strategic Management Journal* and the *Journal of Marketing*

State-owned enterprises (SOEs) in China (Ralston et al., 2006). They compared the organizational cultures of state-owned enterprises with private-owned enterprises and foreign-owned businesses in order to decide whether SOEs are dinosaurs or dynamos for China's economic future.

Should multinational enterprises (MNEs) adapt their marketing strategy to each market or standardize across markets? (Katsikeas, Samiee and Theodosiou, 2006). They looked at the international marketing strategies of US, Japanese and German MNEs operating in the UK. They found that standardization only makes sense when there is a good fit to the market environment.

Knowledge transfer in business-to-business relationships (Dyer and Hatch, 2006). They found that Toyota were much better than US car companies (GM, Ford and Chrysler) in getting better quality out of their suppliers. They concluded that there can be specific capabilities within relationships between customers and suppliers that are not easily transferable to other relationships.

How to influence a company on environmental issues (Eesley and Lenox, 2006). They used a database of secondary stakeholder actions to check out what it takes to get positive responses out of companies.

Home or away? – where to put your HQ (Birkinshaw et al., 2006). They found that MNEs put their business unit headquarters overseas when it made sense for *internal* reasons; while the location of their corporate HQ was influenced most strongly by the demands of *external* stakeholders – global financial markets and shareholders.

Is corporate social responsibility (CSR) smart as well as good? (Luo and Bhattacharya, 2006). They used secondary data archives to test the link between CSR activities such as cash donations and employee volunteerism, customer satisfaction and the market value of the firm. They found that CSR can be smart – good for the company – but there is a dark side too.

What do website visitors value on a manufacturer's site? (Steenkamp and Geyskens, 2006). The authors found that the answer depends on the country where the consumers live. They looked at over 8,000 consumers from 23 countries, visiting the sites of 16 consumer packaged goods companies.

the plot, the temperatures of 30°C and higher are grouped under the stem labelled as '3', the temperatures of 20–29°C are grouped under the stem labelled '2', and so on. The lowest temperatures of −10°C and below are grouped together at the top of the plot under the stem labelled '−1'. In this plot, there are six stems, and the column to the left shows how many leaves there are attached to each stem. There are four locations in the coldest category (stem value '−1'), and the leaf shows the second digit of the temperature for each one: Prague (−10°C), Stockholm (−12°C), Oslo (−14°C) and Moscow (−15°C). The next stem is labelled '−0' and holds the leaves showing locations with temperatures between −1°C and −9°C. The frequency column shows that there are 16 of these locations, and with the exception of Chicago and Reykjavik they are all in Europe. As some UK readers may remember, December 2010 was a period of record low temperatures. At the other end of the distribution, the plot shows six locations with temperatures of 30°C or more: Bangkok, Mumbai, Buenos Aires, Kuala Lumpur, Singapore and Mombasa.

Having introduced the dataset, we now turn to describe different ways of summarizing key features of the data.

SUMMARIZING AND DESCRIBING DATA

There are three sections to this part of the chapter. The first looks at ways of showing the shape of data distributions, and it capitalizes on the highly developed capabilities that

TABLE 10.2 Maximum midday temperatures for 94 world locations, Thursday 2 December 2010

(THE TIMES, 3 DECEMBER 2010)

Location	Temp	Location	Temp
Alicante	13	Madeira	18
Amsterdam	−6	Madrid	5
Athens	23	Majorca	14
Auckland	19	Malaga	15
Bahrain	24	Malta	20
Bangkok	33	Melbourne	23
Barbados	29	Mexico City	15
Barcelona	9	Miami	28
Beijing	4	Milan	1
Beirut	25	Mombasa	31
Belgrade	8	Moscow	−15
Berlin	−8	Mumbai	32
Bermuda	20	Munich	−4
Bordeaux	2	Nairobi	25
Brussels	−5	Naples	15
Bucharest	0	New Orleans	12
Budapest	1	New York	15
Buenos Aires	30	Nice	10
Cairo	22	Nicosia	24
Calcutta	26	Oslo	−14
Canberra	24	Paris	−2
Cape Town	26	Perth	24
Chicago	−4	Prague	−10
Copenhagen	−2	Reykjavik	−2
Corfu	0	Riga	−8
Delhi	22	Rio de Janeiro	29
Dubai	28	Riyadh	22
Dublin	−1	Rome	14
Faro	14	San Francisco	9

Florence	12	Santiago	21
Frankfurt	–7	Sao Paulo	26
Geneva	–1	Seoul	12
Gibraltar	13	Seychelles	25
Harare	18	Singapore	31
Helsinki	–3	St Petersburg	–9
Hong Kong	23	Stockholm	–12
Honolulu	28	Sydney	25
Istanbul	21	Tel Aviv	28
Jerusalem	28	Tenerife	21
Johannesburg	26	Tokyo	21
Kuala Lumpur	30	Toronto	16
Lanzarote	20	Vancouver	7
Las Palmas	21	Venice	4
Lima	21	Vienna	0
Lisbon	11	Warsaw	–8
Los Angeles	19	Washington	6
Luxor	27	Zurich	–3

humans have for seeing visual patterns. The second section considers a variety of measures that summarize data in terms of different attributes. The third section draws out two formal characteristics of summary measures that we can use to help us understand why alternative measures work the way that they do. These formal characteristics give the criteria for making smart choices about which summary measures to use in practical situations.

FIGURE 10.1
Stem and leaf plot for world temperature data

Showing the shape of data distributions

Although Table 10.2 reports the temperature scores, the general shape of this set of data is really hard to visualize from a table of numbers. Many of the characteristics of data distributions that have important consequences for analysis and interpretation can be seen very easily provided that data can be displayed informatively. Two obvious forms of data display are provided by most statistical packages: bar charts and histograms. A **bar chart** summarizes the distribution of a category variable: bars are drawn to represent each category and the length of the bar reflects the number of cases in the category – the more people, the longer the bar. If variables are measured on an ordinal scale, then it would be strange to do other than order the bars in the chart accordingly. For variables on a nominal scale, where the categories are not ordered, it makes sense to apply some thought to how to order the bars on the chart. A **histogram** is a bar chart drawn for a continuous variable, after grouping adjacent scale points together.

Bar charts

Figure 10.2 shows a bar chart for the temperature data from Table 10.2. Along the bottom of the chart is the measurement scale for the variable, the temperature in Celsius, and runs from −15°, the lowest value recorded in this dataset through to +33°, the highest value recorded for these data. Essentially, the bar chart is a visual representation of the frequency table. Each figure in the **frequency distribution** is translated into the height of a bar in Figure 10.2. The height of each bar is marked by the vertical axis of the figure, labelled 'frequency'; and this shows how many respondents gave each alternative response. The higher the bar, the more respondents recorded this answer.

Histograms

A histogram is a special form of bar chart, with the points on the scale grouped into a smaller and more manageable number of categories. The histogram in Figure 10.3 shows the temperature data with the 94 different scores grouped together into 15 categories instead of 45. The labels on the horizontal axis are the mid-points of the categories shown by each bar. Histograms have immediate visual appeal, and show gross features of data very

FIGURE 10.2
Bar chart for the temperature data from Table 10.2

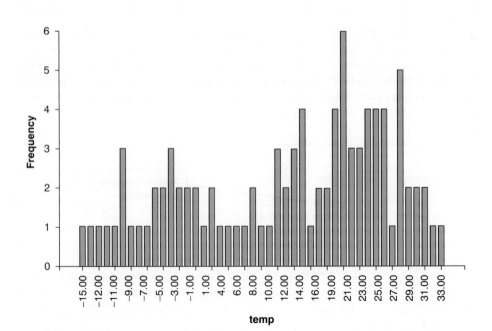

easily. The peak in the data around 20°C is more obvious, and the 'holes' in the data have been hidden by combining categories together. The shape is thus smoother to the eye. We can also see that there are more values at the top end of the scale than there are at the bottom. These data thus are not completely symmetrical.

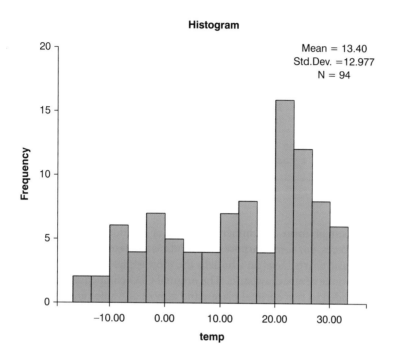

FIGURE 10.3

Histogram for temperature data from Table 10.2

This chapter started with a table showing 94 temperature values, but it is obviously impossible to carry all that information around in one's head (some values stick in the memory: the lowest and highest values, temperatures in one's favourite holiday locations etc.). Instead, it is much more efficient to capture some key features of the data in convenient summary form. This section covers three features of data that are most informative and most useful: location, spread and symmetry. We will describe summary measures of some of these key features of data, and following that we will examine a number of formal properties of summary measures that will make it easier to make choices between alternatives.

Summary measures of location

The obvious starting point for summarizing a large set of data is with an index that locates the data as a whole on its measurement scale: in general *high, middling* or *low*. For example, if there is a risk to consumers due to contamination of a batch of chocolate during manufacture (as in the case of Cadbury's chocolate early in 2006), then how big is the risk? Is it so minute that any impact on community health would be hard to detect, as the company argued when challenged by the UK Health and Safety Executive? Whatever the researcher is interested in measuring, and however large or small the dataset, most people would be interested in where on its measurement scale the data as a whole are located. Four summary measures of location are commonly used – the mode, the median, the mean and the midmean – and we now consider each one in turn, using data on the pay for Chief Executives of US companies. Overall compensation data for the 200 highest-paid CEOs in the USA in 2009 are reported in www.Forbes.com, and summarized in Figure 10.4. The lowest total compensation is $6.86 million, and the highest compensation is a scarcely believable $556.98 million.

FIGURE 10.4
Stem and leaf display for CEO compensation data

```
$million Stem and Leaf

Frequency   Stem and Leaf

  63.00     0 . 666677777777777777777777777778888888888888889999
            999999999999999
  49.00     1 . 000000000000011111111111111122222222222222333333444
  28.00     1 . 55555556666677788888888899999
  12.00     2 . 001223333444
  13.00     2 . 5555666788899
   9.00     3 . 000123334
   8.00     3 . 56668899
   3.00     4 . 224
  15.00 Extremes    (>=48)

Stem width:      10.00
Each leaf:       1 case(s)
```

Mode

The **mode** is a simple form of summary measure of location: it is the commonest value among a set of scores. For some purposes, the mode as a measure of location can be informative (i.e. the music charts focus on who sells the most copies of their work), but the mode does have some quite severe drawbacks. The original CEO compensation data are reported in $million rounded to two decimal places; and almost all values are unique – there is no single modal value. However, the stem and leaf plot (Figure 10.4) shows the scores as whole numbers, and the modal compensation value is $7m. Grouping the scores together in different ways would create a different modal value depending on how the grouping is done. Thus, a problem with the mode as a summary of location for data on a continuous scale is that it depends upon how scores are grouped. A second problem is that it ignores the rest of the data and conveys nothing at all about what other values there might be in the data. Finally, there may be more than one mode, so that this measure of location need not have a unique value. All in all then, the mode is rarely a serious tool for summarizing location of data in business and management research.

Median

The **median** is the middle value once scores have been placed in rank order, either from largest to smallest or from smallest to largest. It is the value that divides a set of data in half. Where there is an even number of data points, the median is halfway between the middle two, in this case $12.86m. For an odd number of data points, the median is simply the middle one, counting in from either end. The median has some important properties, which are easy to grasp intuitively:

1. Every observation in the data contributes something to determining the value of the median, unlike the mode. That makes the median more meaningful as a summary measure of location because it uses more of the information in the data in estimating location.

2. Most of the data points do not contribute much – it is the rank position of a data point that matters rather than its precise value. That makes the median less efficient than it might be (it throws away the values of each observation and replaces them with rank-order information), but it has the great advantage that the median is insensitive to odd things happening to extreme scores. Adding a million to the largest data point (perhaps by forgetting to put in the decimal point when entering

the data) does nothing to the median because it does not change the fact that this is still the largest data point. It also makes the median useful where the measurement scale is not particularly precise, and the researcher cannot be certain of the accuracy of the numbers.

3. The median works better for data where the category at the top of a grouped continuous scale is open-ended. Examples include:

   ○ Sometimes we judge ability by how quickly people complete a task, but some people may not finish in the time allocated. For those people, we over-estimate their ability because all we know is that they would take at least as long as the maximum time allowed.

   ○ Family size may be judged on the basis of the number of children, and it often happens that the largest category is recorded as more than three (or four or five) children. These data will under-estimate the actual number of children in a sample of families.

   ○ Data on survival rates following exposure to toxic hazards in the workplace will typically be over-estimates if they include people who were exposed to the hazard but are still alive at the time that data are collected.

4. This kind of grouping of data at one end of the scale is called *censoring*. It gives no trouble at all for calculating the median, whether the censoring is at the bottom of the scale (left censoring) or at the top of the scale (right censoring).

Mean

The **mean** is the average value formed by adding all the scores and dividing by how many data points there are. The formula for the mean is:

$$M = \Sigma(X) / n$$

where M stands for the mean, X represents each data value, n indicates how many data points there are, and the Σ symbol is a summation sign. The mean CEO compensation level for top US CEOs is $23.4m. Just like the median, every score contributes to forming the mean, but the mean differs because it takes into account how big each score is. This can be both a benefit and a disadvantage. By using the mean as a summary measure of location, the researcher can be confident of making the most of the information in the data about where the data are centred. However, using the mean assumes that each data point is accurately recorded.

Mid- mean

The **mid-mean** is an average formed by first removing scores equally from both extremes of a dataset and then working out the mean of the remainder. It is part of a family of summary measures called **trimmed means**, which differ in how much is trimmed from each end of the distribution of data points. The mean is a zero per cent trimmed mean (with nothing trimmed), while the median is a 50 per cent trimmed mean. The mid-mean is a 25 per cent trimmed mean, the mean of the middle half of the data. It uses rank order information (like the median) to select data points to ignore, but then uses the data values themselves (like the mean) to calculate the summary index.

Comparing summary measures of location

The different summary measures of location for the CEO compensation data in Figure 10.4 are:

Mode: $7m (data rounded to nearest whole number of millions)

Median: $12.86m

5 per cent trimmed mean: $17.37m

Mean: $23.44m

There are substantial differences between these estimates of where the centre of the data lies. The modal (or commonest) value is around $7m, while the median shows that half of the top 200 CEOs earn $12.86m or more (of course the other half of the sample earn less than $12.86m). The mean gives the highest value of all, $23.44m, which is more than three times as much as the modal value.

Why do the summary measures of location differ so much? A clue is given in Figure 10.5, which shows that the data for the top CEOs are highly skewed. Three-quarters of the top 200 CEOs earn less than $30m, while those at the very top of the ranking list earn substantially more than that, with Lawrence Ellison, CEO of Oracle, alone earning $556.98m (the same total compensation package as the bottom 65 CEOs in the sample combined). The median is based on the ranks of the scores, while the mean takes the size of each data point into account. Thus Ellison's salary influences the mean but not the median.

Which of these summary measures is most useful? The answer is that all of them are useful but for different purposes, while none of them is universally useful. Each summary measure captures different aspects of the data, which contain information about the feature of locatedness. When researchers calculate one of these summary measures to report where a dataset as a whole is located on its measurement scale, they are implicitly making a judgement about what matters in the data. If they want to emphasize what is typical (in the sense of commonest), they might prefer the mode. However, attention on inequalities in income in an organization, for instance, might lead someone to choose the median, which will show that half of the organization earns less than £x, while another group might prefer the mean because it takes into account the much higher pay of the most senior officials in the organization, which makes the pay levels look generally higher.

FIGURE 10.5

Histogram for CEO compensation data from Figure 10.4

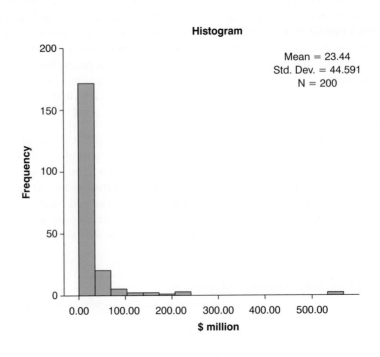

The most widely used summaries of location are the mean and the median. Less common, but useful, are the mid-mean and other forms of the trimmed mean. An important point to note is that even something so simple as working out an average is a choice. The consequences of making different choices about summary measures of location depend very much on the characteristics of a specific dataset, and which features of the data the researcher wishes to emphasize.

Summary measures of spread

Of course, most samples of data will contain variability around a central value, with some people scoring higher than others. How much spread there is around a measure of location is a valuable way of capturing something extra about a dataset as a whole. Three common measures of spread are: the range, the mid-range and the standard deviation. Like the measures of location considered in the previous section, each one captures different aspects of data.

Range

The **range** is the distance between the largest and the smallest scores. For the temperature data in Table 10.2, the lowest recorded midday temperature was −15°C and the highest was 33°C, so the range is 33 − −15 = 48°C. On a single day then, the spread of temperatures across a sample of locations in the world was enormous. The range of CEO compensation scores in Figure 10.4 is also large ($556.98m − $6.86m = $550.12m). While the range is easy to calculate, it is also potentially very misleading. Most people have seen the banner headlines in shop windows 'Up to 50 per cent off'. This means that at least one item is discounted by this much, but says nothing about how many other items are treated in the same way. The same goes for the advertisements for cheap seats on airlines, where there is no mention of how many of the seats on a given flight are actually available at that price. Any summary index based on an extreme statistic (either largest or smallest) can be dangerously misleading.

Mid-range (interquartile range)

The **mid-range** is the range of the middle half of the data, calculated by dividing the data into quarters. The values in the data that mark the boundaries between four equal-sized segments are called 'quartiles', and the mid-range is the difference between the first quartile and the third quartile. It is often given the name **interquartile range**. The second quartile is the median, with two quarters below and two quarters above. Calculating the mid-range starts in the same way as calculating the mid-mean: trim off the top and bottom quarter of the data values. Then, the mid-range is the difference between the largest and the smallest values in the middle half of the data: for the CEO compensation data in Figure 10.4, the mid-range is $14.98m. The mid-range gives a better indication of how diverse the data are, especially where the data are skewed by a few extreme scores at either end. Note that the compensation package for the highest paid CEO has a dramatic effect on the range, but none at all on the mid-range.

Standard deviation

The **standard deviation** (SD) measures the average spread around the mean; it is the most typical distance (or deviation) of scores from the mean. The formula for the standard deviation is:

$$SD = \sqrt{(\Sigma(X-M)^2 / n-1)}$$

where SD stands for the standard deviation, $\sqrt{}$ is the square root symbol and the other symbols are the same as in the formula for the mean.

The SD is calculated by working out the average squared deviation around the mean (this is called the **variance**) and then taking the square root. For each data point in turn, first work out how far it is above or below the mean (these are called 'deviations'). The mean of the scores in Figure 10.4 is 23.44, so the deviations around the mean are calculated like this:

556.98 – 23.44 = 533.54

222.64 – 23.44 = 199.20

....

6.87 – 23.44 = –16.57

6.86 – 23.44 = –16.58.

Next, each of the deviations is squared to remove the ± sign, and the average squared deviation is calculated by dividing by the number of items minus one. This gives the variance. The reasoning behind subtracting one before calculating the mean deviation is technical – dividing by $n-1$ rather than n makes the sample SD an unbiased estimate of the population SD. Finally, take the square root of the variance to give the standard deviation. For these data, the variance (based on 200 – 1 = 199 as the sample size) is 1988.38, and the standard deviation is 44.59.

Comparing summary measures of spread

Just as we argued for summary measures of location, there is no single answer to the question of which measure of spread is most useful. The range is a measure of how much of the measurement scale is covered by sample data, from largest to smallest. This is sometimes useful to know, but is heavily influenced by a few extreme scores, while the mid-range is more informative especially for data that are distributed symmetrically and follow roughly a bell-shaped curve.

The most widely used summaries of spread are the standard deviation and the mid-range, and measures of location and spread tend to be paired together. Thus, the mean and the standard deviation are the basis for many parametric significance tests, while the median and the mid-range are the basis for many non-parametric significance tests. Both types of test are described in the next section of this chapter.

The importance of symmetry

A third characteristic of the shape of a set of data is the extent to which scores are distributed evenly around a central value; that is, whether the data are symmetrical. *Positively* skewed data have many small values concentrated together and few large values strung out to the right, and the long tail of the data is to the right. The CEO compensation data in Figure 10.4 are positively skewed. Most of the data are located at the low end of the distribution, while 15 CEOs out of 200 receive extremely high pay packages. By contrast, *negatively* skewed data have many large values concentrated together at the top of the distribution and few small ones strung out at the bottom; the long tail of the data is to the left.

Why pay attention to symmetry in data? This feature is important for two reasons. Extreme values at either end of a distribution (but most likely at the high end of the range) may indicate gross errors, for which reason they should be sought out (perhaps by looking to a completed questionnaire in order to correct transcription errors, or by returning to the source of derived data) and correct values inserted instead. Data that are strongly asymmetrical are less naturally described in terms of summary measures of location. When data are symmetrical the mean and median will tend to coincide, while a symmetrical and unimodal distribution will tend to have the modal value (the most frequently occurring one) at the same point as the mean and median. When data are skewed, the different summary measures will not coincide. The mean will be influenced by the relatively small number of extreme scores, while the median will not be because it simply records the value below which 50 per cent of the scores lie.

Formal features of summary measures

This section looks at two characteristics of summary measures, robustness and efficiency, which give a stronger conceptual basis for the choices that a researcher makes between alternative summary measures of location or spread.

Robustness

The extent to which a summary measure is sensitive to disturbances in data quality is known as **robustness**. There has been a lot of work by statisticians examining the consequences of robustness (or the lack of it) for commonly used summary indices and analyses which are based on them (see Jackson, 1986). Disturbances in data quality can arise either from small changes to many data values (e.g. by grouping of values on a measurement scale into a few categories) or by large errors in a few data values (e.g. by transcription errors). A summary measure is robust if disturbances like these do not greatly alter its value, while summary measures that are very sensitive to such disturbances are not robust.

We now examine three of the summary measures of location: the mean, the median and the mid-mean. Since the *mean* is the total of all the data points divided by the sample size, changing even a single data point through a transcription error would alter the mean. The more extreme the value introduced in error, the bigger would be the influence on the value of the mean. Similarly, small changes to all of the data values through, for example, grouping adjacent scores together on the measurement scale, would also alter the mean. It is obvious, therefore, that the mean is not very robust.

Since the *median* is based on the ranked scores, the effect of a single transcription error would be small, and if the error were made with either the largest or the smallest data value the median would not change at all. Changes such as coarse grouping of adjacent scores on the measurement scale would also have little effect on the value of the median. The *mid-mean* uses rank-order information to define the middle half of the data, and so extreme scores introduced in error will not have a major impact on its value, and in this respect it is robust like the median. Both the mid-mean and the median are thus more robust than the mean, and using either in preference to the mean would protect the researcher against disturbances in measurement quality.

Efficiency

Think of getting the juice out of a lemon. First you have to cut the lemon in half. After that there are options. However, the way that Jamie Oliver (a British celebrity chef) uses is to squeeze each half in his hand; this has high screen appeal but does not extract all the juice that is there – its efficiency is quite low. Another way is to use a juicer to macerate the flesh of the lemon and then filter out the juice. The juicer does not look so appealing on the TV, but it is more efficient because it yields more juice. Applying this principle to statistical analysis, **efficiency** refers to how much a summary measure captures all the information within the data that is relevant to what is summarized. For summary measures of location, the mean is the most efficient index we know because it uses everything about the data that is relevant to summarizing where the data are located on their measurement scale. Of course, that is the very reason why we sometimes do not use it, because some scores are suspiciously large or because we do not trust the fine detail. The median is much less efficient than the mean, since it replaces scores with their ranks, while the mid-mean (as well as other varieties of trimmed mean) is almost as efficient as the mean.

Summary of formal features of summary measures

The two characteristics of summary measures tend to work in opposite directions: the mean is generally preferable to the median because it is more efficient, but the median is more robust. A lot then depends on the quality of data that the researcher has available and on how well variables are measured. Researchers who have confidence in the quality of their data will tend to prefer using summary measures, which are high in efficiency, such as the mean for location and the standard deviation for spread. These will work particularly well for data that are broadly symmetrical and do not have rogue values which are more extreme than the bulk of the data. However, where data are more rough and ready, and the researcher may be less confident about measurement quality, summary measures based on ranks (the median for location and the mid-range for spread) may be used with more confidence.

GOING BEYOND A SAMPLE

Relationships versus differences

Most introductory statistical texts organize their presentation of significance tests into two categories, according to whether the focus of attention is on differences between groups or on relationships between variables. This book is no different, and so we explain the basic idea behind each of them and then explain why the difference is actually an artificial one.

The idea of *group differences* is a simple one. It addresses questions such as:

1. Are small start-up businesses more innovative than large bureaucratic ones?
2. Are there more men than women on the boards of companies?

Each of these can be translated into a question about whether groups differ on a summary measure of a dependent variable (for question 1 the dependent variable is the level of innovation, while for question 2 the dependent variable is the percentage of women at board level). Tests have been developed to deal with variations in the number of groups and also in the kind of dependent variable (see later in this chapter).

The idea of *relationships between variables* is also quite a simple one. It addresses questions such as:

1. Is there a link between sunny weather and how people feel at work?
2. Does greater company use of social media (such as Facebook and Twitter) increase their reputation with customers?

Each of these questions is concerned with a pattern of association between two variables: are high levels of one variable (e.g. the number of hours of sunshine per day) associated with high levels of another variable (e.g. the morale of employees in an office)? There are specialist tests that have been developed for dealing with different kinds of relationship for a variety of types of variable.

Relationships and differences – what's the difference?

While the distinction we just described is pretty straightforward, it can actually be quite misleading. Consider the question above about whether there are more men than women on the boards of companies. We just stated this in terms of a difference between two groups, but we could just as easily have expressed it in the language of relationships: is there a relationship between gender and board membership? Those are just two ways of talking about the same thing.

There was a time when statistical work was done using a calculator or even pen and paper, and in those days researchers looked for the easiest way of doing their work. This led them to develop shorthand techniques, which were custom-made for each specific configuration of data. So, we have separate procedures in packages, such as SPSS for looking at either group differences or relationships. However, statisticians have realized over the last 40 years or so that there are deep similarities between methods that were up to then regarded as quite different. Thus we now have methods called **generalized linear models**, which use a common language (albeit a rather inaccessible algebraic one) to express research hypotheses, whether they be relationships or group differences. We won't spend much time in this book on these general models, but it is useful to remember that any hypothesis about differences between groups can also be expressed as a relationship involving the concept that underlies the group distinction.

The rationale of hypothesis testing

Every piece of empirical management research involves analysis of data from a sample of some kind at two levels: first, to identify patterns in that sample data; and second, to use the conclusions drawn from those patterns to make claims that go beyond the sample itself. The greatest part of the craft of quantitative data analysis lies in defining the limits to which it is appropriate to generalize beyond a specific sample. The studies listed in Table 10.1 at the start of this chapter each used quantitative data to address important research questions. The authors of those studies presented their data, but their conclusions relate not just to the specific sample but also to claims about theory based on the data. In general, scholars do not theorize on the basis of specific datasets alone; instead, theories are statements about relationships between concepts, about boundary conditions for when those relationships occur, and about causes and consequences. **Hypothesis testing** is about making inferences about populations based upon data drawn from samples. Because we want to go beyond a sample, there is always an element of judgement or guesswork involved, and mistakes can be made. Hypothesis testing allows the researcher to define how safe it is to go beyond a specific sample of data.

Specifying a hypothesis

EXAMPLE 10.1

Bloom and van Reenen (2006) claim that family-owned firms are better run (and perform better) when the CEO is a professional manager and not chosen because he or she is a family member. Their claim is based on comparisons of management practice between groups of firms that differ in ownership and the status of the CEO. Having made statistical comparisons within their data, they go on to make broad statements about such things as the reasons for the rise of the USA in the early part of the twentieth century compared to the UK (something their data do not address directly).

As part of a long-lasting collaboration between one of the authors and a large pharmaceutical company, data from company bi-annual employee opinion surveys were made available for research. One of the regular questions in the surveys is about the speed of decision making within the company (it isn't really surprising to find that snail-like bureaucracy is a concern in a big company). Here we take a look at what two groups of employees think: those who have been in the company less than two years; and those with longer organizational tenure (more than two years).

In the survey questionnaire respondents were offered three response alternatives: 1 = too fast; 2 = about right; and 3 = too slow. The mean scores for the two groups are:

Short tenure (< 2 years; n = 802): mean = 2.40

Long tenure (2 or more years; n = 6993): mean = 2.59

We can see that there is a higher mean score for longer-tenure employees, and this indicates that they are more likely to feel that decision making is too slow. Taking another perspective, 44 per cent of short-tenure employees reported that decision making is *too slow*, compared to a much higher proportion (64 per cent) of longer-tenure employees. It would appear that opinions about the speed of organizational decision making differ according to how long employees have been within the company. But how confident can we be about that claim? The purpose of hypothesis testing is to enable the researcher to draw conclusions like that.

Formal steps in hypothesis testing

Whatever the statistical procedure that is applied, the underlying logic is the same. This chapter concentrates on the **univariate test** (taking one dependent variable at a time) while the next chapter looks at the **multivariate test** (where many variables are considered at once). However complex the dataset, the steps are the same. We spell out the five steps using the decision-making data as an example, and then set out in more general form what choices the researcher has in setting out to test hypotheses with data.

Step 1: defining a research hypothesis to be tested

The initial research question reflects the purpose of the study: to explore sample differences in speed of organizational decision making as reported by company employees. The researchers had reason to believe that the two samples of employees might see decision-making speed differently, but observation of the data alone does not allow any firm conclusion to be drawn. In general, we are interested in two states of affairs: what the data would look like if there is a real difference between the two samples, and if there really is no difference between the samples. The research hypothesis, called H_1, is that there is a real difference between the two samples in reputation ratings. Note that making a decision about whether to accept this hypothesis or not does nothing to explain *why* such a difference might occur.

Step 2: defining a null hypothesis

In the absence of any evidence to the contrary, the simplest starting point is to assume that it makes no difference how the data were collected. This defines a **null hypothesis** (called H_0) that the responses for short tenure employees are generated by the same process as the responses from long-tenure employees. If the evidence in favour of the **alternative hypothesis** (H_1) is inconclusive, then the reasonable conclusion to draw is the starting position (H_0). On the other hand, strong evidence of a difference in decision-making speed scores between the two samples would allow the researcher to modify this initial position.

It is important to note the logic here. The null hypothesis has nothing to do with what the researcher *wants* to be true, and neither is it anything to do with a specific theory. Instead, it reflects a simple agnostic position that the data from the two samples were generated by the same process unless there is strong evidence otherwise.

Step 3: deriving a summary measure of a characteristic of interest

Having defined a null hypothesis, the third step is to calculate a summary index based on the characteristic of interest. In this case, the natural way to express the hypotheses is in terms of summary measures of the location of the data on the decision-making speed measurement scale. Earlier in this chapter we described three summary measures of location that could be used to test the research hypothesis: the median, the mean and the mid-mean. Whichever summary measure is chosen, the null hypothesis is that the difference between the location measures for the two samples is zero, while the alternative research hypothesis is that the difference is not zero. Thus the hypothesis test is expressed in terms of the group difference in a measure of location. The previous section showed that the mean decision-making speed scores for the two groups are 2.40 and 2.59, with a group difference of 0.29. Of course, it is unrealistic to expect a difference of precisely zero in a specific study even if it can be guaranteed that the method of collecting data makes no difference. Repeated studies with the same structure would be expected to show differences in means (or medians or mid-means) between samples, but the differences would be expected to be small most of the time and very different only infrequently. The problem that the researcher faces is: what does similar mean? How different is very different? For these data, is a mean difference of 0.29 a large or a small difference? Addressing this problem is the job of the reference distribution in the next step.

Step 4: choosing a reference distribution and calculating a test statistic

The logic of hypothesis testing is that convincing evidence is needed from the study data before the researcher is prepared to move away from the null hypothesis in favour of an alternative. If the null hypothesis were true, how likely is the outcome observed in the study data? Quantifying the answer to this question requires the use of a **reference distribution**, which summarizes the alternatives available if the null hypothesis were true. Text books often refer to this as a **sampling distribution**, but we prefer the more general term to reflect the process of calibrating a result from one study against a reference standard. The reference distribution is not the distribution of the observations in a dataset, but rather it is the distribution of the hypothesis summary index for all possible outcomes, of which the one from a specific study is just one.

Sources of reference distributions   Selecting a reference distribution involves either using extra data (over and above that from a sample) or making assumptions about the data and the process that generated it. We consider three different sources of reference distributions:

1. *Standard reference distributions* are drawn from statistical theory, and choosing them is the commonest way of testing hypotheses. There are many families of reference distributions derived from theorizing about different kinds of idealized situations. For example, the **normal distribution** is the distribution of the sum of independent measures where the standard deviation of the reference distribution is known. The *t*-distribution is the same as the normal distribution, but differs only in that the standard deviation of the reference distribution is estimated from sample data. The **binomial distribution** is the distribution of entities that are binary (present/absent, success/failure). These distributions are used for testing hypotheses about differences in location. The **chi-square distribution** is the

distribution not of means but of variances, and is used for testing hypotheses about spread. The *F-distribution* is the distribution of ratios of variances, and is used for testing hypotheses about group differences in the spread of mean scores. All standard reference distributions share a number of characteristics:

a. *They are mathematically well defined* – their shape reflects a few features called parameters (this is the reason why tests using standard reference distributions are called parametric tests). For example, the precise form of the normal distribution depends only upon just two quantities: the mean and standard deviation.

b. *Their theoretical properties are well worked out.* For example, the normal distribution is symmetrical and bell-shaped. For a normal distribution with a mean of zero and a standard deviation of one, two-thirds (68 per cent) of the area under the curve lies in the range between −1 and +1 on the measurement scale: 34 per cent on either side of the mean. A further 13 per cent of the area under the curve lies either side of the mean in the range between −1 and −2 and between +1 and +2 on the measurement scale.

c. *They are theoretical entities* that do not exist in the real world, but researchers can use them as approximations to their own data. Thus, many of the tests described below (see Tables 10.4 and 10.7) are said to assume normally distributed data. Since real data never follow precisely any of the standard reference distributions, this assumption is almost never valid. However, the practical issue is whether the approximation to normality is close enough to allow reliable inference. Statisticians agree that most statistical tests that use standard reference distributions are robust in the face of departures from the ideal assumptions provided that sample sizes are more than about 50 and that the distribution of sample data is approximately symmetrical. Small samples and 'wild' distributions should lead the researcher to consider one of the options below.

2. *Permutation distributions* are reference distributions formed by finding all possible **permutations** of ranked data. For example, consider tossing two dice. Overall, there are six different outcomes for each die, making 36 outcomes in all, and the distribution of all of these 36 alternatives is the permutation distribution. There is only one way of achieving a total score of 12, by throwing two sixes; similarly, there is only one way of achieving a score of 2, by throwing two ones. However, there are six ways of achieving a score of 7 (1+6, 2+5, 3+4, 4+3, 5+2, 6+1), and this is the commonest total score from throwing two dice. As the dice example shows, permutation distributions are derived by taking all possible alternative outcomes for a specific setting, and they do not rely on assuming anything about an underlying theoretical parametric distribution for data. As a result, tests using them are called non-parametric tests. Examples include the Mann-Whitney U test and the Kruskal-Wallis test for differences between groups, and Kendall's rank order correlation test of association (see Tables 10.4 and 10.7).

3. *Bootstrap distributions* are reference distributions formed by treating the available data as all there is, and drawing repeated samples from it. The bootstrap procedure has been around for more than 40 years, but has only recently become easy to use (it is included as a standard option within SPSS version 20). For well-behaved data, the bootstrap will usually lead to the same conclusions as standard methods, but there are circumstances where bootstrapping is the only option (significance tests involving medians and tests for indirect effects in mediation analysis are two of them). Examples of how it works are given by Jackson (1986) and Wood (2005).

The next step in the hypothesis testing process is to calculate the difference between the two summary measures – either medians or means – for the two samples.

Step 5: drawing a conclusion

What is the probability of getting a difference as big as this if the null hypothesis were true? If the probability is small enough (the conventional criterion that is used is 1 in 20, equivalent to 5 in 100 or 5 per cent), then the researcher can conclude that the observed outcome is too surprising for the null hypothesis to be true, or stated another way, that the evidence from the data is convincing enough to modify the starting position. This is usually stated as: reject the null hypothesis at the 5 per cent level, or the difference between the groups is significant at the 0.05 level.

When someone makes a claim about how the world is on the basis of data, there are two kinds of mistakes that can be made, which are shown in Table 10.3. In the case of the example of the two sets of data collected for short- and long-tenure employees, there are two conclusions that could be drawn: either that there is a difference between the two groups in how employees see the speed of organizational decision making, or that there is no difference. If there really is no difference between the groups but the researcher uses sample data to make the false claim that there is a difference, this is called a **type I error**. A type I error is made when someone claims a difference where none exists. However, if there really is a difference between the groups but the researcher falsely concludes that there is none, then this is called a **type II error**.

The convention is that type I errors are more serious than type II errors, since the type II error is the same as retaining the initial starting point before the data were collected. The type I error amounts to changing the initial state of affairs in falsely claiming something new about the world based on data. After all, it is possible to correct an error of omission by gathering more data, while making false positive claims on the basis of a single sample is altogether different. From time to time there are dramatic examples of such type I errors reported in the press. These include claims of finding so-called 'cold fusion' (offering potential for unlimited free energy for the world), emissions from PC screens as harmful to unborn babies, the triple MMR vaccine as a cause of autism. All of these claims were subsequently found to be false, but each one was a source of confusion for researchers and sometimes alarm for members of the public.

Selecting the right kind of statistical test

So far, we have set out the general principles of hypothesis testing, using as an example the case of comparing the means of two samples of data. We next turn our attention to deciding how to choose the right significance test for a given situation.

For each type of test, two versions are listed: a *parametric test*, which assumes that the variables are measured on continuous scales, and also that the data are at least approximately bell-shaped, like the normal distribution; and a *non-parametric test* which makes the simpler assumption that the variables are measured on ordinal category scales. Thus, the choice between tests depends on what the researcher is prepared to assume about the

TABLE 10.3   Options in drawing conclusions from data

	True State of Affairs	
Conclusion from data	**Groups do not differ**	**Groups are different**
Data shows no difference between groups	Correct conclusion from sample data	Type II error
Data shows a difference between groups	Type I error	Correct conclusion from sample data

TABLE 10.4 Selecting the right kind of test for group differences

Purpose	Measurement Scale	Characteristic of Data	Test	Null Hypothesis	Test Statistic	Reference Distribution
Compare 2 groups	Continuous	Location: means	*t*-test	Groups are from a single population	*t*-value	t
	Ordered category	Location: medians	Mann-Whitney U test	Groups are from a single population	U statistic	All combinations of ranks
Compare 3 or more groups	Continuous	Location: means	Analysis of variance (ANOVA)	Groups are from a single population	*F*-ratio	F
	Ordered category	Location: medians	Kruskal-Wallis test	Groups are from a single population	W statistic	All combinations of ranks

measurement scale for the variables involved (see Chapter 8). Sometimes the answer is very straightforward. When a study asks whether there are more men than women employed at top level in a company, gender cannot be anything but measured on a *category scale*: male versus female. At other times, the issue is more a matter of judgement about the quality of measurement. When measurement quality is high, the researcher will probably be confident to think of the measurement scale as *continuous* and use the mean as a measure of location (choosing the mean because it is very efficient). This leads to choosing a parametric test such as the *t*-test or ANOVA for testing group differences. When there is more uncertainty about measurement quality, it is probably wiser to treat the scores as no more than ranked (an *ordinal* scale) and then rely on the median as a measure of location. This then leads to choosing non-parametric tests, which are more robust (because the summary measures they use are less influenced by extreme scores) but less efficient (because they throw away information that is in the data).

Testing for group differences – comparing groups

Table 10.4 lists procedures that can be used to test hypotheses about group differences in location. We distinguish between tests for comparing two groups, and tests for more complex datasets involving three or more groups. Table 10.5 picks out research questions that involve comparing groups from some of the studies listed in Table 10.1. Where there are only two groups to compare, the choice is between the *t*-test for comparing means and the **Mann-Whitney U test** for ranked data. For each, the table sets out how the groups were defined and what variable was involved in the group comparison. The second two examples concern hypotheses about differences between three groups, and the appropriate choice here is between the **analysis of variance** (**ANOVA**) for comparing means and the **Kruskal-Wallis test** based on ranked data. We illustrate the process of using the *t*-test for testing for differences between two groups; though the general principles apply to analysis of variance too.

Worked example of two-group comparison tests for the CEO compensation data

The data for this example come from the CEO compensation data summarized in Figures 10.4 and 10.5. Here we examine the relationship between pay level and the age of the CEO. We have created two groups: the larger group (n = 164) consists of those under 63 years of age, and a smaller group (n = 36) are 63+ years old. We use different forms of significance test to make a more precise inference about whether the two groups of employees differ in their level of pay. The null hypothesis is that there is no difference, such that two groups could have been defined by splitting the sample randomly into two groups. The null hypothesis is accepted unless there is sufficient evidence from the data to discard it in favour of the alternative that the two sets of observations are drawn from different populations. Figure 10.5 shows that pay is highly positively skewed, with one individual receiving over $500m. One question that we will explore is whether the shape of the data will have an influence on the conclusions drawn from the different ways of testing the same hypothesis.

The appropriate summary index that captures the relevant feature of the data depends on the type of test: the difference between the group means is used for the *t*-test and for the bootstrap test, while the ranked scores are used for the Mann-Whitney test (and so medians are reported in Table 10.6).

First, we explain the logic of the *t*-test, and then we show what happens when different forms of significance test are used. Table 10.6 shows that the mean (M_1) for the younger group is 19.55 (*n* = 164) and the mean (M_2) for the older group is 41.17 (*n* = 36). The difference in group means is 41.17 − 19.55 = 21.62 and the null hypothesis is that this group difference is zero. The formula for the *t*-test is a ratio:

$$t = M_1 - M_2 / SE (diff)$$

TABLE 10.5   Examples of research questions that involve comparing groups

Study	Groups to Compare	Dependent Variable
a) Testing for group differences – comparing two groups		
B2B relationships (Dyer and Hatch, 2006)	Two car companies – Toyota versus US	quality of supplier products
Locating your HQ (Birkinshaw et al., 2006)	Two types of HQ – business unit versus corporate	satisfaction of stakeholders
b) Testing for group differences – comparing three or more groups		
SOEs in China (Ralston et al., 2006)	Three categories – privately-owned versus foreign-owned versus state-owned	culture
MNEs' marketing strategies (Katsikeas, Samiee and Theodosiou, 2006)	Three groups of MNEs – US versus German versus Japanese	marketing strategies

TABLE 10.6   Summary statistics of CEO pay level (in millions of dollars) for two samples defined by age of the CEO, and results of significance tests.

	Age under 63 years (n = 164)	Age 63+ years (n = 36)	Significance tests
Mean	19.55 (SD = 18.93)	41.17 (SD = 96.14)	t-test: t = 2.68, df = 198, p < .01 Conclusion: groups do differ
			Bootstrap test: 95% CI (-2.06, 58.25), p = 0.273 Conclusion: groups do not differ
Median	12.56 (IQR = 14.37)	13.90 (IQR = 19.89)	Mann-Whitney test: U = 2551.50, Z = -1.27, p = 0.203 Conclusion: groups do not differ

The top line is the difference between the group means (21.62), and the bottom line (which makes it possible to judge how big a difference this is) is the standard error of the difference (8.08). The standard error is calculated from the standard deviation and the sample size in each group. The smaller the spread of scores around the group mean and the larger the sample size, the smaller is the standard error. Applying this formula gives a t-value of $21.62 / 8.08 = 2.68$.

If the null hypothesis (H_0) is true, the difference in means will be close to zero most of the time, and far from zero seldom. If the alternative hypothesis (H_1) is true, the difference in means will be far from zero most of the time and close to zero seldom. Where there is prior expectation about the direction of difference between the groups, the test is called a **2-tailed test**; and where one group is expected to have a higher mean than the other, the test is called a **1-tailed test**.

In order to get an idea of how big the observed difference actually is, it is necessary to locate it on the t-distribution. The shape of the t-distribution is defined by two parameters: the mean as an estimate of location and the standard deviation as an estimate of spread. The mean of the reference distribution is estimated from the difference between the group means under the null hypothesis. The standard deviation of the reference distribution, also called the **standard error** (SE) of the difference in group means, forms the bottom line of the t-test formula. It is a scaling factor that allows us to say whether a given difference is large or small. The size of the standard error depends on the sample sizes in the groups and on the spread of scores around the mean in each of the groups. The standard error is inversely related to the total number of observations in the study, and this makes sense because most people would have more confidence in means based on large samples. It also depends on the spread around the group means in the observed data (as measured by the standard deviations of the two groups), and this too makes sense. If data points are widely dispersed around their respective group means, then the mean is a less precise indicator of where the data in each group lie on the measurement scale. Overall then, the size of the t-value obtained depends upon three things:

1. The difference in group means.
2. The spread around group means.
3. The sample size in each group.

In general, convincing evidence about whether groups differ comes from big differences between means, small spread around those means (thus increasing their precision) and large sample sizes.

The bigger the t-value obtained, the more convincing is the evidence from the data that the initial starting position of two samples from a single population is incorrect, and needs to be modified in the light of evidence from the data. The final step is to select a significance level (conventionally $p < .05$), and find in the test tables the value of t that would be necessary to achieve the desired significance level. If the researcher finds that the actual t-value is greater than the tabulated value, then he or she will reject the null hypothesis that the groups are random samples from a single population at that level of significance, in favour of the alternative hypothesis that they are sampled from different populations.

The shape of the reference distribution depends on a quantity called **degrees of free-dom** (or df). For the two-sample t-test, this is calculated as the total sample size (200) minus the number of groups (2), giving the value of 198 shown in Table 10.6. The probability of achieving a t-value as big as 2.68 if the null hypothesis were really true is 1 in 1,000, shown in the table as $p < .01$. This is a small probability, and the conclusion is that the null hypothesis is very unlikely to be true and is rejected in favour of the alternative that the groups really do differ. Based on the t-test result, we would conclude that the younger group receive a lower level of pay than the older group. So far, so good, but remember that the CEO pay data are highly skewed (and this means that the normality assumption of the t-test is not very plausible).

The t-test compares group means (which are reported in the first row of Table 10.6), and it appears that the very high mean score for the older group is influenced by the single extreme outlier of $557m. Note that the difference in median scores for the two groups is much smaller than the difference in the means (we saw earlier that the median is not influenced by a few extreme scores). Next, we consider two different types of significance test that do not rely on the implausible assumption of normality.

The Mann-Whitney U test is a non-parametric test which works with the ranked scores, just as the median does. With the pay scores ranked from smallest to largest, the null hypothesis is that the two age groups are distributed evenly throughout the ranked scores.

The most extreme version of the alternative hypothesis is that all of the members of one age group are distributed at one end of the ranked data, and the other group are distributed at the other end. For this data, the test statistic, U, is 2551.50, with an associated z score of −1.27, and a probability level which is higher than the convention 0.05 level. The conclusion from this test is that the ranked pay levels for the younger group are not different from those for the older group. The bootstrap test follows a different logic, drawing repeated samples from the data itself, but the conclusion is the same as for the non-parametric test.

What do we conclude then from these three forms of significance test? The parametric test indicated that the groups do differ, but the other two tests do not. The safest conclusion is that pay level for CEOs (at least in this data) does not relate to the age of the CEO. The *t*-test seems to have been highly influenced by a single atypical data point, and so the result using this method is not representative of the data set as a whole. This shows the wisdom of looking at the shape of data and being prepared to look at the same data in different ways.

Testing association between variables

Table 10.7 lists procedures that can be used to test hypotheses about association between variables. If there is an **association** between two variables, then knowing how someone responds on one variable carries information that can be used to predict their response on the other. This definition applies regardless of the measurement scale of the variables being considered. Where the scale is at least ordered (either ordinal or continuous), we can be more precise and talk about the direction of the relationship in terms of a correlation. There is a *positive* correlation between two variables when high scores on one tend to occur with high scores on the other, and similarly for low scores. A *negative* correlation is shown by people responding with high scores on one variable but low scores on the other. A *zero* correlation indicates that knowing about one variable does not help in telling us anything about the other. Table 10.8 shows examples of association between variables from the studies in Table 10.1.

Different kinds of association between variables can be illustrated using data from a study of the impact of social support networks among unemployed adults. The study involved repeated interviews, and the figures below show data from measures of clinical anxiety and depression taken at the first and second interviews for 208 adults.

Figure 10.6 shows a *positive* association between two variables. The horizontal axis shows anxiety scores at the first interview, with low scores to the left and high scores to the right. The vertical axis shows the anxiety scores at the second interview, with low scores at the bottom and high scores at the top. In this plot there are more data points than there are circles, and the darker circles show multiple data points with the same combination of values. The drift of the data is from bottom-left to top-right: for the most part, people who reported being anxious at the first interview tended also to report high scores at the second interview (and vice versa). The correlation is 0.63, n = 208, p < .01. The high correlation is not surprising: levels of anxiety tend to be quite stable over time, reflecting either individual personality or stability in circumstances.

Figure 10.7 shows a *negative* association between two variables. The horizontal axis shows depression scores at the first interview, with low scores to the left and high scores to the right. The vertical axis shows the change in depression between the first interview and the second (calculated as time$_2$ score minus the time$_1$ score). A positive change score towards the top of the plot indicates someone reporting an increase in depression at the second interview, and a score towards the bottom of the plot indicates someone reporting a reduction in depression. Each data point is shown by a circle in the plot (with multiple overlapping points shown in darker circles), and the drift of the data is top-left to bottom-right. The top-left quadrant consists of people who reported low depression initially but an increase in depression at the second interview. The bottom-right quadrant consists of people with high depression at the first interview but whose depression score dropped at

TABLE 10.7 Selecting the right kind of test for association

Purpose	Measurement Scale	Characteristic of Data	Test	Null Hypothesis	Test statistic	Reference Distribution
Association in a contingency table	Two nominal category scales	Co-variation of scores on two variables	Chi-square test	Independence – overall distribution applies to all groups	χ^2 (chi-square)	χ^2 distribution
	Two binary category scales (0 / 1)	Co-variation of scores on two variables	Phi coefficient	Independence – overall distribution applies to all groups	Φ (phi)	R distribution
Correlation between variables	Two continuous scales	Co-variation of scores on two variables	Pearson product-moment correlation	Independence	r	R distribution
	One continuous scale and one binary category scale	Co-variation of scores on two variables	Point bi-serial correlation	Independence	r	R distribution
		Consistency of ranking	Rank-order correlation (Kendall);	Independence	τ (tau)	R distribution
	Two ordered category scales	on two variables	Rank-order correlation (Spearman)	Independence	ρ (rho)	R distribution

TABLE 10.8 Examples of research questions that involve testing association between variables

Study	Association Between:	
Influencing companies on environmental issues (Eesley and Lenox, 2006)	Different stakeholder actions	Positive corporate responses
MNEs' marketing strategies (Katsikeas, Samiee and Theodosiou, 2006)	Standardization of marketing strategy	Market environment
Locating your HQ (Birkinshaw et al., 2006)	HQ – business unit/corporate	Satisfying stakeholders
Is CSR smart as well as good? (Luo and Bhattacharya, 2006)	CSR activities of companies – cash donations/employee volunteering	Market value of company/customer satisfaction

FIGURE 10.6

A positive association between two variables

the second interview. This pattern is reflected in a negative correlation of −0.40, n = 208, p < .01. The negative correlation is not surprising: people with extreme scores at the first interview will tend to report scores which are closer to the mean second time around (this is called 'regression to the mean').

The specific test for association between two variables depends on the measurement scale. For variables measured on nominal category scales, the **chi-square test** (χ^2) is appropriate. Where the measurement scale is either ordinal or continuous, association between

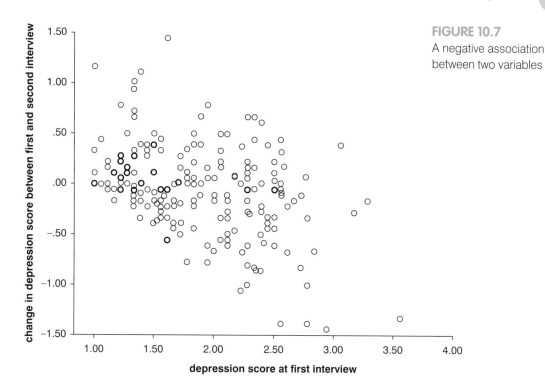

FIGURE 10.7

A negative association between two variables

variables is assessed by a *correlation coefficient*. The correlation coefficient for continuous scales is the Pearson **product-moment correlation**. For data measured in the form of ranks, the Kendall **rank-order correlation** is used.

Testing association for nominal category measurement scales: the chi-square test

While it is possible to draw a scatterplot for looking at association between variables measured on category scales, it is generally more convenient and informative to use a contingency table to show how a sample is divided up according to each person's score on the two variables we are interested in. Contingency tables do not have to be two-way, but they get much harder to read when we use more than two variables to divide up the sample. The chi-square test is used to test association between two category variables measured on nominal scales.

An example of a contingency table is shown in Table 10.9, which is taken from a study by Anya Johnson, a doctoral student. She carried out a worldwide survey (18 countries) of over 3,000 professional managers (both men and women) who had been made redundant by their company and then enrolled in a career transition programme to help them get another job. One of the things that the student looked at was the effect of job loss on family relationships, and she asked the following question: *What is the effect of job loss on your relationship with your partner/spouse?* They could select from three responses: *bringing you closer together, having no effect at all* and *causing relationship difficulties.* She wondered whether unemployed men and women would answer this question differently, and the contingency table below shows the two variables together. The table shows the counts, and also the row percentages: each count as a percentage of the row total. The first row shows how men answered the question, and the second row shows responses for women.

The bottom right-hand corner of the table shows that 2,861 people answered the relationship question and also reported their gender. The right-hand column with the row

TABLE 10.9 Contingency table showing frequencies of men and women according to the reported effect of job loss on the relationship with their partner

NOTE: PERCENTAGES ARE BASED ON THE ROW TOTALS

	Effect of Job Loss on Relationship with Partner			
	Brings them closer together	No difference to the relationship	Causes difficulties in the relationship	Total
Men	952 (43%)	874 (39%)	406 (18%)	2232 100%
Women	223 (35%)	276 (44%)	130 (21%)	629 100%
Total	1175 (41%)	1150 (40%)	536 (19%)	2861 100%

totals shows that there are 2,232 men in the analysis, and 629 women. The bottom row of the table shows how people answered the question about the effect of job loss on their relationship, and the effect seems to be mostly either positive or neutral. About four out of ten people (1,175 out of 2,861: 41 per cent) say that the experience has brought them closer together, and about the same number (1,150 out of 2,861: 40 per cent) say it has not affected their relationship. Only a minority (536 out of 2,861: 19 per cent) say that job loss has caused relationship difficulties.

One of the key questions that Johnson asked was whether the effect of the experience was different for men and women. In other words, is there an association between gender and the effect of job loss on the quality of the relationship with partner? An initial step in addressing this question is to look at the pattern of responses for men and women separately, using the row percentages. For men, 43 per cent say that job loss has brought them closer together compared to 35 per cent for women – so men tend to be more positive about how job loss has affected the relationship with their partner. Corresponding to this, 18 per cent of men say that job loss has caused relationship difficulties, compared to 21 per cent of women – men are less negative than women. Overall then, there does seem to be an association between gender and impact of job loss on partner relationship.

Interpreting this result is quite complicated. It could be that losing a job is really more damaging to the family relationships of women than it is for men; it could also be that harm is equally strong for both sexes, but that women are more aware of it than men. From semi-structured interviews that Johnson carried out she suspected that the second interpretation was more likely. These tended to show that men are less aware of their own feelings and those of their partner than are women, and so do not notice when relationship problems exist.

Having looked at the data, it would appear that there is an association between gender and the effect of job loss on the relationship, but this can be tested formally using the chi-square (χ^2) test of association. The null hypothesis for the chi-square test of association is that there is no relationship between the two variables. For a contingency table this means that the distribution of responses for the total sample (shown by the percentages in the bottom row of the table) applies equally to both men and women. The alternative hypothesis is that the distribution of responses is different for men and women, and that seems to be the case for these data.

Just as with any significance test, the purpose is to estimate how likely would be the pattern observed in the data if the null hypothesis were true, and the test statistic, χ^2, for this table is 10.52. The degrees of freedom for the test with these data are 2: for χ^2 this is calculated as (number of rows – 1) times (number of columns – 1) = 2. The probability of getting a distribution of data like this if there really is no association between gender and the effect on relationship is 0.005, or 5 in 1,000. This is a small number, so the odds of the null hypothesis being true are small, and the null hypothesis is rejected at the 0.005 level. Johnson concluded that there is a gender difference in how people see the effect of job loss on the relationship with their partner.

Contingency table analysis

EXERCISE
10.1

Below is a contingency table presenting data from a large pharmaceutical company showing the number of men and women employed by the company divided into five regions where they operate.

		Gender		Total
		Female	Male	
Region	Middle East & Africa	315	401	716
	Asia Pacific	4304	5923	10227
	Europe	13618	12138	25756
	North America	2072	1771	3843
	Latin/Central America/Caribbean	1576	2085	3661
Total		21885	22318	44203

First of all, explore the table in order to decide whether there are gender differences between the regions (hint: work out the row percentages, which will show you the proportion of women employed in each region). Then carry out a chi-square analysis in order to test whether there are significant gender differences between regions.
    Answer the following questions:

1. What is your conclusion?
2. What further information would you need in order to help you interpret the reasons behind your finding?

Testing association for continuous and ordered category scales: correlation between variables

For variables measured on scales that are at least ordered, association can be tested using a correlation coefficient. For continuous scales (whether interval or ratio), the test of choice is the Pearson product-moment correlation (r), while the test of choice for ordinal category scales is a rank-order correlation coefficient developed by Kendall (**Kendall's tau**) though there is another one developed by Spearman (**Spearman's rho**), which is less commonly used. Pearson's r is the extension of the variance to cover the co-variance between two variables: the extent to which variation in one variable is associated with variation in the other. Spearman's *rho* is the product-moment correlation of the ranked scores for two variables. Kendall's *tau* is an index of consistency of the two sets of ranked scores – how many swaps of scores are necessary to bring the two into consistency.

CONCLUSION

The material we have covered in this chapter is:

 Methods of looking at data and the key features that the researcher should pay attention to before summarizing those features using summary statistics.

 Measures of location and spread, and we have argued that choosing one form of summary measure rather than another has the effect of emphasizing some features of data and neglecting others.

 Making inferences about population characteristics based on data from samples. We described the common steps involved in testing hypotheses about group differences and about association between variables, using tests for variables taken one at a time.

The next chapter builds on the principles of hypothesis testing, applying them to the multivariate case where variables are considered together.

FURTHER READING

Buglear, J. (2012) *Quantitative Methods for Business and Management Students*. Harlow: Pearson.
  Less comprehensive (and perhaps less amusing) introduction into quantitative research methods. Tailored to the needs of business and management researchers, this textbook is well written and includes chapters on presenting, summarizing and investigating quantitative data.
Field, A.P., Miles, J. and Field, Z. (2012) *Discovering Statistics Using R*. London: Sage.
Field, A. (2013) *Discovering Statistics Using IBM SPSS Statistics. And Sex and Drugs and Rock 'n' Roll*, 4th edn. Los Angeles, CA: Sage.
  The focus of this book is getting the statistical work done rather than the dry statistical theory itself. It is accessible (provided you can tune into the author's sense of humour and his liking for selfies), and covers much of the material in this chapter and the next, plus a lot more. A different version of the book introduces statistics using the increasingly popular software tool R:
Howell, D. (2013) *Statistical Methods for Psychology*, 8th edn. Belmont, CA: Wadsworth.
Howell, D. (2013) *Fundamental Statistics for the Behavioral Sciences*, 8th edn. Nashville, TN: Broadman and Holman.
  Both books go into more detail on the logic of hypothesis testing and describe a much more extensive set of statistical tests for comparing groups or testing association between variables. The strengths of the author's approach are that he emphasizes the importance of looking at data intelligently before making decisions about forms of analysis, and he also explains clearly the conceptual underpinnings of the methods that are covered.

Want to know more about this chapter? Visit the ⓈSAGE edge™ website at **https://edge.sagepub.com/easterbysmith** to access practice questions, selected journal articles, useful web links and much more.

MULTIVARIATE ANALYSIS

11

THE DOMAIN OF MULTIVARIATE ANALYSIS

The social world that we all live in is a complex system, and cannot really be understood just by looking at one thing at a time: causes interact with each other in complex ways; effects are not always simple to measure. Table 11.1 lists studies from the management literature which use **multivariate methods** to test theoretical propositions.

The complication arises because most of the interesting things researchers want to look at are correlated with each other. The tools and methods that we considered in the previous chapter are basic ones for working with quantitative data, but they are not enough to deal with the complexities of the world of work. This chapter on multivariate analysis builds on the previous two, but it is more advanced because it deals with analytical methods for looking at complex data, and these are intrinsically more difficult than the univariate methods that were considered in the previous chapter.

The purpose of multivariate analysis is to find a way of summarizing the relationship between variables, which is simpler than the original data but also captures the essence of that relationship. In that respect, working with quantitative data is no different from working with research evidence in any other form (see Chapter 8): research seeks out a conceptual model that is both simpler and richer. Simplicity is desirable so that the model is understandable; richness is desirable so that the model can stimulate new ways of thinking about the world. The models that are used in multivariate analysis are mathematical models, and a full understanding of multivariate statistics requires a fair amount of facility with matrix algebra. However, in this chapter we give a conceptual introduction to some of the methods, which can then be built on in a more advanced way.

Forms of interdependence in management research

There are many kinds of interdependency among concepts within the domain of management research. The first kind of interdependence is **interaction effects** where variables have different effects depending on the context, and these have been examined in the form of contingency theories. Examples of contingency theories can be found in cross-cultural management (e.g. what works well in a US business negotiation would cause deep offence among Arabs), in organizational design (different forms of organizing are needed to deal with rapidly changing markets compared to the stable bureaucracies that most people work in (Brown and Eisenhardt, 1998)), and in guidance on how organizations can effectively manage worker stress (Jackson and Parker, 2001).

The second kind of interdependency is that of **synergy**, one of the favourite buzzwords of the management change consultant. The idea is a simple one: plant a seed, give it both warmth and water and it will grow. Water alone will make it rot, warmth

TABLE 11.1   Examples of studies using multivariate statistical methods

Coyle-Shapiro and Kessler (2000): Commitment of employees to the organization (DV) as a function of fulfilment of the psychological contract (PV).
Brouthers and Brouthers (2003): Mode of entry into foreign markets (DV) by service and manufacturing organizations (PV).
Thompson (2004): Decline in national competitiveness (DV) as a function of cost factors or institutional arrangements (PV).
Filatotchev (2006): The entry of forms into public ownership (DV) according to the characteristics of executives and involvement of venture capital (PV).

alone may lead the seed to become dormant; but both together can achieve the miracle of making a new plant. This is the logic behind many organizational mergers where the capabilities of different partners are brought together with the intent of making a step change in performance.

The third kind of interdependency is that *influences on performance tend to occur together*, either because they affect each other or because they have common causes. Several of the studies in Table 11.1 share the same feature; that is, they control for organizational size in their analysis (e.g. Brouthers and Brouthers, 2003; Filatotchev, 2006). Looking at the Brouthers and Brouthers study first, their logic was simple – they were not directly interested in differences between large and small firms but they know that size makes a difference to lots of things, so ignoring it would probably bias answers to questions they were interested in. They wanted to study how service and manufacturing firms went about their internationalization through entering new foreign markets. If the service firms in their sample were smaller (or larger) on average than the manufacturing ones, then conclusions based on a comparison between the two sectors would be confounded by differences in size. As a result, including the size of the firm in statistical analysis makes sense. Filatotchev used the same logic in his efforts in explaining what happens when entrepreneurial firms first go into public ownership through initial public offerings (IPOs).

Ways of dealing with interdependence within quantitative analysis

In this section, we consider four ways of dealing with interrelated influences (see Table 11.2). Three of them involve simplification: through design, through selecting sub-samples and through statistical control. The final method is multivariate analysis, and this forms the main focus of this chapter. While all four methods are useful, most people develop a preference to suit their own style or the options open to them in their research area.

Simplification through design

The first way of dealing with interrelated influences is to design the study so that relevant causal factors are made independent of each other through the design itself (see also Chapter 4). Consider the case of age and salary level: as people get older their experience grows and their salary level tends to go up. Thus there is an association between age and salary, which can be summarized by a positive correlation (see Chapter 10). If a researcher picks employees at random, then the sample will be likely to reflect this association. However, another approach would be to divide the potential sample into groups based on age, and then select equal numbers of people at a number of salary levels within each age range. Even though age and salary may be correlated within the organization as a whole, the effect of this sampling strategy would be to create a sample of respondents

TABLE 11.2 How to deal with interrelated factors

Method	Action
1 Simplification through design.	Sampling – select equal numbers within sub-groups.
2 Simplification through selecting sub-samples.	Restrict sample to one level of a key variable.
3 Simplification through statistical control.	Take variables two at a time, and use partial correlations to achieve statistical control.
4 Multivariate analysis.	Use multiple predictors and consider their joint influence.

where the two are independent of each other. The linkage between the two variables would not then be present in the sample.

The craft of research design (Shadish et al., 2002) is about developing imaginative ways of achieving simplicity of inference through creating a study design within which factors are orthogonal, where they are not independent of each other in the world at large. Such study designs are linked to statistical methods called *analysis of variance*, and designs with multiple factors are called **factorial designs**. Because they make analysis and inference simple even in research areas with many interrelated complicating factors, they have developed a strong appeal for some kinds of people. Experimental approaches based on structured research designs are widely used, particularly in work psychology, marketing and information systems research.

Simplification through selecting a sub-sample

The second way of dealing with interrelated influences is through selecting samples to be equal on potentially confounding factors. It is common to find that women are paid less than men, and one of the reasons is that men and women tend to do different jobs, which in turn command different pay levels. In random samples of men and women at work then, there will be different mixes of jobs for the two groups as well as differences in pay levels, and it is difficult to disentangle the relative influence of gender and job type. However, restricting a study sample to people doing the same job would mean that any gender difference cannot be attributed to job type but must be due to something else. The same logic was used by Hofstede (1991) in his research on national culture, where he gathered data only from IBM employees working in many countries across the world rather than by drawing random samples in each country. The differences he found led him to conclude that there were four basic dimensions of national culture: power distance, masculine-feminine, individual-collective and uncertainty avoidance (he later added long-term orientation). Relying on samples drawn from only one company means that he is controlling for differences in labour markets across the world.

Simplification through statistical control

The third way to deal with interrelated influences is through a form of **statistical control** called **partial correlation**. We have already seen in Chapter 10 that a correlation is a way of summarizing the extent to which people respond to two variables in consistent ways. A partial correlation is a correlation between two variables (we call them A and B) where the value of a third variable (we call this S) is adjusted statistically as if it were equal to the sample mean for everybody (this is usually referred to as *holding constant* a third variable). The correlation between A and B is written as r_{AB}. The symbol for the partial correlation is $r_{AB|S}$. The method of partial correlation allows the researcher to see how much of an observed correlation, say between A and B, can be accounted for by the relationship that both variables have with a third variable, S.

Table 11.3 presents three possible patterns for r_{AB} and $r_{AB|S}$. We will use an example to explain the three patterns. Social media technologies such as blogs (Scoble and Israel, 2006) are rapidly becoming popular, and it would not be surprising to find correlations between willingness to use blogs for external marketing (B) and both age (A) and salary level (S). A correlation between age and blogging (r_{AB}) could be interpreted in terms of the conservatism of older people when it comes to embracing new technologies. A correlation between blogging and salary (r_{BS}) could be interpreted in terms of more senior people in the organization having fewer direct links with customers. We have already suggested that a correlation between age and salary is plausible (r_{AS}), and so all three variables are likely to be correlated. The partial correlation of age and blogging with salary held constant identifies that part of the total correlation is independent of salary. Pattern 1 shows a high AB correlation and also a high AB|S partial correlation, and here the S variable has not altered the correlation between A and B. Pattern 2 shows a high AB correlation but a zero AB|S partial correlation, and in this case the researcher would conclude that A and B are not really correlated at all. The relationship suggested by the AB correlation is spurious. Finally, pattern 3 shows an unusual but interesting case, where the AB correlation is zero, suggesting that A and B are not related at all. However, a high partial correlation implies that there really is a relationship between the two, but one that has been masked by the third variable S.

TABLE 11.3 Example of possible relationships between correlation and partial correlation

Pattern	Interpretation
1 r_{AB} is high; $r_{AB|S}$ is high	A and B are related; and S is irrelevant to both
2 r_{AB} is high; $r_{AB|S}$ is zero	A and B are not really related at all; but S has contributed to the appearance of a relationship between A and B
3 r_{AB} is zero; $r_{AB|S}$ is high	S is masking the 'real' relationship between A and B

Multivariate analysis

The final way of dealing with many interrelated factors builds on this logic of statistical control but extends it to many variables, and also to predictive relationships rather than simple associations as measured by correlations. Multivariate statistical methods are designed to allow researchers to include many variables in a single analysis and to assess the separate contribution of each variable within an overall model. These methods are the focus of the rest of this chapter. Their main feature is the specification of a conceptual model that expresses the researcher's hypotheses about the relationships among variables. The variables to be included in a model will be defined by the focus of the research. Researchers in business and management get excited in their work by very different things. For example, in some of the studies considered already in this chapter, the size of the firm is treated as a 'nuisance' factor, which gets in the way of finding clear answers to interesting questions. However, there are other scholars for whom understanding the factors that make firms grow is the very focus of their work, and the size of the firm is not a nuisance factor at all.

Once a decision is made about which variables to include in a model, the next step is to specify what role each variable has in the model, usually as a cause (a predictor variable) or as an effect (a dependent variable). Making a decision about whether something is a dependent variable or a predictor variable is really a decision about how a variable is treated in the researcher's thinking. It is not an intrinsic characteristic of a variable, but instead a function of how it is used in a particular circumstance. This will depend to a large extent on the focus of a specific research project. Note that the role that a variable plays in statistical analysis reflects its position in the researcher's thinking, not something about the variable itself. The role that a variable plays in a researcher's model may even change within a study. Thus the paper by Coyle-Shapiro and Kessler (2000) reports one analysis where perceived organizational support is treated as a dependent variable, and later in the paper the authors use the same variable as a predictor of organizational commitment. So, its role changes from dependent variable to predictor variable.

Multivariate models can be specified using matrix algebra, for those with a strong mathematical training, and also represented graphically for those without such a background. We will use the graphical representation in this chapter for the sake of simplicity (see Figure 11.1). Variables are shown by boxes, which may be either rectangular or elliptical, and relationships among variables are shown by either single-headed or double-headed arrows. The variables used in multivariate models may be of two kinds: those that are measured directly by the researcher, called **observed variables**; and **latent variables,** which are not measured directly but are inferred from observed variables. Observed variables are shown by rectangular boxes, and latent variables are shown by elliptical boxes.

Figure 11.1(a) shows a model for observed variables, with a single dependent variable to the right (DV1) and two predictor variables (PV1 and PV2). The assumed causal relationship between the PVs and the DV is indicated by the single-headed arrows. The double-headed arrow connecting the two PVs indicates an association between them, which may or may not reflect a causal relationship (this relationship is called **exogenous**, because the specified model does not concern itself with its origins: it is taken as a given). Figure 11.1(b) shows a model with two observed variables (DV1 and DV2) and one latent predictor variable (LV). The LV is assumed to be a cause of both DV1 and DV2.

The next sections give an introduction to multivariate analysis methods for analysing **causal models**. Measurement models explore the relationship between observed variables and latent variables. Causal models are of two kinds: those that involve only observed variables, and those that involve both observed and latent variables.

MULTIVARIATE ANALYSIS OF CAUSAL MODELS

Rationale for causal models

Causality cannot be proved
Using multivariate statistical methods to test causal models is a very powerful technique that is widely used within management research. Its major value is that it forces the researcher to define very precisely both the variables to be included and the way in which they relate

FIGURE 11.1
Graphical representation of multivariate models

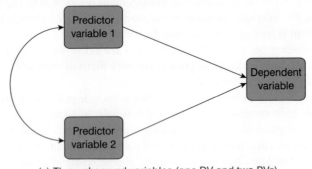

(a) Three observed variables (one DV and two PVs)

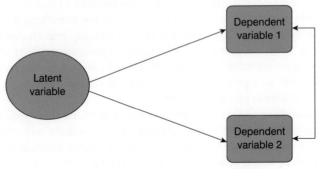

(b) Two observed DVs and one latent PV

to each other. In return, the statistical methods offer specific tests of hypotheses that can allow the researcher to judge how good those models are. However, what causal modelling methods cannot do is prove a causal relationship. Instead, they allow decisions to be made about whether a given model is consistent with observed data. The plausibility of a particular model needs first to be established conceptually from theory, and then quantitative evidence can be used to assess whether the model is consistent with data. Consider again the study by Coyle-Shapiro and Kessler (2000) from Table 11.1. In their article, they developed a theoretical rationale for treating employee commitment as a dependent variable and psychological contract fulfilment as a predictor variable. Unless they have longitudinal data, with variables measured on more than one occasion, it is impossible for them to prove that this assumption is correct. Instead, all they can do is assess whether the conceptual model that they formulated is consistent with their data.

Defining what variables to include in the model

This step is important because any causal model will estimate the best values that it can for the contribution of each variable that is included. However, the estimation procedure can only take into account the information it has available to it. If the researcher leaves out (by accident or by design) a factor that is critically important, then the modelling procedure cannot find it, and the results obtained can be misleading. Studies that leave out important variables are very likely to produce misleading conclusions. Almost every week, some survey is reported in the newspapers showing that red wine is good/bad for health, or that chocolate/chips help you diet. Such studies almost always suffer from small and idiosyncratic samples, and their big failing is that the true causal factors behind good health or weight loss were not even included in the study. For the most part, the findings are either chance results that cannot be replicated, or are the spurious consequence of some other more important variable.

Specifying causal models

Research propositions should be translated into formal causal models that can be tested statistically, either as a single model or as a sequence of models of increasing complexity. Comparing a simple model with a more complex one is a powerful way of testing research hypotheses, but it is important to remember that a more complex model, one that includes more variables or has more complex relationships among them, will always give a better fit to a given dataset. So, **goodness of fit** alone is not the most important criterion in selecting the best model. Instead, the researcher needs to take into account what the gain in the quality of the model is relative to the added complexity needed to achieve it. An example of the development of a series of causal models is shown in Example 11.1.

EXAMPLE
11.1

Stakeholder relationship management and corporate financial performance: formulating alternative causal models

This example considers different accounts of how stakeholder relationship management links to corporate strategy and to the performance of the organization (Freeman et al., 2010; Cornelissen, 2011). Berman et al. (1999) propose two kinds of model, the normative model and the instrumental model, and show how they can be tested empirically. The **normative** model states that looking after the interests of stakeholders is the right thing to do, and that the strategic goals set by

(Continued)

(Continued)

senior management will be determined by a need to protect and promote the interests of their stakeholders. So principles of stakeholder relationship management guide how the organization formulates its corporate strategy, and strategy in turn has some influence on financial performance. Figure 11.2 expresses the normative model using blocks for the key variables and arrows to show the hypothesized causal relationships among them.

The *instrumental* model (Figure 11.3) states that organizations should pay attention to their stakeholders because they will benefit financially; thus the model proposes that both stakeholder relationship management and corporate strategy

SOURCE: (ADAPTED FROM BERMAN ET AL, 1999)

FIGURE 11.2
The normative model of stakeholder relationship management and corporate financial performance

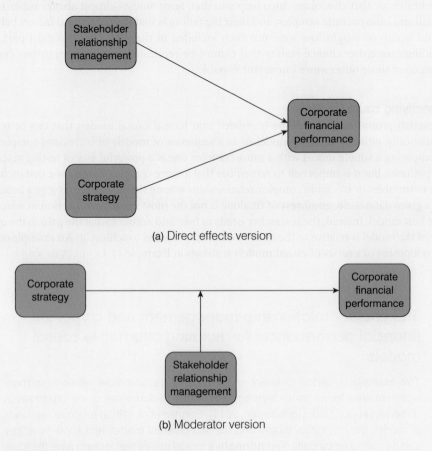

(a) Direct effects version

(b) Moderator version

FIGURE 11.3
The instrumental model of stakeholder relationship management and corporate financial performance

influence corporate financial performance. Berman et al. propose two variants of the instrumental model: the direct effects model shown in Figure 11.3(a) and the moderation model shown in Figure 11.3(b). The direct effects model differs from the normative model in that there is no path between corporate strategy and stakeholder relationship management, but there is a direct path from stakeholder relationships to financial performance. The moderation model is a more sophisticated version of the direct effects model, which proposes a different mechanism for the role of stakeholder relationship management, as modifying the link between strategy and performance. The logic behind this form of the model is that companies will find it easier to put their strategic goals into practice and benefit from them if they foster good relationships with their stakeholders.

Sample size

The trustworthiness of a model depends on how stable it is, and that means the sample size needs to be large enough to give confidence that the results could be replicated in new samples. Analyses based on small samples tend to give quirky results that may not be repeatable. The adequacy of a sample depends on the complexity of the model that is fitted to the data: complex models need larger samples. As a useful rule of thumb, multiplying the number of observed predictor variables by ten gives a minimum sample size (though this really is a minimum, and other factors such as the reliability of measurement would lead us to recommend larger samples than this).

Assessing the appropriate form of a causal model

Once the researcher has defined the conceptual model in a form that can be tested statistically, the next step is to check that the data available are expressed in a form which is appropriate for the assumptions required by the statistical method. This involves assessing both measurement quality and that the form of the statistical model is appropriate. The input for all multivariate analysis methods is a matrix containing the variances of each variable (indicating the spread of scores: see Chapter 10) and the covariances among them (these reflect the associations among each pair of variables and are used to calculate correlations). It is important therefore that there are no extreme scores on any of the study variables (outliers) that can distort the value of the variance as a measure of spread (see Chapter 10). It is also important to check the form of the association among each pair of variables to ensure that relationships are linear. We showed in Chapter 10 that correlation coefficients can be seriously misleading if relationships between variables are not linear.

Assessing the quality of fitted causal models

All multivariate methods for analysing causal models share common characteristics. They give a summary measure of how good the prediction is for the model as a whole, generally expressed in terms of the proportion of variance in the dependent variable(s) accounted for by a set of predictors. They also report specific measures for components of the model, indicating the separate contribution of each predictor variable.

Generalized linear models

The multivariate methods considered in this chapter – multiple regression analysis, MANCOVA, MANOVA and **logistic regression** – have the same formal structure and they are all referred to as 'generalized linear models'. The technical details are beyond the scope of this book, but the management researcher benefits from these theoretical developments in statistics because they provide both a theoretical 'cleanness' to the models and also the basis for the computational algorithms used by statistical packages such as SPSS.

Analysis of causal models for observed variables

Three general classes of multivariate model for observed variables are described in this section in order to illustrate how researchers can approach the analysis of causal relationships. Our purpose is to demonstrate what the methods have in common rather than their differences, and to show part of the craft of multivariate modelling. The main features of each class of model are summarized in Table 11.4. The table is in four parts for each method in turn. Part (a) shows what kinds of variables are appropriate for the method, according to the number of dependent variables used and the measurement scale for both DVs and PVs. Part (b) describes how the quality of the model as a whole is assessed in that method. Part (c) lists how the individual elements of the model are represented in the model. Part (d) outlines alternative options that are available within each method. First, we consider the multiple regression and analysis of covariance models whose characteristics are shown in column 1.

Multiple regression analysis (MRA)

The basic **multiple regression model** consists of a single dependent variable measured on a continuous scale and a set of predictor variables, which may be measured on continuous or category scales (see Table 11.4(a)). The model for two predictor variables can be expressed algebraically like this:

$$Y = a + b_1X_1 + b_2X_2 + e$$

where the symbol Y is used for the dependent variable, while the symbol X is used for each predictor variable, a is called the intercept or the constant (it is the value of Y when each X is zero), b is called a regression weight, and e is a residual (or error) term. On the predictor side of the model above, there are two kinds of variables. The PVs (shown here by X_1 and X_2) are the systematic part of the model chosen by the researcher. All other factors that influence the spread of scores on the DV are combined together into the residual term, e. The graphical form of this regression model is shown in Figure 11.4.

The quality of the regression model as a whole (Table 11.4(b)) is summarized by the **squared multiple correlation**, R^2, whose value varies between 0 and 1 and shows how much of the spread in DV scores can be accounted for by the predictors in the model. In MRA, the measure of spread that is used is the variance (see Chapter 10), and the R^2 measure is the proportion of variance in the DV accounted for by the PVs collectively. It is often multiplied by 100 to give a percentage of variance accounted for, from 0 per cent to 100 per cent. R^2 indicates the relative importance of the PVs and the residual term, which is shown to the right in Figure 11.4. Thus where a set of predictors account for 20 per cent of the variance in a DV, this means that 80 per cent of the variance is accounted for by all other causal factors combined into the residual term. An F-test is used to test the null hypothesis that the proportion of variance accounted for by the PVs is zero against the alternative hypothesis that it is greater than zero. The individual components of the model are summarized in Table 11.4(c). The regression weights indicate the size of the independent contribution that each PV makes to predicting the spread in scores on the DV. When predictor variables are measured on different scales, the relative size of regression weights for different variables cannot be compared. So it is usual to transform each of the variables in MRA to a common measurement scale (this is called 'standardizing'), and then the regression weights are referred to as either standardized regression weights or β (beta) weights. The significance test for regression weights gives a t-value, and the null hypothesis tested is that the regression weight is zero against the alternative that it is different from zero.

TABLE 11.4 Multivariate methods for analysis of causal models for observed variables

	MRA / ANCOVA	MANOVA / MANCOVA	Logistic Regression Analysis
(a) Variables	DV – a single continuous variable. PVs – MRA – one or more continuous variables. ANCOVA – one or more category variables and one or more continuous variables.	DVs – two or more continuous variables. PVs – MANOVA – one or more category variables (factors). MANCOVA – one or more category variables and a one or more continuous variable (covariates).	DV – a single dichotomous category variable. PVs – one or continuous and/or category variables.
(b) Assessing quality of the model as a whole	Multiple R shows the validity of the model as a whole; multiple R^2 shows the proportion of variance in the DV accounted for. An F-ratio tests whether the multiple R is significantly different from zero.	Wilks' Lambda – multivariate test for each effect (category and continuous variable) shows the significance level for all DVs jointly. An F-ratio tests the significance of Lambda.	Model χ^2
(c) Contribution of individual elements of the model	Regression weights show the independent contribution of each PV; beta weights are regression weights standardized onto the same measurement scale for all variables. A t-test assesses whether a regression weight is significantly different from zero.	Separate tests for each dependent variable: ● Univariate tests (which ignore correlations among the dependent variables). ● Stepdown tests (which partial out the effects of dependent variables entered according to a pre-determined sequence).	Regression weights and odds ratios for each predictor variable
(d) Options available	● Simultaneous entry of all predictors. ● Hierarchical regression – entry of variables in a sequence determined the researcher. ● Stepwise regression – sequential entry of variables determined by the predictive value of variables.	● Stepdown tests require a pre-determined sequence for the dependent variables. ● Tests could be performed with and without covariates in the model.	● Simultaneous entry of all predictors. ● Hierarchical logistic regression – entry of variables in a sequence determined by theory. ● Stepwise logistic regression – sequential entry of variables according to their predictive value.

FIGURE 11.4
Graphical
representation of a
multiple regression
model

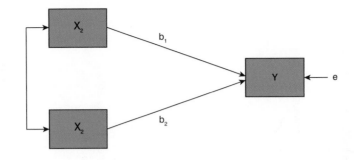

EXAMPLE
11.2

Multiple regression analysis of predictors of quality commitment

Jackson (2004) reported a study of one aspect of employees' commitment to the values of their organization: their commitment to quality. There were three stages to the research: defining the concept of quality commitment itself; formulating a way of measuring it; and developing and testing a conceptual model of how quality commitment relates to both personal and organizational variables. Here, we focus on the third stage where a sequence of regression analyses were used to test the conceptual model.

Table 11.5 shows a matrix of correlations for quality commitment, demographic variables (age, company tenure and gender) and a number of measures of work design. Row 10 of the table shows the correlation between quality commitment and each of the other variables in the study. There is a strong relationship with age ($r = 0.30$, $p < 0.001$), indicating that older workers show higher quality commitment; and the relationship with company tenure is much lower but also significant ($r = 0.14$, $p < 0.001$). Gender differences are significant but small in size ($r = 0.09$, $p < 0.05$), with women showing higher quality commitment. Table 11.5 also shows, not surprisingly, that age and company tenure are correlated: those who have been employed longer with their company tend to be older. There are also consistently strong correlations between quality commitment and work design characteristics. Workers with more control over the timing and methods aspects of their jobs report higher quality commitment ($r = 0.21$, $p < 0.001$ and $r = 0.24$, $p < 0.001$ for timing and method control respectively); workers whose jobs are more mentally demanding in terms of problem solving ($r = 0.11$, $p < 0.001$) and system monitoring ($r = 0.23$, $p < 0.001$) also report higher quality commitment; and quality commitment is correlated with production responsibility ($r = 0.16$, $p < 0.001$): workers reporting more expensive consequences if they make a mistake have higher quality commitment.

However, interpreting these relationships is not simple, because the table shows that there are strong correlations among many of the study variables. For example, people who have been employed in the company for longer tend to report higher levels of the work design variables, presumably because they have jobs with more responsibility. We have also seen that age and company tenure are correlated. Testing the conceptual model means that it is necessary to tease out these relationships, and that is the purpose of multiple regression analysis.

In the analyses reported in Table 11.6, the DV is quality commitment, and the predictors are the demographic and work design variables. Two steps in hierarchical regression analysis are shown in the table. In the first step, column 1, the demographic variables are used as PVs and the results show that both age and gender are significant predictors of quality commitment, while company tenure is not. This suggests that the correlation between company tenure and quality commitment arises because both variables are correlated with age: it would appear that quality commitment reflects a person's age

(JACKSON, 2004)

TABLE 11.5 Correlations among study variables

	1	2	3	4	5	6	7	8	9	10
1 Organization	–									
2 Age	.13	–								
3 Gender	-.43	-.09	–							
4 Company tenure	.02	.48	-.11	–						
5 Individual timing control	.28	.26	-.23	.23	–					
6 Individual method control	.29	.19	-.28	.24	.67	–				
7 Monitoring demands	-.08	.11	-.03	.17	.16	.28	–			
8 Problem-solving demands	.09	.00	-.22	.21	.20	.34	.52	–		
9 Production responsibility	.00	.02	-.11	.05	.02	.15	.42	.34	–	
10 Quality commitment	.02	.30	.09	.14	.21	.24	.23	.11	.16	–
Mean	.22	30.78	.78	5.74	2.83	3.09	3.85	3.00	3.19	3.97
Standard deviation	.62	11.12	.41	6.16	1.21	.93	.84	.88	1.06	.51

(Continued)

(Continued)

rather than the length of employment with the employer. The second step (column 2) adds the work design predictors in order to test how much each one adds independently to predicting quality commitment, but also how important work design factors are relative to demographic factors. The regression weights shown here give a different picture from the correlations. Although all five work design variables were significantly correlated with quality commitment (Table 11.5), only three of the five regression weights are significant. Interpreting how important each individual work design variable is on the basis of how strongly it correlates with quality commitment is clouded by the correlations among the work design variables themselves. The difference in interpretation between pairwise correlation analysis and multiple regression analysis in this example shows how important it is to consider variables together.

An example application of multiple regression analysis is shown in Example 11.2. It illustrates the basic elements of MRA, but also shows the value of a variant of MRA called **hierarchical regression** (see Table 11.4d) where predictors are entered sequentially in more than one block. Hierarchical regression allows the researcher to test hypotheses not just about the importance of individual predictors but also about variables entered into a model as groups. Table 11.6 (bottom row) shows that it is possible to compare the overall fit of one model to another with one or more predictor variables added. Each model has an R^2 value

TABLE 11.6 Hierarchical regression analysis for predicting quality commitment from demographic and work design variables

	Step 1	Step 2
Organization	.04	.02
Demographics		
Age	.30 **	.27 **
Gender	.14 **	.19 **
Company tenure	.01	χ.05
Work design		
Individual timing control		.07
Individual method control		.15 **
Monitoring demands		.12 **
Problem-solving demands		.00
Production responsibility		.10 **
Multiple R^2	.10	.18
Change in Multiple R^2	.10	.08
F-ratio for test of change in R^2	36.03 **	18.47 **

(ADAPTED FROM JACKSON, 2004) NOTE: ** p<0.01

and the same F-test that was used to assess each individual R^2 can be used to test the change in R^2 between models.

Figure 11.5 shows two versions of a hypothetical regression model for three observed variables. In both models, the variable PV1 is assumed to be a cause of PV2, shown by the single-headed arrow between them, and PV2 in turn is assumed to be a cause of DV. The difference between the models lies in how PV1 relates to DV: in (a) there is a direct path between the two, while in (b) there is no path and any causal influence of PV1 on DV would have to work through PV2. Such a causal influence would make PV2 a mediator between PV1 and DV, and the model is called a **mediational model**. Hierarchical regression analysis could be used to test the mediational model as follows. First, model (a) is tested using both PV1 and PV2 as predictors of DV. The multiple R^2 shows what proportion of the variance in DV is accounted for by both predictors. Second, model (b) is tested by dropping PV1 from the set of predictors of DV, and again multiple R^2 is calculated. The only difference between model (a) and model (b) is the removal of PV1, so the difference between the two values of R^2 shows whether PV1 is a significant predictor of DV and therefore the path between them in Figure 11.5(a) is necessary.

There are other forms of regression analysis, called **stepwise regression**, which involve an automatic process of adding or subtracting variables according to how well they contribute to predicting the dependent variable. However, they rely on a blind search among predictors in order to identify those that make the greatest contribution to predicting the dependent variable, and such methods rarely have a place in management research.

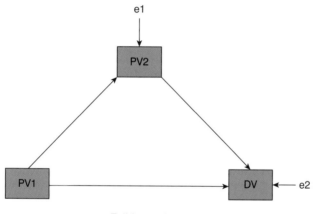

(a) Full form of the model

FIGURE 11.5
Hierarchical regression analysis for testing mediational effects

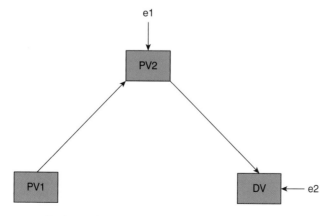

(b) Reduced form of the model with one path removed

Analysis of covariance (ANCOVA)

ANCOVA is the name given to a form of multiple regression analysis where some of the predictors are continuous variables and others are category variables. It is a generalization of the methods for assessing differences between groups that were considered in Chapter 10, which allows the researcher to include predictors measured on continuous scales (these are called the **covariates**). Conclusions based on hypothesis tests about group differences can be seriously misleading if groups differ on variables other than the dependent variable. **Analysis of covariance (ANCOVA)** adjusts the dependent variable scores to what they would have been had the treatment groups been equal on the covariate. ANCOVA achieves a statistical matching between treatment groups by adjusting groups' means on the DV to what they would have been had the groups scored the same on the covariates. The next class of methods that we consider are **multivariate analysis of variance** (MANOVA) and **multivariate analysis of covariance** (MANCOVA), and their characteristics are listed in column 2 of Table 11.4.

MANOVA/MANCOVA

These methods bring together a number of methods that we have already considered, generalized to the situation where the researcher is interested in assessing the predictability of more than one dependent variable. MANOVA is used for comparing groups that are classified on the basis of one or more category variables. MANCOVA is the multivariate generalization of ANCOVA, which includes one or more continuous variables as covariates as well as at least one category variable.

The practical problem addressed by this class of methods is that of interpreting the causal influences of predictors on dependent variables that are correlated among themselves. Taking correlated dependent variables singly can be misleading because each one carries not just information about the thing it measures but also something of what it shares with other dependent variables.

The quality of the model as a whole is shown by a multivariate test for the whole set of DVs taken together. There are several test statistics available, but the one most frequently used is called **Wilks' Lambda** (this varies between 0 and 1 and a small value is better), and an *F*-ratio tests the significance of Lambda. Having looked at each of the effects for the set of DVs taken together, the next step is to explore individual components of the model, and there are two options here. The first option is the **univariate *F*-test** and this is the same test as if the analysis had been performed for each DV separately, but with an adjustment in significance level made to take account of the number of dependent variables in the model. The univariate *F*-test thus ignores correlations among the DVs, and so its usefulness depends on how high those correlations are. Another option is a **stepdown *F*-test**, where the DVs are tested in a sequence decided upon by the researcher. In effect it is a form of analysis of covariance, which holds constant previous DVs. The first test is carried out ignoring the other DVs, the second test adjusts for the first DV and so on. Stepdown tests are preferable to univariate tests because they take into account the correlations among the DVs, but their value is dependent on whether the researcher can give a justifiable ordering of the dependent variables. While the results from the univariate tests will be the same regardless of which order the DVs are listed, this is not true of stepdown tests. Univariate tests and stepdown tests will only give the same answers when the DVs are completely uncorrelated with each other.

EXAMPLE
11.3

Worked example of MANOVA

This example uses the same data as Example 11.2 from a developmental study of employees' commitment to quality (Jackson, 2004). Earlier, we used gender and a number of work design characteristics as predictors of individuals' quality commitment, and this example tests the hypothesis that there are gender differences in work design. Table 11.5 shows that there are correlations among the work design variables, so it may be misleading to ignore these relationships by taking each variable alone. Table 11.7 gives the main results from MANOVA with gender as a category variable predictor and five work design characteristics as dependent variables.

TABLE 11.7   Results of multivariate analysis of variance: gender differences in five work design characteristics ($n = 967$)

	Male (n = 209)	Female (n = 758)	t-test
(a) Univariate tests for each variable separately			
Individual timing control	3.37	2.69	7.24 **
Individual method control	3.60	2.96	9.25 **
Monitoring demands	3.89	3.84	0.76
Problem-solving demands	3.37	2.89	7.16 **
Production responsibility	3.41	3.12	3.51 **
(b) Multivariate test for all variables together			
Wilks' Lambda = 0.87, F = 27.73 **			

NOTE: ** INDICATES SIGNIFICANT AT 0.01 LEVEL

The mean scores for males and females on each work design variable are shown in Table 11.7(a), together with the results of univariate t-tests (ignoring the correlations among the DVs). This shows that women report significantly lower scores on four out of the five work design characteristics: they have less control over work timing and methods; the problem-solving demands on them are lower; and their responsibility for production mistakes is lower. These results would suggest that women's jobs in this sample are more routine and undemanding than those of the men in the sample.

However, the individual tests ignore the fact that there are correlations among the work design variables, and the multivariate test of the gender effect is shown in Table 11.7(b). This shows the Wilks' Lambda coefficient and its associated significance test, an F-ratio. The null hypothesis being tested is that there is no gender difference in the set of DVs taken together, and this is rejected with a high level of confidence. There is clear evidence for a gender difference in work design in general, confirming what was observed for the analysis of the individual DVs.

Follow-up analyses could go in a number of directions, depending on the interests of the researcher. One direction would be to examine in more detail what job titles the men and women in this sample actually hold in order to determine whether men have higher-grade jobs in this sample or whether the observed effects reflect gender differences among people doing the same jobs. A different avenue to explore is whether there is a common factor underlying the work design variables (see the earlier section on measurement models), which might give a greater conceptual clarity to this analysis. Finally, we focused here on gender, but there may be other influential demographic differences between men and women, such as age or organizational tenure, which have been ignored. If so, any interpretation that focuses purely on gender would be misguided.

The final class of multivariate methods that we consider for causal analysis of observed variables is logistic regression analysis.

Logistic regression analysis

This addresses the same questions as multiple regression analysis, except that the DV is a dichotomous category variable rather than a continuous variable (Table 11.4, column 3). Like MRA, predictor variables may be continuous or category variables or any mix of the two. Examples of dependent variables that might be used in logistic regression analysis include: the presence or absence of a risk factor for stress; the success or failure of a merger; the survival or not of a joint venture partnership. The dependent variable in logistic regression analysis is based on an **odds ratio**, which expresses the relative likelihood of the two possible outcomes. For example, if 20 per cent of mergers in a dataset of companies succeed while 80 per cent do not, then the odds of success are 4:1 against (20 per cent/80 per cent). It is the log of these odds that is used as the DV in logistic regression:

$$\log p / (1-p)$$

where p is the probability of succeeding and $1-p$ is the probability of failing. The model is used to assess the independent contribution of several predictor variables to the prediction of these odds.

Because the DV in logistic regression is a complex function of the probability of being in one category rather than another, the method used to fit the model is different from that used in multiple regression. This method gives a different test statistic for the quality of the model as a whole, a **likelihood ratio chi-square**. Despite this difference from multiple regression, the significance test tells the same story: whether the set of predictors as a whole account for significant variation in the DV. The individual components of the model are also evaluated by their regression weights, and each is tested by comparing its size relative to the standard error. In logistic regression, the result is called a **Wald test**, but its meaning is the same as in multiple regression. A worked example of logistic regression analysis is shown in Example 11.4.

EXAMPLE
11.4

A worked example of logistic regression analysis

This example uses data from the study by Sprigg and Jackson (2006) of stress in call-centre staff. The DV is whether or not the respondent had experienced musculoskeletal disorder (MSD) caused by his or her work in the previous seven days (this includes back pain, aches in the wrist or shoulders etc.). Logistic regression is appropriate because the DV is a category variable with two levels. The two predictors that we focus on here are: workload, a continuous variable assessing aspects of the demands of the job; and scripting, a three-point ordered category variable assessing to what degree call handlers followed a strictly worded script when they answered calls. The sample size for this analysis was 836, and of these 520 (62 per cent) reported MSD in the previous seven days. MSDs are thus relatively common in this sample of call handlers. The odds in favour of MSD are 62 relative to 38, and the odds ratio is calculated as:

$$\text{Odds ratio} = p / (1 - p) = 0.622 / 0.378 = 1.65.$$

Logistic regression takes the log of this odds ratio as the DV, and the hypothesis being tested is whether the predictor variables either increase or decrease the risk of experiencing MSD while working as a call handler.

Table 11.8 shows the results of logistic regression. The quality of the model as a whole is shown by a chi-square test statistic, and its value is 5.46, with 2 degrees of freedom (because there are two predictors). This is statistically significant, so we conclude that the two predictors together do account for a difference in the relative risk of MSDs.

The separate contribution of each predictor variable is shown by the standardized regression weights (labelled as **beta weights** in Table 11.8), just as in multiple regression. The hypothesis that the beta weight is zero is tested by a Wald statistic rather than a *t*-value for testing significance, but otherwise the interpretation of the coefficients is the same as for multiple regression. Both beta weights are positive in sign and statistically significant, indicating that higher workload is associated with an increased risk of MSDs and more use of a set script is also associated with an increase in risk. These influences are independent, so that someone who has high workload *and* greater use of a set script will tend to experience greater risk of MSD than someone who is high on only one predictor.

TABLE 11.8 Results of logistic regression analysis for MSD as a function of workload and following a set script

Overall fit of the model: chi-square = 5.46 (df = 2), p <.01		
Variable	Beta weight	Wald statistic
Workload	.50**	29.90
Script	.28*	5.31

The options available to the researcher within logistic regression are exactly the same as for multiple regression analysis (see Table 11.4(d)). Predictor variables may be entered in a single block, or the researcher may have theoretical reasons for defining a sequence of models to be fitted hierarchically. Finally, stepwise logistic regression can be used to enter predictor variables purely on the basis of how well they predict the dependent variable. Just as for stepwise options in multiple regression analysis, we see limited scope for this within management research.

Analysis of observed and latent variables – structural equation modelling

Structural equation modelling (SEM) (Blunch, 2008; Hair et al., 2010; Tabachnick and Fidell, 2014) brings together the two kinds of multivariate methods that we have considered so far: **measurement models** for assessing hypotheses about relationships between observed and latent variables (Chapter 9), and **structural models** of the causal relationships among both observed and latent variables. As such, they provide within the same framework a way of expressing and estimating many of the different kinds of model that are used by management researchers. There are several statistical packages available for fitting structural equation models, and the best known are: LISREL (www.ssicentral.com), EQS (www.mvsoft.com), Mplus (www.statmodel.com) and AMOS (www-03.ibm.com/software/products/en/spss-amos). While the detailed characteristics differ among them, they all share the same underlying models and the graphical interface used to develop the model. AMOS has a reputation for being easier to use than the others, but the craft of SEM involves the same five steps whatever software is used (see Table 11.9).

The first step in SEM is to *define model hypotheses*, specifying what variables are included within the model (both measured and latent variables), and what the relationships are among them. Any model fitting procedure will use the relationships among the variables that are included to estimate the parameter in the hypothesized model. There is no substitute for careful consideration of which variables to include in a model: leave out something important and the model obtained can be seriously biased and misleading. Furthermore, the use of latent variable

TABLE 11.9   Steps in structural equation modelling

1   Define model hypotheses
2   Specify the model
3   Estimate model parameters
4   Evaluate the quality of the model
5   Consider alternative models

models places the responsibility onto the researcher to think carefully about what indicators to use for each latent variable and to ensure that they are measured reliably. The most sophisticated of statistical treatment cannot overcome the deficiencies introduced by sloppy thinking or poor measurement practice.

The second step in SEM is to *specify the model*, including either fixed or free parameters. Free parameters are those elements of the model whose values are to be estimated from data, while fixed parameters have a pre-defined value allocated to them (usually, but not always, zero). Fixed parameters are usually necessary to make a model identifiable, and they also give the basis for testing theoretical propositions by comparing different models where fixed parameters are set free. The full structural equation model has both measured variables and latent variables, and may also include causal relationships among the latent variables. The model in Figure 11.6 looks quite different from the ones considered so far in this chapter, but it is almost the same as the model in Figure 9.2. Both models have three kinds of variable: observed variables shown in rectangles, latent variables (we called these common factors earlier) and specific factors both shown in ellipses. Apart from a cosmetic change in layout, the only difference is that there is a causal arrow linking the two latent variables in the centre of the model.

The left-hand side shows the measurement model for the latent variable labelled as PV (see the earlier section of this chapter). This model hypothesizes that the PV is a common factor that accounts for the correlations among observed variables 1–3, while the specific factor associated with each of the observed variables captures all influences on observed variable scores which are specific to that variable. The right-hand side shows the equivalent measurement model for the DV. At the centre of the figure is the structural model showing the hypothesized causal link between the two latent variables.

Each of the arrows in the figure represents a path between two variables and also a parameter to be estimated from the data. For measurement models, these parameters are called **factor loadings**, while for causal models, they are called **regression weights** or **path coefficients**. Since (by definition) latent variables cannot be measured directly, the only information the researcher has about them comes from the observed variables. For a structural equation model, there are two kinds of parameter that need to be defined. The first is the covariance among the latent and observed variables. The second is the variance of each latent variable, so that its measurement scale is defined. The variance of an observed variable indicates the spread of scores around the mean on its measurement scale and thus defines the scale, and the same is true of the variance of a latent variable. However, the scale of a latent variable is unobservable and so it has to be defined in another way. One common option is to assume that the measurement scale of a latent variable is the same as that of one of its indicator variables (it does not matter which one), and another is to assume that the scale is a standardized one with a variance of one. For each parameter, the researcher can either define a fixed value for a parameter (as shown in the CFA example in Chapter 9) or estimate a value from data. The commonest fixed values are zero for paths between variables, and 1 for variances of latent variables.

The input to a model fitting procedure consists of:

- The variances of the observed variables, which define their measurement scale.

- The covariances among the observed variables.

If there are p observed variables, then the number of items of information available for model fitting is p variances and $p*(p-1)/2$ covariances. The model in Figure 11.6 contains six observed

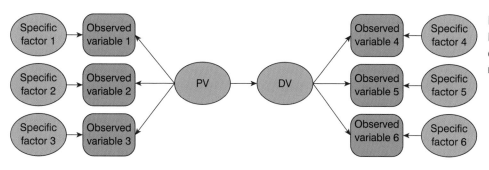

FIGURE 11.6
Full structural
equation
model

variables, so the number of items of information available is 6 + 6*5/2 = 21. There are three possibilities for the relationship between the number of parameters to be estimated and the information available to do it, and together they define the **identifiability** of a model:

1. *Just identified* – there are the same number of parameters to estimate and information available. A just-identified model will always fit the observed data perfectly. Unique values for the parameters of the model can be estimated and their significance tested, but the model is as complex as the original data.

2. *Under-identified* – there are more parameters to be estimated than information available to define unique values for them, and it is then impossible to fit a model.

3. *Over-identified* – there are fewer parameters to be estimated than items of information. Here, the fitted model is simpler than the original data, and it is possible to calculate a significance test for the model as a whole as well as unique values for the individual parameters.

The third step in SEM is to *estimate model parameters*. All the programs work broadly in the same way. First, starting values for model parameters are formed, and these are used to calculate the initial estimate of the population covariance matrix (Σ). The difference between this and the sample **covariance** matrix (S) is called the **residual** matrix. The initial parameters are modified, and a new Σ matrix is formed. This procedure is repeated until no further improvements in goodness of fit can be achieved. The logic of SEM is to find estimates of the parameters in the statistical model in order to produce a population covariance matrix that is a close fit to the covariance matrix from the sample data. A close fit indicates that the hypothesized model is a plausible way of describing the relationships within the sample data. The goal of SEM therefore is to achieve a good fit between hypothesized model and the data – shown by a small and non-significant index of goodness of fit.

A goodness of fit index is calculated based on the estimated population covariance matrix (Σ) and the sample covariance matrix (S). A common estimation method is called maximum likelihood, and the goodness of fit index that is minimized is called chi-square (χ^2). The value of χ^2 depends on a function of the S and Σ matrices and on the sample size. This means that large values of χ^2 reflect either poor model fit or a large sample size, or both. Studies with large samples (e.g. over 1,000 participants) will almost always show significant χ^2 values regardless of how good the fitted model is. As well as indices for the model as a whole, it is also important to look at the individual parameters within the model. A significance test for each parameter is reported by all of the programs, testing the null hypothesis that the population value of the parameter is zero.

The fourth step is to *assess the fit of a model*. The quality of the overall fit between a hypothesized model and the data can be assessed in a variety of ways; indeed, one version of AMOS has 24 different fit indices, and most published papers report three or four different indices (see Jaccard and Wan, 1996). They fall into three broad categories:

● *Discrepancy-based indices*. The commonest index is the chi-square value, which is reported by every SEM program. It indicates the goodness of fit between the observed covariance matrix from the data and the predicted covariance matrix from the hypothesized model. A small value of chi-square indicates a close fit between the two, and suggests that the hypothesized model is a good one. However, there are problems with the chi-square index since a large value need not mean that the model is poor because chi-square varies with sample size.

- *Relative fit compared to a null model.* As well as the hypothesized model, most of the SEM programs also fit a null model, which assumes that all the covariances among the observed variables are zero (this is often called the 'independence' model). A number of fit indices have been developed that adjust the chi-square value for a specific model according to how much better it is than the null model and also take into account the complexity of the model (the number of parameters needed to achieve fit). One of these is the non-normed fit index (NNFI), whose values can vary between 0 and 1, and a value above 0.95 is regarded as acceptable (Bentler and Dudgeon, 1996).

- *Relative fit adjusted for the complexity of the model.* Complex models will fit data better than simple models, and some indices assign a cost to this extra complexity; in other words, they reward **parsimony**. On these criteria a model that achieves a reasonable fit with few parameters is better than a model that gives a marginally better fit achieved at the cost of a large increase in complexity. One of these measures is **RMSEA** (the root mean squared error of approximation), which adjusts chi-square according to the degrees of freedom of the model and the sample size.

The fifth step in SEM after examining the fit of a particular model is to *consider alternative models*, and it is most unusual to fit only a single structural equation model to a set of data. Almost all SEM work involves modifying the model in some way, either to improve the fit of an initial model or to test hypotheses derived from theory. The logic of SEM is strictly confirmatory, since the method requires that the researcher define a set of observed and latent variables together with a hypothesized model for the relationships among them. However, many tests of theoretical propositions involve comparisons between models rather than fitting a single model. We have already considered two examples in this chapter. Example 11.1 presented three models of the impact of stakeholder relationship management on corporate financial performance. Testing these alternatives involves fitting a sequence of models. Similarly, mediational models (see earlier section) can most effectively be tested by comparing a model including direct paths with a model that fixes the value of all these paths to zero. Model comparison tests like these are done by chi-square difference tests, the difference in goodness of fit between two models, in exactly the same way that we have seen already in hierarchical regression.

However, most researchers find that their a priori model does not fit the data to an acceptable degree and so they often undertake an exploration of alternatives using **modification indices**. The **Lagrange multiplier (LM) test** corresponds to forward stepwise regression, and tests what would happen if each one of the fixed parameters in the model were to be set free. The second type of index is called the **Wald test** and this corresponds to backwards stepwise regression. It tests which parameters currently included in the model have a value so small that they could be dropped from the model. The logic behind these procedures is similar to that used in the stepwise options available in the methods for multivariate analysis of causal models among observed variables (e.g. multiple regression and logistic regression). They involve a search through fixed parameters to see what the effect would be if fixed parameters were allowed to be free.

For example, the CFA model in Figure 11.7 (repeated from Figure 9.2) has six free parameters representing the loading of each observed variable on a single latent common factor. However, there are also an additional seven fixed parameters, which are implied by the model in Figure 11.2. They are shown by dotted lines in Figure 11.7: six additional arrows linking observed and latent variables, and also a double-headed arrow between the two common factors indicating a correlation between them. There are even more implied fixed parameters, because the model also assumes that the specific factors to the left of the diagram are uncorrelated with each other. We have not drawn the double-headed arrows for those because it would complicate the diagram considerably.

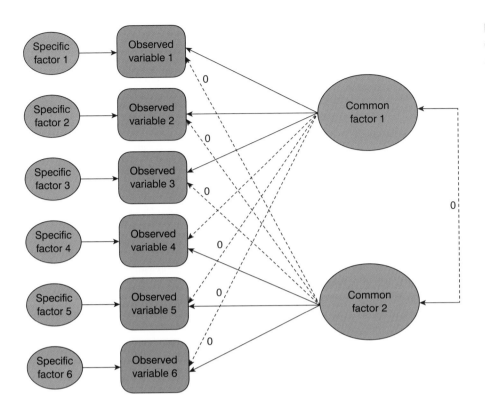

FIGURE 11.7
CFA model showing free parameters (solid lines) and fixed parameters (dotted lines)

If the hypothesized CFA model does not fit the data well, the researcher might decide that at least one of the items should load on both common factors, and thus relax the constraint of a fixed zero loading for that path. If this process is guided firmly by conceptual considerations, there could be a strong justification, but blind searching through multiple alternative models in the hope of finding one that is 'best' violates both the statistical requirements that underpin the SEM method and also the principles of sound research practice that we have described in this book. Theory development should be guided both by conceptual rigour and by the weight of evidence from data. Holding to theory regardless of what the data say is not good practice, but neither is blindly following data regardless of the theoretical justification.

Advanced features

The SEM area of statistics is developing rapidly, and each update of the programs adds features and options:

- New goodness of fit indices for assessing the quality of models.
- New estimation procedures for fitting the parameters in a hypothesized model.
- Additional methods for the preliminary assessment of data characteristics before fitting SEMs.
- New models; for example for analysing multiple groups, for longitudinal designs, for testing differences in the means of latent variables, for complex sampling designs.

Going further

Researchers interested in keeping up with developments in SEM can go to the software distributors' websites listed at the start of this section. There is also the journal *Structural Equation Modeling* published by Taylor and Francis, but be aware that the articles here tend to be quite technical.

CONCLUSION

This chapter has introduced a number of methods for analysing the complexity of the world of business and management using quantitative data:

 Methods for working with complex concepts which often cannot be measured directly but have to be inferred from observed variables.

 Conceptual introduction to ways of modelling causal relationships among both observed and latent variables, particularly using structural equation models.

The most important point that we would like to make is that the process of multivariate model fitting must be guided firmly by conceptual considerations. Fitting statistical models to quantitative data is not an automated process of blindly finding the 'best' model. Good-quality models are grounded both in rigorous conceptualization guided by existing literature as well as in an evidence base of data collected according to sound design and measurement principles.

FURTHER READING

Atinc, G., Simmering, M.J. and Kroll, M.J. (2011) 'Control variable use and reporting in macro and micro management research', *Organizational Research Methods*, 15, 57–74.
Helpful discussion on the use of control variables in management research.

Blunch, N.J. (2008) *Introduction to Structural Equation Modelling Using SPSS and AMOS*. London: Sage.
This is a readable book, which introduces both SEM and the key concepts underlying measurement models (such as reliability). The examples are based on the AMOS package, which is now an add-on to SPSS, but could easily be adapted for use with other software.

Hair, J.F., Black, B., Babin, B., Anderson, R.E. and Tatham, R.L. (2010) *Multivariate Data Analysis*, 7th edn. Upper Saddle River, NJ: Prentice Hall.
This is an excellent book on the use of multivariate methods in social science. The strength of the book is the applications it uses as illustration of the methods covered, and the focus on preparatory work to examine the properties of the data first before embarking on complex multivariate analysis. Again, see also Field listed at the end of the previous chapter.

Kaplan, D. (2004) *The SAGE Handbook of Quantitative Methodology for the Social Sciences*. Thousand Oaks, CA: Sage.
Collection of chapters covering a wide range of quantitative methods for an advanced readership.

McWilliams, A. and Siegel, D. (1997) 'Event studies in management research: theoretical and empirical issues', *Academy of Management Journal*, 40, 626–57.
Examination of a range of event studies in management research.

Tabachnick, B.G. and Fidell, L.S. (2014) *Using Multivariate Statistics*, 6th edn. Boston, MA: Pearson Education.
This too is an excellent and thorough text on multivariate statistical methods for social science researchers. Its approach is practical rather than theoretical, and the authors cover all of the methods described in this chapter as well as others not covered here. For each method, they give its rationale, practical guidelines about how to use it, worked examples using a variety of statistical packages, and show how to present the results of analysis.

Want to know more about this chapter? Visit the ⓈSAGE edge™ website at **https://edge.sagepub.com/easterbysmith** to access practice questions, selected journal articles, useful web links and much more.

WRITING MANAGEMENT AND BUSINESS RESEARCH

12

LEARNING OBJECTIVES

 To develop personal strategies for writing.

 To appreciate different structures for writing.

 To recognize the needs and interests of different audiences.

 To develop awareness of the requirements of different forms of output.

 To develop skills in publishing and disseminating research.

The skills of writing

The content of reports and dissertations

Writing up the literature review

Outputs and evaluation

Dissemination strategies

Conclusion

Further reading

This book has examined the various ways of designing and conducting research: it has looked at how to choose and use the methods that will provide the relevant data; it has considered how to analyse, interpret and use data; and it has offered insights into the political and ethical sides of doing research. This last chapter, then, focuses on how to write up research findings, and how and where to disseminate research.

There are many potential audiences, including tutors, clients, academics, policy-makers and the general public, and these audiences correspond roughly to the stakeholders that we discussed in Chapter 5. However, as there are many ways of effecting dissemination, we think it is important to consider communication early in the research process, preferably at the design stage. Although the written word dominates in the form of reports, articles and books, there are other important ways of getting the message across, including presentations, videos and media interviews. A dissemination strategy, therefore, may include the use of different media at different points of time during the research, and after it has been completed.

We start the chapter with writing, and argue that there are generic skills that apply to any context. Second, we look at different forms of output, concentrating on how evaluative criteria vary, and discuss the stylistic differences between, for example, positivist and constructionist forms of research. Third, we provide guidance on the main elements of a report or dissertation, including literature reviews. Fourth, we consider different audiences and the media available for communication. Fifth, we look at the thorny subject of plagiarism, explaining the different forms that it can take, and providing advice on how to ensure that you won't be accused of plagiarism. Finally, we draw the threads together by looking at dissemination strategies.

THE SKILLS OF WRITING

The main aim in writing about research is to communicate with an audience, and to persuade them that the research is serious, important and believable. This means that it is important to be clear about the potential *readership* to which the paper or report is aimed. One technique used by a number of successful authors is to hold two or three 'typical' readers in mind while writing something. Gerry Johnson, the lead author of a best-selling book on corporate strategy (Johnson et al., 2008), writes his books with two imaginary individuals in mind: a lecturer at Kingston University called Theresa, and a third-year student called Charles who is bright but more interested in rugby than his studies. These imaginary people help him to focus on the potential readership and also to communicate with co-authors about the appropriateness of new material in new editions (personal communication).

A second point is that readers will be more interested in the document if it relates to their ongoing concerns, and this is where Huff (1999) stresses the importance of trying to link into an existing 'conversation'. So it is important to start a journal article with a summary of the main debate that has appeared up to that point, and upon which the current paper intends to build. Here the researcher needs to be aware of who are the main contributors in the field. Similarly, when writing a client report it is important to start with a brief statement of how the client has articulated the problem.

Third, in order to increase the credibility of the research there are a number of rhetorical strategies that may be used in written accounts. Positivist authors often write in the third person so that the researcher seems distanced from the research, and this gives an impression of greater objectivity; they may cite papers by famous authors in order to give credibility to the present research; and present the research as a linear process that was designed in advance and executed precisely to plan. However, constructionist authors often go to great lengths to be reflexive, indicating their engagement with the research setting and their influence on the research material; they often write up the research as it actually happened, indicating the problems that they encountered along the way, and how they tackled (sometimes heroically) these problems.

Writing as a habit

Woody Allen, the American comedian, director and author, has remarked that 90 per cent of the success in writing lies in getting started and finished on time, and the bit in the middle is easy. There is a key implication: don't wait until the end before starting to write. Get into the writing habit from the beginning, and sustain it throughout the research. Normally, reviews of the literature and research designs should be written up in the early stages of the research and 'banked' for later use. Of course they will have to be edited and rewritten later on, but they provide critical foundations upon which other parts can build. This ability to edit material is one of the joys of computers – which were not available when the authors of this book wrote their doctoral theses in longhand!

Most people experience writing blocks at some stage or another: the blank page can be exhilarating or intimidating. Many different strategies can be adopted to overcome writing blocks. The American author John Steinbeck (1970) adopted an interesting strategy when writing *East of Eden*. He always began his daily sessions by writing a letter to his editor about what he planned to say that day. The letters were written on the left-hand pages of a large note book (and not sent); on the right-hand pages he wrote the text of the book. He found this a useful way of starting his thought processes, and overcoming his own writing block.

Various academic authors offer advice on how to get into the flow of writing, including creating sufficient time and space for writing, setting modest goals on a daily basis and providing rewards for oneself, such as coffee breaks or Liquorice Allsorts after the next paragraph or section is completed (Saunders et al., 2009). Murray and Moore (2006) emphasize the need to take time out from writing for exercise or social activities: it is fine if the writing is flowing, but if not, take a break and do something completely different for an hour or so.

Developing structures

It is also important to develop an appropriate structure for the report or thesis, which can be done in a number of ways. First, an *emergent* structure comes from writing anything in order to get started, and once you have worked out what you are trying to say, deleting the initial paragraphs that may be a lot of rubbish. A *patchwork* structure comes from writing self-contained chunks of text and then starting to stitch them together into a coherent narrative. A *planned* structure involves trying to work out all the main sections and paragraphs in advance.

A good way of starting the planning process is to develop a 'mind-map'. This has the advantage that no commitments to linearity are required – one can simply type in ideas and then experiment to see how they group together. We used this in an early plan for this chapter (see Figure 12.1).

Mind-maps can help groups of researchers share their sense-making of research data, and they are also useful for authors when planning books and reports. But there is a limit to the amount of information that can be displayed on one page, and so it is generally best to move to PowerPoint in order to work out the details of a report. Figure 12.2 shows a PowerPoint slide that provides the overall structure for the current chapter. The first slide summarizes the main subheadings, and then later slides (not shown) provide further detail on each of the sections.

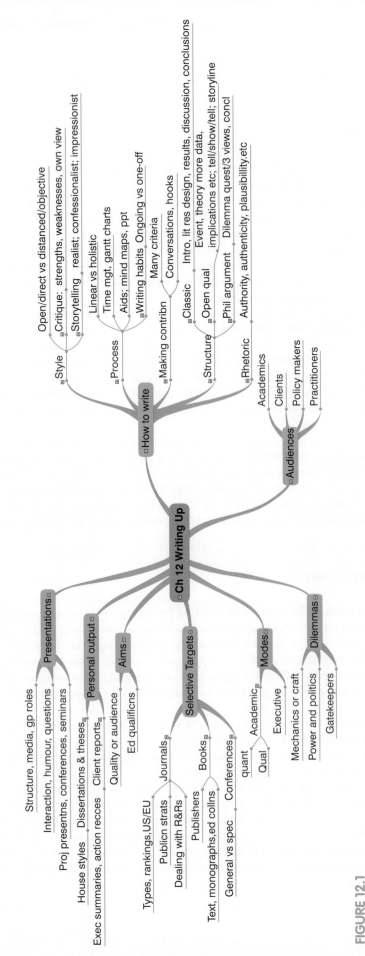

FIGURE 12.1

Early mind-map for writing Chapter 12

Chapter 11 – Writing up

- Introduction
- The skills of writing
    - Getting into the habit
    - Developing structures
    - Positivist and constructionist styles
    - Client reports

- The content of reports and dissertations
    - Starting and finishing
    - The middle bits

- Writing up the literature review
    - Structures
    - Styles
    - Conclusions of literature reviews

- Outputs and evaluation
    - Unpublished outputs
    - Conferences, journals and books

- Dissemination strategies
- Conclusions

FIGURE 12.2
PowerPoint outline of Chapter 12

It should be noted that this PowerPoint screen performs an intermediate stage between the mind-map and the final version of the chapter, because once we started to write we realized that we needed to make some further changes both to the subheadings and the content in order to make the argument flow. This flexibility is important; it is also a good way of communicating when you are trying to write with other people.

Generic structures for writing papers and research reports

Although research papers and reports conducted under different traditions may look quite different, there is much consistency in the basic issues and topics that they need to cover. The main differences come in the style and language used. In Table 12.1, we have therefore summarized the main questions that need to be answered in academic research in column 1. In the other two columns we summarize the way each of these questions gets operationalized, respectively in positivist or constructionist research reports.

As can be seen, there is much similarity in the earlier and later parts; the main differences come in the articulation of the central research questions and in the handling of data. Although most positivist studies follow the list of subheadings in column 2, there is often more flexibility in how qualitative reports and client reports are presented, especially in the presentation of qualitative data. In this case there is an opportunity for the researcher to exercise some creativity depending on the needs of the situation, the actual research and the audience. Hence we provide further comment below on ways of presenting qualitative data.

Where the research makes deliberate use of mixed methods, the normal solution is to structure the outer parts of the report according to whichever method is dominant, and then to present the data in two separate sections. Alternatively, where qualitative data is used to explain *why* various quantitative results are obtained, then it may be appropriate to present some qualitative data in relation to each of the quantitative hypotheses. However, as we said in Chapter 4, it is important to articulate in the research design/methodology section how the qualitative and quantitative data are supposed to be supporting each other.

TABLE 12.1   Typical report structures

Principle	Positivist Research	Constructionist Research
What is the research about?	Abstract.	Abstract.
What is already known?	Review of literature and previous studies.	Review of literature and relevant theories.
What is new about this study?	Statement of aims and hypotheses.	Identify the gap or research question(s).
How was the research done?	Description of procedures, samples and methods used.	Research design and methods.
What did it find out?	Data tables and summary of results.	Descriptions of data and interpretations.
What are the implications?	How far the hypotheses are supported.	How the data adds to existing theory.
Next steps?	Limitations and suggestions for future research.	Limitations and suggestions for future research.
Addenda	References, questionnaires, etc.	References, sample transcripts and analytic process.

Client reports

Reports of projects conducted for clients usually have a different structure to the more academic reports and dissertations. Essentially, these need to be shorter, with more emphasis on the identification of the problem and the practical courses of action to be taken. There needs to be some explanation of methodology because this has a bearing on the quality of evidence underpinning the recommendations, but there is much less need for a literature review, which might be restricted to half a dozen references that have informed both the focus and methods of the study. In Table 12.2 we summarize the elements that will typically feature in a client report.

TABLE 12.2   Generic structure for a client report

Sections of Client Report	Contents
Executive Summary	Aims, conclusions and recommendations.
Introduction	What is the problem, and what are the potential solutions? How will this study help?
Methodology	What data was gathered, and from what sources?
Results	Tabulations and presentation of data.
Discussion and Conclusions	Using the results to evaluate alternative actions.
Recommendations	List of practical recommendations.
Appendices	References and background data.

THE CONTENT OF REPORTS AND DISSERTATIONS

Following Woody Allen's comment, we will begin with 'starting and finishing', and then move on to discuss how to craft the middle bits of research reports.

Starting and finishing

Most experienced writers and editors agree that the start and end of a report or article are crucial. Reviewers, examiners and editors often form provisional judgements by reading the first and last pages, on the assumption that if the authors are able to communicate their message clearly in the first page, the rest of the document will be of similar quality; but if the initial page is unclear or confusing, this bodes badly for the rest of the document.

Locke and Golden-Biddle (1997) provide a very interesting analysis of the way successful academic authors structure their introductory paragraphs. They conducted an analysis of 82 papers that had appeared in two leading journals (*Academy of Management* and *Administrative Science Quarterly*) over the 20 preceding years and identified two factors that were always present. First, the authors provided a coherent overview of the previous literature using one of three strategies: they either produced *progressive coherence*, showing how concepts and literature developed cumulatively over time; or *synthesized coherence*, where they identify links between streams of research or theory that have not been spotted before; or *non-coherence*, where the field is characterized by arguments, debates and general fragmentation. Second, authors try to identify a new niche that demonstrates how they can add to previous research. Again, three methods appeared to be most commonly used, either through introducing new data, or new theory or new research methods.

In Table 12.3 we show the frequency with which different strategies were adopted in the 82 papers. As can be seen, the most common way of developing a new niche was to claim that new theory was being introduced, and the least common way was through introducing new methods. Progressive coherence was the most common way of characterizing past research, and this was most likely to be linked to the introduction of new theory.

TABLE 12.3 Academic introductions (after Locke and Golden-Biddle, 1997)

		Finding the new niche		
		New data	New theory	New methods
	Progressive coherence	13	18	3
Past research	Synthesized coherence	11	11	3
	Non-coherence	6	13	2

It is possible to summarize the four key elements that need to be in the introduction of an academic paper as follows:

1. Establish the *theoretical field* and why this particular topic is important.
2. Summarize previous research.
3. Identify the *niche*. What is the problem/question that is to be addressed?
4. State what the present study will *contribute* to this problem/question, and how it is tackled in this paper.

Exercise 12.1 provides an opportunity to test out skills in writing a credible academic introduction. This can be done either individually or as a small group exercise.

EXERCISE 12.1

Writing academic introductions

The following text was written on the back of a bottle of pesto.[1] Try to rewrite this piece of text as if it is the introduction of an academic article. You will have to use your imagination with regard to references. Use the four key elements listed above as the basic structure, and limit the introduction to a maximum of two paragraphs. Think about how you are going to characterize the past research and establish your niche using the categories in Table 12.3. Add a title that in your view encapsulates the essence of the paper. Present the finished product on a flip chart or computer projector for critique by tutors and colleagues.

> "Pesto is a mainstay of Italian cooking, yet surprisingly it is little known in the UK. The inviting ease with which *Sainsbury's Pesto* can be used belies the difficulty with which it is made. The fresh basil that gives the sauce its distinctive colour and flavour is by far the most troublesome ingredient.
>
> It occupies some of the most desirable real estate in Europe: the Ligurian hills that frame the Italian Riviera. Here, a unique mix of soil and sea breezes infuse the herb with an aroma and texture unmatched in any other part of Italy. Throughout June and July the farmers brave the summer sun to survey the maturing crop. They wander from bush to bush, sniffing and chewing the young leaves until the day they are deemed to be perfect. Then, to ensure that the leaves are harvested at their aromatic peak, the whole crop is picked within the space of a few days."

In Exercise 12.1 we suggested writing a title that captured the essence of the paper. Good titles are short and memorable. In academic work it is very common to write a title in two parts, separated by a colon. The first part summarizes the topic of the research, and the second part indicates the argument that the paper is taking, or the question that it is addressing. Sample titles for the example in Exercise 12.1 might be: 'The marketing of exotic foods: the role of image and metaphor' or 'The globalization of food products: can local production methods survive?' Once you have a good title the rest should be easy! Conversely, lengthy and convoluted titles usually indicate that the author is unclear about the central topic and main message of his or her document. Given the importance of the title we would recommend developing a provisional title very early in the writing process. This should evolve as the work develops, but at any point in time it provides a point of reference against which to check the coherence of what has already been written.

Then we have the conclusions. As we have indicated in Table 12.1, the precise form of the conclusions may vary with different kinds of work: essentially they need to summarize the nature of the research, the main findings or contributions, provide an indication of the limitations of the work, and make suggestions for future research directions. Once again, they need to be clear and reasonably succinct (three or four paragraphs is enough for an academic paper, and 10 to 12 pages is enough for a doctoral thesis).

The middle bits

One recurrent dilemma with constructionist studies is about how to achieve a balance between qualitative data in the form of quotations, and discussions of the theoretical

---

[1]Thanks to Nickie Hedge for drawing our attention to this example.

implications. Golden-Biddle and Locke (2007) suggest different strategies for combining data and theory. They distinguish between 'showing' the data/evidence and 'telling' what it means. Although some authors might be tempted to show large amounts of data, there is a limit to how far it will hold the attention of the reader without being put into the context of the wider narrative. Consequently one of the preferred strategies is to start with a theoretical point, then illustrate it with a quote, and then explain further what it all means (tell-show-tell). Another way of grabbing the imagination of readers is to provide a sneak preview of the data right at the start of the paper followed by setting the theoretical context, and then adding more sections of quotations and discussions (show-tell-show-tell).

WRITING UP THE LITERATURE REVIEW

Literature reviews have many features in common with other forms of writing, plus some features that are distinct, and hence there is some justification for considering the writing of literature reviews as the distinct art. In this section we cover five features of literature reviews that are often regarded as problematic: selection of material; different ways of structuring literature reviews; styles of presenting literature; the issue of criticality; and the endpoint of a literature review. In doing this we also build from Chapter 2 on conducting literature reviews.

Selection of source material

In most topics the quantity of existing literature is almost limitless, and the problem for the researcher is to decide which bits to include and which bits to leave out. We have two main criteria that can determine the selection of literature for the review: importance and relevance. By *importance*, we mean the extent to which a particular book or article is regarded as central to the particular field on which you are working. A quick search on Google Scholar, using the title or central topic of your work as the search item, will normally yield a list of the key books and some of the main articles that have been cited by others. Similarly, searches through ISI Web of Science using the same search terms will yield the primary journal articles that have addressed the topic. Since these indexes accumulate over time, the books and articles that come to the top of the list will be the older, classical, works. A few of these will have to be mentioned, but not too many because they will not take account of more recent developments in the field.

For example, a search within Google Scholar using the term 'absorptive capacity' leads immediately to the most influential paper in this field and written by Cohen and Levinthal (1990). This one paper had 23,910 citations, at the time of writing this sentence (7 December 2014) which is over 4 times as many as the next most cited paper. So the work of Cohen and Levinthal would need to be mentioned in any literature review of absorptive capacity, perhaps with a few other foundational works on the subject. But the issue of whom else to include depends very much on the *relevance* to the line of argument that you are trying to develop in your work. If you consider that the foundational works on absorptive capacity pay too little attention to the inner processes of knowledge absorption and transformation, then you would need to continue through the work of Zahra and George (2002) and Todorova and Durisin (2007), and then follow up on more recent work that has cited these authors.

There is always a dilemma in deciding how many sources to quote in a literature review, and this partly depends on the depth versus breadth of coverage decision. In general, dissertations and theses need to contain a wide coverage of literature. This helps you to demonstrate to tutors and examiners that you are fully aware of the breadth and range of the field, and the more focused coverage comes towards the latter end of the review. If you are seeking to publish an article in a journal, then it is less important to demonstrate that you know everything about the field, because a general level of familiarity will normally be assumed by the reader, and unless you have anything especially new to say about the traditional literature it is likely that it will be seen as boring to have to wade through material that is familiar to everybody.

Structures

Structures refer to the way that you decide to marshal your literature, and the logic behind different ways of grouping the material. Although the framework of Locke and Golden-Biddle (1997) was derived from analysis of how the literature was presented in academic papers, the principles are still relevant to literature reviews conducted in dissertations. The idea of progressive coherence implies that literature should be organized within a timeline in order to demonstrate how the particular field evolved chronologically. Within the overall timeline there may be additional structures, such as characterizing different periods of time (e.g. decades) or organizing discussion of the literature around a few key works or turning points.

With synthesized coherence you may try to demonstrate how two or three different perspectives on the subject may be combined because they are able to make up for the weaknesses of each other. However, non-coherence is most often associated with broad mapping exercises, which show, for example, that different disciplines have tackled a particular topic without demonstrating much awareness of what each other has been doing.

EXAMPLE 12.1

Structuring the Literature Review

Stephen Allen was reviewing the literature on sustainability for his PhD. He identified seven main bodies of literature that had tackled the topic of sustainability, and which he characterized as follows: history; engineering; social movements; philosophy; economics; corporate social responsibility; and natural science (including ecology and botany). Since these were rooted in distinct disciplines with their own languages and internal debates, which paid minimal attention to writings in the other disciplines, this represented the literature as being non-coherent. He therefore decided to structure his review around the concepts of complexity, production of knowledge and scale – which enabled him to cut across the seven disciplinary areas.

Styles

With regard to style, there are still a few dilemmas, but there is a reasonable amount of agreement between authors and experts regarding what is desirable or less desirable in the writing of a literature review (see Table 12.4). First, it is important to avoid producing an 'annotated bibliography'. This usually takes the form of a series of paragraphs each of which starts with the names of the authors of the works cited, then summarizes the main points made by those authors, possibly with a brief critique of what they have said. Then in the next paragraph another author is introduced, and so on. The problem here is that there is rarely any clear linkage between successive paragraphs, and it is very difficult for the readers to identify the thread or argument that the author might be wishing to make. This is where a thematic structure to the literature review is preferable because it enables the links and relationships between the contributions to be identified.

Second, the references cited in the text need to be selected on the grounds of relevance. In other words, each reference needs to make a distinct contribution to the general argument. It is generally best for authors/references to be mentioned in the middle of sentences, rather than being added at the end of a sentence to provide 'decoration' and an air of authority over what has just been said. In particular, when trying to develop an argument, it adds precision if you indicate the page numbers of the book or article where the particular elements of the argument are being made.

Third, and especially with constructionist research, we think it is important for the *author's voice* to be heard. In general it is better to summarize what you think other writers are saying, rather than simply dropping quotations from these writers into your text. There is no problem with the occasional quote, if it is central to your argument, but there is a danger if there are lots of short quotes from other authors that the review will seem like a patchwork quilt. There is also a dilemma here between depth and breadth. A good literature review will contain some of both. In other words, it will pay considerable attention to the more important and relevant works, but it will also demonstrate a reasonable awareness of related literature. Thus in a journal article one might expect to see five or six major pieces of work discussed in some depth, but with brief reference made perhaps to 50 or 60 other pieces of work. Of course, in longer documents such as dissertations or theses these numbers could be doubled or tripled.

Being critical

The literature review needs to demonstrate *criticality*. This does not mean being negative about everything that has previously been written. Far from it. It means demonstrating discernment about what is good and bad about the previous literature, and explaining why you have reached these judgements. This is where the voice of you, the author, is particularly important. One dilemma with regard to critical literature reviews is where the critique should be placed within the overall structure. For example, if you have divided your topic into five major themes, then it might make sense to summarize the views and contributions of the main contributors to each theme, and then provide a critique at the end. But if there are major works contained within that overall theme, it may be better to interleave summaries of each work, with the main critiques produced by other people of that work, and then give your own view.

TABLE 12.4   Stylistic features in literature reviews

Stylistic Features	Incorporate	Avoid
Framework for literature review	Thematic structure; progressive coherence.	Annotated bibliography; no links between paragraphs.
Selection of references	Clear relevance; functional; focused on argument development.	Decorative use; long strings that are vaguely linked.
Voice	Focus on key works; paraphrase others' arguments.	Patchwork of quotes from other authors.
Criticality	Explain what you like/dislike about other authors' work; build on others' critiques.	Sweeping dismissal of others' work.

Conclusions of literature reviews

Sometimes, when a student or author gets to the end of the literature, they are often so exhausted, or short of time, that they simply present material and then move on to the next chapter. But the whole point of the literature review, other than demonstrating that you have in-depth knowledge of the field you are investigating, is to provide a platform for the work that is yet to come within the research project. This normally requires two elements. First, there needs to be a summary of the main features and arguments covered in the literature review, which may take the form of a diagram, a model, a table, a set of propositions, or hypotheses. Second, it is essential to identify some sort of gap, or weakness, or limitation in the previous work, which provides a justification for the work that you will be describing in the following chapters.

OUTPUTS AND EVALUATION

What, then, are the different forms of output that can be generated by research, and how may they be evaluated? To some extent, the answer builds upon the discussion of political issues in Chapter 5. Here we can distinguish two main types of output: *unpublished outputs*, such as reports and dissertations, which are generally targeted at a very small number of people such as clients and examiners; and *published outputs*, such as articles and books, which are intended to be widely disseminated.

Unpublished outputs: reports, dissertations and theses

Reports and dissertations are initially aimed at a small number of people, and although some may eventually get published, this is the exception rather than the rule. The immediate audience are often involved in the evaluation of the work (possibly supplemented by a presentation), and this will result in the award of grades and educational qualifications. We will start with research reports, and then discuss dissertations and theses.

Client reports

Projects are increasingly being incorporated into undergraduate and postgraduate degree schemes where small groups of students tackle a real problem located in a company or other organization. Normally a senior manager will act as the client and will make arrangements or appropriate access to people and documents. Since the client project is being conducted as part of an educational qualification, those working on the project will face two different kinds of evaluation: first, they must come up with results or recommendations that satisfy the client; and second, they must produce a written document that satisfies the academic tutors and examiners.

The written output from the project can seek to resolve the potential tension of expectations in three ways: (a) as a single report for the client, which has sufficient elements of reflection and critical thought to pass academic muster; (b) as a distinct consultancy report, which can be sandwiched within a more academic commentary that reflects on choices made, evaluates experiences, and develops relevant theoretical insights; or (c) as two completely separate documents tailored to the distinct needs of the client and the academic assessors. The first two options are pedagogically appealing, since they require integration between academic and practical discourse; they are more feasible nowadays since a growing proportion of 'clients' are former students of business and management courses, and therefore have a greater understanding of the mutual contribution of theory and practice. Nevertheless, the third option is increasingly appealing since it provides greater clarity for students uncomfortable with ambiguous evaluation criteria.

Funded research projects

Funded research projects are normally carried out by small teams of established academics working with research associates employed on fixed-term contracts. All of these projects require full reports at the end, which describe the conduct of the research, any problems encountered in doing it, and give an overview of the theoretical and practical contributions provided by the project. Research reports are sent out to external referees with expertise in the area of the project for evaluation, and who will be expected to comment on the degree to which the project achieved its original objectives, whether any departures from the original proposal have been adequately justified, and the quality of the public academic output. In general the academic output needs to include conference papers, journal papers (at least under submission), and perhaps an edited book.

Dissertations

For BBA and Masters' courses the required dissertations are often longer than research reports (perhaps 10,000 to 20,000 words), and are the product of individual rather than group efforts. In most cases they are written solely for academic evaluation, and therefore do not have the potentially competing objectives of project reports. In general it is worth following the suggested report structure in Table 12.1, although there is less of a requirement to demonstrate theoretical contribution than in the case of a doctoral thesis (see below). Evaluative criteria will depend both on the nature of the dissertation and on the formal expectations of tutors and examiners. A general guide to criteria is given in Table 12.5, which summarizes seven features that should normally be present in a good dissertation. The list is based on Bloom's *Taxonomy of Educational Objectives* (Bloom and Krathwohl, 1956) and is organized hierarchically in terms of the increasing complexity of each feature. Thus, demonstrating knowledge of the field and comprehension of the problem to be addressed are relatively basic elements; the evaluation of literature and ideas and clear argumentation are regarded as more complex processes, which will therefore gather more brownie points when the dissertation is being evaluated.

There is some uncertainty at the moment about whether it is more important for management dissertations to demonstrate evidence of application or analysis. As we noted in Chapter 1, there is a long-standing debate in the UK about whether management education should emphasize practical or academic training (Whitley et al., 1981), and this has translated into the debate between mode 1 and mode 2 forms of research (Tranfield and Starkey, 1998; Huff, 2000). The rise of the MBA puts greater emphasis on practical relevance and application, while academics are likely to value the analytic and evaluative elements of the dissertation. Since most degrees are awarded by academics, it is prudent to include some elements of analysis and synthesis in the work submitted.

Doctoral theses

Doctoral theses are similar to Masters' dissertations in that they require a synthesis of ideas and data. In addition they must provide critical evaluation of relevant work, and demonstrate some kind of original *contribution* to the field. This contribution can be provided in three main forms: as new knowledge about the world of management (**substantive contribution**), as new theories and ideas (**theoretical contribution**), or as new methods of investigation (**methodological contribution**). In each case the contribution needs to be stated explicitly in the conclusions, and there also needs to be a clear link back to the early part of the thesis where the existing theories and methods were reviewed and evaluated. The theoretical contribution is most important, although it may be supplemented by each of the others.

The final award of a doctorate depends on the judgement of independent examiners (though practice in this respect varies surprisingly widely across Europe and North America), and it is very important that the right choices are made. Not only do the examiners need to be conversant with the field of study, but they should also be sympathetic to the worldview and methodology of the researcher. In this context it is worth developing a provisional list of examiners early on in the period of study, which gets refined and updated as the theoretical and empirical work develops. If the candidate has done sufficient networking through conferences and learned societies (such as the British Academy of Management or the US-based Academy of Management), he or she should be clear about who the best examiners would be.

TABLE 12.5 Hierarchy of evaluative elements

7) Quality of argumentation

6) Evaluation of concepts

5) Synthesis of ideas and concepts

4) Analysis of data and evidence

3) Application of theories/ideas to practise

2) Comprehension of the problem addressed

1) Knowledge of the field

Published outputs: conferences, journals and books

Nowadays it is essential for aspiring academics to get their research into the public domain. It is advisable to attempt publication from doctoral research while the work is being conducted, and occasionally it is possible to publish results from Masters' dissertations. In each of these cases the evaluation takes place before the final copy of the work is produced, and this acts as a filter on the quality of work that appears in public. In general, it is easier to get a paper accepted for a conference than for a journal, although significant hierarchies exist within both categories. Hence many researchers will take an incremental approach, submitting the results of their work to a conference, and then on the basis of feedback rewriting the paper and submitting it to a journal.

With some conferences it is possible to submit extended abstracts, which are evaluated by two or three referees, and the feedback from the referees can be incorporated into the paper before the conference takes place. Other conferences, such as the Academy of Management, will only accept submission of full papers, but in these cases the feedback from referees can be more focused, and this can be combined with discussion and feedback at the conference itself in helping the authors revise the paper for submission to a journal. As we have mentioned earlier, participation at conferences is very important for publishing contacts and building up research networks. However, conference papers per se have limited value for academics wishing to build up their careers or to gain tenure. The 'gold standard' is acceptance of papers in academic journals, and preferably the more highly rated ones.

Sometimes edited books and special issues of journals are initiated at conferences, and the conference organizers often take on the editorial roles for these publications. Although peer review is normally used to support decisions, one of the easiest ways of getting included in such publications is to offer to co-edit the proceedings. You too can become a gatekeeper! But this is by no means the end of the road, because conference proceedings and book chapters only achieve modest ratings in the increasingly hierarchical world of academic publishing. The gold standard is the academic journal, and this is where some of the strictest hierarchies operate.

There are very clear hierarchies in the reputation of different journals. Most countries have their own journal ranking systems,[2] and internationally the ISI Impact Factor and the *Financial Times* (FT) list are the most widely recognized indicators of quality. There are a number of factors that help to sustain the position of the top journals: they get large

---

[2]The dominant system in the UK is provided by the Association of Business Schools (the ABS List). It rates over 2,000 journals from 1 up to 4*, and the list is updated biennially in April.

numbers of submissions and are therefore able to be very selective; people will usually only submit their very best work to the top journals; and the reviewing process is conducted with such rigour that the finally published paper is often significantly better than the initial submission. There are two simple ways of judging in advance the standing of an academic journal. First, submission and rejection rates indicate how much demand there is to get into the journal. Top journals will have rejection rates of over 95 per cent, lesser journals may be around 50 per cent. Journals that take almost everything will not be considered as serious journals (but then they are unlikely to publish their rejection rates). Second, the citation index *ISI* **Web of Knowledge** produces annual rankings of journals based on the frequency with which papers from a given journal are cited by papers published in other respectable journals (see http://wok.mimas.ac.uk/). These rankings use 'impact factor' as the key criterion. This is calculated as the number of citations appearing in *ISI* journals during the target year that refer to papers published in the focal journal during the two previous years, divided by the total number of papers published in the focal journal during the two previous years.

Calculating the 2013 impact factor for *Journal of Management Studies*

EXAMPLE 12.2

Number of citations			Number of articles		
to articles published in:	2012	122	published in:	2012	63
	2011	327		2011	74
	Sum:	449		Sum:	137
Calculation: Divide citations to recent articles by number of recent articles					
	449 ÷ 137 = 3.3				

Journals with impact factors over 3.00 are generally considered 'world class'; those between 1.5 and 3.0 are seen as very good international journals; those between 0.5 and 1.5 are respectable international journals; and those below 0.5 are in danger of relegation. Of course, interpretation of these ratings depends greatly on where your favourite journals fall, and it is also important to look at trends over several years since these ratings can be quite volatile!

Beyond that, you must make up your own mind, by reading past papers in the journal or by submitting something to it. If you want to get something published quickly or easily, then start with one of the more lowly journals. Top journals have much greater lead times, often running into several years. This is not because they are slow or inefficient, more that they will be dealing with a very large volume of material and they will be very exacting in their standards. For example, a paper that Mark Easterby-Smith published in the *Academy of Management Journal* (Easterby-Smith and Malina, 1999) was initially submitted in March 1996 (and that was based on earlier conference papers given in 1993 and 1995). The initial rewrite offer from the *AMJ* arrived 11 weeks after submission and contained eight single-spaced pages of comments and advice from the editor and referees. Over the next two years the paper went through four rewrites, and on each occasion the guidance from the editorial office ran to four or five pages. Thus by the time the paper was accepted in July 1998, the length of comments from the editorial office was greater than the eventual length of the paper. On occasions such as this, as Golden-Biddle and

Locke (2007) comment, one starts to wonder whether the referees should be included as co-authors of the paper!

Our general advice regarding publication strategies is to aim for good journals wherever possible, and perhaps seek to submit papers with others (supervisors, examiners, people met at conferences) who have already been successful in getting published in the target journal.

It is important for people carrying out academic management research to understand some of the hidden rules and procedures, because these may determine whether they are eventually successful. Despite efforts to be fair and transparent, these hidden rules and procedures are inevitable. In general it is easier for North Americans to get accepted in North American journals, and for Europeans to get accepted in European journals, because of the institutional and human networks that support these journals. American journals tend to prefer quantitative papers based on survey data; European journals often prefer qualitative papers based on in-depth case studies. But there are always exceptions to these rules, and therefore it is important to be alert and not to accept stereotypes too easily.

In order to get published in a peer-reviewed academic journal it is essential to understand the decision-making process for most journals, especially the role of referees. In Figure 12.3 we summarize the decision-making process of a typical journal. In this figure the numbers indicate the percentage of the original submissions that move to each of the successive stages. A number of papers (perhaps 60 per cent) will be rejected by the editors without being sent to the referees, a further number will be rejected after receipt of referees' reports, and most of the remainder will be sent an offer to revise and resubmit (R&R). It is extremely rare for a paper to be accepted outright by a good journal. For those lucky enough to have been sent an R&R, they then move on to the critical stage of responding to the criticisms/recommendations of reviewers and the editors. Frequently the reviewers will provide conflicting advice, and a good editor will notice the conflicts and provide guidance on which lines to follow.

The resubmitted paper needs to be accompanied by a letter to the editor (and referees) explaining how recommendations have been implemented and providing a rationale where the authors feel that the recommendations are not appropriate. Sometimes these letters can get very lengthy, perhaps 10 to 20 pages, but long letters can irritate editors and make it difficult for referees to see how their suggestions have been implemented, so the advice is to deal with every point the editors and reviewers have made, but only discuss the critical issues at any length.

Finally, there is the possibility of publishing a book. Although in some subjects, such as history, it is quite normal to turn theses into books, this is relatively rare in the management field. Publishers have a preference for textbooks and handbooks because they have more general and sustained appeal than research monographs. In order to develop a book proposal with broad appeal, it is generally necessary to collaborate with other scholars who can provide complimentary perspectives, and this may not be a sensible option until several years after the PhD is completed. In the short term there are few academic credits for publishing books in the management field. Nevertheless, in the longer term they can contribute substantially to personal reputation and visibility, and this can also be measured in terms of 'hits' in Google Scholar.

Peters and Waterman (1982) are reputed to have received royalties of $1.8 million in the first year of their book's publication, and Mintzberg (1973) did well out of his book (unusually, based on his PhD thesis). But these are the exception: for most people the direct financial rewards are not great. Fortune is most likely to follow the fame of being a published author, and academic careers depend on both the reputation of the publisher and the quality of the reviews that ensue. The nice thing about books is that it is usually possible to develop ideas over a period of time with the help of the publisher. Once again, contacts with publishers are most easily established at conferences, where more of the relevant firms are represented.

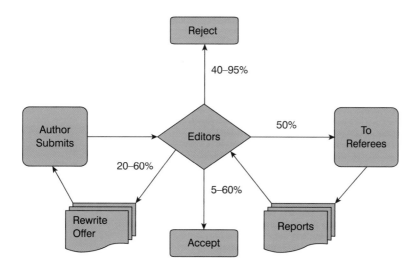

FIGURE 12.3
Flowchart
of journal
decision
making

PLAGIARISM

It is important to be aware of plagiarism, because over the years there has been a steady growth in cases of, and discussions about, plagiarism among students, which often reveal uncertainty and doubt about its significance. Acknowledging work and referencing sources means that the student or researcher knows his or her topic, has read and searched for sources, and knows how to acknowledge the work of others. Plagiarism generally involves presenting the work and ideas of other people and passing them off as your own, without acknowledging the original source of the ideas used.

Although plagiarism is not a new issue, its existence has been less easy to detect and it is only through the advent of information technology and packages such as Turnitin (www. turnitin.com) that plagiarism can be detected relatively easily. While internet search engines may make information easier to acquire, they also serve to provide students with endless sources of material from which to 'cut and paste'. What were once cases of minor infringements have become a problem of epidemic proportions (Duggan, 2006). Similarly, while there may be naïve use and sloppy referencing, Leask (2006) observes that there is a growth in deliberate plagiarism, especially as it relates to the Internet. He draws attention, however, to ambiguities that can exist between interpretations, arguing that plagiarism has different meanings, depending on the context; for example, whether plagiarism relates to research in the context of a report or an exam. For the progress of this book, discussions on plagiarism centre on conscious attempts by individuals to steal the work of others. Also under this heading are those without due recognition or reference, researchers who memorize ideas that originate from other sources, and after a degree of assimilation then go on to make the very same ideas their own and as a consequence fail to add an appropriate acknowledgement (Park, 2003). A screenshot of how Turnitin works is illustrated in Figure 12.4.

Examples of plagiarism

The recurring themes as to what constitutes plagiarism include, as we have already identified: copying another person's material without proper acknowledgement or reference; paraphrasing others without acknowledgement, thereby giving others the impression that the work represents your own original formulation; and of course buying ready-made material from professional writers. There is an increasing number of

FIGURE 12.4
Turnitin
software

websites that offer such services and some of those being offered are extremely sophisticated. Payment relates to the level of degree but individual topics can be specific. Of course for those who have to undergo oral defence of their work, the fact they are not attached to the literature soon means they are caught out, while references that are not in the university libraries also raise suspicion. In preparing this book use has been made of the work of others, but references or acknowledgement will be seen in the text. Where researchers have provided data or material for incorporation or critical feedback obtained from colleagues, they have been acknowledged by name at the front of the book. Park (2003: 475) synthesized four different forms of plagiarism found to be common among students:

1. Stealing material from another source and passing it off as their own, for example:

   - Buying a paper from a research service, essay bank or term paper mill (either pre-written or specially written).
   - Copying a whole paper from a source text without proper acknowledgement.
   - Submitting another student's work, with or without that student's knowledge (e.g. by copying a computer disk).

2. Submitting a paper written by someone else (e.g. a peer or relative) and passing it off as their own.

3. Copying sections of material from one or more source texts, supplying proper documentation (including the full reference) but leaving out quotation marks, thus giving the impression that the material has been paraphrased rather than directly quoted.

4. Paraphrasing material from one or more source texts without supplying appropriate documentation.

In order to avoid plagiarism, students should ensure that they have clearly referenced where others' words and concepts have been used but also where others' ideas have influenced their thought process. This involves keeping up-to-date and precise references about where you have accessed material from, as even accidental plagiarism is considered a serious issue. Given the increase in plagiarism, universities are employing a zero-tolerance policy and students are increasingly being penalized over this issue. In an attempt to combat this problem, institutions are beginning to run courses that aim to educate students to ensure that they are aware of what constitutes plagiarism. Given that plagiarism is a difficult and confusing area, it may be worthwhile checking if any such courses are available at your institution, where you will most likely be given clear examples of both deliberate and accidental plagiarism to ensure that you are aware of the potential perils of careless referencing.

DISSEMINATION STRATEGIES

In the previous section we concentrated on dissemination mainly to academic audiences, and here we focus on other audiences, especially policy-makers and practitioners. We start with some general comments on making public presentations (although this applies equally to client and conference presentations), then discuss publishing in practitioner journals and making the best use of the public media.

We hesitate to provide much advice on the technicality of presentations since most of our students nowadays are very expert and professional at structuring and presenting data using PowerPoint. However, a common mistake is to provide too much material, especially in the form of slides, which puts the presenters under considerable time pressure and makes it extremely difficult for them to introduce any kind of interaction into the presentation. Our preference is to use a minimal number of slides (four or five for a ten-minute presentation) to provide a basic structure, and then provide stories and vignettes to illustrate the points that are being made. If it is a team presentation, then people can take different roles according to their strengths: providing introductions, telling stories, making jokes, encouraging interaction and dealing with questions. If the presentation is being made by an individual, it is often worth recording the session because you may be so focused on providing answers to questions that you do not listen to what people are really saying!

Publications in practitioner journals are also important because they reach much wider audiences and demonstrate that you are engaging with potential 'users'. However, it can be very difficult to get into the famous practitioner journals, such as *Harvard Business Review*, *Sloan Management Review* or *California Management Review*, because the majority of papers are written by established academics, who may have been invited by the editors to submit because they have recently published some interesting material in a top academic journal. So, there is a virtual cycle operating, and it may be quite difficult to break in.

Another way to increase the exposure of one's research results is to approach the media. This can most easily be done through a press release, which is circulated to relevant newspapers and radio stations. Most universities and learned societies have considerable experience in dealing with the media and should be able to provide advice on whom to contact. In Example 12.2 we provide some general guidance on writing press releases.

Guidance on writing press releases

EXAMPLE
12.2

Press releases should be quite short, with a maximum of 600 words printed on two sides of a single sheet of paper. From the outset, you have to convince the reader that you have something interesting to say, perhaps a new fact about the world or a new way of looking at an important issue that has topical relevance. The press release should start with the conclusions, and then provide the supporting evidence – which is opposite to the normal way of writing academic papers, which end with the conclusions. In summary:

(Continued)

(Continued)

- Begin with a catchy headline.
- Provide a general statement that sums up the main finding.
- Distil into three or four points the essence of the research.
- Back up these points with facts and figures.
- Finish with the main policy implications or the 'way forward'.
- Add your contact details, including e-mail address and phone numbers.
- Above all, keep the language intelligible and jargon-free.

Source: Personal communication from Romesh Vaitilingam.

Naturally there is much competition about getting access to the media, and those academics who excel in this respect generally build up excellent relationships over time with journalists and make themselves available 24/7. There are also wider political implications of building up reputations: credit for research should not be taken for granted; it depends very much on how much the researcher is able to exploit his or her work through contacts, publications and other forms of dissemination. We will now use the story of the discovery of penicillin by Alexander Fleming to illustrate how politics and public relations can have a major impact on research reputations (see Example 12.3).

EXAMPLE
12.3

The politics of reputations

Alexander Fleming was a biologist specializing in immunology and anti-bacterial agents who studied and then worked at St Mary's Hospital in London during the first half of the twentieth century. He is credited with the discovery of penicillin in 1928 about which he published a paper in the *British Journal of Experimental Pharmacology* the following year. But little interest was shown in his paper, and after undertaking only one experiment when he injected penicillin into a mouse and found that it disappeared from the blood stream within 30 minutes, he concluded that it would have little therapeutic application. Ten years later, Howard Florey and Ernest Chain, working with a team at the Radcliff Infirmary in Oxford, uncovered Fleming's description of penicillin following a systematic review of the literature (Macfarlane, 1985). Although the paper ignored previous literature on bacteriological inhibition and was vague about the chemical properties, it did note that the therapeutic potential might be worthy of further investigation. Florey and Chain concentrated on penicillin and eventually produced sufficient quantities to be able to demonstrate its life-saving properties. The results were published in a leading article in *The Times*. Following this, Sir Almroth Wright, the head of Fleming's department, saw an opportunity to increase charitable contributions to St Mary's, and wrote a letter to the editor claiming credit for penicillin for Fleming. The upshot was that Fleming was given the major credit in the form of a Nobel Prize, a knighthood, 25 honorary degrees, 15 civic freedoms and 1140 major honours, despite the fact that he had conducted no further research during the 11 years following his experiment with the mouse.

It is important to develop a dissemination strategy at the outset of any funded research projects, and perhaps halfway through doing a doctoral thesis. This should normally include two or three conferences with a brief synopsis of the possible paper in each case, and potential target journals for the next phase of each paper. It is also worth thinking about potential media strategies, including developing press releases towards the end of the research period. As with all forms of publishing, it is important to believe that you have something worth saying.

Putting Dissemination into Practice

1   Prepare a table of contents for your dissertation or thesis.

2   Develop a short press release for either (a) the research project you are currently engaged upon, or (b) the piece of research that you developed for the pesto example above. Share the results with colleagues for critique and suggestions.

3   Debate the proposition that: 'The public dissemination of social science results is harmful to the integrity and progress of research.' This can be done with different groups taking the *pro* or *anti* line.

CONCLUSION

We see the publication and dissemination of ideas not merely as a means to the researcher's own ends, but as an obligation that each researcher has to the wider community. That being said, it is important to understand how appropriate forms of writing and dissemination vary with the audience, the type of research and the form of output that is envisaged. In this chapter we have tried to provide advice on:

   Core skills in writing academic reports

   Strategies and templates for developing appropriate structures.

   How to structure literature reviews.

   Criteria for evaluating different forms of output.

   The complex political processes involved in publishing and dissemination.

Overall, we hope that this book will have provided some of the armoury both to complete worthwhile research and capitalize on it.

FURTHER READING

Golden-Biddle, K. and Locke, K. (2007) *Composing Qualitative Research*, 2nd edn. London: Sage.
    A delightful book that looks at strategies for presenting qualitative research. It also provides good examples from the authors' own experiences of how to handle the complex politics of the review process when submitting papers to journals.

Hart, C. (1998) *Doing a Literature Review: Releasing the Social Science Research Imagination*. London: Sage.
The final chapter provides guidance on writing up literature reviews, with an emphasis on how to develop arguments and guidance on the elements that need to be included.

Murray, R. (2002) *How to Write a Thesis*. Milton Keynes: Open University Press.
This book provides lots of advice and guidance on the technicalities of writing including grammar, style and structure. It is also very helpful on the more strategic and emotional aspects of academic research and writing.

Phillips, E.M. and Pugh, D.S. (2005) *How to Get a PhD: A Handbook for Students and their Supervisors*, 4th edn. Maidenhead: Open University Press.
This is a thoughtful and practical book with lots of advice on how to manage and complete research work, especially at the doctoral level. Lots of examples and good humour from the authors.

Wallace, M. and Wray, A. (2011) *Critical Reading and Writing for Postgraduates*, 2nd edn. London: Sage.
An accessible and well-written book on how to develop a reflective and critical approach to academic reading and writing which can be helpful for both practitioners and more experienced academics.

Want to know more about this chapter? Visit the ⓈSAGE edge™ website at **https://edge.sagepub.com/easterbysmith** to access practice questions, selected journal articles, useful web links and much more.

ANSWERS TO EXERCISES

CHAPTER 2

Exercise 2.4 Performing literature searches

b) Individual exercise: *Test your searches on one specialized database (such as Web of Science, ABI (ProQuest), Business Source Premier or JSTOR), on SRRN and on Google Scholar. Have you found what you expected? What were the problems? How do the results of the scholarly database compare with those listed by SRRN and Google Scholar?*

While many scholarly databases are only available through subscription, there are a growing number of free databases as well as online repositories available on the Internet. It is important to note, however, that these databases rarely offer access to the same kind of material. The full text of many of the most reputable journals cannot be accessed without subscription. Therefore, a thorough systematic review of peer-reviewed articles usually requires access through a library that has made the appropriate subscriptions to the journals being sought. Free databases can help to identity relevant journal articles (i.e. citations) but they rarely provide access to the full text of these articles. In contrast to most subscription-based services, free databases (such as Google Scholar) search journal articles as well as other types of publications including books, conference proceedings, working papers and reports. Some free online repositories (such as SRRN) specialize on the rapid dissemination of working papers. These papers are uploaded but many have not been peer-reviewed. Whilst interest in the journal papers held can to some extent be ranked by the number of downloads, there is no formal evaluation process. Revised drafts of the same papers may (or may not) subsequently become reviewed and published at a later stage. Free databases and repositories however, offer early access to the latest current research – but they also perhaps require the reader to assess more carefully the quality of the material. Some of our readers will find that searches on free databases can also lead to more inter-disciplinary outcomes, which can be a good thing. Journals tend to frame debates within disciplinary boundaries, whereas the scope of Google Scholar or large repositories can lead to surprising and interesting results, highlighting the developments taking place in neighbouring disciplines. Depending on the intention of the literature search, this can be inspiring, distracting or even frustrating. More generally, it is probably safe to say that the convenience of free databases is offset by the significant amount of time which is then needed to assess the quality and standing of a fair proportion of the results. It can also be time-consuming to compare and integrate different lists of results. With this in mind, searching of peer-reviewed articles may appear at first glance to limit the search, but it does offer a relatively quick way of accessing well-established knowledge in a field. A subsequent search on free databases could then be used to complement the review process by adding material published in other formats (e.g. books) and providing insights into more recent and ongoing research in the area (repositories of working papers). For more information about different academic databases and their strengths and limitations, look up the following website: http://en.wikipedia.org/wiki/List_of_academic_databases_and_search_engines.

f) **Interactive exercise**: In pairs, discuss the advantages and disadvantages of using systematic searches compared to a more personally directed approach to the identification of appropriate sources.

Systematic literature searches identify a *maximum number of relevant publications* for a given research project. They are therefore the method of choice if you want to gain a *comprehensive, if not complete, overview* of a specific body of literature and avoid missing any key publications. However, in order to retrieve *relevant* publications, your research topic has to be clearly delineated. Otherwise, all a systematic literature search will do is lead to information overload: when 2,000 papers all appear as equally relevant, where do you start?

At the early stages of a research project, when the topic is not entirely clear, a more personally directed approach can be useful. Using literature searches to follow up and clarify emerging ideas can be a fruitful and inspiring exercise. Such searches encourage researchers to transgress disciplinary boundaries and to learn about a topic in a less comprehensive but perhaps more intuitive or innovative way. However, without a system for doing this, a literature search can turn into a Sisyphean undertaking. As the topic becomes clearer in your own mind, searches may have to be repeated, and if there is no clear record made of the word combinations and databases that have already been used much time can be lost. Comparing dozens of outputs and lists which list only a few new articles among hundreds of

duplicates is a painstakingly tedious activity.

CHAPTER 3

Exercise 3.1 Spotting the epistemology

1. Positivist: 'empirically validating'.
2. Constructionist: 'holistic model'; 'perspectives'.
3. Constructionist: 'drawn from a longitudinal study'.
4. Positivist: 'has a stronger influence on'.
5. Positivist: 'when both LMX quality and empowerment were low'; 'both variables were high'; 'positive outcomes resulted'.
6. Constructionist: 'our longitudinal, inductive study'.
7. Strong constructionist: 'a discussion of the credibility performance'; 'the very structure of a corporation can be seen as …'

CHAPTER 4

Exercise 4.1 Questions for discussion about the Hawthorne experiment

Q1 What are the physical working conditions that contribute to increasing productivity of workers?

Q2 Research design includes incremental changes to supposed key variables; continual comparisons against predicted variable; and continuous observation.

Q3 The selection of workers is not random; there is no parallel control group; open observation takes place throughout, including interaction with the subjects.

Exercise 4.2 Designing a call centre

Q1 From the list of general factors, is there a best combination? You would need to include cost in the equation – the best design might also be impossibly expensive.

Q2 You would have to start with any constraints on design and layout that are imposed by the proposed building itself. Then it makes sense to prioritize factors, perhaps on the basis of impact or cost. You might consider a sequence of studies which varies one factor at a time, in order to identify whether there is an optimal combination of design features. Some factors (such as density and layout) would be the same for everyone taking part in a particular study, while you could vary the ergonomics of the workstation for different workers within the same study.

Exercise 4.3 Which supermarket gives the best deal?

Q1 Every supermarket will choose a comparison which makes it look good, and it is probably not possible to define 'the best deal' in a way that will suit every consumer. An answer to this question would require an analysis of different ways of defining 'best': quality, price, convenience, customer service.

Q2 Comparing the prices of products is inevitably complicated. The approach of using a 'typical' shopping basket is common (it is how the UK defines the Retail Price Index), but no shopper is really typical, so the approach taken by Which! is probably not a good guide for many people. Comparing branded goods is easier than own-label goods, but again is not necessarily a good guide for people who buy supermarket own-brand products.

Exercise 4.4 A longitudinal case study

Q1 The study involved gathering data from multiple sources over a period of time, and this was appropriate

to studying the complex inter-relationships and processes within the company. But also the feedback to key actors in the company also added to the validity of the conclusions we drew.

Q2 Because this is a unique study, the findings can only be generalized theoretically. That is, the case study needs to be able to demonstrate something about dynamic capabilities, knowledge management, or the relationship between the two of them, which supports, contradicts, challenges or adds to current theories in the literature.

Q3 They do make sense if you want to publish the results of the study in an academic journal. However, there are plenty of stories that came out of the study which can provide useful anecdotes to illustrate decision-making processes, group dynamics and so on – which we had not expected in the first place, but which made good stories in their own right.

Exercise 4.5 How grounded is this? A letter from a doctoral student

h) Q1 This depends on whose version of grounded theory Suzanne follows. She uses open coding, which leads to a central category (see Chapter 7), but there is no theoretical sampling, nor saturation. The interplay between external theory/literature and data is more complex than as outlined in Glaser and Strauss.

i) Q2 We think this deviation is quite appropriate, provided Suzanne is able to articulate what and why. Reasons include the constraints of the research setting/access, the nature of the theory she is looking at, and the conscious combination of theory development and deduction.

Exercise 4.6 Discussion questions (for small group in class)

	Ontology	Epistemology	Methodology	Method
Grounded theory	*	***	**	*
Unobtrusive measures		*		***
Narrative	*	*	**	*
Case method		*	***	*
Ethnography	*	**	**	
Critical realism	***	**	*	
Participant observation			**	*
Experimental design		***		
Falsification		***		
Theoretical saturation		*	**	**

CHAPTER 5

Exercise 5.2 Political dilemmas in conducting student project (group discussion)

Q1 Persist, ask for the manager; start observation of departments; phone your tutor; find the administrative head; say that you will return next morning.

Q2 Sign it; try to renegotiate; refuse to sign.

Q3 The dilemma is whether your commitment to confidentiality overrides everything, or whether you have a duty to expose wrong-doing? How confident would you be in the quality of data?

Q4 Choices include full, partial or zero disclosure; buy time by arguing that you will need to reflect on this rather than giving an off-the-cuff opinion.

Q5 Confront him as soon as it first happens, or later on? Work with others to apply group pressure? Shop him to the tutor?

CHAPTER 6

Exercise 6.3 Exploring the potential of qualitative interviews

a) **Individual exercise**: There are various types of qualitative interviews, not all of which are discussed in this chapter. Conduct a literature search for more information on different types of qualitative interviews, using the resources and search strategies introduced in Chapter 3 on literature reviews. Identify at least five types of qualitative interviews. Prepare a short briefing (1,000 words) on the more specific features, advantages and disadvantages of expert interviews, narrative interviews and ethnographic interviews.

In the table below we have listed some of the key features, advantages and disadvantages of expert interviews, narrative interviews and ethnographic interviews. We encourage our readers to browse through methods textbooks, handbooks as well as the Internet to find out more about these techniques so that they can add to this table themselves.

Exercise 6.4 Conducting individual and group interviews

Interactive exercise: In groups of two to four, discuss the advantages and disadvantages of individual interviews and focus groups. For what kind of research would you choose to conduct individual interviews? What kinds of projects would benefit from the use of focus groups? Prepare a list of three projects (title and short abstract) that should be undertaken using just one of these two approaches (individual interviews or group interviews) without stating the approaches you have

Type of Interview	Key features	Advantages	Disadvantage
Expert interview	– Interviewer selects interviewees based on their expertise. – Interviews focus on the knowledge or expertise of interviewees, not on the interviewees themselves. – Little is known about the more specific context of the interview. – Depending on the expert, interviews may or may not be audiotaped.	– Fast way of accessing specific knowledge, good and early orientation of a field or to learn about ongoing developments. – Not very time consuming. – Access is easier than with other techniques (less intrusive than observation; most people enjoy being treated like 'experts'). – Depending on the research design, you may be able to use the same questions in various interviews.	– Expert knowledge is not neutral. When there is little information on the context of what is being said, it is more difficult to identify bias or detect lies. – Some interviewees feel offended by not being treated as a person but rather as a 'brain with legs'. – It can be difficult to get an appointment with an 'expert'.
Narrative interview	– Interviewer asks questions which stimulate interviewees to tell them a story about a significant event or experience they have made. – Label derived from the Latin word *narrare* (to tell a story). – The focus is not on the reported 'fact' (expert interview) but how the interviewee makes sense of the fact.	– Allows for the in-depth exploration of what is thought about a social phenomenon and how it is experienced. – Helps to reconstruct the sequential unfolding of an event as experienced by the interviewee. – Information is more contextualized than in an expert interview. – Interviews are usually audiotaped.	– Time consuming: narrative interviews tend to be very long interviews; it can take some time to get to the actual event/story. – Requires flexibility and attentive listening on the side of the interviewer. – Interviews can develop in different ways which makes it more difficult to prepare and compare them. – Information appears as more biased as it is openly based on peoples' perceptions rather than 'abstract knowledge'.
Ethnographic interview	– Informal and usually unstructured interview that is conducted as a 'friendly conversation' in the context of ethnographic research. – Information is obtained through observation and conversation.	– Interview situation appears more natural and is hence more appealing to many interviewees. – Information revealed in the interview is highly contextualized (observation and interaction). – Conversation can take place while interviewee performs other tasks. – Interviewer can ask questions along the way (e.g. how, why something is done).	– Unstructured interviews require more flexibility and focus (thinking on the spot). – Usually recorded in interview notes, which then have to be written up. – Like most ethnographic approaches, this is a very time-consuming method; (participant) observation leading up to the conversation can take weeks if not months. – More difficult to analyse within a comparative framework.

chosen on your list. Exchange the list with another group. Can you guess whether the list suggests projects for individual interviews or focus groups? Which group did a better job in identifying suitable projects? Why?

In the table below we summarize some of the main advantages and disadvantages of individual interviews and focus groups. Again, this should be understood as an indicative rather than exhaustive list of features.

Method	Advantages	Disadvantages
Individual interviews	– Useful for investigating complex topics as they leave more room for in-depth explanations. When probing and/or laddering techniques are required, individual in-depth interviews are the method of choice. – More useful for exploring individual perceptions and decision-making processes. – Relatively easy to set up. – Make it easier to address sensitive issues which interviewees might not wish to share with a group. – More flexibility for the interviewer, easier to alter the interview guide along the way.	– Series of rather similar interviews can become boring for the interviewer. – Interviewers usually avoid challenging the opinions of individual interviewees, whereas peers (focus group) might initiate a more critical, and as such more revealing discussion. – It can be difficult to make sense of conflicting accounts of events forwarded by different interviewees.
Focus groups	– Useful for exploring a wider scope of opinions and experiences as well as group dynamics, relationships and collective decision-making processes. – Group dynamics can be helpful for identifying trends, exploring conflicting opinions, and for building consensus. – Multiple stakeholders can be involved which can make this method more attractive to some research participants. – Focus groups make it easier for participants to engage in the research process.	– Not useful for topics that require long or complex responses. – Peer pressure can inhibit the responses of some individuals. – Logistics can be complicated. – Facilitation of focus groups can require a lot from the interviewer who might require assistance.

Exercise 6.6 Interviewing

b) *Interactive exercise*: *Think about which of your own characteristics and traits could affect your relationship with research participants. In pairs, discuss these traits and write them down. What*

characteristics or traits are likely to have a positive or negative impact on your data collection?

Before entering a field, it is useful to think about one's presence and develop a greater sense of self-awareness about how others might perceive you and how behaviours/activities might be likely to be perceived in this field. This involves reflecting on our own identities and on the identities of potential research participants. Aristotle refers to the importance of pathos, ethos and logos when communicating with others: pathos refers to how well individuals are at making an emotional connection with the person they are communicating with; ethos refers to how credible and authentic the person comes across, in this case, interviewer to the interviewee and logos, refers to how coherent, reasonable and intelligible, in this case the questions, are that are being made. Depending on the project, demographic markers such as nationality, ethnicity, age or gender can impact on our research. Attributes such as social class, shared hobbies or pastimes and religion also shape the ways in which we engage with others, including research participants. Then there are also more personal characteristics which should be considered. The way researchers engage with research participants varies depending on whether they are perceived to be shy, confident, arrogant, intimidating, defensive, nervous, reluctant or bored. It is therefore important to reflect on how we tend to come across when we meet others in a self-critical way. It can be helpful to discuss this issue with a friend who can provide some feedback on our appearance. This might not turn out to be a particularly pleasurable discussion – but is certainly one worth having!

In some fields it is essential to exhibit a sense of fashion or to follow a particular dress code. While researchers should always behave in a polite and respectful manner, some research participants expect a very formal and 'professional' behaviour whereas others could feel rejected or ridiculed when confronted with the same appearance. We are not trying to encourage researchers to be inauthentic or to attempt to always blend in come what may, as in some cases it could be a useful strategy to stand out. What is important, however, is to be aware of the reasons as to why one would (not) like to stand out, and whether it is within our abilities to make a choice in this regard.

d) *Individual and interactive exercise:* *Search online for information about your university's ethical-review process. What is the procedure at your university? Who assesses the applications? What issues are covered? Look online for some templates of consent forms (e.g. here: http://www.lancaster.ac.uk/research ethics/1-4-samples.html). What issues are covered in these templates? Discuss the merits and challenges created by the use of consent forms.*

Most consent forms follow the same design. They require the researcher to provide some general information on the study and its purpose, followed by a description of what the research involves and whether there are any risks associated with participation. It then lists the potential benefits of the study, including personal benefits such as compensation or reimbursement (if appropriate). Most importantly, the form then clarifies the conditions for withdrawal or termination and covers issues around anonymization and data protection, including whether fellow academics will have access to the data, what kind of outputs will be published, and how long the data will be archived for, and what will happen to the data if a participant decides to withdraw. A standard text then emphasizes that the decision to participate (or not participate) is solely up to the research participant who has to declare that he/she has been informed about the nature and purpose of the research and his/her rights as a participant. Finally, the researcher provides contact information for follow-up questions. Signature lines indicate where the researcher and research participant may sign.

Views about the value of such consent forms are often mixed. An increasing number of research institutions expect researchers to produce signed consent forms based on the assumption that the use of such forms increases transparency, protects researchers and research institutions, and ensures that research participants understand their rights in relation to participation and issues in relation to such things as confidentiality. However, in practice the process of obtaining signed consent can be fraught with difficulties. The use of consent forms can be more or less appropriate depending on the context in which the research is conducted. Consent forms can be off-putting for a range of people who wonder why such complex procedure is needed for an involvement they consider to be relatively benign. In some overseas cultures for example, the very production of a form that has to be signed to say the researcher promises to be ethical and trustworthy might suggest to the respondent there may be something they ought to be concerned about! In addition, language issues and illiteracy can make the procedure rather awkward. In these cases consent may be obtained in the form of a tape-recoded statement. Another issue arises from the common requirement to give research participants sufficient time to decide on whether or not they are willing to sign such a form. This can make the initial contact with the field more difficult. Some participants may also perceive the existence of consent forms as a threat to confidentiality and anonymity as they represent written evidence of a respondent's involvement in a study. In the case of research on illegal activities, this can also be problematic for the researcher. Despite these difficulties, it seems that in most cases the advantages of using consent forms outweigh the disadvantages. In any case, consent forms are an instrument for ensuring the ethical conduct of research and they are here to stay. Researchers may be best advised to focus their efforts on how they can best comply and put them into practice.

CHAPTER 7

Exercise 7.2 Exploring the role of the researcher in observational research

a) **Interactive exercise**: Burawoy (2009: 204) notes that as participant observers, 'we don't have access to some Archimedean standpoint' [a hypothetical vantage point from which an observer can objectively perceive the subject of inquiry]: instead we are always located somewhere 'in the site, which has grave

consequences to what we say'. In groups or pairs, discuss how this statement relates to the four types of observational research presented above. What are the implications of the different standpoints for researchers and research participants? What kind of observational research is the most useful/the most problematic?

As with many of our exercises, this exercise aims mainly at generating debate – and it is safe to say that there is no observational standpoint that is perfect in every respect. Depending on the research question and the field under study, it can be appropriate (or useful) for us to minimize our interaction with the field, in this way aiming at a position which comes close to being 'outside the field' (complete observer). Some scholars favour such a standpoint because they feel that it is likely to produce more objective (i.e. less biased) research. While this may or may not be true, it is important to remember that as researchers investigating social phenomena, we will never be able to take a fully 'objective' stance. Our presence will always make an impact on the field, even when we try hard to obscure our presence. As observers we are an intrinsic part of what we observe – not least because our interpretations are informed by our own experiences of engaging with others. Acknowledging this fact, many researchers prefer to follow their fields (observer-as-participant) or to engage with their field in an active way (participant-as-observer; complete participant). Full participation allows us to develop a level of in-depth understanding which can never be achieved by complete observation. At the same time, however, such understandings can lead to a situation where we become lost in the field and our own subjective experience of it, unable to reflect upon the conditions and implications of what we are doing. Taking a more active role also allows us to experiment. For example, we can develop a theory of how a field might react to a certain stimulus and then see if we are right. This can be useful, but it also begs the question of whether the field would ever have reacted in such way if it had not been for our input. This is not to say that the observations resulting from this input do not lend themselves to the development of valid and useful knowledge derived in this way.

Exercise 7.8 Thinking about fieldwork

Individual exercise: *Imagine your-self conducting interactive research. What kinds of situations might you find particularly challenging? A sneering inter-viewee? Being left aside? Think about how you would react to such situations. Now try to put yourself into the position of your research participants. What kind of behaviour could be challenging for them? Do you have any habits or personal traits that could make it more difficult for them to engage in your research? Make a personal list of rules that could help you with your own fieldwork. Don't forget to consider ethical aspects as well as practical ones.*

Table 7.5 gives an overview of some of the most important rules for conduct-ing fieldwork. A more personalized list should be based on these rules whilst taking into account potential practical or ethical issues that come about as a consequence of being in the field. For example, an organizational culture of excessive alcohol consumption may require rules about alcohol consump-tion and interviewing people under the influence of alcohol; or, reflecting on personal traits and issues, a shy person might want to create a rule about mak-ing an effort to socialize more, whereas a very outgoing person should consider expanding on rule 3 on the importance of listening.

CHAPTER 8

Exercise 8.1 Preparing your data

Interactive exercise: *In pairs, prepare a list of issues you need to consider when preparing qualitative data for analysis. Discuss how you would organize your data (chronologically, thematically, by type of data etc.) and how you would label them.*

Data preparation usually addresses the following concerns:

1. Are my data stored in a way that is safe, secure and in line with the current data protection laws and protocols? Do I have sufficient backups? While these questions might appear so obvious that they needn't even be stated, experience has shown that in the excitement of conducting research they can easily be overlooked.

2. Are my data stored in a way that makes it easy for me to find individual files when I need them? It can take hours to organize data in a coherent way. However, even more time can be saved by developing a consistent system for labelling files and folders. For example, a short file name like O1_P2_140212_I2T can reveal that the file labelled in this way is the transcript (T) of the second Interview (I2) with person 2 (P2) in organization 1 (O1) which took place on 12 February 2014 (120212). Having all your data labelled in this way and organized in folders (whether these are structured around types of data or organizations/persons) allows for a more systematic and often a more enjoyable experience when you come to analyse your data. Make sure that you create a spreadsheet that provides you with an overview of all of your data and indicates how you have labelled them, and where they are stored.

3. Are my data stored in a format that facilitates the analysis? Depending on the type of data and on the methods used to analyse them (e.g. software package), some data might have to be converted into a different format (e.g. mp3), transcribed (e.g. audiotaped interviews) or require formatting (e.g. header with data/time, page and line numbers, margins for coding etc.). Some researchers anonymize their data at this stage, others leave it to later in the research process. Whenever you

anonymize data make sure that you keep the list that identifies each of the anonymized participants/organizations in a safe place (i.e. in line with data protection guidelines).

Exercise 8.3 Coding and memo-writing

Interactive exercise: *Discuss what kind of information should be included in a code book and how it should be organized.*

Codebooks provide a structured overview of the codes developed for a particular project or analysis. Codebooks improve consistency in the coding, in particular when multiple researchers work on the same project. Depending on the research design, codebooks listing pre-determined codes can be used to index data and they can also guide the analysis. However, most qualitative approaches involve the incremental development of a codebook, which then traces the development of the analysis. Without a codebook, researchers can easily get lost in their analysis as codes begin to accumulate. By making researchers think more about their codes, and the relationships between their codes, the creation of a codebook can enhance the analytic process. Codebooks are often presented as tables which include the following information: the label of the code, a brief definition, guidelines for when (not) to use the code, a few examples, and, in the case of more important codes, more detailed memos on the development and meaning of this code. Codebooks are usually organized around themes or types of codes. For example, there might be a section on codes for different kinds of respondents or organizations, another for codes labelling different activities or viewpoints. For more elaborate projects it can be useful to create a codebook using a database management program such as Access. This facilitates the production of different versions of the codebook and can be useful as you might want to organize your codes in different ways. Some database formats can then be imported into qualitative data analysis software packages.

CHAPTER 9

Exercise 9.1 Advantages and disadvantages of alternative survey strategies

1. *A project in a small business to assess views on introducing charging employees for car parking.*

The target group here is employees, and a small business presumably has relatively few employees, and they obviously work on-site (otherwise they would not be parking a car). A face-to-face survey would be the easiest to carry out, and would be the best way to get responses from the highest number of employees. A telephone survey would make sense for employees who work from home (e.g. sales staff) and do not come into the company premises frequently. A postal survey would only make sense if employees need to have formal notification of the change. A web survey relies on employees having good access to technology, which cannot be taken for granted in a small business.

2. *A worldwide survey in a multinational company of staff attitudes to HRM practices.*

The target group here is employees, and the organization is multinational. Presumably, employees work in more than one country (with perhaps different native languages). If a large sample is required, then face-to-face or telephone interviews will be difficult and expensive. Postal or web surveys would allow for different language versions to be developed, so that employees can answer in their preferred language. Most multinational companies routinely use email, and so a web survey would be the most cost effective. For employees without internet access at work, a paper copy could be made available at the workplace or through the post.

3. *An investigation to understand the nature of bullying within the Social Services Department of a local authority.*

Bullying is a very sensitive issue, and one which would be very difficult to examine in any other way than a face-to-face interview. Trust would be the most important issue to consider: who it is who carries out the survey, and how employees can be persuaded to trust those involved. A single department of a local authority would be relatively small, and the high cost of face-to-face interviews would be offset by the quality of information obtained.

Exercise 9.2 Types of questions that observational data can answer

Research question	What data to collect	How to sample
Do people buy more cold drinks in hot weather, and more soup in cold weather?	Number of different kinds of drink.	Select a sample of locations, and times of day.
Does the presence and type of background music in a store alter customers' buying behaviour?	Customers – time spent browsing, trying on garments, items bought.	Select days of the week/times of day. Define target customers, and define a quota sample size per day.
How do people use online help sources?	Web pages – pages accessed, time spent per page, click-through from one page to another, content of searches made.	The sampling strategy depends on which people are of interest and which help sources they may use.
When do people who work in different places (virtual teams) switch between media (instant messaging, email, video-conferencing, and phone) in order to manage a project?	The unit of analysis could be the team member or the communication episode. For each episode, you will need data on what work is being done, and what media are used during the episode.	Select a relevant project, and then sample (or select all) teams working on that project. Sample different stages within the project, and tasks within those stages.
How does the conversational style adopted by a call handler influence the effectiveness of telephone helplines?	Conversational style needs to be assessed (this could include factors such as friendliness, manner of eliciting information about the problem, ability to listen to the user). Effectiveness could be measured by ratings of the extent to which the problem is solved, user satisfaction.	The simplest approach is to select a sample of call handlers who adopt different styles, then select a sample of their calls (over several days, times of day, types of user problems).
In negotiations, how do same-sex and mixed-sex groups differ?	It is important to define relevant characteristics of the negotiation task, so that gender-mix differences are not confounded by differences in the task itself. Relevant style characteristics would include: team role characteristics of group members, ways of managing conflict. Some studies will also consider outcomes – success in completing a task etc.	First define what kind of negotiation is of interest, and decide how many same-sex and mixed-sex groups are required. Then select a sample of negotiation episodes (this would be easiest to do in an experimental study in a laboratory).

CHAPTER 10

Exercise 10.1 Contingency table analysis

The contingency table from SPSS shows the row percentages.

The bottom row shows for the company as a whole that there are almost the same number of men and women.

The percentages within regions do differ quite a lot: there are more women than men in Europe and in North America, and there are fewer women than men in the other three regions. The lowest percentage of women is in Asia Pacific at 42.1 per cent, compared with 53.9 per cent in North America. The chi-square test is highly significant ($\chi^2 = 441.82$, df $= 4$, p < 0.01).

region * gender Crosstabulation

			Gender		
			Female	Male	Total
Region	Middle East & Africa	Count	315	401	716
		% within region	44.0%	56.0%	100.0%
	Asia Pacific	Count	4304	5923	10227
		% within region	42.1%	57.9%	100.0%
	Europe	Count	13618	12138	25756
		% within region	52.9%	47.1%	100.0%
	North America	Count	2072	1771	3843
		% within region	53.9%	46.1%	100.0%
	Latin / Central America / Caribbean	Count	1576	2085	3661
		% within region	43.0%	57.0%	100.0%
Total		Count	21885	22318	44203
		% within region	49.5%	50.5%	100.0%

There could be many reasons for regional variations in the proportions of men and women employed within the company, although it is unlikely that there is any difference in the relative percentage of women and men from one region to another. It would be important to find out what jobs are being done by employees in the different regions, in order to check out the possibility that gender is related to the kind of work being carried out. Gender could also be related to qualifications or job level, so it would be useful to investigate regional gender differences in the qualifications that the company requires of its employees.

CHAPTER 12

Exercise 12.1 Writing academic introductions

An example of a response that ticks most of the boxes!
Can English Basil be Romantic?

Supermarket shelf space is limited and merchandisers only select products based on brands they believe will sell. The field of consumer behaviour is important because it contributes significantly to understanding how product selection is made from the shelf in the supermarket. Early research has shown that the romantic association of characteristics of the country of origin influences consumer behaviour (Romeo and Juliet, 1574). More recently, it has been argued by Berlusconi (2010) that romantic associations are linked to linguistic origins. But the evidence to support this claim is thin, and furthermore, as pointed out by Sarkozy (2011), it is not clear which language provides a romantic association with which product.

This study focuses on the case of pesto because of its association with basil production, which takes place both in the romantic Ligurian hills of Italy and in the lesser-known valleys in the South Downs of England. Using matched English and Italian focus groups, we examine perceptions and stereotypes of basil quality in both countries. The study reported in this paper contributes to the field of consumer behaviour by identifying the interactions between product origin, language and romantic associations in both countries, and thus resolves the limitations in the work of Berlusconi (2010) and Sarkozy (2011).

Source: Based on initial draft by Andrei Kovacs, Fionnuala Runswick and Paula Higson on the Executive Doctorate, Cranfield Management School

GLOSSARY

1-tailed test refers to a directional alternative hypothesis relative to the null hypothesis; a prediction of a positive association between variables, or that one group mean will be bigger than another

2-tailed test refers to a non-directional alternative hypothesis relative to the null hypothesis; association between variables may be either positive or negative, or that the means of two groups will differ in either direction

academic theory explicit ideas developed through exchanges between researchers to explain and interpret scientific and social phenomena

action research an approach to research that seeks understanding through attempting to change the situation under investigation

alternative hypothesis (H_1) position adopted during hypothesis testing if the evidence from data is strong enough to reject the null hypothesis (see also null hypothesis)

analysis of covariance (ANCOVA) a form of test of group differences on a continuous dependent variable which also includes continuous variables as predictors (covariates)

analysis of variance (ANOVA) a form of hypothesis test for comparing the means of two or more groups which may be classified on the basis of other variables

applied research studies that focus on tackling practical problems in organizations where the desired outcome will be knowledge about how to solve the problem

archival research collection and analysis of public documents relating mainly to organizational or governmental strategies

argument analysis an approach to the analysis of natural language data that identifies the data used in making claims, the premises made and the conclusions drawn by individuals about issues of relevance

association two variables are associated where knowing a value on one variable carries information about the corresponding value on the other; can be measured by a correlation coefficient

ATLAS.ti a software package that assists in the building and testing of theories through the creative assembly of qualitative analysis of textual, graphical and audio/visual data; available from www.atlasti.com

auto-ethnography a form of insider research often conducted by those studying in the organization in which they work

bar chart a form of graphical summary for category scales, with bars whose length indicates the frequency of responses for each category

beta weight see standardized regression weight

bias in sampling design, a biased sample is one that does not represent the features of the population from which it is drawn (see representativeness)

binomial distribution a form of reference distribution; the distribution of entities that are binary (present/absent, success/failure)

bootstrap a way of forming a reference distribution by repeated sampling from a specific dataset; used in hypothesis testing

CAQDAS computer assisted qualitative data analysis software

case method a research design that focuses in depth on one, or a small number of, organizations, events or individuals, generally over time

category scale a form of measurement scale where responses are recorded in a small number of discrete units, for example, makes of car purchased (cf. continuous scale)

causal model a class of multivariate models of the causal relationships among a set of variables which can be fitted to data

chi-square distribution a form of reference distribution; the distribution of variances used for testing hypotheses about spread

chi-square test a form of hypothesis test for testing association between two variables measured on nominal category scales

cluster sampling a modification of random sampling where the population is first divided into convenient units, called clusters, and then all entities within a cluster are selected

cognitive mapping a method of spatially displaying data in order to detect patterns and by so doing better understand their relationship and significance

common factors a class of latent variables in a measurement model, which are assumed to account for the covariances among a set of observed variables (see also specific factors)

confirmatory factor analysis (CFA) a multivariate method for testing measurement models of the relationship between a set of observed variables and a hypothesized set of latent variables (see also exploratory factor analysis)

content analysis a relatively deductive method of analysis where codes (or constructs) are almost all predetermined and where they are systematically searched for within the data collected

continuous scale a form of measurement scale where responses are recorded in a large number of discrete units, for example, age recorded in months (cf. category scale)

convenience sampling a form of non-probability sampling design where entities are included in a sample on the basis of their ease of access

conversation analysis an analysis of natural language data used with naturally occurring conversations to establish linguistic patterns through the detailed examination of utterances

cooperative inquiry a form of action research where the research 'subjects' not only play a part in sense-making, but also are encouraged to determine the main questions to be researched

covariance a measure of association between two continuous variables expressed in the units of the measurement scales of the variables; its square root is the correlation coefficient

covariates variables measured on continuous scales, which are included as predictors in analysis of group differences

critical action learning a group-based inquiry that takes account of the viewpoint and feelings of members within a social and political context. The agenda and process are determined largely by members, rather than by academics

critical discourse analysis the analysis of natural language data, which emphasizes the power relations and ideologies that are both created and conveyed

critical incident technique a method of teasing out information often employed within interviews, which goes to the heart of an issue about which information is sought

critical realism an approach to social research with an explicit ontological position, which combines features of both positivism and constructionism

critical theory a philosophy that critiques the structures and outcomes of capitalist society, and examines how powerful members of society maintain their dominance over the less powerful members

Cronbach's alpha coefficient an index of the internal consistency of a composite variable formed by combining a set of items; a common measure of reliability

cross-sectional surveys these usually involve selecting different organizations, or units, in different contexts, and investigating the relationships between a number of variables across these units

Decision Explorer a software program for collecting, conveying and managing ideas and other kinds of qualitative information that surround complex and uncertain situations; available from Banxia software (www.banxia.com)

degrees of freedom (*df*) the value that defines the shape of a standard reference distribution in hypothesis testing; for example, in testing association, *df* = sample size minus one

dependent variables the factors that research is trying to predict (see independent variables)

discourse analysis covers a range of analysis approaches that focus on data in the form of language. This could be the language used or the context in which the forms of language is used. Researchers focus on the development of and contribution to aspects of social theory and social action

dominance in the context of mixed methods research this refers to whether, or not, one method uses significantly more time and resource than the other

efficiency the extent to which a summary measure captures all the information within the data which is relevant to what is summarized

eigenvalues the term used in exploratory factor analysis for the summary measure of the amount of variance in the observed variables accounted for by a factor

embedded case a case within a larger case, for example, the A&E department within a hospital that was the primary case

emic insights into communities, societies or organizations as seen from the perspective of insiders

engaged research involves close collaboration between academics and practitioners in determining the research aims, its implementation, and the practical implications

epistemology views about the most appropriate ways of enquiring into the nature of the world

ethnography approaches to research and data collection that emphasize gaining access to the perspectives and experiences of organizational members

etic insights into communities, societies or organizations as seen from the perspective of outsiders

evaluation research is research which has, as its focus, the systemic and rigorous assessment of an activity or object such that the information and insights gleaned can provide useful feedback

everyday theory the ideas and assumptions we carry round in our heads in order to make sense of everyday observations

exogenous variables those variables that are part of a multivariate model, but whose causal influences are taken as given and do not form part of the model itself

experimenter effect the idea that the act of observing or measuring any social process actually changes that process

exploratory factor analysis (EFA) a multivariate method for fitting measurement models, which describes the covariances among a set of observed variables in terms of a set of latent variables (see also confirmatory factor analysis)

exploratory surveys these are similar to cross-sectional surveys, but tend to focus on identifying patterns within the data through the use of factor analysis or principal components analysis (see Chapter 10)

external validity whether the results of the research can be generalized to other settings or contexts

factor loading the weight allocated to the path between a latent variable and an observed variable in a measurement model

factorial designs a form of experimental design which includes combinations of more than one independent variable

factual surveys involve collecting and collating relatively 'factual' data from different groups of people

falsification a research design that seeks evidence to demonstrate that the current assumptions or hypotheses are incorrect

F-distribution a form of reference distribution; the distribution of ratios of variances used for testing hypotheses about group differences in means

feminism a philosophy that argues that women's experiences and contributions are undervalued by society and by science; also an emancipatory movement to rectify these inequalities

financial databases archives of records about companies or other entities, which contain financial data, such as income data, cash flow, profit and loss, share prices

focused codes codes that are directed, conceptual and analytical

framing the theoretical lens or device which guides and shapes the way research is conducted. Framing can apply equally well to research design, data collection and analysis

frequency distribution a summary representation of a sample of data containing the number of responses obtained for each alternative on the measurement scale

generalizability the extent to which observations or theories derived in one context can be applicable to other contexts

generalized linear models a class of multivariate statistical models within which the relationships between DVs and PVs are linear, and DVs can be expressed through a transformation called a link function; it includes multiple regression analysis, ANOVA and logistic regression

goodness of fit a summary measure of the discrepancy between observed values and the fitted values derived from a hypothesized model

grand theory a coherent set of assumptions intended to explain social or physical phenomena; may or may not be empirically testable

grey literature academic literature that is not formally published in journals. As a consequence it is usually considered to be not widely accessible or available e.g. reports or working papers. However, with the internet, this is increasingly less the case

grounded analysis the linking of key variables (theoretical codes) into a more holistic theory that makes a contribution to knowledge in a particular field or domain

grounded theory an open (and inductive) approach to analysis where there are no a priori definitional codes but where the structure is derived from the data and the constructs and categories derived emerge from the respondents under study

hermeneutics a philosophy and methodology about the interpretation of texts. Stresses that textual materials should be understood in the context within which they are written

hierarchical regression a form of multiple regression analysis, which involves entering predictor variables sequentially in blocks

histogram a form of bar chart for continuous scales, where scale points are first grouped together and the length of bars indicates the frequency of responses for each category

human relations theory assumes that performance of both individuals and organizations is dependent on the commitment and involvement of all employees, and hence managers need to foster positive relationships with, and between, employees

hypothesis testing the process of making inferences about populations based upon data drawn from samples

identifiability the characteristic of a hypothesized model defined by the relationship between the number of parameters in a model to be estimated and the information available to do it; a model is identified if there are fewer parameters to be estimated than there are items of information available

independent variables the factors that are believed to cause the effects that are to be observed; also called predictor variables (see dependent variable)

in-depth interview an opportunity, usually within an interview, to probe deeply and open up new dimensions and insights

inference drawing conclusions about a population based on evidence from a sample

inferential surveys surveys that are aimed at establishing relationships between variables and concepts

interaction effects where the effect on a variable depends on the context defined by another variable

internal realism a philosophical position which assumes that reality is independent of the observer, but that scientists can only access that reality indirectly

internal validity assurance that results are true and conclusions are correct through elimination of systematic sources of potential bias

interquartile range see mid-range

interval scale a form of continuous scale that has no true zero point, so that ratio calculations are not meaningful, for example temperature (cf. ratio scale)

interview bias occurs when the process of questioning influences the interviewee's response

Kendall's tau a test of association between two variables based on the ranks of the scores for each variable

Kruskal-Wallis test a form of hypothesis test for comparing two or more groups that uses rank-order data

laddering up a method of questioning which can be employed within interviewing which can elicit the values that underpin statements or actions made by respondents

laddering down a method of questioning which can be employed within interviewing which can elicit examples which evidence general statements, views or values expressed in interview responses

Lagrange multiplier test a form of modification index in SEM that indicates the value of a fixed parameter if it were to be set free

latent variables a class of variables within a multivariate model, which are not measured directly but are inferred from observed variables

leading question a form of wording of a question that leads the respondent to give the answer preferred by the questioner

likelihood ratio chi-square an index of the overall quality of a model fitted by the maximum likelihood method; used in logistic regression analysis

Likert scale a form of ordinal category scale for measuring attitudes from very positive to very negative

local knowledge ideas and principles that are relevant to the setting of a particular organization or social setting, but which may not apply in other contexts

location a characteristic of a set of data that summarizes where the data are located on the measurement scale; measured by the mode, median, mid-mean or mean

logistic regression a form of multivariate analysis of causal relationships among observed variables where the dependent variable is measured on a binary category scale

Mann-Whitney U test a form of hypothesis test for comparing two groups that uses rank-order data

mean a summary measure of location that uses all the values in a dataset in its calculation; the sum of all data points divided by the sample size

measurement model a multivariate model for the relationship between observed variables and latent variables

median a summary measure of location that uses the ranks of all the values in a dataset in its calculation; the middle value in an ordered set of data points

mediational model a form of causal model in which the causal influence of a predictor variable on a dependent variable is indirect, operating through an intermediary variable (called a mediator)

methodological contribution this is achieved where an academic report or paper develops new methods of inquiry, or extends existing methods into new contexts

methods and techniques the instruments and processes for gathering research data, analysing it and drawing conclusions from it

middle-range theory a set of ideas and concepts relevant to explaining social or physical phenomena within relatively specific contexts, normally empirically testable

mid-mean a summary measure of location; the mean of the middle half of the data

mid-range a summary measure of spread; the range of the middle half of the data (also called the interquartile range)

mode a summary measure of location; the most frequently occurring value in a dataset

mode 1 research the generation of theoretical knowledge through detached scientific research

mode 1½ research the generation of useful knowledge through combining scientific research methods with practical engagement

mode 2 research the generation of practical knowledge through direct engagement with practice

modification index an estimate in SEM of the change in goodness of fit of a fitted model if a fixed parameter were allowed to become free

multiple regression model a multivariate method that includes a single dependent variable measured on a continuous scale and a set of predictor variables that may be measured on continuous or category scales

multi-stage sampling a process of dividing up a population into hierarchical units, such as countries, regions, organizations, work groups, and applying random sampling at each level

multivariate analysis of covariance (MANCOVA) a class of statistical methods for testing group differences for two or more dependent variables simultaneously, which also includes one or more continuous variables as predictors

multivariate analysis of variance (MANOVA) a class of statistical methods for testing group differences for two or more dependent variables simultaneously

multivariate methods a class of statistical methods that analyses the covariances among a number of variables simultaneously

multivariate test a test of a study hypothesis that involves consideration of several dependent variables simultaneously

narrative analysis focuses on stories or accounts of individuals (or groups) in order to capture within social science research and management the accounts of individuals

narrative methods ways of conducting research that concentrate on collecting the stories told among organizational members

natural language data the term is used in this book to signify data that is presented in the form of words (spoken) or text (written). These data can be analysed and interpreted in a variety of different ways in order to make inferences in relation to such things as content, meaning and practice

nominal scale a form of category scale where the scale units have no natural ordering, for example makes of car purchased (cf. ordinal scale)

nominalism an ontological view that objects in the world are 'formed' by the language we use and the names we attach to phenomena

non-experimental designs positivist research conducted through comparing groups for which the members have not been assigned at random; similar to quasi-experimental designs

non-parametric test a form of hypothesis test that uses a reference distribution derived from all possible permutations of study outcomes using the ranking of data (cf. parametric test)

non-probability sampling designs sampling designs where the likelihood of each population entity being included in the sample cannot be known

non-proportional stratified random sampling a form of sampling where the population is divided into subsets (called strata) and different sampling proportions are used for each stratum for selecting a sample

normal distribution a form of standard reference distribution; the distribution of the sum of independent measures where the standard deviation of the reference distribution is known (its shape is sometimes called the bell-curve)

normative theory describes how organizations should be structured and managed

null hypothesis (H_0) the initial position adopted during hypothesis testing, which may be modified on the basis of evidence from data; for tests involving comparing groups, the null hypothesis is that the groups are nothing but random samples from a single population (see also alternative hypothesis)

null model a model within structural equation modelling which assumes that all the covariances among the observed variables are zero; used as the baseline for calculating incremental fit indices

NVivo a software package that assists in the building and testing of theories by classifying, sorting and arranging information; available from QSR International (www.qsrinternational.com)

observational methods ways of collecting data that involve direct sampling of aspects of behaviour

observed variables a class of variables in a multivariate model that are directly measured; they can be used to estimate latent variables

observer effects influences on behaviour that result from study participants knowing that they are being observed

odds ratio the relative likelihood of the two possible outcomes for a binary category variable; used to form the dependent variable in logistic regression analysis

ontology views about the nature of reality

ordinal scale a form of category scale where the scale units have a natural ordering, for example social class (cf. nominal scale)

paradigm a consensual pattern in the way scientists understand, and inquire into, the world

parametric test a form of hypothesis test that uses a standard reference distribution derived from probability theory whose form is defined by a small number of parameters (cf. non-parametric test)

parsimony the extent to which a fitted model in SEM can account for observed data with fewer parameters

partial correlation a correlation between two variables that is adjusted to remove the influence of a third variable

participant observation a form of ethnography where there is close involvement in the organization in order to gain a detailed understanding of other people's realities

path coefficients see regression weight

permutations all possible ways of rearranging a set of entities; used in forms of non-parametric testing of hypotheses

population the set of entities about which a researcher wishes to draw conclusions

positivism the key idea of positivism is that the social world exists externally, and that its properties should be measured through objective methods

postal questionnaire survey a form of survey distribution that involves postal distribution, and relies on respondents to complete a survey themselves and return it to the researcher

postmodernism a collection of philosophies that are opposed to realism, and are generally critical of scientific progress

pragmatism a philosophical position that argues that knowledge and understanding should be derived from direct experience

precision the level of confidence that the researcher has in estimating characteristics of the population from evidence drawn from a sample; it depends on sample size but not on the sampling proportion

predictor variables the factors that are believed to cause the effects that are to be observed; also called independent variables (see dependent variable)

primary data new information that is collected directly by the researcher

principal components analysis a mathematical procedure that assists in reducing data and by so doing indicates possible relationships between a number of uncorrelated variables: the first principal component accounts for as much of the variability in the data as possible, successive components (of which there may be two, three or four) account for as much of the remaining variability as possible

probability sample designs sampling designs where the likelihood of each population entity being included in the sample is known

probe a device used as an intervention technique to improve and sharpen the interviewees' response

product-moment correlation a test of association between two variables measured on continuous scales

proportional stratified random sampling a form of sampling where the population is divided into subsets (called strata) and within strata the same sampling proportion is used for selecting a sample

pure research research for which the primary objective/output is the development of theory

purposive sampling a form of non-probability sampling design where the criteria for inclusion in a sample are defined, and entities are first screened to see whether they meet the criteria for inclusion; those entities that meet the criteria are included in the sample

qualitative data the authors of this book see the logic or framing that defines the research questions of social scientists as little different whether structural equation models are used or methods of discourse analysis. Qualitative data requires relevance to be identified, categories and concepts to be defined and theories developed, as well as the development of particular truths. In addition, data is usually (but not always) gathered through the engagement of the researcher

qualitative interviews offer ways by which rich and detailed information can be gathered from respondents to reveal aspects of their lives, understandings or experience.

quasi-experimental design the use of multiple measures over time in order to reduce the effects of control and experimental groups not being fully matched

quota sampling a form of non-probability sampling design where the population is divided into units and a target sample size (quota) is defined for each unit; entities that meet the criteria for a specific unit are added to the sample until the target sample size for the unit is achieved

random assignment where the objects of the experiment (e.g. people) are assigned at random to either the experimental treatment or to the control (non-treatment) groups

range a summary measure of spread; the difference between the largest and smallest data values

rank-order correlation a test of association between two variables measured on ordered category scales

ratio scale a form of continuous scale that has a true zero point, so that ratio calculations are meaningful, for example height (cf. interval scale)

realism an ontological position which assumes that the physical and social worlds exist independently of any observations made about them

reference distribution the distribution of all alternative values of a test statistic based on the assumption that the null hypothesis is true; used in hypothesis testing

reflexivity where researchers think about the effects they have had or may have on the outcome and process of research

regression weight the value of the independent contribution of a predictor variable to predicting a dependent variable in multiple regression analysis. Also called a path coefficient

relativism an ontological view that phenomena depend on the perspectives from which we observed them; also an epistemological position that observations will be more accurate/credible if made from several different perspectives

reliability the consistency of measurement in a composite variable formed by combining scores on a set of items; can be measured by Cronbach's alpha coefficient

repertory grid a tool for uncovering an individual's (or group's) view of the world based on the constructs they develop and hold

representativeness in sampling design, this refers to how much the characteristics of a sample are the same as the characteristics of the population from which the sample is drawn

residual the value of that portion of the variance of a dependent variable that cannot be accounted for by a set of predictor variables

RMSEA (root mean squared error of approximation) an index in SEM of the goodness of fit of a hypothesized causal model adjusted for the complexity of the fitted model

robustness the extent to which a summary measure is sensitive to disturbances in data quality

sample a subset of the population from which inferences are drawn based on evidence

sample size the number of entities included in a sample

sampling distribution a form of reference distribution derived from probability theory based on repeated sampling from a theoretical population; used in hypothesis testing

sampling frame the list of all of those eligible to be included in a sample

sampling proportion the size of a sample relative to the size of a population

scholarship this is a term given to the development of high levels of knowledge about a particular issue or topic, largely on the basis of secondary data

search engine a program that will find text relating to the word(s) input

secondary data research information that already exists in the form of publications or other electronic media, which is collected by the researcher

secondary visual data relates to the analysis of verbal accounts that respondents give in response to visual images

semi-concealed research a form of ethnography where there is negotiated access with research agendas that the researchers are not always willing to reveal to all those they meet

semi-detached design a mixed methods design where there are no direct linkages between the two parts of the study

sequencing in the context of mixed methods research this refers to whether or not the methods are used in a discernable order

simple random sampling a form of sampling where every entity in the population has an equal chance of being included in the sample

snowball sampling a form of non-probability sampling design where the criteria for inclusion in a sample are defined; entities that meet the criteria are included in the sample and then asked whether they know others who also meet the criteria

social constructionism the idea that 'reality' is determined by people rather than by objective and external factors, and hence it is most important to appreciate the way people make sense of their experience

social desirability where people adjust their answers to a survey in order to project a positive image of themselves to the interviewer

Spearman's rho a test of association between two variables: the product-moment correlation of the ranked scores for the two variables

specific factors a class of latent variables in a measurement model, which is assumed to account for idiosyncratic aspects of an observed variable (see also common factors)

spread a characteristic of a set of data that summarizes how much the data vary around a measure of location; measured by the range, mid-range or standard deviation

squared multiple correlation an overall measure of the quality of a multiple regression model; the proportion of variance in a dependent variable accounted for by a set of predictor variables

standard deviation a summary measure of spread; based on the average deviation of scores around the mean

standard error the standard deviation of a sampling distribution used in hypothesis testing; estimated from the standard deviations and the sample size within groups in a sample

standardization the process of transforming a variable in order to express it on a scale with a mean of zero and a standard deviation of one; often carried out for variables measured on interval scales (with no true zero point) so that regression weights can be compared between predictor variables

statistical control a way of simplifying inference about the relationships among variables by adjusting for their covariance with another variable

stepdown F-test the test statistic in a multivariate analysis of variance of group differences, where the DVs are tested singly in turn in a sequence decided upon by the researcher holding constant DVs earlier in the sequence

stepwise regression a form of multiple regression analysis where predictor variables are automatically entered or dropped sequentially on the basis of the extent of their independent contribution to predicting the dependent variable

stratified random sampling a form of sampling where the population is divided into subsets (called strata) and within strata every entity in the population has an equal chance of being included in the sample

structural equation model a multivariate model of the hypothesized causal relationships among a set of variables, which may include both observed and latent variables

structural models a multivariate model of the hypothesized relationships among a set of variables, which may include both observed and latent variables

structuration theory an epistemology that assumes that social structure and individual behaviour are interlinked, and that each is produced and reproduced by the other

structured interview surveys a form of survey where an interviewer locates each participant, and completes the survey face-to-face by asking structured questions

structured interviews where the interviewer follows a prescribed list of questions each of which may have predetermined response categories

substantive contribution this is achieved when the research throws new light onto the subject of study, whether it is a particular kind of organization or aspects of employee or managerial behaviour

summarizing describing a characteristic of a dataset such as location or spread based on aggregating data from all respondents

survey feedback the collection of opinions about the management of an organization, which is then fed back to all employees to stimulate change and improvements

symmetry a balanced distribution of data points around a central value

synergy a form of interaction between variables, where their joint effect is different from the sum of their individual effects

systematic random sampling a process of random sampling where every nth entity from the population is selected

systematic review a means of synthesizing research on a topic or within a field in such a way that is both transparent and reproducible

t-distribution a form of standard reference distribution; a form of the normal distribution where the standard deviation of the reference distribution is estimated from sample data

telephone interview surveys a form of survey where an interviewer locates each participant, and completes the survey by telephone by asking structured questions

template analysis a method of qualitative data analysis that enables a systematic, thematic analysis of text

testing effect where changes observed in individual behaviour or attitudes over time are caused by the measures having been made in the first place

theoretical contribution this is achieved when new concepts are developed, or existing concepts are extended, in order to understand or explain behaviour and organizational phenomena

topic guide a prepared list of areas (rather than specific questions) that need to be covered during the course of an interview

transcendental realism a philosophical position which assumes that the objects of scientific inquiry exist and act independently of the observer triangulation using different kinds of measures or perspectives in order to increase the confidence in the accuracy of observations

trimmed mean a family of summary measures of location where a proportion of the largest and smallest values are ignored in calculating a mean; the mid-mean is a 25 per cent trimmed mean, the median is a 50 per cent trimmed mean

t-test a form of hypothesis test for comparing mean scores of two groups

type I error a false conclusion from a hypothesis test involving a claim that an effect exists (an association between variables or a group difference) when there is no such effect in the population

type II error a false conclusion from a hypothesis test involving a claim that no effect exists (an association between variables or a group difference) when there is an effect in the population

unit of analysis the main level at which data is aggregated: can be individuals, groups, events, organizations, etc: within relativist studies researchers look for relationships between attributes that vary across different units of analysis

univariate F-test the test statistic in multivariate analysis of variance for group differences in a single dependent variable ignoring others

univariate test a test of a study hypothesis, which involves consideration of a single dependent variable

universal theories theories that may be derived in one social organizational setting, and which are applicable in any other setting or context

validity the extent to which measures and research findings provide accurate representation of the things they are supposed to be describing

variance a summary measure of spread used in calculating the standard deviation; the average deviation of scores around the mean

verification a research design that seeks evidence to demonstrate that the current assumptions or hypotheses are correct

visual analysis a combination of research traditions that come together to analyse various forms of visual data, typically characterized by its volume, homogeneity and dynamic nature

visual metaphors an approach to eliciting the views of individuals or groups with the notion of metaphors in order to get individuals (or groups) to draw and describe issues or events as they currently see them or would like to see them in the future

Wald test the test statistic in logistic regression analysis expressing the independent contribution of a predictor variable

Web of Knowledge a database that provides a single route to journals in the Social Sciences Citation Index

web-based surveys a form of survey where a website link is sent to each potential participant, respondents complete the survey by recording their answers on online; answers may be checked for consistency and then stored on a database for analysis

Wilks' Lambda the test statistic in multivariate analysis of variance for group differences in a set of two or more dependent variables

Zetoc a current awareness service for higher education institutions in the UK; the service gives access to the British Library's table of contents database and a Zetoc alert can provide users with information on the contents of new journals as soon as they are issued

FURTHER READINGS

CHAPTER 1: GETTING STARTED AND WRITING THE RESEARCH PROPOSAL

Alvesson, M. and Willmott, H. (eds) (2003) *Studying Management Critically*. London: Sage.
   A collection of chapters for readers who are exploring areas for critical research in business and management.

Bartunek, J.M., Rynes, S.L. and Daft, R.L. (2001) 'Across the Great Divide: knowledge creation and transfer between practitioners and academics', *Academy of Management Journal*, 44, 340–55.
   This article discusses the role of relationships between practitioners and academics in generating and disseminating knowledge across 'the Great Divide.'

Grey, C. (2005) *A Very Short, Fairly Interesting and Reasonably Cheap Book About Studying Organizations*. London: Sage.
   As it says on the label, this book provides a succinct overview of theories of management and organization, and it is reasonably priced. It adopts a critical view in the sense that it has a slight preference for the perspectives of those who are managed, rather than the managers themselves.

Marshall, S. and Green, N. (2007) *Your PhD Companion: A Handy Mix of Practical Tips, Sound Advice and Helpful Commentary to See You Through Your PhD*, 2nd edn. Oxford: Cromwell Press.
   A handy guidebook for readers embarking on doctoral study – and a good read.

Thomas, A. (2004) *Research Skills for Management Studies*. New York: Routledge.
   A comprehensive overview of skills required to conduct management research.

CHAPTER 2: REVIEWING THE LITERATURE

We recommend in particular the following textbooks on literature reviews:

Hart, C. (1998) *Doing a Literature Review: Releasing the Social Science Research Imagination*. London: Sage.
   Excellent introduction to how to plan a literature review, which also offers important guidance on how to read and critically evaluate research publications (with a focus on traditional literature reviews).

Jesson, J., Matheson, L. and Lacey, F.M. (2011) *Doing Your Literature Review. Traditional and Systematic Techniques*. London: Sage.
   An extremely helpful textbook that covers both traditional and systematic reviews.

The following three publications focus more specifically on systematic reviews:

Fink, A. (2005) *Conducting Research Literature Reviews: From the Internet to Paper*. Thousand Oaks, CA: Sage.
Petticrew, M. and Roberts, H. (2006) *Systematic Reviews in the Social Sciences: A Practical Guide*. Malden, MA: Blackwell.
Tranfield, D., Denyer, D. and Smart, P. (2003) 'Towards a methodology for developing evidence-informed management knowledge by means of systematic review', *British Journal of Management*, 14 (3): 207–22.

Published reviews of literature can be seen in specialist review journals such as *International Journal of Management Reviews*, *Academy of Management Review*, *Annual Review of Organizational Psychology and Organizational Behavior* and *Psychological Review*. The following three articles were chosen to illustrate different kinds of literature reviews:

Easterby-Smith, M. (1997) 'Disciplines of organizational learning: contributions and critiques', *Human Relations*, 51 (9): 1085–116.

Shalley, C.E. and Gilson, L.L. (2004) 'What leaders need to know: a review of social and contextual factors that can foster or hinder creativity', *The Leadership Quarterly*, 15 (1): 33–53.

Thorpe, R., Holt, R., Macpherson, A. and Pittaway, L. (2005) 'Knowledge within small and medium-sized firms: a review of the evidence', *International Journal of Management Reviews*, 7 (4): 257–81.

CHAPTER 3: THE PHILOSOPHY OF MANAGEMENT AND BUSINESS RESEARCH

Ackroyd, S. and Fleetwood, S. (eds) (2000) *Realist Perspectives on Management and Organizations*. London: Routledge.
A useful collection of readings that cover both the theoretical assumptions of critical realism and their applications to organizational research in different contexts, such as medicine and high-technology companies. Authors emphasize different features of critical realism and do not follow a single party line.

Alvesson, M. and Deetz, S. (2000) *Doing Critical Management Research*. London: Sage.
One of the few books that articulates what 'critical' management research looks like, and how it can be conducted, for example through increasing sensitivity to the aspects of organization life that normally lie hidden. Also provides a much deeper review of critical theory and why it is important.

Blaikie, N. (2007) *Approaches to Social Enquiry*, 2nd edn. Cambridge: Polity Press.
This book provides an excellent overview of different philosophical approaches to social research, with particular attention to the question of whether the research methods in the natural sciences are appropriate for the social sciences. It is quite comprehensive and very useful, provided you are prepared to put in the effort!

See also:

Hassard, J. and Parker, M. (eds) (1993) *Postmodernism and Organizations*. London: Sage.
Since postmodernism is such a wide and disparate field, it is probably best to start with edited collections. This book is one of a number of edited works on postmodernism, but has the advantage that it focuses on the relevance and application of postmodernism to organization and management theory. Contributors include many of the leading European management scholars with expertise in postmodernism.

Johnson, P. and Duberley, J. (2000) *Understanding Management Research: An Introduction to Epistemology*. London: Sage.

CHAPTER 4: DESIGNING MANAGEMENT AND BUSINESS RESEARCH

Charmaz, K. (2014) *Constructing Grounded Theory: A Practical Guide Through Qualitative Analysis*, 2nd edn. London: Sage.
A good textbook that introduces how to design and conduct a grounded theory study. Charmaz is a prominent advocate for constructionist approaches to grounded theory, distancing herself from the more positivist leanings of the founders of grounded theory.

Creswell, J.W. (2003) *Research Design: Qualitative, Quantitative and Mixed Methods Approaches*, 2nd edn. Thousand Oaks, CA: Sage.
A great beginner's overview of the three different paradigms.

Locke, K. (2001) *Grounded Theory in Management Research*. London: Sage.
This is an excellent overview of the origins of grounded theory including the differences of opinion between Glaser and Strauss, the key methods and approaches as currently practised, and the specific adaptations that may be required when conducting organizational or management research.

Miller, D.C. and Salkind, N.J. (2002) *Handbook of Research Design & Social Measurement*, 6th edn. Thousand Oaks, CA: Sage.
A useful, albeit slightly dated, handbook for further reference with excellent chapters on how to develop a research design, formulate a research problem and compose a research proposal. It also includes a section on applied and evaluation research.

Shadish, W.R., Cook, T.D. and Campbell, D.T. (2002) *Experimental and Quasi-Experimental Designs for Generalised Causal Inference*. Boston, MA: Houghton Mifflin.
An updated version of the classic book on experimental forms of social research.

Teddlie, C. and Tashakkori, A. (2009) *Foundations of Mixed Methods Research: Integrating Quantitative and Qualitative Approaches in the Social and Behavioral Sciences*. London: Sage.
  Chapter 7 of this authoritative text on mixed methods research considers research designs for studies which combine quantitative and qualitative methods.

CHAPTER 5: POLITICS, ACCESS AND ETHICS

Bell, E. and Bryman, A. (2007) 'The ethics of management research: an exploratory content analysis', *British Journal of Management*, 18 (1), 63–77.
  The authors suggest that management researchers face ethical issues that are distinct from those encountered by other social science researchers. They provide a review of ethics codes formulated by nine social scientific associations, and argue that reciprocity is a central principle for management research.

Boje, D. (2001) *Narrative Methods for Organizational and Communication Research*. London: SAGE.
  An authoritative book on the use of stories as a source of understanding of organizational life. It provides eight different ways of making sense of stories using the idea of 'anti-narrative', which recognizes that organizational stories are not necessarily complete, that they can be fragmented and can vary with the times and purposes of the story-teller.

Buchanan, D. and Badham, R. (2008) *Power, Politics and Organizational Change: Winning the Turf Game*, 2nd edn. London: Sage.
  This edition, which focuses on how managers can act as internal change agents, emphasizes the contexts in which they initiate and achieve change. It provides an accessible overview of organizational politics, which is useful for the researcher both in conducting and implementing research.

Buchanan, D.A. and Bryman, A. (2009) *The SAGE Handbook of Organizational Research Methods*. Los Angeles: SAGE.
  Textbook that provides a rich resource for researchers in management and business studies and includes chapters on important ethical and political issues.

Israel, M. and Hay, I. (2006) *Research Ethics for Social Scientists. Between Ethical Conduct and Regulatory Compliance*. London: SAGE.
  A useful and well-written textbook on research ethics in the social sciences which includes an overview of how research ethics are regulated in different parts of the world.

Morrill, C., Zald, M.N. and Rao, H. (2003) 'Covert political conflict in organizations: challenges from below', *Annual Review of Sociology*, 29, 391–415.
  This review identifies different forms of covert political conflict in organizations and examines different explanations for their occurrence.

Saunders, M., Lewis, P. and Thornhill, A. (2012) *Research Methods for Business Students*, 6th edn. Harlow: Pearson.
  This is a competitor textbook which provides an extensive discussion of ethics and access in Chapter 6 (pp. 208–57). Somewhat less coverage of politics, though.

CHAPTER 6: CRAFTING QUALITATIVE DATA THROUGH LANGUAGE AND TEXT

Alvesson, M. (2003) 'Beyond neopositivists, romantics, and localists: a reflexive approach to interviews in organisation research', *Academy of Management Review*, 28 (1): 13–33.

Bourne, H. and Jenkins, M. (2005) 'Eliciting managers' personal values: an adaptation of the laddering interview method', *Organizational Research Method*, 8 (4): 410–28.

Cassell, C. and Symon, G. (2004) *Essential Guide to Qualitative Methods in Organizational Research*. London: Sage.
  Useful guide with chapters on how to use different methods and techniques in organizational research (including interviews, critical incident technique, repertory grids, cognitive mapping and other methods).

Fielding, N., Lee, R.M. and Blank, G. (2008) *The SAGE Handbook of Online Research Methods*. London: Sage.
  Useful collection of chapters on how to conduct research using the Internet, including a chapter on internet-based interviewing. Also:

Gubrium, J.F., Holstein, J., Marvasti, A.B. and McKinney, K.D. (2012) *The SAGE Handbook of Interview Research: The Complexity of the Craft*, 2nd edn. Thousand Oaks, CA: Sage.
  Excellent resource with chapters on all aspects of interviewing.

Krueger, R.A. and Casey, M.A. (2009) *Focus Groups: A Practical Guide for Applied Research*, 4th edn. Los Angeles, CA: Sage.
Explains in detail how to plan and moderate focus groups. Similarly useful:

Kvale, S. and Brinkmann, S. (2009) *InterViews: Learning the Craft of Qualitative Research Interviewing*, 2nd edn. Thousand Oaks, CA: Sage.
Useful overview of different interview methods.

Nadin, S. and Cassell, C. (2006) 'The use of a research diary as a tool for reflexive practice: some reflections from management research', *Qualitative Research in Accounting & Management*, 3 (3): 208–17.
Tracy, S.J. (2013) *Qualitative Research Methods: Collecting Evidence, Crafting Analysis, Communicating Impact*. Chichester: Wiley-Blackwell.
Excellent textbook for students planning to conduct a qualitative study; Chapters 7 and 8 cover many practical aspects of interview planning and interview practice.

The following references provide a useful starting point for those interested in critical incident technique, repertory grids and cognitive maps:

Butterfield, L.D., Borgen, W.A., Amundson, N.E. and Maglio, A.T. (2005) 'Fifty years of the critical incident technique: 1954–2004 and beyond', *Qualitative Research* 5 (4): 475–97.
Eden, C. (1992) 'On the nature of cognitive maps', *Journal of Management Studies*, 29 (3): 261–65.
Rogers, B. and Ryals, L. (2007) 'Using the repertory grid to access the underlying realities in key account relationships', *International Journal of Market Research*, 49 (5): 595–612.

CHAPTER 7: CRAFTING QUALITATIVE DATA THROUGH OBSERVATION AND INTERACTION

Banks, M. (2008) *Using Visual Data in Qualitative Research*. London: Sage.
A helpful overview of visual methods. See also:

Coghlan, D. and Brannick, T. (2014) *Doing Action Research in Your Own Organization*, 4th edn. London: Sage.
Practical manual on how to prepare for action research in your own organization. See also:

Cunliffe, A.L. (2003) 'Reflexive inquiry in organizational research: questions and possibilities', *Human Relations*, 56 (8): 983–1003.
Cunliffe, A.L. (2010) 'Retelling tales of the field: in search of organizational ethnography 20 years on', *Organizational Research Methods*, 13 (2): 224–39.
Eden, C. and Huxham, C. (1996) 'Action research for management research', *British Journal of Management*, 7 (1): 75–86.
Emerson, R.M., Fretz, R. and Shaw, L.L. (2011) *Writing Ethnographic Fieldnotes*, 2nd edn. Chicago, IL: University of Chicago Press.
Very helpful guidance on how to write – and work with – fieldnotes.

Galman, S.C. (2007) *Shane, the Lone Ethnographer. A Beginner's Guide to Ethnography*. Lanham, MD: AltaMira.
Entertaining (cartoon) introduction to ethnography for novice researchers.

Karra, N. and Phillips, N. (2007) 'Researching "back home": international management research as autoethnography', *Organizational Research Methods*, 11 (3): 541–61.
Margolis, E. and Pauwels, L. (2011) *The SAGE Handbook of Visual Research Methods*. Los Angeles, CA: Sage.
Excellent collection of chapters on a broad variety of methods and techniques for creating (and analysing) visual data, including participatory approaches.

Reason, P. and Bradbury, H. (2006) *Handbook of Action Research: The Concise Paperback Edition*. Thousand Oaks, CA: Sage.
Concise student version (400 pages) of the most comprehensive compendium on action research.

van Maanen, J. (2011) 'Ethnography as work: some rules of engagement', *Journal of Management Studies*, 48 (1): 218–34.
Ybema, S., Yanow, D., Kamsteeg, F.H. and Wels, H. (eds) (2009) *Organizational Ethnography: Studying the Complexity of Everyday Life*. London: Sage.
Collection of chapters in which authors explore the particular challenges faced by scholars and students conducting ethnographic research in and with organizations. To be complemented by:

CHAPTER 8: FRAMING AND INTERPRETING QUALITATIVE DATA

Banks, M. (2008) *Using Visual Data in Qualitative Research*. London: Sage.

> Discusses a wide range of visual data produced by researchers and research participants, whereas the following Chapter focuses more on the analysis of video data:

Boje, D.M. (2003) 'Using narratives and telling stories', in D. Holman and R. Thorpe (eds), *Management and Language*. London: Sage.

> Offers a guide for researchers to examine alternative discourse-analysis strategies. The book sets out eight options for use in organization and communication research. See also:

Charmaz, K. (2014) *Constructing Grounded Theory: A Practical Guide Through Qualitative Analysis*, 2nd edn. London: Sage.

> Seminal textbook on how to conduct data creation and data analysis using Grounded Theory.

DeCuir-Gunby, J.T., Marshall, P.L. and McCulloch, A.W. (2011) 'Developing and using a codebook for the analysis of interview data: an example from a professional development research project', *Field Methods*, 23 (2): 136–55.

> Details steps on how to create a codebook for coding interview data.

Duriau, V.J., Reger, R.K. and Pfarrer, M.D. (2007) 'A content analysis of the content analysis literature in organization studies: research themes, data sources, and methodological refinements', *Organizational Research Methods*, 10 (1): 5–34.

> A great example for applied content analysis and a useful overview of how it has been used in organization studies.

The following website is a great starting point for readers wanting to find out more about template analysis:

Flick, U. (2014) *SAGE Handbook of Qualitative Data Analysis*. London: Sage.

> Comprehensive collection of chapters on a wide range of approaches, methods and techniques for analysing qualitative data.

Galman, S.C. (2013) *The Good, the Bad, and the Data: Shane the Lone Ethnographer's Basic Guide to Qualitative Data Analysis*. Walnut Creek, CA: Left Coast Press.

> Comic-style textbook for novices to qualitative analysis.

King, N. (2014) *Template Analysis Website*, University of Huddersfield. Available at www.hud.ac.uk/hhs/research/template-analysis/ (last accessed 14 August 2014).

Knoblauch, H., Tuma, R. and Schnettler, B. (2014) 'Visual analysis and videography', in U. Flick (ed.), *SAGE Handbook of Qualitative Data Analysis*. London: Sage, pp. 435–49.

The following four publications give useful introductions into discourse analysis and conversation analysis:

Bergmann, J.R. (2004) 'Conversation analysis', in U. Flick, E. Kardorff and I. Steinke (eds), *A Companion to Qualitative Research*. London: Sage, pp. 296–302.

Cunliffe, A.L. (2008) 'Discourse analysis', in R. Thorpe and R. Holt (eds), *The SAGE Dictionary of Qualitative Management Research*. London: Sage.

Leitch, S. and Palmer, I. (2010) 'Analysing texts in context: current practices and new protocols for critical discourse analysis in organisational studies', *Journal of Management Studies*, 47(6): 1194–212.

Sidnell, J. (2011) *Conversation Analysis: An Introduction*. Malden, MA: Wiley-Blackwell.

Lawler, S. (2002) 'Narrative in social research', in T. May (ed.), *Qualitative Research in Action*. London: Sage, pp. 242–58.

Some examples of applied narrative analysis:

Boje, D.M. (1995) 'Stories of the story-telling organization: a postmodern analysis of Disney as "Tamara-land"', *Academy of Management Journal*, 38 (4): 997–1035.

Dawson, A. and Hjorth, D. (2012) 'Advancing family business research through narrative analysis', *Family Business Review*, 25 (3): 339–55.

Silver, C. and Lewins, A. (2014) *Using Software in Qualitative Research: A Step-by-step Guide*, 2nd edn. Los Angeles, CA: Sage.

> A comprehensive introduction into how to use CAQDAS packages with text, video and mixed data. For readers working with Atlas.ti and NVivo we also recommend their online tutorial along with:

Bazeley, P. (2007) *Qualitative Data Analysis with NVivo*. London: Sage.

Flick, U. (2007) *Managing Quality in Qualitative Research*. London: Sage.

> In this slim volume, Flick goes a long way in explaining how to distinguish good from bad qualitative research. See also Barbour and Maxwell and Chmielin in Flick's *SAGE Handbook of Qualitative Data Analysis*.

Friese, S. (2012) *Qualitative Data Analysis with ATLAS.ti*. London: Sage.

Locke, K. (2001) *Grounded Theory in Management Research*. London: Sage.

> Offers a comprehensive overview of the debates and possibilities available to researchers when considering grounded approaches to data collection and analysis.

Miles, M.B., Huberman, A.M. and Saldaña, J. (2014) *Qualitative Data Analysis*, 3rd edn. Thousand Oaks, CA: Sage.
One of the leading textbook on qualitative data analysis in the social sciences. Miles, Huberman and Saldaña cover a wide range of methods for exploring, describing, analysing and explaining qualitative data as well as drawing and verifying conclusions.

Saldaña, J. (2009) *The Coding Manual for Qualitative Researchers*. Los Angeles, CA: Sage.
A practical introduction into coding which also provides an excellent overview of different frameworks for coding qualitative data.

Suddaby, R. (2006) 'From the Editors: what grounded theory is not', *Academy of Management Journal*, 49 (4): 633–42.
Article that discusses common misconceptions of what constitutes 'grounded theory'.

Tracy, S.J. (2010) 'Qualitative quality: eight "big-tent" criteria for excellent qualitative research', *Qualitative Inquiry*, 16 (10): 837–51.
A more recent compilation of quality criteria for qualitative research.

CHAPTER 9: CRAFTING QUANTITATIVE DATA

The following two texts describe the System of Multiple Level Observation of Groups (SYMLOG), which is a more detailed elaboration of the IPA:

Bales, R.F., Cohen, S.P. and Williamson, S.A. (1979) *SYMLOG: A System for the Multiple Level Observation of Groups*. New York: The Free Press.
Bales, R.F. (1988) 'A new overview of the SYMLOG system: measuring and changing behavior in groups', in R.B. Polley, A.P. Hare and P.J. Stone (eds), *The SYMLOG Practitioner*. New York: Praeger, pp. 319–44.

Couper, M.P. (2008) *Designing Effective Web Surveys*. Cambridge: Cambridge University Press.
This is a useful source for web-based surveys.

DeVellis, R.F. (2012) *Scale Development: Theory and Applications*, 3rd edn. Thousand Oaks, CA: Sage.
Covers the foundations of scale construction and measurement in an accessible manner.

The following two books offer a comprehensive introduction to different kinds of sampling design for social science research and the principles that inform how a researcher might choose between them.

Dillman, D.A., Smyth, J.D. and Christian, L.M. (2009) *Internet, Mail, and Mixed-Mode Surveys: The Tailored Design Method*, 3rd edn. Hoboken, NJ: Wiley.
Sapsford, R. (2006) *Survey Research*, 2nd edn. London: Sage.

George, G., Haas, M.R. and Pentland, A. (2014) 'Big data and management', *Academy of Management Journal*, 57, 321–6.
Discussion of emerging trends around 'big data' in business and management research.

Miller, D.C. and Salkind, N.J. (2002) *Handbook of Research Design & Social Measurement*, 6th edn. Thousand Oaks, CA: Sage.
A comprehensive handbook with a useful introduction to assessing social variables, scales and indexes.

Waters, C.D.J. (2011) *Quantitative Methods for Business*, 5th edn. Harlow: Financial Times/Prentice Hall.
A practical introduction into quantitative methods for beginners with a helpful part on data collection.

CHAPTER 10: SUMMARIZING AND MAKING INFERENCES FROM QUANTITATIVE DATA

Buglear, J. (2012) *Quantitative Methods for Business and Management Students*. Harlow: Pearson.
Less comprehensive (and perhaps less amusing) introduction into quantitative research methods. Tailored to the needs of business and management researchers, this textbook is well written and includes chapters on presenting, summarizing and investigating quantitative data.

Field, A.P., Miles, J. and Field, Z. (2012) *Discovering Statistics Using R*. London: Sage.
Field, A. (2013) *Discovering Statistics Using IBM SPSS Statistics. And Sex and Drugs and Rock 'n' Roll*, 4th edn. Los Angeles, CA: Sage.
The focus of this book is getting the statistical work done rather than the dry statistical theory itself. It is accessible (provided you can tune into the author's sense of humour and his liking for selfies), and covers much of the material in this chapter and the next, plus a lot more. A different version of the book introduces statistics using the increasingly popular software tool R:

Howell, D. (2013) *Statistical Methods for Psychology*, 8th edn. Belmont, CA: Wadsworth.

Howell, D. (2013) *Fundamental Statistics for the Behavioral Sciences*, 8th edn. Nashville, TN: Broadman and Holman.

> Both books go into more detail on the logic of hypothesis testing and describe a much more extensive set of statistical tests for comparing groups or testing association between variables. The strengths of the author's approach are that he emphasizes the importance of looking at data intelligently before making decisions about forms of analysis, and he also explains clearly the conceptual underpinnings of the methods that are covered.

CHAPTER 11: MULTIVARIATE ANALYSIS

Atinc, G., Simmering, M.J. and Kroll, M.J. (2011) 'Control variable use and reporting in macro and micro management research', *Organizational Research Methods*, 15, 57–74.

> Helpful discussion on the use of control variables in management research.

Blunch, N.J. (2008) *Introduction to Structural Equation Modelling Using SPSS and AMOS*. London: Sage.

> This is a readable book, which introduces both SEM and the key concepts underlying measurement models (such as reliability). The examples are based on the AMOS package, which is now an add-on to SPSS, but could easily be adapted for use with other software.

Hair, J.F., Black, B., Babin, B., Anderson, R.E. and Tatham, R.L. (2010) *Multivariate Data Analysis*, 7th edn. Upper Saddle River, NJ: Prentice Hall.

> This is an excellent book on the use of multivariate methods in social science. The strength of the book is the applications it uses as illustration of the methods covered, and the focus on preparatory work to examine the properties of the data first before embarking on complex multivariate analysis. Again, see also Fields listed at the end of the previous chapter.

Kaplan, D. (2004) *The SAGE Handbook of Quantitative Methodology for the Social Sciences*. Thousand Oaks, CA: Sage.

> Collection of chapters covering a wide range of quantitative methods for an advanced readership.

McWilliams, A. and Siegel, D. (1997) 'Event studies in management research: theoretical and empirical issues', *Academy of Management Journal*, 40, 626–57.

> Examination of a range of event studies in management research.

Tabachnick, B.G. and Fidell, L.S. (2014) *Using Multivariate Statistics*, 6th edn. Boston, MA: Pearson Education.

> This too is an excellent and thorough text on multivariate statistical methods for social science researchers. Its approach is practical rather than theoretical, and the authors cover all of the methods described in this chapter as well as others not covered here. For each method, they give its rationale, practical guidelines about how to use it, worked examples using a variety of statistical packages, and show how to present the results of analysis.

CHAPTER 12: WRITING MANAGEMENT AND BUSINESS RESEARCH

Golden-Biddle, K. and Locke, K. (2007) *Composing Qualitative Research*, 2nd edn. London: Sage.

> A delightful book that looks at strategies for presenting qualitative research. It also provides good examples from the authors' own experiences of how to handle the complex politics of the review process when submitting papers to journals.

Hart, C. (1998) *Doing a Literature Review: Releasing the Social Science Research Imagination*. London: Sage.

> The final chapter provides guidance on writing up literature reviews, with an emphasis on how to develop arguments and guidance on the elements that need to be included.

Murray, R. (2002) *How to Write a Thesis*. Milton Keynes: Open University Press.

> This book provides lots of advice and guidance on the technicalities of writing including grammar, style and structure. It is also very helpful on the more strategic and emotional aspects of academic research and writing.

Phillips, E.M. and Pugh, D.S. (2005) *How to Get a PhD: A Handbook for Students and their Supervisors*, 4th edn. Maidenhead: Open University Press.
This is a thoughtful and practical book with lots of advice on how to manage and complete research work, especially at the doctoral level. Lots of examples and good humour from the authors.

Wallace, M. and Wray, A. (2011) *Critical Reading and Writing for Postgraduates*, 2nd edn. London: Sage.
An accessible and well-written book on how to develop a reflective and critical approach to academic reading and writing which can be helpful for both practitioners and more experienced academics.

BIBLIOGRAPHY

AACSB (2013) *The Promise of Doctoral Education: Setting the Pace for Innovation, Sustainability, Relevance and Quality.* Tampa, FL: AACSB International.

Abrahamson, M. (1983) *Social Research Methods.* Englewood Cliffs, NJ: Prentice Hall.

Ackermann, F. and Eden, C. (2011) *Making Strategy. Mapping Out Strategic Success*, 2nd edn. London: Sage.

Ackroyd, S. and Fleetwood, S. (2000) 'Realism in contemporary organizational and management studies', in S. Ackroyd and S. Fleetwood (eds), *Realist Perspectives on Management and Organizations.* London: Routledge, pp. 3–25.

Agar, M.H. (1986) *Speaking of Ethnography.* Beverly Hills, CA: Sage.

Ahmed, S. (1998) *Differences that Matter: Feminist Theory and Postmodernism.* Cambridge: Cambridge University Press.

Ahuja, G. (2000) 'Collaboration networks, structural holes, and innovation: a longitudinal study', *Administrative Science Quarterly*, 45: 425–55.

Aiken, H.D. (1956) *The Age of Ideology.* New York: Mentor.

Alvesson, M. (1990) 'Organization: from substance to image', *Organisation Studies*, 11: 373–94.

Alvesson, M. (1998) 'Gender relations and identity at work: a case study of an advertising agency', *Human Relations*, 51 (8): 969–1005.

Alvesson, M. (2003) 'Beyond neopositivists, romantics, and localists: a reflexive approach to interviews in organisation research', *Academy of Management Review*, 28 (1): 13–33.

Alvesson, M. and Deetz, S. (2000) *Doing Critical Management Research.* London: Sage.

Alvesson, M. and Kärreman, D. (2011) 'Decolonializing discourse: critical reflections on organizational discourse analysis', *Human Relations*, 64 (9): 1121–46.

Alvesson, M. and Sköldberg, K. (2000) *Reflexive Methodology: New Vistas for Qualitative Research towards a Reflexive Methodology.* London: Sage.

Alvesson, M. and Willmott, H. (eds) (2003) *Studying Management Critically.* London: Sage.

Amis, J. and Silk, M.L. (2008) 'The philosophy and politics of quality in qualitative organizational research', *Organizational Research Methods*, 11: 456–80.

Anderson, L. (2008a) 'Participant observation', in R. Thorpe and R. Holt (eds), *The SAGE Dictionary of Qualitative Management Research.* London: Sage, pp. 150–2.

Anderson, L. (2008b) 'Reflexivity', in R. Thorpe and R. Holt (eds), *The SAGE Dictionary of Qualitative Management Research.* London: Sage, pp. 183–5.

Anderson, L.M. (2008) 'Critical action learning: an examination of the social nature of management learning and development', unpublished PhD thesis, University of Leeds, Leeds University Business School, April.

Anderson, M.L. (1993) 'Studying across difference: race, class and gender in qualitative research', in J.H. Stanfield and R.M. Dennis (eds), *Race and Ethnicity in Research Methods.* London: Sage, pp. 39–52.

Aristotle, with Brown, L. (ed.) and Ross, D. (trans.) (2009) *The Nicomachean Ethics.* Oxford: Oxford University Press.

Ashton, D.J.L. and Easterby-Smith, M. (1979) *Management Development in the Organisation.* London: Macmillan.

Astley, W.G. and Zammuto, R.F. (1992) 'Organisation science, managers, and language games', *Organisation Science*, 3: 443–60.

Atinc, G., Simmering, M.J. and Kroll, M.J. (2011) 'Control variable use and reporting in macro and micro management research', *Organizational Research Methods*, 15, 57–74.

Atkinson, P. (2010) *Handbook of Ethnography.* Reprinted. Los Angeles, CA: Sage.

Austin, J.H. (1978) *Chase, Chance and Creativity.* New York: Columbia University Press.

Ayer, A.J. ([1936] 1971) *Language, Truth and Logic.* Harmondsworth: Pelican.

Back, L. (2006) *ESRC Research Development Initiative Conference.* London: Royal College of Physicians.

Bailey, J. (2008) 'First steps in qualitative data analysis: transcribing', *Family Practice*, 25 (2): 127–31.

Baker, C.D., Emmison, M. and Firth, A. (2005) *Calling for Help.* Amsterdam: John Benjamins.

Baker, S. (1996) 'Consumer cognitions: mapping personal benefits relating to perfume purchase in the UK and Germany', 207th ESOMAR Seminar, Capturing the Elusive Appeal of Fragrance: Techniques, Experiences, Challenges. Amsterdam.

Baker, S. and Knox, S. (1995) 'Mapping consumer cognitions in Europe', in M. Bergadaa (ed.), *Marketing Today for the 21st Century*. Proceedings of 24th EMAC Conference, Cergy-Pontoisse, France, 1: 81–100.

Bales, R.F. (1950) *Interaction Process Analysis*. Cambridge, MA: Addison-Wesley.

Bales, R.F. (1970) *Personality and Interpersonal Behavior*. New York: Holt, Rinehart & Winston.

Bales, R.F. (1988) 'A new overview of the SYMLOG system: measuring and changing behavior in groups', in R.B. Polley, A.P. Hare and P.J. Stone (eds), *The SYMLOG Practitioner*. New York: Praeger, pp. 319–44.

Bales, R.F., Cohen, S.P. and Williamson, S.A. (1979) *SYMLOG: A System for the Multiple Level Observation of Groups*. New York: The Free Press.

Bancroft Library Oral Histories (2014) *Venture Capitalists Oral History Project*. Edited by Project Director and Interviewer: Sally Smith Hughe. Regional Oral History Office (ROHO), The Bancroft Library, University of California, Berkeley. Available at: http://bancroft.berkeley.edu/ROHO/projects/vc/transcripts.html (last accessed 14 August 2014).

Banks, M. (1995) 'Visual research methods', *Social Research Update*, 11: 1–6.

Banks, M. (2008) *Using Visual Data in Qualitative Research*. London: Sage.

Bannister, D. and Fransella, F. (1971) *Inquiring Man: The Theory of Personal Constructs*. Harmondsworth: Penguin.

Barbour, R.S. (2014) 'Quality of data analysis', in U. Flick (ed.), *SAGE Handbook of Qualitative Data Analysis*. London: Sage, pp. 496–509.

Barley, S.R. (1986) *The Innocent Anthropologist: Notes from a Mud Hut*. Harmondsworth: Penguin.

Barry, C.A. (1998) 'Choosing qualitative data analysis software: Atlas/ti and Nudist compared', *Sociological Research Online*, 3 (3). Available at: www.socresonline.org.uk/3/3/4.html (last accessed 27 October 2008).

Barry, L.R. (2004) 'NVivo 2.0 and ATLAS.ti 5.0: a comparative review of two popular qualitative data-analysis programs', *Field Methods*, 16: 439–64.

Bartunek, J.M. and Louis, M.R. (1996) *Insider/Outsider Team Research*. Thousand Oaks, CA: Sage.

Bartunek, J.M., Rynes, S.L. and Daft, R.L. (2001) 'Across the Great Divide: knowledge creation and transfer between practitioners and academics', *Academy of Management Journal*, 44: 340–55.

Barwise, P., Marsh, P., Thomas, K. and Wensley, R. (1989) 'Intelligent elephants and part-time researchers', *Graduate Management Research*, Winter: 12–33.

Bazeley, P. (2007) *Qualitative Data Analysis with NVivo*. London: Sage.

Bell, E. and Bryman, A. (2007) 'The ethics of management research: an exploratory content analysis', *British Journal of Management*, 18 (1): 63–77.

Bennis, W.G. and O'Toole, J. (2005) 'How business schools lost their way', *Harvard Business Review*, 83 (5): 1–9.

Bentler, P.M. and Dudgeon, P. (1996) 'Covariance structure analysis: statistical practice, theory and direction', *Annual Review of Psychology*, 47: 563–92.

Berger, P.L. and Luckman, T. (1966) *The Social Construction of Reality*. London: Penguin.

Berger, R. and Rosenberg, E. (2008) 'The experience of abused women with their children's law guardians', *Violence Against Women*, 14: 71–92.

Berghman, L., Matthyssens, P. and Vandenbempt, K. (2006) 'Building competences for new customer value creation: an exploratory study', *Industrial Marketing Management*, 35 (8): 961–73.

Bergmann, J.R. (2004) 'Conversation analysis', in U. Flick, E. Kardorff and I. Steinke (eds), *A Companion to Qualitative Research*. London: Sage, pp. 296–302.

Berman, S.L., Wicks, A.C., Kotha, S. and Jones, T.M. (1999) 'Does stakeholder orientation matter? The relationship between stakeholder management models and firm financial performance', *Academy of Management Journal*, 42 (5): 488–506.

Bernard, H.R. (2011) *Research Methods in Anthropology: Qualitative and Quantitative Approaches*, 5th edn. Lanham, MD: AltaMira.

Berrone, P., Fosfuri, A., Gelabert, L. and Gomez-Mejia, L.R. (2013) 'Necessity as the mother of "green" inventions: institutional pressures and environmental innovations', *Strategic Management Journal*, 34: 891–909.

Bessant, J., Binley, S., Cooper, C., Dawson, S., Gernard, J., Gardiner, M., Gray, A., Jones, P., Mayer, C., Magee, J., Pidd, M., Rowley, G., Saunders, J. and Stark, A. (2003) 'The state of the field in UK management research: reflections of the Research Assessment Exercise (RAE) Panel', *British Journal of Management*, 14: 51–68.

Bettis, R.A. and Prahalad, C.K. (1995) 'The dominant logic: retrospective and extensions', *SMJ*, 16 (1): 5–14.

Beynon, H. (1973) *Working for Ford*. Harmondsworth: Penguin.

Beynon, H. (1988) 'Regulating research: politics and decision making in industrial organisations', in A. Bryman (ed.), *Doing Research in Organisations*. London: Routledge, pp. 21–33.

Bhaskar, R. (1978) *A Realist Theory of Science*. New York: Harvester Press.

Bhaskar, R. (1989) *Reclaiming Reality: A Critical Introduction to Contemporary Philosophy*. London: Verso.

Billig, M. (1988) 'Review of: *Murderous Science: Elimination by Scientific Selection of Jews, Gypsies and Others in Germany, 1933–1945* [B. Muller-Hill, Oxford: OUP]', *The Psychologist*, December: 475–6.

Billig, M. (1991) *Ideology and Opinions: Studies of Rhetorical Psychology*. London: Sage.

Billig, M. (1999) 'Whose terms? Whose ordinariness? Rhetoric and ideology in conversation analysis', *Discourse & Society*, 10(4): 543–82.

Birkinshaw, J., Braunerhjelm, P., Holm, U. and Terjesen, S. (2006) 'Why do some multinational corporations relocate their headquarters overseas?', *Strategic Management Journal*, 27 (7): 681–700.

Blaikie, N. (2007) *Approaches to Social Enquiry*, 2nd edn. Cambridge: Polity Press.

Bloom, B.S. and Krathwohl, D.R. (1956) *Taxonomy of Educational Objectives*. London: Longman.

Bloom, N. and van Reenen, J. (2006) 'Measuring and explaining management practices across firms and countries', CEP Discussion Paper No. 716. London: London School of Economics.

Blunch, N.J. (2008) *Introduction to Structural Equation Modelling Using SPSS and AMOS*. London: Sage.

Boissevain, J. (1974) *Friends of Friends*. Oxford: Blackwell.

Boje, D.M. (1991) 'The storytelling organization: a study of storytelling performance in an office supply firm', *Administrative Science Quarterly*, 36: 106–26.

Boje, D.M. (1995) 'Stories of the story-telling organization: a postmodern analysis of Disney as "Tamara-land"', *Academy of Management Journal*, 38 (4): 997–1035.

Boje, D.M. (2001) *Narrative Methods for Organizational and Communication Research*. London: Sage.

Boje, D.M. (2003) 'Using narratives and telling stories', in D. Holman and R. Thorpe (eds), *Management and Language*. London: Sage.

Boje, D.M. (2008) 'Storytelling in management research', in R. Thorpe and R. Holt (eds), *The SAGE Dictionary of Qualitative Management Research*. London: Sage, pp. 213–15.

Borgatti, S.P. (2006) 'Identifying sets of key players in social network', *Computational and Mathematical Organisation*, 12 (1): 21–34.

Borgatti, S.P., Everett, M.G. and Freeman, L.C. (2002) *Ucinet for Windows: Software for Social Network Analysis*. Harvard, MA: Analytic Technologies. Available at: www.analytictech.com (last accessed 24 November 2011).

Borgatti, S.P., Mehra, A., Brass, D.J. and Labianca, G. (2009) 'Network analysis in the social sciences', *Science*, 323: 892–95.

Bourne, H. and Jenkins, M. (2005) 'Eliciting managers' personal values: an adaptation of the laddering interview method', *Organizational Research Method*, 8 (4): 410–28.

Bouty, I. (2000) 'Interpersonal and interaction influences on informal resource exchanges between R&D researchers across organizational boundaries', *Academy of Management Journal*, 43: 50–65.

Bowey, A.M. and Thorpe, R. (1986) *Payment Systems and Productivity*. Basingstoke: Macmillan.

Box, G.E.P., Hunter, S.J. and Hunter, W.G. (2005) *Statistics for Experimenters: Design, Innovation, and Discovery*, 2nd edn. Chichester: Wiley.

Boyacigiller, N.A. and Adler, N.J. (1991) 'The parochial dinosaur: organizational science in a global context', *Academy of Management Review*, 16: 262–90.

Boyatzis, R.E. (1982) *The Competent Manager: A Model for Effective Performance*. New York: Wiley.

Brandi, U. and Elkjaer, B. (2008) 'Pragmatism', in R. Thorpe and R. Holt (eds), *Sage Dictionary of Qualitative Management Research*. London: Sage, pp. 169–71.

Brass, J.B., Galaskiewicz, J., Greve, H.R. and Tsai, W. (2004) 'Taking stock of social networks and organizations: a multi-level perspective', *Academy of Management Journal*, 47 (6): 795–817.

Brewer, J.D. (2000) *Ethnography*. Buckingham: Open University Press.

Brouthers, K.D. and Brouthers, L.E. (2003) 'Why services and manufacturing entry mode choices differ: the influence of transaction cost factors, risk and trust', *Journal of Management Studies*, 40 (3): 1179–204.

Brown, S.L. and Eisenhardt, K.M. (1998) *Competing on the Edge: Strategy as Structured Chaos*. Boston, MA: Harvard University Press.

Bryman, A. and Bell, E. (2003) *Business Research Methods*. Oxford: Oxford University Press.

Bryman, A. and Bell, E. (2007) *Business Research Methods*, 2nd edn. Oxford: Oxford University Press.

Bryman, A. and Cramer, D. (2004) *Quantitative Data Analysis with SPSS 12 and 13: A Guide for Social Scientists*. London: Routledge.

Buchanan, D.A. (1980) 'Gaining management skills through academic research work', *Personnel Management*, 12 (4): 45–8.

Buchanan, D.A. (1999) 'The role of photography in organisation research: a re-engineering case illustration', *Journal of Management Inquiry*, 10: 151–64.

Buchanan, D.A. and Badham, R. (2008) *Power, Politics and Organizational Change: Winning the Turf Game*, 2nd edn. London: Sage.

Buchanan, D.A. and Bryman, A. (2007) 'Contextualizing methods choice in organizational research', *Organizational Research Methods*, 10 (3): 483–501.

Buchanan, D.A., Boddy, D. and McCalman, J. (1988) 'Getting in, getting on, getting out, getting back: the art of the possible', in A. Bryman (ed.), *Doing Research in Organisations*. London: Routledge, pp. 53–67.

Buglear, J. (2012) *Quantitative Methods for Business and Management Students*. Harlow: Pearson.

Bulmer, M. (1988) 'Some reflections upon research in organization', in A. Bryman (ed.), *Doing Research in Organizations*. London: Routledge, pp. 151–61.

Burawoy, M. (2009) *The Extended Case Method: Four Countries, Four Decades, Four Great Transformations, and One Theoretical Tradition*. Berkeley, CA: University of California Press.

Burgess, R.G. (1982) *Field Research: A Source Book and Field Manual*. London: Allen and Unwin.

Burgoyne, J. and James, K.T. (2006) 'Towards best or better practice in corporate leadership development: operational issues in Mode 2 and design science research', *British Journal of Management*, 17: 303–16.

Burgoyne, J. and Stuart, R. (1976) 'The nature, use and acquisition of managerial skills and other attributes', *Personnel Review*, 15 (4): 19–29.

Burkhardt, M.E. (1994) 'Social interaction effects following a technological change: a longitudinal investigation', *Academy of Management Journal*, 37: 869–98.

Burrell, G. (1993) 'Eco and the Bunnymen', in J. Hassard and M. Parker (eds), *Postmodernism and Organizations*. London: Sage, pp. 71–82.

Burrell, G. and Morgan, G. (1979) *Sociological Paradigms and Organisational Analysis*. London: Heinemann.

Butterfield, L.D., Borgen, W.A., Amundson, N.E. and Maglio, A.T. (2005) 'Fifty years of the critical incident technique: 1954–2004 and beyond', *Qualitative Research* 5 (4): 475–97.

Buzan, T. (2004) *Mind Maps: How to Be the Best at Your Job and Still Have Time to Play*. New York: Plume.

Calder, A. and Sheridan, D. (1984) *Speak for Yourself: A Mass-Observation Anthology 1937–49*. London: Cape.

Calhoun, M.A., Starbuck, W.H. and Abrahamson, E. (2011) 'Fads, fashions and the fluidity of knowledge: Peter Senge's *The Learning Organization*', in M. Easterby-Smith and M. Lyles (eds), *Handbook of Organizational Learning and Knowledge Management*, 2nd edn. Chichester: Wiley, pp. 225–48.

Calori, R., Johnson, G. and Sarnin, P. (1994) 'CEOs' cognitive maps and the scope of the organization', *Strategic Management Journal*, 15 (6): 437–57.

Cassell, C. and Symon, G. (2004) *Essential Guide to Qualitative Methods in Organizational Research*. London: Sage.

Castells, M. (2000) *The Rise of the Network Society*, 2nd edn. Oxford: Blackwell.

Charmaz, K. (2000) 'Grounded theory: objectivist and constructivist methods', in N.K. Denzin and Y.S. Lincoln (eds), *SAGE Handbook of Qualitative Research*, 2nd edn. Thousand Oaks, CA: Sage, pp. 509–35.

Charmaz, K. (2014) *Constructing Grounded Theory: A Practical Guide Through Qualitative Analysis*, 2nd edn. London: Sage.

Checkland, P.B. (1989) 'Soft systems methodology', *Human Systems Methodology*, 8 (4): 273–89.

Chen, C-Y. (2008) 'How virtual teams use media to manage conflict', unpublished PhD thesis, University of Manchester.

Chia, R. (2008) 'Postmodernism', in R. Thorpe and R. Holt (eds), *Sage Dictionary of Qualitative Management Research*. London: Sage, pp. 162–3.

Chouliaraki, L. and Fairclough, N. (2010) 'Critical discourse analysis in organisational studies: towards an integrationist methodology', *Journal of Management Studies*, 47 (6): 1213–18.

Churchill, J. (1990) 'Complexity and strategic decision making', in C. Eden and J. Radford (eds), *Tackling Strategic Problems: The Role of Group Decision Support*. London: Sage, pp. 11–17.

Clarke, J. (2007) 'Seeing entrepreneurship: visual ethnographies of embodied entrepreneurs', unpublished PhD thesis, University of Leeds, Leeds University Business School, June.

Clarke, J. (2011) 'Revitalizing entrepreneurship: how visual symbols are used in entrepreneurial performances', *Journal of Management Studies*, 48 (6): 1365–91.

Coch, L. and French, J.R.P. (1948) 'Overcoming resistance to change', *Human Relations*, 1: 512–33.

Coffey, A. and Atkinson, P. (1996) *Making Sense of Qualitative Data*. London: Sage.

Coghlan, D. and Brannick, T. (2014) *Doing Action Research in Your Own Organization*, 4th edn. London: Sage.

Cohen, W.M. and Levinthal, D.A. (1990) 'Absorptive capacity: a new perspective on learning and innovation', *Administrative Science Quarterly*, 35: 128–52.

Coleman, J.S. (1988) 'Social capital in the creation of human capital', *American Journal of Sociology*, 94: S95–S120.

Collier, J. and Collier, J. (1986) *Visual Anthropology: Photography as a Research Method*. Albuquerque, NM: University of New Mexico.

Collins, H.M. (1983) 'An empirical relativist programme in the sociology of scientific knowledge', in K.D Knorr-Cetina and M. Mulkay (eds), *Science Observed: Perspectives on the Social Study of Science*. London: Sage, pp. 3–10.

Collinson, D.L. (1992) *Managing the Shop Floor: Subjectivity, Masculinity, and Workplace Culture*. New York: de Gruyter.

Collinson, D.L. (2002) 'Managing humour', *Journal of Management Studies*, 39: 269–88.

Comte, A. (1853) *The Positive Philosophy of Auguste Comte* (trans. H. Martineau). London: Trubner.

Conan Doyle, A. (1982) *The Adventures of Sherlock Holmes*. London: George Newnes.

Cook, S.D.N. and Brown, J.S. (1999) 'Bridging epistemologies: the generative dance between organizational knowledge and organizational knowing', *Organization Science*, 10 (4): 381–400.

Cooper, R. (1992) 'Formal organization as representation: remote control, displacement and abbreviation', in M. Reed and M. Hughes (eds), *Rethinking Organization*. London: Sage, pp. 254–72.

Cooper, R. and Burrell, G. (1988) 'Modernism, postmodernism and organizational analysis: an introduction', *Organization Studies*, 9 (1): 91–112.

Corbin, J.M. and Strauss, A. (2008) *Basics of Qualitative Research: Techniques and Procedures for Developing Grounded Theory*. London: Sage.

Corbin, J.M. and Strauss, A. (2015) *Basics of Qualitative Research: Techniques and Procedures for Developing Grounded Theory*, London: Sage Publications.

Cornelissen, J.P. (2006) *Metaphor in Organization Theory: Progress and the Past, Academy of Management Review*, 31 (2): 485–8.

Cornelissen, J.P. (2011) *Corporate Communications: A Guide to Theory and Practice*, 3rd edn. London: Sage.

Cotterill, P. (1992) 'Interviewing women: issues of friendship, vulnerability and power', *Women's Studies International Forum*, 15 (5/6): 593–606.

Cotterill, S. and King, S. (2007) 'Public sector partnerships to deliver local e-government: a social network study', paper presented at the Sixth International EGOV Conference, Regensburg (Germany), 3–7 September. Available at: www.springerlink.com/content/a646737037n18g70/ (last accessed 24 November 2011).

Couper, M.P. (2008) *Designing Effective Web Surveys*. Cambridge: Cambridge University Press.

Couper, M.P., Traugott, M.W. and Lamias, M.J. (2001) 'Web survey design and administration', *Public Opinion Quarterly*, 65 (2): 230–53.

Coyle-Shapiro, J. and Kessler, I. (2000) 'Consequences of the psychological contract for the employment relationship: a large scale survey', *Journal of Management Studies*, 37 (7): 903–30.

Crawford, S.D., Couper, M.P. and Lamias, M.J. (2001) 'Web surveys: perceptions of burden', *Social Science Computer Review*, 19 (2): 146–62.

Creswell, J.W. (2003) *Research Design: Qualitative, Quantitative and Mixed Methods Approaches*, 2nd edn. Thousand Oaks, CA: Sage.

Creswell, J.W. (2013) *Qualitative Inquiry and Research Design: Choosing Among Five Approaches*, 3rd edn. Los Angeles, CA: Sage.

Creswell, J.W. (2014) *A Concise Introduction to Mixed Methods Research*. London: Sage.

Crotty, M. (1998) *The Foundations of Social Research: Meaning and Perspective in the Research Process*. London: Sage.

Cryer, P. (2000) *The Research Student's Guide to Success*. Buckingham: Open University Press.

Cukier, W., Trenholm, S., Carl, D. and Gekas, G. (2011) 'Social entrepreneurship: a content analysis', *Journal of Strategic Innovation and Sustainability*, 7 (1): 99–119. Available at: www.na-businesspress.com/jsis/cukierweb. pdf (last accessed 14 August 2014).

Cunliffe, A.L. (2001) 'Managers as practical authors: reconstructing our understanding of management practice', *Journal of Management Studies*, 38: 351–71.

Cunliffe, A.L. (2002a) 'Reflexive dialogical practice in management learning', *Management Learning*, 33 (1): 35–61.

Cunliffe, A.L. (2002b) 'Social poetics as management inquiry: a dialogical approach', *Journal of Management Inquiry*, 11 (2): 128–46.

Cunliffe, A.L. (2003) 'Reflexive inquiry in organizational research: questions and possibilities', *Human Relations*, 56 (8): 983–1003.

Cunliffe, A.L. (2008) 'Discourse analysis', in R. Thorpe and R. Holt (eds), *The SAGE Dictionary of Qualitative Management Research*. London: Sage.

Cunliffe, A.L. (2010) 'Retelling tales of the field: in search of organizational ethnography 20 years on', *Organizational Research Methods*, 13 (2): 224–39.

Cunliffe, A.L. (2011) 'Crafting qualitative research: Morgan and Smircich 30 years on', *Organizational Research Methods*, 14 (4): 647–73.

Curran, J. and Downing, S. (1989) 'The state and small business owners: an empirical assessment of consultation strategies', paper presented at the 12th National Small Firms Policy and Research Conference, Barbican, London.

Cyert, R.H. and March, J.G. (1963) *A Behavioral History of the Firm*. Englewood-Cliffs, NJ: Prentice Hall.

Czarniawska, B. (1998) *A Narrative Approach to Organization Studies*. London: Sage.

Daft, R.L. and Lengel, R.H. (1986) 'Organisational information requirements, media richness and structural design', *Management Science*, 32: 554–71.

Daiute, C. and Lightfoot, C. (2004) *Narrative Analysis: Studying the Development of Individuals in Society*. Thousand Oaks, CA: Sage.

Dalton, M. (1959) *Men Who Manage: Fusion of Feeling and Theory in Administration*. New York: Wiley.

Dalton, M. (1964) 'Preconceptions and methods in *Men Who Manage*', in P. Hammond (ed.), *Sociologists at Work*. New York: Basic Books, pp. 50–95.

Davies, G., Chun, R., Da Silva, R. and Roper, S. (2002) *Corporate Reputation and Competitiveness*. London: Routledge.

Davies, J. and Easterby-Smith, M. (1984) 'Learning and developing from managerial work experiences', *Journal of Management Studies*, 21: 169–82.

Davila, C. (1989) 'Grounding management education in local research: a Latin American experience', in J. Davies, M. Easterby-Smith, S. Mann and M. Tanton (eds), *The Challenge to Western Management Development: International Alternatives*. London: Routledge, pp. 40–56.

Dawson, A. and Hjorth, D. (2012) 'Advancing family business research through narrative analysis', *Family Business Review*, 25 (3): 339–55.

DeCuir-Gunby, J.T., Marshall, P.L. and McCulloch, A.W. (2011) 'Developing and using a codebook for the analysis of interview data: an example from a professional development research project', *Field Methods*, 23 (2): 136–55.

Deem, R. and Brehony, K. (1997) 'Research students' access to research cultures: an unequal benefit?', paper presented at Society for Research in Higher Education Conference, University of Warwick.

Denzin, N.K. (1994) 'The Art and Politics of Interpretation', in N.K. Denzin and Y.S. Lincoln (eds) *Handbook of Qualitative Research*. Thousand Oaks, CA: Sage.

Denzin, N.K. and Lincoln, Y.S. (eds) (2006) *SAGE Handbook of Qualitative Research*, 3rd edn. Thousand Oaks, CA: Sage.

Derrida, J. (1978) *Writing and Difference*. London: Routledge and Kegan Paul.

Detert, J.R. and Edmondson, A.C. (2011) 'Implicit voice theories: taken-for-granted rules of self-censorship at work', *Academy of Management Journal*, 54 (3): 461–88.

DeVellis, R.F. (2012) *Scale Development: Theory and Applications*, 3rd edn. Thousand Oaks, CA: Sage.

Dewey, J. (1916) *Democracy and Education*. London: Collier Macmillan.

Dhanaraj, C., Lyles, M.A., Steensma, H.K. and Tihanyi, L. (2004) 'Managing tacit and explicit knowledge transfer in IJVs: the role of relational embeddedness and the impact on performance', *Journal of International Business Studies*, 35 (5): 428–43.

Dillman, D.A. (2007) *Mail and Internet Surveys: The Tailored Design Method*, 2nd edn. New York: Wiley.

Dillman, D.A., Smyth, J.D. and Christian, L.M. (2009) *Internet, Mail, and Mixed-Mode Surveys: The Tailored Design Method*, 3rd edn. Hoboken, NJ: Wiley.

Ditton, J. (1977) *Part-time Crime*. London: Macmillan.

Dobson, A.J. (2001) *Introduction to Generalized Linear Models*, 2nd edn. London: Chapman and Hall.

Douglas, J.D. (ed.) (1976) *Investigative Social Research*. Beverly Hills, CA: Sage.

Drisko, J.W. (2004) 'Qualitative data analysis software: a user's appraisal', in D. Padgett (ed.), *The Qualitative Research Experience*. Belmont, CA: Wadsworth, pp. 193–209.

Dubois, A. and Gadde, L.-E (2002) 'Systematic combining: an abductive approach to case research', *Journal of Business Research*, 55 (7): 553–60.

Duggan, F. (2006) 'Plagiarism: prevention, practice and policy', *Assessment & Evaluation in Higher Education*, 31 (2): 151–4.

Duriau, V.J., Reger, R.K. and Pfarrer, M.D. (2007) 'A content analysis of the content analysis literature in organization studies: research themes, data sources, and methodological refinements', *Organizational Research Methods*, 10 (1): 5–34.

Dyer, J.H. and Hatch, N.W. (2006) 'Relation-specific capabilities and barriers to knowledge transfers: creating advantage through network relationships', *Strategic Management Journal*, 27 (8): 701–19.

Easterby-Smith, M. ([1986] 1994) *Evaluation of Management Education, Training and Development*. Aldershot: Gower.

Easterby-Smith, M. (1997) 'Disciplines of organizational learning: contributions and critiques', *Human Relations*, 51 (9): 1085–116.

Easterby-Smith, M. and Ashton, D. (1975) 'Using repertory grid technique to evaluate management training', *Personnel Review*, 4 (4): 15–21.

Easterby-Smith, M. and Lyles, M. (2011) *Handbook of Organizational Learning and Knowledge Management*. Oxford: Blackwell.

Easterby-Smith, M. and Malina, D. (1999) 'Cross-cultural collaborative research: toward reflexivity', *Academy of Management Journal*, 42 (1): 76–86.

Easterby-Smith, M., Graca, M., Antonacopoulou, A. and Ferdinand, J. (2008) 'Absorptive capacity: a process perspective', *Management Learning*, 39 (5): 483–501.

Easterby-Smith, M., Li, S. and Bartunek, J. (2009) 'Research methods for organizational learning: the transatlantic gap', *Management Learning*, 40 (4), 439–47.

Easterby-Smith, M., Thorpe, R. and Holman, D. (1996) 'The use of repertory grids in management', *Journal of European Industrial Training*, 20 (3): 1–30.

Easterby-Smith, M., Thorpe, R. and Holman, D. (2010) 'Using repertory grids in management', in F.B. Birks and T. Macer (eds), *Marketing Research*, Vol. 2. London: Routledge, pp. 448–90.

Eden, C. (1990) 'Strategic thinking with computers', *Long Range Planning*, 23 (6): 35–43.

Eden, C. (1992) 'On the nature of cognitive maps', *Journal of Management Studies*, 29 (3): 261–65.

Eden, C. and Ackermann, F. (1998) *Making Strategy: The Journey of Strategic Management*. London: Sage.

Eden, C. and Huxham, C. (1995) 'Action research for the study of organisations', in S. Clegg, C. Hardy and W. Nord (eds), *Handbook of Organisation Studies*. Beverley Hills, CA: Sage, pp. 526–42.

Eden, C. and Huxham, C. (1996) 'Action research for management research', *British Journal of Management*, 7 (1): 75–86.

Eden, C. and Huxham, C. (2002) 'Action research', in D. Partington (ed.), *Essential Skills for Management Research*. London: Sage, pp. 254–72.

Eden, C. and Huxham, C. (2007) 'Action research and the study of organisations', in S. Clegg, C. Hardy and W. Nord (eds), *Handbook of Organisation Studies*. London: Sage, pp. 526–42.

Eden, C., Jones, S. and Sims, D. (1983) *Messing About in Problems: An Informal Structured Approach to their Identification and Management*. Oxford: Pergamon.

Eesley, C. and Lenox, M.J. (2006) 'Firm responses to secondary stakeholder action', *Strategic Management Journal*, 27 (8): 765–81.

Eisenhardt, K.M. (1989) 'Building theories from case study research', *Academy of Management Review*, 14 (4): 532–50.

Eisenhardt, K.M. and Graebner, M.E. (2007) 'Theory building from cases: opportunities and challenges', *Academy of Management Journal*, 50 (1): 25–32.

Emerson, R.M., Fretz, R. and Shaw, L.L. (2011) *Writing Ethnographic Fieldnotes*, 2nd edn. Chicago, IL: University of Chicago Press.

Engeström, Y. (1999) 'Activity theory as a framework for analysis and redesigning work', *Ergonomics*, 43 (7): 960–74.

Engeström, Y. (2000) 'Activity theory and the social construction of knowledge: a story of four imports', *Organisation*, 7 (2): 302–10.

Ernst, P. (1996) 'The nature of mathematics and teaching', *Philosophy of Mathematics Education Journal*, 9. Available online at: http://people.exeter.ac.uk/PErnest/pome/pompart7.htm (last accessed 25 February 2015).

ESRC (2009) *Postgraduate Training and Development Guidelines*. Swindon: Economic and Social Research Council.

Evers, F.T. and Rush, J.C. (1996) 'The bases of competence: skill development during the transition from university to work', *Management Learning*, 27 (3): 275–300.

Fahy, K.M., Easterby-Smith, M. and Lervik, J.E. (2014) 'The power of spatial and temporal orderings in organizational learning', *Management Learning*, 45 (2): 123–144.

Fairclough, N. (1992) *Discourse and Social Change*. Cambridge: Polity Press.

Fairclough, N. and Hardy, G. (1997) 'Management learning as discourse', in J. Burgoyne and M. Reynolds (eds), *Management Learning: Integrating Perspectives in Theory and Practice*. London: Sage, pp. 144–60.

Fairhurst, E. (1983) 'Organisational rules and the accomplishment of nursing work on geriatric wards', *Journal of Management Studies*, Special Issue, 20 (3): 315–32.

Fayol, H. ([1916] 1950) *Administration Industrielle et Generale*. Paris: Dunod.

Fendt, J. and Sachs, W. (2007) 'Grounded theory method in management research: users' perspectives', *Organizational Research Methods*, 11 (3): 430–55.

Field, A. (2009) *Discovering Statistics Using SPSS*, 3rd edn. London: Sage.

Field, A. (2013) *Discovering Statistics Using IBM SPSS Statistics. And Sex and Drugs and Rock 'n' Roll*, 4th edn. Los Angeles, CA: Sage.

Field, A.P., Miles, J. and Field, Z. (2012) *Discovering Statistics Using R*. London: Sage.

Fielding, N.G. and Fielding, J.L. (1986) *Linking Data*. Beverly Hills, CA: Sage.

Fielding, N.G., Lee, R.M. and Blank, G. (2008) *The SAGE Handbook of Online Research Methods*. London: Sage.

Filatotchev, I. (2006) 'Effects of executive characteristics and venture capital involvement on board composition and share ownership in IPO firms', *British Journal of Management*, 17: 75–92.

Finch, J. (1986) *Research and Policy: The Uses of Qualitative Methods in Social and Educational Research*. London: Falmer Press.

Fink, A. (2005) *Conducting Research Literature Reviews: From the Internet to Paper*. Thousand Oaks, CA: Sage.

Firth, J.R. (1957) *Papers in Linguistics, 1934–1951*. London and New York: Oxford University Press.

Flanagan, J.C. (1954) 'The critical incident technique', *Psychological Bulletin*, 1: 327–58.

Flick, U. (2007) *Managing Quality in Qualitative Research*. London: Sage.

Flick, U. (2009) *An Introduction to Qualitative Research*, 4th edn. London: Sage.

Flick, U. (2014) *SAGE Handbook of Qualitative Data Analysis*. London: Sage.

Flick, U., Kardorff, E. and Steinke, I. (2004) *A companion to qualitative research*. London: Sage.

Foucault, M. (1979) *Discipline and Punish*. Harmondsworth: Penguin.

Fournier, V. and Grey, C. (2000) 'At the critical moment: conditions and prospects for critical management studies', *Human Relations*, 52 (1): 7–32.

Freeman, R.E. (1984) *Strategic Management: A Stakeholder Approach*. London: Pitman.

Freeman, R.E, Harrison, J.S., Wicks, A., Parmar, B.L. and de Colle, S. (2010) *Stakeholder Theory: The State of the Art*. Cambridge: Cambridge University Press.

Friese, S. (2012) *Qualitative Data Analysis with ATLAS.ti*. London: Sage.

Gadamer, H-G. (1989) *Truth and Method*, 2nd rev. edn (trans. J. Weinsheimer and D.G. Marshall). New York: Crossroad.

Galman, S.C. (2007) *Shane, the Lone Ethnographer. A Beginner's Guide to Ethnography*. Lanham, MD: AltaMira.

Galman, S.C. (2013) *The Good, the Bad, and the Data: Shane the Lone Ethnographer's Basic Guide to Qualitative Data Analysis*. Walnut Creek, CA: Left Coast Press.

Gash, S. (2000) *Effective Literature Searching for Research*. Aldershot: Gower.

Gatewood, J.B. (1983) 'Deciding where to fish: the skipper's dilemma in Southeast Alaskan salmon seining', *Coastal Zone Management Journal*, 10 (4): 347–67.

Geary, L., Marriott, L. and Rowlinson, M. (2004) 'Journal rankings in business and management and the 2001 Research Assessment Exercise in the UK', *British Journal of Management*, 15: 95–141.

George, G., Haas, M.R. and Pentland, A. (2014) 'Big data and management', *Academy of Management Journal*, 57: 321–6.

Gergen, K.J. (1995) 'Relational theory and discourses of power', in D-M. Hosking, H.P. Dachler and K.J. Gergen (eds), *Management and Organization: Relational Alternatives to Individualism*. Aldershot: Avebury, pp. 29–49.

Gergen, K.J. (1999) *An Invitation to Social Construction*. London: Sage.

Ghauri, P. and Grønhaug, K. (2010) *Research Methods in Business Studies*. Harlow: Prentice Hall.

Gibbons, M.L., Limoges, C., Nowotny, H., Schwartman, S., Scott, P. and Trow, M. (1994) *The New Production of Knowledge: The Dynamics of Science and Research in Contemporary Societies*. London: Sage.

Gibbs, G.R. (2014) 'Using software in qualitative analysis', in U. Flick (ed.), *SAGE Handbook of Qualitative Data Analysis*. London: Sage, pp. 277–94.

Gibbs, G.R., Friese, S. and Mangabeira, W.C. (2002) 'The use of new technology in qualitative research', Introduction to *Forum Qualitative Sozialforschung/Forum: Qualitative Social Research*, 3 (2), Art. 8. Available at: http://nbn-resolving.de/urn:nbn:de:0114-fqs020287 (last accessed 29 October 2008).

Giddens, A. (1984) *The Constitution of Society: Outline of the Theory of Structuration*. Cambridge: Polity Press.

Glaser, B.G. (1978) *Theoretical Sensitivity*. Mill Valley, CA: Sociological Press.

Glaser, B.G. (1992) *Basics of Grounded Theory Analysis: Emergence versus Forcing*. Mill Valley, CA: Sociology Press.

Glaser, B.G. (1998) *Doing Grounded Theory: Issues and Discussions*. Mill Valley, CA: Sociology Press.

Glaser, B.G. and Strauss, A.L. (1967) *The Discovery of Grounded Theory: Strategies for Qualitative Research*. New York: Aldine.

Glenn, P. and LeBaron, C. (2011) 'Epistemic authority in employment interviews: glancing, pointing, touching', *Discourse & Communication*, 5 (1): 3–22.

Gold, J. (2008) 'Postcards', in R. Thorpe and R. Holt (eds), *The SAGE Dictionary of Qualitative Management Research*. London: Sage, pp. 157–60.

Gold, J., Hamblett, J. and Rix, M. (2000) 'Telling stories for managing change: a business/academic partnership', *Education through Partnership*, 4 (1): 36–46.

Gold, J., Holman, D. and Thorpe, R. (2002) 'The role of argument analysis and storytelling in facilitating critical thinking', *Management Learning*, 33 (3): 371–88.

Gold, J., Thorpe, R. and Holt, R. (2007) 'Writing, reading and reason: the "three Rs" of manager learning', in R. Hill and J. Stewart (eds), *Management Development: Perspectives from Research and Practice*. Abingdon: Routledge, pp. 271–84.

Goldacre, M.J., Davidson, J.M. and Lambert, T.W. (2004) 'Country of training and ethnic origin of UK doctors: database and survey studies', *British Medical Journal*, 329 (11): 597–600.

Golden-Biddle, K. and Locke, K. (1993) 'Appealing work: an investigation of how ethnographic texts convince', *Organisation Science*, 4 (2): 595–616.

Golden-Biddle, K. and Locke, K. (2007) *Composing Qualitative Research*, 2nd edn. London: Sage.

Goodall, H.L. (1989) *Casing a Promised Land: The Autobiography of an Organizational Detective as Cultural Ethnographer*. Carbondale, IL: Southern Illinois University Press.

Goodall, H.L. (2007) *Need to Know: The Clandestine History of a CIA Family*. Walnut Creek, CA: Left Coast Press.

Goodwin, C. and Goodwin, M.H. (1996) 'Seeing as a situated activity: formulating planes', in Y. Engeström and D. Middleton (eds), *Cognition and Communication at Work*. Cambridge: Cambridge University Press, pp. 61–95.

Goodwin, M.H. (1995) 'Assembling a response: setting and collaboratively constructed work talk', in P. Have and G. Psathas (eds), *Situated Order: Studies in the Social Organization of Talk and Embodied Activities*. Lanham, MD: University Press of America (Studies in ethnomethodology and conversation analysis, No. 3), pp. 173–86.

Goulding, C. (2002) *Grounded Theory: A Practical Guide for Management, Business and Market Researchers*. Thousand Oaks, CA: Sage.

Granovetter, M. (1973) 'The strength of weak ties', *American Journal of Sociology*, 78: 1360–80.

Green, S. and Li, Y. (2011) 'Rhetorical institutionalism: language, agency and structure in institutional theory since Alvesson 1993', *Journal of Management Studies*, 48 (7): 1662–97.

Gremler, D.D. (2004) 'The critical incident technique in service research', *Journal of Service Research*, 7 (1): 65–89.

Grey, C. (2005) *A Very Short, Fairly Interesting and Reasonably Cheap Book about Studying Organizations*. London: Sage.

Guba, E.G. and Lincoln, Y.S. (1989) *Fourth Generation Evaluation*. London: Sage.

Gubrium, J.F. and Silverman, D. (eds) (1989) *The Politics of Field Research*. London: Sage.

Gubrium, J.F., Holstein, J., Marvasti, A.B. and McKinney, K.D. (2012) *The SAGE Handbook of Interview Research: The Complexity of the Craft*, 2nd edn. Thousand Oaks, CA: Sage.

Gummesson, E. ([1988] 1991) *Qualitative Research in Management*. Bromley: Chartwell-Bratt.

Gummesson, E. (1992) *Case Study Research in Management: Methods for Generating Qualitative Data*. Stockholm: Stockholm University Press.

Gunn, H. (2002) 'Web-based surveys: changing the survey process', *First Monday*, 7 (12). Available at: www.firstmonday.dk/issues/issue7_12/gunn/#note3 (last accessed 24 November 2011).

Habermas, J. (1970) 'Knowledge and interest', in D. Emmett and A. Macintyre (eds), *Sociological Theory and Philosophical Analysis*. London: Macmillan, pp. 36–54.

Habermas, J. (1971) *Towards a Rational Society*. London: Heinemann.

Hair, J.F., Black, B., Babin, B., Anderson, R.E. and Tatham, R.L. (2010) *Multivariate Data Analysis*, 7th edn. Upper Saddle River, NJ: Prentice Hall.

Hales, C.P. (1986) 'What do managers do? A critical review of the evidence', *Journal of Management Studies*, 23 (1): 88–115.

Hamer, B. (Director) (2003) *Kitchen Stories (Salmer fra kjøkken)* [Motion picture]. Norway: IFC Films.

Handy, C. (1996) *Beyond Certainty: The Changing Worlds of Organizations*. London: Arrow Books.

Hanneman, R.A. and Riddle, M. (2005) *Introduction to Social Network Methods*. Riverside, CA: University of California Press. Available at: http://faculty.ucr.edu/~hanneman/ (last accessed 24 November 2011).

Hansen, M.T. (1999) 'The search-transfer problem: the role of weak ties in sharing knowledge across organization subunits', *Administrative Science Quarterly*, 44: 82–111.

Hardy, C. (1996) 'Understanding power: bringing about strategic change', *British Journal of Management*, 7 (Special Issue): S3–S16.

Harper, D. (1989) 'Visual sociology: expanding sociological vision', in G. Blank, J. L. McCartney and E. Brent (eds), *New Technology in Sociology: Practical Applications in Research and Work*. New Brunswick, NJ: Transaction Books, pp. 81–97.

Harper, D. (1994) 'On the authority of the image: visual methods at the crossroads', in N.K. Denzin and Y.S. Lincoln (eds), *Handbook of Qualitative Research*. Thousand Oaks, CA: Sage, pp. 403–12.

Harris, K.J., Wheeler, A.R. and Kacmar, K.M. (2009) 'Leader-member exchange and empowerment: direct and interactive effects on job satisfaction, turnover intentions, and performance', *Leadership Quarterly*, 20: 371–82.

Hart, C. (1998) *Doing a Literature Review: Releasing the Social Science Research Imagination*. London: Sage.

Hart, C. (2005) *Doing a Literature Review: Releasing the Social Science Research Imagination*. Reprinted. London: Sage.

Harvey, C., Morris, H. and Kelly, A. (eds) (2007) *Association of Business Schools Academic Journal Quality Guide*. London: Association of Business Schools.

Harzing, A-W. (ed.) (2007) *Journal Quality List*, 27th edn. Available at: www.harzing.com (last accessed 24 November 2011).

Hassard, J. and Parker, M. (eds) (1993) *Postmodernism and Organizations*. London: Sage.

Hatch, M.J. (1996) 'Irony and the social construction of contradiction in the humor of a management team', *Organization Science*, 8 (3): 275–388.

Hayano, D.M. (1979) 'Auto-ethnography paradigms, problems and prospects', *Human Organisation*, 38: 99–104.

Hayes, R.H. and Abernethy, W.J. (1980) 'Managing our way to economic decline', *Harvard Business Review*, 58: 67–77.

Heath, C. and Hindmarsh, J. (2002) 'Analyzing interaction: video, ethnography and situated conduct', in T. May (ed.), *Qualitative Research in Action*. London: Sage, pp. 99–122.

Heisenberg, W. (1927) 'Über den anschaulichen Inhalt der quantentheoretischen Kinematik und Mechanik', *Zeitschrift für Physik*, 43: 172–98. (English translation: J. A. Wheeler and H. Zurek (1983) *Quantum Theory and Measurement*. Princeton, NJ: Princeton University Press, pp. 62–84.)

Heritage, J. and Maynard, D.W. (2006) *Communication in Medical Care: Interaction between Primary Care Physicians and Patients*. Cambridge: Cambridge University Press.

Heritage, J., Robinson, J.D., Elliott, M.N., Beckett, M. and Wilkes, M. (2007) 'Reducing patients' unmet concerns in primary care: the difference one word can make', *Journal of General Internal Medicine*, 22 (10): 1429–33.

Heron, J. (1996) *Co-operative Inquiry: Research into the Human Condition*. London: Sage.

Herzberg, F., Mausner, B. and Snyderman, B.B. (1959) *The Motivation to Work*. New York: Wiley.

Hickson, D.J. (1988) 'Ruminations on munificence and scarcity in research', in A. Bryman (ed.), *Doing Research in Organizations*. London: Routledge, pp. 136–50.

Hobday, M. and Rush, H. (2007) 'Upgrading the technological capabilities of foreign transnational subsidiaries in developing countries: the case of Thailand', *Research Policy*, 36: 1335–55.

Hofstede, G. (1980) *Culture's Consequences: International Differences in Work-Related Values*. Beverly Hills, CA: Sage.

Hofstede, G. (1991) *Cultures and Organizations: Software of the Mind*. Maidenhead: McGraw-Hill.

Holman, D. (1996) 'The experience of skill development in undergraduates', PhD thesis, Manchester Metropolitan University.

Hong, J., Easterby-Smith, M. and Snell, R. (2006) 'Transferring organizational learning systems to Japanese subsidiaries in China', *Journal of Management Studies*, 43 (5): 1027–58.

Howell, D. (2013a) *Fundamental Statistics for the Behavioral Sciences*, 8th edn. Nashville, TN: Broadman and Holman.

Howell, D. (2013b) *Statistical Methods for Psychology*, 8th edn. Belmont, CA: Wadsworth.

Hsieh, H.F. and Shannon, S.E. (2005) 'Three approaches to qualitative content analysis', in *Qualitative Health Research*, 15 (9): 1277–88.

Huczynski, A.A. (1996) *Management Gurus: What Makes Them and How to Become One*. London: International Thomson Business Press.

Huff, A.S. (1999) *Writing for Scholarly Publication*. Thousand Oaks, CA: Sage.

Huff, A.S. (2000) 'Changes in organizational knowledge production', *Academy of Management Review*, 25 (2): 288–93.

Huff, A.S. (2009) *Designing Research for Publications*. London: Sage.

Huff, A.S. and Jenkins, M. (2002) *Mapping Strategic Knowledge*. London: Sage.

Humphreys, M. and Brown, A.D. (2002) 'Dress and identity: a Turkish case study', *Journal of Management Studies*, 39 (7): 927–52.

Humphreys, M. and Brown, A.D. (2008) 'An analysis of corporate social responsibility: a narrative approach', *Journal of Business Ethics*, 80 (3): 403–18.

Hutchby, I. and Wooffitt, R. (2008) *Conversation Analysis*, 2nd edn. Cambridge: Polity Press.

Huxham, C. (2003) 'Action research as a methodology for theory development', *Policy and Politics*, 31 (2): 239–48.

Hyder, S. and Sims, D. (1979) 'Hypothesis, analysis and paralysis: issues in the organisation of contract research', *Management Education Development*, 10: 100–11.

Ibarra, H. (1992) 'Homophily and differential returns: sex differences in network structure and access in an advertising firm', *Administrative Science Quarterly*, 37: 422–47.

Irwin, A. (1994) 'Science's social standing', *The Times Higher Educational Supplement*, 30 September: 17–19.

Jaccard, J. and Wan, C.K. (1996) *LISREL Approaches to Interaction Effects in Multiple Regression*. Thousand Oaks, CA: Sage.

Jackson, M.C. (2000) *Systems Approaches to Management*. New York: Klewer Academic/Plenum.

Jackson, P.R. (1986) 'Robust methods in statistics', in A.D. Lovie (ed.), *New Developments in Statistics for Psychology and the Social Sciences*. London: British Psychological Society and Methuen, pp. 22–43.

Jackson, P.R. (1989) 'Analysing data', in G. Parry and F.N. Watts (eds), *Behavioural and Mental Health Research: A Handbook of Skills and Methods*. London: Lawrence Erlbaum, pp. 55–79.

Jackson, P.R. (2004) 'Employee commitment to quality: its conceptualisation and measurement', *International Journal of Quality & Reliability Management*, 21 (7): 714–30.

Jackson, P.R. and Parker, S.K. (2001) *Change in Manufacturing: Managing Stress in Manufacturing*. London: HSE Publications.

James, W. ([1907] 1979) *Pragmatism*. Cambridge, MA: Harvard University Press.

Janesick, V.J. (2003) 'The choreography of qualitative research design: minuets, improvisations, and chrystallization', in N.K. Denzin and Y.S. Lincoln (eds), *Strategies of Qualitative Inquiry*. Thousand Oaks, CA: Sage, pp. 46–79.

Jansen, J.P., Van den Bosch, F.A.J. and Volberda, H.W. (2005) 'Managing potential and realised absorptive capacity: how do organizational antecedents matter?', *Academy of Management Journal*, 48 (6): 999–1015.

Jarzabkowski, P., Balogun, J. and Seidl, D. (2007) 'Strategizing: the challenges of a practice perspective', *Human Relations*, 60 (1): 5–27.

Jefferson, G. (2004) 'Glossary of transcript symbols with an introduction', in G.H. Lerner (ed.), *Conversation Analysis: Studies from the First Generation*. Amsterdam: John Benjamins, pp. 13–31.

Jesson, J., Matheson, L. and Lacey, F.M. (2011) *Doing Your Literature Review. Traditional and Systematic Techniques*. London: Sage.

Jick, T.D. (1979) 'Mixing qualitative and quantitative methodologies: triangulation in action', *Administrative Science Quarterly*, 24 (4): 602–11.

Jobber, D. and Horgan, I. (1987) 'Market research and education: perspectives from practitioners', *Journals of Marketing Management*, 3 (1): 39–49.

Johnson, G., Scholes, K. and Whittington, R. (2008) *Exploring Corporate Strategy*, 7th edn. London: Prentice Hall.

Johnson, P. and Duberley, J. (2000) *Understanding Management Research: An Introduction to Epistemology*. London: Sage.

Johnson, S., Cooper, C.L., Cartwright, S., Donald, I., Taylor, P. and Millet, C. (2005) 'The experience of work-related stress across occupations', *Journal of Managerial Psychology*, 20 (2): 178–87.

Jones, O. (2006) 'Developing absorptive capacity in mature organizations: the change agent's role', *Management Learning*, 37 (3): 355–76.

Jones, S. (1985) 'The analysis of depth interviews', in R. Walker (ed.), *Applied Qualitative Research*. Aldershot: Gower, pp. 56–70.

Kalaitzidakis, P., Mamuneas, T.P. and Stengos, T. (2001) *Ranking of Academic Journals and Institutions in Economics*. Available at: www.le.ac.uk/economics/ research/rankings/econ-rankings.html (last accessed 24 November 2011).

Kaplan, D. (2004) *The SAGE Handbook of Quantitative Methodology for the Social Sciences*. Thousand Oaks, CA: Sage.

Karra, N. and Phillips, N. (2007) 'Researching "back home": international management research as autoethnography', *Organizational Research Methods*, 11 (3): 541–61.

Katsikeas, C.S., Samiee, S. and Theodosiou, M. (2006) 'Strategy fit and performance consequences of international marketing standardization', *Strategic Management Journal*, 27 (9): 867–90.

Kelly, G.A. (1955) *The Psychology of Personal Constructs*. New York: Norton.

Kendall, G. (2007) 'What is critical discourse analysis? Ruth Wodak in conversation with Gavin Kendall', *Forum: Qualitative Social Research*, 8 (2). Available at: www.qualitative-research.net/index.php/fqs/article/view/255/561 (last accessed 14 August 2014).

Kilduff, M. and Brass, D.J. (2010) 'Organizational social network research: core ideas and key debates', *The Academy of Management Annals*, 4 (1): 317–57.

King, N. (1998) 'Template analysis in qualitative methods and analysis', in G. Symon and C. Cassell (eds), *Organizational Research: A Practical Guide*. London: Sage.

King, N. (2004) 'Using templates in the thematic analysis of text', in C. Cassell and G. Symon (eds), *Essential Guide to Qualitative Methods*, 2nd edn. London: Sage, pp. 118–34.

King, N. (2014) *Template Analysis Website*, University of Huddersfield. Available at: www.hud.ac.uk/hhs/research/template-analysis/ (last accessed 14 August 2014).

King, N. and Horrocks, C. (2010) *Interviews in Qualitative Research*. Los Angeles, CA: Sage.

Knoblauch, H., Baer, A., Laurier, E., Petschke, S. and Schnettler, B. (2008) 'Visual analysis: new developments in the interpretative analysis of video and photography', *Forum: Qualitative Social Research*, 9 (3): Visual Methods. Available at: www.qualitative-research.net/index.php/fqs/article/view/1170 (last accessed 14 August 2014).

Knoblauch, H., Tuma, R. and Schnettler, B. (2014) 'Visual analysis and videography', in U. Flick (ed.), *SAGE Handbook of Qualitative Data Analysis*. London: Sage, pp. 435–49.

Knorr-Cetina, K.D. (1983) 'The ethnographic study of scientific work: towards a constructivist interpretation of science', in K.D. Knorr-Cetina and M. Mulkay (eds), *Science Observed: Perspectives on the Social Study of Science*. London: Sage, pp. 115–40.

Knox, H., O'Doherty, D., Vurdubakis, T. and Westrup, C. (2008) 'Enacting airports: space, movement and modes of ordering', *Organization*, 15 (6): 869–88.

Koenig, T. (2008) 'CAQDAS comparison'. Available at: www.lboro.ac.uk/research/mmethods/research/software/caqdas_comparison.html (last accessed 29 October 2008).

Kolb, D.A. (1984) *Organisational Psychology: An Experimental Approach to Organisational Behaviour*. Englewood Cliffs, NJ: Prentice Hall.

Kolb, D.A. (1986) *Experiential Learning*. Englewood Cliffs, NJ: Prentice Hall.

Konopásek, Z. (2008) 'Making thinking visible with ATLAS.ti: computer assisted qualitative analysis as textual practices', *Forum Qualitative Sozialforschung/Forum: Qualitative Social Research*, 9 (2), Art. 12. Available at: http://nbn-resolving.de/urn:nbn:de:0114-fqs0802124 (last accessed 29 October 2008).

Kotter, J. (1982) *The General Managers*. Glencoe, IL: Free Press.

Krech, D., Crutchfield, R.S. and Ballachey, E.L. (1962) *Individual in Society*. London: McGraw-Hill.

Krueger, R.A. and Casey, M.A. (2009) *Focus Groups: A Practical Guide for Applied Research*, 4th edn. Los Angeles, CA: Sage.

Kuhn, T.S. (1962) *The Structure of Scientific Revolution*. Chicago, IL: University of Chicago Press.

Kunda, G. (1993) *Engineering Culture: Control and Commitment in a High-tech Corporation*. Philadelphia, PA: Temple University Press.

Kvale, S. (1996) *InterViews*. London: Sage.

Kvale, S. and Brinkmann, S. (2009) *InterViews: Learning the Craft of Qualitative Research Interviewing*, 2nd edn. Thousand Oaks, CA: Sage.

Kwon, W., Clarke, I. and Wodak, R. (2009) 'Organizational decision-making, discourse, and power: integrating across contexts and scales', *Discourse and Communication*, 3 (3): 273–302.

Labov, W. (1972) *Language in the Inner City*. Oxford: Blackwell.

Latour, B. (1988) 'The politics of explanation: an alternative', in S. Woolgar (ed.), *Knowledge and Reflexivity: New Frontiers in the Sociology of Knowledge*. London: Sage, pp. 155–77.

Latour, B. and Woolgar, S. (1979) *Laboratory Life: The Social Construction of Scientific Facts*. Beverly Hills, CA: Sage.

Law, J. (1994) *Organizing Modernity*. Oxford: Blackwell.

Lawler, S. (2002) 'Narrative in social research', T. May (ed.), *Qualitative Research in Action*. London: Sage, pp. 242–58.

Lawrence, P.R. (1986) *Invitation to Management*. Oxford: Blackwell.

Lawrence, P.R. and Lorsch, J.W. (1967) *Organisational Environment: Managing Differentiation and Integration*. Boston, MA: Division of Research, Graduate School of Business Administration, Harvard University.

Lawrence, T.B., Dyck, B., Maitlis, S. and Mauws, M.K. (2006) 'The underlying structure of continuous change', *MIT Sloan Management Review*, 47 (4): 59–66.

Lawrence, T.B., Mauws, M.K., Dyck, B. and Kleysen, R.F. (2005) 'The politics of organizational learning: integrating power into the 4I framework', *Academy of Management Review*, 30 (1): 180–91.

Leask, B. (2006) 'Plagiarism, cultural diversity and metaphor – implications for academic staff development', *Assessment & Evaluation in Higher Education*, 31 (2): 183–99.

Lee, F.S. (2007) 'The Research Assessment Exercise, the state and dominance of mainstream economics in British universities', *Cambridge Journal of Economics*, 31: 309–25.

Lee, R.M. (2000) *Unobtrusive Methods in Social Research*. Buckingham: Open University Press.

Legge, K. (1984) *Evaluating Planned Organisational Change*. London: Academic Press.

Leitch, S. and Palmer, I. (2010) 'Analysing texts in context: current practices and new protocols for critical discourse analysis in organisational studies', *Journal of Management Studies*, 47(6): 1194–212.

Lervik, J.E., Fahy, K.M. and Easterby-Smith, M. (2010) 'Temporal dynamics of situated learning in organizations', *Management Learning*, 41 (3): 285–301.

Lewin, K. (1948) 'Frontiers in group dynamics', *Human Relations*, 1: 5–41.

Lewins, A. (2008) 'CAQDAS: computer assisted qualitative data analysis', in N. Gilbert (ed.), *Researching Social Life*, 3rd edn. London: Sage, pp. 394–419.

Lewins, A. and Silver, C. (2007) *Using Software in Qualitative Research: A Step-by-Step Guide*. London: Sage.

Lewins, A. and Silver, C. (2009a) *QSR NVivo 8 Distinguishing Features and Functions*, Working Paper No. 004, 1–5, CAQDAS, Guildford: University of Surrey.

Lewins, A. and Silver, C. (2009b) *ATLAS.ti 6 Distinguishing Features and Functions*, NCRM Working Paper. Guildford: University of Surrey.

Lewins, A. and Silver, C. (2009c) *Choosing a CAQDAS Package*, NCRM Working Paper. Guildford: University of Surrey.

Liebow, E. (1993) *Tell Them Who I Am: The Lives of Homeless Women*. New York: Penguin.

Locke, K. (1997) 'Re-writing the discovery of Grounded Theory after 25 years?', *Journal of Management Inquiry*, 5: 239–45.

Locke, K. (2001) *Grounded Theory in Management Research*. London: Sage.

Locke, K. and Golden-Biddle, K. (1997) 'Constructing opportunities for contribution: structuring intertextual coherence and "problematizing" in organization studies', *Academy of Management Journal*, 40 (5): 1023–62.

Locke, T. (2004) *Critical Discourse Analysis*. London: Continuum.

Löfgren, K. (2013) *Qualitative Analysis of Interview Data: A Step-by-Step Guide*. Tutorial published on YouTube on 19 May 2013. Available at: www.youtube.com/watch?v=DRL4PF2u9XA (last accessed 14 August 2014).

Lofland, J. and Lofland, L.H. (1984) *Analyzing Social Settings: A Guide to Qualitative Observation and Analysis*, 2nd edn. Belmont, CA: Wadsworth.

Lok, J. and Rond, M. de (2013) 'On the plasticity of institutions: containing and restoring practice breakdowns at the Cambridge University Boat Club', *Academy of Management Journal*, 56 (1): 185–207.

Lowe, A. (1998) 'Managing the post merger aftermath by default remodelling', *Management Decision*, 36 (2): 102–10.

Lu, Y. and Heard, R. (1995) 'Socialised economic action: a comparison of strategic investment decision-making in China and Britain', *Organization Studies*, 16: 395–424.

Luff, P., Hindmarsh, J. and Heath, C. (eds) (2000) *Workplace Studies: Recovering Work Practice and Informing System Design*. Cambridge: Cambridge University Press.

Luker, K. (2008) *Salsa Dancing into the Social Sciences: Research in an Age of Info-glut*. Cambridge, MA: Harvard University Press.

Luo, X. and Bhattacharya, C.B. (2006) 'Corporate social responsibility, customer satisfaction, and market value', *Journal of Marketing*, 70 (4): 1–18.

Lupton, T. (1963) *On the Shop Floor: Two Studies of Workshop Organization and Output*. New York: Macmillan.

Lyles, M.A. and Salk, J.E. (1996) 'Knowledge acquisition from foreign parents in international joint ventures: an empirical examination in the Hungarian context', *Journal of International Business Studies*, Special Issue, 27: 877–903.

Lyotard, J-F. (1984) *The Postmodern Condition: A Report on Knowledge*. Manchester: Manchester University Press.

Macbeth, D. (2001) 'On "reflexivity" in qualitative research: two readings, and a third', *Qualitative Inquiry*, 7 (1): 35–68.

Macbeth, D. (2004) 'The relevance of repair for classroom correction', *Language in Society*, 33: 703–36.

Macdonald, S. (2010) 'British social anthropology', in P. Atkinson (ed.), *Handbook of Ethnography*. Reprinted. Los Angeles, CA: Sage, pp. 60–79.

Macfarlane, G. (1985) *Alexander Fleming: The Man and the Myth*. Oxford: Oxford University Press.

Mackinlay, T. (1986) 'The development of a personal strategy of management', Dissertation, Master of Science Degree, Manchester Polytechnic, Department of Management.

Maclean, D., Macintosh, R. and Grant, S. (2002) 'Mode 2 management research', *British Journal of Management*, 13: 189–207.

Macmillan, K. (2005) 'More than just coding? Evaluating CAQDAS in a discourse analysis of news texts' (57 paragraphs), *Forum Qualitative Sozialforschung/Forum: Qualitative Social Research*, 6 (3): Art. 25. Available at: http://nbn-resolving.de/urn:nbn:de:0114-fqs0503257 (last accessed 29 October 2008).

Macpherson, A. (2006) 'Learning to grow: the evolution of business knowledge in small manufacturing firms', PhD thesis, Manchester Metropolitan University.

Macpherson, A., Kofinas, A., Jones, O. and Thorpe, R. (2010) 'Making sense of mediated learning: cases from small firms', *Management Learning*, 41 (3): 303–23.

Madden, R. (2010) *Being Ethnographic: A Guide to the Theory and Practice of Ethnography*. London: Sage.

Mangham, I.L. (1986) 'In search of competence', *Journal of General Management*, 12 (2): 5–12.

Margolis, E. and Pauwels, L. (2011) *The SAGE Handbook of Visual Research Methods*. Los Angeles, CA: Sage.

Marshall, C. (2000) 'Policy discourse analysis: negotiating gender equity', *Journal of Education Policy*, 15 (2): 125–56.

Marshall, S. and Green, N. (2007) *Your PhD Companion: A Handy Mix of Practical Tips, Sound Advice and Helpful Commentary to See You Through Your PhD*, 2nd edn. Oxford: Cromwell Press.

Mason, J. (1996) *Qualitative Researching*. London: Sage.

Mauch, J.E. and Birch, J.W. (1983) *Guide to the Successful Thesis and Dissertations: A Handbook for Students and Faculty*. New York: Marcel Dekker.

Maxwell, J.A. and Chmiel, M. (2014) 'Generalization in and from Qualitative Analysis', in U. Flick (ed.), *SAGE Handbook of Qualitative Data Analysis*. London: Sage, pp. 541–53.

Mayo, E. (1949) *The Social Problems of an Industrial Civilisation*. London: Routledge and Kegan Paul.

McCann, L., Granter, E., Hyde, P. and Hassard, J. (2013) 'Still blue-collar after all these years? An ethnography of the professionalization of emergency ambulance work', *Journal of Management Studies*, 50 (5): 750–76.

McClelland, D.A. (1965) 'Achievement and enterprise', *Journal of Personal Social Psychology*, 1: 389–92.

McClelland, D.A. (1967) *The Achieving Society*. Princeton, NJ: Van Nostrand.

McCullagh, P. and Nelder, J. (1989) *Generalized Linear Models*. London: Chapman and Hall.

McLaughlin, H. and Thorpe, R. (1993) 'Action learning – a paradigm in emergence: the problems facing a challenge to traditional management education and development', *British Journal of Management*, 4: 19–27.

McWilliams, A. and Siegel, D. (1997) 'Event studies in management research: theoretical and empirical issues', *Academy of Management Journal*, 40, 626–57.

Mehra, A., Kilduff, M. and Brass, D.J. (1998) 'At the margins: a distinctiveness approach to the social identity and social networks of underrepresented groups', *Academy of Management Journal*, 41: 441–52.

Mehrabian, A. (1981) *Silent Messages: Implicit Communication of Emotions and Attitudes*, 2nd edn. Belmont, CA: Wadsworth.

Miles, M.B. and Huberman, A.M. (1984) *Qualitative Data Analysis: A Sourcebook of New Methods*. London: Sage.

Miles, M.B. and Huberman, A.M. (1994) *An Expanded Sourcebook: Qualitative Data Analysis*, 2nd edn. London: Sage.

Miles, M.B., Huberman, A.M. and Saldaña, J. (2014) *Qualitative Data Analysis*, 3rd edn. Thousand Oaks, CA: Sage.

Miller, D. (1993) 'The architecture of simplicity', *Academy of Management Review*, 18 (1): 116–38.

Miller, D.C. and Salkind, N.J. (2002) *Handbook of Research Design & Social Measurement*, 6th edn. Thousand Oaks, CA: Sage.

Mintzberg, H. (1973) *The Nature of Managerial Work*. London: Harper and Row.

Mintzberg, H. (2005) *Managers not MBAs: A Hard Look at the Soft Practice of Managing and Management Development*. San Francisco, CA: Berrett-Koehler.

Moeran, B. (2005) 'Tricks of the trade: the performance and interpretation of authenticity', *Journal of Management Studies*, 42: 901–22.

Moingeon, B. and Edmondson, A. (1997) *Organizational Learning and Competitive Advantage*. London: Sage.

Moreno, J.L. (1934) *Who Shall Survive?* Washington, DC: Nervous and Mental Disease Publishing.

Morgan, D.L. (1997) *Focus Groups as Qualitative Research*, 2nd edn. Thousand Oaks, CA: Sage.

Morgan, G. and Smircich, L. (1980) 'The case for qualitative research', *Academy of Management Review*, 5: 491–500.

Moser, C.A. and Kalton, G. (1971) *Survey Methods in Social Investigation*, 2nd edn. London: Heinemann.

Munir, K.A. and Phillips, N. (2005) 'The birth of the "Kodak Moment": institutional entrepreneurship and the adoption of new technologies', *Organization Studies*, 26 (11): 1665–87.

Murray, R. (2002) *How to Write a Thesis*. Milton Keynes: Open University Press.

Murray, R. and Moore, S. (2006). *The Handbook of Academic Writing: A Fresh Approach*. Maidenhead: McGraw-Hill.

Nadin, S. and Cassell, C. (2006) 'The use of a research diary as a tool for reflexive practice: some reflections from management research', *Qualitative Research in Accounting & Management*, 3 (3): 208–17.

Nguyen, P. (2005) 'Public opinion polls, chicken soup and sample size', *Teaching Statistics*, 27 (3): 89–91.

Nonaka, I. (1988) 'Toward middle-up-down management: accelerating information creation', *Sloan Management Review*, Spring: 9–18.

Nonaka, I. and Takeuchi, H. (1995) *The Knowledge-Creating Company: How Japanese Companies Create the Dynamics of Innovation*. Oxford: Oxford University Press.

Nor, S.M. (2000) 'Privatisation and changes in organization: a case study of a Malaysian privatised utility', PhD thesis, Lancaster University.

Norman, M. (2006) 'Student teachers' perceptions of becoming teachers and their experiences of confidence during their transition to teaching', PhD thesis, University of Manchester.

O'Connor, H., Madge, C., Shaw, R. and Wellens, J. (2008) 'Internet-based interviewing', in N. Fielding, R.M. Lee and G. Blank (eds), *The SAGE Handbook of Online Research Methods*. London: Sage, pp. 271–89.

O'Reilly, D. and Reed, M. (2010) '"Leaderism": an evolution of managerialism in UK public service reform', *Public Administration*, 88 (4): 960–78.

Obstfeld, D. (2005) 'Social networks, the tertius iungens orientation, and involvement in innovation', *Administrative Science Quarterly*, 50: 100–30.

Oliver, P. (2012) *Succeeding with your Literature Review: A Handbook for Students*. Maidenhead: Open University Press.

Padgett, D.K. (2008) *Qualitative Methods in Social Work Research*. Thousand Oaks, CA: Sage.

Park, C. (2003) 'In other (people's) words: plagiarism by university students – literature and lessons', *Assessment & Evaluation in Higher Education*, 28 (5): 471–88.

Parry, O. and Mauthner, N.S. (2004) 'Whose data are they anyway? Practical, legal and ethical issues in archiving qualitative research data', *Sociology*, 38 (1): 139–52.

Patriotta, G. (2003) *Organizational Knowledge in the Making*. Oxford: Oxford University Press.

Pears, D. (1971) *Wittgenstein*. London: Fontana.

Peters, T.J. and Waterman, R.H. (1982) *In Search of Excellence: Lessons from America's Best Run Companies*. New York: Harper and Row.

Petticrew, M. and Roberts, H. (2006) *Systematic Reviews in the Social Sciences: A Practical Guide*. Malden, MA: Blackwell.

Pettigrew, A.M. (1985) *The Awakening Giant: Continuity and Change in Imperial Chemical Industries*. Oxford: Blackwell.

Pettigrew, A.M. (1990) 'Longitudinal field research on change: theory and practice', *Organization Science*, 1 (3): 267–92.

Phillips, E.M. (1984) 'Learning to do research', *Graduate Management Research*, 2 (1): 6–18.

Phillips, E.M. and Pugh, D.S. (2005) *How to Get a PhD: A Handbook for Students and their Supervisors*, 4th edn. Maidenhead: Open University Press.

Phillips, N., Sewell, G. and Jaynes, S. (2008) 'Applying critical discourse analysis in strategic management research', *Organizational Research Methods*, 11 (4): 770–89.

Pike, K.L. (1954) *Language in Relation to a Unified Theory of the Structure of Human Behavior.* Glendale, CA: Summer Institute of Linguistics.

Pink, S. (2001) *Doing Visual Ethnography: Images, Media and Representation in Research.* London: Sage.

Platt, J. (1976) *Realities of Social Research: An Empirical Study of British Sociologists.* Brighton: Sussex University Press.

Popper, K. (1959) *The Logic of Scientific Discovery.* London: Hutchinson.

Porter, L.W. and McKibbin, L.E. (1988) *Management Education and Development: Drift or Thrust into the 21st Century?* New York: McGraw-Hill.

Potter, J. and Wetherell, M. (1987) *Discourse and Social Psychology Beyond Attitudes and Behaviour.* London: Sage.

Potter, J. and Wetherell, M. (1988) *Social Psychology and Discourse.* London: Routledge.

Potter, S. (2006) *Doing Postgraduate Research.* London: Sage.

Prasad, P. and Elmes, M (2005) 'In the name of the practical: unearthing the hegemony of pragmatics in the discourse of environmental management', *Journal of Management Studies,* 42 (4): 845–67.

Prieto, I.M. and Easterby-Smith, M. (2006) 'Dynamic capabilities and the role of organizational knowledge: an exploration', *European Journal of Information Management,* 15: 500–10.

Pritchard, K. (2011) 'From "being there" to "being […] where?": relocating ethnography', *Qualitative Research in Organizations and Management: An International Journal,* 6 (3): 230–45.

Psathas, G. (1995) *Conversation Analysis: The Study of Talk-in-Interaction.* Thousand Oaks, CA: Sage.

Pugh, D.S. (1983) 'Studying organisational structure and process', in G. Morgan (ed.), *Beyond Method.* Beverly Hills, CA: Sage, pp. 45–55.

Pugh, D.S. (1988) 'The Aston research programme', in A. Bryman (ed.), *Doing Research in Organisations.* London: Routledge, pp. 123–35.

Pugh, D.S. and Hickson, D.J. (1976) *Organisation Structure in its Context: The Aston Programme.* Farnborough: Saxon House.

Punch, K.F. (1998) *Introduction to Social Research: Qualitative Approaches.* London: Sage.

Punch, M. (1986) *The Politics and Ethics of Fieldwork.* Beverly Hills, CA: Sage.

Putnam, H. (1987) *The Many Faces of Realism.* La Salle, IL: Open Court.

Ralston, D.A., Terpstra-Tong, J., Terpstra, R.H., Wang, X.L. and Egri, C. (2006) 'Today's state-owned enterprises of China: are they dying dinosaurs or dynamic dynamos?', *Strategic Management Journal,* 27 (9): 825–43.

Ram, M. and Trehan, K. (2010) 'Critical action learning, policy learning in small firms: an inquiry', *Management Learning,* 41 (4): 414–28.

Rappoport, R.N. (1970) 'Three dilemmas in action research', *Human Relations,* 23 (4): 499–513.

Reason, P. (1988) *Human Inquiry in Action.* London: Sage.

Reason, P. and Bradbury, H. (2001) *Handbook of Action Research: Participative Inquiry and Practice.* London: Sage.

Reason, P. and Bradbury, H. (2006) *Handbook of Action Research: The Concise Paperback Edition.* Thousand Oaks, CA: Sage.

Reason, P. and Bradbury, H. (2013) *The SAGE Handbook of Action Research: Participative Inquiry and Practice,* 2nd edn. Thousand Oaks, CA: Sage.

Rerup, C. and Feldman, M. (2011) 'Routines as a source of change in organizational schemata: the role of trial-and-error learning', *Academy of Management Journal,* 54 (3): 577–610.

Richards, L. and Morse, J.M. (2013) *Read Me First for a User's Guide to Qualitative Methods,* 3rd edn. Los Angeles, CA: Sage.

Ricoeur, P. (1981) 'What is a text? Explanation and understanding', in J.B. Thompson (ed.), *Paul Ricoeur, Hermeneutics and the Human Sciences.* Cambridge: Cambridge University Press, pp. 145–64.

Ridley, D. (2012) *The Literature Review: A Step-by-step Guide for Students.* London: Sage.

Riessman, C.K. (1996) *Narrative Analysis.* Newbury Park, CA: Sage.

Riessman, C.K. (2003) 'Narrative analysis', in M.S. Lewis-Beck, A. Bryman and T. Futing Liao (eds), *The SAGE Encyclopedia of Social Science Research Methods.* Thousand Oaks, CA: Sage, pp. 705–9.

Roberts, K.A. and Wilson, R.W. (2002) 'ICT and the research process: issues around the compatibility of technology with qualitative data analysis' (52 paragraphs), *Forum Qualitative Sozialforschung/Forum: Qualitative Social Research,* 3 (2), Art. 23. Available at: http://nbn-resolving.de/urn:nbn:de:0114-fqs0202234 (last accessed 29 October 2008).

Roethlisberger, F.J. and Dickson, W.J. (1939) *Management and the Worker.* Cambridge, MA: Harvard University Press.

Rogers, B. and Ryals, L. (2007) 'Using the repertory grid to access the underlying realities in key account relationships', *International Journal of Market Research,* 49 (5): 595–612.

Rose, G. (2001) *Visual Methodology: An Introduction to the Interpretation of Visual Materials.* London: Sage.

Rouleau, L. (2005) 'Micro-practices of strategic sensemaking and sensegiving: how middle managers interpret and sell change every day', *Journal of Management Studies,* 42 (7): 1413–41.

Roulston, K. (2010) *Reflective Interviewing: A Guide to Theory and Practice.* London: Sage.

Roy, D. (1952) 'Quota restriction and goldbricking in a machine shop', *American Journal of Sociology,* 57: 427–42.

Roy, D. (1954) 'Efficiency and "the fix": informal intergroup relations in a piecework machine shop', *American Journal of Sociology,* 60 (3): 255–66.

Roy, D. (1970) 'The study of southern labour union organising campaigns', in R. Haberstein (ed.), *Pathway to Data.* New York: Aldine, pp. 216–44.

Rubin, H.J. and Rubin, I. (2012) *Qualitative Interviewing: The Art of Hearing Data*, 3rd edn. Thousand Oaks, CA: Sage.

Rugg, G. and Petre, M. (2004) *The Unwritten Rules of PhD Research*. Maidenhead: Open University Press.

Runco, M.A. (2004) 'Creativity', *Annual Review of Psychology*, 55: 657–87.

Ryan, G.W. and Bernard, H.R. (2003) 'Data management and analysis methods', in N.K. Denzin and Y.S. Lincoln (eds), *Collecting and Interpreting Qualitative Materials*. Thousand Oaks, CA: Sage, pp. 259–309.

Ryan, G.W. and Bernard, H.R. (2006) 'Testing an ethnographic decision tree model on a national sample: recycling beverage cans', *Human Organization*, 65 (1): 103–14.

Ryave, A.L. and Schenkein, J.N. (1974) 'Notes on the art of walking', in R. Turner (ed.), *Ethnomethodology: Selected Readings*. Harmondsworth: Penguin, pp. 265–74.

Said, E. (1978) *Orientalism*. London: Routledge and Kegan Paul.

Saldaña, J. (2009) *The Coding Manual for Qualitative Researchers*. Los Angeles, CA: Sage.

Sapsford, R. (2006) *Survey Research*, 2nd edn. London: Sage.

Saunders, M., Lewis, P. and Thornhill, A. (2006) *Research Methods for Business Students*, 4th edn. Harlow: Pearson Education.

Saunders, M., Lewis, P. and Thornhill, A. (2009) *Research Methods for Business Students*, 5th edn. London: FT Prentice Hall.

Saunders, M., Lewis, P. and Thornhill, A. (2012) *Research Methods for Business Students*, 6th edn. Harlow: Pearson.

Saunders, M.N.K., Lewis, P. and Thornhill, A. (2003) *Research Methods for Business Students*, 3rd edn. Harlow: FT Prentice Hall.

Sayer, A. (2000) *Realism and Social Science*. London: Sage.

Scarbrough, H. (ed.) (2008) *The Evolution of Business Knowledge*. Oxford: Oxford University Press.

Scarbrough, H. and Swan, J. (1999) 'Knowledge management and the management fashion perspective', Proceedings of British Academy of Management Conference, Manchester, Vol II: 920–37.

Schegloff, E.A. and Sacks, H. (1973) 'Opening up closings', *Semiotica*, 8 (4): 289–327.

Schmitt, N. and Stults, D.M. (1985) 'Factors defined by negatively keyed items: the results of careless respondents?', *Applied Psychological Measurement*, 9 (4): 367–73.

Schon, D.A. (1983) *The Reflective Practitioner: How Professionals Think in Action*. London: Maurice Temple Smith.

Schyns, B., Kiefer, T., Kerschreiter, R. and Tymon, A. (2011) 'Teaching implicit leadership theories to develop leaders and leadership – how and why it can make a difference', *Academy of Management Learning and Education*, 10 (3): 397–408.

Scoble, R. and Israel, S. (2006) *Naked Conversations: How Blogs are Changing the Way Businesses are Talking to Customers*. Hoboken, NJ: Wiley.

Scott, M. (1997) 'PC analysis of key words – and key key words', *System*, 25 (1): 1–13.

Scott, M. (2001) 'Comparing corpora and identifying key words, collocations, and frequency distributions through the WordSmith Tools suite of computer programs', in M. Ghadessy, A. Henry and R.L. Roseberry (eds), *Small Corpus Studies and ELT: Theory and Practice*. Amsterdam: John Benjamins, pp. 47–67.

Scott, M. (2002) 'Picturing the key words of a very large corpus and their lexical upshots – or getting at the *Guardian*'s view of the world', in B. Kettemann and G. Marko (eds), *Teaching and Learning by Doing Corpus Analysis*. Amsterdam: Rodopi, pp. 43–50 (see also CD-ROM).

Scott, M. (2010) 'What can corpus software do?', in A. O'Keeffe and M.J. McCarthy (eds), *Routledge Handbook of Corpus Linguistics*. London: Routledge, pp. 136–51.

Seale, C. (2000a) 'Resurrective practice and narrative', in M. Andrews, S.D. Sclater, C. Squire and A. Treacher (eds), *Lines of Narrative*. London: Routledge, pp. 36–47.

Seale, C. (2000b) 'Using computers to analyse qualitative data', in D. Silverman (ed.), *Doing Qualitative Research: A Practical Handbook*. London: Sage, pp. 154–74.

Secrist, C., Koeyer I., de Bell, H. and Fogel, A. (2002) 'Combining digital video technology and narrative methods for understanding infant development', *Forum: Qualitative Social Research*, 3 (2). Available at: www.qualitative-research.net/fqs-texte/2-02/2-02secristetal-e.htm (last accessed 14 August 2014).

Selvin, H.C. and Stuart, A. (1966) 'Data-dredging procedures in survey analysis', *American Statistician*, 20: 20–3.

Senge, P. (1990) *The Fifth Discipline: The Art and Practice of the Learning Organization*. London: Century.

Shadish, W.R., Cook, T.D. and Campbell, D.T. (2002) *Experimental and Quasi-Experimental Designs for Generalised Causal Inference*. Boston, MA: Houghton Mifflin.

Shalley, C.E. and Gilson, L.L. (2004) 'What leaders need to know: a review of social and contextual factors that can foster or hinder creativity', *The Leadership Quarterly*, 15 (1): 33–53.

Shotter, J. (1993) *Conversational Realities*. London: Sage.

Shotter, J. (1995) 'The manager as a practical author: a rhetorical-responsive, social constructionist approach to social-organizational problems', in D. Hosking, H.P. Dachler and K.J. Gergen (eds), *Management and Organization: Relational Alternatives to Individualism*. Aldershot: Avebury, pp. 125–47.

Shrader, C.B., Lincoln, J.R. and Hoffman, A.N. (1989) 'The network structures of organizations: effects of task contingencies and distributional form', *Human Relations*, 42: 43–66.

Sidnell, J. (2011) *Conversation Analysis: An Introduction*. Malden, MA: Wiley-Blackwell.

Siggelkow, N. (2007) 'Persuasion with case studies', *Academy of Management Journal*, 50 (1): 20–4.

Silver, C. and Lewins, A. (2014) *Using Software in Qualitative Research: A Step-by-step Guide*, 2nd edn. Los Angeles, CA: Sage.

Silver, M. (1991) *Competent to Manage*. London: Routledge.

Silverman, D. (1993) *Interpreting Qualitative Data: Methods for Analysing Talk, Text and Interaction*. London: Sage.

Silverman, D. (2000) *Doing Qualitative Research: A Practical Handbook*. London: Sage.

Silverman, D. (2003) 'Analyzing talk and text', in N.K. Denzin and Y.S. Lincoln (eds), *Collecting and Interpreting Qualitative Materials*. Thousand Oaks, CA: Sage, pp. 340–62.

Simon, H.A. (1959) *Administrative Behaviour*, 2nd edn. London: Macmillan.

Simpson, B. (1995) 'A university: an organisation for learning … but a learning organisation?', unpublished MSc dissertation, Manchester Metropolitan University.

Sims, D. (1993) 'Coping with misinformation', *Management Decision*, 3: 18–21.

Sims, D. (2003) 'Between the millstones: a narrative account of the vulnerability of middle managers' storying', *Human Relations*, 56: 1195–211. Doi: 10.1177/00187267035610002.

Slater, D. (1989) 'Corridors of power', in J.F. Gubrium and D. Silverman (eds), *The Politics of Field Research*. London: Sage, pp. 113–31.

Smeyers, P. and Verhessen, P. (2001) 'Narrative analysis as philosophical research, bridging the gap between the empirical and the conceptual', *International Journal of Qualitative Studies in Education*, 14 (1): 71–84.

Snell, R.S. (1993) *Developing Skills for Ethical Management*. London: Chapman and Hall.

Spector, P.E. (1992) *Summated Rating Scale Construction: An Introduction*. Newbury Park, CA: Sage.

Sprigg, C.A. and Jackson, P.R. (2006) 'Call centers as lean service environments: well-being and the mediating role of work design', *Journal of Occupational Health Psychology*, 11 (2): 197–212.

Stake, R.E. (2006) 'Qualitative case studies', in N.K. Denzin and Y.S. Lincoln (eds), *SAGE Handbook of Qualitative Research*, 3rd edn. Thousand Oaks, CA: Sage, pp. 443–66.

Starbuck, B. (2004) *Journals Ranked by Citations per Article*. Available at: http://pages.stern.nyu.edu/~wstarbuc/ (last accessed 24 November 2011).

Starkey, K. and Tiratsoo, N. (2007) *Business Schools and the Bottom Line*. Cambridge: Cambridge University Press.

Steedman, P. (1991) 'On the relations between seeing, interpreting and knowing', in F. Steier (ed.), *Research and Reflexivity*. London: Sage, pp. 193–209.

Steenkamp, J-B.E.M. and Geyskens, I. (2006) 'What drives the perceived value of web sites? A cross-national investigation', *Journal of Marketing*, 70 (3): 136–50.

Steers, R.M., Bischoff, S.J. and Higgins, L.H. (1992) 'Crosscultural management research: the fish and the fisherman', *Journal of Management Inquiry*, 1 (4): 321–30.

Steinbeck, J. (1970) *Journal of a Novel: The East of Eden Letters*. London: Pan.

Stewart, R. (1967) *Managers and their Jobs*. Maidenhead: McGraw-Hill.

Stewart, R. (1982) *Choices for the Manager: A Guide to Managerial Work and Behaviour*. London: McGraw-Hill.

Stewart, V., Stewart, A. and Fonda, N. (1981) *Business Applications of Repertory Grid*. Maidenhead: McGraw-Hill.

Stokes, D. and Bergin, R. (2006) 'Methodology or "methodolatry"? An evaluation of focus groups and depth interviews', *Qualitative Market Research: An International Journal*, 9 (11): 26–37.

Strauss, A.L. (1987) *Qualitative Analysis for Social Scientists*. Cambridge: Cambridge University Press.

Strauss, A.L. and Corbin, J. (1990) *Basics of Qualitative Research: Grounded Theory Procedures and Techniques*. Thousand Oaks, CA: Sage.

Strauss, A.L. and Corbin, J. (1998) *Basics of Qualitative Research: Techniques and Procedures for Developing Grounded Theory*, 2nd edn. Thousand Oaks, CA: Sage.

Suddaby, R. (2006) 'From the Editors: what grounded theory is not', *Academy of Management Journal*, 49 (4): 633–42.

Tabachnick, B.G. and Fidell, L.S. (2014) *Using Multivariate Statistics*, 6th edn. Boston, MA: Pearson Education.

Tashakkori, A. and Teddlie, C. (1998) *Mixed Methodology: Combining Qualitative and Quantitative Approaches*. Thousand Oaks, CA: Sage.

Tashakkori, A. and Teddlie, C. (eds) ([2003] 2010) *Handbook of Mixed Methods in Social and Behavioral Research*. Thousand Oaks, CA: Sage.

Taylor, B. (1999) 'Patterns of control within Japanese manufacturing plants in China: doubts about Japanisation in Asia', *Journal of Management Studies*, 36 (6): 853–73.

Taylor, F.W. (1947) *Scientific Management*. London: Harper and Row.

Taylor, S.J. and Bogdan, R. (1984) *Introduction to Qualitative Research Methods*. New York: Wiley-Interscience.

Teagarden, M.B., von Glinow, M.A., Bowen, D.E., Frayne, C.A., Nason, S., Huo, Y.P., Milliman, J., Arias, M.E., Butler, M.C., Geringer, J.M., Kim, N.M., Scullion, H., Lowe, K.B. and Drost, E.A. (1995) 'Toward a theory of comparative management research: an ideographic case study of the best international human resources management project', *Academy of Management Journal*, 38: 1261–87.

Teddlie, C. and Tashakkori, A. (2009) *Foundations of Mixed Methods Research: Integrating Quantitative and Qualitative Approaches in the Social and Behavioral Sciences*. London: Sage.

Tesch, R. (1990) *Qualitative Research, Analysis Types & Software Tools*. New York: Falmer.

Thomas, A. (2004) *Research Skills for Management Studies*. New York: Routledge.

Thomas, W.I. and Thomas, D.S. (1928) *The Child in America: Behavioural Problems and Progress*. New York: Knopf.

Thompson, E.E. (2004) 'National competitiveness: a question of cost conditions or institutional circumstances?', *British Journal of Management*, 15: 197–218.

Thorpe, R. (1980) 'The relationship between payment systems, productivity and the organisation of work', MSc thesis, Strathclyde Business School.

Thorpe, R. and Cornelissen, J. (2003) 'Visual media and the construction of meaning', in D. Holman and R. Thorpe (eds), *Management and Language: The Manager as Practical Author*. London: Sage, pp. 67–81.

Thorpe, R. and Danielli, A. (1996) 'Oldham Town Park', unpublished study conducted for Oldham Borough Council.

Thorpe, R. and Holloway, J. (2008) *Performance Management: Multidisciplinary Perspectives*. Houndsmill: Palgrave Macmillan NC.

Thorpe, R. and Holt, R. ([2008] 2009) *The SAGE Dictionary of Qualitative Management Research*. London: Sage.

Thorpe, R., Holt, R., Macpherson, A. and Pittaway, L. (2005) 'Knowledge within small and medium-sized firms: a review of the evidence', *International Journal of Management Reviews*, 7 (4): 257–81.

Tilly, C. (2006) *Why?* Princeton, NJ: Princeton University Press.

Todd, D.J. (1979) 'Mixing qualitative and quantitative methods: triangulation in action', *Administrative Science Quarterly*, 24: 602–11.

Todorova, G. and Durisin, B. (2007) 'Absorptive capacity: valuing a reconceptualization', *Academy of Management Review*, 32 (3): 774–86.

Toulmin, S. (2001) *The Uses of Argument*. Cambridge: Cambridge University Press.

Tracy, S.J. (2010) 'Qualitative quality: eight "big-tent" criteria for excellent qualitative research', *Qualitative Inquiry*, 16 (10): 837–51.

Tracy, S.J. (2013) *Qualitative Research Methods: Collecting Evidence, Crafting Analysis, Communicating Impact*. Chichester: Wiley-Blackwell.

Tranfield, D. (2002) 'Formulating the nature of management research', *European Management Journal*, 20 (4): 378–82.

Tranfield, D. and Starkey, K. (1998) 'The nature, social organization and promotion of management research: towards policy', *British Journal of Management*, 9: 341–53.

Tranfield, D., Denyer, D. and Marcos, J. (2004) 'Co-producing management knowledge', *Management Decision*, 42 (3/4): 375–86.

Tranfield, D., Denyer, D. and Smart, P. (2003) 'Towards a methodology for developing evidence-informed management knowledge by means of systematic review', *British Journal of Management*, 14 (3): 207–22.

Tsai, W. and Ghoshal, S. (1998) 'Social capital and value creation: the role of intrafirm networks', *Academy of Management Journal*, 41 (4): 464–76.

Tsang, E.W.K. (1997) 'Learning from joint venturing experience: the case of foreign direct investment by Singapore companies in China', PhD thesis, University of Cambridge.

Tsang, E.W.K. (1999) 'Internationalisation as a learning process: Singapore MNCs in China', *Academy of Management Executive*, 13 (1): 91–101.

Tsang, E.W.K. (2002) 'Acquiring knowledge by foreign partners from international joint ventures in a transition economy: learning-by-doing and learning myopia', *Strategic Management Journal*, 23: 835–54.

Tsoukas, H. and Hatch, M.J. (1997) 'Complex thinking, complex practice: the case for a narrative approach to organisational complexity', paper presented to the American Academy of Management.

Turner, B.A. (1988) 'Connoisseurship in the study of organisational cultures', in A. Bryman (ed.), *Doing Research in Organisations*. London: Sage, pp. 108–21.

Ullman, J.B. (2006a) 'Structural equation modeling', in B.G. Tabachnick and L.S. Fidell (eds), *Using Multivariate Statistics*. Boston, MA: Allyn & Bacon, pp. 653–771.

Ullman, J.B. (2006b) 'Structural equation modeling: reviewing the basics and moving forward', *Journal of Personality Assessment*, 87 (1): 35–50.

Uzzi, B. (1997) 'Social structure and competition in interfirm networks: the paradox of embeddedness', *Administrative Science Quarterly*, 42: 35–67.

Van de Ven, A.H. and Johnson, P.E. (2006) 'Knowledge for theory and practice', *Academy of Management Review*, 31 (4): 802–21.

van Maanen, J. (1991) 'The smile factory: work at Disneyland', in P.J. Frost, L.F. Moore, M.R. Louis, C.C. Lundberg and J. Martin (eds), *Reframing Organizational Culture*. Newsbury Park, CA: Sage, pp. 58–76.

van Maanen, J. (2011) 'Ethnography as work: some rules of engagement', *Journal of Management Studies*, 48 (1): 218–34.

Von Bertalanffy, L. (1962) 'General systems theory – a critical review', *General Systems*, 7: 1–20.

Walker, G.B. and Sillars, M.O. (1990) 'Where is argument? Perelman's theory of values', in R. Trapp and J. Schuetz (eds), *Perspectives on Argumentation*. Long Grove, IL: Waveland Press, pp. 121–33.

Walker, R. (1985) *Applied Qualitative Research*. Aldershot: Gower.

Wall, T.D., Jackson, P.R. and Davids, K. (1992) 'Operator work design and robotics system performance: a serendipitous field experiment', *Journal of Applied Psychology*, 77: 353–62.

Wall, T.D., Kemp, N.J., Jackson, P.J. and Clegg, C.W. (1986) 'Outcomes of autonomous workgroups: a long-term field experiment', *Academy of Management Journal*, 29 (2): 282–304.

Wallace, M. and Wray, A. (2011) *Critical Reading and Writing for Postgraduates*, 2nd edn. London: Sage.

Walsh, G. and Beatty, S.E. (2007) 'Customer-based corporate reputation of a service firm: scale development and validation', *Journal of the Academy of Marketing Science*, 35 (1): 127–43.

Walsh, G., Mitchell, V-W., Jackson, P.R. and Beatty, S.E. (2009) 'Examining the antecedents and consequences of corporate reputation: a customer perspective', *British Journal of Management*, 20 (2): 187–203.

Wansink, B. (2003) 'Using laddering to understand and leverage a brand's equity', *Qualitative Market Research: An International Journal*, 6 (2): 111–18.

Warr, P.B., Cook, J.D. and Wall, T.D. (1979) 'Scales for the measurement of some work attitudes and aspects of psychological well-being', *Journal of Occupational Psychology*, 52: 129–48.

Waters, C.D.J. (2011) *Quantitative Methods for Business*, 5th edn. Harlow: Financial Times/Prentice Hall.

Watford, A.J. (1980–87) *Watson's Guide to Reference Material: Vol. 2 – Social and Historical Sciences, Philosophy and Religion*. London: Library Association.

Watson, T.J. (1994) *In Search of Management: Culture, Chaos and Control in Managerial Work*. London: Routledge.

Watson, T.J. (2011) 'Ethnography, reality, and truth: the vital need for studies of 'how things work' in organizations and management', *Journal of Management Studies*, 48 (1): 202–17.

Watzlawick, P. (ed.) (1984) *The Invented Reality*. London: Norton.

Weick, K.E. (1989) 'Theory construction as disciplined imagination', *Academy of Management Review*, 14 (4): 516–31.

Weick, K.E. (1995) *Sense-making in Organisations*. London: Sage.

Weitzman, E.A. (1999) 'Analyzing qualitative data with computer software', *Health Services Research*, 34 (5/2): 1241–63.

Wertsch, J.V. (1991) *Voices of the Mind: A Socio Cultural Approach to Mediated Action*. Cambridge, MA: Harvard University Press.

Whitley, R., Thomas, A. and Marceau, J. (1981) *Masters of Business?* London: Tavistock.

Winter, S.G. (2003) 'Understanding dynamic capabilities', *Strategic Management Journal*, 24: 991–5.

Wittgenstein, L. (1953) *Philosophical Investigations*. Oxford: Blackwell.

Wood, M. (2005) 'Bootstrapped confidence intervals as an approach to statistical inference', *Organizational Research Methods*, 8, 454–70.

Wright, R.P. (2006) 'Rigor and relevance using repertory grid technique in strategy research', *Research Methodology in Strategy and Management*, 3: 295–348.

Ybema, S., Yanow, D., Kamsteeg, F.H. and Wels, H. (eds) (2009) *Organizational Ethnography: Studying the Complexity of Everyday Life*. London: Sage.

Yin, R.K. (2013) *Case Study Research: Design and Methods*, 5th edn. Thousand Oaks, CA: Sage.

Zahra, S.A. and George, G. (2002) 'Absorptive capacity: a review, reconcepualisation, and extension', *Academy of Management Review*, 27 (2): 185–203.

Zimmerman, D. (1992) 'The interactional organization of calls for emergency assistance', in P. Drew and J. Heritage (eds), *Talk at Work: Interaction in Institutional Settings*. Cambridge: Cambridge University Press, pp. 418–69.

INDEX